creating Nordic capitalism

'This welcome volume stresses the micro-economic perspective: including case stories of important firms, remembering the comparative aspect, and not least using a theoretical framework which is very useful for understanding the dramatic changes in economic development.'

— **Per Boje**, *Professor of Business History,*
University of Southern Denmark

'The world has a lot to learn from the recent success of 'Nordic Capitalism' and this book has a lot to teach. With leading companies such as Nokia, ABB and Carlsberg at the centre, the authors offer an authoritative and nuanced account, with rich materials for students, policy-makers and teachers alike'.

— **Richard Whittington**, *Professor of Strategic Management,*
Oxford Saïd Business School, UK

creating Nordic capitalism

the business history of
a competitive periphery

Edited by

Susanna Fellman, Martin Jes Iversen,
Hans Sjögren and Lars Thue

First published 2008 by
PALGRAVE MACMILLAN
Houndmills, Basingstoke, Hampshire RG21 6XS and
175 Fifth Avenue, New York, N.Y. 10010
Companies and representatives throughout the world

PALGRAVE MACMILLAN is the global academic imprint of the Palgrave Macmillan division of St. Martin's Press, LLC and of Palgrave Macmillan Ltd. Macmillan® is a registered trademark in the United States, United Kingdom and other countries. Palgrave is a registered trademark in the European Union and other countries.

ISBN-13: 978–0–230–54553–3
ISBN-10: 0–230–54553–X

This book is printed on paper suitable for recycling and made from fully managed and sustained forest sources. Logging, pulping and manufacturing processes are expected to conform to the environmental regulations of the country of origin.

A catalogue record for this book is available from the British Library.

A catalog record for this book is available from the Library of Congress.

10   9   8   7   6   5   4   3   2   1
17   16   15   14   13   12   11   10   09   08

Printed in China

contents

list of figures

list of tables

list of photographs

acknowledgements

We wish to express our deep appreciation to everyone who contributed at different stages of this project, reading and discussing various draft chapters, attending seminars and giving constructive feedback, commenting on particular subjects, giving new insights and submitting the content to thorough inquiry. In particular we thank Per Boje, from University of Southern Denmark, Andrea Colli, from Bocconì University and Geoffrey Jones, from Harvard Business School for all the constructive comments. We would also like to thank the Nordic Council's educational Nordplus Programme for supporting the research financially. As the title of our book indicates, a particular inspiration came from Thomas K. McCraw's book, *Creating Modern Capitalism* (Harvard University Press, 1996); we would like to thank Thomas K. McCraw and the whole team affiliated to Harvard Business School who developed the original book.

The final gratitude is for our efficient and patient research assistants Lisa Conibear and Meriam Kaddoura and our publishers Ursula Garvin and Mark Cooper from Palgrave Macmillan who have been extremely patient and helpful in the complex process of creating an international textbook on Nordic business history.

notes on the contributors

Steen Andersen is Assistant Professor of Business History at Copenhagen Business School. He has written extensively on Danish business in the 1930s and 1940s and his wrote his dissertation on multinational Danish construction companies in crisis and in war, 1919–47. This work is about to be published in English as *Working for the Axis and the Allies*.

Andrew Arnold is managing partner of Native Edge, a public relations consultancy in Copenhagen. He has twenty years' experience as a business journalist and has written for *The Grocer*, AFX News, The Economist Intelligence Unit and the *Financial Times*. He was employed by Carlsberg A/S in Copenhagen as a public relations consultant from 1998 to 2004. His work at Native Edge includes advising Danish companies on their international communications strategy and tactics.

Susanna Fellman is Adjunct Professor in the Department of Social Science History at University of Helsinki. Her special interest is in business history and the history of management in Finland. Currently she is also working on a project on cartels, having previously done work on industrial relations and on labour market issues.

Martin Jes Iversen is Associate Professor of Business History at Copenhagen Business School. He is the author of several business history books including *GN Store Nord – A Company in Transition* (CBS Press, 2005). This work was based on his PhD dissertation on the changing managerial regimes in a long-term perspective. Currently he is studying the strategic responses to European integration among the largest companies in a number of European countries. His teaching experience includes the development of new business courses for the Globe Programme, which is a BA co-operation between State University of Hong Kong, Kennan–Flagler Business School, North Carolina and Copenhagen Business School.

Sverre Knutsen is Associate Professor of Economic and Business History at Norwegian school of Management BI in Oslo. His main areas of research and teaching have been financial history, transport history and financing of entrepreneurial ventures, and he has written several books, articles and chapters on themes from this research fields. Currently he is working on the history of Norwegian road building in the nineteenth century and an institutional and comparative study of Nordic financial crises.

Juha-Antti Lamberg is Professor of Strategic Management at Helsinki University of Technology, Institute of Strategy and International Business. His research interests include organizational change, history and theory of strategy and institutional theory.

Mats Larsson has been Professor of Economic History at Uppsala University since 1997. He has mainly within the fields of business and financial history, including two monographs on the Swedish media company Bonniers. Larsson is also the head of the newly established Uppsala Centre for Business History.

Håkan Lindgren has been Professor of Economic History at Stockholm School of Economics since 1995. He is head of The Institute for Research in Economic History (EHFF) and former chairman of the board of directors of The Economic Research Institute (EFI) of the School. His *alma mater* is Uppsala University, where he held office as associate professor and head of the Financial History Unit of the Department of Economic History. His main research area is financial and business history with, several extensive works on the Wallenberg group.

Anders Melander is Associate Professor of Business Administration at Jönköping International Business School (JIBS). He defended his thesis, Industrial Wisdom and Strategic Change in the Swedish Pulp and Paper industry 1945–90 in 1997. Since then the wood processing sector has been the empirical setting for his research on strategic change, industrial networks and customer orientation. In the period 2000–6 Anders managed a national business development program targeting small and medium sized companies (see more on www.krAftprov.nu). Today, he is director of business development at JIBS.

Mads Mordhorst is Assistant Professor of Business History at Copenhagen Business School. He has published several books and articles in varied of historical fields. His current research is focused on how history is used by companies and companies' impact on the shaping of national identity. His teaches in subjects as strategy, business history, branding and philosophy of science.

Daniel Nyberg has done research mainly on media economics, particularly on issues connected with ownership structure and business behaviour, governing systems and family business.

Jari Ojala is a professor of history at the Department of History and Ethnology of the University of Jyväskylä. His research includes long-term development in business enterprises, maritime history, international trade and the co-evolution of business and society.

Hans Sjögren is Professor of Economic History and Institutional Economics in the Department of Management and Engineering at Linköpings University and Research Fellow at the Stockholm School of Economics. His research focuses on economic change, where he has used institutional analysis to explain structural transformation and behaviour in markets, sectors and orga-nizations. Three current research fields, in which he also teaches courses and supervises doctoral students, are normative behaviour in relation to economic crime, Nordic financial crises and corporate governance.

Mika Skippari is a research associate in the department of marketing and management at Helsinki School of Economics. He has earned his doctoral degree at Tampere University of Technology. He has published widely in international journals, such as the *International Studies of Management & Organization, Business & Society* and the *Scandinavian Economic History Review*. His research interests include industry evolution, business–society relations and institutional theory.

Knut Sogner is Professor of Economic History at Norwegian School of Management. He is the author of several books, articles and chapter, focus-ing particularly on industrial history in the twentieth century. He is currently head of the Business History Unit at Norwegian School of Management.

Fredrik Tell is Associate Professor in Management at the Department of Management and Engineering, Linköping University. He has also been a lec-turer in economic history at the London School of Economics and Political Science as well as a visiting research fellow at University of Sussex and Stanford University. Tell's main research interests are innovation and industry dynam-ics, management of complex technologies and standards, organizational knowledge and learning, history of technology and business history.

Lars Thue is Professor of Modern History at the Centre for Business History, Department of Innovation and Economic Organization, Norwegian School of Management. He has written extensively on the history of Norwegian infrastructures, such as telecommunications, postal services and electricity. He has been responsible for many years for a graduate course on comparative business systems. He is currently participating in an international project 'The Emergence and Governance of Critical Transnational European Infrastructures', financed by the European Science Foundation.

list of abbreviations

AMS   Swedish Labour Market Board
AMV   Swedish Labour Market Authority
CEO   chief executive officer
CET   common external tariff
CIA   Central Intelligence Agency (US)
CWS   Co-operative Wholesale Society
DOK   Commission for Extraordinary Measures (Denmark)
dwt   deadweight
EAC   East Asian Company
EC   European Community
ECA   Marshall Plan Administration
EEA   European Economic Area
EEC   European Economic Community
EFTA   European Free Trade Association
EMU   European Monetary Union
EPU   European Payment Union
ERM   Exchange Rate Mechanism
EU   European Union
FDI   foreign direct investment
FPMA   Finnish Paper Mills Association (Finnpap)
FTA   free-trade area
GATT   General Agreement on Tariffs and Trade
GDP   gross domestic product
ha   hectare
hp   horsepower
hl   hectolitre
ICT   information and computer technology
IMF   International Monetary Fund
IT   information technology
LO   Swedish Confederation of Trade Unions
M&As   mergers and acquisitions
MNC   multinational corporation

MNE	multinational enterprise
MP	Member of Parliament
MTK	Agricultural producers (Finland)
NATO	North Atlantic Treaty Organization
NIEO	New International Economic Order
NPM	New Public Management
NYSE	New York Stock Exchange
OECD	Organisation for Economic Co-operation and Development
OEEC	Organization for European Economic Co-operation
OMO	open-market operations
OPEC	Organization of Petroleum Exporting Countries
R&D	research and development
SAF	Swedish Employers' Confederation
SAJ	Finnish Federation of Trade Unions
SAK	Confederation of Finnish Trade Unions
SDFI	State's Direct Financial Interest
SEA	Single European Act
SEB	Stockholms Enskilda Bank
SEV	Socialist trade block (Finland)
SME	small- and medium-sized enterprise
SOE	state-owned enterprise
SSEEs	Small Successful European Economies
STK	Confederation of Employers in Finland
TNC	transnational corporation
TWh	billion kilowatt hours
TWI	Training Within Industry
UK	United Kingdom
US	United States
VAT	value added tax
WTO	World Trade Organization

creating Nordic capitalism – the business history of a competitive periphery

Martin Jes Iversen and Lars Thue

Introduction

This book illustrates the development of the capitalist business systems in four Northern European countries: Denmark, Finland, Norway and Sweden. During recent years these Nordic business systems have served as exemplary models for leading politicians, economists and businessmen. Though small and placed on the periphery of Europe, these Nordic countries rank among the world's wealthiest and most economically competitive nations. The Nordic nations combine their successful capitalistic systems with well-developed welfare systems and a successful and large public sector. Furthermore, they each have a long democratic tradition and a well-functioning and orderly civil society. These qualities have contributed to worldwide interest among economists and politicians in Nordic general development, the Nordic welfare model and leading Nordic multinationals (MNCs) such as Nokia and IKEA.[1] Since the mid-1990s, Nordic countries have been among the world's most competitive nations, according to the World Economic Forum's rankings. In 2005–6, five of the ten most competitive nations globally were Nordic. According to Chief Economist and Director of Global Competitiveness Programme, World Economic Forum, Lopez Claros Augusto, 'the Nordics have entered virtuous circles where various factors reinforce each other to make them among the most competitive economies in the world, with world class institutions and some of the highest levels of *per capita* income in the world'.[2]

This book explains the historic backgrounds behind these 'virtuous circles' – an analysis of the interrelated factors which have made the Nordic economies the most competitive in the world. The book is a comparative analysis. We acknowledge that the Nordic region consists of four different countries, each with their own national business systems formed by their countries' national histories, cultures and values. On the other hand, it is our hypothesis that the four Nordic business systems have some fundamental common characteristics, which makes it possible to speak of a 'Nordic model of capitalism'.[3] The main question is thus: what similarities and differences can we identify between the four Nordic capitalistic business systems and what factors have caused these systems to develop as they have? In the Conclusion (Chapter 14) we will try to identify differences and similarities and discuss whether we may speak of a specific Nordic capitalist business system and, if so, how it emerged and what it consists of.

The success of the Nordic welfare societies is by no means a given fact. In the post-war decades, the Swedish *folkhem* model, in particular, was studied and admired by scholars and politicians for its success in combining high welfare with strong economic performance. But in the mid-1980s the Nordic welfare model seemed less attractive and books were published with titles such as *Paradise Lost* and *Remaking the Welfare State*.[4] Analysts argued that strengthening global competition and de-industrialization would lead to pressure on the fundamental pillars of the welfare state system. In the years before the Single European Market in 1993, scholars believed that political and economic decision-making processes would gradually move from the national level towards international forums such as the WTO and the EU. As a result, organized labour would be weakened and the typical small-state national consensus between industry, state and labour would be limited. This scepticism about nationally grounded welfare states was further strengthened by a number of real economic events in the early 1990s, when the largest Nordic banks were all shaken by a fundamental financial crisis. The crises were particularly deep in Sweden and Finland, and both countries experienced three consecutive years of negative economic growth. The result was substantial national budget deficits, major unemployment and a wave of corporate bankruptcies. The Nordic societies were confronted with severe challenges: liberalization of financial markets, movement of production towards low-wage countries and an important new geo-political situation with the disappearance of the Nordic 'Sonderweg' between American-influenced western liberal societies and the Soviet Union-dominated socialist countries.[5] Considering this background, it seems surprising and unexpected that the Nordic countries economically outperformed most of world between 1995 and 2005. It is worth noting that as recently as 1973, Norway's GDP *per capita* was well below the western European average – but today Norway is one of the richest countries in the world. The point of departure of this book is an attempt to analyse the historical explanations behind this distinctive Nordic economic growth and its strong competitiveness.

Even though this 'Nordic Miracle' is apparently a phenomenon of the 1990s and 2000s we have decided to follow the Nordic capitalist economies from the outset in the mid-nineteenth century. We believe in the 'path dependency' phenomenon, meaning that all current realities have traceable historical roots. For example, if we attempt to unveil a relationship between government, labour organizations and employers in the Nordic region during the 1990s, we would need to follow this relationship back in time in order to understand its background and content. The wish to understand and describe the above-mentioned 'virtuous circles' of the Nordic countries thus requires tracing different aspects of the capitalist business systems back in time to see how and why these important aspects occurred and developed. It is our ambition to identify particular 'formative phases' in the development of Nordic capitalism when crucial political and economic decisions were taken and thus analyse how, when and by whom the recent Nordic growth and competitiveness has been formed.

This book has been written during a period when the Nordic system and capitalist societies are competitive and strong, but our intention is not to show that the Nordic systems are the best possible. The recent interest in the Nordic welfare model can be compared to the interest in the neo-liberal model of the US and the UK in the 1990s, the Japanese Keiretsus at the end of the 1980s, the German 'Wirtschaftswunder' in the 1960s and the American mass production paradigm, or 'Fordism', in the 1950s. The Keiretsu structure did not attract much attention in the late 1990s when the Japanese economy stagnated, and the Nordic capitalistic model might face the same fate and lose its current attraction in a few years. All such models should be handled cautiously when used as economic structures. Models successful in one context and period may not be as effective in others. Despite this fact, leading 'hype' models have inspired political and economic decision-makers, who have a general tendency to make predictions based on the current situation. Well-thought-out insights into different capitalistic business systems are thus important for high-quality decision-making. The reason is two-fold: on one hand we need comparative analysis, as this book provides, to understand how other capitalist business systems differ from the Nordic model. Similarly, we endeavour to provide inspiration that can make Nordic and non-Nordic readers better prepared to analyse and perhaps even reform aspects of their future national business systems. The three key words in the title of the book

CREATING NORDIC CAPITALISM • PROLOGUE • SWEDISH WELFARE CAPITALISM • THE BONNIER AND WALLENBERG BUSINESS GROUPS • FROM ASEA TO ABB

1

3

are 'Creating', 'Nordic' and 'Capitalism', and this Introduction is centred on these three terms. First, there is a short introduction to the most important economic system in the western world: capitalism. Then follows a description of the Nordic region, and finally the introduction is rounded off by a discussion of the difficult but important concept: change.

Capitalism: business systems and varieties

According to the neo-liberal Nobel Prize winner Milton Friedman the present liberal democratic époque is rather exceptional. In general, the long history of mankind has been dominated by tyranny, servitude and misery. The western world of the nineteenth and twentieth centuries thus stand outs as exceptional and according to Friedman 'History suggests only that capitalism is a necessary condition for political freedom'.[6]

It is on the other hand important to stress that political democracy and capitalistic principles do not necessarily accompany each other. The economy in Nazi Germany, for instance, was marked by the importance and growth of large private enterprises such as IG Farben, Siemens and Volkswagen while Chinese development after 1990 shows that economic capitalist principles can be introduced to a political system marked by a one-party system. Extraordinary growth, as in recent Chinese and South Korean development, does not imply that capitalism is by definition good – or even that capitalism by definition leads to richer and better societies. On the contrary, it most often exalts material values over spiritual ones and market forces may have harsh consequences.

Capitalism differs over time and between countries. The four national business systems analysed in this book thus represent different varieties of capitalism. Despite the differences, however, we believe these four characteristics are central to any capitalist systems:

■ Capitalist systems are market economies and a substantial part of the economic co-ordination within the system should be market-based.
■ Private property is protected and there is widespread private ownership of the means of production.
■ Labour is a commodity and wages are paid in money.
■ Accumulated wealth is, to a large extent, reproductively employed.

Besides these more formal characteristics, capitalism certainly has its cultural and psychological aspects. The interaction of these elements gives capitalist systems their restless dynamic, their crises and periods of growth: what the

Austrian economist, Joseph Schumpeter, labelled 'creative destruction'. 'Stabilized capitalism is', stated Schumpeter already in 1939, 'a contradiction in terms'.[7]

Capitalism as a system gradually grew out of the European feudal societies, having roots back to about the eleventh century in the city-states of northern Italy. Under the protection and support of the strong mercantilist state, a more significant commercial capitalist class emerged in the Netherlands, the UK and France. During the first industrial revolution emerging in Britain from the 1760s, capitalism got a strong foothold in the production of goods. During the nineteenth century industrial capitalism also spread to the Nordic countries – as will be studied closer in later chapters.

The company as the fundamental institution

In the centre of this dynamic economic system we find one particular institution, namely 'the company'. The company, although essential to an analysis of capitalist development, should be analysed in the context of the surrounding society. Thus this book on the capitalist development of the Nordic countries from roughly 1850 to 2005 consists of a combination of country chapters and company cases. Researchers from various disciplines have tried to explain the existence and importance of the company as a key economic organization – we can thus find corporate *raison d'être* arguments based on juridical, philosophical and economic disciplines.

A juridical explanation is that an officially registered company possesses some of the legal rights of a human being (it can own property, register patents, employ people, etc.) but in contrast to people it is theoretically immortal.[8] Companies can exist for centuries and reinvent themselves over and over again. One example is the Finnish company, Nokia, founded in 1865 as a pulp and paper producer. In the 1960s Nokia became an industrial conglomerate and in recent decades has been transformed into the world's dominant producer of cellular phones.

The American economist Milton Friedman has a more ideological view on the strengths of the company. According to Friedman, the strength of the capitalist company *per se* built upon its single *raison d'être*, namely, profitability. In Friedman's words: 'The corporation is an instrument of the stockholders who own it', and the 'instruments' can organize thousands and in some cases hundreds of thousands of employees who accept this primary aim and work for it. Prior to capitalism, large organizations had religious, political or cultural *raison d'êtres*. In contrast to the religious orders or the state-controlled administrations, companies fight for more profitability, and this competition causes endless technological, organizational and commercial innovation. In the 1990s the neo-liberal 'shareholder value' approach was widely debated and the so-called 'stakeholder value' school suggested that the existence – and strength – of the company relied on its relationship to various stakeholders including employees, customers, the broad society including the environment, etc.[9]

Joseph Schumpeter has suggested a third explanation of the success of the company. According to Schumpeter, it was through this institution that entrepreneurs changed societies by developing new technologies and new organizational methods. It is essential to any capitalist society that entrepreneurs have the right to found companies and have access to capital. These rights and options may sound obvious today. But most societies before the 1850s were based on centrally controlled privileges to establish firms and shops. The financial infrastructure based on privately owned banks was in place only in the most advanced societies such as Great Britain, the US and Germany by the end of the nineteenth century.

In this book we have decided to illustrate the characteristics of Nordic business systems in different periods by two extensive company cases from each country. These companies are not necessarily archetypical for the nations, but they all exemplify important issues of one or more particular phases in the national business system at a particular time.

Analysing capitalism with the 'business systems' concept

Even though early capitalism had its specific national forms, these variations were given little attention. Differences between socialist economic systems and capitalist economic systems were, however, a main theme in many textbooks. Only following the breakdown of communism in the late 1980s has the study of varieties of capitalism been given a more systematic consideration. Alfred D. Chandler, Jr is one of the business historians who has contributed most to our understanding of how capitalist systems vary, primarily between nations. In his book *Scale and Scope*, he conceptualizes capitalism in the US as 'competitive managerial capitalism', in Britain as 'personal capitalism' and in Germany as 'co-operative managerial capitalism'.[10] Inspired by Chandler, the Norwegian historian Francis Sejersted has called Norwegian capitalism 'democratic capitalism'.[11] Democratic capitalism mirrored a high degree of equality and participation within the decision-making processes, in the private, the economic and the political spheres.

While Chandler's different types of national capitalism are based on descriptive characteristics, the 'business system' approach takes a step further and tries to map and explain how capitalist systems work. The business system is a core concept in our book. Systems consist of elements and the relationships between them. In a business system, the main elements are those who make, manage and regulate business: firms, banks, infrastructural operators, consumers, public authorities and organizations such as labour unions and industrial associations. A special focus is given to the co-ordination of transactions and the interaction between them. A business system is a system of co-ordination for economic transactions.

Transaction co-ordination depends on the institutions that make up the structure of business systems. The economic historian Douglass C. North has defined institutions as 'the rules of the game in a society' or, 'the humanly devised constraints that shape human interaction'.[12] As North has stated, the institutions in society can be compared to the rules of the games in a football match. A football match is based on a long series of formal and informal rules, and the game only makes sense because all players are aware of these rules and behave according to them – and if they don't, the referee can punish the illegal act – just as in society. Competition laws, EU directives, technical standards and formal and informal rules for the conduct of negotiations between trade unions and employers' organizations are only a few such institutions in society. Institutions define and limit the set of choices for an individual, or group, but also reduce uncertainty. Institutions are decisive for the relative significance of markets, networks and hierarchies in the co-ordination of transactions between business systems. Differences in the relative significance of these co-ordination mechanisms make up an important distinction between national business systems (see Figure 1.1). Because many of the institutions

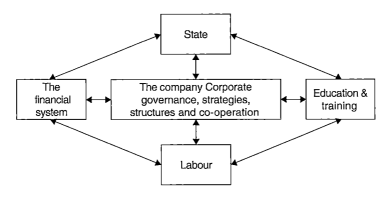

Figure 1.1 **The business systems of the Nordic countries**

that make up the environment of business are created or ratified by the nation-state, national organizations or politics at a national level, business systems are mostly considered as national systems. Nonetheless, there is no a *priori* reason that the most important institutions will always have such a primarily national character. The most internationalized Nordic telecommunication companies, for instance, are probably more dependent on international and global institutions than on national regulation and policy.

Inspired by the British sociologist Richard Whitley, the main contributor to the comparative business system approach, the analysis of the Nordic capitalism in this book builds on four major contextual arenas regarded as important for the structuring of the business system: the state, the financial system, education and training, and the labour market. The core of the business system approach consists of the essential institution in any capitalist economy – the company.

Primarily, Whitley is concerned with the extent to which companies are dependent on a strong, cohesive *state*. He focuses on the states' commitment to industrial and economic development. According to Whitley, states that were established before the industrial revolution – as for instance in Great Britain – have often been less committed to industrial development than states established in line with industrialization. The late-movers Germany and the US are more committed to playing an active role in the industrialization process. The comparative nature of this book makes it possible to unveil differences in the role of the state between the old Nordic countries, Sweden and Denmark, and the younger states Norway (1905) and particularly Finland, which only got its independence in 1917.

The second important arena is the *financial system*. In the continental credit-based financial system, such as in France and Germany and the Nordic countries, the banks have traditionally played a very active role as investors, owners and occasionally board members. For instance, the Finnish banking system resembled the Germanic universal bank system, with the banks being an important source of credit financing, but also an important actor in the entrepreneurial development of Finnish big business through board membership and concrete influence on, for example, mergers and acquisitions (M&As). In the Anglo-Saxon capital market-oriented systems, such as the US and Great Britain, the role of the banks has been more limited, while shareholders and institutional investors have played a larger role in, for instance, corporate structural changes such as M&As.

The third arena – the *education and training system* – concerns the organization and structure of educational institutions and their relation to the labour market. Education plays a key role for companies' recruitment, promotion and organization. As emphasized by the American economic historian, Joel Mokyr, small, open economies in particular rely on investments in human capital, as companies from these countries needs to define niches in which they can be competitive – even on foreign markets and often against larger competitors.[13]

Finally, the fourth contextual aspect in the business system is the *labour market* and the strength of *skill-based trade unions*. The labour market affects the firm's management practices and ways of structuring employment relations. According to Whitley, societies with strong employment and personnel practices are much more homogeneous and standardized, while societies with weak unions are more dependent on the worth of a particular employer than on the collective organization to which the individual belongs.

The state of the Nordic region

The Nordic countries (Denmark, the Faroe Islands, Greenland, Finland, Åland, Iceland, Norway and Sweden) have a combined population of around 25 million compared with nearly 313 million for the twelve Euro countries and nearly 300 million in the US. Despite the dissimilarities in size, the Nordic economies belong to the very richest in the world in terms of *per capita* income. GDP *per capita* in 2005 was €29,300 compared with €24,800 in the twelve Euro countries and €34,800 in the US.[14] Around 1850 – when the analysis in this book begins – the Nordic region was on the economic periphery of Europe, with the centre consisting of early-industrialized countries such as Great Britain, the Netherlands and the German states. The Nordic countries were marked by large unexploited and underdeveloped areas, such as Norrland in Sweden, the long and rough coastline in Norway and the flat and sparsely inhabited interior of Finland. Denmark was the exception – this country was small, densely populated and well connected through trade routes to the important markets in the German states, the Netherlands and Great Britain. In the early capitalist period, Denmark was the only Nordic country that was above or close to the average size of western European *per capita* GDP. Denmark had its industrial breakthrough in the late part of the nineteenth century, while the other Nordic countries had theirs in the early part of the twentieth century.[15] Finland had a fairly strong performance during the inter-war years compared to the rest of western Europe, but the Civil War (1918)

Table 1.1 **GDP per capita (1990 international $): the Nordic countries, UK and western Europe, 1820–2006**

Country	1820	1870	1913	1950	1973	1990	1998	2006[1]
Denmark	1274	2003	3912	6946	13,945	18,463	22,123	24,871
Finland	781	1140	2111	4253	11,085	16,868	18,324	23,191
Norway	1104	1432	2501	5463	11,246	18,470	23,660	27,774
Sweden	1198	1664	3096	6738	13,493	17,680	18,685	23,870
UK	1707	3191	4921	6907	12,022	16,411	18,714	22,933
Western Europe	1270	2086	3688	5013	12,159	16,872	18,742	21,582

Note: 1. www.gdc.net.
Source: Maddison (2001), p. 185.

and the Second World War meant heavy losses for the economy, which makes the growth figures for this period fairly modest. In the tumultuous years of 1913–50 Sweden and Norway had the highest annual growth rates in GDP *per capita* in the western world. As shown in Table 1.2 (p.11), the average annual growth rate was 2.13 per cent in Norway and 2.12 per cent in Sweden in contrast to 0.83 in western Europe, which experienced two world wars during this period. In Denmark, the agricultural sector continued played an important role, while the manufacturing corporations played a key role for the Swedish economy in the first half of the twentieth century. High growth in Sweden was based on a combination of the success of large export-oriented corporations such as L.M. Ericsson, ASEA and Bofors and a rich forest of small- and medium-sized manufacturing enterprises (SMEs). In Norway, growth was based on export and improvement of natural resources such as timber, mineral ores and fish, combined with an extensive commercial fleet. Finland's take-off in the late nineteenth century was also heavily dependent on resource-based industries, particularly forest resources, and their export.[16]

Table 1.1 illustrates the economically peripheral position of the Nordic countries in the period known as the 'second industrial revolution', the late 1800s. Nevertheless, Table 1.1 reveals two interesting characteristics of Nordic development after 1950. First of all the Norwegian development is notable, especially from a GDP *per capita* viewpoint, from being below the western European average in 1973 to one of the highest GDP *per capita* in 2006. This 'Norwegian Miracle' is a direct cause of the successful exploitation of natural resources – particularly the Norwegian oil policy of state-owned oil funds and state-controlled oil companies. Political institutions and decision-making are important in this case. As the experience of some South American and Middle Eastern countries shows, access to oil resources does not automatically lead to

Country	1820–70	1870–1913	1913–50	1950–73	1973–98
Denmark	0.91	1.57	1.56	3.08	1.86
Finland	0.76	1.44	1.91	4.25	2.03
Norway	0.52	1.30	2.13	3.19	3.02
Sweden	0.66	1.46	2.12	3.07	1.31
UK	1.26	1.01	0.92	2.44	1.79
Western Europe	1.00	1.33	0.83	3.93	1.75

Source: Maddison (2001), p. 186.

top performance on a national economic level. Another important lesson from Table 1.1 is that the economic development in the Nordic countries differed. The GDP *per capita* of Finland was below the western European average in all benchmark years from 1814 to 1998, while the Swedish GDP *per capita* was close to, or above, the average since 1950. At the end of the twentieth century, the Nordic countries were four of the richest and most successful countries in Europe, with two countries well above and two countries just below the western European GDP *per capita* average. Additionally, as Table 1.2 shows, three of the four Nordic countries maintained a GDP *per capita* average growth rate above the western European average in the period 1973–98.

The strong economic performance of the Nordic economies in the last decades of the twentieth century was marked by a strong growth in international trade and capital flows. This development took place simultaneously with important international trade agreements such as the European Common Market in 1993, the European Monetary Union in the late 1990s and the various WTO agreements. Traditionally, foreign trade with large powers has been the preferred explanation for the capitalist growth of small- and medium-sized West European countries.[17] Notwithstanding, in more recent research foreign trade has only been regarded as the 'fuel' for the real 'engine' of the economies, namely the essential internal factors. In Denmark, Norway, Sweden and Finland these internal factors also included institutional elements such as the agricultural enclosure reforms – which stimulated urbanization – and the early liberal market reforms in the 1860s and 1870s, which created a domestic market based on private property and the freedom to establish businesses. The role of the educational reforms in the early twentieth century should also be stressed as they resulted in growing general literacy and thus, industrial production and innovation, including inward transfer of foreign technology. Finnish basic education also developed in the late nineteenth century, but a general, compulsory primary education lasting six years did not take root until 1921. This did not mean that all the children went to school for six years. Particularly in the countryside the length of school attendance were often shorter. However, the educational level rose gradually after the declaration of independence in 1917, although the development clearly occurred later than in the other Nordic countries.

Our assumption that capitalism in the Nordic countries was based on internal institutional factors fuelled by international trade is reflected in the structure of this book. The four country chapters on Sweden, Finland, Denmark and Norway (Chapters 2, 5, 8 and 11) include important political, cultural, legal and economic institutional factors while the essential 'fuel' of a capitalist economy, namely the company and its trade and technological innovation, is included and elucidated via the eight company cases.

History and the 'formative' periods of change

So far, this book has treated business systems as if they were rather stable phenomena – with no reference to time. And indeed the business system approach has been criticized for not taking change seriously enough and certainly not from a historian's point of view.[18] No matter which business system approach we use, we must look to the past for its origins. It is implicit that some formative periods in the past, when the main structure of the business system was set, must have had a lasting influence. Formative periods are periods of change when the development of a business system takes a new direction; it is a time of crossroads, where there could have been multiple possible outcomes. Formative periods are important time-arenas for strategic economic and political decisions. The business system structure developed in a formative period could have a long life. Formative periods create institutional 'lock-ins' or path dependence, and are usually followed by more stable periods.[19]

Formative periods are often the combined result of internal and external pressures acting on the established economic structure. Wars, economic and political crises, or occupation by foreign powers are examples of challenges to established orders that demand economic and political responses. Such responses may have lasting imprints on a national business system. The Allied occupation of Japan after the Second World War had some significant effects on the Japanese business system, even if the result was far from what the Americans had aimed for. On the other hand, the Japanese occupation of Korea has definitely had an impact on the South Korean business system. Some business system characteristics are connected to pre-industrial periods. The lack of any heavy pre-capitalist societal organization in the Nordic countries may explain some of the differences between the four countries and part of the European continent – that is, the more egalitarian values connected to the social democratic aspects of the business systems.

Our intention is to combine the 'business system model' and 'formative periods' perspectives. We might accept that modern Nordic business systems of today could be classified as co-ordinated market economies. We might also accept that within this class of business system they are what Whitley calls 'collaborative business systems' and the regulation school calls 'social democratic business systems'. But we want to show how the system characteristics were formed, to identify the formative periods of the four Nordic business systems. And since history matters, what sort of economic organization preceded the co-ordinated market economy, or the collaborative model, or the social democratic model? For some period of time, the business systems of the Nordic countries were closer to the liberal market economy than today, and the whole establishment of a liberal, industrial-based market economy has a history of its own in the four countries.

To describe and explain how Nordic business systems, through different paths, developed some important common traits is, however, only one of the aims of this book. We are just as eager to show the significant differences between our four business systems, to show the different paths and time periods in which these business systems developed. Only with this historic and dynamic approach can we understand how the Nordic capitalism evolved.

Dealing with change: three industrial revolutions, five 'Kondratiev waves', or economic evolution?

This book is about the development of capitalism in the Nordic countries from approximately 1850 to 2000. The development in these 150 years was obviously a very complex process, with innumerable actors, events and facts. Historians make order out of historical facts through periodization, and in economic and business history one of the most used periodizations is the distinction between the first, second and third industrial revolutions. The 'revolution' metaphor is rather misleading: there is no economic equivalent to the French revolution in 1789 or the Russian revolution in 1917. Economies developed through a gradual, slow-moving and highly complex process. On the other hand the total outcome of this process was rather revolutionary. The creation of the first machine-based industries – and later human societies – substituted inanimate for animate sources of power. One steam-driven train could transport more goods than hundreds of packhorses, one textile factory based on a division of labour was 100-fold more efficient than the previous home-based production while the telegraph even in the 1860s made it possible to communicate transcontinentally in real time. According to the British historian, Paul Kennedy, these changes were just as fundamental as the transformation of savage Palaeolithic hunting people to domesticated Neolithic farming people.[20]

The characteristics of the three industrial revolutions can be divided in three categories: chronology and geography, industrial processes and typical new products.

The first industrial revolution began in the 1780s. It was lead by Great Britain with the Netherlands, France and the German-speaking regions following. The first factory-based mechanization of production was introduced, particularly in the cotton and pottery industries. In 1831 the first railway between Manchester and Liverpool was opened and along with steam ships these new technologies transformed the infrastructure of western societies in the following decades.

The second industrial revolution took off in the 1880s with Germany and the US as the leading countries of science-based mass production. The most important principles were mass production, mass distribution and mass marketing. These phenomena were made possible by a combination of new technologies based upon the invention of electricity and the gasoline-powered engine and new large organizations. 'Big business' appeared, including the need for professional managers – and thus business schools. The third industrial revolution, very much based on information and communication technology (ICT), began in the 1970s. The most important new aspect was probably the IT-based new internet-related infrastructure and the new production methods based upon microprocessors. These new technologies changed almost any advanced organization often towards more decentralization, outsourcing and network-based relations.

The industrial revolutions provide a helpful overview but do not explain how and why each different industrial revolution emerged, developed and disappeared. Another type of periodization, which tries to conceptualize economic development, is the five 'Kondratiev waves'.[21] According to the techno-economic 'Kondratiev wave' theory the economic development in

Table 1.3 The five "Kondratiev waves" 1870–1973

The paradigm	Core industries	Infrastructure	New organizations	Time (Up-down-swing)	Place
1. Water-powered mechanization of industry	Cotton spinning Textiles Iron products	Canals Turnpike roads Sailing ships	Factory systems Partnerships	1780–1815 1815–48	GB
2. Steam-powered mechanization of industry & transport	Railways Steam engines Machine tools Electrical equip.	Railways Telegraph Steam ships	Joint stock companies Subcontracting to craft workers	1848–73 1873–95	GB US Ger
3. Electrification of industry, transport and the home	Heavy engineering Heavy chemicals Steel products Automobiles	Steel railways Steel ships Telephone	Professional management 'Taylorism' Giant firms	1895–1918 1918–40	US Eur
4. Motorization of transport, civil economy and war	Trucks and tractors Diesel engines Aircraft Refineries Computers	Radio Motorways Airports Airlines	Mass production and consumption 'Fordism' Giant firms	1941–73 1973	US Jap Eur
5. Computerization of entire economy	Software Telecoms. Biotechnology	'Information highways' Internet	Networks–internal, local and global		US China EU

Source: Freeman and Louçã (2001), p. 141.

industrialized societies has followed a wave-like movement in which different technical and organizational paradigms have succeeded each other.[22] Each technical and organizational paradigm has an upswing and a downswing, and in the centre of these paradigms we find a specific technology, new type of infrastructure, and one or a few new core industries and new types of organizations. The first wave is labelled the 'water-powered mechanization' of industry, it was primarily a British phenomenon and its upswing was from the 1780s to 1815 and the downswing from 1815 to 1848. This wave was based on improvements in water-powered technology, which made it possible to introduce water power on a large scale in industrial production particular in the British textile industry. The dynamic in the model consists of the idea that each old paradigm is being challenged by the new succeeding one. Water-powered production was then challenged by steam-powered technology in the mid-nineteenth century. Later on, steam power was replaced by electrification, etc. Old technologies and infrastructures do not necessarily disappear (railways and electricity still exist) but the dynamic in the societies is the new technological paradigms which established new types of work, companies, etc. and also changed the old companies and their way of organizing themselves (Table 1.3).

Alfred D. Chandler, Jr once wrote: 'a historian's task is not merely to borrow other people's theories or even to test their theories for them. It is to use existing concepts and models to explore the data he has collected in order to answer his own particular questions and concerns.'[23] We will not use this book to test the idea of three industrial revolutions or the techno-economic revolution in relation to the Nordic countries. We use these chronological categories only to place the development of the Nordic countries' economies and business systems in a larger context. In this way, these concepts may help our understanding of the particular national development of capitalism in the Nordic countries.

Structure of the book
This book intends to explain how the Nordic capitalist systems could historically bridge two apparently conflicting situations, namely, the expensive welfare systems and highly competitive economies. The explanation is posited on three fundamental assumptions:

- The Nordic countries have a number of common characteristics, which make it possible to speak of a 'Nordic model of capitalism'.

- The company is the core institution of capitalism. The company should be analysed in the context of the surrounding societies – that is, as an essential part of the broad business systems.
- The content and construction of Nordic capitalism can be understood only through a historical understanding of how different parts of the capitalist systems developed over time.

The four country chapters describe and analyse the capitalist development of, respectively, Denmark, Sweden, Norway and Finland in the 150 years from 1850 to 2000. Each country chapter touches upon the particular aspects of the business systems that we find in the different nations in different periods: companies and the contextual factors in terms of the state, the financial system, education and training and the labour market. In each country chapter we will define specific time periods and the formative periods that shaped the business systems.

As we believe that companies and entrepreneurs were essential to the capitalist development in the Nordic countries, we give case studies a key role in this book. Each country chapter will be followed by two case studies. Even if we have not been able to mirror all important aspects of the national business systems, these cases mirror and explain some important characteristics of each system. It would hard to explain the development of Danish capitalism without reference to the agricultural sector. The dairy company, Arla (Chapter 9), reflects a self-understanding from within the agricultural sector based on terms such as 'democratic' management, co-operative ownership and a distinct contrast to industrial urbanization. In the Finnish case, the large role of the forest industry, particularly the pulp and paper industry, obviously makes the selection of Stora-Enso (Chapter 6) as a case study quite natural. The Finnish business system and the economic policy was during the most of the twentieth century until today, organized in order to secure a favourable working environment for the large-scale export industry, a feature we will develop further in the country chapter. The Swedish case of Wallenberg (Chapter 3) on the other hand, reflects the political, economical and cultural power of a Swedish industrial dynasty, while the development of Norwegian capitalism would be difficult to understand without an analysis of the relationship between the Norwegian state and crucial resource-based industries such as Elkem (Chapter 12).

The title of the book consists of three key concepts: 'Creating', 'Nordic' and 'Capitalism'. 'Creating' refers to the importance of history and the importance of understanding change. 'Nordic' is the geographical focus of the book, while

'Capitalism' is regarded as the national economic system and thus the subject and essential focus of the book. In the preceding sections we have defined these three keywords in depth and thus prepared the reader for a journey through more than 150 years of capitalism in the world's most competitive and egalitarian periphery.

Notes

1. An illustrative example can be found in Thomas K. McCraw's biography of Joseph Schumpeter. McCraw mentions the world's most well-known innovative twenty-first-century companies: Microsoft, IKEA, Nokia, and Google, two of which two have origins in the relatively small Nordic region (McCraw, 2007, p. 179).
2. *Global Competitiveness Report 2005–2006*: Interview with Lopez Claros Augusto, September 29 2005.
3. Lindert (2004).
4. Marklund (1988)
5. Francis Sejersted has described the Nordic capitalist systems as a particular type of 'democratic capitalism', see n. 11.
6. Friedman (2002), p. 10.
7. Schumpeter, (1939), pp. 90, 1033.
8. Micklewait and Wooldridge, (2001), p xv.
9. Met Blair (1995), and Kelly *et al.* (1997).
10. Chandler, Jr (1990), p. 59.
11. Sejersted (1993), p. 269.
12. North (1990), p. 208.
13. Mokyr (2006).
14. *Nordic Statistical Yearbook 2006*, Nordic Council of Ministers.
15. Krantz in Kryger-Larsen (2001), p. 40.
16. Kryger-Larsen (2001).
17. Kryger-Larsen (2001), p. 12.
18. Morgan *et al.* (2005), pp. 3–4.
19. David (1986).
20. Kennedy (1988), p. 186.
21. See Freeman and Louçã (2001) for a comprehensive introduction to 'Kondratiev waves'.
22. Freeman and Louçã (2001).
23. Chandler (1971), p. 305.

References

Blair, M., *Ownership and Control: Rethinking Corporate Governance of the Twenty-First Century* (Washington, DC: Brookings Institution, 1995).

Chandler, A. D. Jr, 'Business History as Institutional History', in Rogers Taylor, G. and Ellsworth, L. F. (eds), *Approaches to American Economic History* (Charlotsville, VA: University Press of Virginia for the Eleutherian Mills–Hagley Foundation, 1971).

Chandler, A. D. Jr, *Scale and Scope: The Dynamics of Industrial Capitalism* (London: The Belknap Press, 1990).

David, P. A., 'Understanding the Economics of QWERTY', in Parker, William N, *Economic History and the Modern Economist* (Oxford: Basil Blackwell 1986).

Freeman, C. and Louçã, F., *As Time Goes By: From the Industrial Revolutions to the Information Revolution* (New York: Oxford University Press, 2001).

Friedman, M., *Capitalism and Freedom* (Chicago: University of Chicago Press, 40th Anniversary Edition, 2002).

Kelly, G., Kelly, D. and Gamble A, *Stakeholder Capitalism* (Basingstoke: Macmillan, 1997).

Kennedy, P., *The Rise and Fall of the Great Powers: Economic Change and Military Conflicts from 1500 to 2000* (London: Fontana, 1988).

Krantz, O. 'Industrialisation in Three Nordic Countries: A Long-term perspective', in Hans Kryger Larsen (ed.), *Convergence? Aspects of the Industrialisation of Denmark, Finland and Sweden 1870–1940* (Helsinki: Finska Vetenskaps-Societeten (Suomen Tiedeseura), 2001).

Kryger Larsen, H. (ed.), *Convergence? Aspects of the Industralisation of Denmark, Finland and Sweden 1870–1940* (Helsinki: Finska Vetenskaps-Societeten (Suomen Tiedeseura), 2001).

Lindert, P. H., *Growing Public: Social Spending and Economic Growth Since the Eighteenth Century* (Cambridge: Cambridge University Press, 2004).

Maddison, A., *The World Economy: A Millennial Perspective* (Washington, DC: Brookings Institution, 2001), pp. 185, 186, www.ggdc.net.

Marklund, S., *Paradise Lost?: The Nordic Welfare States and the Recession, 1975–1985* (Lund: Arkiv forlag, 1988).

McCraw, T., *Creating Modern Capitalism: How Entrepreneurs, Companies and Countries Triumphed in Three Industrial Revolutions* (Cambridge, MAC Harvard University Press).

Micklewait, J. and Wooldridge, A., *The Company* (New York: Modern Library, 2001).

Mokyr, J., 'Successful Small Open Economies and the Importance of Good Institutions', in Ojala, J., Eloranta, J. and Jalava, J. (eds), *The Road to Prosperity: An Economic History of Finland* (Helsinki: Suomalaisen Kirjallisuuden Seura, 2006).

Morgan, G., Whitley, R. and Moen, E., *Changing Capitalisms? Internationalization, Institutional Change, and Systems of Economic Organization* (Oxford: Oxford University Press, 2005).

North, D., *Institutions, Institutional Change and Economic Performance* (Cambridge: Cambridge University Press, 1990).

Schumpeter, J., A, *Business Cycles: A Theoretical, Historical, and Statistical Analysis of the Capitalist Process. Vol.II* (New York: McGraw-Hill, 1939).

Sejersted, F., *Demokratisk Kapitalisme* (Oslo: Universitetsforlaget, 1993).

Whitley, R., *European Business Systems: Firms and Markets in their National Contexts* (London: Sage, 1992).

prologue to the Swedish chapter

We start this journey by analysing the factors behind welfare capitalism in Sweden. The development has not been straightforward, but there are some elements that make it possible to talk about continuity back to the mid nineteenth century, where certain social–liberal institutions re-shaped business and society. Naturally, Sweden has a lot in common with other small European economies, such as the Netherlands and Switzerland, in terms of cultural orientation, number of MNCs and type of governance. However, a geographical location in the periphery of Europe brings about both advantages and disadvantages – for example, vast natural resources but high transportation costs. The country chapter will also show how firms have been clustered in certain capital-intensive industries, where they have played the same role as in larger economies.

Sweden was once admired by many experts for a constructive, smooth combination of private and public resources, including a labour market with nearly no strikes at all. In fact, this middle way, balancing between socialism and capitalism by taking the best from both regimes, was for a long time seen as ideal model for democratic capitalism. The country chapter (Chapter 2) describes what happened after the golden age, when the land of milk and honey was hit by several structural crises. Finally, the Swedish story is a good example of the capacity of a state to adapt to a changing environment, re-shape the institutions and support new types of businesses. Thus, this country chapter provides us with an insight into the linkages between creative destruction, flexibility of institutions and internationalization processes, all captured in the on-going transformation of the business system.

The case chapter on Bonnier and Wallenberg (Chapter 3) treats two types of family capitalism. We often think of family firms as small- and medium-sized. Another view is that mature industrial firms are owned and governed by large institutions or more or less anonymous and dispersed owners. This is, of course, not true. Sweden is the country of origin for many international large family firms operating in a wide range of sectors – for example, Tetra Pak, IKEA and Hennes & Mauritz. The Wallenberg group is also a good example of traditional family-based ownership that still plays a role in international business. While the active long-term minority-based ownership in the Wallenberg group ranges over many different industrial and service sectors, the holdings by the Bonnier group are both wholly owned and concentrated on just one sector, the media sector. These two contrasted types of co-ordination of family activities, in the fifth and sixth generations from the founder, give us an excellent view on how family values can be used to build strong entrepreneurship and take the lead in the transformation of business.

In the country chapter you will see that one reason behind the success of Swedish welfare capitalism is the many MNCs in the forefront of new technology, which has guaranteed a high level of employment, new skills and economic performance. The case of ASEA (Chapter 4), stemming from the inventions of Jonas Wenström and continuously thriving on new innovations in electro-mechanics, is chosen to illustrate this common track in Swedish business history. Since the domestic market is small, all these technology-based companies became internationalized very early. ASEA is good example of an MNC, internationalized almost from its inception, evolving through a spectacular merger in 1988 into a globally active MNC, namely Asea Brown Boveri, ABB. The case on ASEA/ABB illustrates how managerial, strategic and organizational capabilities can be created both endogenously and in interaction with the socio-economic context and, not least, how state-owned and private companies in Sweden very often have collaborated in large-scale investments and successful innovations.

WELFARE CAPITALISM: THE SWEDISH ECONOMY 1850–2005 ● ENTREPRENEURSHIP AND OWNERSHIP: THE
LONG-TERM VIABILITY OF THE SWEDISH BONNIER AND WALLENBERG FAMILY BUSINESS GROUPS ● FROM
ENTREPRENEURSHIP TO MANAGERIAL INCREMENTALISM: THE SWEDISH INVESTMENT FINNISH
CAPITALISM, 1850S–2005 ● FROM STATE OWNERSHIP TO MULTINATIONAL CORPORATION: THE PATH OF
ENSO-GUTZEIT TO STORA-ENSO ● BUILDING AND TAKING A CONGLOMERATE FIRM: THE STRATEGIC
PATHS OF NOKIA AND TAMPELLA IN THE LIBERALIZING FINNISH ECONOMY AFTER THE SECOND WORLD
WAR ● CO-OPERATIVE LIBERALISM: DENMARK FROM 1857 TO 2007 ● ARLA – FROM DECENTRALIZED INDUSTRY
TO MULTINATIONAL ENTERPRISE ● CARLSBERG AND THE SELF-REGULATION OF THE DANISH BEER MARKET
● NORWAY: A RESOURCE-BASED AND DEMOCRATIC CAPITALISM ● CONSTRUCTIVE POWER: ELKEM 1904–2004
● FINANCE AND THE DEVELOPMENT OF NORWEGIAN CAPITALISM – THE CASE OF CHRISTIANIA BANK

2

welfare capitalism: the Swedish economy, 1850–2005

Hans Sjögren

Introduction

Sweden has a reputation of being a highly industrialized country with an extensive welfare system. This apparently modern phenomenon has deep roots, however, and current economic performance is to a large extent still based on innovations emanating from the industrial take-off in the late nineteenth and early twentieth century. Traditionally, Sweden has been the home of resource-based and capital-intensive industries – for example, mining, forest industries and metal industries – with strong representatives such as Grängesberg, LKAB, SCA and Stora Kopparberg. Some of the manufacturing firms from this period, such as AGA, Alfa-Laval, ASEA, Ericsson and SKF, rapidly reached a prominent position in the world market. Later on, the business system was enlarged by multinationals as Astra, Tetra-Pak, IKEA and Hennes & Mauritz, reflecting a continuously high rate of innovation in emerging markets. In an international perspective, considering the size of Sweden's population and economy, the proportion of large MNCs is unique. There is no single cause for this development and this chapter will discuss the institutional, economic and technical factors behind Sweden's wealth today.

Another key feature of Swedish welfare capitalism has been the balancing of capitalism and socialism, a middle way sometimes labelled the 'Swedish model'.[2] Concepts such as corporatism, compromise thinking, consensual democracy, low corruption, high taxes and an egalitarian spirit are often associated with the Swedish type of welfare economy. Another characteristic is close co-operation between government, trade unions, commercial banks and business elites. This indicates an active modern state, but also a national culture that has roots in early agrarian society (peasant proprietors instead of a feudal system). The choice of the 'middle way' has had an impact on all parts of the business system. The financial system may be characterized as a control- or bank-oriented one, while the labour market has been heavily regulated and the education and training system has been adjusted to political and economic goals.

The welfare capitalism we see today is a result of path dependency and co-existing historical layers, as successive institutional and techno-economic regimes have been put on to the original platform. Institutionally the welfare capitalism in the mid-nineteenth century was based on liberal principles, which remained an under-layer when social democratic policies and a regulated economy appeared in the mid-1930s, a regime that began to dominate after the Second World War. From the 1980s, a neo-liberal regime was established as a new institutional layer on top of the two former ones. Viewing the techno-economical side, welfare capitalism underwent – as in most western countries – a structural transformation from an agricultural society to an industrial one, which has recently been transformed to a service society. These layers correspond to two waves of globalization, the first from 1880 to 1929, followed by a period of disintegration and protectionism, which in the late 1970s turned into a new wave of globalization.[3]

The chapter is divided in four sub-chapters, reflecting four more or less distinctive periods in the transformation of the Swedish economy and business system from 1850 to 2005. Every period is distinguished by a certain institutional setting, economic structure and economic performance. The point of departure for every period is a change of institutions and technology that alters the possibilities for doing business. This has been referred to in Chapter 1 as a 'formative phase'. The direction of the institutional change reflects both the demand-side and supply-side of the economy, while the techno-economic paradigm that follows exploits the commercial possibilities created by the institutional change. Consequently, the change in the business system is seen as a combination of more or less simultaneous technical push, economic needs and political movement. The formative phase is followed by a sub-period characterized by institutional stability and economic rationalization, when the new political and business setting makes use of the new technological paradigm. There have been four main periods:

- Liberalism and early industrialization within agricultural society, 1850–90 – the foundation era
- Industrial society and financial capitalism, 1890–1935

- The Swedish model, mature industries and welfare economy, 1935–1975
- Neo-liberalism and internationalization within the service society, 1975–2005.

At the core of the analysis are the economic and business structures, including the Swedish companies' strategies, governance structures and various co-operative networks. The many variations and particularities of Swedish modern capitalism are difficult to cover in just one chapter: this chapter will highlight only the key features of every period. This is somewhat compensated, however, by the two case studies that follow, where ownership principles in family-controlled MNCs and changing management systems in the electricity company ASEA are treated. Both case studies also highlight the strong entrepreneurial leadership that has been a hallmark of the Swedish business system and a contributing factor to high economic growth.

Liberalism and early industrialization within agricultural society 1850–90 – the foundation era

The chronological description starts here, but we should keep in mind that the business system, and even the welfare capitalism of Sweden, has roots back to the medieval age. Thus, Swedish multinational firms grew out of the existence of the continuous exploitation of natural resources, primarily iron ore and forest products. Productivity steadily increased thanks to mechanization and water power. Stora Kopparberg in Dalacarlia is said to be the oldest company in the world still operating. Its history goes back to 1288, when Bishop Peter acquired one-eighth of the Kopparberg Mountain. The Deed of Exchange was signed by a large number of prominent people, including King Magnus Ladulås. The enterprise was extended in 1347 with a Royal Charter, one of the oldest surviving royal charters written in Swedish, issued after King Magnus Eriksson had visited the copper mine. At the beginning of the sixteenth century, all chambers of the mine were being operated, but it was not until the seventeenth century that it became systematically exploited. King Karl IX emulated German methods in an attempt to create a model mine in terms of technology and organization. In many mines at this time in Sweden, Walloon and Dutch entrepreneurs introduced advanced techniques, which put them in better shape than ever before. In 1650, more than 3,000 tonnes of raw copper were produced in Dalacarlia. Excavation continued day and night and the mine went deeper and deeper. Sweden's total export of iron rose from about 6,000 tons in 1620 to more than 30,000 tonnes at the end of the century, leaving Sweden with probably the largest iron industry in Europe at that time.

The early story of Stora Kopparberg and the Swedish mining industry gives a representative picture of what continue to be cornerstones of the business system. The supply of natural resources absorbed both local and international entrepreneurs, encouraged export-related firms and gave incentives for the state to found technical schools for fostering further innovation processes. The institutional creation of business-relevant human capital, resulting in the highest literacy in the world, was effectively combined with knowledge transfer from abroad, mainly Germany. The skills for building large enterprises and implementing hierarchical organizations were taken from the nobility, who had centuries of experience of military operations in Europe. Such management and strategy skills, together with the factors above, were enough to piggyback on the UK, Germany and the US in the second industrial revolution.

The formative phase that began in the mid-nineteenth century was characterized by liberal reforms, railways, export trade and strong mechanization. It was a parallel process, as politics and institutions changed at the same time as industrialization and economic growth geared up. The transformation was driven by domestic and international factors. On the supply side, agricultural society reached its climax and high labour productivity led to a surplus of labour for emerging factories to absorb. On the demand side, domestic markets for various mechanical products grew as workers' wages increased. Internationally, continued industrialization in combination with free trade treaties in Europe led to increasing Swedish exports of raw material and mechanical products.

Increasing foreign trade and market integration in Europe were underpinned by a liberalization of the key institutions of business life. A modernization of the public sector also took place, with new reforms for municipalities and the state. A new banking system was born that paved the way for a stronger industrialization. Part of the institutional change was directly related to the construction of railways and was introduced to encourage the state and private financiers to raise the necessary investment capital. The railways had a central role in the expansion of export trade, carrying products from saw mills and iron mills to the nearest harbour for further transport by sea to the rest of Europe.

These changes, though, still took place within agricultural society. In terms of employment and economic value, agriculture was still the dominant sector, and industrial production still took place in the countryside or in small cities. To a large extent, industry was focused on certain raw materials, such as timber and iron in the case of the export-oriented industry. The dependence on raw materials also meant that energy sources and labour were concentrated in the countryside. Thus, the period 1850–90 did not mean a radical break in relation to agricultural society. However, it was an irreversible evolutionary process that led to a general industrial breakthrough and made the establishment of industrial cities possible later on.

Political economy and institutional change

A cornerstone in the wave of liberalistic reforms was the abolition of the guild system in 1846. This was followed in 1864 with a reform of the general freedom of trade, which enabled Sweden to take advantage of international market integration. The government of 1856–8 exempted various agricultural products from duty and lowered the duty rate on many consumer products. At the same time, the remaining prohibitions on imports and exports were lifted.[4] The education system had been reformed in 1842 with the introduction of a compulsory six years of schooling. However, Sweden had already an internationally high adult literacy rate and in many economically advanced regions – for example Skåne and Bergslagen – education being provided to the majority of children long before 1842. Thus, the new system should be seen more as a codification than a radical reform. The high adult literacy rate had other implications for Swedish society, not least at economically. It made the general public capable of absorbing and communicating new ideas, which speeded up the process of technical and organizational innovations in society. There were no restrictions on capital, but nevertheless, the adoption of the gold standard and the establishment of a Scandinavian Currency Union in 1873 lent stability to the flow of financial transactions and gave international trade an extra push. So, by the mid-1870s there was thus free movement of labour, goods and services and capital, both within the country and across its borders.

The business system was renewed with the Company Act in 1848, enabling companies with share capital and limited liability for shareholders to operate in the market. The new institution opened up possibilities for private organizations to raise capital on a large scale and to take part in the industrialization process. Many old companies were converted to joint stock companies, but new ones also registered as a consequence. From the late 1860s to the mid-1890s, about 200 new joint stock companies were founded every year, with the exception of the years around the 1878–9 banking crisis (see p. 33). The majority of the new firms were industrial, while transport and trade firms together represented a third of all new establishments.[5] The joint stock companies lent emphasis to the element of property rights in the economy and gave entrepreneurs a strong incentive to pursue their commercial ideas on a long-term basis. However, for infrastructure investments it was not always enough to co-ordinate private capital. In the case of new technical systems such as railways, telegraph and gas, the involvement of the state was a prerequisite for large investments as well as for the running of the system. Infrastructure projects in relation to urbanization, such as roads, water supply and drains, also depended on the activities and resources of the public sector.

Railways and early industrialization

After some less successful private attempts to build railways, the government took full responsibility in the 1850s for a national network of so-called trunk lines. The private lines took their place inside the national network and had their routes and operations adjusted to the interests of public railway policy. Colonel Nils Ericson, with experience from an earlier infrastructural project – a waterway through Sweden (the Göta Kanal) – became the chief designer of the new transport system. He was supported by the finance minister Johan August Gripenstedt, who convinced his colleagues in the cabinet to pursue the project. Certain policy factors guided the construction of the network: the possibility of connecting various regions of Sweden; support for reclamation in poor areas and thereby an increase in the value of land; and the need to link Stockholm with other commercial and industrial districts in Sweden.

The national railway network included direct lines between Stockholm and the three main industrial and commercial districts – Göteborg, Malmö and Norrköping. Along the lines, new cities emerged that successively attracted viable craft, industry and services. Thus, the new transport system provided regional commercial vitality, which made it important for entrepreneurs and local government officers in cities placed in the shadow of the main railways to invest in branch lines connected to the new rail artery. Private railways were a specially important complement in regions with heavy transport needs, for example dairy goods in Skåne, products from mines and sawmills in Bergslagen and Göteborg and mechanical products from Västerås and Stockholm. In the latter case, the development of new railways was prolific in the 1870s and contributed significantly to giving this part of Sweden a prominent position economically and culturally.

A prerequisite for the new transport system was financial capital: a sparsely populated country with long distances between cities implied substantial investment. In a European perspective, the costs of constructing nationwide railways were relatively high in a sparsely populated and far-flung country such as Sweden. Since domestic financial resources were too small to cover these costs, the state decided to issue bonds on the international market. In 1857, the National Debt Office placed the first international railway loan, in Germany, and from the 1860s the state co-operated on this matter with private commercial banks. Since the foreign capital was placed as deposits in the banking system, the private banks began to expand on the credit market and make revenues on the interest market. This capital import continued to play a key role in Swedish investments until the early twentieth century – in 1913 Sweden had the highest foreign debt/*per capita* rate in the world.

Mechanization, export trade, the working class and product innovation

The industrial transformation from the 1850s onwards meant both a higher degree of mechanization and larger industrial organizations than before. Steam engines and water turbines became the heart of the power system that provided growing factories with energy. Energy consumption in industry multiplied in terms of horsepower. Thus, early industrialization also implied a technical shift in production (Table 2.1).

Of the export industries, sawmills grew most and became the leading processing industry from 1850 to 1890, with an annual growth rate of 5.4 per cent (fixed prices). At the same time, the forestry industry became highly important for the agricultural sector. The paper industry had an annual growth in 1870–90 of 8.4 per cent, while the pulp industry reached an annual growth rate of over 15 per cent during the same period. The iron industry also underwent technological change, with new processes and concentration of production in larger units. However, since this transformation was relatively slow, the iron industry fell back *vis-à-vis* total industrial production. By the end of the period, there were some examples of natural resource-based export, primarily within the pulp and paper industry and the dairy industry. On the expanding domestic market, certain fast-growing industries were noticeable, such as cotton mills, match factories and chemical–technical factories, with annual growth rates in 1850–90 of 8 per cent, 11 per cent and 13 per cent, respectively. During later decades joinery shops, glass factories, porcelain factories and sugar mills entered to this segment. In fact, food,

Sector	1850–60	1860–70
Industry excl. handicraft	4.0	3.3
Export of industrial goods	3.8	8.3

Source: Schön (2000), p. 168.

beverage and tobacco industries, including flour mills, breweries, distilleries and tobacco factories, represented a large part of total industrial production.

Demographic changes were considerable. A wave of emigrants had started before 1850, but grew in later decades. Between 1850 and 1930, about 1.15 million Swedish people emigrated, most of them to the US. The peak of emigration was reached in the 1880s. Some of the emigrants returned home, but a majority chose to stay. Many were young industrious people and came from agriculturally poor areas, mostly Småland and Värmland. Considering that the total population in 1850 was 3.5 million inhabitants, this emigration had a large impact on society. Even those who choose to stay received higher living standards and real wages, since fewer people had to share food and other resources.

Around the emerging factories, a new social class was formed, consisting of people more or less dependent on industrial work. In the early 1850s, the number of people working in factories, at various mills and with handicrafts was close to 100,000. By the 1870s, this group had increased to about 140,000. To these numbers should be added further thousands of people relying on seasonal industrial activity. During the 1870s and 1880s, the number of workers grew rapidly and in 1890 the total number of industrial workers was estimated to be 320,000. From the 1870s, the industry generally became more specialized because of a higher degree of mechanization.

As urbanization took off, seasonal occupations more or less faded away in the labour market. As a consequence, the structure of the working class became more homogeneous, as new industrial workers were recruited directly from the families of existing workers. In the 1890s industrial workers could be viewed as one distinctive social group in society. To strengthen socialistic ideas, increase salaries and implement collective agreement on the labour market, workers formed the Swedish Confederation of Trade Unions (Landsorganizationen, LO) in 1898. Employers responded in 1902 with the foundation of Swedish Employers' Confederation (Svenska Arbetsgivareföreningen, SAF).

The growth and modernization of export industries, continuous positive trade conditions within agriculture and the expansion of railways gradually created a strong mechanical industry. Engineering became one of the most expansive industries in the early industrialization and some of the innovations from the 1870s and the 1880s established a platform for the later general industrial break-through. Three examples of such product innovations are the dairy separator, the telephone and electricity transmission. The function of the separator was to mechanically separate milk from cream and the consumption of dairy products guaranteed growing markets. The inventor Gustaf de Laval and the risk capitalist Oscar Lamm experienced a large commercial success for their product in Northern Europe and in the US.[6] Another inventor was Lars Magnus Ericsson, who started production of telephones in 1878, which were the origin of a 'development bloc' around the telecommunication industry and the success story of the world-wide company Ericsson. In both cases, there were strong international influences, mostly from Germany and the US, behind the product development, reflecting the chronology of the industrialization process in the Western world. The third example is Allmänna Svenska Elektriska Aktiebolaget (ASEA). Thanks to inventions within electricity transmission, ASEA provided Swedish industry with modern power plants and effective electrification of machines. In both ASEA and Ericsson, the state played a decisive role in product development by ordering certain technical systems through its public affiliates Vattenfall and Televerket, a combination of private and public actions sometimes called 'technological procurement'.

This general expansion was temporarily interrupted in the late 1870s by a financial crisis and railway bond crisis in 1878–9. The crisis started when revenues from the earlier export of iron ore to England disappeared; England had increased its own production and no longer required large imports of iron ore. The result was a fall in price and a crisis for assets in Sweden associated with iron. Large investments had been made in areas that failed to be profitable in a short-term perspective. The crisis symbolized a turning-point and marked an end to optimistic investments in infrastructure and natural resource-based areas that had carried the early industrialization since the 1850s, and it was followed by consolidations and rationalization in the 1880s, in line with the European pattern. At the same time, there were clear indications of new powers of growth, less dependent on natural resources and more focused on industrial technology than previously.

Foundation of a modern financial system

Technical progress often goes hand in hand with financial innovation. Therefore, not surprisingly, the growth of new industries with higher grain and timber export prompted the need for a more effective credit market. So far, the financial system had been the National Bank of Sweden, founded in 1668, and savings banks and mortgage institutes, created in the 1820s and 1830s, respectively. In the formative phase 1850–70, this was complemented with commercial banking, which fuelled the credit market. The prototype was the Scottish system, concentrated on bill discounting and short-term lending, attracting mainly liquid and short-term deposits. In both Scotland and Sweden, commercial banks were organized as joint stock banks with unlimited liability for all shareholders. In both countries they worked with both note issues and deposit acquisition as basis for lending. Owing to a less developed deposit market in Sweden, however, note issuing became more important to Swedish *enskilda* banks than to their Scottish counterparts.

In the beginning, both the National Bank of Sweden and influential private moneylenders in Stockholm – the capital and hub of Swedish commercial life – fiercely opposed new banking establishments in the Swedish capital. Finally, in 1856, Stockholms Enskilda Bank (SEB) was established, and soon became a trendsetter in operational respects.[7] Though the new bank was an ordinary *enskilda* bank chartered with the privilege of note issue, it managed to capture a large part of the Stockholm deposit market by introducing new instruments for deposit. For the first time the operations of a Swedish bank were largely based on stockholders' equity and deposits from the general public. Moreover, the new bank introduced innovative ways to manage real and efficient payment transfers within the economy. The regional *enskilda* banks were allowed to open free-of-charge transfer accounts in SEB. A network of commercial banks was built up which brought distant regions together into a national system for clearing and paying, making possible transfers from surplus to deficit regions. In the 1860s, extensive branch banking further stimulated this process of integration. The development of financial intermediation and various systems for transferring payments and credits was a natural development due to an underdeveloped financial infrastructure and the need for transactions in a growing economy.

In a situation of shortage of legal tender and credits, the issuing of *enskilda* bank notes replaced earlier promissory notes and filled a gap on the currency market, rather than competing with the function of the central bank.

Instead of holding reserves in silver and gold, the *enskilda* banks choose to hold reserves in central bank notes. Since the costs of exchange were partly carried by the banks, notes were circulated to at par value against the central bank notes. As a consequence, an exchange rate system was created that was based on the reserves of the central bank. Since bank notes were accepted in all banks, including the central bank, the foundation was created for a deposit-based banking system in Sweden. In an international comparison, the uniqueness of the private note issuing demonstrated how a poor country could increase its monetary base and the liquidity in the economy without risking the fixed exchange rate. Between 1834 and 1873, the exchange rate system was based on a silver monetary standard, which was replaced by a gold standard with the establishment of a Scandinavian Monetary Union in 1873. The Union led to a common currency market in Scandinavia and further increased the monetarization of the capital market that followed wider note-issuing.[8]

In the 1860s, commercial banking developed rapidly, encouraged by the wave of liberal economic policies and the monetarization of the capital market. The 1864 banking law allowed not only unrestricted interest rates, but also the right to set up joint stock banks and establish branches in cities other than where the head office was located. In the following year, eight new joint stock banks were set up. The first non-issuing joint stock bank was also formed in 1864, Skandinaviska Kredit AB (later Skandinaviska Banken). By 1879, twenty-one private banks were using Skandinaviska Banken as their agent of exchange. Until the 1890s, both Skandinaviska Banken and SEB performed the central bank function. The success story of the commercial banks relied on legal and ideological support from the state: convinced ministers and radical liberals such as Johan August Gripenstedt, Mortimer Agardh and André Oscar Wallenberg together contributed significantly to the implementation of a new banking system (Table 2.2).

The success story of commercial banking was temporarily halted by the crisis of 1878–9. Many railway companies were unable to pay interest rate

Table 2.2 **Loans and credits affiliated to various credit organizations 1850, 1875 and 1900 (per cent)**

	National Bank of Sweden (Riksbanken)	Commercial banks	Savings banks	Mortgage institutes	Others	Total
1850	35	16	11	33	5	100
1875	7	38	16	30	9	100
1900	6	50	18	17	9	100

Source: Nygren (1985), p. 140.

on the bonds issued, at the same time as they needed external finance and had non-saleable bonds in their own portfolios. The bonds fell in value and railway companies and lenders became financially distressed. In the case of Bergslagernas Järnvägsaktiebolag, a railway company hit early on in the crisis, the state decided to take over the bonds at a high value. However, when the crisis was spread to the entire sector, the government was no longer interested in financially supporting distressed railway companies: as the situation worsened in 1879 many firms ended up in bankruptcy.

While the crisis in railway bonds was the immediate cause of the banking crisis, the liberalization of the banking system was the underlying one. Many commercial banks experienced substantial losses and the risk of bankruptcy was particularly graver one for them, SEB, where bond placements amounted to 36 per cent of total financial assets. To avoid a collapse of vital parts of the banking system, Parliament, at the suggestion of the government, established the so-called Railway Mortgage Fund, where banks were able to pledge their unmarketable railway bonds. The Fund was administrated at the National Debt Office. After this intervention by the state, the financial distress gradually disappeared from the market. The debate in Parliament whether the state should take the role as a lender of last resort or not had been intense, but it was clear afterwards that the intervention had led to a rapid stabilization of the financial system.

Swedish commercial banking thus developed as a response to the demand stemming from the growth in domestic and foreign trade. Gradually, new functions in relation to the finance of railways, industries and transfer systems were added. At the end of the period 1850–90 the commercial banks dominated the financing of the non-financial sector in Sweden, having replaced merchant and trading houses, private banking firms and bankers as the main providers of financial capital. The resources of the latter players were too small, not sufficiently co-ordinated or technically inadequate to finance the increasing demand for external capital. Nor had they enough financial muscle to stand up to the strains of recurring financial crises in an agricultural society standing on the threshold of becoming an industrial one.

Industrial society and financial capitalism, 1890–1935

At the turn of the century, Sweden had a leading position in the industrial world in terms of productivity growth, economic growth and increase in real

CREATING NORDIC CAPITALISM • PROLOGUE • SWEDISH WELFARE CAPITALISM • THE BONNIER AND WALLENBERG BUSINESS GROUPS • FROM ASEA TO ABB

2   33

wages – a position that lasted for the next sixty years. A characteristic feature of the industrial transformation were the many 'genius companies' within engineering firms based on technical inventions and brought to production in close co-operation with entrepreneurs, private investors and commercial banks. The innovation processes and the rapid economic growth were stimulated by hectic financial capitalism, including the foundation of new commercial banks and extensive corporate finance – about fifty new banks were founded in 1896–1910. But the process also involved an element of risky speculation. Viewing the many financial and industrial innovations together with the institutional changes, it is reasonable to see the first two decades of the period 1890–1935 as a formative phase in the transformation of the Swedish business system.

In an international context, Sweden was industrially a late-comer, lagging behind both the UK and Germany. This meant that the business system was adjusted to the fact that other western countries were well ahead in terms of technology, production volumes, customer markets and financial capital. Germany, in particular, stood as a role model for building up industrial capitalism, including a certain engineering culture, strong universal banks and various cartels. There was also a strong component of nationalism behind the striving for market expansion and economic growth. The industrial take-off in Sweden at the turn of the century meant a breakthrough for the organization of an industrial society and resulted in structural changes in the labour market, together with further urbanization. Employment in agriculture decreased in relative terms, while industrial employment and private services increased. Old cities grew and new ones emerged. Between 1880 and 1900 the fifteen fastest-growing cities were home to more than half of the Swedish population: in many cities the number of inhabitants doubled during these two decades. These demographic changes led a new social situation for many people. Employees and employers organized on a national basis and a right–left polarization was established on the political scene, where universal suffrage became one of the key issues. Urbanization also broke up the traditional job and gender roles within families that had been formed in the agricultural society.

In the inter-war period, economic growth slowed as the effects of lower demand for goods and services, institutional disintegration and economic protectionism in the whole industrialized world were felt. The constructive formative phase was fading away. Inter-war Europe was characterized by political and economical instability, surrounded by a severe financial crisis directly after the First World War and the Great Depression in the first half of the 1930s. As in other European countries, the Great Depression had long-term consequences for the distribution of income and private property. However, since the rationalization and reorganization of industry was relatively profound during the 1920s, Sweden was better off than many other countries. Nevertheless, the pressure on industry, finance and society led to substantial difficulties and hardship. In the mid-1930s, highly competitive industries such as iron and steel, pulp and paper, engineering and shipping helped the Swedish economy to grow. The new economy also benefited from innovations and a changing consumption pattern, which was reflected in development blocs around the car industry, media, wholesale and retail trades and electrical domestic appliances.

Structure and performance

In the 1890s, the economy started to grow significantly: the annual increase in industrial volume was 5.5 per cent between 1890 and 1910. Considering all the economic sectors between 1890 and 1930, the annual increase in GDP per capita was 2.4 per cent. The pace of the growth was slower during the second half of the period, due to the First World War and the subsequent crisis. In spite of this, industrial volume was six times as large in 1930 as in 1890. This impressive GDP growth gave Sweden a prominent position on the world-ranking list (Table 2.3).

The strong economic growth was not limited to industry. The transport sector and private services increased at an annual rate of 3.8 and 3.3 per cent respectively (fixed prices), while the corresponding figure for industry was 4.7 per cent. Within the transport and service sector, railways, telecommunication, postal service, banking and insurance and international shipping all

Table 2.3 **Annual change of GDP per capita in the industrialized world, 1870–1930 (per cent)**

Country	1870–90	1890–1910	1910–30
Sweden	1.0	2.4	2.0
Denmark, Finland, Norway	0.8	1.7	1.8
Great Britain	0.9	0.9	0.0
Rest of Europe	0.8	1.4	1.4
North America	1.7	2.0	1.6
Japan	1.1	1.4	2.1

Source: Schön (2000), p. 223.

showed annual growth rates over 5 per cent during 1890–1910. The combination of expanding trade and new technology paved the way for a strong increase within communication and transport. This is illustrated by the way the shipping industry was reorganized and specialized in order to meet the demand for global transport of various goods. Many new shipping companies were founded and new international and national trade lines opened. This restructuring process was broad in range and led to discussion of the scope of the industrial break-through. An important lesson to learn is that a narrow view of industrial take-off, with a focus on manufacturing industry, tends to overshadow the fact that industrial society was based on a co-existence of many growing economic sectors, not least transport and services.

The main feature of these fast-growing sectors was technical innovation, often related to motorization. In turn, this gave rise to the growth of industrial cities and new markets, but also changing social patterns. Around the turn of the century, the strongest growth could be seen in branches such as energy, pulp and paper, printing and engineering, which all had annual growth rates above 10 per cent until 1910. Similar rates were shown in parts of other industries, such as ready-to-wear clothing and shoemaking, and cement works. Another expanding branch was media, where the Bonnier family established a large company within newspaper and publishing. Famous Swedish authors – Gustaf Fröding, Verner von Heidenstam, Selma Lagerlöf and August Strindberg – chose Bonniers to publish their books. In 1909, the family business was complemented by the daily newspaper *Dagens Nyheter* and in 1929, after acquisition of Åhlén & Åkerlund, with literary magazines and periodicals. The Bonnier business is analysed in the case study in Chapter 3.

It was symptomatic of the second industrial revolution that iron mills and sawmills, previously leading branches, now showed the relatively lowest growth rates. The timber industry and sawmills stagnated substantially during the whole period, while iron and steel experienced a difficult situation after the First World War, mainly because of increasing international competition. It was also symptomatic that these stagnating branches were based on natural resources, export-oriented and located in the countryside, while emerging expansive branches in the formative phase were based on refined products, located in industrial cities and dependent on a strong domestic market. The mining industry was an exemption to this rule, as new methods in steel making meant an upswing for regions like Grängesberg and Norrbotten, especially after a railway between Swedish Kiruna and Norwegian Narvik was built in

1902. Trafik AB Grängesberg-Oxelösund (Grängesberg) became the largest company in Sweden at this time, while Luossavaara-Kirunavaara (LKAB) was based on the exploitation of ore fields.

After the First World War, industrial growth generally declined, especially in the branches that had carried earlier industrialization. The difference in growth rates between various branches was equalized. Innovation-based structural transformation became less evident and the dynamic forces changed from expansion towards concentration and rationalization. The concentration of industry had an early peak in 1918, when every other company on the stock and share dealer list pursued a merger. A second strong wave occurred in the late 1920s, when 15 per cent of the listed firms accomplished a merger. Almost one-third of the mergers in 1913–38 took place in the metal and machine industry, namely 136 out of 397 mergers. Other branches with a relatively high proportion of mergers were paper and pulp and chemical–technical firms – in the latter case, more than half of the mergers were related to a concentration of match factories. The industrial concentration process, including both vertical and horizontal integration, created a new industrial structure with a clear dominance of large firms in every branch. .

In terms of production volumes and sectoral contribution to total GDP, the period 1890–1935 was an industrial one, although agriculture still dominated employment until 1930: one-third of the professional population was employed in the sector compared to one-quarter in the industrial sector. As noticed earlier, the strong industrialization included a break-through of related sectors, such as building and construction, transport and communication and services. The productivity rate was highest in the industrial sector – the annual volume of production per occupation doubled between 1890 and 1930, despite the reduction in hours worked. Together with a rapid decline of employees in the economically stagnated agriculture sector, these circumstances suggest that we should label this dynamic period in Swedish economic history as an 'industrial society' after all (Table 2.4). In the next period, the industrial society became mature and fully extended.

The most important single product innovation for Swedish industrialization was probably the electric motor. From the very beginning of electrification, Swedish technicians and companies were highly active in the further development and diffusion of the innovation. The electric motor and electricity quickly gathered the best of Swedish knowledge capital including technicians, entrepreneurs and bankers. Many of the investments were explorative, complex and far-reaching, lacking a clear pay-off period.

Table 2.4 **Shares of employment in various sectors and change in absolute numbers, 1890–1930**

Sector	1890	1930	Absolute change 1890–1930
Agriculture and related activities	58	34	−165,000
Industry and craft	17	26	+400,000
Building and construction	7	9	+120,000
Transport and communication	3	6	+110,000
Private services	11	19	+290,000
Public services	5	6	+70,000
Total employment	**100**	**100**	**+825,000**

Source: Schön (2000), p. 233.

Sometimes they needed legitimacy from the state, which gave an incentive for civil servants and politicians to be involved in the development. In fact, some of the investments were made to order for the state (technical procurement). One of the companies operating in the centre of this development bloc was ASEA (see the case study in Chapter 4).

Launching and pursuing large investment projects not only required networks between industry, financial capital and the state, but also an appropriate education system. Inspired by Germany, the Swedish system of higher education was designed on a hierarchical model, with the Royal Institute of Technology (KTH) and Chalmers at the top, followed by technical elementary schools, and vocational schools at the bottom of the pyramid. KTH in Stockholm started technical education in 1826, although the roots of the institute goes back to 1697 and Christopher Polhem's *Laboratorium mechanicum*. Chalmers in Göteborg started in 1829, after a financial donation by William Chalmers, director of the Swedish East India Company. Germany was the basic model for most technical schools, as well as the engineering culture that was created in Sweden at this time.

The demand for proper accountancy led to the foundation of the Stockholm School of Economics in 1909 followed by one in Göteborg in 1923. But the historical root of business schools goes back to the mercantilist ideas of Professor Anders Berch in Uppsala in the eighteenth century. As the professionalization of business leaders and management continued in the twentieth century, new subjects were added and new business schools established. The students, and also the managers of manufacturing firms, were educated in the principles of Taylorism, pursuing the success story of the Model T-Ford and the process innovation of assembly lines in the US.

A key feature of the business system in many industrialized countries was cartels, i.e. contractual arrangements between firms aiming to reduce competition. These could be designed as agreements on prices, quotas on production volume, or market operations. Since the free right of negotiations gave approval to cartels, the arrangement became an undisputable part of organized capitalism with a substantial impact on the economy. Swedish cartels were to be found in many sectors, most frequently in domestic-oriented branches that were protected by tolls and had a substantial fixed capital. Arrangements among breweries, distilleries and sugar mills were especially common. Strategically positioned in the business system, as the hub of various firms, the commercial banks played a central role in developing cartels. One motive for banks to co-ordinate cartels was the opportunity to protect and secure long-term investments, based on capital provided or guaranteed by the banks. A related activity for universal banks was to initiate, co-ordinate and force restructurings of old branches characterized by many small and unprofitable companies.

Vibrant financial capital

At the end of the nineteenth century, the entire financial system was formalized for the first time. It was given a sectoral logic conferring specialization in various credit organizations. The institutional setting, the outcome of protracted political debate, was designed in order to specify the relative functions of the central bank, the savings banks, the commercial banks and the mortgage institutes. New laws in the 1890s and the first decade of the twentieth century reduced previously overlapping functions. For customers, too, this clear distinction made the market structure more transparent and predictable than before. For example, the function of lender of last resort was given exclusively to the state, the monopoly of note issuing to the National Bank of Sweden, while commercial banks were to invest in industry.

The shift in how banking functions were viewed at the turn of the century was a consequence of the shortage of domestic capital, lofty national ambitions to catch up with more industrially advanced countries and an acute awareness of the need to find answers to social problems. The prohibition against commercial banks owning shares became a subject of public controversy. Developments in Germany provided a considerable spur to this change in attitudes. The impressive growth in the German economy made contemporary Swedish experts and politicians see the participation of German universal banks in the industrialization process as an ideal way of using idle bank funds as venture capital to promote growth and economic transformation.

A review of the entire question of share purchase by commercial banks formed the part of the public debate preceding the Government's new banking bill in 1911. With its enactment in 1912, certain freedom to purchase and own shares was granted to all large joint stock commercial banks. Although there were limitations laid down by law, they were no serious impediment to the large-scale involvement of big banks in providing venture capital during the boom years of the First World War. The new provisions allowed the banks to establish subsidiary companies for the purpose of acquiring shares and real estate, which were then deposited with the parent bank. This indirect ownership by the banks circumvented regulations limiting share ownership. In the 1910s, the commercial banks, by combining loan operations with ownership responsibilities, became venture capitalists of considerable importance.

The fundamental cause of the implementation of German universal practices into the Scottish-influenced banking system is to be found on the demand side in the rapid industrial transformation of the economy during the prolonged 1895–1913 boom. Shortage of domestic capital for long-term investment rapidly increased capital transfers from abroad. The commercial banks responded to the new business opportunities, by exploiting the advantage they held concerning information about various surplus capital markets in Europe, and through their traditional networking relationships with foreign banks, the Swedish commercial banks gained a strong foothold as intermediaries when the state and city bonds were floated on international capital markets. The outbreak of the First World War, however, dramatically changed Sweden's position on the international capital market. Thanks to growing export surpluses during the war, a substantial part of the foreign debt was paid off and Sweden emerged from the war as a capital exporting country.

The hyped war economy with its inflation boom led to a deflationary crisis in 1920–1. Demand decreased sharply and stocks in trade were overfilled with unmarketable goods. In fixed prices, GDP decreased in 1921 by 5 per cent. The falling prices hit the share-issuing subsidiary companies severely. Repayments on loans were suspended and collateral shares were transferred to banks as protection for credit claims. In the mid-1920s, about 75 per cent of credit in the large-companies' sector was granted to more or less bank-owned enterprises. The adequacy of bank ownership in industry was discussed in length, but it was not until after the collapse of the Kreuger Group in 1932 that the banks' industrial holdings were restricted.

In the late 1920s, Ivar Kreuger had created a globe-spanning organization that had come to control the once-fragmented international match industry. At the time of its collapse, the Group controlled three-quarters of the world's match business. Kreuger's business idea was to make loans to countries in exchange for a monopoly in match production and selling. In 1930 Kreuger lent $125 million to the German government, the largest in series of similar loans he had made to governments in Europe, Latin America and Asia since 1927. The famous economist John Maynard Keynes called Kreuger 'perhaps the greatest financial intelligence of this time' and said that he seems to have 'deemed it his task amid post-war chaos to create a channel between the

Photograph 2.1   In the inter-war years Ivar Kreuger (1880–1932) was one of the most powerful businessmen in Europe, and he thus symbolized Sweden's gradual transition from the periphery to the economic centre. The Kreuger Corporation gained a match monopoly across Europe by combining economic concentration with legislative acts of European governments. But Kreuger also forged signatures on loan papers, faked financial records, created imaginary banks to hold imaginary money, and was engaged in innumerable other fraudulent business transactions. The economic crisis following 1929 left Kreuger facing bankruptcy and criminal exposure. All attempts to restructure his holdings failed, and on March 12, 1932, he shot himself with a handgun.
Source: Scanpix.

countries with abundance of capital and those in bitter need of it [until he] was crushed between the ice-bergs of this frozen world'.[9] Even before the collapse of the Group it was not clear whether the 'Swedish Match King' was a genius or a swindler, and it is still disputed. He shot himself on 12 March 1932 in Paris after failing to convince banks and ministers about the solidity of the Group.[10]

Indisputably, Kreuger was an extraordinary person, with substantial influence not only on the match industry, but also the structure and content of the financial market in the 1920s and early 1930s. His invention of a new instrument, a debenture, enabled a firm to increase its equity without giving away voting rights, something that helped him expand his operation without inviting more or new people on the board of 'his' companies. A map of his match monopolies was indeed impressive. In the early 1930s, Swedish Match owned manufacturing operations in thirty-six countries, had monopolies in sixteen countries, and controlled 40 per cent of the world's match production. The stocks and bonds of Kreuger companies were the most widely held securities in the US and in the world. In Sweden, the Group controlled the four largest industrial enterprises and its operations were mainly financed with foreign capital. By the time of Ivar Kreuger's death in 1932, about 15 per cent of the total assets of Swedish banks were lent to the Group, while the claim of the Skandinaviska Banken represented half of the Swedish banks' credits to the concern. In the subsequent collapse, shares were taken over by banks as protection for credit claims.[11]

The state acted in a similar way at the end of the deflationary crisis and the banking crisis following the Kreuger crash. It did not only guarantee depositors' money, but also the stability of the financial system. Second, large and small actors were treated equally concerning their need for public financial support. The argument for making no differentiation was not to change the structure of competition in the market. When the banks' industrial holdings were restricted, the banks sold their shares to allied investment companies, some of them invented for the purpose of taking care of industrial shares, in contrast with floating them on the market. This guaranteed a continuous tight grip of large firms and was a consolidation of bank 'spheres' of ownership, which thereafter became typical for the Swedish business system. The most prominent examples are the Wallenberg sphere with SEB (later, Skandinaviska Enskilda Banken), the investment company Investor and minority holdings in, for example, ASEA, Ericsson, Stora Kopparberg, SKF and Swedish Match, and the Handelsbanken sphere including the investment company

Industrivärden and key holdings in AGA, Ericsson, MoDo, Sandvik and SCA, among others. There were also links between the spheres through common key holdings. For example, after the collapse of the Kreuger Group ownership and credit relations in the 'homeless' Ericsson were divided equally between the Handelsbanken sphere and the Wallenberg sphere, a circumstance that has lasted since.

Economy and society in the mid-1930s were totally different to that of forty years earlier. Merely the fact that production *per capita* had more than doubled meant a lot to the living conditions of the new generation. Many innovative firms had been established, while some old ones had been reorganized, reconstructed, or even liquidated. The transformation had also reached the banking sector and the resulting concentration meant fewer organizations than before. The break-up of the Scandinavian Monetary Union in 1924 and abandonment of the Gold Standard in 1931 had led to a new monetary situation. Real wages had increased for workers and various markets for consumer products had been established and were expanding rapidly. The rapid transformation at the turn of the century had been followed by rationalization and consolidation after the First World War. This trend was common in all sectors, with the largest consequences for branches that had been subject to expansion during an earlier stage.

The Swedish model, mature industries and welfare economy, 1935–75

The years 1935–50 represent a formative phase in the transformation of the Swedish business system. The Great Depression revealed structural imbalances in all industrialized countries and led to various programmes to help economic sectors. In many European countries, the recovery of the economy went hand in hand with the adoption of Keynesianism as the major economic policy. In Sweden, even before Keynes' ideas had become widespread, there was a consensus among economists and politicians about the long-term benefits of state intervention to manage employment and reduce fluctuations in the economy. By encouraging the public sector, investing in infrastructure and giving subsidies to housing, new jobs were created. The introduction of more or less state intervention in Sweden took place at the same time as social democracy was established as the dominant political ideology. Economic achievements after the Second World War did not stem from pure socialism or from economic liberalism. The mix of state regulation and market forces was essentially reformed capitalism, with roots in both traditions. By the 1970s, some institutional changes, especially in relation to resource allocation, labour and industrial policies (particularly nationalization) carried the stamp of Marxist ideas. However, Sweden continued to walk the middle way, avoiding contemporary international alternatives as strong market orientation in the US and the UK, communism in Soviet Union and Eastern Europe and authoritative regimes in Germany, Italy and Spain.

'Mixed economy' is sometimes used as a term to characterize this package of policies. Within this framework, the function of the private sector is to obey the institutional rules that constitute the market, which in turn is conditioned by overriding macroeconomic goals decided by the government. In order to keep control over the mixed economy, the political system regulated the market heavily. Although the low interest rate policy from the inter-war years was abandoned, a fiscal policy of high income taxes, higher duties and compulsory savings was established. To direct the flow of credit and investments, restrictions were imposed on the capital market: until the early 1980s, there were, for example, restrictions on bank borrowing, bond issues and foreign loans. The government directed support to certain favoured sectors – mainly housing, infrastructure and the industrial sector. From the early 1970s, most public institutions were identified with left-of-centre policies with the implied objective of protecting the numbers of jobs. However, in many cases, industrial and financial policy was counterproductive, as the state was simply throwing good money after bad and disguising the seriousness of the situation.

The extensive welfare state was possible because of the large revenues in the private sector. Having rationalized industry in the 1920s and 1930s, Sweden was better off than many other European countries after the Second World War. By choosing neutrality, the adaptation to peacetime was smooth compared with the rest of Europe. A large part of the Swedish industrial production remained intact during the war, which gave Sweden a strong competitive advantage after the war, and for a long time this kept the economic growth rate at an internationally high level. Nevertheless, the state feared the same situation as after the First World War. Since a substantial downturn never occurred, the recovery accelerated and some Swedish firms quickly reached a prominent position in the industrialized world. For many years the Swedish version of Keynesianism went hand in hand with the image of the perfect welfare state. Economic growth in the 1950s and 1960s gave an illusion of an ever-faithful couple and outside observers frequently looked to Sweden as *the* model of welfare capitalism. However, the 'marriage' broke down during recession from the mid-1970s – the structural crisis following OPEC I and OPEC II – when substantial budget and balance of payments deficits appeared.

The 'Swedish model'

The Swedish model was essentially a pragmatic model, not a theoretical but a practical one. Its main characteristics were a strong belief in social engineering, a corporatist state, economic growth and political stability through the hegemony of a powerful Social Democratic Party.

After the Great Depression, many argued that the market left to its own devices could not secure growth and full employment and that these required a stronger state role in the economy.[12] Substantial elements of the new regime were interventionist social measures, including housing programmes and active labour market policies. 'The People's Home' (Folkhemmet) was used as a metaphor to emphasize the important welfare targets to achieve for the good of the family. In the labour market, certain agreements, above all the *Saltsjöbadsavtalen* (1938–48), guaranteed smooth relations between employers and employees, a co-operative climate that did not provoke either lock-outs or strikes. The economic parts of the model were informed by a Keynesian approach to macro management. The Stockholm School of economists – most prominently Bertil Ohlin, Gunnar Myrdal, Erik Lundberg and Erik Lindahl – had in the early 1930s anticipated some of the ideas Keynes was to put forward.[13] Thus, the academic and political opinion was predisposed to Keynesianism, and hence this approach was very influential in the formulation of policy.[14]

A key feature of the model was stable party government operating with a bias towards consensus. Although the operation of the model coincided with a long period of social democratic hegemony (1945–76), the essential principles were supported by most non-socialist parties. In addition, the existence of a nexus of neo-corporatist institutions was important for the introduction and implementation of new ideas, both inside and outside Parliament. A further basic feature was the pragmatic trade-off between capitalist and socialist values. This phenomenon involved accepting a strong relationship between the financial–industrial elite and the major political parties. There was consensus among most institutions, including the unions, that the economy as a whole benefited from extended social security and a wage policy based on solidarity with employees with low incomes. In 1948, the public labour policy was embodied in a new public authority and board, the Swedish Labour Market Authority (Arbetsmarknadsverket, AMV) and the Swedish Labour Market Board (AMS). These organizations launched reforms in the 1950s and early 1960s such as the three-week summer holiday, a common labour market in the Nordic countries, financial help when moving to another job and finally the five-day week. The solidaristic wage policy emanated from the Rehn–Meidner Model for Wage Bargaining, approved by LO at their congress in 1951. Since high wage claims on behalf of the Confederation forced business to rationalise to increase labour productivity, this model contributed greatly to the structural transformation of Swedish industry. The Swedish model reached its zenith in the mid-1960s. The seven core economic goals of the Swedish model can be summarized as:

- Full employment, the unemployment rate varying between 1.5 and 2.5 per cent.
- Low inflation – about 3 per cent.
- High degree of cyclical stability.
- No balance of payment troubles.
- Rapid rise of the public sector.
- No visible structural imbalances between various economic sectors.
- Rate of growth of total output about 4 per cent.

The government took advantage of the long boom to implement further social reforms to the framework of the welfare system. For example, the state decided it was able to finance a rapid growth of the public sector. From 1960 to 1980, total public expenditure in relation to GDP increased from 31 to 62 per cent. Unfortunately, however, it was becoming clear that there was a substantial difference in productivity growth between those sectors of the economy subject to external competition and the sheltered, largely public, sector. It was demonstrated that productivity was growing at twice the rate in the competitive sector, but this was not reflected in wage policy. Thus, costs rose sharply and taxation started to take a progressively larger proportion of GDP.

Economic features of the 'Golden Age'
Sweden had the highest economic growth rate among all industrial countries from 1930 to 1950 – 2.6 per cent compared to 1.8 per cent in the rest of Scandinavia, 0.9 per cent in the rest of Europe and 2.1 per cent in North America. During the first five years after the Second World War, the Swedish economy grew at an annual rate of close to 5 per cent. Between 1950 and the

Table 2.5 **Annual growth in GDP per capita: Sweden, 1800–1995 (per cent and fixed prices)**

Years	Annual growth
1800–1850	0.4
1850–1890	1.5
1890–1930	2.1
1930–1975	3.2

Source: Schön (2000), p. 13.

mid-1970s, other countries caught up with Sweden and achieved annual rates over 3 per cent, with Japan at the top of the list with 7.6 per cent. Annual growth in Sweden was not only extremely high, it was also regular and stable without the interruption of serious crises. Additionally, the inflation rate was at a relatively low level, between 2 and 4 per cent. The Swedish model was definitely one of the key factors behind this 'Golden Age' in the country's economic history. Other reasons were new and stable international institutions, a striving to fill the technological gap with the US by making further investments in R&D at home and abroad, and finally the generous supply of factors of production. Institutions such as the Bretton Woods system, GATT and later on EFTA guaranteed the benefit from monetary stability and free trade, while the technical gap gave a direction and predictability to the pattern of growth in the whole of Europe. Concerning factors of production, Swedish development – high economic growth *and* low inflation rate – was underpinned by an elastic supply of labour and capital (Table 2.5).

Three sectors were the focus of the strong economic growth during the first decades of the 'Golden Age': transport, industry and public service. In transport and industry, the growth was accompanied by both increasing employment and productivity as a consequence of modernization. The reason behind high production volumes in public service was primarily increasing employment. The engineering and chemical industry showed extraordinary figures, with an annual average growth rate over 7 per cent from 1930 to 1950. Engineering was relatively the most important, and included extensive production of electrical devices, machines, ships, cars, office machines, radios and refrigerators. The chemical industry presented many new and fast growing sub-branches within refining, paints and coatings, cellulose lacquer, washing powder and rubber.

In terms of relative shares of total employment, agriculture was surpassed by both the industrial and the service sector (including transport, other private services and public service) in the early 1930s. After the Second World

Table 2.6 **Shares of employment in various sectors, 1931–5, 1951–5, 1971–5 (per cent)**

Sector	1931–5	1951–5	1971–5
Agriculture and related activities	34.2	18.6	6.8
Industry and craft	26.2	34.6	29.4
Building and construction	8.1	8.4	8.6
Transport and communication	5.8	7.5	7.5
Private services	18.9	20.4	23.9
Public services	6.7	10.5	23.7
Total employment	**100**	**100**	**100**
Salaried work and work for sale	68.6	67.5	74.8
Unsalaried housekeeping	31.4	32.5	25.2
Total	**100**	**100**	**100**

Source: Schön (2000), pp. 339, 379.

War, the rate of decline in agriculture grew and by around 1950 private services exceeded the agriculture sector as relative share of total employment, while industry occupation increased to more than one-third. Society was dominated by industry and service (Table 2.6). A deficit of labour appeared, which called for active recruitment of unskilled and skilled workers from less industrialized regions in Europe. Thus, immigrants from Finland, the Baltic countries and southern Europe seeking a better living standard were easily absorbed by the expanding industries in Sweden. After a peak in 1968, industrial employment began to decline in relative terms, while the production of public services showed a strong increase. Between 1950 and 1975, the public sector grew by 600,000 workers.

The growth of the public sector was connected to a breakthrough for women on the labour market. In 1950, about 1.5 million women were employed in unpaid housekeeping, which made this the largest economic sector. In 1975, the number had decreased by 500,000, i.e. about the same number as the increase in the public sector. In this early period of the growth of the public sector, a large part of women's work was to take care of children for other women employed in the public sector, and to take care of the parents of the women who were looking after their children. However, there was an important difference in relation to previous periods. This time, the job was valued and salaried. Besides, the labour market for women went beyond the demand of public services, and comprised needs in consumer-related industries, such as textile, but also retailing. Thus, the new labour market meant more paid work for women in both the private and the public sector.

The first bill to regulate gender discrimination on the labour market appeared in 1970, but did not lead to any law. Nevertheless, the labour market was institutionally reformed in many other ways during the 1970s. Financial help was provided by the state in order to give unemployed people an incentive to move or take jobs in other geographical regions. In 1971, the AMS had sixty-nine district offices and 166 local offices, to give effective service to job applicants. In 1974, a law for security of employment and promotion of employment opportunities (Lagen om anställningsskydd och anställningsfrämjande åtgärder), education for distressed private businesses and labour market cash support (Kas) were introduced. Two years later, a law for the registration of vacant jobs was passed, while the first year of retirement was set to 65 years and partial retirement was introduced as an alternative to a full-time job. For the first time, financial support was given to firms that could recruit new people to replace employees taking part in an education programme. To cover the costs for the enlarged and generous education system on the labour market, a tax called the Arbetsgivaravgift (payroll tax) was introduced.

The liberalization of world trade and economic growth after the Second World War led to a four-fold increase of Swedish exports in the following two decades. As a consequence, the Swedish economy became much more internationally dependent than before. Furthermore, international specialization became an important factor in the further growth of the economy. Some Swedish firms developed as MNCs with a presence on all continents. The 'Golden Age' turned out to be a harvest time for the industrial structure settled in the late nineteenth and early twentieth century and thereafter transformed and modernized. Compared to earlier periods, the new element in exports from 1930 to 1975 was a higher proportion of processed products. Raw materials and semi-products related to timber, pulp and paper, and iron industries were losing ground, while refined products from manufacturing industry increased in importance. The share of the latter products doubled to represent more than 40 per cent of total exports in the early 1970s. The expansion of exports also included machines and transport vehicles, which grew on an annual basis of more than 10 per cent. During a short period of time, exports of cars and new ships became an important part of the economy.

Expanding businesses

Despite the relatively small size of its population and economy, Sweden is home to an impressive number of successful MNCs. One branch that has created internationally strong products is the car industry. Swedish production of cars increased more than five times from 1950 to 1975, with SAAB and Volvo as the two dominant firms. Apart from cars, these two firms also covered a substantial production of trucks and buses. In 1970, Volvo was, together with ASEA, the largest Swedish employer. Successful models such as the PV 444/544 during the 1950s and the Amazon during the 1960s created a strong business climate in industrial cities such as Göteborg and Skövde. SAAB was the result of a diversification process from the aeroplane industry, which explains some of the high-technology arrangements and aerodynamic design in the early models. SAAB's car production was located at Trollhättan, on the western side of the country, while the aerospace industry was established in Linköping, on the eastern side.

Other expanding branches were shipbuilding and shipping, both established as important export industries. With an increasing demand for tonnage, shipbuilding was expanding and gave high returns on invested capital until the late 1960s, when competition from Japan somewhat changed the situation. However, in spite of declining profitability, Swedish firms kept a high share of the market and had about 10 per cent of the world production of tonnage from 1950 to 1975. Geographically, the firms were concentrated on the west coast of Sweden, with Kockums in Malmö, Öresundsvarvet in Landskrona, and Eriksberg, Götaverken and Lindholmen in Göteborg and Uddevallavarvet. From the 1960s, ships became larger, especially the fleet carrying oil. Consequently, shipyards gradually became larger, too. Due to decreasing profitability in the 1960s, new investments were more or less dependent on credit guarantees from the state.

Increasing world trade after the Second World War gave this export-oriented transport and service sector a lift. Apart from the established Broströmrederiet and Johnsonrederiet, relatively new shipping firms also experienced many years of expansion and high profitability. Salénrederiet increased its fleet and specialized in refrigerated transport, in which it became the world's largest shipping firm. The niche market of Walleniusrederiet was car transport on specially built vessels, and contracts with Japanese car industries made this a large commercial success. The Stena Line was expanding thanks to profitable ferry lines in the west and east coast.

Other branches performing well were to be found in the engineering industry, which was benefiting from cheaper electricity. The pace of innovation was extremely high within the machinery and electricity industries, where the use of electrical devices provided complete automatic production processes.

On the consumption side, increasing real wages led to a spread of new electrical appliances to the household sector, where white goods meant a rationalization of housekeeping. Electrolux, founded in the 1910s and developed by the entrepreneur Axel Wenner-Gren over four decades, was a leader in this sector.

The growth in public health care and clinical research at university hospitals provided a solid base for growth for firms in the pharmaceutical industry, especially Astra and Pharmacia. Thanks to product innovations, such as Xylocain and Seloken in the case of Astra, these two firms became large and profitable players in the international market.

The forestry industry (wood, paper and pulp), the second largest after the metal industry, showed a mixed development. While wood and pulp developed more slowly than the Swedish industrial average, paper showed a strong volume expansion from the 1950s. Due to a perceived shortage of timber, Billerud, SCA and Stora Kopparberg started to invest in forests and production lines overseas, in Portugal, British Columbia and Nova Scotia. In the 1970s, the pulp industry had become an integrated stage in the processing of paper, which continued to grow thanks to a strong demand for tissue and other types of paper.

The development of leading international companies was closely related to a certain type of governance system, distinguished by corporate groups, ownership spheres and dynastic families. This symbiotic relationship between commercial banking (corporate finance) and non-financial business, originated from the industrial breakthrough and further deepened during the inter-war years, continued to be a key factor behind the transformation and rationalization of firms in the post-war period. Notably, family ownership was not limited to small firms or traditionally strong family industries such as shipping and trade, but continued to be vital within large industries such as engineering, the forestry and pharmaceutical industries. For example, mature firms as ASEA, Astra, Electrolux, Ericsson, SAAB, Scania-Vabis, Separator (Alfa-Laval), SKF, Stora Kopparberg and Swedish Match industry were more or less controlled by the Wallenberg group, through a combination of minority shareholdings and the family bank, SEB, being the largest creditor in each firm. The existence of ownership spheres, with a combination of dual voting shares, long-term credit relationships and personal networks, could be seen both as an advantage and disadvantage for the renewal of the industrial society during the 'Golden Age'.

The growth of the large-firm sector lent stability and predictability to the economy and was supported by leading politicians who argued for strong employment growth within the concept of the Swedish model. SAAB and Volvo developed rapidly thanks to tariffs, import restrictions and the support of tax subsidies for firms to buy trucks and cars. But they also benefited from certain regional subsidies and public investments in the national traffic system. Both firms integrated backwards and developed a vital network of decentralized suppliers. Not surprisingly, the transport industry soon became a large employer and a significant export industry. Very often it was said that what was good for Volvo was good for Sweden.

However, strong market regulations and tax reductions had many disadvantages, since the concentration of mature industries led to so-called 'lock-in' effects. Investment capital did not spill over to new entrepreneurs and SMEs in emerging markets, which meant a continuation of the existing business structure. Thus, the ownership structure hindered single entrepreneurship and prevented small firms growing, while mature capital- and labour-intensive companies became highly modernized. This made Sweden especially vulnerable during the structural crisis of the 1970s.

The post-war period had created new growth patterns and distinctive geographical nodes of knowledge capital. In the early 1970s, business leaders and economic experts were optimistic about the future. Together with generous financial and monetary policies, this optimistic attitude laid the ground for a wave of new investments in Swedish industries in the first half of the 1970s. The most extensive investments involved steelmaking, shipping and pulp and paper, affecting both Swedish plants and production lines overseas. The outcome of these substantial investments, however, was not the expected one.

Neo-liberalism and internationalization within the service society, 1975–2005

The strong export market in the first half of the 1970s, with high profits for Swedish international business, was followed by a deceleration as a result of the two oil price shocks (OPEC I and OPEC II). Relative to the other Nordic countries, Sweden performed extremely poorly. The average growth rate decreased substantially and deep-seated problems affected most industries and households. In the industrial sector, textiles, shipyards and shipping suffered, and the structural crisis left many of the companies in these branches in bankruptcy after years of losses. The period turned out to be the worst structural crisis since the inter-war period. The steel industry, with shipyards as their large customers, experienced severe financial difficulties, as steel production fell by 30 per cent from 1975 to 1977. The value of total industrial production fell by more than 10 per cent from 1976 to 1978. It would take a decade to get back to the same production value as 1975. To avoid bankruptcies of large plants, the state was active in restructuring whole industries. However, the result was not impressive and due to increasing budget deficits, Sweden had to depreciate the krona four times between 1976 and 1982. In 1981–2, total depreciation reached 26 per cent.

Because of the comparatively slow growth and the poor productivity record, the dismantling of the large public sector became a major concern. The questioning of the 'Swedish model', after years of welfare programmes, exposed certain disadvantages of the system. One was the substantial use of real resources in the public sector that, in combination with free provision of these services led to over-consumption and waste of resources. Because of the state's substantial subsidising of the housing sector, the real costs of these services never became clear to either entrepreneurs or households. Obviously, there was a gap between the real costs and the direct consumer price in many economic sectors. These imbalances, which made production prices inelastic, put a lot of pressure on the state budget. To keep up the growth of subsidies following a certain percentage of the prices, the state had to borrow internationally to cover the budget deficit.

The main structural problems remained, although the short-lived strong economic boom of the mid-1980s gave the illusion that the difficulties had blown over. The budget was in balance, wages began to increase and export-oriented industries were flourishing thanks to the devaluations in the early 1980s. A return to growing prosperity seemed assured, as there was an expectation of steadily increasing values in all kinds of assets. By the 1990s it became clear that this was simply an illusion, and an ensuing financial crisis forced a major rethink. For three years in row, Sweden experienced negative GDP growth. It was also obvious that the public sector was too large for the economy. Consequently, the state began to dismantle vital parts of the public sector. This process was accompanied by a right-wing government selling out some of the state-owned companies. Although the prime motive was to break up monopolies and improve efficiency through competition, it also had an effect of improving the state budget.

In 1995, Sweden joined the European Union (EU) and policy-making was changed to match EU requirements. For example, monetary policy, fiscal policy and structural policy was gradually adjusted to the goals decided within the EU. The new reforms seemed to have had a positive impact on economic growth in Sweden, as the annual growth rate in GDP varied between 3 and 4 per cent from 1997 to 2000, above the EU average. The leading industrial sector during the boom was ICT and Stockholm soon became one of the leading ICT regions in the world. The boom ended when the 'dotcom bubble' burst in 2001, leaving the ICT sector to struggle through a process of 'creative destruction', while some entrepreneurs in Stockholm found themselves in the lucky position of having sold their patents for millions of dollars before the crash. Looking back at this turbulent time, it is quite clear that the outcome of the structural transformation was partly successful, since the ICT sector was at the centre of the strong productivity and economic growth that followed. Between 1995 and 2004, real annual growth of GDP *per capita* was 2.6 per cent in Sweden, compared to 2.1 per cent in the US and 1.9 per cent in the EU.

Neo-liberalism and re-regulation in key sectors

In the 1980s, the impact of neo-liberalism and monetarism on the decision making of the government was evident. The adoption of a new economic policy resulted in a series of deregulations in several economic sectors. These substantial deregulations began a distinctive formative phase in the trans-formation of the Swedish business system. In the financial sector, constraints associated with a regulated economy were lifted and new financial instruments were introduced to cover budget deficits and to pave the way for open-market operations (OMOs) by the central bank. The deregulation process – or the re-regulation process, since the rules of the game were merely transferred from the state to the market organizations – was initiated and implemented by the Social Democrats. The process was a real break with traditional policy and the strategy was heavily criticized by trade unions and left-wing fractions within the Social Democratic party. During the right-wing government of 1991–4 the process of re-regulation became stronger than before. The market-orientation process continued with the left-wing government that followed, not least with a reform that constituted an independent central bank that had mainly to consider inflationary goals.

As indicated above, the shift toward liberalism embraced sectors other than the financial one. Various types of controls were lifted from the trans-port, building and housing sectors. Monopolies were broken up and replaced by a competitive environment, for example in railways, the postal service, energy, media and telecommunications. The adoption of 'Reaganomics' and

'Thatcherism' meant privatization of state-owned companies, although the state kept its influence in some of the private enterprises that followed. Clearly, the re-regulation process and the privatization movement changed the structure of the Swedish economy. The state more or less waived the right to maintain central collective services in society, but also deprived itself of revenues from these organizations and firms. The labour market became more flexible and fragmented, with increasing differentiation of wages and project-based appointments. There was also a tendency towards weaker labour unions where membership in a union was not viewed as compulsory.

The structural crisis activated the role of the AMV, although the restrained state budget meant a larger obstacle to generous reforms than previously. In 1980, certain institutes were established within Swedish Labour Market Authority to co-ordinate the rehabilitation of workers, while special community firms were founded to absorb some of the surplus of labour. In 1986, the labour market education system was reorganized and a commission authority (Uppdragsmyndighet, AMV) was founded. Another key feature of the system was the increasing focus on higher education. Both internationalization and specialization in business contributed to various competence programmes and strong links were created between business and the system of higher education, including the foundation of new colleges and universities, each surrounded by a science park.

The liberalization movement was temporarily interrupted in the early 1990s, when Sweden, like many other countries in Europe, was hit by a deep recession and a crisis in the financial system. The deregulation of the capital market functioned as a trigger for greater speculation and moving market positions forward. When many credit institutions, including some of the largest commercial banks, became insolvent in the subsequent slump, the state had to step in as a lender of last resort to rescue the monetary and credit system. Despite a re-activation of the state, negative effects on the labour force could not be prevented. The unemployment rate increased at the same time as economic growth declined substantially. As in the 1930s, efforts were made by the state to increase the labour demand in some sectors by implementing subsidies on goods and services for customers, and by initiating national investments in infrastructure, principally railways and motorways. By introducing various programmes for the unemployed, some of the many negative effects of the depression were reduced.

The strong emphasis on public investment in sectors with high labour intensity was strategic and reflected a return to an earlier form of

Keynesian-inspired policy. However, the return to an older policy did not mean an end to the trend of neo-liberalism. Instead, the process of re-regulation was transferred to other areas of the public sector, such as education, medicine and care of the elderly. However, in the early twenty-first century, after more than ten years of re-regulation, the high tide of privatization seemed to have ebbed away.

End of the 'Swedish model?'

In the 1980s, the Swedish model was really questioned for the first time since the Second World War. This was the result of the overloading of government, imbalance and tension between the private and public sectors and the effects of the internationalization of the economy. For example, the model abandoned the original Rehn–Meidner commitment, made in the late 1940s, to tight monetary policy and failed to keep down effective demand arising from private consumption and public expenditure during the booms. A secular trend of steadily growing public expenditure was not a feature of the original Keynesian theory. Instead, higher expenditure during recessions should have been offset by lower expenditure during booms so that, over the economic cycle, the budget was balanced. Although deviations were considered in a new model (the EFO model), problems remained. Given the slowdown of productivity growth from the mid-1970s, the norms of wage determination previously regarded as satisfactory disappeared. The incompatibility between a less productive competitive private sector and growing expenditure in the public sector required action.

In spite of this, trade unions kept imposing costs upon the system by demanding higher salaries and increasing social expenditure. As a consequence, the losses in the industrial sector became even higher. This negative spiral hit labour-intensive industries most, such as textile, iron and steel and shipping industries. The trade unions, supported by the government, seemed to assume that welfare capitalism was capable of carrying indefinitely burdens in the form of private consumption (wages) and public consumption. However, in the absence of substantial productivity growth, these demands imposed intolerable burdens on the real economy.

Obviously, a drawback of the model was the low incentive to increase productivity. Instead of changing the wage policy, negotiators in the labour market simply pushed for high wage increases. Given the egalitarian aspirations that had been a feature of Swedish society, these wage increases would be generalized throughout the economy. However, a solidaristic wage policy

Photograph 2.2   *Olof Palme was the leader of the Swedish Social Democratic Party from 1969 to 1986 and was the Prime Minister of Sweden from 1969 to 1976 and from 1982 until his assassination by an unknown gunman near Segelstorget in the centre of Stockholm in February 1986. As leader of a new generation of Swedish Social Democrats, Olof Palme was often described as a 'revolutionary reformist'. Domestically, his socialist views – especially the Social Democrat drive to expand Labour Union influence over business – engendered a great deal of hostility from more conservatively inclined Swedes. Shortly before his assassination, Palme had been accused of being pro-Soviet and not sufficiently safeguarding Sweden's national interest. Palme's murder shocked the Swedish nation and had an impact across the Nordic region.*
Source: Scanpix.

and egalitarianism were only possible as long as consensus reigned and individuals were prepared to pay higher taxes. Until the early 1970s everyone seemed to benefit from better social, health and educational services. But in the 1980s negative effects began to appear. As the marginal tax rate for persons in the upper income groups approached 100 per cent, they became reluctant to contribute to a continually growing public sector without increasing their marginal utility. Even ordinary workers faced marginal rates of tax of 60–80 per cent.

The egalitarian spirit, a crucial feature of the model, seemed to be dissipating. The difficulties of maintaining wage policies while striving for common goals and social provision in many areas of life were reflected in growing suspicions of politicians and a stronger emphasis on individual choice and spending. The free-rider problem was obvious as there was a strong temptation to cheat the state in one way or another. Thus, informal markets and tax evasion went hand in hand with lower incentives to search for jobs, given how extensive the social security system was. As a result the model was becoming counterproductive because it had lost its central driving feature – consensus and collective responsibility.

One reason for the original success of the Swedish model is related to the size of the economy. Since the population was small and homogeneous, the implementation of new rules set up by the government was rather easy. Neo-corporatist institutions, together with an extensive and organized bureaucracy, guaranteed that various asymmetries were efficiently adjusted to changes in the environment. However, when the long tradition of government by Social Democrats was broken in 1976,[15] some parts of the machinery began to break down. The stability in government, which was characteristic of the 'Golden Age', turned into a period of confrontation and unpredictability. Domestic instability was accompanied by growing international influences. As well as the forces of competition, there were major domestic reasons for internationalization. For example, because of tax policy, nationalization of key branches, and rigidities in the labour market, private firms felt less loyal to Sweden. To get cheaper labour and get away from an unfavourable business climate, some firms increased their foreign direct investments (FDI). Another reason for overseas investment was to surmount the common external tariff (CET) of the European Community (EC).

To sum up, the 'Swedish model' could be defined and interpreted in at least three ways. Depending on the definition, the answer to whether it has faded away or is still alive will differ. Using a strict definition, the model embraced the efforts to establish a solidaristic wage policy (the Rehn–Meidner Wage Bargaining Model), where centralized wage negotiations between the two actors representing the employees and employers were essential. From the political side, the incentive was to avoid open class conflicts which, in the event of success, would benefit both private and public interests. The economic ideas of full employment, high economic growth and price stability had been the inspiration for the model, but from the mid-1970s it became progressively more difficult to attain these objectives. When the representatives of employees and employers abandoned central negotiations in the 1980s, the 'Swedish model', in this operational form, had apparently come to an end.

If we then consider the welfare state as the crucial element of the 'Swedish model', we may come to a different conclusion. It emerged during the recession in the 1930s as a successful method to bring people back to work, by subsidising investments in housing and infrastructure. During the post-war period, it continued as a giant project where unemployed and women could more easily get access to the labour market and where many services in society became nationalized and channelled within an expanding state bureaucracy. In this definition the 'Swedish model' is distinguished not by a special wage policy but by the range and size of the public sector. Taking the level of welfare as an indication of the persistence of the model, the Swedish version of the mixed economy is still alive, albeit under threat, today.

If by the 'Swedish model' we mean a specific mentality of compromise thinking and a middle way between socialism and capitalism, we will get a similar answer. The tradition of compromise goes back a long way in the history of Scandinavia and has not disappeared from the scene, although it has recently been undermined by the globalization of industry and services. To maintain relations with the opposition and obtain mutual advantage has been a common objective in the behaviour of parliament, trade unions and industrial leaders since the Second World War. This could be interpreted as a type of corporatism where the state is centralized but still open, the bureaucracy professional but not authoritarian, and where the policies are differentiated but have a central co-ordination. In this respect, the Swedish model has sometimes been viewed as a nearly ideal-typical case of corporatism. The labour market policy has been characterized as a form of paternalistic corporatism, where it has been legitimate to force people to move from the countryside to the cities, then from areas with high unemployment to regions with better prospects.

In this latter view, the key features of the Swedish model are a tradition of consensual democracy, a multiparty political system, an extensive welfare system including a large public sector, a low level of corruption in the state administration, close links between state, banks and industry (including public ownership in some sectors) and a high level of organization, flexibility and efficiency in both the public and the private sphere. In that perspective, it might be true to say that the Swedish model is still present and relevant in the twenty-first century.

Structure and strategy in international business

The relative importance of both agriculture and industry decreased from the 1970s to the 1990s, illustrated as changes in shares of employment (Table 2.7). These long-term trends corresponded to a growth in services, both private

Table 2.7   **Shares of employment in various sectors, 1971–5 and 1991–5 (per cent)**

Sector	1971–5	1991–5
Agriculture and related activities	7.1	3.9
Industry	28.5	20.5
Building and construction	8.6	6.1
Transport and communication	6.6	7.0
Trade	15.5	15.3
Private services	9.7	13.8
Public services	24.0	33.4
Total employment	**100**	**100**

Note: The statistical sources for 1971–5 are different from those in Table 2.6.
In contrast with Table 2.6, this table also has a category for trade.
Source: Schön (2000), p 476.

and public. In the mid-1990s, nearly half of total employment belonged to the service sector, compared to one-third in the mid-1970s. Evidently, main production was no longer associated with industrial goods, but public and private services. The industrial society had been transformed into a service society.

The industrial sector decreased partly as a consequence of the structural crisis of the 1970s. It became obvious that many Swedish industries were incapable of competing with more productive international firms. For example, textiles and the shipping industry experienced severe losses due to higher labour productivity and lower wages in Iberia, Greece, Japan and South Asia. One reason behind these problems was substantial state subsidies that altered the conditions of competitiveness in the world market. Another element of the increasing internationalization of business was higher specialization, especially in exporting industries such as iron and steel, pulp and paper, engineering, food and dairy, and the consumer industry. Therefore, there was a growing recognition within business that further specialization, diversification and foreign investments were necessary to keep positions internationally.

To gain a position in the growing international markets, the Swedish business climate had to change and become more export-oriented. Swedish outward FDI began to grow rapidly and in the early 1990s Sweden accounted for 4 per cent of global FDI, while its contribution to world trade was less than 2 per cent. However, since inward FDI (investments in Sweden made by non-domestic firms) was less, the net result of investment flows across the border was slightly negative. In 2002, outward FDI amounted to 60 per cent of

Country	1–19	20–199	200–499	500–	Total
Sweden	18	17	7	58	100
France	29	21	16	34	100
Germany	26	19	18	37	100
UK[2]	33	16	17	34	100

Notes: 1. Private economy except for extractive industries.
2. 0–19 instead of 1–19.
Source: Central Statistical Office (SCB), Företagarregistret.

GDP, which could be compared to the relatively less internationally oriented Norwegian economy, with 20 per cent of GDP. Sweden's high proportion of outward FDI was consistent with the investment policies in the late nineteenth century, which more or less lifted the economy from poverty to wealth. Like the Netherlands and Switzerland, two other small European economies with a long record of high degree of outward FDI and high GDP per capita, Sweden continued to be a persistent foreign investor in the twenty-first century.[16]

The process of globalization of Swedish business also reflected a gradual liberalization of foreign exchange control. This allowed the players not only to invest in financial and real assets abroad, but also to take advantage of benefits abroad through an increasing capital inflow back home. Among the largest Swedish firms, a minority of the employees work inside the country. To some extent, the process of internationalization of large firms hindered further enlargement of the public sector, since the state lost control over the firms' activities and tax incomes when markets became globalized and activities were located overseas.

There is a metaphor for the Swedish business structure that uses the idea of a schnapps' glass – a wide top, a thin neck and a small base. In 2000, twenty-one of the fifty largest listed firms were founded before 1914, only eight in the post-war period and none after 1970. Such a dominant large-firm sector is, even in an international perspective, quite unusual (Table 2.8). Taking into account the effects of global competition, such an asymmetric formation might be a disadvantage: financial problems in only one or two major firms mean difficulties for the whole economy, not at least all the small and medium sub-contractors to the large financially distressed firms. This was illustrated with the crisis in the telecommunication company Ericsson in 2000–2. Obviously, earlier industrial policies have led to an ageing economy with a high proportion of old and large firms with well-defined owners in control. However, current statistics do not consider the existence of unlisted and relatively new large firms owned by Swedish families tax-registered abroad, such as IKEA and Tetra Pak.

For a long period of time, the political focus has been on the performance of large firms in mature industries, even though their contribution to domestic employment and the tax economy has diminished. Domestic manufacturing employment decreased by approximately 100,000 people in Sweden from 1960 to 1986, while the employment rate in foreign branches of Swedish MNCs increased by 150,000 persons. If we add the number of people occupied in other Swedish affiliates overseas, the MNCs in 1986 employed nearly as many abroad as in Sweden. In 1998, 66 per cent of the workforce in Swedish firms was occupied abroad. With regard to sales, the domestic market for these firms halved in importance between 1974 and 1998, from 59 to 29 per cent of total sales. This illustrates the increased international dependency for Swedish business in this period, as well as the process of further integration of the international economy.

Photograph 2.3 *Ingvar Kamprad, born 1926, Swedish entrepreneur and founder of the retail chain IKEA. The successful development of IKEA has made Kamprad one of the richest men in the world. On the other hand, he keeps a low-budget profile, combined with a branding of Swedish egalitarian values.*
Source: Scanpix.

In terms of strategic thinking, the Swedish business system in the post-war period has gradually been more influenced by the US business system, which has taken over from the strong inspiration from the German system prevalent since the industrial breakthrough. New management ideas in the 1960s led to increasing diversification (conglomerates), which shifted to a wave of outsourcing and downsizing from the 1980s onwards. This was followed by a focus on shareholder value, strong leadership, institutional ownership and short-term profits, including a market for corporate control. Although the débâcle of the so-called 'new economy' changed the focus, the US system continued to be the guiding light for the Swedish business system in the early twenty-first century. Nevertheless, there are remaining layers from the industrial break-through, making the Swedish system a distinctive one in the international context. First, the role of the state is stronger than in many other countries, although membership in the EU has to some extent reduced the possibility of taking independent reforms and actions. Second, the labour unions are relatively strong and also allied with the Social Democratic party. Third, there are no elite schools and a strong focus on vocational training. Fourth, the financial system is highly credit-based with ownership spheres and family capitalism in the large-firm sector.

In the on-going globalization of business, certain sectors have played a vital role. The fastest-growing branch has been ICT, where innovations such as the AXE switchboard and mobile telephony (GSM standard) have made a fortune for Ericsson and its sub-contractors. Other expanding branches have been pharmaceutical and biotech. The innovation processes in these sectors were related to a substantial increase in R&D (Table 2.9). With the motive to increase R&D budgets and keep their position in the highly competitive international market, both Astra and Pharmacia merged in the 1990s, becoming AstraZeneca and Pharmacia-UpJohn.[17] Astra experienced a commercial success with Losec (gastric ulcers), while an important product for Pharmacia in the 1990s was Genotropin (for people short in stature), the latter highlighting an increasingly importance of linkages between pharmacology and

Table 2.9   *R&D intensity according to different measures: Swedish MNCs, 1965–94 (per cent)*

	1965	1974	1986	1994
Total R&D/total MNC	2.08	2.08	3.83	4.65
Total R&D/Swedish parent sales	2.59	2.93	6.71	9.72
Swedish R&D/Swedish parent sales	2.37	2.51	5.83	7.32

Source: Swedenborg (2001), p. 120.

biotech. In the area of medicine technology, another company - Gambro – reached a strong international position. The world-leading company within packaging industry – Tetra Pak – originated from the same business elite in Skåne. Since the shares are not floated on the stock market, the Rausing family has total control of the firm. Another world-leading family business is IKEA, which was founded by Ingvar Kamprad in 1943 and has had a major impact on the furniture industry, from consumption patterns and design to logistics and distribution systems.

The neo-liberalistic re-regulation in key sectors led to many new markets, for example within energy, telecommunication and television. Kinnevik, for example, controlled by the Stenbeck family, rapidly took a grip on satellite-based television and new forms of media. The entrepreneur and CEO Jan Stenbeck introduced an aggressive US style of management that challenged both the rigid structures and principles of business ethics. Other expanding firms in the international context have been attached to clothing, retailing, design and entertainment, where new development blocs have been created around firms such as Hennes & Mauritz and Lindex. Within the music industry various pop groups have followed the track pioneered by ABBA and Roxette. In fact, today the music industry makes a larger contribution to GDP than the agricultural sector does, which illustrates the substantial transformation of the Swedish economy and society since the first industrial revolution.

Conclusion

A reasonable assumption is that the welfare capitalism we find in Sweden is embedded in a certain national culture. Its outward-looking nature could be traced back to the Vikings and the engineering culture back to the vast exploitation of natural resources in medieval times. Sweden has never been colonial, but shares with other small economies – for example, Switzerland – a long tradition of involvement in international trade and foreign exposure.[18] Thus, the three largest cities (Stockholm, Göteborg and Malmö) have always been great ports and well integrated in the mercantile world. Two other components of the outward orientation are multilingual abilities and migration flows. To be able to take part in knowledge transfer and made FDI it soon became vital for Swedish professionals to be educated in first German and later English. The strong multilingualism in Sweden is also currently viewed as a key factor in the expanding tourist industry. About 25 per cent of the population emigrated in 1850–1930, mainly to the US, a phenomenon that broke cultural barriers and helped to increase trade across national borders, especially the Atlantic Ocean. In the post-war era, a substantial immigration of industrial workers took place during the booming 1950s and 1960s. Together with a generous policy towards refugees, new migration flows from the 1980s and onwards have broken remaining cultural barriers and further reshaped Swedish city-communities.

Sweden has a lot in common with other small European economies in terms of cultural orientation, number of MNCs and type of governance. As in the Netherlands and Switzerland, firms have been 'clustered' in certain capital-intensive industries, where they have played the same role as in larger economies. Due to the size of the home market, they started to export quite early and some of them soon became global giants. Thus, the limitation of the national market does not seem to have been the reason for strong economic growth in Sweden. The key factor was rather having a unique product to offer.[19]

The question is whether the Swedish case is reminiscent of the British type of personal capitalism, German co-operative capitalism or American competitive capitalism. Some scholars are inclined to link the Swedish case to the German type of capitalism, which is correct if you only have these three options. Since many Swedish blue chips are still controlled by families and the US highly competitive market has always been important for Swedish MNCs, we should suggest a mixture of the three types of capitalistic modes. In order to be more precise in our views and labelling, we also have to consider the extensive welfare system built up as part of the Swedish model, with roots going back far into history. Since this component makes a difference to the pattern observed in other western countries, we suggested the term 'welfare capitalism'. The fact that the latest wave of re-regulations and globalization has swept away some principles of the Swedish middle way is not enough to make us think that earlier layers do not have an impact on cultural orientation and business behaviour. As an example, Sweden continues to have an extensive re-distribution of income and a large public sector, based on the highest income taxes in Europe.

Once we have accepted the term 'welfare capitalism' to cover the essence of the Swedish economy and society, we are ready to approach the next and lower level of our analysis. Here, the concept of business system provides us with an analytical framework of factors that have to be considered in order to discuss driving forces during each formative phase of the various industrial revolutions. The business system could be labelled as a collaborative one, but has a higher dominance of MNCs and a more re-distributive state than, for example, the German collaborative system.

On the level of the business system

The Swedish story is characterized by many turning points and choices of páth, although welfare capitalism has been evident during the long transformation of the economy. One way to focus on changes in the business system is to divide the history into periods. Every period starts with a formative phase featuring a certain structural transformation, an outcome of the interplay between institutional change and a new techno-economic paradigm, and is followed by a contrasting period of institutional stability and economic rationalization. Figures 2A.1–2A.4 in the Appendix (p. 71) give a compressed view of four periods in Swedish economic and business history. Although each period could be seen as one type of business system, there are many continuities that challenge such an interpretation. Therefore, we are inclined to interpret the Swedish collaborative business system from 1850 until today as one theme with four variations.

In the formative phase of the foundation era (*Gründerzeit*) liberal ideas remoulded the economic and the political spheres. The radical reforms totally reshaped the incentive structure for many players, not at least for entrepreneurs that received new and better possibilities for doing business. The state took an active role beyond regulation and supervision – for example, by importing capital from abroad to build a national network of railways. The agricultural sector still dominated in terms of employment and GDP, but the rate of growth was in fact stronger in other sectors. Operations within the industrial sector were concentrated on various extractive activities, such as sawmills and ironworks. The richness of unique natural resources and a limited home market gave birth to an extensive export of more or less pro-cessed natural products. Along the coastline, merchant houses and transport companies were set up to handle risks and practical matters connected to export industries.

In the late nineteenth century, the state was highly active in promoting economic growth. The state co-ordinated investments in post, telegraph, tele-phone, roads and railways services by building up hierarchical and centralized organizations on a large scale. According to the production function, public investments in railways and roads were also motivated by the possibility of increasing export trade. In the formative phase 1890–1910, the activity of the state was enlarged to technical procurement, where civil servants co-operated with private actors to pursue innovative processes. The state gave orders to a company to come up with a certain product innovation or a complete technical system, for example, within energy, electricity and telephony. This type of arrangement led to extensive networks between representatives from the state, industrial firms and universal banks. A strong entrepreneurial leadership was established connected to the emerging capital-intensive industries. Thanks to low taxes some entrepreneurs were able to accumulate substantial wealth, which also led to donations and new foundations later on.

In the early twentieth century, the formation of centralized labour unions stabilized the links between the state and private capitalists. Another institutional shift took place in the financial system, when corporate finance in combination with cartels was used for the interest of organized capitalism. A long period of high growth rates and rampant financial capitalism was replaced in the early 1920s by a period of monetary instability, low growth rates, high unemployment rates and substantial restructuring of industry and trade. However, in the 1930s it was clear that the creative destruction had led to a rationalized and modernized industrial economy with a great many innovations in emerging markets.

Key characteristics in the subsequent period, 1935–75, were high economic growth, low unemployment rates, low inflation, extensive public services, a state-regulated capital market and internationalization of private businesses. Sweden had the highest economic growth rate among all industrialized countries from 1930 to 1950, and continued to keep a strong international position until the structural crisis in the 1970s, which hit the Swedish business system extremely hard. During the formative phase, the Swedish model, with strong connections to Keynesianism, gave predictability and transparency for economic actors to act upon. A key institution was the *Saltsjöbadsavtalen*, which guaranteed certain stability in the labour market. Also other rules of the game gave stability to the economy and began a harmonious relationship between employees and employers. The establishment of the AMV and the AMS during a long-lived dominance of Social Democratic governments opened the way for many reforms in the labour market, hand in hand with a solidaristic wage policy. Thanks to strong economic growth, the state could invest in infrastructure, housing programmes and health care. Consequently, the public sector grew significantly, illustrating a gradual shift from industrial society to service society. The financial system was still characterized by tight relationships between certain (mature) large industries and ownership spheres, now underpinned by a favourable tax policy and strong regulation of capital flows.

Since the late 1970s, the Swedish business system has changed considerably. In a long perspective the main features have been – in chronological order – creative destruction following the structural crisis in the 1970s, relatively low growth rates, stagflation, devaluations, re-regulation in key sectors (financial, energy, transport, communication, telephony, etc.), financial crisis, EU reforms, FDI, internationally based M&As, a new monetary regime and mass university education. The service society has matured and expanded to a variety of forms, from immigrant-based family networks to hierarchical global concerns. Deregulations and further internationalization of business has made the labour market more fragmented and flexible, while the financial system has received a higher degree of market orientation.

The core of the Swedish business system is still the old innovative companies that have been able to compete internationally on the basis of on-going technical innovations. However, in terms of employment, they are challenged by young and fast-growing concerns in sectors featuring distributional and market innovations. Politically, the direction of the Swedish business system has been subordinated to the political process within the EU, putting a restriction on independent national fiscal and labour policies. Economically, the direction of the Swedish business system is even more dependent on the international market than before and the identity of the firm is not primarily European but rather a result of where in the world the market happens to be. In a way, the new global economy is a reminiscent of a world that lifted the Swedish business system to a certain height more than a hundred years ago.

QUESTIONS 1. We suggest that Swedish economic history could be divided into four periods of more or less distinctive paths in terms of institutional settings, economic structure and economic performance. The point of departure for every such period is a change of institutions and technology that alters the possibilities for doing business. This first part of a long period of change has been referred to in Chapter 1 as a 'formative phase'. Try to pinpoint key features in the four formative phases observed in Sweden, compare them and discuss which of them has been the relatively most important in terms of structural changes and economic performance.

2. Give examples of the core principles of the 'Swedish model'. To what extent is it still relevant to talk about a 'Swedish model', as a label for Swedish contemporary political economy? What happens to the answer if you vary the definition of the 'Swedish model' (narrower–broader), in line with the three definitions put forward by the chapter author above?

Notes

1. Special thanks to Håkan Lindgren for many useful comments.
2. The Swedish way of handling the problems was internationally known already in the 1930s, from a book by Michael Childs, entitled *Sweden: The Middle Way* (1936).
3. For the role of multinationals during and between the waves of globalization, see Jones (2005).
4. The need for a passport was abolished in 1860, which made a free movement of individuals across the border possible. Before that there were, as in many other countries, restrictions on travelling between domestic cities and overseas. During the First World War, compulsory passports for international travel was introduced.
5. Broberg, (2006), pp. 80–98.
6. AB Separator was founded in 1883 and merged with the two largest Swedish competitors in 1928. In 1963 the name was changed to Alfa-Laval.
7. Nilsson (2005).
8. Ögren (2003), ch. 4 and Talia (2004). Norway joined the Scandinavian Union in 1875.
9. Shaplen (1960), p. 9.
10. See also Harvard Business School, Case No. 9-804-078, p. 1.
11. Hildebrand (1985).
12. Olsson (1991).
13. The older Stockholm School included Erik Lindahl, Gunnar Myrdal and Bertil Ohlin, whilst the younger generation involved Dag Hammarskjöld, Alf Johansson, Erik Lundberg and Ingvar Svennilson.
14. The School diverged from pure Keynesianism on four issues (Lundberg, 1985, pp. 7–8). Firstly, stabilization of the price level was taken as a primary aim of stabilization policy. Secondly, the Stockholm School put relatively more attention on the cyclical instability and disequilibrium economics, and stressed the expansion possibilities of the economy. Thirdly, the policy orientation, such as pros and cons of expansionary fiscal policies, was more extensive compared to Keynes. Finally, the treatment of international relations differed. The problems facing a small open economy like Sweden had to be treated in another way compared to the analysis of a closed economy in General Theory.
15. After not having the majority of votes between 1973 and 1976, the power was lost to a non-socialist government in 1976. This period lasted for six years, until the Social Democrats recovered the governance for a period of nine years. In 1991, the governance moved to a bloc of non-socialist parties, while a voting minority based on the Social Democratic Party had power between 1994 and 2006.
16. Jones (2005), p. 232.
17. The first major merger in contemporary Swedish business (and European business) occurred in 1988, when ASEA merged with the Swiss company Brown Boveri.
18. Jones (2005), p. 242.
19. Schröter (1997).

References

Andersson-Skog, L. and Krantz, O. (eds), *Omvandlingens sekel: Perspektiv på ekonomi och samhälle i 1900-talets Sverige* (Lund: Studentlitteratur 2002).

Broberg, O., *Konsten att skapa pengar: Aktiebolagens genombrott och finansiell moderniser-ing kring sekelskiftet 1900*, Meddelanden från Ekonomisk-historiska institutionen, 95 (Göteborg: Göteborgs universitet, 2006).

Childs, M. W., *Sweden, The Middle Way* (New Haven: Yale University Press, 1936).

Gershenkron, A., *Economic Backwardness in Historical Perspective* (Cambridge, MA: The Belknap of Harvard University Press, 1966).

Harvard Business School, Case 9-804-078 (Kreuger, Ivar and the Swedish Match Empire).

Henrekson, M., Jonung, L. and Stymne, J., 'Economic Growth and the Swedish Model', in Crafts, N. and Toniolo, G. (eds), *Economic Growth in Europe since 1945* (Cambridge: Cambridge University Press, 1996).

Hildebrand, K.-G., *Expansion, Crisis, Reconstruction: The Swedish Match Company, 1917–1939* (Stockholm: Liber Tryck, 1985).

Högfeldt, P., 'The History and Politics of Corporate Ownership in Sweden', in Morck, R. (ed.), *A History of Corporate Governance Around the World: Family Business Groups to Professional Managers* (Chicago: University of Chicago Press, 2005).

Jones, G., *Multinationals and Global Capitalism* (Oxford: Oxford University Press, 2005).

Lane, J.E. (ed), *Understanding the Swedish Model* (London: Frank Cass, 1991).

Larsson, M., *Staten och kapitalet: Det svenska finansiella systemet under 1900-talet* (Stockholm: SNS förlag, 1998).

Larsson, M., 'Storföretagande och industrikoncentration', in Isacson, M. and Morell, M. (eds), *Industrialismens tid* (Stockholm: SNS förlag, 2002).

Lindgren, H. and Sjögren, H., 'Banking Systems as 'Ideal Types' and as Political Economy: The Swedish Case, 1820–1914', in Forsyth, D. J. and Verdier, D. (eds), *The Origins of National Financial Systems: Alexander Gerschenkron Reconsidered* (London: Routledge, 2003).

Lundberg, E., 'The Rise and Fall of the Swedish Model', *Journal of Economic Literature,* 23 (1985), pp. 1–36.

Maddison, A., *Dynamic Forces in Capitalist Development* (Oxford: Oxford University Press, 1991).

Maddison, A., *Monitoring the World Economy* (Paris: OECD, 1995).

Mjöset, L. (ed), *Norden dagen derpå: De Nordiske økonomisk-politiske modellene og deres problemer på 70- og 80-talet* (Oslo: Universitetsforlaget, 1986).

Nilsson, G. B., *The founder: André Oscar Wallenberg (1816–1886); Swedish Banker, Politician and Journalist* (Stockholm: Almqvist & Wiksell, 2005).

Nygren, I., *Från Stockholms Banco till Citibank: Svensk kreditmarknad under 325 år* (Stockholm: Liber, 1985).

Ögren, A., *Empirical Studies in Money, Credit and Banking: The Swedish Credit Market Transition under the Silver and the Gold Standards, 1834–1913* (Stockholm: Institute for Research in Economic History, 2003).

Olsson, U., 'Planning in the Swedish Welfare State', *Studies in Political Economy, Economic Outlook,* (Pans: OECD, Spring 1991), pp. 147–71.

Olsson, U., 'Securing the Markets: Swedish Multinationals in a Historical Perspective', in Jones, G. and Schröter, H. (eds), *The Rise of Multinationals in Continental Europe* (London: Edward Elgar, 1993a).

Olsson, U., 'Industrilandet', in *Äventyret Sverige: En ekonomisk och social historia* (Stockholm: Utbildningsradion och Bra Böcker, 1993b).

Pettersson, L. and Nilsson, A., 'Utbildning, ekonomisk omvandling och tillväxt', in *Äventyret Sverige: En ekonomisk och social historia* (Stockholm: Utbildningsradion och Bra Böcker, 1993).

Rothstein, B., 'State Structure and Variations in Corporatism: The Swedish Case', *Scandinavian Political Studies,* 14(2) (1991), pp. 139–71.

Sandberg, L. G., 'The Case of Impoverished Sophisticate: Human Capital and Swedish Economic Growth before World War I', *Journal of Economic History,* 39(1), (March 1979).

Shaplen, R., *Kreuger: Genius and Swindler* (New York: Alfred A. Knopf, 1960).

Schön, L., *En modern svensk ekonomisk historia: Tillväxt och omvandling under två sekel* (Stockholm: SNS förlag, 2000).

Schröter, H., 'Small European Nations: Cooperative Capitalism in the Twentieth Century', in Chandler, A. D., Jr, Amatori, F. and Hikino, T. (eds), *Big Business and the Wealth of Nations,* (Cambridge: Cambridge University Press 1997).

Sjögren, H., 'Scandinavia', in Foley, B. J. (ed), *European Economies Since the Second World War* (London: Macmillan, 1998).

Swedenborg, B., 'Svenska multinationella företag', *Sveriges Industri* (Stockholm: Industriförbundet, 1992).

Swedenborg, B., 'Determinants and Effects of Multinational Growth: The Swedish Case Revisited', in Blomström, M. and Goldberg, L. S. (eds), *Topics in Empirical International Economics* (Chicago: University of Chicago Press, 2001).

Talia, K., *Scandinavian Currency Union 1873–1924: Studies in Monetary Integration and Disintegration* (Stockholm: Institute for Research in Economic History, 2004).

appendix: the transformation of the Swedish business system

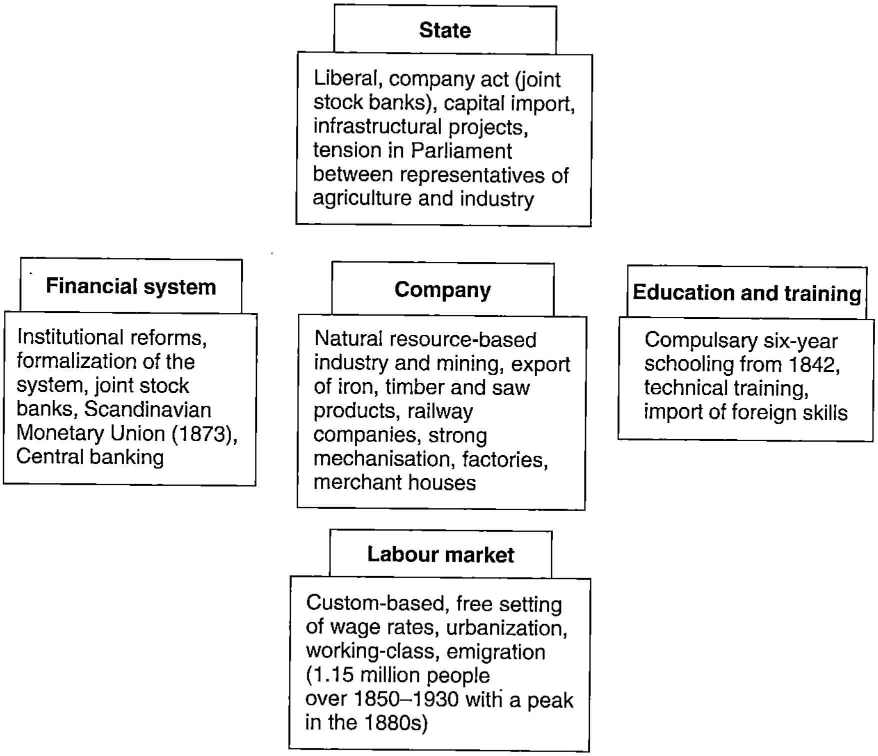

```
                    ┌──────────────────────┐
                    │        State         │
                    ├──────────────────────┤
                    │ Liberal, company act (joint
                    │ stock banks), capital import,
                    │ infrastructural projects,
                    │ tension in Parliament
                    │ between representatives of
                    │ agriculture and industry
                    └──────────────────────┘

┌─────────────────┐  ┌──────────────────────┐  ┌────────────────────────┐
│ Financial system│  │       Company        │  │ Education and training  │
├─────────────────┤  ├──────────────────────┤  ├────────────────────────┤
│ Institutional reforms, │ Natural resource-based  │ Compulsary six-year
│ formalization of the   │ industry and mining, export │ schooling from 1842,
│ system, joint stock    │ of iron, timber and saw │ technical training,
│ banks, Scandinavian    │ products, railway       │ import of foreign skills
│ Monetary Union (1873), │ companies, strong
│ Central banking        │ mechanisation, factories,
│                        │ merchant houses
└─────────────────┘  └──────────────────────┘  └────────────────────────┘

                    ┌──────────────────────┐
                    │    Labour market     │
                    ├──────────────────────┤
                    │ Custom-based, free setting
                    │ of wage rates, urbanization,
                    │ working-class, emigration
                    │ (1.15 million people
                    │ over 1850–1930 with a peak
                    │ in the 1880s)
                    └──────────────────────┘
```

Figure 2A.1 **Liberalism and early industrialization within agricultural society, 1850–90 – the foundation era**

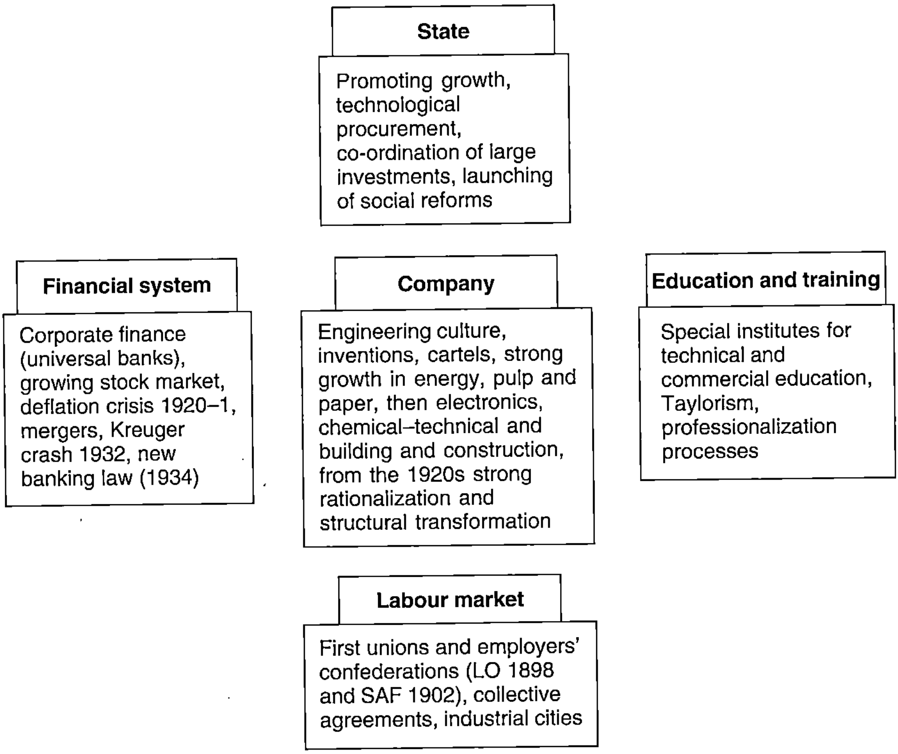

State
Promoting growth, technological procurement, co-ordination of large investments, launching of social reforms

Financial system
Corporate finance (universal banks), growing stock market, deflation crisis 1920–1, mergers, Kreuger crash 1932, new banking law (1934)

Company
Engineering culture, inventions, cartels, strong growth in energy, pulp and paper, then electronics, chemical–technical and building and construction, from the 1920s strong rationalization and structural transformation

Education and training
Special institutes for technical and commercial education, Taylorism, professionalization processes

Labour market
First unions and employers' confederations (LO 1898 and SAF 1902), collective agreements, industrial cities

Figure 2A.2   Industrial society and financial capitalism, 1890–1935

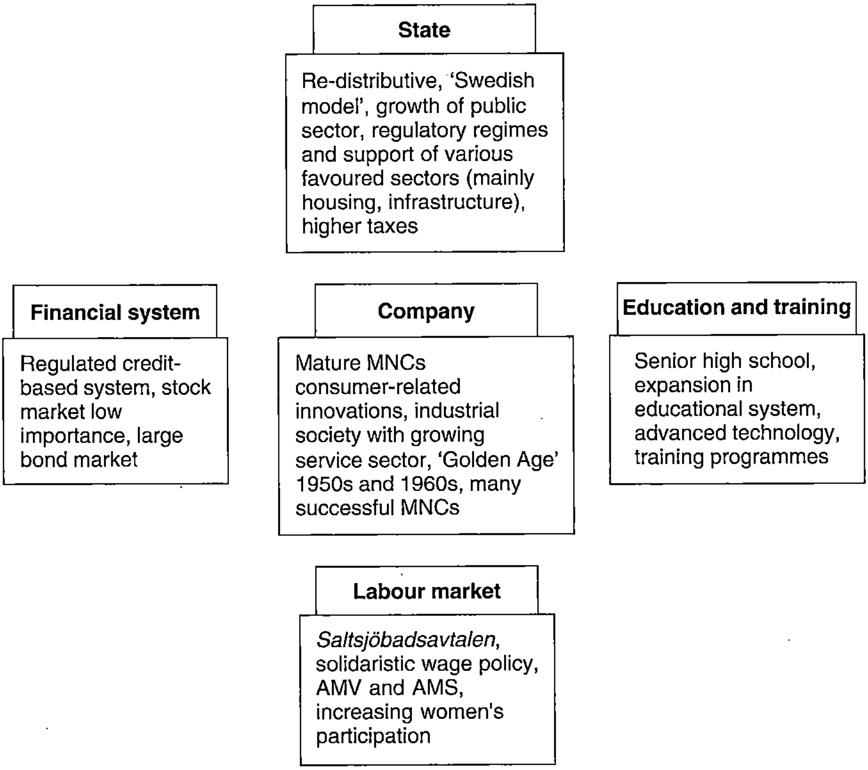

State
Re-distributive, 'Swedish model', growth of public sector, regulatory regimes and support of various favoured sectors (mainly housing, infrastructure), higher taxes

Financial system	Company	Education and training
Regulated credit-based system, stock market low importance, large bond market	Mature MNCs consumer-related innovations, industrial society with growing service sector, 'Golden Age' 1950s and 1960s, many successful MNCs	Senior high school, expansion in educational system, advanced technology, training programmes

Labour market
Saltsjöbadsavtalen, solidaristic wage policy, AMV and AMS, increasing women's participation

Figure 2A.3   The 'Swedish model', mature industries and welfare economy, 1935–75

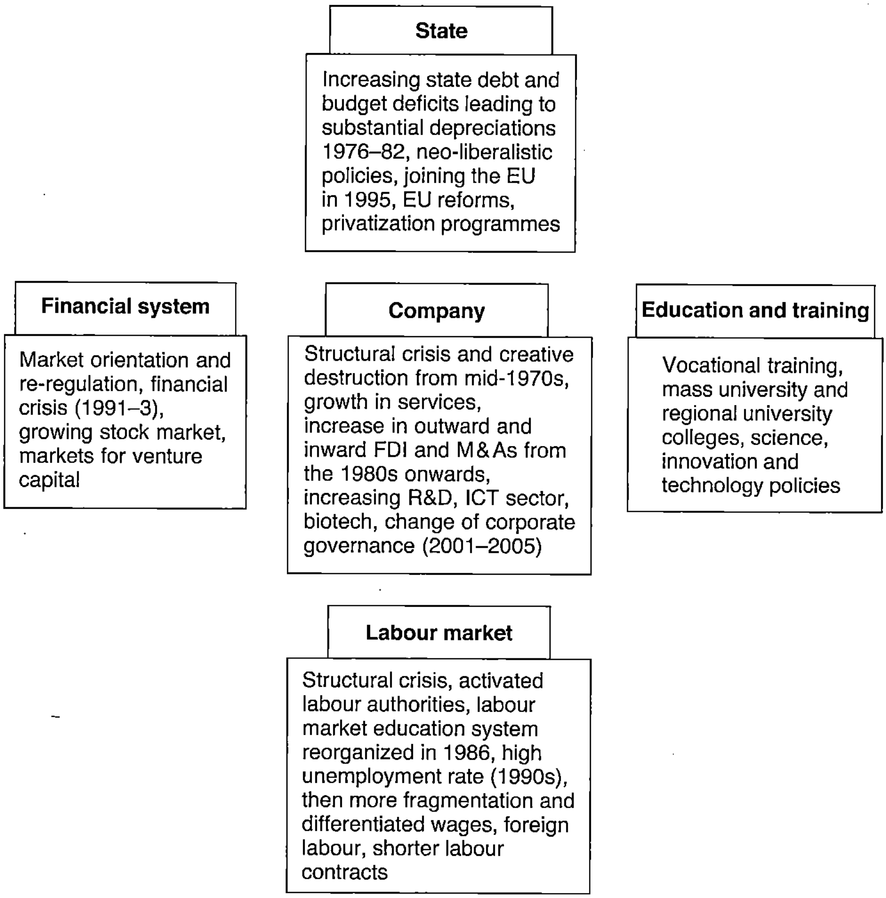

State
Increasing state debt and budget deficits leading to substantial depreciations 1976–82, neo-liberalistic policies, joining the EU in 1995, EU reforms, privatization programmes

Financial system	Company	Education and training
Market orientation and re-regulation, financial crisis (1991–3), growing stock market, markets for venture capital	Structural crisis and creative destruction from mid-1970s, growth in services, increase in outward and inward FDI and M&As from the 1980s onwards, increasing R&D, ICT sector, biotech, change of corporate governance (2001–2005)	Vocational training, mass university and regional university colleges, science, innovation and technology policies

Labour market
Structural crisis, activated labour authorities, labour market education system reorganized in 1986, high unemployment rate (1990s), then more fragmentation and differentiated wages, foreign labour, shorter labour contracts

Figure 2A.4 **Neo-liberalism and internationalization within the service society, 1975–2005**

WELFARE CAPITALISM: THE SWEDISH ECONOMY 1850–2005 • ENTREPRENEURSHIP AND OWNERSHIP: THE ERM VIABILITY OF THE SWEDISH BONNIER AND WALLENBERG FAMILY BUSINESS GROUPS • FROM ABB CAPITALISM, 1805–2005 • FROM STATE OWNERSHIP TO MULTINATIONAL CORPORATION: THE PATH OF ENSO-GUTZEIT THE STRATEGIC PATHS OF NOK AND TAMPELLA IN THE LIVING FINNISH ECONOMY AFTER THE SECOND WORLD WAR • CO-OPERATIVE LIBERALISM: DENMARK FROM 1857 TO 2007 • A – FROM DECENTRALIZED INDUSTRY TO MULTINATI... THE SELF-REGULATION OF THE DANISH BEER MARKET • NORWAY: A RESOURCE-BASED AND DEMOCRATIC CAPITALISM • CONSTRUCTIVE POWER: ELKEM 1904–2004 • FINANCE AND TH...

entrepreneurship and ownership: the long-term viability of the Swedish Bonnier and Wallenberg family business groups

Mats Larsson, Håkan Lindgren and Daniel Nyberg

Introduction

This chapter deals with family firms, business groups and big business. None of these concepts is easy to define as their content varies over time and space. A 'family firm' is usually considered as an enterprise that is owned and controlled by a single family. This does not necessarily mean that the family directly administers the business. Nor does it mean that the family necessarily owns a majority of the shares. What is required, however, is that the family acts as an active principal owner and that it has the will and the competence to control and steer the firm's evolution, even if policies are actually implemented by salaried administrators. This definition separates the concept of the family firm from that of the small business: the former can be both large and publicly traded and still be considered a family firm.

According to Mark Granovetter, a business group is 'a collection of firms bound together in some formal and/or informal ways, characterized by an "intermediate" level of binding'.[1] This definition allows the inclusion of stable cartels and conglomerates, provided that the ties among the companies are personal and operational. It thus includes the Korean Chaebols and the Japanese Keiretsus. It is also convenient to include holding company groups and trusts controlled directly or indirectly by a common parent company or by a family. Such a broad definition, however, makes it extremely difficult to pinpoint business groups, since they are neither a legal entity nor a census category. The more practical and operational approach utilized in this chapter is to limit the definition of a business group to a collection of firms linked by ownership ties. It will permit a comprehensive analysis of actual group behaviour and corporate governance.

What, then, is 'big business'? It is one thing in the huge American economy and something else in a small country such as Sweden. Inspired by the Chandler thesis, observers have drawn countless comparisons between European (mainly British) and American business performance. These have mainly focused on the size and the organizational structure of individual firms. Too often, big business and manufacturing are synonymous. As noted by Youssef Cassis, however, 'big business is a matter of large-scale operations, of money and power, whatever the type of activity or the forms of organization'.[2] From this perspective, a family business group may be part of big business, and the pertinent family member representatives of their home country's business elite.

As in other countries, Sweden's industrialization during the nineteenth century was largely built up by family-owned companies. Even after the breakthrough of joint stock companies with limited liabilities in the late nineteenth century, family ownership kept its position. Managerial capitalism with a spread ownership was still unusual among the largest Swedish companies in the early twentieth century. The two families, Wallenberg and Bonnier, analysed in this chapter, both entered Swedish business as owners in the nineteenth century. During the twentieth century, their companies gradually grew and attained central positions in the Swedish economy.

In the early twenty-first century, family capitalism is still of the greatest importance in Sweden, as well as the other Nordic countries. In fact, the large financial families are regarded as one of three major networks or ownership groups in Sweden's big business – the others being bank groups and managerially-run large companies. When official Swedish investigations in 1963–4 scrutinized the ownership in Sweden's big business sector, fourteen of the seventeen largest owner groups were families – the Wallenberg family being the largest and the Bonnier family the ninth largest. Later research has shown that family ownership also maintained a strong position in Sweden's big business in the 1980s.[3]

Problems of the study

The intent of this chapter is to compare the strategies of two of present-day Sweden's most important family business groups, those of the Bonnier and the Wallenberg families. Both of these groups have an impressive record of longevity: heading into the new millennium they were governed by the sixth (Bonnier) and the fifth (Wallenberg) generations. This long-term viability is proof of an ability to adapt to changing structures and conditions.

By necessity, they must have chosen effective strategies in the past. The point of comparative business history, however, is to reveal both the similarities and the dissimilarities in the strategic behaviour of firms. It can demonstrate how identical objectives (in this case, the survival and consolidation of the family group) can be achieved by differing means. It can also show how variations in the institutional setting (in this case, mainly at the industrial level) can decisively influence the choice of strategies to reach the given objective.

The focus here is on three areas of strategic behaviour: (1) how change has been balanced with continuity in business group behaviour, i.e. the role of family tradition within the business groups; (2) how active versus passive ownership and centralization versus decentralization have been balanced in group decision-making; and (3) how entrepreneurship was handled in the two groups during the twentieth century.

From our analysis, we can learn not only how two of the most important business families in Sweden managed to survive as leaders within their branch of industry for over 150 years, but also what preconditions were important for that development. The chapter also gives us a more general insight into the role of entrepreneurship within larger companies and how active ownership can be combined with entrepreneurship. Knowledge of how ownership has been exercised also helps us to understand the mechanisms of economic development and success.

The Bonnier and the Wallenberg group of companies

Sweden has two types of business groups, distinguishable by their historical roots. One of these is family groups, originating in a single entrepreneur and a single firm, which have grown powerful thanks to incremental investment in various activities. Sometimes these have evolved into important conglomerates that are active in a number of unrelated fields. Several such groups hold prominent positions within the Swedish business elite: the Johnsons, the Rausings, the Lundbergs, the Stenbecks and the Bonniers, to name but a few.

The second major type is those business groups that evolved around the principal commercial banks, starting just before and during the First World War. Most of these were impersonal spheres of interest, not family groups. For a long time, they dominated big business in Sweden, and some of them are still quite important. By contrast with the other major Swedish banks and banking groups, however, one of them, in fact, was family-controlled, even if through a minority stock holding – the Wallenberg family-controlled Stockholms Enskilda Bank group (SEB).

The choice of the Bonnier and the Wallenberg groups as cases in this chapter is not explained only by their different organization of family ownership, but also by their different lines of business. The Wallenberg group has since the 1920s had a strong position in Swedish industry, with approximately 23 per cent of the industrial workforce in 1979 employed in companies controlled by the Wallenberg group – including the SEB bank.[4] Even though the Bonnier group for a period also included industrial production, the group's focus has since its establishment been on media. For example, the Bonnier magazine group held nearly 50 per cent of the Swedish magazine market in the early 1950s, while the Bonnier publishing house was at the same time the most prestigious book publisher. However, with the diversification and internationalization of media industry during the last decades, the role of Bonnier on the Swedish market decreased. Still, in an international perspective, the Bonnier group in the early twenty-first century was the twentieth largest family-owned media company in the world – larger, for example, than Italy's Berlusconi group.[5]

The growth of a media group

The Bonnier family's involvement in publishing began during the turbulent years of the Napoleonic Wars, when Gutkint Hirschel, the twenty-two-year-old son of a Dresden banker, moved to Denmark together with his French wife. Having changed his name to Gerhard Bonnier, he opened a bookshop in 1804, later supplemented with both a lending library and a publishing business in Copenhagen. The Swedish branch stretches back to 1827, when Gerhard's oldest son Adolf opened a bookshop in Gothenburg, later supplemented by shops in Stockholm and Uppsala. Encouraged by his success, Adolf expanded into publishing. He also accepted both economic and social responsibility for the education of his younger brothers. One of these, Albert Bonnier, was to become the founder of today's Bonnier media conglomerate (see Figure 3.1). Having moved to Stockholm, Albert began a hands-on apprenticeship, which included training abroad at publishing houses belonging to the family's business network. After returning to Stockholm in 1837, he opened his own publishing house, Albert Bonniers förlag.[6]

During the following decades, the new firm's publishing activity was put on a solid footing. Starting in the mid-1850s, however, an expansion phase began. The firm expanded vertically with the addition of compositing and

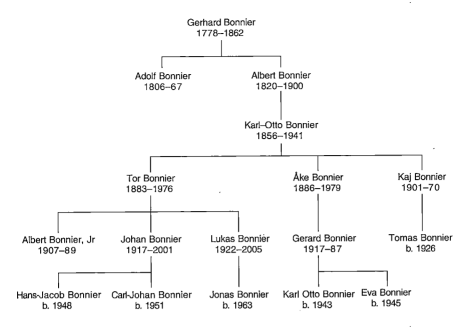

Figure 3.1 **Members of the Bonnier family active in the Bonnier group**
Note: Other Bonnier family members are or have been active within the group.

printing functions. Towards the end of the century, Albert Bonnier's son Karl-Otto Bonnier took over the leadership of the firm and, following his father's death in 1900, became the sole owner. This situation continued until 1914, when Karl-Otto's three sons, Tor, Åke and Kaj Bonnier, began to participate as managers and owners. During the pre-First World War period, Albert Bonniers förlag developed into Sweden's premier book publisher, thanks to a considerable extent to its close contacts with leading Swedish authors. The firm has succeeded in retaining this position to the present day.

In addition to publishing and printing books, the Bonnier family developed an early interest in newspapers and magazines. Towards the end of the nineteenth century, they acquired an initial block of shares in *Dagens Nyheter*, one of Sweden's largest dailies. The family became the newspaper's principal owner during the 1920s.[7] After consolidation during the inter-war period, *Dagens Nyheter* became the country's largest daily newspaper during the Second World War. The family's domination of newspaper publishing was strengthened from 1944 by the introduction of the evening paper *Expressen*, which was also incorporated into the *Dagens Nyheter* business.

During the inter-war and post- Second World War periods, Tor Bonnier was the principal representative, of both the concern and the family. He was also the driving force behind the 1929 purchase of the Swedish magazine publisher Åhlén & Åkerlund. This firm had earlier published pulp fiction, as well as serials. For a time during the 1920s, it had even experimented with radio transmissions. When the firm was incorporated into the Bonnier concern, it concentrated on weekly magazine publication and soon established a prominent position. Tor Bonnier's son, Albert Bonnier, Jr played a particularly important role in this process. During the post war-period, Åhlén & Åkerlund also developed an extensive publication of both comic books and special-interest magazines. In addition, the purchase of other magazine publishers also permitted expansion into the other Nordic markets.[8]

During the early 1950s, the concern was re-organized, with the newly formed Bonnierföretagen becoming the holding company for media and other activities. An exception was newspaper publishing which, together with some other ownership interests, was moved out of the concern. During the 1950s, there was also a broader investment in industrial activities. Initially, firms with a certain vertical relation to the publishing companies, such as paper producers, were started or acquired. Over time, however, the industrial commitment became broader. During the 1960s and 1970s, it came to include, for example, the production of furniture, disposable tableware, packaging, engineering products and even a ferry service.[9]

This diversification was partially motivated by a desire to spread risks. In addition, however, the concern encountered difficulties in expanding its national media holdings. Bonnier's strong position on the Swedish media market had led, as early as the 1950s, to intensive discussion of the consequences of media concentration. To try to expand the concern's Swedish media holdings in such a situation might have been not just unwise but, perhaps, impossible. The industrial commitment thus became one among several possible ways of managing the family fortune.

Starting in the late 1980s, however, the transformation of the media market created new opportunities for the Bonnier concern. The industrial assets were successively sold and attention re-concentrated on media activities. These included increased internationalization and entry into new areas, especially movies and broadcasting.

At the time of the establishment of Bonnierföretagen in 1952, the Bonnier group was owned by three different parts of the family, represented primarily by the brothers Tor, Åke and Kaj Bonnier. They had to a smaller or larger extent turned over their ownership to their children – Tor Bonnier's sons Albert Jr, Johan and Lukas, Åke Bonnier's son Gerard, and Kaj Bonnier's son Tomas (see Figure 3.1).

The creation of Bonnierföretagen was initially intended to be a part of the succession from one generation to another, but turned out to be much more dramatic, when the antagonism between Albert Bonnier, Jr and his uncle Kaj Bonnier became evident. Albert Bonnier, Jr in charge of the profitable Bonnier magazine publication, openly criticized Kaj Bonnier – the director of the book publishing house – for extensive losses in the publishing business. Kaj Bonnier argued that the family must be prepared to support book publishing financially in order to maintain the family's cultural position. The situation worsened during the discussion of how the Bonnier concern would be organized to meet future demands. Finally, in December 1952, Kaj Bonnier made it clear that he wanted to be bought out by the other owners, with the exception of his ownership in the newspapers *Expressen* and *Dagens Nyheter*. This was also accepted. As a result, the administration of these newspapers was separated from the rest of the Bonnier concern, and a special holding company – Deni – was created to co-ordinate the newspaper holdings of the various family branches.[10]

During the following 35–40 years after the establishment of Bonnierföretagen, this part of the Bonnier group was dominated by three representatives from the Bonnier family – the brothers Lukas Bonnier (from 1957 director of the magazine group), Albert Bonnier, Jr (general manager and chairman of the board at Bonnierföretagen) and their cousin Gerard Bonnier (in charge of book printing). Albert Bonnier, Jr had the main responsibility for the administration of the family fortune. From his central position in the holding company, Bonnierföretagen, he could exercise control over all activities in the business, including the publishing of books and magazines. Albert Bonnier, Jr was also the driving force behind Bonnierföretagen's industrial activities.

The Wallenberg dynasty

From the founding of SEB in 1856 until its merger with Skandinaviska Banken in 1972, the Wallenberg family maintained intact, and passed down through three generations, a dominant block of shares in the bank. The bank's founder, A.O. Wallenberg, was a naval officer and a devoted liberal who worked hard to modernize the Swedish banking system. It was the second-generation half-brothers, K.A. Wallenberg and Marcus Wallenberg, Sr, however, who shaped SEB's distinctive character as a banking house and industrial bank during their tenure as managing directors (1886–1920). With the third generation, especially during the period 1930–60, the Wallenberg sphere of influence in Swedish industry grew substantially. Under the leadership of Jacob and Marcus Wallenberg, both sons of Marcus Wallenberg, Sr, SEB became the centre of the most influential business group in Sweden and co-ordinated the activities of an extensive network of financial and industrial firms. As an influential owner – during the 1970s, more than 10 per cent of all employees in the Swedish private sector worked for Wallenberg companies – the Wallenberg group secured a unique position in Swedish high finance. A number of investment companies were affiliated with SEB, the most important of which were Investor, established in 1916, and Providentia, established in 1946. The principal task of these investment companies, supported by the Wallenberg foundations, was to provide an ownership platform for the business activities of the family.[11]

Following the merger of Skandinaviska Banken and SEB in 1972, the new S-E Banken came to be dominated by a company culture and management style that had its roots in the old Skandinaviska Banken. Furthermore, restrictions on voting rights in the new bank caused the Wallenberg family to lose its dominant minority ownership position for more than two decades. When Marcus Wallenberg died in 1982 and the fourth generation, in the person of his son Peter Wallenberg, took charge, the family business group was centred round the family's ownership base of investment companies and charitable foundations (see Figure 3.2). The two investment companies, Investor and Providentia, were given new identities. The administrative, research and

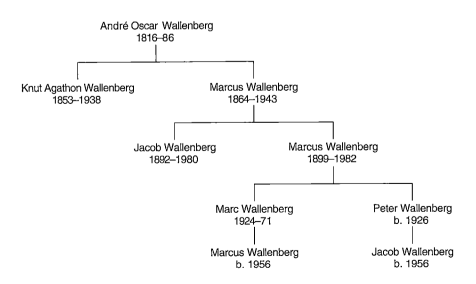

Figure 3.2 **Members of the Wallenberg family active in the Wallenberg group**

finance departments were reinforced and new divisions for mergers, acquisitions and share issue (corporate finance) were created to serve the needs of the group's industrial companies. These efforts accelerated during the stock market boom and financial market expansion that characterized the 1980s.

From being a traditional investment company with a highly diversified portfolio, Investor evolved into a holding company with controlling positions that allowed it to exercise active ownership in a limited number of large firms. During the early 1990s, Investor acquired the other Wallenberg investment companies and took over the central role previously played by the old SEB. Investor now became the hub for co-ordinating the family's business activities. Following the financial crisis of 1992–3 that brought S-E Banken to the brink of bankruptcy, the Wallenberg family increased its holding in the bank. Once more, they became a dominant and active minority owner. In 1996, two years after the voting rights restrictions had been lifted, the Wallenberg group could mobilize 17 per cent of the share capital and votes in the bank. By 1999, the time was ripe for S-E Banken to be renamed SEB, the time-honoured abbreviation used by the family bank prior to 1972.[12]

Equally striking, the Wallenberg family's control of its 'new but old' bank includes strong personal participation. Several of the holdings included fifteen of Sweden's best known telecom and engineering firms, such as L.M. Ericsson, Scania (until 2008), Atlas Copco, SKF, Electrolux and the Finnish–Swedish forest company Stora Enso.

Succession strategies

One problem associated with family enterprises is that of succession, and it is often presented as a major drawback and an important explanation for why SMEs have relatively short life expectancies. Indeed, most family enterprises end with the retirement of the founder, and barely one in ten is thought to survive the second generation.[13] A different problem may arise if the older generation chooses to remain too long in strategic positions within the firm or group. This can hamper the training of the next generation, as well as risking a loss of company dynamism even before the inevitable transition.

During its first three generations, a male member of the family led the Bonnier family business in Sweden, although not necessarily the eldest son. The existing leadership trained those of the children who expressed an interest in carrying on the business. A change in this tradition, however, occurred with the transfer from the third to the fourth generation. Of Karl-Otto Bonnier's six children, three were interested in joining the family enterprise. All three were sons, and neither of the two daughters was expected to be involved in the business. The growth of the enterprise, through the addition of newspaper and magazine publishing, had also increased the number of high-ranking positions available.[14]

Karl-Otto Bonnier's eldest son, Tor, assumed an overall responsibility for the entire concern, while Åke Bonnier, until 1940 when Albert Bonnier, Jr succeeded him, was responsible for the magazines. Kaj Bonnier was placed in charge of book publishing. As already noted, this arrangement was not problem-free. The conflict between Tor's son Albert Bonnier, Jr and his uncle Kaj caused the latter to sell out when the Bonnier concern was formed in 1952. At the time, Tor Bonnier was seventy years old and was starting to cut down his business involvement. Despite his role in the family split, Albert Bonnier, Jr was the natural heir to overall responsibility for the group. For a few years, he combined the leadership of magazine publication with his work as head of the business. Starting in 1957, however, he devoted himself entirely to the latter task.

Albert Bonnier, Jr also played an active role in placing other family members in leading positions. When Kaj Bonnier left, Albert, Jr recruited his cousin Gerard Bonnier as head of book publishing. To replace himself in the magazine business, Albert, Jr hired his brother Lukas Bonnier. Compared to other firm leaders, Gerard and Lukas Bonnier seem to have enjoyed greater freedom in administering their activities. With the changes that occurred during the 1950s, all the top positions in the concern were held by members of the fifth Bonnier generation.

In 1978, Albert Bonnier, Jr left his position as president to become instead a working chairman of the board. At that point, there was no natural heir within the family. Instead, it was decided that a non-family member from within the business would fill the position. Since Albert Bonnier, Jr was a distinctly active chairman, who could use his ownership position to halt or alter any board decision, it was crucial that the new president could co-operate with him. During the following twelve years, the group had two non-family presidents. The family's position was assured by the fact that first Albert, Jr, until 1988, and then Lukas Bonnier, until 1992, was chairman of the board.

During the entire period when the group was led by an external president, it was clear that this was just an interlude. Once a member of the sixth generation had displayed sufficient competence, that person would assume the leadership. Who that might be, however, was not clear. Rather, the plan was to let as many members of the family's various branches as possible be trained. Their work would show who might be suitable for the post. The change occurred in 1992 when Carl-Johan Bonnier – the nephew of Albert Bonnier, Jr – took over as president while the serving non-family president became chairman of the board. One additional transfer has since occurred; Carl-Johan Bonnier has become chairman of the board and a new non-family president has been appointed.[15]

Events since the late 1980s have clearly demonstrated how the Bonnier concern has been able to engineer a relatively smooth succession by combining family involvement with the recruitment of outsiders. This strategy has also involved persons in leading positions in other parts of the group. Meanwhile, a well-functioning board has guaranteed the family insight into, and control of, the business.

The succession in Deni and *Dagens Nyheter* followed a pre-established plan. Within each branch of the family, it was decided which of the other owners and persons associated with the group were to represent the family on the board of the newspaper. In many regards, these family leaders also became the bearers of tradition. Especially during times of crisis, they had to convince the other owners to stay the course. Using Deni as a bridge between the Bonnier enterprises and *Dagens Nyheter* allowed the family to maintain a tight grip on the newspapers. Through Deni, the family came to dominate *Dagens Nyheter*, even though some of the family owners sold out and the government threatened action against their dominant position within the Swedish media.

Ownership succession in the Wallenberg group has been conditional both on the inter-generational preservation of controlling blocks of shares in the companies within the group's sphere, and on the appearance in the next generation of someone with both the ability and the desire to assume family leadership. The Wallenberg foundations have been the depositories of the fortunes of earlier family generations. They have strong ownership positions in Investor, and they support Investor's function as the ownership platform for the group's business activities. The most important of these foundations is the Knut and Alice Wallenberg Foundation, established in 1917 to administer that childless couple's wealth. These foundations, it should be noted, are the largest private donors to a number of Swedish universities and research institutes.

The investment companies, together with the increasing number of Wallenberg foundations supporting scientific and cultural activities, have made it possible for the family to maintain its ownership-based business activities. The transfer of the family leadership mantle, on occasion, has been more turbulent. By tradition, the Wallenberg aspect was expected to dominate the family business. Thus the recruitment principle for CEOs and middle managers, namely that competence, independence and reliability trumps family and social origin, did not apply to the group leadership position. The eldest son was predestined to carry the torch forward, assuming only that he possessed the will and the competence to shoulder the responsibility.

When the dynasty's founder, A.O. Wallenberg (AO), died in 1886, the succession had been long arranged, and the precedent set then was to become the accepted rule for later generations. The oldest living son, Knut Agathon (KA) had in 1874, aged only twenty-one, been elected to the board of SEB and had started working there. On his father's death, Knut Agathon became the bank's CEO. All of AO's many children, even the girls, had, by the standards of the day, received excellent educations. Since women at that time played no active role in important businesses, however, the daughters were not expected, nor did they wish, to participate in the family's inner circle. Even today, there is an almost total absence of women family members among the Wallenberg group's leading managers. Upon completing his legal education, KA's younger half-brother Marcus Wallenberg accepted his offer of a legal position with the bank. Marcus then began working his way towards a leading position by accumulating expertise in the financial and industrial reconstruction of client firms. He eventually succeeded KA as CEO in 1911, when the latter assumed the chairmanship of the bank's board. KA remained childless, while Marcus' marriage was blessed with four girls and two boys.

In two later generations, two close relatives have shared leadership of the Wallenberg business group: two brothers in the third generation and two male cousins in the fifth. The great crisis for the dynasty occurred during the 1970s and 1980s, when a family tragedy suddenly destroyed the existing succession plans and led to a number of improvisations. Jacob Wallenberg of the third generation remained unmarried, and for a long time lacked an heir. The younger brother, Marcus Wallenberg, Jr, however, had two sons, Marc, Jr and Peter. With Marc working in the bank, advancing to CEO in 1958, and Peter working abroad for the foreign subsidiaries of Atlas Copco, the succession seemed assured.

The merger talks that led to the formation of the new S-E Bank in 1972 created great tension between the two brothers, Jacob and Marcus. Jacob was opposed to the whole idea of 'selling the family bank', while Marcus

Photograph 3.1 *Jacob Wallenberg (standing), Marc Jr and Marcus Wallenberg during the historic annual meeting of shareholders at Stockholm's Enskilda Bank on 15 October 1971, when the decision to merge with Skandinaviska Banken was taken.*
Source: SEB archive.

supported the merger. Marc, Jr was torn between his father and his uncle, a situation that is believed to have contributed to his decision to take his own life in November 1972. The future succession now depended entirely on Peter, whose position in the family group was not improved by his brother's death. The personal chemistry between father and son was bad, and conflicts and tensions between them led to Peter being deliberately held back by his father.

At his death in 1982, Marcus Wallenberg had begun an alliance with Volvo and its chief, Pehr G. Gyllenhammar, at that time thought to be Sweden's industrial leader par excellence. Peter Wallenberg, however, did not approve of all his father's measures, which had included letting Volvo obtain partnership status in some of the Wallenberg sphere's most dearly held firms. A few years later, Peter launched a counter-offensive that, during the boom of the 1980s, succeeded in consolidating the family sphere once again. He also laid the basis for the succession of the fifth generation, Marc, Jr's son Marcus (Husky) and his own son Jacob.

Thus, we can see both differences and similarities between the Bonnier and the Wallenberg succession strategies. Until the early 1900s, the Bonnier succession was also rather strict and reminiscent of the Wallenberg's. However, the strategy changed during the 1900s. In contrast to the Wallenbergs, the door was opened to all family members – initially the men, but later also including the women. All could find a place in the business, and the one most capable and suitable would assume the responsibility of heading the concern. While this approach created a certain degree of uncertainty, it also allowed for maximum utilization of the family's talent pool.

Change and continuity

Tradition and reactive ownership

Since its inception in the 1830s, the Bonnier group has focused on the media sector. Originally limited to book publishing, it soon expanded to include newspapers and magazines. More recently, during recent decades, it has extended its reach to broadcasting. The commitment to these activities was never questioned, even when, as in the case of book publishing during the period 1940–60, large losses were incurred. The name Bonnier was so closely associated with the Albert Bonnier publishing house that it was unthinkable to cease publishing books. Thus, for decades, more profitable lines such as magazines had to subsidise book publishing.

The group's long-term involvement in media included both newspapers and magazines. While the newspaper publishing business remained relatively stable, however, there were continual changes in the publication of magazines, all intended to satisfy readers' tastes. The long-term view, however, did result in a marked reluctance to drop individual magazines.

The long-term attitude towards the media does seem to contrast with the attitude towards the industrial commitments. From a long-term perspective, and in retrospect, the latter seems to have been a thirty-year digression. Even here, however, looking at the individual firms reveals evidence of strong ownership involvement. Investments in development firms, by their very nature, are long term. Such firms could incur losses for a decade without being dropped. The principal advocate of industrial involvement was the head of the concern, Albert Bonnier, Jr and his great passion for new technology and business. This, in turn, made it hard for him to sell or liquidate a project or firm. Instead, Albert Bonnier, Jr preferred to take the offensive and transform the firm's activity. Especially during economic downturns, this approach was severely tested and resulted in lock-in effects.[16] The goal for Albert Bonnier, Jr was that industrial production would stand for half of the business groups' turnover. Not putting all their eggs in one basket would reduce the risks connected with media activities – especially the risk of governmental interfering in the Bonnier's strong media position.

In contrast to the Wallenberg group, the Bonnier sphere wished to maintain total control of its various businesses. This, in turn, led to the reluctance to list firms on the stock exchange. It was felt that going public would interfere with active ownership policies. In this regard, the Bonniers better fit the traditional picture of a family business.

The *Dagens Nyheter* business is an interesting example of how ownership could be handled. Because of the dissent in the Bonnier family in 1952, the business came to be controlled and overseen by the holding company Deni, which was jointly owned by all the branches of the family. While this arrangement lasted, the ownership situation was stable, thus guaranteeing against a hostile takeover. With the stock market introduction of *Dagens Nyheter* in 1965, however, the shares became much more liquid, thus increasing ownership uncertainty. This, in turn, created strategic and financial problems for the holding company Deni. In order to more closely tie Deni's shares in *Dagens Nyheter* to the Bonnier sphere, a partnership agreement that allowed Deni to sell shares to the Bonnier firms was concluded, at Albert Bonnier's instigation. In due course, the Bonnier firms took over Deni's role vis-à-vis *Dagens Nyheter*.[17]

The ownership of *Dagens Nyheter* has been characterized by a consistent strategy. The intent has been to maintain majority control of Sweden's leading newspaper, while simultaneously developing the firm by, among other actions, expansion outside the media sector. Over time, *Dagens Nyheter*'s strategy has evolved to make it an increasingly integrated part of the Bonnier sphere. Since 1998, the business, once again, has been wholly owned by the family.

This legacy is of decisive importance in the case of family firms that have persisted for several generations. A particularly strong connection between family and firm can be observed at both Wallenberg and Bonnier. An extremely long time horizon has been combined with a strong sense of family. Unity and continuity have in many ways been at the core of the family's ownership philosophy. Thus, preserving the legacy for the next generation has become an important and inherent part of the family's exercise of ownership.

The business has also been the family's face to the outside world. This has especially been the case with the Bonnier publishing house and *Dagens Nyheter*. The poor financial results of book publishing were tolerated just because it was the family's traditional activity, associated with freedom of expression and the name of Bonnier.

Neither the weekly, or other magazines, nor the industrial firms were of decisive importance for the image of the Bonnier family. These businesses have also experienced much greater turbulence; firms and magazines have changed names, altered their activities and been liquidated. Even though Albert Bonnier, Jr defended the industrial firms, considering that the Bonnier businesses originated during the early nineteenth century, they were little more than a parenthesis. Thus, whether or not a firm contributed to creating the Bonnier family image was a matter of its area of interest and traditions rather than whether or not it was wholly family-owned.

This legacy has clearly affected the family's ownership philosophy – i.e. how the owner views the enterprise and its role. This is most obvious in that the family's representatives in the firms have had a legacy to preserve for future generations, thus directly drawing them towards a long-term ownership perspective. Since some of the firms were essential to the family's image, these could hardly be sold or liquidated. The Bonnier's ownership was sometime nostalgic and, in many ways, non-rational. A great deal of emotional involvement with the firms characterized their ownership philosophy. These emotions were not limited to book publishing and the newspapers, but extended even to the industrial firms. No Bonnier firm could be allowed to fail and go bankrupt since that would have a negative effect on the family.

Albert Bonnier, Jr's strong interest in the companies of the Bonnier group also resulted in sometimes very active ownership. As long as the companies developed in accordance to plan and profits were stable, he used his right to appoint persons at leading positions, but did not interfere actively in the management. However, if something went wrong he soon became engaged in restructuring the companies' activities. In all companies, whether they were successful or not, he made unannounced visits to the factories and at the offices. This could result in concrete measurements, but more often in confidential notes that he archived for future use.[18]

Stable ownership or lock-In?

From a long-term perspective, it is apparent that the Wallenberg ownership policy was designed, as group ownership contracts often put it, to 'ensure the steady development of the enterprises'. Having its roots in banking, and consequently with experience of client firms in crisis, the Wallenberg group had early on accumulated knowledge concerning the nature of industrial development. Its first test came with the reconstruction of the Hofors iron works during 1878–95, following the grave crisis of the late 1870s. The Wallenbergs learned in particular that the financial and industrial reconstruction of firms in crisis requires patience. As a result, Wallenberg industrial ownership has been a stabilizing factor, having tended to offset stock market turbulence driven by short-term expectations and profits.[19] Its principles of active ownership, often referred to by family members, include the support of, and participation in, the evolution and organizational development of firms. This is normally accomplished from its position as board chairman, and it is intended to offset the potentially stultifying effects of long-term ownership.

There are numerous examples of how the active ownership practised by the Wallenberg group accelerated the transformation of enterprises and 'whole' branches of industry. Today's Atlas Copco, for example, has very little in common, in terms of products, technology or internationalization, with the company created in 1917 through the Atlas–Diesel merger. Many group enterprises have in this way changed their 'contents' even though their legal form, or even their name, have remained unchanged.

Thus, the Wallenberg ownership policy has been characterized by a complicated interplay between loyalty, patience and support to firms in crisis, on the one hand, and an understanding of the necessity to undertake changes and restructuring, on the other. However, when conflict between these competing goals has been consciously and deliberately weighed, priority has always been given to change rather than continuity.

This choice became very clear when the group disposed of its old railway interests during the 1930s and the 1940s. Halmstad-Nässjö Järnvägar (HNJ) was a railway investment that was not only a major component of Investor's strategic portfolio but also played a strong emotional role in family tradition. The emotional aspect had its roots in the fact that the railway had been reconstructed in the 1880s under the direction of KA and SEB. When the bus and railway businesses were sold to the national government in 1945, the Wallenbergs reorganized the HNJ company as a venture capital firm dedicated to supporting new enterprises and entrepreneurship within the old railway's regional area of activity. The new company, however, began its work with an investment that seemed only tangentially related to its assigned task. It purchased a block of shares in SILA, the company that later was to become the principal Swedish participant in Scandinavian Airlines. This transaction was the basis for a comment by Marcus Wallenberg, Jr that deserves to be cited: 'To sell a railway and to invest in an airline, that is to shift from the past to what is coming, that was the motto of earlier generations of our family, the only tradition worth maintaining and the one our forefathers surely would want us to preserve.'[20]

Stable ownership provided the group companies with a degree of security even in crises. For the same reason, however, there was an obvious risk that stable ownership and security might lead to 'lock-in effects' within a firm. According to one of the strong beliefs of the Wallenberg family tradition, which was carried forward from one generation to the next, the most important check on lock-in effects was effective competition. According to both Marcus and Peter Wallenberg, one way to stimulate firm efficiency within the group was to internationalize the business in order to expose the firm to international competition.

The Wallenbergs have followed the principle that their companies should be introduced to the stock exchange as soon as each business was sufficiently consolidated to make a public offering possible. Stock market exposure has two important advantages. First, it makes it possible to develop a 'box within the box' or 'pyramid' ownership structure, thus reducing capital requirements by controlling group companies through a series of minority holdings. Conversely, however, it exposes family ownership to corporate raiders and hostile takeovers. This was most apparent during the boom years of the late 1920s and during the 1980s. Second, the market's response, at least in the medium and long run, provides valuable information on how outside observers judge a firm, and put the management continually under pressure to perform. At an early stage, the Wallenberg family thus recognized the importance of the stock market as a check on, and an evaluator of their enterprises.

Corporate governance in family business groups

Regardless of their size, family-owned firms are characterized by a corporate culture that distinguishes them from management-controlled firms with anonymous owners. In addition to active ownership, a long decision-making horizon and a certain insularity, the literature maintains that family firms are characterized by a high degree of self-financing, tendencies towards nepotism and paternalism, together with an inter-weaving of ownership, board work and strategic planning. Together, these give the family firm a centralized structure with short decision paths.

Direct and indirect Bonnier ownership

Until the reorganization in the 1950s, members of the Bonnier family held leading positions within the group. As the business grew and the number of firms controlled increased, it became impossible to continue operating the group in this direct manner. The simultaneous growth of the number of passive family members also required the development of new ways to maintain owner control.

Before the mid-1970s, the board of the entire concern was largely a paper phenomenon. It never met, and important decisions were taken elsewhere, either by a special administrative council that included most of the family members active in the business, or else at informal get-togethers, possibly over lunch. Legislation granting the employees representation on company boards, however, necessitated a change in the decision-making process. The board, at least theoretically, was given more weight. In practice, the family had already taken many important decisions before the board met.

Thanks to his position, first as president and then as working chairman, Albert Bonnier, Jr, until his death in 1989, was the leading representative of the family. He held the group together, while also being involved in the various separate activities. In some respects the magazine publishing businesses and especially the book publishing, both led by family members, had greater independence than did the other activities. With regard to these activities, Albert Bonnier, Jr mainly reacted. That is, he became directly engaged only when they encountered financial or other difficulties. Compared to the more directly administered industrial activities, publishing was thus indirectly controlled by the group administration. Group headquarters included a division principally dedicated to supporting, developing and controlling the various industrial enterprises. Albert Bonnier, Jr was heavily engaged in these activities.[21]

On the surface, the owner's ability to appoint the CEO of the industrial enterprises was the most important control mechanism. In addition, however, Albert Bonnier, Jr had direct personal contacts with administrators at various levels in the firms. Through these contacts, as well as personal visits, he accumulated direct knowledge both of the firms and of their executives.

In several regards, Albert Bonnier, Jr was a dynamic entrepreneur. He welcomed new ideas and tried as much as possible to follow, and exploit, market opportunities resulting from social change. Through his efforts to act as an entrepreneur, Albert Bonnier, Jr also created opportunities for others to be entrepreneurs and innovators. Contacts with such persons, at least periodically, endowed the industrial firms with a degree of dynamism.

The workings of Deni (the holding company for *Dagens Nyheter*) clearly demonstrated how the Bonnier family sought to control the newspaper business while preserving ownership from generation to generation. The large number of part-owners in Deni, around thirty in all, could freely discuss strategic questions and take important decisions concerning *Dagens Nyheter* and *Expressen*. These included the composition of the board and the appointment and dismissal of administrative and editorial leaders. These activities made Deni a source of cohesion among the owners and a bridge between the generations and family branches. The heads of the family served as chairman and vice-chairman of the newspaper firm's board and were the family's public spokesmen. On most questions, they made the ownership decisions, but they always needed the support of the other owners. By actively participating in the work of the board and maintaining contact with the CEO of *Dagens Nyheter*, it was possible to present viewpoints and to quickly react to and discuss problems with the administration, without having to be directly involved in the organization.[22]

The Wallenberg family and their managers

The necessity of adapting to continuously changing economic circumstances was the cornerstone of Wallenberg corporate governance policy. It was frequently repeated as a moral imperative within the family, and it was recognized as a pre-condition for the survival, and the generation-to-generation growth, of the family's wealth and influence. Indeed, keeping their companies at the technological and organizational forefront, and thereby developing the Swedish industrial economy, was seen as the family's historical mission. Early on, the concept of entrepreneurship took a place at the very top of the family's hierarchy of values. The financial resources of the family were conscientiously applied to exploiting new scientific and technological advances. To 'transform technology into business' was a frequently used metaphor for the family's business strategy. In these efforts, the personal contacts and information network of the Wallenberg family, industriously cultivated by family members, played an important role. Not only was it a source of valuable information, it also helped to create markets for, and to stimulate co-operation among, group companies.

A readiness to accept change and stimulate entrepreneurial activity was combined with a centralized control structure. Centralized decision-making made even brutal and painful restructuring schemes possible. Thus, the flexibility of the entire group was increased. Within this general structure of centralized governance, however, the managers of group companies sometimes enjoyed great innovative freedom. The extent of the authority given to managing directors varied over time, even within the same generation of the Wallenberg family. This is most clearly apparent in the third generation of the family, when the two brothers Jacob (1892–1980) and Marcus Wallenberg, Jr (1899–1982) led the group. Conflicting personalities and interests between the two brothers make it possible to separate two distinct spheres of interest within the group, one made up of those companies with Jacob as chairman of the board and one including those where Marcus was chairman. Jacob Wallenberg had a much softer touch than did Marcus and, despite his aura of great personal authority, he related to his managing directors very differently from his younger brother. The company managing directors had decidedly more independence and freedom of action in Jacob's firms. Even though there was no doubt as to who had the final say, the Jacob Wallenberg sphere was more decentralized, giving it a more federalist stamp than was the case in the Marcus Wallenberg sphere.

During the 1980s and the fourth generation, following the conscious policy of Peter Wallenberg, it was the federalist organizational structure, permitting the individual firms more independence, that developed and came to characterize the entire Wallenberg group. A clear expression of this development was the fact that the decision-making centres of the group, for the first time in the family's history, were opened to the managing directors of the group's core enterprises. They were elected members of the boards of the investment companies of Investor and Providentia, and the board meetings, to a much greater degree than previously, involved a true exchange of views and ideas.

Group leadership authority was very selectively allocated, even within the Wallenberg family. Ability was a badge of honour, often mentioned in family conversations and in public debates. The wholehearted confidence of the Wallenberg leadership in an inventor or a company's management was a prerequisite before funds for developing a new idea, purchasing a new ownership position in an existing company, or reorganizing and reconstructing a group firm were forthcoming. The importance of good leadership for business success was stressed in many contexts, and changing the CEO was usually the first action to be considered when a firm in crisis faced them. Finding suitable CEOs was a major concern. Marcus Wallenberg, Jr, of the third generation, even kept a notebook labelled 'suitable CEOs'. Here the personal qualifications of the mid-level managers he encountered while visiting group companies were listed. These included his first impressions, not least his sense of their level of charisma.

Compared to the Bonnier group, exercise of ownership was to a larger degree concentrated on board meetings and strategic decisions, while decisions in the group were mostly taken in informal owner meetings. Both Marcus Wallenberg, Jr and Albert Bonnier, Jr also had a personal involvement in production at different companies and made direct contacts with representatives at different levels. However, it looks as if Albert Bonnier, Jr had more personal contacts with the factory workers and production than Marcus Wallenberg, Jr.[23] This is not surprising since several of the firms within the Wallenberg group were very large and hardly could be handled in the same personal way as the smaller Bonnier companies.

Entrepreneurship and the 'Swedish model'

Regulations and governmental involvement have played an important role for both the activities of companies and entrepreneurship especially after the Second World War. Governmental legislation from the early twentieth century could hardly be accused of being too detailed, and during the inter-war period restrictions gradually increased, resulting in limitations on companies' development possibilities.

The centralization of wage negotiations for industry and trade in 1938 was an important step towards a 'Swedish model' for handling business activities and firms. During the Second World War restrictions on economic activities were introduced at a much greater speed than before, motivated by political as well as economic reasons. This policy continued also after the war when political guidance and control increased in importance. The introduction of new regulative measures for the financial market, given shape by the Central Bank (Riksbanken), was of great importance for economic life.[24] This meant that lending was largely controlled by these new measures, and that banks and other financial intermediaries could only with difficulty compete for new customers. As a result, big firms in particular had to depend on their own assets to a larger extent, since credits were hard to obtain. For a company like Bonnierföretagen, this was of minor importance, at least during the 1950s and 1960s. The ability to create capital for investments was good, and so was the situation for other larger companies during this 'Golden Age' for industrial production. However, with the crises in the 1970s and 1980s the need for external capital became more important. A solid bank connection was thus of great value. Companies within the Wallenberg group in this case probably had an advantage compared to other firms. At the same time the possibilities to support new entrepreneurs were diminished. Thus, to some degree, restrictions on the capital market probably hampered the development of new companies. At the same time, however, already established companies had the possibility to develop their activities and consolidate their finances.

Social democratic policy in the 1950s, 1960s and early 1970s also promoted large-scale solutions in production and trade. Rationalization in the economy would make the total national product larger and with an appropriate fiscal policy it would be possible to distribute wealth more evenly. One example of this policy was the principle of solidarity in wage policy that promoted efficiency and large-scale production.

Another aspect of social democratic policy was the desire to democratize decision-making within companies. The most important step in this direction was the introduction of workers' rights to be consulted in company decision-making in the MBL law of 1974. One of the effects of this legislation was that employees should be given representation on the board. For Bonnierföretagen, this had an immediate effect. Before this legislation was adopted, the board did not in fact meet. Albert Bonnier, Jr no doubt saw the importance of controlling the board, but he could hardly be chairman and managing director at the same time. Therefore, in 1978 he left his position as CEO of Bonnieföretagen to become the working chairman of the board.

However, it was not only through legislation that social democratic policies affected the activities of Bonnierföretagen. There is at least one good example where the entire strategic development of the group was hampered by the fear of legislative measures. Already from the early 1950s, Albert Bonnier, Jr feared an intrusion from the social democratic government to limit the family's strong position in the media. Since the late inter-war period, criticism had been put forward against the family's governing role in the Swedish media. This resulted in the introduction of self-regulation by the Bonnier group especially in the newspaper market. For fear of a nationalization or a *Lex Bonnier* limiting ownership in the media, Albert Bonnier, Jr could not until the late 1980s accept that the family should increase its position on the Swedish newspaper market. Instead, he promoted the diversification of the Bonnier group into other industrial areas and the establishment of media activities on international markets.[25] A side effect of this strategy was an early interest in foreign media markets, even though several of these activities were not especially profitable.

During the preparatory work for the business paper *Dagens Industri* (*Today's industry*) in the 1970s, contacts were made with the Social Democratic Prime Minister Olof Palme in order to get his acceptance for the introduction of this new paper. Even though he supported the idea and gave his word that he would not act against the business, Albert Bonnier, Jr maintained his position that the family should not increase its activities on the newspaper market. This halted the establishment of *Dagens Industri* for several years.[26]

Political constraints were also shown in other areas of economic life. The threat of nationalization was present in several parts of Swedish industry. The increased radicalization of Swedish society in the 1960s raised support for a stronger governmental control of, for example, the medical industry, in which the Wallenberg group had a strong interest (in Astra). The situation became increasingly difficult when the minister for industry in the late 1960s gave his support for the nationalization of the medical industry. This was regarded as an obvious blow to this branch of industry, even though it was never realized in its most radical form. Instead, the government decided to purchase a private biochemical company (Kabi) and a pharmacy company (Vitrum) to create a state-owned medical industry with a research capacity to compete with the private firms.[27]

However, this did not eliminate all political risks connected with the medical industry. To avoid this, private medicinal companies – among them, Astra – increased their participation on international markets in both research and production and diversified their production. Thus, the situation for the Wallenberg-controlled Astra showed large similarities with that of the Bonnier group.

Although there were similarities between the handling of institutional barriers between the Wallenbergs and the Bonniers, there were also important differences. Since the Wallenberg family controlled companies employing over 20 per cent of the Swedish industrial workforce, they were of the greatest importance to national economic development. After the Second World War the Wallenberg group became, more or less, too large to fail. Therefore, it was of the greatest importance that the Social Democratic government could co-operate with the Wallenbergs, or at least accept their position in Sweden's economy. Moreover, even though radical left-wing representatives often attacked the Wallenbergs, the Social Democratic government avoided that kind of confrontation. The Bonnier group, on the other hand, was in constant opposition to the Social Democratic government. In the liberal Bonnier-owned newspapers *Dagens Nyheter* and *Expressen*, social democratic policy was frequently attacked and it was no secret that Albert Bonnier, Jr in particular supported the political opposition. On the other hand, social democratic politicians were in strong opposition against the Bonnier family's control over the Swedish media market, which they believed could suppress free speech. Thus, while the Wallenberg group became a part of the Swedish model, Bonnier was in a more clear opposition to social democracy.

Conclusions

In this chapter, we have shown the importance of family firms in modern Swedish big business. Even though the organization of family ownership exhibits large differences over time and between countries, family firms are not obsolete constructions, in Sweden or on the international market.[28]

In our examples from the Wallenberg and the Bonnier groups, we can see that family-owned big business contains elements of both strong traditions and entrepreneurship. The long time frame and patience inherent in the Wallenberg ownership policy was combined with a readiness to re-evaluate and sell holdings, even among the traditional core enterprises. From the group's earliest days, to simply expand and refuse to contemplate the sale of a holding had been considered an untenable ownership policy. Like other parts of the oral family tradition, however, the principles for how active ownership should be pursued within the group had to be adjusted in the face of reality. There are numerous examples of how emotional considerations, or even commitments, influenced individual Wallenberg family members in their stand vis-à-vis strategic business decisions. Economic rationality and wealth maximization stood highest in the family's hierarchy of values, but they were by no means always decisive. Room also existed for decisions motivated by other, socially and culturally based, values.

The Bonnier sphere did not display the same clear insistence on rational business logic as the Wallenbergs. Naturally, firms were expected to make a profit and the family fortune was expected to grow. Beyond this expectation, however, there were also strong tendencies towards traditionalism and economic irrationality. The name Bonnier was connected with certain activities, especially book publishing, and the tolerance for losses was great. Moreover, Albert Bonnier, Jr had a strong emotional attachment to the industrial group he had worked to build up. It pained him to sell or liquidate any of these firms.

The remarkable continuity of the Wallenberg's influence on Swedish business, together with the ongoing consolidation of its interests, has contributed to a tradition-dominated corporate culture. Today, Wallenberg ownership, both inside and outside the group, involves industrial involvement and large-scale participation in the evolution of firms. This perception has consolidated strong normative standards within the group. Key employees share a feeling of commitment and loyalty to the family and its 'historical mission'. While difficult to measure, the value of this firm-specific 'asset', consisting of strong personal relations among core employees, should not be underestimated. The economic values that have evolved within the Wallenberg group represent a clear case of path dependence. Here, historical experience and tradition determine not just what to do, but also how to do it.

Like the Wallenberg group, the Bonnier sphere was characterized by an almost extreme long-sightedness. While the Wallenbergs influenced the industrial climate in Sweden, the Bonniers had a very strong, long-standing effect on the country's cultural life. The leading position established during the late nineteenth and early twentieth century, to a considerable extent, rested on a policy of understanding and tolerance towards the authors and journalists that belonged to the Bonnier network. This also seems to have been the case with the industrial firms that were developed after the Second World War. The leadership of the Bonnier concern often granted substantial freedom to the industrial leaders, permitting them to develop their businesses and to function as entrepreneurs. The Bonnier family has listened to people with new ideas, whether cultural or industrial.

The most interesting question about the Bonnier and Wallenberg ownership is perhaps their long-term viability as dominant company owners. How have they managed to keep and develop their positions in Swedish economy during over 150 years? This question cannot be answered that easily. However, one reason might be that both company groups have developed strong family traditions, as both entrepreneurs and dominant controlling owners, without being hampered by these traditions. This has made the family groups too large to fail – especially the Wallenbergs. At the same time both family groups have during the last 50 years proved to be open enough to allow non-family members to act as managers, entrepreneurs or specialists. This probably has helped the groups to renew their activities.

SEB was a vital source of capital for the entire Wallenberg group. It not only financed new investments and entrepreneurial activities, but also the group's defence against corporate raiders and hostile takeovers. At an early stage, the family was forced to deal with financial crises and defaulting corporate clients. It thus accumulated competence in financial, as well as in industrial, reconstruction work. The bank's management developed a broader frame of reference and a wider set of contacts than would have been possible had they been limited to a single level of industry. No doubt, this served as an important resource in strategic decision-making at the group ownership level. Clearly, the resulting reduction in transactions costs was an essential element in the package of comparative advantages that the group possessed.

This study of two of the largest Swedish family business groups demonstrates that successful long-term ownership in a market economy requires both willingness and an ability to adapt to change, as well as a continuous effort to develop new resources in competition with other actors. It supports the belief that economic activity can be organized successfully without large bureaucratic structures. In particular, institutional settings, and comparative advantages based mainly on low information costs, may even make a business group more efficient for organizing long-term, profit-generating enterprises.

QUESTIONS
1. Analyse the reasons for why the Bonnier and Wallenberg families have managed to keep their positions as long-term owners in Swedish business for over 150 years?
2. What differences and similarities are there between the ownership performance (active, re-active, passive ownership) in the Bonnier and Wallenberg groups?

Notes

1. Granovetter (1994, 1995).
2. Cassis (1999).
3. SOU 1968:7; 1988:38, Glete (1994).
4. Lindgren (1991).
5. Albinsson (1962); Koulouvari (2004).
6. Bonnier (1974).
7. Sundin (1996).
8. Larsson (2003).
9. Larsson (2001).
10. Larsson (2001); Nyberg (2002).
11. Lindgren (1987, 1994).
12. Olsson (1997); Carlsson (2000).
13. Karlsson-Stider (2002).
14. Sundin (1996); Bonnier (1974).
15. Larsson (2001).
16. Larsson (2001).
17. Nyberg (1999, 2002).

18. Larsson (2001).
19. Gårdlund (1976).
20. Lindgren (1994).
21. Larsson (2001).
22. Nyberg (2002).
23. Sjögren (2005).
24. Larsson (1998).
25. Larsson (2001).
26. Larsson (2003).
27. Sjögren (2005).
28. Sjögren (2006).

References

Albinsson, G., *Svensk populärpress 1931–61* (Stockholm: Almqvist & Wiksell, 1962).

Bonnier, Å., *Bonniers: En släktkrönika 1778–1941* (Stockholm: Bonniers förlag, 1974).

Carlsson, R. H., *Ownership! Strategic Corporate Governance in the New Economy* (New York: John Wiley, 2000).

Cassis, Y., *Big Business: The European Experience in the Twentieth Century* (Oxford: Oxford University Press, 1999).

Glete, J., *Nätverk i näringsliv* (Stockholm: SNS förlag, 1994).

Gårdlund, T., *Marcus Wallenberg 1864–1943: Hans liv och gärning.* (Stockholm: Norstedt & söner, 1976).

Granovetter, M., 'Business Groups', in Smelser, N.J. and Swedberg, R. (eds), *The Handbook of Economic Sociology* (Princeton: Princeton University Press, 1994).

Granovetter, M., 'Coase Revisited: Business Groups in the Modern Economy', *Industrial and Corporate Change*, 4(1) (1995).

Karlsson-Stider, A., *Familjen & Firman*, PhD thesis, EFI, The Economic Research Institute at the Stockholm School of Economics (2002).

Koulouvari, P., *Family-Owned Media Companies in the Nordic Countries*, JIBS, Working Paper Series, 2004-4 (2004).

Larsson, M., *Staten och kapitalet* (Stockholm: SNS Förlag, 1998).

Larsson, M., *Bonnierföretagen: förlag, konglomerat, mediekoncern, förlag, konglomerat och mediekoncern* (Stockholm: Bonniers förlag, 2001).

Larsson, M., *Å&Å drömfabriken: Från fiction till fakta 1906–90* (Stockholm: Bonniers förlag, 2003).

Lindgren, H., *Bank, investmentbolag, bankirfirma: Stockholms Enskilda Bank 1924–45* (Stockholm: Institute for Economic History Research, Stockholm School of Economics, 1987).

Lindgren, H., 'Affärsbankerna – Näringslivets herrar eller tjänare', *Pecvina, skrifter i mynt och penninghistoriska ämnen: Skrifter utgivna av Kungl. Myntkabinettet*, 1 (Stockholm, 1991).

Lindgren, H., *Aktivt ägande: Investor under växlande konjunkturer* (Stockholm: Institute for Economic History Research, Stockholm School of Economics, 1994).

Nyberg, D., *Stockholms tidningsmarknad 1953–88*, Licentiate thesis (Stockholm: Stockholm School of Economics, 1999).

Nyberg, D., *Marknad, företag, ägande: Familjen Bonniers ägarstyrning i Dagens Nyheter 1953–88* (Stockholm EHF: Stockholm School of Economics, 2002).

Olsson, U., *At the Centre of Development: Skandinaviska Enskilda Banken and its Predecessors 1856–1996* (Skandinaviska Enskilda Banken, informationsavdelningen, 1997).

Sjögren, H., *Den uthålliga kapitalismen: Bolagsstyrning i Astra, Stora Kopparberg och Svenska Tändstickbolaget* (Stockholm: SNS förlag, 2005).

Sjögren, H., 'Family Capitalism within Big Business', *Scandinavian Economic History Review*, 54(2), (2006).

SOU, Ägande och inflytande inom det privata näringslivet, 1968: 7, Stockholm.

SOU, Ägande och inflytande i svenskt näringsliv: Huvudbetänkande från utredningen, 1988: 38, Stockholm.

Sundin, S., *Från bokförlag till mediekoncern: Huset Bonnier 1909–29, Publications of the Department of Economic History*, University of Gothenburg 70 (1996).

WELFARE CAPITALISM: THE SWEDISH ECONOMY 1850–2005 • ENTREPRENEURSHIP AND OWNERSHIP: THE
...ERM VIABILITY OF THE SWEDISH BONNIER AND WALLENBERG FAMILY BUSINESS GROUPS • FROM
ABB ... ...MENT: FINNISH
CAPITALISM, 1850–2005 • FROM STATE OWNERSHIP TO MULTINATIONAL CORPORATION: THE PATH OF
ENSO-GUTZEIT ... ...OMERATE FIRM: THE STRATEGIC
PATHS OF NOKIA AND TAMPELLA IN THE LIBERALIZING FINNISH ECONOMY AFTER THE SECOND WORLD
WAR • CO-OPERATIVE LIBERALISM: DENMARK FROM 1857 TO 2007 • ARLA – FROM DECENTRALIZED INDUSTRY
TO MULTINATIONAL ENTERPRISE • CARLSBERG AND THE SELF-REGULATION OF THE DANISH BEER MARKET
• NORWAY: A RESOURCE-BASED AND DEMOCRATIC CAPITALISM • CONSTRUCTIVE POWER: ELKEM 1904–2004
• FINANCE AND THE DEVELOPMENT OF NORWEGIAN CAPITALISM – THE CASE OF CHRISTIANIA BANK

from ASEA to ABB: managing big business the Swedish way

Fredrik Tell

Introduction

There are many salient features of capitalism as it has evolved in Sweden, some of which will be investigated in this chapter by using the case of one large and important firm: ASEA. First, the so-called 'genius enterprises' (snilleföretagen) have formed a conspicuous backdrop for research into big-business entrepreneurship in Sweden. These firms, many formed out of techno-logical innovations during the second industrial revolution, grew steadily during the twentieth century. The modern corporate landscape at the millennium was still dominated by the big businesses created out of this early entrepreneurship[1]. The ability of these enterprises to build on early innovations and develop new products is a particularly interesting feature, suggesting that they may have succeeded in creating the institutionalized entrepreneurship alluded to by Joseph Schumpeter in *Capitalism, Socialism and Democracy* (1942). ASEA is an example of such a technology-based snilleföretag, stemming from the inventions of Jonas Wenström and continuously thriving on new innovations in electro-mechanics.

Second, since the domestic market available for utilizing new products was small, Swedish industry internationalized early. While the pattern of internationalization was a gradual process, usually starting with 'pure export' through sales agents abroad, successful companies evolved (often through several stages) into multinational corporations (MNCs), with sales and manufac-turing in many countries. ASEA is an example of an MNC, internationalized almost from its inception, evolving through a merger in 1987 into a globally active MNC, namely Asea Brown Boveri (ABB).

Third, the composition of Swedish industry has been one of many large firms and many small firms, but rather few medium-sized companies, relative to the size of the country.[2] The concentration of firms is partly due to policy reasons (the 'Swedish model') but also due to agreements among owners and managers to allow mergers and sectoral specialization of large firms. This makes it especially pertinent to investigate further the evolution of big business in the Swedish context. ASEA is an example of a large firm that rapidly grew into a big business, specializing in heavy electrical machinery (Ericsson specializing in lighter goods and, later, Electrolux in appliances): it became a 'small giant' in the electrical equipment industry.[3]

Big business has, ever since Alfred Chandler, Jr's seminal work on the evolution of modern American capitalism (1962), been a focal point for analysis and debate in business history. According to Chandler, the large, vertically integrated, industrial enterprise directed by professional managers became the most important economic institution in capitalist economies.[4] One organizational innovation was the multidivisional form (M-form), emerging first in the US and then spreading throughout the western world.[5] In Oliver Williamson's phrase (1975): markets were supplanted with hierarchies. This thesis has been debated over the years.[6] While this case study does not purport to confirm or refute Chandler's hypotheses, it may cast some light on the management of Nordic big business. In many respects, ASEA/ABB typifies the large industrial enterprise. It is large (virtually monopolistic in its home market), vertically integrated, professionally managed (rather than owner-managed) and has made three-pronged investments in distribution, manufacturing and managerial hierarchies.

Capitalism as it evolved in Sweden came to be heavily influenced by the 'Swedish model'.[7] Some of ASEA's managers became involved in the decision process affecting Swedish industrial policy, partly due to the fact that big business was a part of the 'Swedish model'.[8] Under the auspices of this model, co-operation among managers in networks such as horizontal cartels and user–producer interaction became part of a certain management style.[9] It may be argued that a particular Nordic (or even Swedish) way of managing big business has appeared.[10] ASEA belongs to those firms that have had particularly visible and forceful managers, exemplified here by J. Sigfrid Edström, Curt Nicolin and Percy Barnevik. Moreover, these managers have had strong links to the Wallenberg group/family, but have also at times acted somewhat independently of the Wallenberg family's interest.

The purpose of this chapter is primarily to discuss the management of one of the most prominent Swedish technology-based firms. In doing so, it will focus on the top management of the company. The chapter covers the period from inception and establishment of ASEA in the late nineteenth century to the end of the 'Swedish era' in ABB, signified by Jürgen Dormann's entry as CEO in 2002.

1878–1918: inception of a domestic dominant and the entry of Edström

The predecessor of ASEA, Elektriska Aktiebolaget i Stockholm (The Stockholm Electrical Co. Ltd), was founded on 17 January 1883 by the former banker, entrepreneur and industrialist Ludvig Fredholm and the engineer and inventor Jonas Wenström. The development in the US of electrical engineering inspired young engineers from Sweden to go abroad to study the new technology, in order to return later on and implement their new-found knowledge domestically. There was further progress in electrical engineering in Great Britain and Germany, where Ludvig Fredholm went to study gas and electric lighting systems in 1881. The same year, Fredholm joined forces with the Wenström brothers, Göran and Jonas, and he persuaded financiers to invest in test equipment for arc lighting, using a brush dynamo. The recently graduated engineer Göran Wenström was appointed test leader, and it was also through him Fredholm got in touch with his elder brother Jonas. That same year, Jonas Wenström visited the World's Fair in Paris, which introduced him to the latest innovations within the field.

Using a Schuckert dynamo, manufactured in Germany, as a prototype, Jonas Wenström developed his own dynamo. In a critical test at the end of 1882, Jonas Wenström's design performed better than the German one, and Wenström and Fredholm decided to continue with their business and established Elektriska Aktiebolaget i Stockholm.

With their head office in Stockholm, the company leased production facilities from a factory in Arboga. One of the main advantages with the Arboga plant was the possibility of making full-scale experiments with the equipment, vitally important in these early stages of a developing technology. The company installed their first municipal lighting system in Västerås in 1888. The company focused on providing and installing lighting equipment, but did not have the resources to finance customers.

Göran Wenström supervised the Arboga plant and in 1889 made a trip to continental Europe to study power transmission systems. Accompanied by Gustaf Abraham Granström, he found no breakthrough discoveries in the field, but saw many instances of electrical power in practical industrial use. This convinced the travellers to develop their knowledge in electricity into industrial usage, in order to exploit the power needs of industrializing Sweden. However, on returning to Sweden, they found Fredholm against diversification into this field and Göran Wenström and Granström therefore founded the company Wenström & Granströms Kraftbolag in October 1889 to pursue their utility interests.[11]

One year later, it became evident that the two companies needed to expand in order to face foreign competition. Therefore, a new company, Allmänna Svenska Elektriska Aktiebolaget (The Swedish General Electric Company) (ASEA) saw the light in December 1890, aiming at exploitation and development of the joint resources of the two firms, by injecting more capital. The headquarters were located in Västerås, where local businessmen were persuaded to invest in the new venture. Göran Wenström was appointed CEO of the new company. Fredholm stepped in as chairman of the board, but when he died in 1896 a local businessman and politician, Oscar Fredrik Wijkman, succeeded him.

In Sweden, important actors in the electro-technical sector were the German firms AEG and Siemens, as well as Swiss firms Brown Boveri (BBC) and Oerlikon.[12] Due to the firm's technological progress and not least because of Jonas Wenström's finding and development of the three-phase alternating current system, ASEA expanded rapidly despite this competition. At this point in time, ASEA manufactured a wide range of heavy electrical apparatus such as rotating machines, transformers, switchgear, instruments, and overload protection devices. In order to further advance new products the company established a design and development department in 1892, led by Jonas Wenström until his death one year later.

At the beginning of the twentieth century, recession struck and competition in Sweden increased. The firm went into a financial crisis, marked by the risky venturing of the Swedish inventor Gustaf de Laval, who together with financier Ernest Thiel had gained control of ASEA. In 1901, the company's management initiated negotiations with the German company Union concerning a German acquisition of SEK 2 million worth of shares. However, Union rejected the offer and instead a reconstruction of ASEA was made with the financial aid of a Swedish commercial bank, Stockholms Enskilda Bank (SEB). It provided new capital as the old share capital was halved in the reconstruction.

The era and management of J. Sigfrid Edström

The manager of the bank, Marcus Wallenberg, Sr, recruited J. Sigfrid Edström as the new executive to lead the company. Edström was well aware of the prospects of the industry, since he had been working for both Swedish and Swiss tramway companies, as well as Westinghouse and General Electric in the US. However, he needed assurance of financial support from the bank to ASEA in order to accept the offer. The bank also provided market contacts in Norway, where the company delivered the world's largest generator set in 1907.

Edström, who succeeded Göran Wenström, was a skilled manager who introduced new accounting principles and rationalized and improved production efficiency.[13] He took on an expansionist course for the ailing Swedish firm, aiming at the creation of a large industrial enterprise.

Strategy and development

In general, Swedish industry developed into sectors where major exporting companies specialized to be able to exploit mass production and organization. Cartels, mergers and structural rationalization were extensions of the specialization arguments in the Swedish debate on the subject. One of Edström's leading principles was indeed that of specialization – that is, ASEA should specialize within certain sectors and gain monopoly positions.[14]

Cartel negotiations with the German manufacturers failed and the chilly response of especially AEG caused ASEA to increase lobbying efforts toward an increase of import tariffs on electrical goods. Domestically, however, the establishment of agreements between the electrical manufacturers proceeded (and with Siemens–Schuckert). These discussions lead to a concentration of the electrical industry in Sweden, similar to that experienced internationally. ASEA became the hub to which a large amount of firms were connected. ASEA often ended up by acquiring competing firms or suppliers as a natural result of cartels and trust arrangements, Edström's brother-in-law, Arthur Lindén, was a driving force in the creation of cartels and finding opportunities for horizontal integration. ASEA's expansion was successful and in 1911 SEB could sell its shares in the company with a profit.

During the first ten years of the twentieth century, ASEA's capacity for manufacturing tailor-made heavy electrical products for utilities was complemented by mass manufactured standard components. The idea was to offset the large risks involved in heavy electrical engineering by profits generated by standardized products. Consequently, the company radically changed its manufacturing processes, moving from batch production to rationalized mass production and increasing vertical integration. ASEA was a Swedish pioneer in rationalizing production in this way. This was in line with developments in leading countries, such as the US and Germany. In 1911, ASEA began building a new factory in Västerås, called Mimer, for mass manufacturing purposes.

ASEA's position in the market for power equipment was strengthened by the acquisition of one of its major domestic competitors, Nya Förenade Elektriska Aktiebolaget (The New Allied Electrical Company) (NFEA). Technologically, NFEA was equal to ASEA, but it still lacked the financial strength of the Västerås-based company. Being ASEA's largest competitor, a merger between the companies would give ASEA a dominant position in the Swedish market. When NFEA neglected to sign a new cartel agreement in 1915, ASEA made an offer for the outstanding shares of the company. The major owners accepted the offer and ASEA acquired NFEA in a wave of M&As conducted in 1916. At the time of the acquisition the number of employees was 550. The annual turnover in 1914 was SEK 6.3 million for NFEA, compared to SEK 19.1 million for ASEA in the same year.

Through the acquisition, the two largest companies in the heavy Swedish electrical industry had merged. After the acquisition, top management from NFEA remained in Ludvika. ASEA, however, restructured the organization and thus the entire industry by dividing production between the factories in Västerås and Ludvika. The manufacturing and development of transformers and some other high-voltage products were put in Ludvika, while the manufacture of rotating machines, low-current components, instruments and special designs was concentrated in Västerås.[15]

The initial stage of ASEA was also important for building market relationships. The most important of these relationships was, without doubt, that with the Swedish State Power Board (Vattenfall). Despite lagging behind foreign competitors in large switchgear when a large contract was to be signed in 1907, ASEA was given a second chance as Vattenfall delayed its decision on procurement for one year. Still not satisfied with the design of the switches, Vattenfall and ASEA jointly continued testing the apparatus.

The beginning of the century was a period that formed the strong ties that were to remain for over fifty years between the engineers of Sweden's major manufacturer and its main utility. Many of these engineers (some subsequently important managers) were the first graduates from Kungliga Tekniska Högskolan (Royal Institute of Technology)(KTH) in electrical engineering. As Vattenfall immediately showed an interest in procurement of Swedish equipment for its power systems, ASEA had acquired a close customer with high demands and great resources.

During the First World War, ASEA acquired a number of electrotechnical firms in Sweden. Apart from NFEA, the company bought STAL, Surahammars Bruk and Liljeholmens Kabelfabrik in 1916. STAL (an acronym for Svenska Turbinfabriks AB Ljungström), located in Finspång, was a newly established manufacturer of steam turbines that made use of Birger Ljungström's patented design. The acquisition caused the two brothers, Birger and Fredrik Ljungström, to leave the company. The acquisition of Surahammars Bruk stemmed from ASEA's need for raw material (mainly iron), manufactured to certain specifications. Surahammars Bruk was an iron works that could provide sheet iron by using a rolling mill installed in 1917. Liljeholmens Kabelfabrik manufactured cables and electrical conductors, and ASEA had need of these products in its development and manufacturing of power equipment. Moreover, cables were sold by ASEA's sales organization. Despite being in the electrical manufacturing industry, these companies were not direct competitors to ASEA, but rather possessed complementary product lines such as turbines, cables and insulation materials. Becoming increasingly 'lighter', the company went from having 42 per cent of its products in heavy electrical products in 1908–10, to a share of 24 per cent in the period 1917–20.[16]

Management and organization

Edström was a paradoxical manager. On the one hand he represented a professionalization of the organization through modern rationalization methods and on the other hand he was keen to involve friends and family. Examples were his brother-in-law Arthur Lindén and his cousin Hugo Edström. He also brought his friend Emil Lundqvist to the company to rationalize production.[17]

The outcome of the rationalization programme was a concentration of manufacturing in Västerås. Manufacturing was separated into electrical and mechanical workshops, and a foundry was established. Lundqvist and his predecessor, Fred Vickers, copied mass manufacturing methods from the US to replace the craft-style production employed before the reconstruction. They also found inspiration in the vertical integration and rational working environment of German manufacturers. Moreover, the company organized sales and installation in four departments based on customers (railway, utility, wholesale and residual work). Edström introduced a management style based on planning, directives and organizational schemes, rather than direct super-vision. His strategy was to decentralize authority to middle management. His management style was quite action-oriented and American-inspired: 'One who never makes a fault, never makes anything else!' was one of his mottos.[18] The initiatives succeeded, and sales increased from SEK 3.7 million in 1903 to SEK 13 million in 1910, while the workforce doubled (from 1186 to 2462 employees).[19] The same year, Sten Anckarcrona, a former naval officer, became chairman of the board. Two years later, in 1913, Arthur Lindén was appointed the closest associate to Edström, and in the years before the First World War ASEA went through an organizational transforma-tion. Management accounting methods were improved with the institution of monthly reports and transfer pricing between departments. The num-ber of departments increased and Edström began delegating authority down the organization. Edström spent much time travelling, as a representative of ASEA but he was also engaged in industry associations and sports asso-ciations. He was chairman of the Swedish Confederation of Manufacturing Industries (Verkstadsföreningen) in 1916–39 and chairman of the Swedish Employers' Confederation (SAF) in 1931–42.[20] He took an active part in the creation of the agreement between the employers' associations and trade unions, the so-called 'Saltsjöbadsavtalet'.[21] He also represented the 'Swedish model' for organizing employers at international conferences. He was essen-tially concerned with establishing peace between employers and unions, but was more reluctant regarding the rights of employees to exert influence over corporate management. As a liberal, however, he believed in everyone's right to vote in parliamentary elections. Moreover, Edström was actively engaged in the political life of the municipalities of Västerås and Ludvika.[22] He also had contacts with leading Social Democrats, on both a local and national level.

Internationalization and export

On the international scene, ASEA had had little impact during its forma-tive years. Since 1893, the company had been represented in Russia and Finland. In 1898, ASEA had entered the British market by establishing Fuller Electrical Manufacturing Co., which was almost considered domes-tic in the British Isles. Financial performance had been poor, however. In 1904, Sigfrid Edström initiated an internationalization strategy. ASEA had manufacturing plants in Göteborg, London and (through minor interests in other companies) in Sundsvall, Helsinki, Christiania and Copenhagen. However, most of these possessions were sold or liquidated in the crisis of

Table 4.1 ASEA sales (thousand SEK) and employees, 1891–1923

	Revenues	Export	Export (%)	Employees
1891	410	NA		62
1892	450	NA		163
1893	493	NA		170
1894	577	NA		185
1895	710	NA		245
1896	1040	NA		400
1897	1830	NA		520
1898	2400	NA		975
1899	3100	NA		1062
1900	3200	NA		1143
1901	2814	NA		968
1902	3205	NA		863
1903	3700	NA		1186
1904	5423	477	9	1416
1905	5089	420	8	1487
1906	9267	485	5	1804
1907	12330	1551	13	2309
1908	12061	1285	11	2167
1909	9110	1247	14	2354
1910	13023	2117	16	2462
1911	12800	3170	25	2527
1912	14000	3980	28	2780
1913	17600	4370	25	3215
1914	21400	5840	27	3001
1915	26300	9010	34	3641
1916	39500	13310	34	3864
1917	66800	16970	25	4787
1918	87400	7690	9	5052
1919	81500	12080	15	5156
1920	65600	14180	22	5343
1921	54100	13820	26	3336
1922	37000	13640	37	3163
1923	30700	10930	36	3413

Source: Glete (1983), pp. 38, 49, 55, 72.

1906–7 (Glete, 1983, p. 50). Export activities did restart in the 1910s, as ASEA opened branch offices for direct sales of Swedish equipment in England (1910), Spain (1912), Denmark (1913), Finland (1913) and Russia (1914). Moreover, the company built a new factory in Norway. Exports rose from SEK 4 million in 1912 to 13 million in 1916, and provided about a third of ASEA's annual sales in that year (Table 4.1).

ASEA was primarily a domestic supplier before the First World War, and despite an upturn during the war, export shares decreased rapidly again as the war ended.[23] Overall, the war caused an increase in sales for ASEA, but as the end approached, there were signs of crisis. The single most important customer for ASEA during the period up to the First World War remained the Swedish state in power plants and railways, and other Swedish customers in, for example, tramways.

1919–42: expansion by Edström, consolidation by Lindén

Strategy and development

ASEA's strategy after the First World War was to build a corporate group to gain increasing sales and a sufficiently broad range of products to be able to compete with foreign full-range manufacturers. The inter-war period was one of consolidation, expansion, group-building and investment in high-technology R&D. ASEA did not run into the same financial difficulties as many of its domestic competitors. Measures were taken to depreciate the value of assets during the war. Moreover, acquisitions of other firms had been made by using ASEA shares as payment rather than cash. ASEA had: (1) solid and large customers and (2) an improved export organization and subsequent increase in export sales. However, the number of employees was reduced by a third (from 7220 to 4853) between 1919 and 1921.[24] Despite the depression at the beginning of the 1920s, the bonds between ASEA and Vattenfall strengthened. There are numerous examples of R&D-based relationships between ASEA and Vattenfall from this time to the mid-1950s, signifying the tight bonds that grew between the two entities (such as joint laboratories, joint product development projects and joint testing facilities).[25] The opportunity of such co-operative development also gave ASEA a very good reference customer in marketing their products.

The rapid growth of electricity in Sweden after the First World War caused ASEA to increase production of its traditional products. The firm also started manufacturing new products and took more interest in delivering complete power systems with complex control equipment. From the 1930s onwards, the company grew increasingly 'heavy' in its product assortment. After the Second World War, the company had around 70 per cent of its products in this segment.[26] New products manufactured by ASEA included welding equipment, batteries, electrical blast furnaces, synthetic diamonds, fibre-glass and military products (during the Second World War). Among the traditional products, ASEA specialized in hydro-generators rather than the steam and turbo generators developed abroad. However, turbines developed at STAL remained a technological spearhead in the 1920s and 1930s. In the inter-war period, ASEA went from a transformer manufacturer lagging far behind its competitors to one of world-class standard. In particular, the parent company of ASEA concentrated on delivering complex heavy engineering projects, while subsidiaries focused on more standardized production. ASEA continued to buy ailing firms in the electrical manufacturing industry throughout the 1930s.

An agreement was made with Telefon AB LM Ericsson (Ericsson) where the two companies divided and regulated their operations into three areas: electrical products, telecommunications, and cables. In the early 1920s, five of the largest industrial enterprises (ASEA, Separator, LM Ericsson, Electrolux and SKF) in Sweden founded 'The Big Five', an interest group that lobbied for industry and export.[27] In 1925, ASEA entered a cartel agreement with AEG and Siemens, guaranteeing Swedish manufacturers 90 per cent of the domestic market.[28] At one time (1929–30) General Electric (GE) showed some interest in acquiring 25 per cent of the shares in ASEA, but nothing came of the negotiations. The main consequence was that the Wallenberg family turned into one of the major shareholders in ASEA, since they bought a great deal of the stocks acquired by GE. Later, in 1939, Westinghouse also showed interest in acquiring shares in ASEA.

Management and organization

As a result of the stable home market, the ASEA organization grew quite considerably during the inter-war period. In 1939, ASEA employed the largest cadre of engineers in Swedish industry: 650 design engineers compared to Bofors (the second-highest-ranked company), which had 300. In addition to periods of increasing demand, a number of acquisitions contributed to this growth. One of the larger industrial manufacturers in Sweden, Luth & Rosén (1500 employees), was acquired in 1931, and ASEA chose to keep the brand name. The cable manufacturing at Liljeholmens Kabelfabrik was expanded, not at least once Ericsson acquired the main competitor, Sieverts Kabelverk, in 1928. The main domestic competitor left was Elektromekano in Helsingborg, run by the former ASEA engineer Iens Lassen la Cour. In the late 1920s, this firm became a part of the Krueger dynasty and its management saw opportunities to challenge ASEA. However, when the Swedish financier and industrialist Ivar Krueger's empire fell apart after he committed suicide in 1932, ASEA acquired Elektromekano, but publicly it was stated that it belonged to Ericsson. The secrecy in ownership was a consequence of the fact that the last domestic competitor to ASEA now had fallen into its hands, a monopoly situation which might scare customers. ASEA continued on the path of secret acquisitions of minor firms during the 1930s to eliminate competition. In 1933 ASEA acquired ventilation equipment manufacturer Svenska Fläktfabriken in Jönköping. Three years later the household appliance manufacturer Elektro-Helios became a part of the ASEA group. In 1938, ASEA began manufacturing electrical welding equipment through the new venture Svenska Svetsmaskiner.

Arthur Lindén succeeded Sigfrid Edström in 1933, and remained CEO until 1942. Edström continued as chairman of the board from 1934 to 1949, and took on the role as an advisor to Lindén and more of a public relations officer. From the 1920s, ASEA had been run centrally by a top management team consisting of Edström and Lindén, together with the departmental managers of manufacturing, sales and engineering. Arthur Lindén was not interested in continuing the decentralization efforts initiated by Edström, but exhibited a more centralized management style. As characterized by contemporaries, he was personally involved in most issues, scrutinizing decisions meticulously, being both rigorous and patient. However, this behaviour also led to some conflicts with other members of the upper management. In 1940–1 ASEA's organization was further centralized, as all assets and debts of subsidiaries were transferred to the parent company (mostly for tax reasons). The idea was to keep subsidiaries running as profit-and-loss centres despite this reorganization, but incentives for subsidiary presidents changed and the initiative was later criticized both internally and externally. One year earlier it had been decided that Thorsten Ericsson was to succeed Lindén when he retired in 1942. Lindén then became vice-chairman of the board, but died in 1944. Financially, ASEA was quite healthy throughout this period.

Internationalization and export

ASEA's largest foreign markets were Russia (Soviet Union), Great Britain and Finland. The Swedish manufacturer had a factory in Jaroslavl that was not confiscated during the revolution, although it was conveyed to the Soviet authorities in 1932. In Great Britain, ASEA had a subsidiary: ASEA Electric (AEL), one of the largest manufacturers of motors and transformers in the British Commonwealth. Moreover, ASEA established a joint venture with the investment group Investor (owned by the Wallenberg family) in 1929, called Electro-invest, to secure and acquire foreign concessions. ASEA also tried to enter the US market, but success was confined to electrical relays.

The economic crisis in the beginning of the 1930s caused ASEA's export share to shrink from 48 per cent (1928–30) to 28 per cent (1937–9) of annual sales; while the domestic market maintained a constant level, export markets weakened. The next upturn in ASEA's sales (1936–9) was almost entirely due to an increase in Swedish demand for electrical equipment. As international markets expanded in the latter part of the 1930s, the Swedish firm was fully occupied with satisfying domestic needs and did not have any capacity for increasing sales abroad. During the Second World War ASEA focused more on the domestic market, and supplies of raw materials (for example, copper) were produced in Sweden. However, domestic demand for electrical apparatus did not explode either (which had been the case during the First World War), and sales were quite stable in 1940–4. During this period, only 12 per cent of sales were exported.[29] – However, in 1944 ASEA's subsidiary Svenska Fläktfabriken acquired a manufacturing unit in France, and the parent company did likewise the year after (the family-owned firm Hillairet) (Table 4.2).

1942–75: new management ideas and the post-war boom

After the Second World War, state ownership of ASEA was being discussed, in particular since the Swedish state after the war owned AEG and Siemens' subsidiaries in Sweden. Nothing came out of these plans. However, ASEA felt the pressure. Due to the anti-monopolistic public opinion, the company was prevented from acquiring further domestic competitors. In 1948, ASEA's chairman of the board, Sigfrid Edström, offered the Vattenfall engineer Åke Vrethem the position of assistant to CEO Thorsten Ericsson. Vrethem accepted and the next year he was appointed the new CEO of ASEA. This strengthened the bonds between ASEA and Vattenfall, where Vrethem's old college friend Åke Rusck had been appointed director general in 1948. Vattenfall's share of ASEA's business rose from 5.2 per cent in 1942–3 to 15 per cent in 1950–2.[30]

Strategy and development
In the mid-1950s, ASEA had to make some major strategic choices. A three-pronged strategy evolved: (1) Investments in R&D to maintain a position

Table 4.2 **ASEA Group sales (million SEK) and employees: Sweden, 1933–59**

	Sales	Employees in Sweden
1933	90.4	10,241
1934	109.4	11,719
1935	128.5	13,599
1936	149.8	15,241
1937	191.3	16,550
1938	206.4	17,360
1939	241.4	18,849
1940	254.7	18,936
1941	280.6	20,464
1942	304.2	21,113
1943	322.4	21,962
1944	345.8	22,938
1945	278.5	23,229
1946	405.8	24,163
1947	431.4	24,974
1948	525.2	25,995
1949	575.3	26,707
1950	675.5	27,428
1951	883.8	29,106
1952	1021.6	28,447
1953	975.3	27,186
1954	1044.7	28,520
1955	1132.9	30,300
1956	1209	30,562
1957	1258	31,940
1958	1332	32,242
1959	1222	28,428

Source: Glete (1983), pp. 220, 227.

as a full-range heavy electrical manufacturer; (2) Increased manufacturing capacity for heavy products; and (3) Establishment of an international sales organization complemented with new foreign manufacturing facilities.[31] Increasing volumes were perceived necessary for continued survival. Sales volumes provided a larger base for covering increased R&D spending, increased labour cost, increased size of each unit sold and less risk through the diversification of products. ASEA reorganized by M&As, more product-orientated manufacturing and, finally, a sector organization of the parent company.

Through acquisitions and investments such as Svenska Transformatorverken in 1956 and AB Hägglund & Söner in 1971, ASEA, became dominant in Sweden. Domestic domination was considered a prerequisite for international success by ASEA's management. In 1956, the company had a domestic market share of more than 50 per cent in the fields of generators, motors, transformers and electrical apparatus. Three years later, in 1959, ASEA sold AB Svenska Fläktfabriken and parts of Skandinaviska Elektricitetsverk AB. This year also saw the merger of turbine manufacturing subsidiary STAL and its competitor DeLaval Ångturbin into STAL-Laval, owned by ASEA.

After all its acquisitions and divestitures, ASEA became quite a diversified company within the electrical industry, embracing a wide range of products. However compared to the international giants it was still specialized.[32]

ASEA's products at the time after the Second World War continued to be for generation, transmission and distribution of electricity and for the use of electricity within industry and the transport sector.

As part of the expansion strategy, ASEA assigned more resources to R&D. R&D's share of sales rose from 2.2 per cent in 1965 to 3.7 per cent in 1970.[33] Nicolin had a rule for product development that it was 1 per cent pre-study (problem definition and indication of possible solutions), 10 per cent finding complete solutions applicable within given cost constraints and 89 per cent development of the path chosen.[34] Therefore, he considered the second and third steps the ones where gains and cost reductions could be made. During his reign at ASEA, he himself had ultimate control of R&D projects. One reason for this increase was the venturing of nuclear power technology. In Sweden there was interest in pursuing this new technology in the 1950s and 1960s. ASEA developed quite successfully a boiling water reactor (BWR) and, somewhat less successfully, turbo-generators for nuclear power plants.[35] However, turbine technology was licensed from BBC. In 1968, ASEA-ATOM was created as a 50–50 joint venture between ASEA and the Swedish state. Three years later, this company was awarded orders for two BWR nuclear power plants, the largest industrial procurement in Swedish history. In 1973–2, the first export order came, two reactors to Finland. Meanwhile, however, ASEA negotiated, unsuccessfully, with foreign manufacturers concerning co-operation in the nuclear business. As the oil crisis appeared, ASEA was unable to find any markets for its nuclear power equipment in Europe, but despite low profitability and political problems ASEA's management still considered nuclear power to be of 'industrial strategic importance'.[36]

In transport as well as in power engineering, electronics would come to play an important role in future technological development. In fact, it was used in most of ASEA's production, through core technologies, procured components with applications in ASEA-designed systems and computerized engineering. The electronics sector (called Y) was established in 1962 and all electronics development and manufacturing was concentrated in the main facilities in Västerås. ASEA's semiconductor operations were in 1969 reformed into ASEA-HAFO, which specialized in integrated circuits in the 1970s using a licence from US company RCA. Semiconductors were also used in control and monitoring devices, a speciality of ASEA since the 1940s. The company management discussed computer manufacturing in the mid-1960s, but opted for buying American-made hardware and software that were tailor-made to the specific requirements of the power industry. In power technology, the main applications were for controlling plants and remote control of power transmission grids. Another use of microelectronics furthered by the Swedish firm was robotics and automation in industry. In the late 1960s, ASEA exchanged its military electronics products for industrial electronics products with Ericsson.

Increasing investments during this period caused ASEA to take on further debt, and solvency decreased quite radically.[37] However, the company was never short of cash. The company's heavy products experienced low profitability from the 1960s and onwards, and ASEA had to rely on the revenues generated by lighter, more standardized equipment.

Management and organization

Following the appointment of Thorsten Ericsson as CEO of ASEA in 1942, the company embarked upon a programme of decentralization and further division of organizational units. One measure taken was the splitting up of the large manufacturing department into two departments: Design and Production. Moreover, smaller units were created within these two departments. Another change was the abandonment of the mechanical department. The work previously conducted here was transferred to the design, production and construction units. The construction department was divided into three sections: Power Stations, Industrial Systems and Traction. Reorganization also took place in the sales department. Three foreign units based on geographical regions were created to complement the central sales office. However, the wholesale organization and the group structure of the subsidiaries were kept intact.[38]

ASEA also started to reorganize in the 1950s. One problem for the firm was the organization of its subsidiaries. Some of them, like AB Svenska Fläktfabriken, Elektriska AB Helios, AB Asea Svetsmaskiner and Skandinaviska Elektricitetsverk AB were quite independent and floatation on the Stockholm Stock Exchange was an alternative. The activities of Svenska Turbinfabriks AB Ljungström (STAL), Surahammars Bruk and Liljeholmens Kabelfabrik had grown increasingly closer to the parent company. Finally, some of the subsidiaries, like Elektromekano and ASEA-Skandia, constituted a minor 'shadow' organization to the parent company, as they produced and sold similar products. Therefore, different rationalization possibilities were ventured, but one problem was the difficulty of absorbing further activities into the parent organization, which already was hard to govern and increasingly bureaucratic.

ASEA had an organization that resisted being divisionalized for a long time. The issue of decentralized 'divisions' where each larger production line should have its own management, designers and marketing people, had been discussed within top management in 1919, but these organizational changes were never implemented. When American consultants (Stanford Research Institute, SRI) were brought into the company at the end of the 1950s, they advised divisionalization, in the same way that most major international companies had done. But the management of ASEA was reluctant. Major organizational changes were implemented when Curt Nicolin took office in 1961, and former CEO Vrethem became group president. The new CEO had been a project leader of ASEA's jet engine project, which ceased in 1952 when the Swedish Air Force opted for a Rolls-Royce engine. Thereafter, Nicolin had been CEO of the ASEA subsidiary STAL.

Nicolin started creating a sector organization. Design offices and factories for specific products were grouped together and responsibility for sales of more standardized products was transferred to the sector level. The responsibility for direct contact with most customers did, however, remain with the domestic sales offices and international sales companies. Departments for power, industrial and traction products assumed responsibility for systems selling, engineering and turnkey delivery, by buying components from the sectors at market prices. This organization meant that both sectors and sales-oriented departments were kept as separate profit-and-loss centres. The explanation given by management as to why the organization was not completely divisionalized and decentralized was that markets and technologies did not coincide in ASEA's operations.

One problem for the reorganization efforts at ASEA was that Scandinavian Airlines (SAS) head-hunted Curt Nicolin in 1961. During his nine months at SAS, Nicolin introduced a rationalization programme, saving SEK 60 million; however, after his rescue operation Nicolin returned to ASEA. The internally controversial 'shadow' subsidiary Elektromekano became a part of this organization in 1962, signifying the increased integration of operations. The same year, the subsidiary Elektro-Helios (domestic appliances) was traded to Electrolux for a large amount of shares in that company, making ASEA Electrolux's principal owner.

Moreover, Nicolin began reorganizing and rationalizing production operations. Already in 1958, he had written a memorandum where he had analysed the indirect costs associated with manufacturing.[39] He aimed for gains in administration and capital expenses rather than direct labour. This meant a decrease in white-collar labour, and the scrapping of several administrative functions. Nicolin pursued an idea that administration had an inherent tendency to grow so target levels of administrative personnel were set below the 'optimal' level. He also suggested an abolition of the very concept 'white-' and 'blue-collar' labour.[40] However, the high-technology strategy had induced a need for qualified engineers, and the share of white-collar labour increased from 31.3 per cent in 1945 to 43.4 per cent in 1960.[41]

In another memo in 1959, Nicolin also pointed to the importance of throughput in manufacturing, which was to be mediated by the 'pull' created by slack resources in the later stages of the manufacturing process.[42] Capital turnover was increased rapidly through inventory control and a manufacturing system based on 'pull' and bottleneck reduction. Nicolin focused on lead times, insisting that 'the more intensive, the less expensive'. Design departments were ordered to increase standardization of products and provide modularity in designs, in a programme to reduce product variety introduced in 1966. Moreover, Nicolin promoted more ad hoc design work, where designers 'were born, lived, and died with their product'.[43] Because ASEA was smaller than its main rivals, the company had to be more efficient, the gospel preached by company management. The aim was to raise profitability by longer product series and new manufacturing philosophies. Another management innovation introduced by Nicolin at ASEA was long-range planning. The function of such planning was to serve as a 'requirements specification' for the corporation. In general, Nicolin believed in deductively generated 'rules of thumb' that could be applied in strategic planning as well as operations management.

Curt Nicolin was very actively involved in the contemporary public discourse on economic and industrial policy in Sweden. In the mid-1960s, he was a board member of SAF for a few years. As a representative of one of the largest industrial firms in Sweden, he often publicly debated with Swedish Minister of Finance, Gunnar Sträng. He also used his position as director of ASEA to influence the firm's attitude towards public relations. For instance, annual reports of ASEA in the 1970s contained public criticism of Swedish industrial policy. ASEA was one of the first Swedish companies to hire a professional Director of Information, and also make him a member of the corporate directorate. ASEA in general, and Nicolin in particular, emerged as the prime example of industrial capitalism (further accentuated by the fact that ASEA was controlled by the Wallenberg family). Nicolin regained a role similar to that of his predecessor Edström.

In 1976, Curt Nicolin resigned as CEO of ASEA and moved on to become chairman of the board. He was also appointed president of SAF, becoming an even more public figure than previously. While SAF had evolved into an organization primarily involved in negotiations with the employees' associations, the selection of Nicolin as its new chairman implied a more active role in debating Swedish economic, industrial and labour market policy.

Folke Westerberg became new president of the ASEA group and the position as CEO was awarded to Torsten Lindström.[44] This new management team continued on a 'more of the same' track, nurturing the technological culture that dominated at ASEA. In the aftermath of the oil embargo, a steel crisis appeared in Sweden. ASEA's subsidiary, Surahammars Bruk, had in 1974 installed a new blast furnace. In the period 1976–81, the subsidiary made a loss of SEK half a billion, the largest deficit in ASEA's history.

Despite management's efforts to internationalize and increase sales, Swedish operations remained more profitable than foreign subsidiaries, for example in Great Britain and Greece, where ASEA made some loss-generating acquisitions. The energy crisis was further complicated by the emerging public debate on nuclear power, which caused severe delays in Swedish utilities ordering nuclear power plants. For ASEA, it was primarily the partly owned ASEA-ATOM that was affected financially. Throughout the 1970s, ASEA negotiated with foreign competitors about co-operation in trading know-how, for instance in nuclear power, but to little avail. Electricity demand decreased in Sweden after the oil crisis, and in the end of the 1970s Nicolin showed impatience with top management's efforts to improve the financial situation of the company.

Internationalization and export

In the 1960s there was a high demand for ASEA's products, when the industrialized countries were building their power generation capabilities. The internationalization of ASEA had been stalled after the Second World War by the huge domestic demand for its products, and it was not until the mid-1950s that the company was again able to seriously enter foreign markets. ASEA was invited to join the international cartels and accepted. However, ASEA aggressively tried to gain market shares on foreign markets, and competitors complained about low prices. In the 1960s, negotiations on a general agreement between the European suppliers led nowhere. ASEA entered into discussions with BBC about a close co-operation in 1968–9, with the outcome being a licence on steam turbine technology from the Swiss company, but little more. Export markets contributed more and more to overall sales volumes for ASEA. Moreover, manufacturing facilities were to a larger extent being placed abroad, mainly due to acquisitions. ASEA also went from a position of selling quite 'standardized' heavy products abroad to 70–80 per cent of exports being complete systems.[45]

The Danish electrical manufacturing firm Titan was acquired in 1965 and was subsequently merged with another Danish company to form the subsidiary Thrige-Titan. The welding operations, AB Asea Svetsmaskiner, were sold to ESAB the same year. By 1969, ASEA-Skandia was the largest wholesaler of electrical products in Scandinavia.

The US grew into ASEA's most important export market in the 1960s and 1970s. The internationalization efforts by ASEA took place through the establishment of manufacturing and sales abroad; the increase was not dramatic, however, and foreign manufacturing went from 8 per cent of total manufacturing to 10–11 per cent in the late 1970s. As the 1970s approached, ASEA secured new contracts by having a number of home markets, where it manufactured some of its products. This became important, as the Swedish market was contracting, and forced the firm to focus further on international sales. In the period 1951–5, the US market accounted for 1.1 per cent of total sales (5.4 per cent of total exports). Twenty years later (1971–5), the US contributed 6.8 per cent of total sales (14.8 per cent of total exports).[46] During negotiations with other manufacturers, ASEA was

Table 4.3 ASEA Group financial performance (MSEK) and employees, 1960–80

	Revenues	Export	Export (%)	Operating profits	Op. profit margin (%)	Employees	Empl. abroad	Foreign empl. (%)
1960	1,353	NA		132	10	30,681	NA	
1961	1,612	NA		139	9	30,928	NA	
1962	1,742	NA		186	11	33,356	3,204	10
1963	1,781	NA	'	192	11	32,216	3,447	11
1964	2,082	NA		246	12	33,398	3,946	12
1965	2,324	878	38	245	11	34,332	4,984	15
1966	2,447	988	40	162	7	34,413	4,894	14
1967	2,765	1,129	41	177	6	32,401	4,473	14
1968	2,728	1,218	45	191	7	32,726	4,717	14
1969	3,333	1,342	40	246	7	34,867	5,502	16
1970	3,690	1,611	44	252	7	36,591	6,105	17
1971	4,001	2,010	50	236	6	37,911	6,166	16
1972	4,996	2,314	46	264	5	38,651	6,040	16
1973	5,249	2,725	52	321	6	39,154	6,870	18
1974	6,917	3,192	46	432	6	41,217	7,398	18
1975	7,863	3,920	50	527	7	43,604	8,395	19
1976	8,400	4,379	52	685	8	44,194	8,370	19
1977	9,718	5,039	52	474	5	41,528	8,511	20
1978	9,814	5,301	54	426	4	40,574	9,193	23
1979	11,830	7,088	60	437	4	40,629	10,534	26
1980	12,557	6,523	52	279	2	39,605	9,762	25

Source: Glete (1983), pp. 227, 264, 345.

accused of dumping prices in foreign markets. Especially in large transformers, an international price war caused a crisis in the 1960s and 1970s, and
profitability for most manufacturers remained low. ASEA had thus devoted
considerable resources to obtain a position at the international forefront
(Table 4.3).

1980–2002: the Percy Barnevik era and beyond

There was a need to become more market-oriented and therefore the board
decided to employ a business school-trained economist and comptroller as a
trouble shooter in the technology-oriented company. The CEO of Sandvik
(which was not controlled by the Wallenberg family) Percy Barnevik was
No. 1 on the list of names. He was hired as CEO and took up the position
on 1 June 1980. In 1980–2 Barnevik, with the help of some young ASEA
managers (all engineers) – 'Percy's Boys' – conducted a major reorganization
of ASEA.[47]

Barnevik's immediate actions at ASEA were first to discontinue the units that had operating losses; secondly to reorganize the corporate bureaucracy; thirdly to increase sales through new products; and finally to expand geographically to new markets.

ASEA also sought increased sales and margins on sold products and therefore tried to expand in its technological spearheads: power transmission, locomotives, robotics, electronics and industrial products. Moreover, some contracts were renegotiated. The market and market activities were also more closely linked to ASEA through the acquisition of all shares in the subsidiaries Skandinaviska Elverk (utility) and Electro-Invest. The latter acquisition was part of a strategy of increasing the share of complete turnkey sales, as Electro-Invest could take part in the financing of such projects.[48] Another previously partly owned subsidiary, the nuclear business ASEA-ATOM, became wholly owned by ASEA in 1982. Moreover, ASEA Innovation, a subsidiary formed for the venturing of frontline research projects, was established in the same year.

The aim was to introduce a pure divisional structure able to work closer to the market than the previous sectors had been able to do. The reorganization meant that the marketing department at the headquarters disappeared and that marketing functions were decentralized to each division. Several other previously centrally organized departments were split up and deployed into the divisions. Central staff numbers decreased from 1655 employees to around 200.[49] With this structure, each division could be held accountable for its profits, and management control principles were thus drastically changed. Within each division, ASEA created profit centres. With a specific aim of decentralizing the company, but also trying to improve the integration of corporate functions, a matrix-like organization was established in 1981.

Not only were profit centres carved out in the manufacturing organization, international companies were established with the plan of boosting exports from 50 per cent to 75 per cent of sales. The organization was also divided in larger sections in two dimensions: Business Areas, that were responsible for continuing R&D and technological development, and Regions, for regional strategies. Finally, headquarters administrative staff was drastically reduced. In all, around 20 units were wound up. The bleeding steel works, Surahammars Bruk, was closed. Operations in the factories in Brazil, Argentina, Great Britain and Greece ceased. Despite these withdrawals, the matrix organization was instituted with the aim of expanding ASEA from an

CREATING NORDIC CAPITALISM • PROLOGUE • SWEDISH WELFARE CAPITALISM • THE BONNIER AND
WALLENBERG BUSINESS GROUPS • FROM ASEA TO ABB

4   125

Photograph 4.1   ASEA's Chairman, Curt Nicolin, and CEO, Percy Barnevik, at the announcement of the ABB merger on 10 August 1987
Source: Courtesy of ABB.

export company to a MNC, as Barnevik's slogan was: 'be an insider, not an invader'.[50]

In 1982, Percy Barnevik succeeded Torsten Lindström as president of the ASEA group. Following this change in CEO, group headquarters were amalgamated with the parent company's headquarters in Västerås.

Barnevik's explained his management 'rules' in 1983 as:[51]

- *5/95*: a change process is 5 per cent analysis and 95 per cent creating an understanding for the need for changes and implementing them.
- *Right direction*: in doing 50 things, it is enough that 35 of them are in the right direction.
- *Action*: initiative is the most important; lack of initiative is not acceptable.
- *Tempo*: high tempo is necessary to avoid the paralysis of uncertainty.
- *Decentralization*: breaking down the organizational structure into smaller units increases employee efficiency and commitment.

In August 1987 it was announced that ASEA and BBC would merge, effective on 1 January 1988 (Photograph 4.1). The company's name was to become Asea Brown Boveri (ABB).

The combine was seen as positive by outside auditors, since it meant a combination of the Swedish firm's advanced marketing and management skills with the technical expertise of BBC. Because of the Swedish firm's higher value on the stock exchange (despite its lower sales and assets), some subsidiaries of ASEA (ESAB, Electrolux, Hägglunds and Skandinaviska Elverk) were kept outside the merger. These companies were transferred to a holding company: Incentive. The organizational changes that had been initiated at ASEA by Barnevik were continued, as he was chosen as the new CEO for the conglomerate. The matrix organization – where the dualities of global versus local, big versus small, decentralized versus centralized were accentuated – were to become famous in the business press.

ABB made rapid acquisitions of AEG's steam turbine business and the Power Transmission and Distribution segment of Westinghouse within a year. ABB also acquired the transmission and distribution division of the Italian manufacturer Ansaldo. In the US, the company bought the nuclear reactor manufacturer Combustion Engineering in 1989. Barnevik's preference for tempo fitted hand in glove as the two 'small giants' were to merge. In what became known as 'Project Manhattan', the strategy after the merger focused first on competitive advantage and profits, then expansion; secondly on a stronger market presence, especially in the US; and thirdly to look ahead, not to the past. This implied that the company first should focus on restructuring and then turn to growth.[52] Restructuring implied, for example, an increased focus on the power business, an orientation towards change and, in particular, further decentralization using the global matrix, in conjunction with a centralized control system.

ABB, with 180,000 employees was not the largest electrical manufacturer, but it was No.1 in the heavy electrical engineering segment. Barnevik, like his predecessor Nicolin was not a big fan of large-scale operations, but broke down the new enterprise into 800 subsidiaries (companies) and 4,000 profit centres. Moreover, Zürich (the former residence of Oerlikon), not Västerås or Baden, was chosen as the location for ABB group headquarters. The new top management group consisted of six members from ASEA (all Swedes) and seven from BBC (five Swiss, one German and one Italian). In contrast to many other electrical manufacturers, ABB was 'walking against the stream' as it chose to concentrate and invest in power engineering. 1989 saw a 50 per cent increase in corporate profits to USD 922 million (SEK 6 billion), and Percy Barnevik's management style was hailed in the business press (e.g. Taylor, 1991). The creation of ABB focused on multiculturalism, integration on a global scale, speed in implementation, preference for action rather than analysis, top management communication and the balance between operating units' freedom and centralized control.[53] The key organizational features of ABB were closely related to the M&A strategy which was most prominent in the five-year period 1987–91. The emphasis on 'being local world-wide' and having 'many home countries' was well suited to reassuring governments and national utilities of a continued national presence.[54]

In contrast to his predecessor, Nicolin, Barnevik's vision was focused on the global scene. Rather than engaging in the domestic debate and SAF, Barnevik aimed for influence in the international sphere. However, Swedish Prime Ministers Olof Palme, Ingvar Carlsson and Göran Persson (all chairmen of the Social Democratic Party) all had very good working relationships with Barnevik, who refrained from publicly criticizing Swedish industrial policy. Barnevik's international outlook was considered a necessity for the global ABB, which needed a presence throughout the world's markets to be 'at home everywhere'. Since procurement of ABB goods was often made by state-owned utilities or agencies, sales were very much a political process. Both the organization of ABB and Barnevik's willingness to travel accentuated this point. This does not mean that he was entirely inactive on the Swedish scene. As chairman of several Swedish companies, and also of Sandvik and Skanska, which did not belong to the Wallenberg group, Barnevik was involved in a number of deals affecting the Swedish industrial structure, but not ABB. When he resigned as CEO of ABB to become its chairman, he increased his active participation in the World Economic Forum in Davos, Switzerland.

The main vehicle for attaining corporate growth at ABB was a concerted effort directed at conquering the Americas and Asia.[55] Expansion was sought through an acquisition frenzy in 1989–94, where ABB made major acquisitions, not only in American markets but also substantial takeovers of manufacturers in Eastern Europe and Asia. At the end of the twentieth century, Barnevik was the most applauded European executive (almost on par with GE's Jack Welch), and ABB was 'the world's favourite case study'. ABB epitomized the truly global multi-domestic corporation, where no country dominated in terms of number of employees (Table 4.4) (Bélanger *et al*, 1999, see also Table 4.5, p. 10).

Barnevik's successor at the helm of ABB was the Swede Göran Lindahl, who had had a long career in the company and was former head of the Power Transmission segment of ABB. When Lindahl took over on 1 January 1997, it signified that corporate management of ABB was to be dominated by Swedes, rather than Germans or Swiss. This succession was secured by Barnevik working in an interim period as both CEO and chairman of ABB.

Table 4.4 *Foreign employees in the electrotechnical industry, 1993*

Company	Country	Employees	Foreign employees	Foreign empl. (%)
ABB	Sweden/Switzerland	213,000	172,000	81
Siemens	Germany	404,000	153,000	38
GEC-Alsthom	France/Britain	80,000	23,000	29
General Electric	US	222,000	59,000	27

Source: Berggren (1999), p. 7.

Table 4.5 **ABB Group financial performance (MUSD) and employees, 1988–2002**

	Revenues	Operating profits	Operating profit margin (%)	Employees
1988	18,732	854	5	169,459
1989	20,560	1,257	6	189,453
1990	29,281	1,790	6	215,157
1991	28,883	1,908	7	214,399
1992	29,615	1,810	6	213,407
1993	28,315	2,181	8	206,490
1994	29,718	2,619	9	207,557
1995	33,738	3,275	10	209,637
1996	34,574	3,026	9	214,894
1997	31,265	1,137	4	213,057
1998	30,872	2,111	7	199,232
1999	24,681	2,416	10	164,154
2000[1]	22,967	1,385	6	160,118
2001[1]	23,726	279	1	156,685
2002[1]	18,295	336	2	139,051

Note: 1. Operating profit measured as EBIT.
Source: Annual Reports, ABB.

As Lindahl took over the position as CEO, Barnevik remained chairman, replacing the previous ABB arrangement with two chairmen (one from ABB and BBC, respectively). At the same time however, both the Swedish Wallenberg family (through the holding company Incentive) and the Swiss Schmidheiny family decreased their number of shares in ABB.[56] The Swiss shares were acquired by the Swiss BZ Group controlled by Martin Ebner, who took an active interest in the proceedings of ABB and was voted on to the board in 1999. Lindahl's background was in sales, and he advocated intensified sales efforts. He more or less shredded the matrix organization in 1998 and opted for 'pure' segments, which meant that the three regional areas were abolished. The reason was to prioritize growth, but also because the matrix was considered too complex with units pulling in different directions, and hence too difficult to manage. The traditional Power products were having problems and Automation had become responsible for the lion's share of ABB profits at the end of the century. This caused top management to commence a new strategy, based on ICT, that was denoted by Lindahl 'knowledge based industrial operations'. Just as predecessor Barnevik (and also Edström), Lindahl spent many working days on the road, meeting politicians and other top managers. But where Barnevik succeeded in managing the distributed organization, Lindahl didn't. His ABB was centralized where he worked alone, without much contact with other senior managers and, indeed, the chairman of the company, Barnevik. Indeed, at the millennium, Lindahl began to plan to become the next chairman of ABB.

However, when the director of ABB's Automation segment resigned in the summer of 2000 it was a turning point. Jörgen Centerman was brought back by Percy Barnevik to become the latest Swedish CEO for ABB in October 2000. The Automation segment was the powerhouse of the 'new' ABB, now that former core segments such as power generation and traction had been divested. The replacement of Lindahl with Centerman accentuated ABB's shift towards a new strategy of turning into a corporation using information-intensive and knowledge-based business models, rather than selling traditional capital goods. Centerman dismantled the last remains of the matrix organization by standardizing processes across the ABB group and by initiating a project aiming at increasing customer focus. In January 2001, the country subsidiaries (one dimension in the matrix) turned into local representatives.[57] In Centerman's reorganization plan, the former segments (based on manufactured products) were to be replaced by four groups based on different types of end customers. Financial Services, Group Processes (standardization) and Group Transformation were placed on top of this arrangement.

Centerman's place at the helm of ABB was to be short-lived. In spring 2000, the stock market valued ABB at SEK 350 billion. In July 2001, it was down to SEK 140 billion. In October 2002, ABB was only valued at SEK 10 billion (see Figure 4.1, p. 131)[58]. What had happened? One explanation is that the entire strategic shift, from capital goods to IT, had failed. In industrial automation, growth disappeared and prices plummeted. But there were also financial reasons. Through 1997–2001 ABB, under the influence of Martin Ebner, bought back its own shares, amounting to approximately USD 450 million, most financed by short-term borrowing. At the same time, the financial reports were translated to the American GAAP standard, following the introduction of ABB's shares on the New York

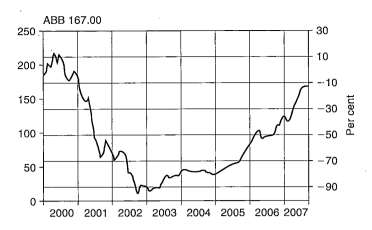

Figure 4.1 **ABB share price (SEK), 1 January 2000–4 September 2007**
Source: DI Stockwatch.

Stock Exchange (NYSE). Provisions for future litigation associated with asbestos skyrocketed, pushing the financial results far below what had previously been presented. Finally, cash flow deteriorated dramatically with the sale of the power generation segment, which had previously brought in advance payments from utilities. Another contributing factor to the changing predicament of ABB was the change of managerial focus. While Nicolin and Barnevik had focused on cost-cutting rationalization programmes (for example, the T50 programme initiated by Barnevik), Lindahl and Centerman had devoted their efforts to increased sales and customer focus. The cost structure of ABB had become a burden on its ability to enhance financial performance. The new ABB organization was criticized internally and in the business press. On top of this, uproar broke out among ABB's owners and the general public when the bonus and compensation packages for Lindahl and Barnevik became known. ABB was in deep crisis, and out went the Swedes.

Despite laying off 12,000 employees worldwide and initiating large cost-cutting programmes, Centerman did not regain the confidence of ABB's owners. The *Annual Report* for 2001 stated that ABB had made a post-tax loss of USD 700 million (see Table 4.5 for ABB group financial pre-tax financial performance).

In March 2002, ABB's credit rating was so low that credit institutions could have obtained control of ABB if they had so wished. The German Jürgen Dormann replaced Percy Barnevik as chairman of the board, and when Jörgen Centerman resigned as CEO in August 2002, Dormann assumed the

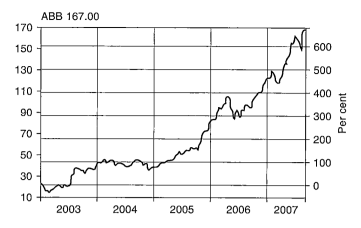

Figure 4.2 **ABB share price (SEK), 1 January 2003–4 September 2007**
Source: DI Stockwatch.

dual position as CEO and chairman. He reorganized ABB into two parts, Automation and Power, and disposed of the customer focus and group process programmes initiated by Centerman. The Swedish list of 'ASEA kings' – Fredholm, Wenström, Edström, Lindén, Nicolin, Barnevik, *et al.* – had come to a halt.

However, the end of the Swedish era did not mark the end of ABB. On the contrary, the company at the beginning of the twenty-first century managed to turn its fortunes around. As indicated in Figures 4.1 and 4.2, while the confidence of the stock market in 2002 in ABB was at an all-time low, the efforts of ABB's management to focus on power and automation paid off. In the quarterly report for the second quarter of 2007, the company boasted a 27 per cent increase in revenues compared to the second quarter of 2006 and an operating profit margin (measured as EBIT margin) of 14.4 per cent. ABB Group annual revenues for 2006 were USD 24,412 million and EBIT USD 2,586 million. Total employees amounted to 108,000. Hence, in addition to having become a truly global company, with Germans, Americans, Swiss, Swedes, Indians, Finns, etc. in the executive committee, ABB by 2007 was financially solid and still at the technology frontier.

The case of ASEA/ABB provides insights into a number of features of the management of Swedish 'big business'. The firm operated in an industry that almost immediately became highly internationalized, and ASEA moved on from a traditional exporting company to being the prime example of a transnational corporation (TNC). An additional feature of ASEA/ABB is its thirst for innovation through technological development. While Edström and

Nicolin were very active in the employers' confederations, and they were of substantial importance in the development (and criticism) of the 'Swedish model', Barnevik refrained from publicly criticizing or debating with the Swedish political establishment. Rather, in his actions on the global political scene he in a sense epitomized ASEA's shift from a domestic 'little giant' to a global enterprise.

QUESTIONS 1. ASEA/ABB has developed as a company concurrent with the emergence of the Swedish welfare state. Is, then, the essence of Swedish capitalism captured in the evolution of ASEA/ABB? Does ASEA/ABB represent a particular Swedish/Nordic way of managing companies, and if so in what sense? In what dimensions have ASEA/ABB been integrated in to the Swedish political economy?

2. ASEA/ABB epitomizes the 'big business' character of the Swedish economy as it emerged from the second industrial revolution and onwards. But is the management of big business in Sweden akin to big business in the US, as described by Alfred Chandler? Were there any relationships between the strategies of AEA/ABB and choice of organizational structure? How did ASEA act with regard to horizontal and vertical integration? Why was ASEA late in adopting the divisional form (M-form) of organizing its activities?

Notes

1. Glete (1994); Henreksson (2001).
2. Henreksson (2001); Larsson (2002).
3. Paquier and Fridlund (1998).
4. Chandler (1977); Chandler and Daems (1980); McGraw (1988); Chandler (1990).
5. See also Sobel (1984); Lazonick (1991); Blackford (1998).
6. See, for example, Fligstein (1985, 1990); Glete (1994); Hounshell (1995); Cassis (1997); Whittington and Mayer (2000); Lamoraux et al. (2003, 2004); Langlois (2004).
7. See, for example, Myhrman (2003); Schön (2000); Sjögren (this volume).
8. Henreksson (2001).
9. Glete (1994); Fridland (1994, 1995); Hasselberg and Petersson (2006).
10. See, for example, Jönsson (1995); Nordlund (2005); Matti (2006).
11. Glete (1983), p. 33.
12. Paquier and Fridlund (1998), p. 239.
13. Matti (2006), p. 89.
14. Glete (1983), pp. 66–7.
15. Wermelin and Ström (1950), p. 51.
16. Paquier and Fridlund (1998), pp. 245–6.
17. Nordlund (2005), pp. 94, 96; Matti (2006), p. 84.
18. Nordlund (2005), pp. 91–2.
19. Glete (1983), p. 49.
20. Nordlund (2005), p. 141.
21. Wallenberg (1970).

22. Nordlund (2005), pp. 278–94.
23. Glete (1983), pp. 72–5.
24. Glete (1983), p. 81.
25. See Fridlund (1999).
26. Glete (1983), p. 159.
27. Matti (2006), pp. 102, 106.
28. Fridlund (1999), p. 114.
29. Glete (1983), p. 104.
30. Glete (1983), p. 138.
31. Glete (1983), p. 237.
32. See, for example, Latham (1969), p. 94; Newfarmer (1980), p. 44.
33. Glete (1983), p. 295.
34. Ehrenurona (1991), p. 193.
35. Glete (1983), p. 305.
36. Glete (1983), p. 318.
37. Glete (1983), pp. 342, 344.
38. Glete (1983), p. 332.
39. Ehrenurona (1991), p. 110.
40. Nicolin (1973), p. 59.
41. Glete (1983), p. 332.
42. Ehrenurona (1991), pp. 111–14.
43. Ehrenurona (1991), p. 152.
44. Ehrenurona (1991), p. 354.
45. Glete (1983), p. 160.
46. Glete (1983), pp. 262–3.
47. Hang and Petersson (1998), p. 105.
48. Glete (1983), p. 357.
49. Ehrenurona (1991), p. 360.
50. Brandes and Brege (1991), p. 6.
51. Haag and Petersson (1998), p. 108.
52. Barham and Heimer (1998), p. 59.
53. Haag and Petersson (1998), pp. 199–206.
54. Berggren (1996), p. 127.
55. Barham and Heimer (1998), p. 93.
56. Carlsson and Nachemson-Ekwall (2003), p. 57.
57. Carlsson and Nachemson-Ekwall (2003), p. 129.
58. Carlsson and Nachemson-Ekwall (2003), p. 217.

References

Barham, K. and Heimer, C. ABB: *The Dancing Giant: Creating the Globally Connected Corporation* (London: Financial Times/Pitman Publishing, 1998).

Bélanger, J., Berggren, C., Björkman, T. and Köhler, C. (eds), *Being Local Worldwide: ABB and the Challenge of Global Management* (Ithaca: Cornell University Press, 1999).

Berggren, C., 'Building a Truly Global Organization? ABB and the Problems of Integrating a Multi-domestic Enterprise', *Scandinavian Journal of Management*, 12(2), pp. 123–37 (1996).

Berggren, C., Introduction: 'Between Globalization and Multidomestic Variation', in Bélanger, J., Berggren, C., Björkman, T. and Köhler, C. (eds), *Being Local Worldwide: ABB and the Challenge of Global Management* (Ithaca: Cornell University Press, 1999).

Blackford, M. G., *The Rise of Modern Business in Great Britain, The United States, and Japan*, 2nd edn. (Chapel Hill: University of North Carolina Press, 1998).

Brandes, O. and Brege, S. *Strategic Turnaround and Top Management Involvement – The Case of ASEA and ABB* (Linköping: Linköping University, 1991).

Bugli, R. W. (ed.), *Electrifying Experience – A Brief Account of the First Century of The ASEA Group of Sweden* (Stockholm: Stenströms, 1983).

Carlsson, B. and Nachemson-Ekwall, S., *Livsfarlig ledning: Historien om kraschen i ABB* (Stockholm: Ekerlids förlag, 2003).

Cassis, Y., *Big Business: The European Experience in the Twentieth Century* (Oxford: Oxford University Press, 1997).

Chandler, A. D., Jr *Strategy and Structure: Chapters in the History of the American Enterprise* (Cambridge, MA: MIT Press, 1962).

Chandler, A. D., Jr *The Visible Hand: The Managerial Revolution in American Business* (Cambridge, MA: The Belknap Press, 1977).

Chandler, A. D., Jr 'The Growth of the Transnational Industrial Firm in the United States and the United Kingdom: A Comparative Analysis', *Economic History Review*, 33 (1980), pp. 396–410.

Chandler, A. D., Jr and Herman Daems, *Managerial Hierarchy: Comparative Perspectives on the Rise of the Modern Industrial Enterprise* (Cambridge: Harvard University Press, 1980).

Chandler, A. D., Jr 'The Beginnings of "Big Business" in American Industry,' in McCraw, Thomas K. (ed.), *The Essential Alfred Chandler: Essays Toward a Historical Theory of Big Business* (Boston, MA: Harvard University Press, 1988).

Chandler, Alfred D., Jr *Scale and Scope: The Dynamics of Industrial Capitalism* (Cambridge, MA: The Belknap Press, 1990).

Ehrenkrona, O., *Nicolin: En svensk historia* (Stockholm: Timbro, 1991).

Fligstein, N., 'The Spread of the Multidivisional Form among Large Firms', *American Sociological Review*, 50 (1985), pp. 377–91.

Fligstein, N., *The Transformation of Corporate Control* (Cambridge, MA: Harvard University Press, 1990).

Fridlund, M., 'En specifikt svensk virtouskonst': Empiriska och teoretiska perspektiv på utvecklingsparet Asea-Vattenfalls historia, *Polhem: Tidskrift för teknikhistoria*, 12 (1994), pp. 106–31.

Fridlund, M., (1995), *Ett svenskt utvecklingspar I elkraft: ASEAs och Vattenfalls FoU Samarbete, 1910–80*, Sandvika, Norway: Senter for Elektrisitetsstudier, Handelshøyskolen BI, Forskningsrapport 1995/2.

Fridlund, M., *Den gemensamma utvecklingen: Staten. Storföretaget och samarbetet kring den svenska elkraftstekniken*, doctoral dissertation (Stockholm/Stehag: Brutus Östlings Bokförlag, Symposion, 1999).

Glete, J., *ASEA under hundra år: En studie i ett storföretags organisatoriska, tekniska och ekonomiska utveckling* (Stockholm: Stenströms, 1983). Bokförlag/Interpublishing AB

Glete, J., *Nätverk i näringslivet: Ägande och industriell omvandling i det mogna industrisamhället 1920–90* (Stockholm: SNS förlag, 1994).

Haag, B. and Pettersson B., *Percy Barnevik: Makten, Myten, Människan* (Stockholm: Ekerlids förlag, 1998).

Hasselberg, Y. & Petersson, T. (eds), *'Bäste Broder!' Nätverk, entreprenörskap och innovation i svenskt näringsliv, (Hedemora: Gidlunds, 2006)'*.

Henreksson, M., 'The Entrepreneur and the Swedish model', in Henreksson, M., Larsson, M. and Sjögren, H. (eds), *Entrepreneurship in Business and Research: Essays in Honour of Håkan Lindgren* (Stockholm: EHF, 2001).

Hounshell, D., *From the American System to Mass Production, 1800–1932: The Development of Manufacturing Technology in the United States* (Baltimore/London: The Johns Hopkins University Press, 1995).

Jönsson, S., *Goda utsikter: Svenskt management i perspektiv*, (Stockholm: Nerenius & Santérus förlag, 1995).

Lamoraux, N. M., Raff, D. M. G. and Temin, P., 'Beyond Markets and Hierarchies: Toward a New Synthesis of American Business History', *American Historical Review*, 108 (2003), pp. 404–33.

Lamoraux, N. M., Raff, D. M. G. and Temin, P., 'Against Whig History, *Enterprise and Society*', 5(3) (2004), pp. 376–87.

Langlois, R. N., 'Chandler in a Larger Frame: Markets, Transaction Costs and Organizational Form in History', *Enterprise and Society*, 5(3) (2004), pp. 355–75.

Latham, J. (1969), *Take-over: The Facts and the Myths of the GEC/AEI Battle* (London: Iliffe Books).

Lazonick, W., *Business Organization and the Myth of the Market Economy* (New York: Cambridge University Press, 1991).

Larsson, M., (2002), 'Storföretagande och industrikoncentration', in Isacson, M. and Morell, M. (eds) *Industrialisment tid. Ekonomisk-historiska perspektiv på svensk industriell omvandling under 200 år*, (Stockholm: SNS förlag, 2002).

Larsson, M. and Sjögren, H. (eds), *Entrepreneurship in Business and Research: Essays in Honoue of Håkan Lindgren* (Stockholm: EHF, 2001).

Matti, T., *Professionella patriarker: Svenska storföretagares ideal, praktik och professionaliseringsprocess 1910–45*, ACTA Universitatis Uppsaliensis, *Uppsala Studies in Economic History*, 75 (Uppsala: Uppsala University, 2006).

McCraw, T. K. (ed.), *The Essential Alfred Chandler: Essays Toward a Historical Theory of Big Business* (Boston, MA: Harvard University Press, 1988).

Myhrman, J. (1994), *Hur Sverige blev rikt*, Stockholm: SNS förlag.

Newfarmer, R., *Transnational Conglomerates & the Economics of Dependent Development: A case of the International Electrical Oligopoly & Brazils Electrical Industry (Greenwich: JAI Press, 1980)*.

Nicolin, C. *Makt och ansvar* (Stockholm: Askild och Kärnekull, 1973).

Nordlund, T. *Att leda storföretag: En studie av social kompetens och entreprenörskap i näringslivet med fokus på Axel Axson Johnson och J. Sigfrid Edström, 1900–50* (Stockholm: Almqvist & Wiksell, 2005).

Paquier, S. and Fridlund, M., 'The Making of Small Industrial Giants: The Growth of the Swedish ASEA and the Swiss BBC through Crises and Challenges Prior to 1914', in Myllyntaus, T. (ed.), *Economic Crises and Restructuring in History: Experiences of Small Countries*, (St Katharinen: Scripta Mercaturae Verlag, 1998).

Schön, L., (2000), *En modern svensk ekomisk historia*, SNS förlag, Stockholm.

Schumpeter, J. A., *Capitalism, Socialism and Democracy* (London: Unwin, 1942/1987).

Sobel, R., *The Age of Giant Corporations: A Microeconomic History of American Business*, 2nd edn.,(Westport, CT: Greenwood Press, 1984).

Spade, B. *Kraftöverföringen Hellsjön-Grängesberg: En 100-årig milstolpe i kraftteknikens historia* (Ludvika: Ludvika 1993).

Taylor, W., ' "The Logic of Global Business": An Interview with ABB's Percy Barnevik', *Harvard Business Review*, March–April, (1991), pp. 91–105.

Tell, F., *Organizational Capabilities: A Study of Electrical Power Transmission Equipment Manufacturers, 1878–1990*, Linköping Studies in Management and Economics, Dissertations, 41, Dissertations from IMIE, 36 (Linköping: Linköping University, 2000).

Wallenberg, M., Jr and J. Sigfrid Edström: *inför hundraårsdagen av hans födelse* (Västerås: ASEA, 1970).

Wermelin, P. G. and Ström, H., *Ludvikaverken 1900–50* (Ludvika: ASEA, 1950).

Whittington, R. and Mayer, M., *The European Corporation: Strategy, Structure and Social Science* (Oxford: Oxford University Press, 2000).

Williamson, O. E., *Markets and Hierarchies: Analysis and Antitrust Implications – A study in the Economics of Internal Organization* (New York: Free Press, 1975).

WELFARE CAPITALISM: THE SWEDISH ECONOMY 1850–2005 • ENTREPRENEURSHIP AND OWNERSHIP: THE

RM VIABILITY OF THE SWEDISH BONNIER AND WALLENBERG FAMILY BUSINESS GROUPS • FROM

ABB **prologue to the Finnish chapter** ESTMENT: FINNISH

CAPITALISM, 1850S–2005 • FROM STATE OWNERSHIP TO MULTINATIONAL CORPORATION: THE PATH OF

ENSO-GUTZEIT TO STORA-ENSO • SUCCESS AND FAILURE OF A CONGLOMERATE FIRM: THE STRATEGIC

PATHS OF NOKIA AND TAMPELLA IN THE LIBERALIZING FINNISH ECONOMY AFTER THE SECOND WORLD

WAR • CO-OPERATIVE LIBERALISM: DENMARK FROM 1857 TO 2007 • ARLA – FROM DECENTRALIZED INDUSTRY

TO MULTINATIONAL ENTERPRISE • CARLSBERG AND THE SELF-REGULATION OF THE DANISH BEER MARKET

• NORWAY: A RESOURCE-BASED AND DEMOCRATIC CAPITALISM • CONSTRUCTIVE POWER: ELKEM 1904–2004

• FINANCE AND THE DEVELOPMENT OF NORWEGIAN CAPITALISM – THE CASE OF CHRISTIANIA BANK

In this chapter we will show that Finland's historical, political and economic development has many similarities with, but also divergences from, the other three Nordic countries included in this volume. Finland has a strong Nordic cultural heritage and some strong common roots, particularly with Sweden, having been a part of Sweden until 1809, which has made institutional and cultural bridging fairly easy. Finland is clearly a Nordic country. However, as a result of being a Russian Grand Duchy between 1809 and 1917, the occasionally politically unstable situation and a more crisis-prone economic structure, the economic and institutional model of the country has had its own distinctive characteristics and partly followed its own development path. We ask if we can talk of a particular 'Finnish model' of capitalism.

In these chapters focusing on Finnish capitalism over a long period, we aim to trace the key factors in – or the 'core' of – something, which could be claimed to be a 'Finnish model' of capitalism. As is stressed in the country chapter (Chapter 5), the model of capitalism has undergone profound and often abrupt transformations over time, often in connection with crises. However, also some persistent features – path dependencies – are discernable, the main ones being a heavy stress on enhancing growth by keeping the investment rate high and by promoting the export sector and big business. In this chapter we will learn more about the roots of this development path and to something called a 'Finnish model'. We will deal in particular with the outline of active growth policies, with the role of the state in the economy and with the significances of crises for institutional change.

In the two case chapters (Chapters 6 and 7) we will examine how 'big business' has been able to adapt to such institutional transformations and ruptures in the model of capitalism, often occurring in relation to crises but also more broadly to institutional change. In the chapter on Nokia and

Tampella (Chapter 7) the adaptation and changing strategies of two key players in Finnish 'big business' during an era of transformation are examined. Top management in Nokia could well orientate in the new global environment and make use of the big institutional transformation and economic turbulence of the 1980s and 1990s in Finland, while Tampella met with huge structural problems after the collapse of Soviet trade and was in the end in practice wiped out. In the second case chapter about the big Finnish forest industry company Enso (Chapter 6), later forming one part of the Nordic corporation StoraEnso, the role of a big state company and its changing profile, changing strategies and changing role in Finnish society are the focus of attention. At the same time the state's changing ownership policies are illustrated from the perspective of one single company. In this chapter the significance of the forest sector for the Finnish economy over a long time period is also illuminated, Enso forming an interesting 'ideal-type' of a Finnish, and later Nordic, forestry corporation.

WELFARE CAPITALISM: THE SWEDISH ECONOMY 1850–2005 • ENTREPRENEURSHIP AND OWNERSHIP: THE
ERM VIABILITY OF THE SWEDISH BONNIER AND WALLENBERG FAMILY BUSINESS GROUPS • FROM
ABB ...STMENT: FINNISH
CAPITALISM, 1850S–200G • FROM STATE OWNERSHIP TO MULTINATIONAL CORPORATION: THE PATH OF
ENSO-GUTZEIT ...ONGLOMERATE FIRM: THE STRATEGIC
PATHS OF NOKIA AND TAMPELLA IN THE LIBERALIZING FINNISH ECONOMY AFTER THE SECOND WORLD
WAR • CO-OPERATIVE LIBERALISM: DENMARK FROM 1857 TO 2007 • ARLA – FROM DECENTRALIZED INDUSTRY
TO MULTINATIONAL ENTERPRISE • CARLSBERG AND THE SELF-REGULATION OF THE DANISH BEER MARKET
• NORWAY: A RESOURCE-BASED AND DEMOCRATIC CAPITALISM • CONSTRUCTIVE POWER: ELKEM 1904–2004
• FINANCE AND THE DEVELOPMENT OF NORWEGIAN CAPITALISM – THE CASE OF CHRISTIANIA BANK

5 growth and investment: Finnish capitalism, 1850s–2005

Susanna Fellman

Introduction[1]

Finnish management and the Finnish business system have received much attention over the past few years, particularly because of Nokia's presence on the world business stage. Finland has been named as one of the most competitive economies of the world, encouraging study of the Finnish economy as an example of a successful adaptor to the perceived challenges arising from the New International Economic Order (NIEO). On the other hand, Finland is perhaps the least familiar Nordic country outside the region and Finnish economic and political history is not even very well known in its home region. One obvious reason is that the Finnish language is different from the Scandinavian ones. Finland is also a small late-comer and perhaps regarded as particularly peripheral. During the post-war era the country was also fairly inwardly close. Nevertheless, Finland experienced a remarkable rapid growth and catch-up in the twentieth century and can boast an average long-run growth rate exceeding that of most other countries, with the exception of, for example, Japan and South Korea. Thus, also in the long run the Finnish economy is an interesting story.

In this chapter we will take a closer look at the 'Finnish model' of capitalism. One point of departure is that the Finnish economy has many features in common with the Nordic countries – for example, it is a small, open economy, dependent on foreign trade. The industrial take-off was mainly a result of exploiting some key – primarily forest – resources, which experienced a growing demand in foreign markets during the late nineteenth century. The Finnish economy has, like the other Nordic countries in the post-war era, also been characterized by a generous welfare state based on the principle of universalism, by extensive public services and by a publicly funded educational system. The labour market has been marked by strict regulation, a high degree of unionization and an elaborate system of collective agreements. However, the 'Finnish model' has also partly followed a different path than in the other Nordic countries and in some cases the motivations and goals behind superficially similar institutional settings and reforms have been somewhat different. The Finnish economy was clearly lagging those of Sweden and Denmark. This is evident from the GDP/*per capita* figures (see Table 5.1 p. 142), but exemplified by for example the fact that Finland in the 1860s experienced the last peace-time hunger crises in western Europe, which had visible effects on population figures.[2]

Also at the institutional level clear divergences can be observed – for example, labour market relations differed substantially from the other Nordic countries. Some of the institutional divergences can be attributed to the lagging economic development, but it would be wrong to conclude that Finland just followed the other Nordic countries with a lag.

Another point of departure is that the Finnish economy appears to have been susceptible to crises. One obvious factor which has made the Finnish economy so crisis-prone is the occurrence of wars, which have made the Finnish situation quite different form its Nordic neighbours, but the economic structure has also given Finland an inherent propensity to crisis. For example, during earlier periods when Finland was still an agrarian society, the harsh climate led to severe crop failures from time to time, while later on the cyclical nature of the main export sector, the forest industry, contributed to deep recessions at regular intervals. The economic policies and the economic model both appear to have contributed to aggravating the business cycles. For example, the depression of the early 1990s was as much a result of shortcomings in economic political decision-making in the 1980s as sluggishness in carrying out necessary transformations earlier. Crises also seem to play a significant role for the model of capitalism, as transformations in the model have often occurred in close connection with crises. Such significant ruptures have also been the case in the other Nordic countries, but they appear to have been more abrupt and sharper in the Finnish case.

Kari Lilja, together with Keijo Räsänen and Risto Tainio, has analysed the Finnish business system during the post-war era on various occasions.[3] They have drawn up a clear picture of the Finnish business system and have characterized it in two distinct periods, with a sharp change in the 1980s and 1990s. In spite of the extensive, or even abrupt, transformations or ruptures in the models of the two periods, Lilja and his colleagues also stress some very persistent features existing in both periods. Moreover, the models have not been 'pure' as the ideal types presented in *Varieties of Capitalism* or in the business systems literature. That is, however, seldom the case anywhere. In the American competitive capitalism extensive co-operation between divergent actors also occurs, while the co-operative models that have marked many European countries have by no means lacked competition and market-based solutions.

One important question I will address in this chapter is whether we can talk about a 'Finnish model'? It has been argued that a 'Finnish model' for growth and economic development has existed, although one cannot speak of a 'model' in the same way as about a 'Swedish model' (cf. Sjögren, Chapter 2 in this volume). There is a common agreement that a 'Finnish model' has existed, when it comes to economic policy (see p. 176).[4] Prominent features of such a Finnish economic model would be strong state involvement, strong collaborative features and a high degree of corporatism, where the aim is to enhance growth and investments. The concrete shape and outline of the model have varied, however, over time, mostly as a result of diverging contemporary views on how to enhance economic growth.

This chapter will to a great extent follow the outline of Lilja and his Finnish colleagues for the post-war era, but I will also go further back in history, connect the models to the larger societal and economic development in the search for the roots of such a 'Finnish model' and, finally, look at its political and ideological foundations. Every section will start with a macroeconomic overview, and then proceed to analyse the model of capitalism and the divergent segments of the economy.

I will divide the capitalistic model into periods and look for the reason behind transformations: when and why does the model change, develop or turn in a new direction? I will also adopt the concept of 'formative phases' or periods – that is, a period when transformations in both the techno-economic paradigm and the institutional setting are rapid, which is then followed by a more stable period (cf. Chapter 1 and Sjögren, Chapter 2 in this volume). In this chapter the concrete periods differ somewhat from the other country chapters, arising from the somewhat different development paths.

The periods will be as follows:

- Transformations and industrial take-off: an era of economic liberalism, 1850–1913.
- War, independence civil war and economic crisis: an interlude, 1914–18.

Table 5.1 *Finnish economic growth in international comparison, 1820–2004*[1]

Year	Finland	UK	US	Sweden
1820	759	1756	1287	1198
1870	1107	3263	2457	1664
1900	1621	4593	4096	2561
1938	3486	5983	6134	4725
1970	9577	10,767	15,030	12,716
2004	21,305	21,847	30,243	22,325

Note: 1. In 1990 Geary Khamis dollars.
Sources: Maddison (1991) and Elorant et al. (2006).

- Nation-building, co-operation and the large scale: an era of qualified liberalism, 1919–38.
- War, reconstruction and regulation: a second interlude, 1939–56.
- State-led growth: an inwardly closed, highly co-ordinated market economy, 1957–81.
- Liberalization, speculative bubble and a delayed structural crisis: a third interlude, 1982–93.
- Towards an inwardly and outwardly open co-ordinated market economy: 1993–2005.

This periodization looks a little different from that of the other countries, as the wars are classified as periods in themselves. This reflects, of course, the prominent role of the wars, which have formed something of interludes or parentheses in Finnish development.

Transformations and industrial take-off: an era of liberalism, 1850–1913

Finland was a part of Sweden until 1809, when it was annexed to Russia as an autonomous Grand Duchy. This long history as an eastern part of the Swedish kingdom left an important cultural and historical heritage. Finland is clearly a Nordic country. One important factor is that the Swedish legislation and institutional setting remained mainly intact after 1809. The economic and social contacts with Sweden continued to be intimate after the separation up until today. This is especially observable in the business sector, where the interaction over the Gulf of Bothnia has been extensive.[5]

Another important factor binding Finland to the other Nordic countries is of course the Swedish language, which has a strong foothold in the country, making cultural bridging easy. The country has had a small Swedish-speaking minority since far back, but the Swedish language has also more broadly a special position in the country, although a certain hostility towards both the Swedish language and the Swedish-speaking minority has occurred from time to time. The Swedish-speaking population, although small, has been important in economic life until today, but particularly so during the early industrialization. The Swedish-speakers constituted a significant share of the early entrepreneurs. Furthermore, the bilinguality of the country also influenced economic development, not the least in the emergence of a Fenno-nationalistic – Fennoman – business life in the late nineteenth century and e.g. in the development of two business schools run according to language.

Coming under Russian rule in 1809 did not mean any abrupt changes for Finland, as Swedish laws and institutions mainly remained in force. Finland also experienced a fairly autonomous position within the Russian empire, particularly with respect to the economic sphere. For example, Finland had its own administration, own tariff and tax policies and, since the 1860s, its own currency. Finland also had a customs border with Russia and the Russian custom duties were fairly favourable for Finland compared with other countries. However, Finland's position in the Russian empire between 1809 and 1917 also made its political and the economic situation somewhat different from the other Nordic countries. In spite of extensive autonomy, there were occasionally Russian attempts to tie the Grand Duchy more closely to the Empire, particularly at the turn of the century. This left some marks on the economic and business development.

Industrialization gathers speed

Finnish society changed extensively during the period of autonomy. Economic progress and modernization started, as well as the building of the modern Finnish nation. Finland also experienced in the last decades of the nineteenth century a very rapid population growth. In 1880s the population exceeded just 2 million, but already in 1910 the population was roughly 3 million. The 'road to prosperity' started with the development of new sectors in the economy, the emergence of the first large-scale firms, new employment opportunities and rising living standards.[6] When industrial take-off actually occurred in Finland is, as in many other countries, much debated in Finnish historiography, but there is a general agreement that the second half of the nineteenth century is a good point of departure, although already in the first half of the century some sort of proto-industrialization was discernible.[7] The

Table 5.2 *Employment shares (% of GDP), main sectors: Finland, 1870–2000*

Year	Agriculture	Industry and Construction	Services
1870	75	16	9
1922	58	22	20
1934	52	26	22
1950	39	32	29
1970	26	32	42
1990	12	31	57
2000	9	28	63

Source: Hjerppe (1989); *Statistical Yearbook*, various years, Statistics Finland.

period from the mid-1880s until the First World War has been called the first period of industrialization.[8] Although industrialization was rapid in some part of the country, Finland was still mainly agrarian. The new industrial plants and the employment opportunities they brought concerned only a small share of the population and certain parts of the economy. In the 1860s, 80 per cent of the labour force worked within the primary sector, which contributed 60 per cent of the GDP (see also Table 5.2). By 1900, the primary sector's share of GDP was already below 50 per cent, although around 70 per cent of the labour input was still in the primary sector.[9]

Although there were no large spurts, a steady growth in the secondary sector is evident, resulting in an increasing share of GDP.[10] Particularly after the 1870s the manufacturing sector developed rapidly, production became more diversified and the exports of manufactured goods and timber grew. An export-led industrialization began. The main export markets for textile and metal industry were in Russia, but the expanding forest production, particularly sawn timber, was to an increasing extent sold on western markets making Finland increasingly dependent on western markets. A rapid emergence of sawmills, and gradually pulp and paper mills, occurred. Many of the companies gaining importance in the Finnish society emerged at this time, such as Kymmene Ab (today part of UPM), W. Gutzeit & Co Ab (today part of StoraEnso) and A. Ahlström Oy (Ahlström Corp.). This was also an era of many legendary innovative entrepreneurs as Antti Ahlström, Fredrik Idestam (Nokia Ab) and Gottfried Strömberg (Oy Strömberg Ab, now part of ABB Corp.), who founded successful corporations.[11] Infrastructure investments, particularly transport, were carried out both on private and public initiative to improve the situation for the rapidly expanding economy. For instance, the Saimaa canal, important for distribution of forest products, opened for traffic in 1856, while the first railway lines began services in the 1860s.

Modernization and commercialization in the primary sector

Although Finnish industrialization has been primarily export-led, these transformations were also induced by developments in the agrarian economy, a feature often neglected when talking about industrialization and early business development. One prerequisite for industrialization is that the agrarian production becomes efficient, allowing it to release labour to other sectors. Moreover, in Finland industrialization and the primary sector were closely linked, as the early industrialization occurred mainly in the periphery, close to the raw material and energy supply, i.e. forests and water resources.

The second half of the nineteenth century meant the beginning of the agrarian revolution and the commercialization of agrarian production in Finland. The modes of production became more efficient, output increased and, more importantly, productivity grew. New technologies, crop rotation and fertilization improved efficiency, but better cattle breeding and increasing skills among farmers also promoted productivity growth. There was also a structural shift from crop to animal husbandry.[12] The commercialization and development of the agricultural sector was greatly promoted by the development of the co-operative movement. Big co-operatives like the dairy co-operative Valio, but also smaller locally bound ones, promoted the accumulation of capital in the agricultural sector, provided important production and distribution channels for the primary products and were important for technological and commercial innovation. These co-operatives became an important factor within the primary sector, but gradually also in other sectors, e.g. in banking (Osuuspankki), in insurance (Tapiola), in retail trade (SOK) and even in forest industry through the strong Metsäliitto Co-operative. The co-operative movement formed during the whole twentieth century an important foundation for the Finnish economic model, although not as significantly as in Denmark (see Iversen and Andersen, Chapter 8 in this volume), perhaps due to the lesser significance of agri-business in the Finnish economy.

The rural population experienced increasing income levels and new consumption opportunities as a result of increasing productivity. Also the increasing exploitation of forest resources by selling timber and developing forest areas and new employment opportunities opening up contributed to higher income levels of the rural population. Forest work (timber work, logging) and the saw mills provided new job opportunities and it became a common pattern to work part of the year in the forest and part of the year within agriculture. The rapid population growth and the increasing productivity at the same time made labour available for the expanding construction work, industry and services.

The big transformations in the Finnish economy in general, and in the agrarian sector in particular, could be seen in agrarian society as a whole. Although the factories and emerging industrial society reached only certain areas, the village centres in the more remote countryside changed remarkably in only a few decades, where railways, shops, banks, schools, etc. emerged at an increasing pace.[13]

This development also had a downside. Primary production was still based on small-scale farming, and the ideal for many Finns was the independent farmer owning his own land and supporting his family. Simultaneously, there was at the same time a rapid growth in the number of sharecroppers without their own farms. Although there was a 'pull' of labour to the growing industrial production, the 'surplus population' or the 'sharecropper question' (*torpparikysymys, torparfrågan*), was seen as worrying. A growing number of underemployed rural and landless people were considered a social problem, later giving rise to social unrest.

Institutional reforms supporting business development

The institutional environment also changed extensively in the second half of the nineteenth century. The main reform from the perspective of the business sector was the abolition the mercantilist system of regulation, which began in the 1850s and was carried through during the 1860s and 1870s. The gradual liberalizing of trade and business activities (*elinkeinovapaus, näringsfrihet*), particularly the freedom to establish steam sawmills and the abolition of the old guild system in 1868, stimulated entrepreneurship in trade and in manufacturing. These reforms were at least partly a response to the increasing economic activity, and a necessity for the rapidly developing sawmills industry. One example often taken as a symbolic measure is the liberalization of the restriction on establishing steam sawmills in 1857. The steam sawmills were much more efficient than the sawmills driven by water power. Technical progress in a way pushed forward these reforms, as the new production methods were more efficient than the old ones.[14] Such liberalizations also furthered economic progress by inspiring new entrepreneurs on the market.

Obviously, these reforms were a part of similar liberalistic reforms in other countries: the Finnish manaufacturers and authorities could observe what was going on elsewhere.

Company law also developed and established an institutional framework within which companies could act. This legislation was primarily an indication of a process of change within the economic sphere.[15] The first Companies Act (*Osakeyhtiölaki, Aktiebolagslagen*) passed in 1864 (revised in 1895), established the rights and obligations of shareholders within the joint stock company and in 1868 the Bankruptcy Act clarified the role of the rights and obligation of creditors and debtors in case of bankruptcy.

The situation on the labour markets went also through extensive transformations, reflecting the new forms of employment and new employee–employer relations as a result of new forms of production in industrial establishments, based on wage labour and regular working hours. The patriarchal master–servant relation was exchanged for the modern free wage-worker based on the liberalist view that employment was a voluntary agreement between free individuals. The obligation to take employment was abolished in 1865, while the liberalization of restrictions on migration enabled labour to move more freely and seek employment. A law providing for freedom of occupation was passed in 1879.[16]

The transitions within the labour market and the liberal reforms led to a new form of collectivism. The first trade unions emerged in the second half of the 1880s, and in 1899 the Finnish Labour party was founded (which changed its name into the Social Democratic Party in 1903). Also the employers organized into federations. In 1907 both the employers and employees founded their own central organizations: the Finnish Federation of Trade Unions (Suomen Ammattijärjestö, SAJ) and the General Confederation of Employers in Finland (Suomen Työnantajain Keskusliitto, STK). Strikes and other kinds of collective action became more common. In the early twentieth century the workers' movement was particularly active. New unions formed and demands for collective negotiations were raised. In 1905, a general strike broke out. Some local agreements were concluded, but these concerned only a small fraction of industrial workers. The unions' position was not very strong among the workers themselves and the number of members varied widely between branches. After 1905, membership decreased, not to recover until the years of unrest in 1917–18.

The educational system also developed. In particular, the supply of primary education grew. The primary school reform in the 1860s has been seen as a landmark. It transferred the responsibility of primary education from the church to the municipalities, which could get support from the state. Unlike the other Nordic countries, however, the educational level remained at a very low level in Finland. Although in principle some primary education should be available for everyone, few Finns participated in more than rudimentary teaching, often provided in so-called 'ambulating' or 'mobile' schools. The result was that most people could read only tolerably, and rarely write. At the turn of the century only around 34 per cent of the age cohort attended regular primary school (*kansakoulu, folkskola*).[17] In 1880, a majority (67 per cent) of the population was only able to read, while 23 per cent were in principle illiterate; thus, only 10 per cent of the population had the ability to both read and write. The situation improved rapidly, however: in 1890, 17 per cent and in 1920 already 58 per cent of the population could both read and write.[18]

The supply of vocational training was still scarce, mostly provided on private initiatives at a rudimentary level. Education at university level, on the other hand, developed fairly rapidly, but this form of education concerned only a small segment of the population. University education was mostly aimed at the civil service, the church and some liberal professions. Some new educational opportunities for manufacturing and trade emerged, however. For example, the opening of the bi-lingual Polytechnic Institute (Polyteknillinen Opisto, Polytekniska Institutet) in Helsinki 1879, which was transformed into a technical university in 1908, and the first two business schools – or rather Handelshochschule (handelshögskola) according to the German model – also in Helsinki in the early twentieth century, improved the supply of trained personnel for a growing business life. Although primarily founded to improve the status of the emerging business elite, the establishment of these schools was also motivated by increasing economic activity.[19] Moreover, looking only at the supply of domestic education underestimates the supply of skilled personnel for business undertakings, as many Finns intending to pursue a business career travelled abroad to study during this period, particularly among young students. Foreign experts were also employed in Finnish firms. Although one of the main reasons for the expansion in university-level education was that the elite wanted to develop an elite education, the expansion of university-level education had favourable 'spill over' effects: the system of higher education developed and technical training in particular became pronounced. The strong emphasis on skill formation and on technical skills has been prominent within the Finnish growth model. The Finnish technical universities were later important for the development of the strong forest 'cluster'.[20] The contacts between the technical university and the private firms were also close from the start.

During this period the basic outline of the Finnish educational system took root, when a system based on three levels emerged: a general primary education, a voluntary secondary education and/or vocational training, and university-level training.

The evolution of a modern financial system

The monetary system and financial markets developed rapidly during this period. A monetary reform of the 1840s, in which the Russian rouble became the sole currency and Finland adopted a silver standard based on its own reserves, was as an important step towards more efficient, organized and independent monetary conditions.[21] But in 1860, when Finland received its own currency, the Markka, the economy became more independent from Russia and its volatile and weak rouble. When Finland joined the international gold standard in 1878, the Finnish monetary system was finally separated from Russia. By joining the international gold standard, the Finnish economy also became more explicitly tied to the West.

New credit regulations and legislative reforms made it possible to establish private commercial banks, which opened up new opportunities for entrepreneurs by improving financial services. The first commercial banks emerged, starting with Föreningsbanken i Finland in 1862, established by prominent entrepreneurs, mainly Henrik Borgström Jr, owner of the trade house Borgström, merchant J.H. Lindroos and some other Swedish-language businessmen and entrepreneurs. This bank was followed by the Nordiska Aktiebanken för Handel och Industri in 1873 and some smaller banks. Previously the Bank of Finland had been the main source for financing business. Already in the 1820s the first savings bank had emerged, and later in the nineteenth century a network of co-operative banks was established. However, the co-operative and savings banks provided primarily financing for smaller undertakings, farmers and individual customers in the countryside and in small towns.

Two decades later, some prominent Fennoman entrepreneurs, such as Alfr. Kihlman, Lauri Kivekäs and Otto Stenroth wanted to have their 'own' commercial bank to promote the emergence of a Finnish-language – 'Fennoman' – 'big business' and started to attract investors interested in furthering their aim.

In 1889 Kansallis-Osake Pankki opened its doors. The legendary figure developing this bank was a banker F.K. Nybom, who came from Nordiska Aktiebanken för Handel och Industri. The share capital was diversified, as the Fenno-nationalistic project mobilized many Fennomans. Among big industrial establishments the Bank of Finland, however, continued to be important until the late nineteenth century, but the commercial banks were successful and in a few years they came to dominate the financial markets and particularly lending to emerging businesses and big business.[22] Within the financial sector, the Finnish system received its basic form during these decades.

However, as the business sector was often so profitable that investments were financed through income financing and share capital – equity was often far above 50 per cent – the role of the banks as power centres within big business was still not strong.[23] An exception was the paper industry, where large investment programmes sometimes demanded extensive lending, increasing the share of outside capital and making the companies heavily dependent on the banks. Actually, the commercial banks aimed to restrict themselves to deposits and lending, and were reluctant to work as general investment banks or to exercise power in manufacturing firms through direct share ownership. For example Jean Cronstedt, managing director of Föreningsbanken in 1872–1907, stated that the bank wanted to avoid being a universal bank, and objected to the bank owning shares.[24] The strongly bank-centred system where two large commercial banks formed 'house-banks' for the large corporations building 'spheres' and where they also directly or indirectly controlled ownership blocks, was a feature of the twentieth century, and particularly of the post-war period.[25]

Actions to improve the trading of shares were also taken in the 1860s and a Stock Exchange Association (*Pörssisäätiö, Börsföreningen*) was founded in 1862. The actual trading did not take place at the meetings of the association, but through informal negotiations. The transactions were completed and confirmed at the meetings and the prices were published in newspapers. In the early twentieth century, the need for a system of public trading of stocks was seen as necessary and the association made an initiative to establish a stock exchange, which started in 1912. Still, also after the opening of the Helsinki Stock Exchange, the markets remained 'thin' as both turnover and the number of firms listed were low. Although the banks were fairly reluctant to act as investment banks and to own stocks in companies during this period, a so-called 'market-based system' – i.e. system where the stock market forms an important mediator of capital – did not emerge.

A weak or a strong state?

This era was clearly liberalistic in every respect. Apart from some stray remarks from the growing socialist movement, there were few voices who wanted any direct interference from the state in the market economy: there should be as little interference in the entrepreneurs' and companies activities' as possible. On the other hand, adverse effects from the ultra-liberalistic era, primarily on the labour market, gradually became evident. The protection of the weakest was as a result necessary and in the 1880s the first employment regulations were enacted, for example, on child labour. In 1889, an act protecting industrial workers was passed, which established a system of factory inspection.[26]

The Finnish historian Viljo Rasila has stressed that the ultra-liberal era remained fairly short, lasting only during a few decades of the late nineteenth century.[27] However, the inter-war period can also be seen as mainly liberalistic, although perhaps not ultra-liberalistic, particularly when it comes to labour and capital markets, although protectionist tendencies, the emergence of state firms and the rapid cartelization marked a move towards a more collaborative form of capitalism (see p. 155).

The role of the state during this period is interesting. Although the transformations on many fronts supported emerging industrialization, no clear agenda for the stimulation of growth or the working environment of the firm by means of a systematic policy existed. The government was, on the one hand, at arm's length, by interfering as little as possible in economic activity in the ultra-liberalistic spirit of the era. On the other hand, there were also direct and explicit actions from the authorities to improve the working environment of business life, not only through legal reforms but also through infrastructure and educational investments. This originated partly in the simple fact that businessmen active in politics and within the Diet based on four Estates used their position to drive reforms that were primarily useful for their own business, but at the same time useful for the whole economy.[28] This would indicate an active but weak state, which was partly in the hands of individual interest groups and sector interests. On the other hand, when introducing the monetary reform, the state was fairly strong, especially as it tied the Markka to the gold standard at a high level, in spite of a severe recession and demands for a devalued currency by the struggling business sectors.

According to Professor Jorma Kalela, the liberal reforms were actually an indicator of a strong and active state, as such reforms promoted the working environment of the 'market forces' when actually no market forces yet existed. These reforms, according to Kalela, emerged prior to economic development.[29] However, although the liberal reforms came early with respect to the stage of economic development, Finnish economic historians agree that economic activity was clearly growing already at the time of the reforms. This would support the argument of the weak, but active state responding to the development. But it has to be stressed that the reason for the fairly early liberalization of the economy was that similar reforms in other countries occurred: the Finnish liberalization was part of a broader phenomenon.

Modernization of society and growing social tension

Beside monetary and other legislative and institutional reforms affecting economic activity, Finnish society changed on many other levels as well. New political parties and political movements emerged. It was an era of political reforms, of which particularly the introduction of a unicameral parliament and universal suffrage in 1906 was an important and radical step towards democratization. The late nineteenth century and the first decades of the twentieth century saw the first steps towards a modern professional society, with the gradual abolishment of a class society hitherto upheld by the system of Estates.

At the same time the country was still also to a great extent a society of the 'old ways'. The primary sector dominated the economy and few people were affected by the new factories, the new schools, the university institutions, the new banks, etc. The severe famine which struck Finland in 1867–8 indicated how dependent the country still was on agricultural production, although the famine was not only a consequence of the two years of disastrous crop failures but also of economic policy, problems in state finances and an international recession, factors which indicate simultaneously an increasing interdependence of the Finnish economy on the international economic order.

At the turn of the century there were increasing pressures in Finnish society both externally, particularly from 'Russification' policies – that is, the efforts to tie Finland more closely to the Russian empire – but also internally from the growing workers' movement. Added to these were the problems of poverty among the landless population, unemployment, or rather underemployment, and increasing gaps in living standards between groups in society; a phenomenon common in periods of turbulence and economic transition. The rapidly transforming society created tensions, but it also disclosed underlying political and social conflicts and a strict stratification in Finnish society in general, and in the rural society in particular, originating further back.

These conflicts, tensions and stratifications formed the basis for the factors that gradually led up to the civil war in 1918.[30]

Not necessarily all groups in society – not even within the elite – were either in favour of promoting big business and large-scale industrialization. Actually also groups within the middle classes, particularly the so-called Fennomans, wanted to promote the development of the agrarian society and small-scale entrepreneurship. The ideal life for a Finn was to have his own piece of land to cultivate in the countryside. The Fennomans also drew much of their support from the large rural, Finnish-speaking population. However, as industrialization progressed and new economic opportunities within trade and industry opened up, the Fennomans turned to promoting the development of a Finnish-language business life, as opposed to the existing big business which hitherto had been dominated by the Swedish-speaking minority. This led to the emergence of a 'cluster' of Fennoman large-scale companies, of which the Kansallis-Osake-Pankki commercial bank and the Pohjola insurance company formed the 'jewels in the crown'. Gradually, as a consequence of economic development, business also became more Finnish-speaking, without ideological connotations.

The Finnish nation and the Finnish capitalism taking shape

So what form and shape did the capitalistic model take during this first period? And what did this period mean for the formation of a possible 'Finnish model' from a long-term perspective? The economy may be characterized as a liberal market economy, but consisting of elements of co-operation and collaboration and even intervention. The system during this period can neither be seen as a strongly co-operative nor as a purely competitive system, but a system in transition – or, perhaps more aptly, in the making – as no clear agenda for a 'growth model' existed. It was a system with elements of both collaboration and unrestricted market forces and a system seeking it's own path. As the elements of co-operation and of state involvement also varied between sectors and segments, not to mention within divergent areas of the country, the system also was also fairly fragmented (see Chapter 1).

The last decade of the nineteenth century was in many respects a significant period for the formation of modern Finnish society, but these decades also laid the foundations for a 'Finnish model'. As has been stressed previously, the ideological and political roots of the development of the Finnish economic – political model can be traced back to this period.[31] Although the capitalistic system transformed significantly over time, simultaneously with the evolvement of the nation called 'Finland', some basic institutional layers took shape. A good example is the role of the state. It was fairly active in the promoting of industrialization by paving the way and smoothing the path for business life – i.e. the role of the state in the economy as a promoter of growth was defined, although the actual policies and actions were transformed in later periods.

Finally, from the perspective of the techno-economic paradigm this era meant the exploitation of forest resources, the increasing use of steam and mechanization of production and an institutional climate supporting the expanding sawmill industry.

War, independence and economic crisis: an interlude, 1914–18

Although the First World War did not affect Finland directly, the war and its aftermath had still extensive effects on the Finnish economy as a part of the Russian empire. The years 1914–16 were fairly beneficial economically, particularly for the manufacturing industries, as many industrial companies exported war materials to Russia at good prices. The financial situation was, however, unstable. As a consequence of the breakdown of the gold standard in 1914 and the shortage of goods, a period of a rapid inflation began. The stock market boomed, but primarily due to a speculative wave. The interruption of western trade was also devastating for some firms.

Furthermore, the years 1917–18 meant a period of severe crisis for the country. In the wake of the Russian revolution, Finland gained its independence in 1917. This meant that exports to Russia ceased more or less instantly. Before the First World War about 45 per cent of exports went to Russia, but during the war the share had risen as high as 94 per cent, due to the interruption of international trade and to the growing war deliveries. Substitute markets were not to be found, due to the ongoing war in Europe. As a consequence of the revolution and the new Bolshevik government in Russia confiscating foreign investments and declaring all foreign debt default, many Finnish firms lost investments they had in the country.

At the same time domestic discontent and unrest in Finland increased. New unions were formed, while strikes, demonstrations and other activities became frequent. Paramilitary organizations, the so called Red (or revolutionary) and White (or civil or bourgeois) Guards mobilized. After the dissolution of Parliament in 1917, re-election, and a new bourgeois Senate which in

January 1918 declared the 'White' Civil Guards as the government's army, civil war broke out, which caused holdups, unrest and both cruel and violent war activity. This caused a sharp decline in industrial production and GDP in 1918, which was aggravated by a bad harvest and food shortages. In the years 1917–18 GDP shrank by 27 per cent. In 1918 Finland actually experienced a real famine. Before the war, self-sufficiency in cereals had been only about 35–40 per cent, but as cereal imports from Russia had been running smoothly this had not been seen as a problem. In 1917 this changed completely with the loss of the Russian trade.[32]

In April 1918, the White Guards, with the support of some German forces, pushed back the Red forces and restored the bourgeois government. The repression of those involved in the Red uproar, but also of other labour movement activists was harsh: executions were carried out and around 80,000 people were interned in prison camps with high death rates, aggravated by epidemics, particularly the Spanish flu.

Apart from the war-time losses, in both economic and humanitarian terms, this period led to deep mental wounds and left a long shadow on Finnish society, influencing particularly labour market relations. The hunger of 1918 also affected agricultural policies in the inter-war period, when self-sufficiency became a key target. The war years cemented the close relations between the political and business elite. Several business managers of the time, like Rudolf Waldén (Yhtyneet Paperitehtaat) and Gösta Serlachius (G.A. Serlachius Ab), had close contacts with the highest political elite and were even active in war management. Later such key figures in Finnish business exercised extensive influence in economic–political agenda-setting, for example in the emergence of favourable attitudes towards cartelization and in the introduction of trade policies that served the interests of the forest industry.[33] Also, the pragmatic decision not to return to pre-war parity for the Finnish Markka (see below) was in the interest of the export industries, which gave the forest industry a competitive advantage when seeking new markets: to resort to devaluation of the currency became an accepted way to solve economic slumps in the post-war era.

Nation-building, co-operation and the large-scale: an era of 'qualified liberalism', 1919–38

After the war, the Finnish economy was in poor shape. The war had led to shortage of many necessities and inflation had been running at a high

Table 5.3 *Main sectors' share of GDP (%): Finland, 1860–2004*

Year	Agriculture	Manufacturing and Construction	Services
1860	61.7	15.9	22.4
1880	56.3	17.7	26.0
1900	48.7	23.2	28.1
1928	33.6	30.8	35.6
1956	21.4	38.4	40.2
1969	13.2	38.5	48.3
1980	9.6	39.4	51.0
1995	4.5	32.5	62.9
2004	3.1	30.2	76.7

Sources: Hjerppe (1989); *Statistical Yearbook*.

level for years. The instability of the First World War was worsened by the Civil War, which had meant a severe decline in production and deficits in both public finances and in the current account. Beside the decline in GDP and the loss of the main export markets, the food shortage, inflation and instability on the financial market were seen as the most problematic issues. The Finnish Markka had lost about 87 per cent of its value during the war years. At the same time the political situation in Finland was by no means stable.

The fairly favourable economic conditions within the Russian Empire before the First World War meant that the independence declaration was not supported by everyone. In particular, many business owners were reluctant. Russia had been the most important export market for the textile and metal industry throughout the latter part of the nineteenth century and the war deliveries had been good business. It was also commonly believed that the political restlessness in Russia would calm down and that the country would return to normal. However, there was no turning back, and Finland had to look for other markets. Immediately after the Civil War, Finland turned politically towards Germany, but this ended when Germany lost the war: Finland started to look west.

Although starting out from such a problematic situation, the inter-war period turned out fairly favourably for the Finnish economy. In the 1920s, the economy recovered rapidly. After the opening up of the trade in Europe, it was easy for the Finnish manufacturing sector to find replacement export markets: in particular the export of timber increased. The recovery of the economy in the early 1920s was also eased by the fact that the Bank of Finland refrained from returning to pre-war parity. Sweden, which chose another currency policy, suffered from a severe economic crisis in the early 1920s (see Chapter 2). Exports also gradually diversified and shifted towards more refined products.

Industrialization experienced a breakthrough, with rapid growth and increasing productivity, and the Finnish 'catching-up process' with the leading economies in Europe began during this period, which for most countries was one of slow growth.[34] Finnish average growth during the period 1920–38 was 4.6 per cent, a very good figure[35] and one, moreover, that gives a much more positive outlook than the figures presented in for example Chapter 2 (see Sjögren, Table 2.3, p. 35), indicating the severity of the war years for the Finnish economy.

The Great Depression, although harsh within certain sectors, was shorter and, measured by GDP figures, not as deep as in many other industrialized countries. The sawn goods industry experienced a deep slump, as did the construction sector, but in the paper industry production grew during every year in spite of the depression. Also the banking sector was fairly severely hit, with bankruptcies or mergers among smaller banks.[36] In 1931, the system of fixed currency was again abandoned, which meant a severe depreciation of the Markka of about 40 per cent but, on the other hand, it led to a rapid recovery in export sectors.

During this period Finland became increasingly integrated in the international economy, but at the same time also more dependent on, and therefore sensitive to, the international economy and its fluctuations, especially as Finnish export was still primarily based on one raw material-based sector: the forest industry. The economic policy and the institutional setting became more systematic and focused on promoting, on the one hand, the export sector and, on the other hand, the exploitation of opportunities on the foreign markets. As the export diversified and shifted towards more refined products (particularly pulp and paper) Finland also succeeded in avoiding the 'staple trap', i.e. becoming too vulnerably to international fluctuations due to a dependence on one single product.[37]

Free capital movements and more influential banks

The First World War had brought with it global financial instability, with the disruption of the gold standard, depreciation of currencies and a rapid inflation in many countries. As their experiences during the classical gold standard had been favourable, most countries wanted to return to fixed exchange rates. The policies adopted differed, however, between countries. In Finland, the restoration of financial stability was one of the main targets after peace was restored. Finland decided, unlike many other countries, not to try to restore pre-war parity and joined the new gold standard as early as 1926 when it was first established: a gold standard and fixed exchange rate were seen as the ideal.

In general, economic policy throughout the inter-war period was liberal when it came to financial and capital markets. Thus, any regulation of financial markets was not favoured. Due to instability, high inflation and shrinking foreign exchange reserves, foreign capital movements were, however, restricted during shorter periods at times of crises. In 1918–20 foreign capital movements were restricted, while in 1919–20 the domestic capital market was also regulated. Interest rates were high. After joining the gold standard, interest rates gradually decreased. The fixed exchange rate had to be abandoned again in 1931 in the midst of the Great Depression and financial markets and capital flows were again regulated for a short period. The currency depreciated severely, but this turned out to be advantageous for the export sector and the recovery from depression started.

Due to the depression and the wave of bankruptcies, particularly in the indebted agricultural sector, voices were raised in demands for interest rate regulation. The banks had a growing amount of problem loans, threatening heavy credit losses. In 1931 a voluntary-interest rate agreement between the banks came about, when a ceiling on the interest on deposits was set in order to depress lending rates. This has been seen as some sort of starting point for the strongly regulated financial markets of the post-war period, where one of the key factors was the regulated (i.e. low) interest rate. Although this was a voluntary agreement between the banks, it also paved the way for future collaboration within the financial sector. In Finland, the interest rate has also during most periods been to some extent regulated – for example, between 1734 and 1892 there was a ceiling of 6 per cent on lending rates. Long-term interest rates were also regulated until 1920. It was actually only between 1920 and 1931 that interest rates were completely unregulated.[38]

The Finnish banking system had taken its basic form already in the late nineteenth century. In the early twentieth century the numbers of commercial banks had grown rapidly, particularly in connection with the speculative wave and boom on the financial markets in the 1910s. In 1920 there were in total twenty-three commercial banks. Some of them were very small, and many experienced huge difficulties in the 1920s. In 1919 the two fairly big commercial banks, Föreningsbanken and Nordiska Aktiebanken för Handel och Industri, were merged into Nordiska Föreningsbanken, Union Bank of Finland, UBF (later a part of the Nordic banking group Nordea), making it a fairly big player. In 1922 the small Privatbanken ran into crisis and was consolidated with UBF, after UBF had taken over its deposits and liabilities: the shareholders lost all their investments. A general banking crisis swept the Finnish banking sector in the late 1920s and early 1930s, which led to a consolidation wave among the smaller commercial banks, and in the mid-1930s there were only nine commercial banks left. Also the co-operative and the savings banks experienced difficulties and their numbers decreased.[39]

In spite of the crises among the smaller banks, the influence of the two big commercial banks, Nordiska Föreningsbanken and Kansallis-Osake-Pankki, over industrial companies grew. Borrowing and outside capital in the companies' balance sheets increased. The banks' direct share ownership in companies also grew. Particularly in times of crisis, the banks from time to time exercised a significant sway. The banks' influence on, for instance, sawmills was occasionally significant, as this sector was volatile and crises occurred frequently and several companies came under administration by the banks. In some cases the banks themselves had been too generous in their lending to certain key companies.[40] The legal system also allowed for the development of universal banks, providing all types of financial services. Although the commercial banks in the late nineteenth century were some-what reluctant to work as universal banks, they gradually became so.[41] The model with 'house banks' and bank spheres, where large industrial compa-nies became dependent on one bank which exercised occasionally a huge influence on the firms, evolved. The division in spheres was partly based on language, where Föreningsbanken financed the 'Swedish-language' business, while Kansallis-Osake-Pankki gathered the Finnish-language firms. The top managers of both these banks gradually gained an extensive economic power in Finnish business, and many of them were key figures in society, such as J. K. Paasikivi (later President of Finland), Rainer von Fieandt and Matti Virkkunen.

The stock market also developed after the opening of the Finnish Stock Exchange in 1912, and during the First World War the turnover was very high, due to a speculative bubble. However, in the 1920s and 1930s the turnover on the stock exchange developed fairly modestly in comparison with the rapid expansion in commercial bank lending to manufacturing companies.[42] The bank-centered system had finally been established and was not threatened until the 1990s.

Increasing collaboration and a stronger state

Signs of a more collaborative environment and more state-led co-ordination in the young nation are observable after the situation returned to normal after the Civil War. The first state-owned firms were established in 1918. The first and symbolically significant acquisition was the one of W. Gutzeit & Co. from its Norwegian owners (later merged with Enso to Enso-Gutzeit Oy, and today part of StoraEnso, see also Chapter 6). Another important state firm emerging in the wake of independence was the Outokumpu copper mill. In neither case did the state take over the whole share capital, but was a majority owner. Outokumpu was, for example, jointly owned by the prominent Hackman family in the 1920s.

The establishing of state companies was a part of the emerging growth goal, of which promoting investment in manufacturing was the core. The motivations behind the foundation of state-owned companies were not outspokenly ideological, in the sense that state ownership was to be preferred to private capital, but primarily pragmatic. In a poor, late-comer country, state capital would secure production within key branches. Ideological views became more important in the post-war era, but also then the growth aspect was the key (see p. 181). Some ideological or political overtones towards state ownership were also traceable, but primarily from a Finnish–nationalistic perspective. The aquiring of the first state companies was part of Finnish nation-building. Gutzeit was foreign-owned, and thus it was in the Finnish interest to buy it. Furthermore, it has been posited that the Fennoman politicians promoted state ownership as it was a new channel for the Fennoman elite and the 'Fennoman capital' to compete with the private 'Swedish-language capital' and the Swedish-speaking elite.[43] The small Swedish People's Party also opposed the acquisition of Gutzeit in Parliament. The party in general favoured a more liberalistic economic policy.

In the post-war period, regional aspects also became important for the location of state companies, but already in the 1920s another forest industry firm, Veitsiluoto, had been established in order to make use of forest resources in the north.

Whether there were nationalistic or ideological overtones or not, the state companies became an important group among the biggest companies and played an important role in Finnish industrialization.

This period also saw an extension and modernization of the public sector. Although Finland had had a fairly extensive autonomy in the Russian Empire, some tasks of the public sector, such as defence and foreign affairs, were naturally taken care of by the Russian government. The establishment of these new administrative areas required new income sources for the state. During this period government income changed, as the role of customs as the primary income source for the central government was replaced by a system of progressive income taxation. A rapid expansion in certain administrative areas occurred. Gradually, services supplied by the municipalities – basic education, health services, etc. – also grew.

The depression of the 1930s led to a more favourable attitude towards government intervention to smooth out both economic downturns and correct the most adverse effects of economic recessions. This was part of an international phenomenon, as the Great Depression launched more active government economic and social policies in many countries. Also the idea of social planning and that society could be developed through active measures gained ground as part of modernization ideologies. Still, a Keynesian counter-cyclical economic policy to smooth out cyclical fluctuations never took root in Finland (see further p. 174). However, although the duties of the the public sector grew, the sector's share of GDP remained at a fairly moderate level: it was around 28 per cent of GDP in 1938.[44]

Another prominent feature in the inter-war period in the Finnish economy and business system was increasing cartelization tendencies. Although cartels had been established already in the late nineteenth century, their number and their scope within divergent branches clearly grew in the inter-war period.[45] For instance, Gösta Serlachius – one of the driving forces behind the formation of the Finnish Paper Mills' Association (Finnpap FPMA), and later also active in the Scandinavian, primarily Finnish–Swedish, paper cartels, the so called 'Scan-family' (Scannews, Scangrease, Scancraft) – had been active in establishing sales organizations and promoting industrial co-operation among the paper producers already before the First World War. However, the founding of the significant and long-standing sales organization of the paper producers, Finnpap in 1918, through which most of the Finnish paper export went, meant co-operation on a new level and a new scope. Finnpap was soon followed by export cartels for cardboard and pulp. Also in other branches cartels emerged, although the co-operation varied in its form and extent. It has been estimated that around 80 per cent of Finnish exports during the inter-war period were sold through the sales organizations and cartels. This figure, however, indicates primarily the major role of the forest industry products in export during this period; in 1920 forest products formed 93.7 per cent and in 1938 81.8 per cent of total exports.[46] But also domestic cartels, like the cotton cartel, dominated many branches and some were fairly effective in fighting import competition and keeping prices and profits high.

The key reason behind the foundation of Finnpap was the problematic situation in 1918 when Finland was tied to Germany after the Civil War. However, this German orientation turned out to be short-lived, as the war came to an end soon afterwards, but Finnpap and the export cartels or common sales associations became an efficient instrument for Finnish export industry when the firms started to seek new markets in Europe, and remained a persistent and prominent phenomenon in the Finnish economy up until 1990s, when the competition legislation changed.

It was not only the cartelization and state companies which indicates an intensified co-operation and co-ordination of the Finnish economy, but new interest and branch organizations, for example the Federation of Finnish Industries, emerged. Also the co-operatives gained more ground. Although the co-operative movement had a somewhat less prominent role than in, for example, Denmark, the co-operatives formed an important link between the producers in the primary sector and the industrial sector.

Weak unions and powerful employers

It has often been stressed that independence and the Civil War had far-reaching effects on certain segments of the economy, while other sectors continued more or less as before the First World War, primarily due to the fact that Finland had been economically autonomous within the Russian Empire. The Civil War particularly affected the labour market and employer–employee relationships. After the end of the war, the trade unions and the socialist movement were severely weakened, while the employers were throughout the inter-war period the stronger party and could more or less dictate labour market practices. The employers were also suspicious of trade unions and strongly opposed to wage bargaining with unions and collective agreements. The employers held firmly to their rights to set wages and decide on working conditions.[47] The lack of trust between employers and employees was mutual, as the workers also had little trust in the employers. The inter-war was characterized by extensive flexibility in wage-setting.[48] This was aggravated by the Great Depression, when wages fell freely in some sectors and unemployment rose.[49] The patriarchal model on the shop floor continued to persist. In the patriarchal firm, employee–employer relations were personal and wage-setting individual, while the patriarchal owner was to take care of housing, education, health care and provide pension schemes for their loyal and long-time employees.

In the 1920s and early 1930s, radical right-wing winds blew in to Finnish society, exemplified by right-wing nationalistic movements such as the Lappo Movement and Isänmaallinen Kansanliike (IKL). Some of the employers within the Employers' Confederation had close connections with these movements. This increased hostility towards the unions. However, after some unlawful actions in the early 1930s, the employers distanced themselves from these organizations' activities. Although the heritage from the Civil War clearly affected practices on the labour market, the little interest in collective bargaining was also affected by the satisfactory supply of (cheap) labour: there was no need to bargain collectively.

The Civil War also had negative effects on the workers' movement itself. Unionization remained low and the unions themselves were weak and suffered from internal conflicts. In the 1920s, the split between left-wing communists and the social democratic wing led to a breakdown of the central organization (SAJ) and to a foundation of a new one, the Confederation of Finnish Trade Unions (Suomen Ammattiyhdistysten Keskusliitto, SAK). The communists lost power and at the same time the Communist Party was abolished. Many members had also difficulties orientating themselves in this conflict between fractions. They wanted to be part of a workers' movement and a member of a trade union, but were not interested in party political activity.[50] The political climate changed in the late 1930s, there was a new upswing in union membership and the attitude towards the unions became more positive.

Moreover, the situation on the labour market and employee–employer relations also varied extensively throughout the inter-war period at the local level. Negotiations between employers and employee representatives occurred frequently within individual firms and industries and local wage agreements were concluded. Employers' attitudes towards collective agreements varied extensively, according to market situation and labour supply.

Even though there was little trust between employers and employees, the situation on the labour markets gradually changed. Both the attitude towards the unions and the economic upswing improved the position and bargaining power of the employees in the late 1930s. Moreover, in some respect labour legislation – for example, concerning child labour – was both strict and fairly 'modern' while the introduction of the 8-hour working day in 1917 meant a step forward in bettering working conditions in the factories. The government and other authorities gradually developed a more conciliatory attitude towards the unions, and wanted to normalise the situation on the labour market and improve working conditions.[51]

Although a fairly modern or protective labour legislation evolved in the inter-war period, social welfare reforms did not yet emerge. During the depression, when unemployment was extremely high in some sectors and no unemployment benefits or other system of social security in case of unemployment existed, the unemployed had to resort to poor relief and relief work. An old-age and sickness pension Act, as well as legislation on maternity allowance, had been passed in the late 1930s, but these systems did not come into force until after the Second World War. An extensive welfare policy, where the aim is to smooth out inequality and to establish equal opportunities, was in the Finnish case a phenomenon of the post-war period, and particularly of the 1960s. One reason for the lack of universal welfare policies was the patriarchal model, where social welfare was taken care of by the employer. Various forms of welfare services initiated by the employers were introduced in the local community. Many employers, for example Gösta Serlachius and Gustaf Herlitz (Arabia Ab), had been inspired by scientific management and the improvement and betterment of working conditions, by means of the Safety First movement, an early American labour protection movement, and had introduced factory inspections.[52]

The situation on the Finnish labour market throughout the inter-war years was, however, significantly different from, for example, the Swedish case (see Chapter 2 Sjögren in this volume). No new system of class compromise which emerged in the Scandinavian countries can be found in Finland.[53] Neither did the idea of the state as a provider of universal welfare protection gain ground.

Educational improvements
The system of education also improved considerably in the inter-war period. In 1921 a law which made a primary education equivalent to six years compulsory for everyone (*oppivelvollisuus*, *läroplikt*) was passed. However, the municipalities were given extensive transition periods to organize the educational system, while those living in sparsely populated areas were exempted from this clause. By no means did the whole age group complete six years of primary education, or the equivalent syllabus. It was not until after the war that primary education reached everyone to this extent. A law on vocational training was also passed, ensuring some government funding to privately provided vocational training. The figures concerning literacy rose sharply during

the first decades of the twentieth century, and in 1930 already 70 per cent of the population could both read and write. However, at the same time this shows that some 30 per cent could only read – or, even worse, barely that.[54] The low level of education is also observable if one looks at the schooling figures: in 1950 39 per cent of the population (over seven years) had had only a partial primary education or received no primary education at all, while 53 per cent had completed the primary education (of six years). Only 4.5 per cent of the population had completed secondary school and only a fraction (2.5 per cent) the matriculation examination.[55] Among the younger age groups the level of basic education rose sharply, but overall the Finnish population still had a very low level of education.

Some advances in further and vocational training can be observed. The business schools and technical universities had started in the early 1900s, and the intermediate technical training, the so-called 'technical institutes', emerged after 1915. In the 1920s two universities in Turku opened up: the Finnish-language University of Turku and a Swedish-language Åbo Akademi University. Vocational schools opened their doors, but such education was often provided by individual companies in industrial areas, like Walter Ahlströms Industriskola, named after the heir to A. Ahlström Oy and, thus, these schools concerned only a minority. It was only after the 1960s, with the educational expansion, that the Finnish population gradually reached a level of education equivalent to that in Sweden.

The primary sector as part of the 'Finnish model'

The primary sector was also influenced by the war years. The food shortage of 1917–18 had a significant impact on the agricultural policies of the inter-war period. The famine, also influencing the outbreak of the Civil War, made self-sufficiency in grain, the most important target of agricultural policy, actually until the 1980s.

In general the agricultural sector developed favourably in the 1920s and 1930s. Agricultural production rose as the amount of arable land grew and productivity increased, while there were growing employment opportunities provided by the intensified use of forest resources.

During the first decades of independence, some of the social problems connected to the landless rural population were also solved, through the so-called *Lex Kallio* in 1922 and a Settlement Act in 1936, which opened up new areas and new opportunities for the landless population to redeem the land they cultivated. Moreover, in 1915 and 1925 laws restricting forest

PROLOGUE TO THE FINNISH CHAPTER • FINNISH CAPITALISM • ENZO-GUTZEIT TO STORA-ENSO • NOKIA AND TAMPELLA AFTER THE SECOND WORLD WAR

5   165

firms' acquisition of forest areas were passed. These reforms prevented the vast and important forest resources coming solely into the hands of the companies. As a result, the growing welfare accumulating from the forest sector in twentieth century Finland 'trickled down' for the benefit of the whole population. This also strengthened the agricultural and Fennoman linkage, which proved important for the development of the corporative model of the post-war era.[56] As the forest industry firms no longer competed for forest areas, they also used their resources to invest in technology.[57]

At the same time, the growth in the secondary and tertiary sectors meant the start of the rapid relative decline of the primary sector. In 1938, the primary sector stood for about one-third of GDP, although still nearly half of the labour force was employed in the primary sector (see Table 5.3, p. 156). The development in the primary sector during the inter-war period was no longer a necessary precondition for the industrialization process, as it was during the take-off phase. The Finnish economy had reached a stage where economic progress was more dependent on other factors, such as export markets, on investments in human and fixed capital, and on technological and organizational developments, than on the supply of surplus labour from the primary sector.

Although a fairly favourable development in output and productivity occurred, Finnish agricultural production was still during this period based on small-scale family farming where the income level was low and technology and production methods old-fashioned. The 1930s' depression had adverse effects on the agricultural sector due to a heavy indebtedness, with bankruptcies and compulsory auctions the result.

Moreover, in spite of a declining share of GDP, the sector retained a strong foothold in the Finnish co-operative model throughout the twentieth century. The agricultural interest organizations and the co-operatives became important players in the co-operative system. This was, of course, primarily due to the significance of the forest sector for manufacturing. Another reason was the recent periods of famine, which made the importance of self-sufficiency evident. The relatively weak position of the small farmers and crofters was also considered a social problem which had, in combination with the famine, been an important reason leading up to the Civil War. It was important to try to improve the standard of living also for these groups in order to avoid future social unrest. Finally, the idea of the self-employed farmer cultivating his own farm was part of a Finnish–nationalist ideology, and continued to be so long after the Second World War.[58]

An era of 'qualified liberalism'?

In many respects the Finnish economy in the inter-war period resembled a liberal market economy, in other respects more of a co-ordinated market economy. The inter-war period has sometimes been labelled a period of 'qualified liberalism' (*varauksellinen liberalismi*).[59] The liberal ideology continued to persist, at least in principle. The prevailing view was that individual innovation and entrepreneurship should not be hindered and, thus, little direct intervention occurred. In particular, the labour and capital markets were little regulated. Although foreign trade and foreign capital movements were restricted during short periods, such reactions were partly an answer to pressures or shocks from abroad. This was largely an era of self-regulation.

At the same time, indications of more co-ordinated and collaborative elements were observable. The role of the state became more prominent as a result of the state companies, but also the promotion of economic development by a policy supporting industrialization became more explicit and more systematic. A belief in the possibilities for steering and directing the path took root. The export industry's interests came into focus, while protectionistic tendencies increased to shelter domestic markets. The big corporations and the powerful (export) cartels' influence on economic policies grew. Such policies had nationalistic overtones, as economic progress could simultaneously promote Finnish nation-building. It has to be remembered that protectionist tendencies, cartelization and state ownership were international phenomena, common in many European countries; but cartelization gained a particularly prominent foothold in the Finnish economy. According to Professor Markku Kuisma, in the inter-war period factors contributing to rapid economic growth and forest-based industrial progress, 'was a successful set of means consisting of government actions coloured by agrarian interests, the establishment of state-owned industrial corporations inspired by economic nationalism and entrepreneurial enthusiasm, and intensive cartelization, led by the family firms of the export sector'.[60]

Finally, a more systematic policy to enhance growth can be traced. The institutional reforms in the 1920s aiming to solve the problems of the big landless population and the restriction of forest industry companies to own forest areas were a clear indication of such advancements. Although the element of low trust between the workers and the employers continued throughout the period, there were also some indications of rapprochement in the late 1930s, although no explicit consensus policies of the post-war decades like those in the other Nordic countries were evident. Finnish society had many inherent tensions, not the least on the labour market.

War, reconstruction and regulation: a second interlude, 1939–56

The outbreak of war in Finland on 30 November 1939 brought with it heavy regulation and state control in the entire economy. The most crucial sectors of the economy were immediately regulated to secure energy and important raw materials for war production and industry. Foreign trade became subject to licences, i.e. the import of goods and raw materials was regulated by the authorities through import licences allocated to firms. Capital movements required permission from the Bank of Finland in order to secure foreign liquidity.[61]

Although the Second World War led to a drastic fall in exports, the year 1939–40 (the 'Winter War') did not yet bring with it any severe economic crisis, due to existing reserves. Domestic production could also substitute for some of the fall in the import of certain goods. However, quite soon problems with energy supply appeared, while the rapid decline in exports meant obstacles for key industries, especially the forest industry. During the period of peace after the end of 'Winter War' in March 1940 until the outbreak of war again, the so called 'Continuance War' in June 1941, the situation recovered a little, but during the years 1941–44, the country suffered increasing shortages of energy, other raw materials and food supplies. Rationing extended gradually also to other products. In 1941 the domestic credit markets were regulated and the shortage of labour became of great concern. The question was how to substitute for those summoned to military service, while war production also raised the demand for labour. In 1939, a law was passed obliging everyone to work. The increase in female labour supply and the re-entry of the ageing population into the labour force made up for much of the labour shortage. The increase in demand for labour in certain sectors was also offset by a decrease in labour demand in others. Resorting to forced labour was seldom needed, but productivity was low, and some sectors experienced a continuous shortage of labour.[62]

A serious problem was the pressure on wages and prices. Price and wage regulation was introduced in 1941, but in spite of this there were continuous inflationary tendencies and wage drift. Although necessary to secure production in certain key sectors and provide a basic standard of living for the whole population, the regulation measures led to a distortion of prices and wages and to tensions between the agrarian population and wage workers.[63]

In autumn 1944 a truce was reached with the Soviet Union. Finland lost the war, but could keep its independence. However, the costs of the war did not end with the armistice. Finland had first to drive out the German troops from the north (the so-called 'Lapland War'), give up large areas of land (around 11 per cent), including areas with some crucial industrial production units. For example the Enso-Gutzeit's headquarters and some of its production units remained on the Soviet side of the new border (see Chapter 6). The country lost 91,500 lives during the war, and had to repatriate 400,000 war refugees. In the peace treaty, Finland was also required to pay heavy war reparations to the Soviet Union. At the same time Finland declined Marshall Aid for political reasons. Finland also decided to stay out of the OEEC (OECD) for the same reason, and joined this organization only in 1969.

Government debt had grown rapidly during the war. After the war the state finances were, moreover, for several years heavily burdened by war reparations. At its height, war reparations devoured around 15 per cent of government expenditures. As a share of GDP, reparations during the first two years amounted to as much as 5–6 per cent.[64] At the same time the political situation was unstable, which labelled the years at the end of the 1940s the 'years of danger' (fi: *vaaran vuodet*), with fears of a communist revolt.

All these factors came to influence the economic policy of the years after the war. Some foreign aid and loans, particularly from Sweden, but later also from the US, were received, which helped the situation. The country also joined the Bretton Woods agreement in 1948, which was seen as politically less problematic. This measure was important in order to stabilise the monetary order and to ensure foreign credits. Finland, in a delicate situation between east and west, also aimed to become more integrated in the western economy.

However, the years were economically difficult and as a result the regulation of the economy remained more or less untouched also until mid-1950s. As a result the years of reconstruction are here grouped as part of the war period. Periodization is always a problematic task, but as the war reparations and recovery and reconstruction influenced so strongly the economy until 1956, they can be seen as a natural extension of the war: the institutional model created during the war was partly 'cemented'. Foreign trade, particularly imports, continued to be restricted by means of the licensing system. Industrial production was organized and directed from the perspective of coping with war reparations. Investments within the metal industry sector were extensive in order to expand production in this sector. For the individual firms, the war deliveries were, on the other hand, often good business, as the orders were secured for many years and the conditions were fairly favourable. Later many large-scale firms involved in war reparations, like Tampella and Wärtsilä were important actors in the Finnish trade with Soviet Union, which evolved after the completion of war deliveries (see p. 181 below and also Chapter 7 in this volume).

One of the biggest problems during the post-war years was the rapid inflation. In 1946 a so-called 'castle peace' (*linnarauha, slottsfreden*) between the unions, the agrarian interest organizations and the employers was signed in order to stop inflationary pressures. However, price and wage drifts continued. and distorted prices and wages even further. Labour shortage was also acute in some sectors, due to production for war deliveries. In 1946 and 1949 the government had to resort to large devaluations of the currency in order to boost exports. Foreign currency from exports to western Europe was desperately needed to cope with war reparations, but in turn increased inflationary pressures.

Gradual opening up

When the war deliveries were completed in 1952, industrial production returned to more normal working conditions. Western export grew, while the first five-year trade agreement with the Soviet Union was signed and opened up exports there. However, the import licensing system continued until the late 1950s.[65]

In 1957, the government resorted to a large devaluation, the gradual liberalization of foreign trade started, and the Finnish economy opened up. The economy entered a favourable era of growth.

In 1955–6 the situation in the domestic economy also gradually returned to more normal conditions. Price and wage regulation came to an end. However, the long regulation, in combination with high inflation, had led to severe imbalances and underlying tensions between various groups, mainly the agrarian population and the wage workers, but also between divergent groups of employees. For instance, wage gaps between white- and blue-collar workers had decreased and the relative wages of white-collar employees and civil servants had declined sharply. As a result, divergent groups wanted to be compensated for their – real or perceived – losses. In March 1956, a general strike broke out, while agricultural producers brought food deliveries to a standstill. This pushed the whole country close to a crisis, although in the end the strike did not last long and the situation returned to normal fairly soon.

It has often been proposed that the war regulation and the institutional environment had long-lasting effects on the Finnish post-war economic model.[66] Although the price and wage regulation was finally abolished and foreign trade gradually opened up, the strict regulation of capital movements and financial markets continued until the 1980s and was as such partly a heritage of the war years. On the other hand, the motivations behind the systems and regulations were, as we shall see below, different and the systems were also transformed over the years. The institutional foundation was, however, laid.

Another long-lasting effect from the war years was in labour market practices. During the 'Winter War' in the name of the interest of the nation and in the unanimity of the country against the foreign threat, the employers announced that they accepted the trade unions as a negotiating party, which led up to the so-called January Engagement (*Tammikuun kihlaus, Januariförlovningen*) in January 1940, which paved the way for centralized collective bargaining. The involvement of SAK in war management in this way forced the trade unions to take responsibility for the war economy and wage regulation, but also the introduction of wage and price regulation demanded state-led collective bargaining.[67]

The war years can, thus, be regarded as the starting point for the tripartite collective bargaining system between central organizations and where the government often played an important role. Although the system of incomes policies ('TUPO'), based on centralized collective bargaining and leading to collective wage agreements, did not emerge until the late 1960s, the basis for such a system can be seen to have evolved when the employers accepted the need to negotiate collectively.

Also some of the government bodies and new activities – for instance, statistics and information-gathering systems – established during the war became permanent, which also proved to be significant tools for the regulation policies later. Perhaps the most important heritage from the war was, however, a general acceptance of strong and direct state involvement.[68]

State-led growth: an inwardly closed highly co-ordinated market economy,[69] 1957–81

After the recovery and reconstruction, the favourable long-run economic growth continued. This period was also in Europe an era of rapid economic development, often labelled as the 'Golden Age'. The average growth during the period 1950–73, was 4.2 per cent in Finland. During this period, Finland experienced a more favourable growth rate than, for example, Sweden. The global recession of the 1970s had severe effects on the Finnish economy, but the recession was not as deep as in many other European countries. Moreover, the growth rate continued to be favourable in the 1980s, when many European countries experienced staggering growth and structural crises. As a consequence, by the mid-1980s, Finland had finally caught up with the western economies.[70] Also structural changes were during the post-war decades extremely rapid, which can be seen on many levels in society, not least in rapid urbanization and in a wave of emigration to Sweden in the 1960s.

In the 1980s, Finland had also passed the stage of the 'traditional industrial society' (*perinteinen teollisuusyhteiskunta*), as the proportion of employment provided by the manufacturing sector showed a rapid decrease.[71] Finland took actually a big – or perhaps – rapid 'leap' from an agrarian to a service society, as only during a few years in the 1950s was the secondary sector, measured as a share of GDP, the largest one. Still, the safeguarding of the interests of the manufacturing sector, and particularly the export industry, was and has been until today a key target in the economic model. In economic–political rhetoric, the emphasis on industrial society and industrial production has been strong.[72] The country's dependence on exports has made the manufacturing sector's role central.

One of the main factors behind the favourable development after the opening up of foreign trade was the growth in exports and a positive development in the terms of trade. Moreover, trade with the other Nordic countries, particularly Sweden, and the rest of western Europe expanded rapidly from 1961, when Finland became an associate member of the European Free Trade Association (EFTA). Finland also developed good trade relations with other European countries, although not participating in the deepening integration in western Europe. In 1974, Finland signed a free trade agreement with the EEC. Finland also developed important trade relations with countries in the socialist trade block (SEV). After the war reparations deliveries had been concluded, the Soviet Union became an important trade partner (see Table 5.4). The trade between the countries was based on five-year bilateral trade agreements drawn up at the highest political level and was administered through a clearing account which had always to be in balance. The import from the Soviet Union consisted primarily of oil, while textile and metal industry products were exported.

The significance of Soviet trade was large, both economically and politically, but its economic effects were, however, ambiguous. Soviet trade had

Table 5.4   **Finland's main trading partners, 1936–2004 (value of exports and imports)**

1936		1950		1965		1980		2004	
Export	Import	Export	Import	Export	Import	Export	Import	Export	Import
UK	Germany	UK	UK	UK	Germany	Sweden	USSR	Sweden	Germany
Germany	UK	US	Germany	USSR	UK	USSR	Sweden	Germany	Russia
US	Sweden	Netherlands	Soviet	Germany	USSR	UK	Germany	Russia	Sweden
Sweden	US	Soviet	Poland	Sweden	Sweden	Germany	UK	UK	China
Netherlands	Be-Lux	Denmark	Sweden	US	US	US	US	US	France

Source: *Statistical Yearbook*, various years.

some clearly positive effects on the Finnish economy, particularly during the oil crises, as Finnish exports to the Soviet Union automatically grew when the oil price increased due to the balance in trade. Although Finland suffered from so-called 'stagflation' problems and experienced a few years of zero growth in the mid-1970s, the country did not experience huge trade balance deficits as a result of the oil price shock, which was common in many countries. Finnish firms also received fairly good prices for their goods on the Soviet market at the same time as they did not have to make any marketing effort, as a result of the political trade agreements. On the other hand, some of the goods exported to the Soviet Union would never have been competitive on the western market. This turned out to have disastrous effects when Soviet trade crashed in the early 1990s.

In spite of a favourable economic growth, the era was also marked by a fairly high volatility in growth rates, and high inflation was a persistent problem. One reason for the fairly big cyclical fluctuations was the country's high dependence on one volatile sector, the forest industry. This was particularly the case during the first decades after the war, when Finnish forest industry exports comprized fairly basic products such as sawn goods, pulp and newsprint. Gradually, when the share of more refined paper products increased and when export overall gradually diversified, the volatility decreased.

High inflation negatively affected competitiveness, which made exports vulnerable. As a result, the Bank of Finland resorted to devaluations of the Markka at regular intervals. This did promote exports, but in turn fed inflation and led to a vicious circle. Finland went through several so-called 'devaluation cycles' after the war until the 1980s, as extensive devaluations occurred in 1945–6, 1949, 1957, 1967, 1977 and 1982. These cycles have sometimes been called 'pulp cycles' (*sellusykli*), arising from the fluctuations in the world market price of pulp, which directly influenced the Finnish business cycle.

The volatility of the economy was, however, also a result of domestic decisions and factors inherent in the economy. During these decades, economic policy and the whole institutional model were constructed to enhance growth. Similar economic models existed in other countries, as there was within economic thinking a strong belief in promoting growth through active measures, strengthened by the growth theories developing rapidly during these decades, and the positive experiences of recovery from the war and from the Great Depression. Many European countries adopted the Keynesian model, where the aim was to smooth out cyclical fluctuations, keep up demand and, thus, employment, and avoid too high interest rates in periods of slumps. In Finland, on the contrary, a Keynesian fiscal and monetary policy model never took root,[73] instead, fiscal policy was often pro-cyclical. In some cases the economic policy actually aggravated business cycles. One reason was that the target of the state bureaucrats in the Ministry of Finance was to keep the budget in balance. Another reason was shortcomings in theoretical economic skills and in economic thinking in the Ministry, which made public spending decrease in slumps and grow in booms. Perhaps more importantly, the growth and investment policy made smoothing out business cycles an inferior criterion to the overall growth target in Finland.[74]

The key in the 'Finnish model' was achieving a high rate of growth by promoting investments. The core of the policy was to keep interest rates low, and all other policy measures were to support this. The main Finnish export sectors – the forest and the metal industries – are both capital-intensive, and as crucial sectors for the economy a high investment rate would promote economic development. Moreover, the significance of investments in fixed capital was also supported by the growth theories. Later, human capital investments also became a key target of economic policy. The investment orientation was the core of this policy but, as we shall see below, an extensive and elaborate co-operative model evolved, where also other sectors of society and other institutional solutions were to strengthen the growth target.

The policy had the intended effects: the interest rate was kept low and the investment rate high until the disruption of this economic model in the 1980s. Investment rates exceeded 20 per cent throughout this period, and sometimes rose above 30 per cent of GDP (Figure 5.1).

In this growth project, the state played a significant role. The Central Bank and the Ministry of Finance in particular became strong bodies in the outlining of the model, constructed and led by civil servants and state bureaucrats. However, in periods of economic boom, politicians could influence fiscal policies to a greater extent by engaging in expansionary policies and inducing welfare reforms.

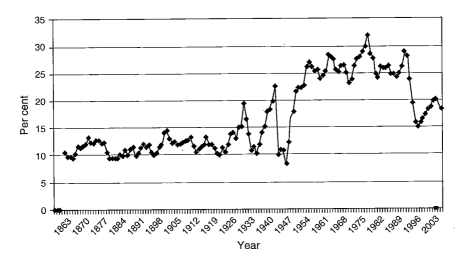

Figure 5.1   Investments as share (per cent) of GDP: Finland, 1860–2005
Sources: Hjerppe (1989); Statistics Finland.

The strong President of the republic between 1956 and 1981, Urho Kekkonen, (Agrarian Party) also took a strong role and interfered personally from time to time in the economic–political leadership. He also had had a great interest before he was elected President in promoting growth, and particularly in regional policies. In the early 1950s, while Prime Minister, Kekkonen had published a pamphlet where he, rhetorically, asked if the country had the 'forbearance it will take to become rich?' (*Onko maallamme malttia vaurustua?*). Many of his proposed measures or policy recommendations were later adopted in some form or another. Kekkonen was also a warm sympathizer of state companies in general, and as an instrument in regional policies in particular. Some important new state companies, like Rautaruukki and Kemijoki, were established with clear regional motivations.

The Soviet trade based on five-year bilateral trade agreements negotiated and signed at the highest political level also strengthened both the role of the President and the state bureaucrats, particularly in economic affairs within the Ministry of Trade and Industry. Moreover, as large companies were important actors in this trade the intimate relationship between the economic and the political elite deepened and reached its height in the 1970s.

Regulated capital markets and a bank-centred financial system

One cornerstone in this investment-oriented growth regime was monetary policy, whose main aim was to keep interest rates low. This policy was also within its narrow parameters successful: the real interest rate was very low until the 1980s. As inflation occasionally was high, real interest rates were actually sometimes even negative. The whole monetary and financial system developed into a complex system of regulation and rationing. One important reason for this was that the low interest rate did not encourage saving. Moreover, each regulation needed additional regulation so that the new rules could not be bypassed. The system changed somewhat over the period, but the basic principles remained the same.[75]

The system was based on lending rates being strictly regulated by the Bank of Finland. Deposit interest rates were agreed by the banks. In the inter-war period the banks had already concluded a voluntary rent agreement, which continued after the war. The low interest rates led to an excessive demand for credit and discouraged savings and as a results credit had to be rationed.

As a result of the interest rate being kept artificially low, a whole set of other regulations and instruments to monitor this policy had to be introduced. One of the most important regulatory instruments was the commercial banks' central bank debt (*keskuspankkivelka, centralbanksskuld*) and the interest rate on it. As the banks' lending and borrowing rates with respect to the public were regulated, the interest rate on central bank lending became an important instrument for steering bank behaviour. Every bank had a certain quota of central bank debt related to a certain basic interest rate (discount or bank rate). If they exceeded this quota, they had to pay a higher penalty interest rate on their whole debt, which in addition was progressive. Furthermore, the issuing of bonds was also restricted, with the government as the sole issuer of bonds.

The Bank of Finland, simultaneously with the low interest rate, aimed to maintain a fixed exchange rate, but to avoid pressures on the balance of payments. As a result foreign capital flows had to be regulated. All foreign capital movements, apart from normal currency transactions like payment for imports, were subject to strict regulation and every application had to be evaluated by the central bank. Foreign currency received from exports abroad was to be repatriated. In the 1960s and 1970s it became a little easier for firms to acquire short-term credits abroad and in particular large companies engaged in exports could fairly easily act on foreign capital markets.

The regulation of foreign capital movements kept outward and inward FDI at a low level. Looking at trade flows, Finland was an open economy, but judging from FDI flows, a significantly closed one. Some foreign MNCs did invest in Finland, while large firms fairly easily also got permission to invest abroad. For instance, Yhtyneet Paperintethaat had subsidiaries in Italy and Israel already in the 1950s, while A. Ahlström Oy had investments in

Italy, Canada and Sweden in the 1960s. While the Italian investments turned out to be a failure for both these firms, Ahlström's investments in Sweden were successful and fairly long-lasting.[76]

Although the low interest rate did not encourage savings, a form of 'forced saving' developed with the establishment of the work pension system in the 1960s (see p. 184 on the welfare state reforms). The work pension system was based on funding in reserves, and thus these pension funds gradually grew large and became important investors on the Finnish market. During this era of 'captive money' (*kahlitun rahan aika*), the pension funds were in particular providing financing to firms by so-called TEL- and LEL-loans.

This system of regulation had extensive effects on both the financial sector and on the financial structure of big business. The banks had a specific and crucial role as financial mediators and as power centres. Finnish banks became also something of credit-rationing institutions, although the rationing was basically directed from the Bank of Finland.[77] Taxation regulation also favoured bank savings and credit financing, as interest on deposits was exempt from tax, while interest rate payments on credits were deductible from taxation.

As this investment-oriented policy promoted financing through borrowing, the share of borrowed capital in business increased substantially and the banks' influence in the manufacturing firms grew. In many cases they actively exercised power, particularly in companies in crisis. The banks were also important shareholders in big business, although the legislation restricting banks' ownership in industrial companies became stricter after 1951, when it became compulsory for banks to get rid of share ownership exceeding 20 per cent of their stock. Such a regulation was actually introduced in 1933, but it had not prevented banks from sometimes holding the majority or even 100 per cent of their stocks in certain industrial firms, as a result of the shares coming into the hands of the bank in times of crises or due to over-indebtedness.[78] As ownership became more and more spread, small minority posts, sometimes amounting to only a few percentage of the total capital stock, gave the banks in the post-war period an important influence as shareholders as well. This model was strengthened by cross-ownership between large firms, banks and insurance companies, a high degree of interlocking directorships and a growing influence of the interest and lobby organizations. Banks were engaged in entrepreneurial activity in many firms: they forced mergers and restructurings and replaced top managers in problem companies. For example, the establishment of the big forest and metal industry conglomerate, Rauma-Repola Oy, was a result of a forced merger in 1952, while Kansallis-Osake-Pankki even succeeded in replacing in 1969 an owner-manager and perhaps the last traditional patron in a family firm, Juuso Waldén in Yhtyneet Paperitehtaat.[79]

The centralization within the banking sector continued, contributing to a polarization of power to the biggest commercial banks. In the post-war period, the two big banks Föreningsbanken i Finland – (Suomen Yhdsy-pankki, Union Bank of Finland) and Kansallis-Osake-Pankki – dominated the market, building up spheres of companies they financed and where they also exercised extensive influence through interlocking directorships. In effect, big business had its own 'house banks', Nokia being an interesting exception where both banks had equal shares (see Chapter 7). The language division became less and less significant in business and in society in general, but the existing division of firms between the banks persisted. The government postal bank (Postipankki) was also important for the financing of state companies.[80] The co-operative and savings banks continued to be important local financiers of private customers, small business undertakings and the agrarian sector.

As a result of the regulatory system, the available financial instruments were few, and no new and more elaborate ones developed. Thus, the period has been labelled as a period of the 'simple financial markets' or of the 'captive money'.[81] The taxation favouring bank savings and bank loans strengthened the bank-centred system, decreasing the role of the stock exchange, and the stock market remained unimportant. The market was thin – that is, the number of firms listed small and the turnover low.

Altough being power centres, the banks' hands were in reality tied due to the strong regulation. The banks remained general banks, with little division of labour, as they were all primarily engaged in obtaining deposits and providing credit to the business and private sector. Competition between banks was in services, mainly by opening new offices. In every small town, offices of all the bank groups could usually be found. This backwardness of the financial markets was also one of the reasons for the overheated financial markets in the 1980s and the severe banking crisis in the 1990s, as neither the banks nor their customers knew how to act on free and open financial markets. One of the key indicators and important steering instruments on the financial markets, the interest rate, was also completely ineffective.[82]

The low real interest rate in combination with a taxation system supporting bank lending, allied to favourable taxation terms for writes-off for investments in company balances, meant that it was more or less unwise for firms not to invest. This favoured particularly the capital-intensive, export-oriented forest and metal industry sector and led to a rapid increase in fixed capital and also investment in new technology, which in turn positively affected growth. In combination with the 'devaluation cycle' supporting the export sector, there was a substantial transfer of resources from the domestic sector to the export sector. However, it has also been concluded that these policies made firms overinvest, and that the return on investments left much to be desired.[83] Some necessary structural changes were retarded. Finally, although the Bank of Finland succeeded in keeping interest rates low, the fixed exchange rate target was more problematic to keep up, as the central bank had to resort to a devaluation of the Markka at regular intervals.

Increasing cartelization and growing importance of state companies

As mentioned earlier, the export industry in particular was already fairly cartelized in the inter-war period, but also producers on the domestic market aimed to restrict prices and/or production through cartel agreements. No regulation concerning cartels, however, existed. During and after the war, business activities were under strict government control and strict regulation and thus the need for separate cartel legislation was not very urgent. After the abolition of the regulation and the opening up of foreign trade, the question about cartel regulation came on the agenda, particularly as such legislation had been passed in many European countries in the inter-war period. In Sweden, a cartel law had been passed in 1946, and this drew attention to the fact that Finland had no law which restricted and steered industrial co-operation. Adverse effects from cartels were becoming evident, and although export cartels were seen as working in the 'interest of the nation',[84] domestic market cartels drove up prices on the home market. The business elite were not necessarily interested in such restrictions: they were often engaged in cartels themselves and their business associations and lobby organizations, like the Federation of Industries, had a strong position in the corporative environment and particularly when it came to economic legislation.

However, a law concerning cartels, voluntary competition restrictions and dominating market position – more or less a copy of the Swedish law of 1946 – came into force in 1958. The only form of cartels declared illegal was tender cartels, while vertical price-fixing agreements could be declared illegal if they were particularly harmful. Perhaps more importantly, cartels and cartel-type agreements had to be notified to the cartel authorities and registered in a cartel register. Export cartels and other types of cartel agreements concerning activities on foreign markets were, on the other hand, excluded as these did not have any effects on the domestic market, and were primarily seen as favourable for the Finnish economy.

The law proved fairly toothless, and the authorities had in reality little power to interfere in single cartel cases, and there was little eagerness to register cartels. The target of the law was, however, not to forbid cartels, but to control and monitor both them and the market situation. Cartels as such were not seen to be harmful, although the most adverse effects should be counteracted. The need for increasing control and monitoring was clearly a part of the new regulative environment.

The law was revised in 1964 and 1973 when it became stricter – when, for example, vertical price-fixing became illegal and cartels 'harmful' to the society could be dissolved. A system of forcing cartels to negotiate gave the authorities more efficient weapons. Also the notification of cartels became stricter and cartels taking the form of associations or companies had to be registered. Still, a large number of cartel agreements still remained outside the register, a fact well recognized by the authorities themselves, while a few cartels were dissolved.[85]

No decartelization started until the 1980s. In many European countries the post-war period had meant decartelization, but this was not the case in Finland in spite of a more or less similar legal framework – in Sweden, tendencies towards decartelization had started after 1968. The reason for slightly diverse outcomes from similar legislation can probably be found in a fairly toothless legislation in combination with the political and intellectual climate. Cartels fitted well into the strongly co-operative model in Finland.

The stronger corporativist environment can also be seen in the growing importance of state companies. Several new ones, like Rautaruukki, were founded while the former ones grew in importance. One reason was the strong connection of some of these big companies to Soviet trade. Enso-Gutzeit, for example, had a significant role in the eastern trade, making the leadership also more political (see Chapter 6 in this volume). Secondly, the active policies to promote industrialization, with a particular focus on regional development, supported the establishing of new state companies, particularly in the periphery. The state companies were also a chief concern of President Kekkonen. Finally, ideologically the decades after the war supported state ownership, although no nationalization of big business occurred. A debate about the nationalization of banks and insurance companies was, however, occasionally on the agenda.

Photograph 5.1 The laying of the foundation stone of the state company Rautaruukki's first blast furnace by the President of Finland, Urho Kekkonen. Rautaruukki was established in 1960 and has been one of the leading state companies in Finland. The company can be seen as having belonged to one of the 'crown jewels' of the Kekkonen era. Among the people gathered around Kekkonen is the CEO of the company, Helge Haavisto (furthest to the right), and the foreign minister of Finland, Ahti Karjalainen (second from the right). The Finnish State still owns nearly 40 per cent of the shares (in 2007).
Source: Rautaruukki Oy, company archives, Helsinki, Finland. Photographer: Foto-Roos.

The Soviet trade also gave the state a large influence on private companies, like Wärtsilä with its strong manager, Wilhelm Wahlforss. As the negotiations were carried out at the highest political level, but private business also took part in the negotiations, the connection between big business and the state was intimate. As the Soviet orders were generally profitable, the private firms were eager to belong to the inner circle around President Kekkonen and the Minister of Trade. At the same time, the political elite most likely benefited among their business connections.

During these decades a very active and strong state was a prominent feature, although the state also compromised with sector interests in the name of the national interest and within the co-operative growth project. This was an era of state-led growth.

Social corporatism and consensus on the labour market

The situation and the practices on the labour markets were transformed greatly during the decades after the war. Female employment grew and the amount and share of white-collar employees increased. This was the period of the 'normalization' of wage work, at the same time as it was the period of an expansion in white-collar employment, as a result of the growing service sector, particularly within the public sector (education, health care and social welfare), but also as a result of increasing skill requirements within administrative and qualified development work in the manufacturing sector.[86] The patriarchal relations between employers and employees eroded, and had finally disappeared by the 1960s. Unionization increased rapidly, real wages grew, while wage gaps decreased. The working conditions improved, with shorter working hours (e.g. the introduction of a 40-hour work week), increasing rights to a vacation and so forth. The level of education among the labour force also grew rapidly.

With the growth in the service sector, particularly public sector welfare employment, women found work on the labour market. Female labour was also common in other types of employment, in private services (banks and office work) and in factory work, for example in the textile and food industry.

Also labour market practices transformed, particularly once the collective bargaining system first seen in the war years became established. Employers had then agreed to negotiate collectively with the unions and to sign collective agreements. However, after the general strike of 1956, agreements between the central confederations of employers and the unions had not yet been concluded. Until the late 1960s, wage agreements varied, but mostly branch agreements were concluded. Strikes and unrest were also fairly common.

In 1968, the first collective agreement between the central employers' organization and employees was signed, the so called 'Liinamaa I', named after the government negotiator. Finland entered the so called 'TUPO era', that is, the era of incomes policies (*tulopoliittikka*). In this system the government often took an active part; it was a tripartite system. Even President Kekkonen interfered occasionally in negotiations in order to force the parties to come to an agreement.

During the following two decades many other issues than wages were included in the negotiation process – for example, taxation, indexation clauses, unemployment benefits, agricultural subsidies and social security reforms were often used as trump cards by the government to conclude an agreement.[87] After this, Finnish labour market practices resembled more closely those of the other Nordic countries.

A more favourable attitude toward collective bargaining had emerged among the employers due to the transformation on the labour market. Collective bargaining was a fairly efficient way of dealing with tensions around employment conditions and wage-setting in an era of increasing skill requirements and wage pressures. The model also suited the labour unions, as it made way for wage policies based on the concept of 'solidarity', i.e. decreasing wage differentials and rapidly increasing real wages for blue-collar workers within key industrial sectors. In this environment the strong export sector unions of the paper industry workers and the metal workers became strong. Beside favourable wage agreements, workers in the paper and metal industry often experienced wage drift during periods of rapid growth in exports. They were an 'elite' of the blue-collar workers – a labour aristocracy.[88] The evolution of a system of collective bargaining also increased the rate of unionization, which now rose to the level of the other Nordic countries.

Collective bargaining and a system of incomes policies also suited the corporate growth project. It was a way to achieve moderate wage increases in slumps and avoid inflationary tendencies after devaluations of the Markka. In times of booms, wage drift was unavoidable.[89] This system also paved the way for consensus in the national interest as it involved the majority of the labour force in the growth project, particularly the strong export sector unions.

However, although a consensus model emerged in the national interest, there were both open and more subtle, underlying conflicts on the labour market throughout the post-war period. As mentioned, strikes had been common in Finland, but the labour movement itself suffered from internal conflicts, particularly between radical left-wing socialist fractions and the social democratic fraction in the 1950s and 1960s.[90]

The welfare state as promoting the 'virtuous circle'

Although Finland today has extensive social security and a system of public welfare services for its citizens, the Finnish welfare state of a 'Nordic model' evolved later than in the other countries. The realization of some reforms carried through already in the inter-war period, like a national pensions system, was interrupted by the war and did not come into effect until 1956. This was complemented by the national, but privately organized, work pension system established in 1961. In the 1960s several welfare reforms were carried through. In 1963, a general sickness insurance act (*kansaneläkelaki*) was introduced. General unemployment benefits, as a result of the unemployment insurance Act in 1960, came into force gradually in the decade.

Until then, relief work – in popular parlance, the so-called 'spade line' (fi: *lapiolinja*) – had prevailed as the sole alternative to getting a living in times of unemployment.

The support for a universal, flat-rate welfare system had taken root. The agrarian population and the Centre Party opposed income-related benefits, but both the Social Democrats and the agrarians were in principle in favour of an extensive welfare system. However, income-related benefits developed slowly and it was not until the 1980s that the Finnish welfare system and social security benefits reached the level, extent and generosity of the other Nordic countries. Only in the 1970s and 1980s did a so-called 'wage-earner' perspective to the social insurance and welfare systems evolve.[91] In line with the importance of human capital investments, and the goal of a high participation rate on the labour market, welfare reforms in general and the support for income-related benefits in particular gained ground. A high participation rate would enhance growth, while such reforms would involve everyone in the joint growth project and, thus, also support the consensus society. Income-related pensions and social security benefits did motivate people to participate in the labour force and both female and male labour participation rates have been high in Finland since the 1960s. The employment rate was around 67–70 per cent during the post-war decades. But for instance among middle-aged cohorts, the participation rate was much higher. Also the female employment rate has been high, and exceeded 60 per cent since the 1980s.[92]

As income-related unemployment benefits were tied to union membership, and membership fees were tax-deductible, they also influenced the unionization rate.[93]

Finnish welfare reforms has been based on an idea that economic growth could be promoted through welfare systems, educational reforms and a fairly equal distribution of incomes. Growth, increasing wealth and egalitarian policies would support each other and the development would lead to continuously increasing prosperity: a 'virtuous circle'.[94] By creating stability and involving all groups in society in the making of the modern, and economically successful, state, radical protest movements could be avoided.

Educational expansion
Although basic education had become compulsory for everyone in the 1920s, the exceptions allowed for the municipalities in providing educational services, the economic harshness during the 1930s depression and the large share of the population still getting a living from the agrarian sector had

made educational levels still low in Finland in the inter-war period. After the Second World War, and particularly since the 1960s, the supply of education increased rapidly on all levels. It is usually believed that Finnish society went through some kind of educational revolution in the 1960s. In the 1970s nine years of compulsory primary education came gradually into force in the whole country, which is usually also seen as the beginning of a truly egalitarian schooling system and the laying of the basis for a knowledge-society. After that, youngsters could go on to the secondary level, either to an institute of vocational training or continue in secondary school, after which they could continue at the tertiary level, either university-level training or some vocational training. This has also been the aim of educational policies since then, supported by student grants and student loans.

However, the late introduction of a truly mass education on all levels meant that the Finnish population still had a significantly lower level of education in the 1960s and 1970s than in the other Nordic countries. For instance, in the 1960s around 90 per cent of the population still had no further education, but only some sort of primary education. By 1970, already 20 per cent of the population had completed some vocational training, and among the younger age groups the level of education started to rise very rapidly.[95] Intergenerational comparisons show this rapid growth: in 1980, already 54 per cent of the youngest cohort (25–29) had completed some further vocational or higher education, but only 13 per cent per cent of those exceeding 65.

This late, but extremely rapid expansion was a result of growing belief among politicians and authorities of the importance of human capital investment as a source of growth. Such ideas were also influenced by the policies during the 'Golden Age', when human capital and growth theories evolved. The idea of equal opportunities in education also became more pronounced, as a consequence of policies to reduce inequality in the post-war decades. This has meant that education on all levels has been publicly funded, and free of charge. In the latter part of the twentieth century, education became an important route for social mobility. Equal opportunities would also have positive effects on growth as no reserves of talents would remain unused.

The educational system has, in the same way as the welfare system, not only been a question of equality of opportunities, but also been seen as promoting growth. The publicly funded educational investments were of great significance with respect to the development of the business sector. In Finland, for example, technical education on all levels, in vocational schools, in technical institutes and in technical universities, was regarded as particularly important.

The proportion of degrees in technical and natural science in relation to all degrees has for a long time been higher in Finland than in other OECD countries.[96] Since the 1960s, business schools and business colleges expanded at a rapid pace. The great belief in education as a source of growth has also been an argument for making education of all types, including higher education primarily intended for business life, publicly funded.

The primary sector in the corporative model

Although the structural change in the Finnish economy was rapid and the primary sector's share of GDP and of employment decreased (in the early 1980s around 10 per cent of GDP and 13 per cent of employment), the primary sector still strongly influenced the economic–political model and ideological thinking. The agrarian interests played a significant role in the building of the welfare society and were an important factor in the corporative model. The interest organization of the agricultural producers, MTK (Maataloustuottajain Keskusliitto) also continued to be strong and influential in spite of a rapidly declining agricultural population. First, as a consequence of the food shortage during the war, self-sufficiency continued to be seen as vital in the national interest. The living standards and the income level of the agricultural population were to be made adequate in comparison with wage earners through welfare policies, food pricing policies and timber prices. Secondly, beside the importance of securing a certain amount of domestic production, many farmers were also owners of forests, and as such vital suppliers of raw material for the main industrial sector. Finally, the ideology of the small farmer owning his farm and supporting his family as the ideal continued to persist. As a result keeping the countryside populated was also seen as important among the urban population. This ideology sprang partly from the rapid transformation from an agrarian to a modern industrialized nation: most Finns still had a close relation to the countryside and to agrarian production.[97] Beside the ideological picture of the independent farmer providing the bread for his family, small-scale farms also went hand in hand with the strong ideology of work typical in Finland.[98] The stress on entrepreneurship today in the public debate can actually be seen as a continuation of this ideological base.

This strong protection of the agrarian interests and self-suffiency led to a complicated and extensive system of subsidies, non-market pricing policies and protectionism, which resulted in both high prices and overproduction. Through set-aside and export subsidies, there were efforts to deal with the overproduction, but it continued until the 1980s. These policies partly prevented, or at least retarded, specialization and efficiency by mergers into larger production units. As a result of EU membership, the backbone of this policy was broken after 1995.

The war and reconstruction years as a 'formative phase'

The war economy has been seen to have had extensive effects on the post-war economic model. On the other hand, at least part of the roots of many of the institutional models taking shape and becoming established during and immediately after the war were actually already to be found earlier.[99] For example, several of the co-operative, collaborative or corporatist features of the Finnish economy, based on close, often personal, relations between big business, politicians and civil servants had been established much earlier.[100] Some models, like state companies and increasing cartel co-operation after independence, also paved the way for a more collaborative model and corporatist features. However, the war years and afterwards elaborated this model further and induced new forms of co-operation and a new acceptance of regulations and state intervention. Some of the institutional settings for carrying out such policies were also established during the war.

Still, the regulation of certain sectors and their corporatist and co-ordinated features would not have been able to survive so long if there had not been a fairly extensive political consensus about such a model, a fairly universal support for the growth project, for the avoidance of tensions and for the bridging of conflicts in society in the national interest. For instance, the highly regulated financial markets, in combination with an investment-oriented economic policy, received support in most sectors of society, although of course difference of opinions about details existed. The national interest had been an outspoken idea during the war, but also during the era of Cold War with its – real or perceived – foreign threats made consensus important. Still, the 'national interest' was not only political, but as much a question of economic advancement: the strong consensus policies leading up to the welfare society and a system of collective bargaining, besides building the modern prosperous welfare society, included an aspect of economic nationalism. This feature was already observed in the inter-war period, although taking new forms and gaining new strength during and after the war.

In this Finnish state-led, corporatist growth model, there was a 'division of labour' between the divergent sectors. The employees' and employers' interest organizations took care of the labour market, and to some extent, welfare state questions, while the financing of big business and rationing of credits were delegated to the banks. Issues concerning cartels, exports, Soviet trade, and state companies were again areas of big business, the industrial lobby and branch organizations. Every segment was, however, strictly directed from above, but this bridged the conflicts and included all sectors in the society.

Moreover, in this model, big business still held a prominent position, not least in the Soviet trade, but also in the emphasis on exports and investments as the source of growth. All policies supported big business in manufacturing. This was the era of the 'smoke-stack industry'. From the perspective of the techno-economic paradigm, the investment-oriented economic model was to support the paper industry, its heavy investments, its need for supply of cheap energy and its dependence on exports.

Although the Finnish post-war growth model had some specific features of its own, similar models existed in many other countries during this period. Social welfare policies, strong unions, collective bargaining systems and income policies and wage-setting supporting decreasing wage differentials were also phenomena found in many European countries. However, the strict regulation within many sectors of the economy, not least the financial markets, had its own features and lasted longer in Finland than in many other western European countries. In the next section we turn to the liberalization and restructuring of the Finnish economy – a rapid but to some extent also painful transformation.

Liberalization, speculative 'bubble' and a delayed structural crisis: a third interlude, 1982–93

The 1980s and 1990s saw some profound and radical transformations in the Finnish economy and the Finnish model of capitalism. In the early 1990s, partly connected to these institutional transformations, the Finnish economy went through one of its worst real economic and financial crises, with negative growth for three subsequent years (1991–3) adding up to a total fall in GDP exceeding 10 per cent.[101]

The 1980s was actually a decade of favourable growth in Finland. The second oil crisis led to only a minor recession in the early 1980s, which was corrected though a small devaluation in 1982, and since the mid-1980s growth figures were good, exceeding 5 per cent in some years. The country had in practice full employment, government finances were in good shape and the state was in principle debt free, and economic activity was high in all sectors.

The welfare system developed, people consumed and firms invested. There was euphoria about this success: Finland had at last become a high-income capitalist society equal to the western European ones.

However, the economy gradually became badly overheated, with an asset price bubble, extremely high indebtedness in the private sector, a growing deficit in the current balance and inflationary pressures leading to problems in the export industry's competitiveness. This favourable but gradually more and more unbalanced period of growth ended in a total crash in the early 1990s: GDP grew by 5.4 per cent in 1989, but the development came to a full stop in 1990, with a total economic collapse, GDP declining by 6.5 per cent in 1991, followed by two additional years of falling growth.

So why did Finland go into its worst peace-time crisis since the 1930s, and the worst in the whole of western Europe since the Second World War? The reasons behind this crisis have been much debated, but it is generally concluded that it was a result of an unfortunate combination of outside shocks in tandem with internal imbalances and a poor economic policy: 'bad luck and bad policies.'[102]

The most obvious reasons for this crisis were two external shocks. First, the general international recession which occurred in the early 1990s hit Finnish exports to western markets hard. Secondly, the Soviet trade more or less collapsed overnight in early 1991, due to the political disintegration of the Soviet Union: the heavy dependence on the eastern trade within some sectors became painfully evident.

Domestic factors also worsened the crises. There were many inherent problems in the economy as a result of the long regulative environment. The regulation of the financial markets and investment-oriented policy had prevented structural changes and caused imbalances within certain sectors. Overinvestment had been going on in manufacturing industries, while the Soviet trade had made some companies inefficient, particularly the textile industry, which produced goods that would have never found markets elsewhere. But the final seeds of the crisis lay in the economic policy of the 1980s, in combination with the rapid and somewhat uncontrolled liberalization of the financial markets starting in the early 1980s.

As the neighbouring Nordic countries, particularly Sweden, had started to liberalise their financial markets and international capital movements somewhat earlier, pressures for such reforms emerged in Finland. An ideological shift in favour of liberalization and a more open and competitive environment occurred in the 1980s. At the same time the availability of new financial

PROLOGUE TO THE FINNISH CHAPTER • FINNISH CAPITALISM • ENZO-GUTZEIT TO STORA-ENSO •
NOKIA AND TAMPELLA AFTER THE SECOND WORLD WAR

189

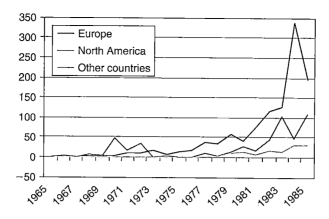

Figure 5.2   Finnish outward FDI, 1965–85 (million Euros)
Source: Balance of Payments Statistics, Bank of Finland.

instruments not covered by regulation also opened up opportunities to operate around the rules: so-called 'grey' financial markets emerged. The regulation started to fall apart from within; such a strict regime was not really possible for a small open economy within an increasingly globalising world economy.

The first step is usually regarded to have been taken in 1981, when banks became free to cover commercial positions. In 1982, lending rate regulation was relaxed and by 1988 interest rates were completely free and determined on the market. Foreign capital flows also began to be liberalized in the early 1980s, and by 1987 all long-term credits were free for all sectors. The last regulation restricting foreign ownership in Finnish companies was abolished in 1993.

Although necessary, this liberalization led to problems. The long period of regulation of the financial markets and capital movements meant that the private sectors – the consumers, the firms and the banks – had little or no experience in acting in an environment with unregulated capital markets and free interest rates. Big business, like Kone Oy, A. Ahlström Oy and Nokia Oy had already had a fairly extensive freedom to operate on the international capital market and their 'path abroad' had also begun before the abolition of the Bank of Finland's restriction on outward FDI.[103] However, when the opportunities also opened up for smaller business and for private persons, it became something of a rush to borrow foreign money or to invest abroad. There was an explosion in Finnish FDI (see Figure 5.2). Companies invested at home and abroad and sometimes in the most unlikely business ideas.

The rapid, but partly uncontrolled, liberalization of the financial markets during an era of favourable growth in the mid-1980s led to extremely rapid credit expansion, with overheating on the housing and stock market, causing a classical asset price 'bubble'. In this overheated situation private consumption grew and the savings rate declined. The expectations of future incomes and profits and rises in asset prices among both firms and households were unrealistic. The private sector was euphoric and the banks shuffled credits around as they competed aggressively for market shares. Thus, apart from 'bad luck and bad policies', 'bad banking' was also an important factor behind the approaching banking crisis. As the the exchange rate at the same time was overvalued, competitiveness declined and exports started to fail. The current balance was negative for several years, adding to the indebtedness of the private sector. This was a ticking time-bomb.

On top of everything, economic policy in the 1980s turned out to be disastrous in the light of rapid deregulation and an overheated economy, as the fiscal policy was extremely stack. As a result of increasing tax revenues, government spending, in line with the tradition of pro-cyclical fiscal policy, was extremely expansionary. At the same time the Finnish authorities wanted to get out of the 'vicious' devaluation cycles. The credibility of the Finnish Markka on the international markets was not particularly strong due to a history of devaluations at regular intervals. In the new economic environment this was a problem for economic and political leaders and the central bank strove to keep the currency fixed. The policy was labelled 'the policy of the stable Markka' (*vakaan markan politiikka*), but was relabelled in the public rhetoric as 'the policy of the strong Markka'. In the midst of overheating, the central bank actually revalued the currency.

When the international recession and the collapse of Soviet trade occurred, the whole bubble burst and the Finnish economy went into a situation best characterized as 'free fall'. Although there were huge problems with the rapid decline in exports, the central bank and the Ministry of Finance wanted to defend the currency at any price, leading to a downward spiral. The crash in the economy meant falling asset prices, high interest rates, bankruptcies and an explosion in unemployment. The collapse of more or less all sectors simultaneously led to an uncontrolled debt-deflation problem, worsening the downward spiral. This in turn led to credit losses and bad debts and after a while a deepening banking crisis, which threatened the stability of the whole financial system. The bank group with the most severe problems, the savings banks, had to be taken over by the Bank of Finland and was later liquidated and sold off to the other bank groups, while the two main commercial banks, Union Bank of Finland, and Kansallis-Osake-Pankki had to resort to government loans and guarantees. Later, they were merged: a symbolic crossing of the old division between the UBF and Kansallis-Osake-Pankki originating in the ancient language division.

There were huge budget deficits and government debt exploded: from having been in reality more or less free from debt, Finnish government debt rose to roughly 70 per cent of GDP in a few years. The speed of the growth in government debt was worryingly swift, particularly in the years 1992–3, and the Finnish credit rating on the international markets fell.

The central bank and the government wanted to stick to the new 'strong currency' policy, although exports were at a standstill. Interest rates rose to defend the currency, adding up to the problems of debt-deflation. However, in the end the Bank of Finland could not avoid the pressures on the Markka, and was forced to devalue by 12 per cent it in autumn 1991, fixing the currency at a new level. But this did not re-establish confidence in the Markka and in September 1992 it was allowed to float freely. The 'market forces' – i.e. international investors – were to determine the value of the Finnish currency in an era of deep crisis.

In 1993 the Bank of Finland instead turned towards an inflation target: to keep inflation at a maximum of 2 per cent. This was a new policy regime partly induced by the efforts to become a member of the EU and particularly to participate in monetary co-operation (ERM).

The extensive depreciation of the currency led to a rapid recovery of exports. The floating exchange rate, which continued for three years, turned out to work favourably. The depression within the domestic sectors continued for much longer, however, and private consumption recovered only slowly.

The seeds of a new regime?

When discussing this period in the Finnish economy, much focus has been placed on the boom and the bust, particularly with respect to the liberalization of the financial markets and the banking crisis. However, also other trans-formations occurred simultaneously during these two decades: a period of regime shift began. This regime shift partly aggravated the crisis, exemplified by the behaviour in the banking sector, but the regime shift later also affected positively the recovery from the crisis. The economic crisis also brought forth changes in old practices, in institutional settings and in the economic model, some of which were already on the way but which were speeded up by the crisis.

For instance, during the 1980s a more competitive environment was accepted overall, which took perhaps its most prominent expression in the renovation of cartel and competition legislation. The cartel legislation was renewed in 1988. Even though the legislation did not change profoundly, yet a more negative attitude towards cartels and industrial co-operation in order to restrict competition was evident and more restrictive polices were introduced to combat efforts to limit competition. The legislation was also renamed 'competition legislation': a symbolic shift. Actually, already in 1982 a committee preparing a renewal of cartel legislation submitted its report. This preparatory work did not lead to any changes in the legislative environment, but a more favourable attitude towards anti-trust policies could be observed in the report.

The economic crisis also affected the welfare system and the public services. The huge problems of financing these services as a result of the growth in unemployment in combination with declining tax revenues forced a reduction in the level of social transfers. Public sector services, such as education and the health service, experienced significant cuts during the recession years, pushing forward reform and reorganization. Efficiency in public service production came to the fore and the public sector came out of the depression more effective and in better shape. However, the cuts in the welfare sector were also a result of a change in the ideological climate in the 1980s, although such measures were easy to blame on the miserable state of public finances.[104]

Finland went through a very swift transition towards a more competitive environment – 'a competition state'[105] – on all levels, but finding its most prominent expression in competition legislation and in the liberalization of the financial markets.

Towards an 'inwardly and outwardly open co-ordinated market economy'[106], 1993–2005

Despite fears of a prolonged crisis, the recovery from the depression turned out to be remarkably rapid in the second half of the 1990s. The average annual growth rate between 1994 and 2000 exceeded 4 per cent. At the turn of the millennium a minor recession occurred, mainly as a result of the end of the so-called 'IT bubble' and the international recession. But also after this, the Finnish growth rate was one of the best in the EU. This remarkable recovery was made possible by several factors. The huge depreciations of the currency in 1991 and 1992 led to a fast recovery of exports. Labour productivity also grew rapidly during the years after the depression. Furthermore, the public sector worked as an important buffer, smoothing the economic crash, taking over a great deal of the costs, not least by supporting the banking sector and maintaining financial stability, but also by absorbing the increasing expenditures coming from the increasing social costs of the crisis. After 1995, EU membership opened up new markets which also contributed to increasing trade and FDI flows between Finland and the other EU countries. Finally, the new environment led to the success of some big Finnish MNCs, not least Nokia, which has expanded rapidly since the mid-1990s. The impact of Nokia and the ICT sector on GDP growth was significant during this period, and it is evident that without this sector the recovery after the crises in the early 1990s would have been much more modest. So when one of the factors behind the depression could be labelled as a case of 'bad luck', Finland experienced in the mid-1990s also a case of 'good luck': in 2000, when Nokia's influence was at its biggest, the company contributed with as much as 1.4 percentage points of the 5 per cent real GDP growth.[107]

Structural transformation between and within sectors was rapid: the service sector grew, while a significant shift within the manufacturing sector from the traditional forest industry towards high-tech industries, primarily the ICT sector, was particularly swift. Electronics export is today larger than exports of forest products.[108] Moreover, the ICT sector also drove structural change and productivity in other sectors and influenced the structure of exports and imports.

EU membership and changes in the corporate environment

One reason for the recovery was EU membership. After Sweden had made their decision to apply for membership in 1991, Finland followed. In the new political environment of Europe – i.e. the collapse of the Soviet Union – this had become possible. The application in 1992 was submitted and in 1995 Finland, simultaneously with Sweden, became a member of the EU. Finland also aimed from the outset to participate in the deepening monetary integration. It was seen as both economically and politically wise: ERM membership would finally put an end to the tradition of devaluation cycles, and politically would mean even closer ties to the West than only an EU membership. The need for a deeper and clearer attachment to western Europe was more urgent in Finland than in the other Nordic countries due to the historical background.[109] In 1996 Finland joined the ERM, putting an end to three years of floating; in 1999 Finland became a member of the EMU and in 2002 the Euro became the sole currency. The membership of EMU led to a period of low inflation and monetary stability, but its long-range effects

Table 5.5   *Finnish outward FDIs abroad, flows, 1985–2000 (Million Euros)*

Year	1985	1990	1995	1998	2000
EU countries	165	1,119	1,097	15,506	12,835
Other European countries	30	262	−130	47	7,489
– of which Russia	–	9	8	16	54
US and Canada	111	314	146	1036	4,862
Other countries	31	187	35	143	855
Not classified	18	−213	−49	27	40
Total	355	1,741	1,100	16,759	26,082

Source: Balance of Payments Statistics, Bank of Finland.

are still to be seen. It also made the Finnish economic situation somewhat different from that of the other Nordic countries.

EU membership also brought with it significant institutional transformations, not the least in competition legislation and competition policies, which had to adapt to EU competition rules. A new competition law came into force in 1992, with a six-month transition period for the business sector to respond and adjust. Since then, cartel agreements and others that affect pricing, hinder business activities, decrease efficiency, and aid the exploitation of a dominant market position became forbidden. In 1998, the competition legislation was harmonized in accordance with union legislation. The transformation of competition legislation and policies must be seen as one of the most significant changes, with immediate consequences from EU membership affecting the corporate environment. The new competition legislation meant that the strong export cartels were abolished. Decartelization was followed by a wave of consolidations and mergers within various branches, not the least in the forest industry, such as the creation of UPM-Kymmene (later UPM). This also induced the big forest companies to go abroad to make acquisitions. The merger wave was, however, also a result of the changing global competitive environment, where mega-mergers were common at the turn of the millennium. Although the new competition legislation was a significant change to the old environment, fifteen years on, secret cartel agreements are still unveiled once in a while: old practices apparently persist.

The opening up of capital markets also meant significant changes in the corporate sector. After the opening up of the foreign capital flows, outward and inward FDI became extensive and foreign ownership in Finnish firms grew remarkably (Table 5.5). The inflow of foreign capital was particularly rapid after the upswing in the late 1990s and the early 2000s. In the early 1990s, only some 10 per cent of the ownership of Finnish companies listed on the stock exchange was in the hands of foreign investors, while ten years later it was nearly 70 per cent.[110] From being one of the most closed economies with respect to foreign capital, Finland became in a decade an economy with extensive foreign ownership. One of the reasons for this is, of course, Nokia, where in the early 2000s around 90 per cent of the shares were foreign-owned; other large corporations, such as UPM, also had had a large share of foreign ownership. It is mainly within 'traditional' family firms that private domestic owners dominate.[111] However, the state is a major investor, as are the the big Finnish pension funds, primarily Varma and Ilmarinen, which are important block owners in both listed and unlisted companies. A significant change is that in many of the listed state companies, foreign owners have also become significant.

Finnish outward investments also grew at a remarkable pace from the late 1990s. The main markets for Finnish FDI since the liberalization were Sweden and other EU countries, but in the early 2000s Asia and the US also became important target areas. The role of Russia became important again in the early 2000s, after the Russian economy has reached a stable growth path. For example, firms in the food industry (Atria Oy) and the retail sector (Stockmann) have successfully entered the Russian market.

The largest Finnish companies became significantly larger in the early 2000s and are today also important in an international comparison. They became truly global. Today not only Nokia, but also the largest forest companies, like UPM and StoraEnso, and also some important corporations in other sectors, like the lift company Kone no longer acted only in response to globalization, but became significant global players. A wave of cross-border, mainly Nordic, mergers occurred in the last decade of the twentieth century, creating large Nordic corporations like StoraEnso, Nordea and TietoEnator.

At the same time, an ideology of self-employment and small-scale entrepreneurship became more pronounced in Finnish society. This went hand in hand with the restructuring of the economies in the industrialized countries, both as a result of the shift from the industrial towards the service sector, and from transformations within the manufacturing industries themselves. The new technology, especially the ICT sector, favoured this transition. As large firms started to organise in new structures, with new ways to communicate, produce and sell, they developed new strategies to increase flexibility and avoid risk.[112]

For Finland the transformation has not only been institutional, but very much a question of a shift in the technological paradigm. New high-tech

Photograph 5.2 **Nokia and Perlos.** *Nokia has been one of the factors behind the rapid Finnish economic development of recent decades. The success of this company led to the upstart of several subcontractors, more or less exclusively dependent on the orders from Nokia. The vulnerability from the high dependence on Nokia is here exemplified by one subcontractor with a long history in Finland, Perlos, which produces plastic shells for mobile phones. In early 2007 Perlos informed that all production in Finland will gradually cease, and thus also the biggest plant in Kontiolahti will, together with the remaining production units in Finland, be closed down.*
Source: Lehtikuva. Photographers: Ismo Pekkarinen and Riikka Hurri.

sectors, particular the ICT sector with Nokia at the forefront, but also in other narrower high-tech sectors, grew extremely fast. This structural change continued also after the crisis. The impact of Nokia and the ICT sector on GDP growth was significant during this period, and it is evident that without this sector the recovery after the crises of the early 1990s would have been much more modest.

It would actually be easy, but also dangerous, to ascribe every positive development and transformation to Nokia's account. As Eli Moen and Kari Lilja claim, the Finnish success was not a single-company story.[113] Nokia's impact was, and still is, enormous, but the Finnish economy is much more than Nokia. Moreover, the success of Nokia has also been a source of extensive myth-building, particularly concerning its most central figure, Jorma Ollila. No doubt Ollila is a remarkable business manager, spotting the opportunities that the digitalization and deregulation of the telecommunications sector could offer.[114] However, many factors in the 1990s paved the way for him to act. The banking crisis and the banks' declining force made way for corporate management to increase its power and take action. Without the opening of the Finnish markets to foreign capital, giving access to the global market, Nokia's growth would not have been possible. Moreover, as the telephone network was never nationalized, the telecommunications equipment market was competitive and fully liberalized by 1994.[115]

Nokia's success was, however, not promoted only by the transformations of the last decade and the overall liberalization of the economy. The foundation for the development of Nokia had been laid in the 'old' Finnish model.[116] For example, the strong emphasis on technical education and a national innovation strategy with the target of building a knowledge-based society had emerged already before the 1990s. Neither was Finland a low-tech country before the growth of Nokia and the IT sector. On the contrary, the forest industry cluster was a high-tech sector in the 1980s. Much of Nokia's success, and the rapid technological and industrial shift that paved the way for the telecommunication and other ICT branches, was also, according to Moen and Lilja, a result of previously existing collaborative features and cross-sector co-ordination. Although a completely divergent institutional setting took shape in the 1990s and 2000s, the idea of co-operation between sectors and between state and companies to enhance development was nothing new.

The more competitive environment of the Finnish companies was also strengthened by allowing for foreign competition in other branches. Agricultural producers and the food industry underwent remarkable transformations as a result of increasing competition from imported goods. This caused extensive pressures on the agricultural cluster's strategies, but it adapted fairly well to the new environment: for example, new markets have been found in the former socialist countries.

Towards a market-based financial system
The financial markets, and particularly the role of the banks, changed remarkably in the wake of the banking crisis. The crisis dealt a hard blow to the banks as power centres. First, the banks in deep crisis could not finance big business. Secondly, the crisis brought with it an extensive restructuring within the banking system. As observed above, one bank group had to be taken over by the Bank of Finland, while the two big commercial banks, Union Bank of Finland and Kansallis-Osake-Pankki, had to resort to government financial support, although they later paid it back. These two banks, previously severe competitors, originating in the language issue within business, were merged in 1995. Although the language division lost most of its significance in the

post-war era, the old split between the two bank spheres had remained intact. Thus, the merging of these two banks was seen as a symbol of a completely new era.[117] The prominent tradition of cross-ownership between financial and non-financial firms was also dissolved after the banking crises.

The diminishing role of the banks during the last two decades was also a result of the capital markets opening up to an inflow of foreign capital. This, in combination with an international trend towards a more 'Anglo-Saxon' market-based system, meant that the importance of the stock market increased significantly in Finland from the mid-1990s. Moreover, the shift from a bank-centred system towards a market-based system was also induced by changes in the legal environment. For example, the taxation regulation favouring banks and bank savings was abolished, while shareholder rights were strengthened.[118] This was part of a broader European phenomenon but, for instance, in a Nordic comparison, Finnish development was particularly rapid. Actually, according to some figures, Finland has the largest stock market measured by market capitalization in relation to GDP in the Euro area.[119] Venture capital markets, having previously been insignificant, also grew in the early twenty-first century, while the biggest pension funds became significant investors in the Finnish corporate sector. The pension funds are today, besides the state, among the biggest Finnish owners of listed firms and are new power centres in the Finnish corporate sector. Today foreign owners also balance the domestic power centres in another way than was the case during the closed era.

Foreign capital inflow and more general changes in the economic environment also had significant effects on corporate governance practices and created an increasing focus on shareholder value. Concrete changes towards a more Anglo-Saxon governance structure occurred: for instance, the traditional system of dual boards – a supervisory and an executive board – lost ground.[120]

Innovation strategies and human capital investments

When investigating the Finnish 'success story', educational and technology policies are usually cited as one of the key issues. Finland is today seen as a model country from the perspective of educational policies, with both an excellent general basic education and a high level of further and vocational training. One of the most significant factors behind the success of the Finnish economy has also been the extensive investments in education and R&D activities. The political and economic elite adapted to the concept of an 'information society' well. Since the 1980s the share of expenditure on education and on R&D increased substantially to one of the highest in the OECD area. In 1980, R&D activities formed around 1 per cent of GDP, while by the end of the 1990s this had risen to 3 per cent.[121] Both publicly funded research and research within firms grew.

These figures are – again – significantly influenced by Nokia's activities. It is estimated that in 2000 Nokia's expenditure on research constituted about one-third of all R&D expenditures, and as much as half of the R&D expenditure in private Finnish companies. As a result of the impact of Nokia's activities, the business sector's share of R&D expenditures is today larger in Finland than in many other countries.[122]

R&D activities grew also within the universities, research institutes and firms themselves, and public research funding increased substantially. The foundation of the national Funding Agency for Technology and Innovation (TEKES) in 1986, and of Sitra in 1967, were important measures for funding applied research within both the academic community and within firms.

An important foundation for lifting the Finnish society into an 'innovation society' was the raising of both the level and extent of basic education and the improvement of further education. In the early 1970s, a basic compulsory education of 9 years (*peruskoulu, grundskola*) was introduced. In the1960s and 1970s, the system of vocational training also developed at all levels, while new universities opened up, both in order to increase the level of education and to promote regional development.

The stress on further and higher education and on scientific achievement became extremely pronounced after the recession. In the 1990s a whole new category of higher education emerged, the so-called polytechnics (*ammattikorkeakoulu yrkeshögskola*) or 'universities of applied science'. Also the universities expanded and in spite of a shrinking youth cohort the number of university students and graduates increased significantly. Also post-graduate education expanded, largely as part of the 'national innovation strategy': a globalized business life would, according to visions repeatedly presented, need highly qualified experts in the future.

The level of education rose extremely swiftly after the 1960s, and continued to do so in the last decades. While the Finnish population's educational level was still low in the 1970s, at the turn of the new millennium educational standards were among the highest in the OECD countries. Today, around 45 per cent of the age group attends some form of higher education. Although the level of education was very high in the early 2000s, the short history of the Finnish 'knowledge society' is shown by the fact that although 86 per cent of the age cohort of 25–29 years old (in 2000) had completed some sort of vocational further education, only 29 per cent of those over 69 years had done so.[123]

The increased funding of research and education did not only affect the number of students, but also the depth of research: the most prominent Finnish universities today compete well internationally in scientific rankings. The emphasis in the late nineteenth century was on technical training and applied natural and technical sciences, and this is still the case. Such strategies, although common in many countries, reached a particularly prominent position in the Finnish official discourse and in research funding.

Pressures on the labour markets

The labour markets changed after the recession both with respect to the types of jobs available and with respect to employment contracts and labour market practices. As a result of the rapid expansion in high-tech sectors and the service sector, new types of jobs emerged, while the relocation of jobs to other parts of the world, particularly within the manufacturing sector, led to a rapid decline in other types of jobs. The new job opportunities were to a growing extent short-term or 'atypical' employment contracts, with increasing wage flexibility and growing wage differentials as a result. Outsourcing and new forms of organizations – for example, network organizations and supply chains – led to a growth in entrepreneurship and in self- and project employment. In spite of rapid economic growth and new job opportunities, however, a fairly persistent and high long-term unemployment among certain groups of employees remained since the depression.

The opening up of the economy and the participation in European integration meant new job opportunities, but also competition from cheap labour in other parts of the world. This has led to growing possibilities for 'regime shopping' for both Finnish companies and for individuals. Also the number of foreigners from other countries (e.g. from Russia) working in Finland became a new phenomen at the turn of the millennium. But, contrary to the other Nordic countries, the share of foreigners on the Finnish labour market was – and still is – low.

These changes also put pressure on labour market practices, on the incomes policy system and on the unions. During the depression, unemployment benefits were cut and the labour law concerning redundancy slackened. There were also some strong efforts during the depression years to abolish the 'old' tripartite system and extensively transform labour law.[124] This was met with firm resistance from the unions, and the plan was withdrawn. However, some reforms were put through in order to fight unemployment by removing rigidities on the labour market. Wage-setting at a local level also became more common, while collective agreements were given more flexibility for local adjustments. After that, a downward trend in unionization rates could be seen. However, in the early 2000s collective agreements covered still over 90 per cent of employees.[125] In 2007 the Confederation of Finnish Industries claimed one-sidedly that there could be no continuation of the old-style comprehensive income policy agreements. However, the future is open. The collective bargaining system was fairly efficient during the depression and after. Although it affected employment figures negatively as the wages were sticky downwards, it turned out to work favourable during the recovery, as wage increases were kept at a moderate level for several years in spite of rapid growth and productivity increases in many sectors.

The role of the state within the 'competition state'

The role of the state in the economy has transformed as well. Direct interference in and regulation of the economy was removed, while an independent monetary policy – a policy segment traditionally strong and active in Finland – disappeared as a result of membership in EMU. The abolition of direct regulation and state interference does not, however, mean that the state took an 'arm's length' strategy, as in the late nineteenth century. The state still plays a fairly active role in the economy as a promoter of growth. Public funding of education and R&D has never been as high as it is today, the system providing the business environment with highly skilled employees and a stable basis for innovations.

In spite of privatization of state companies, state ownership is still large (Table 5.6). Ownership policies also changed significantly: from being the majority owner and in some cases the sole owner, to being one owner among others in listed companies. State companies, or part of them, were sold off, often gradually so as not to distort the market, but also because the state wanted to preserve its influence. Beside a more negative attitude in general towards state ownership, the main reason for the selling off of state companies was pragmatic and often connected to state finances. The profits were, for example, used for paying off government debt and funding start-ups.

Government ownership also decreased through mergers with private companies (e.g. the merger between the Swedish Stora and the Finnish state-company Enso). In this case, the Finnish state came to work side by side with

Table 5.6 **Largest owners of top 10 companies: Finland**

Company	Owners with over 5 per cent of votes
1. Nokia	Widely held
2. Fortum	Finnish state
3. Sampo	Financial investor (foreign), Finnish state, Varma
4. UPM-Kymmene	Widely held
5. Stora Enso	Wallenberg, Finnish state, Varma
6. Neste Oil	Finnish state
7. Metso	Finnish state
8. Outokumpu	Finnish state
9. Kone	Herlin, Antti
10. Rautaruukki	Finnish state

Source: Murto and Fellman (2007).

the influential Swedish Wallenberg group. It appears that the state acts today like any other investor, although still a lot of political and economic power is connected to the state companies.

Finally, the state, instead of regulating and interfering in the economy, has in the new competitive environment taken the role of controlling the actors and enforcing the 'rules of the game' in the liberalized economy: two good examples are the financial supervison and competition authorities, which have extensive power to interfere in any unlawful behaviour of companies.

A system in the making

The 1980s and 1990s was a period of change from an inwardly closed co-ordinated market economy towards an outwardly and inwardly open, co-ordinated or collaborative market economy, dominated by large corporations prepared for global competition.[126] These extensive structural transformations were partly induced and called for by the crisis, while some were a consequence of the changing international environment, outside pressures and the integration process. These radical transformations were also a process within Finnish society, which began long before EU membership was considered: a political and ideological shift had occurred. Moreover, the rapid institutional transformations were also a result of a swift shift in the techno-economic paradigm, away from paper machines and the forest cluster, taking advantage of the investment-oriented policy, to the ICT and electronics sector, taking advantage of the liberalized outward and inward capital flows.

The liberalization and opening up of the Finnish economy, most remarkably in financial markets and foreign capital movements, were part of a new regime that both required and promoted other reforms. The new environment emerged on more or less all fronts in line with the idea of institutional complementarity – i.e. some institutional solutions demand other solutions, while others are incompatible.[127] The Finland of today is very different from the Finland entering the 1980s. The 1980s and 1990s was a formative period towards a different institutional and economic environment. But it appears that we are still in the midst of this formative phase: the 'Finnish model' capitalism of today is a system in the making.

There are still many collaborative features in Finnish society. Labour market practices are a good example, but collaboration also occurs both between and within sectors with more competitive elements. Some sectors transformed less than others, although pressures have been put on all segments.

Although the state plays a significant role today, it is perhaps at the moment partly seeking a role in the open, globalized economy. At the same time as the state is called on to improve working conditions for the companies, at the same time there are pressures for less interference, more liberalization and further privatization.

The growth project of the post-war decades and the realization of a 'virtuous circle' demanded a certain amount of steering from above and suited a fairly closed economy. As a result, such a growth project was severely challenged by globalization and the new economic environment of the late twentieth century. However, something of the state-led – or, at least, 'top-down – approach' is still apparent today. The policies and instruments changed, but the top-down agenda is evident. The National Innovation Strategy and its emphasis on innovation, business–university relations and applied sciences as a road to prosperity provide a good example. Actually, the transformation of the economy and the institutional model from a very co-ordinated to a more liberal market-based system was in itself a state-led, co-ordinated process in itself, in order to build a favourable working environment for the corporate sector in a new global environment.[128] Also EU membership brought with it a model where reforms were implemented from above.[129]

The basic structure of the welfare system and public health care has also remained intact, although there have been significant cuts in income transfer levels and in public services. Demands for radical transformation in the social security system, often motivated by pressures from globalization and 'economic necessity', have grown, although at the same time the welfare system and the public services have a strong and broad legitimacy among the majority of the population.[130]

The educational system appears to be one of the most persistent ones in the 'Finnish model'. No strong pressures for change of the basic education exist. Within higher education changes are, however, evident. The traditional Finnish university training has adapted to the European system, as a result of the so-called 'Bologna process'. The traditional universities are facing greater competition from the new polytechnics and growing opportunities to go abroad and complete a foreign education. Competition for students and funding is an everyday issue in today's universities. In some fields, primarily business training, privately funded training has taken root. The American-type MBA training, emerging in Finland in the late 1980s, is today significant business, although hitherto only taking the form of complementary training to a 'traditional' university-level training.[131]

What the future will be for the trade unions, for the centralized bargaining system and government-funded further education is of course difficult to forecast. It is possible that the old practices and models will turn out to function well within the new environment with only minor modifications. And although there are some strong pressures for change in these sectors, it does not necessarily mean that the models will converge to resemble those in the traditional 'liberal market economies' like the US, but instead that some totally new models for wage bargaining or for funding and organising education and research will develop.

Conclusion

This chapter has dealt with the Finnish model of capitalism over a long period of time in connection with economic development and structural change. It has hopefully brought with it a more profound understanding and given a richer picture of the country's development. The Finnish case looks a little different from the other Nordic countries, although also some clear 'Nordic features' are observable. We have also learned that the Finnish economy and its economic success are not only a story of the last two decades, and especially not only a result of Nokia and some other large firms.

Furthermore, we have observed that the significance of the outside world on the Finnish development was remarkable. Finland efficiently exploited opportunities in the export markets, and was during the 'catch-up' phase a good adapter and copier of foreign models. Lately, deepening integration and globalization has been a lottery ticket for big business and a window of opportunity well taken advantage of. At the same, small size and openness contributed to a certain instability in the Finnish economy.

It is also evident that domestic factors affected the development positively. The pragmatic growth orientation with a strong emphasis on investment in fixed and human capital doubtless had beneficial effects.

On the other hand, Finland was a society with fairly low elements of trust in the inter-war period and it also appears to have had more – both underlying and evident – conflicts and tensions than the other Nordic countries until the last decades of the twentieth century. However, the policies and institutional solutions of the post-war decades, especially on the labour market, but also the efforts to include the agrarian interests in the corporative project, built and enforced trust in Finnish society. Labour market practices, in combination with strongly collaborative features, made growth policies generally accepted and, thus, decreased tensions in society. These policies contributed to a stable working environment for business life, at the same time as they led to increasing real wages and living standards for all employees and the agrarian population.[132] Such policies were also carried through in the name of the national interest. The threat from outside during the Cold War era, but also from inside (communism), made such a national cohesion desirable. Although ideological features influenced how the growth model was perceived in the post-war period, economic and political pragmatism has in general been fairly typical in Finland.

On a broader level, the Finnish development, in comparison to the other countries presented in this volume, has been marked by severe economic and political crises, which have had a significant impact on the political, institutional and economic environment. It is interesting to discuss to what extent institutional settings have evolved slowly over a long period of time or have been more a result of crises, causing the development to take a new path. There has been a common view that crises have created breaks and ruptures in the Finnish economic model, working more or less as 'formative periods'. The Finnish economic and societal discourse has also been very crisis-focused, and crises have often been used to motivate reforms and sometimes even as a force, or even a pretext, to bring about reforms. This made us place the wars and the 1990 crises as interludes with respect to institutional development. The significance of crises has, however, also been exaggerated in Finnish historiography. Because of that, we avoided calling them 'formative periods'. Although a crisis can finally trigger reforms, or at least speeds up the process, the start of the processes can usually be traced in earlier periods. For instance, it has often been claimed that the Second World War had extensive effects on the formation of the Finnish growth model of the post-war era. During the war years significant institutional and policy reforms came about that affected the institutional setting long after the war, particularly on the labour and financial markets. The war forced the healing of the division between employer and employees. However, the ideological roots for many of the institutional reforms of the war years and after can be found already in the inter-war period, or even earlier.[133] This *problematique* concering crisis as ruptures versus long-run changes needs, however, to be studied further and in more depth, the Finnish case with its long history of crisis offering a basis for fruitful research.

The actual 'formative periods' as we define them in this book are longer periods, dependent on transfomations in techno-economic paradigms, although in most cases also overlapping periods of crisis. We can observe three clear 'formative periods' in Finland: the first period was the decades of the late nineteenth century with the growth of the sawmill industry, the growing integration with western markets and the liberalization and legislative reforms supporting this development. The second 'formative period' could be dated to the Second World War and extending until the 1960s, when the growth-oriented policies evolved and collaborative labour market practices took shape, originating in the increasing importance of the pulp and paper industry in the Finnish economy. The third 'formative period' began with the liberalization of capital markets and ended with EU membership radically altering competition policies. This shift was linked to global development, but also to the rapid shift from forest industry to the high-tech sector. However, this 'formative period' is still not complete in all respects.

Another interesting related question is how much of the Finnish crisis and the pressures for transformation have come from internal, and how much from external, pressures. There is a tendency to see crisis as a result of outside shocks and international development and it is a fact that Finland has been highly dependent on external developments. But the severity of the 1990s depression also shows that this crisis in Finland can not be blamed solely on outside factors. External shocks have been combined with internal – and often more long-ranging and deep-rooted – factors and processes, often originating in shifts in the techno-economic paradigm.

We started out talking about a 'Finnish model' in the introduction to this chapter. So what can we say about the existence of such a model? In spite of changing institutional frameworks and market solutions, a belief that the promotion of growth can be achieved through active measures, particularly by promoting investments, has been a prominent feature both in Finnish growth discourse and in actual policies.[134] This model reached its most coherent form during the post-war period up until the 1980s. The 'hard core' consisted at that time of a strongly investment-oriented monetary and fiscal policy in order to promote investments, growth and industrialization, but all other segments of the economy and institutional solutions also supported this growth model. This growth paradigm has, moreover, been fairly lightly based on ideologies, but primarily on pragmatism. Finnish society, with a tradition of coalition governments in the post-war era, not uncommonly including both non-socialist and socialist parties, paved the way for such a pragmatic economic policy.

Although the view of the state's role in this growth-promoting project varied and changed over time, the idea that at least some market co-ordination and some active action from the state are necessary for economic progress generally received support. The state was during the whole period an important actor in paving the way for economic progress by providing a good working environment and carrying out infrastructural investments. Other important features of the Finnish model were the promotion of the interests of big business, particularly the export industry, and the close relationships between the government and big business. Such policies are understandable, due to Finland's status as a late-comer with industrialization heavily dependent on one cyclical export sector and on large-scale firms. The close relation between government and business became even more intimate during the period of Soviet trade.

The Finnish growth model and growth process appear to have followed to a great extent the lines of development of late-comers drawn up by Alexander Gerschenkron.[135] Late-comers, in order to catch-up with the leading countries, have to resort to active growth policies, while the government often takes an active role in industrialization by mobilising capital and taking care of key industries. The significance of state companies in big business stemmed in Finland less from political–ideological perspectives than from a pragmatic growth-oriented perspective.

Furthermore, the growth and industrialization goal has in Finland been strongly connected to nation-building, not an uncommon feature in small, late-comer countries with a fairly long history of dependency on some larger nations.[136] The goal to promote economic growth and industrialization as part of nation-building became particularly pronounced after the declaration of independence. In a way, industrialization and economic progress was for long considered equal to nation-building. This was probably strengthened by the fact that the formtion of Finland as a nation and independence occurred simultaneously with industrial take-off.

Finally, one argument often put forward in Finnish public debate is that both the system and its citizens are inflexible. Labour market practices and labour law make wage-setting and employment conditions rigid, while the welfare system is too extensive, making the citizens uninterested in self-employment and entrepreneurship. However, lately, due to the success of Finland in the globalising world, there are voices claiming that Finland is in fact a fairly flexible society, as shown by the rapid adaptation to global trends. This argument commonly stresses that the flexibility arises from the new regime – i.e. the liberal market economy of today. It is also generally agreed that changes in technological regimes and sector shifts occur more swiftly in liberal market economies than in co-ordinated ones. In a market-based environment, no extensive bargaining processes between sector interests have to be undertaken. This argument is supported by Finland's swift shift to high-tech sectors from the raw materials-based 'forest cluster' that dominated the exports and industrial production of the country until the 1980s.[137]

On the other hand, it can be argued that a certain adaptability is actually one of the inherent strengths of the Finnish economy and was so already early on. Reforms and transformations – also swift ones – although often at times of economic crises, took place fairly smoothly. The rapid structural change that Finland experience during the twentieth century would not have been possible without a profound inherent flexibility at all levels and in all segments of society. Both companies and individuals were during the twentieth century subject to repeated crisis, continuous structural transformations and transforming techno-economic paradigms, bringing about new demands from new market situations, new modes of work and new skill requirements. As a result of the long experience of rapid growth and ongoing structural change, a certain adaptability has become inherent in the Finnish economy and among its actors. Actually, the co-ordinated model also supported this process, as such a system formed a platform to handle change between various groups and interests – and, more importantly, to smooth conflicts and tensions arising from these changes.

QUESTIONS 1. Discuss the role of the State in Finnish capitalism during the various periods. How has it changed? Which divergences and similarities can you find between the periods? How has this influenced the individual companies? (Use also the Finnish case chapters.)

2. Discuss divergences in labour market practices and institutions between Finland and the other Nordic countries? How can these divergences be explained?

Notes

1. The author wishes to thank Professor Kari Lilja, for useful comments on a preliminary draft of the and for interesting discussions on the Finnish economy and business system. I also owe gratitude to Professor Riitta Hjerppe for providing funding for the writing of the Finnish country chapter.
2. The Finnish population decreased during these four years, the total population in 1865 being 1,843,000.
3. Lilja (2006).
4. Pekkarinen and Vartiainen (1993).
5. Aunesluoma and Fellman (2006).
6. For a recent book on the Finnish economic development see Ojala *et al.* (2006): A classic work is Hjerppe (1989).
7. Schybergson (1973–4).
8. Rasila (1982).
9. Ojala and Nummela (2006).
10. Krantz (2001).
11. Hjerppe (1979).
12. Peltonen (2004); Ojala and Nummela (2006).
13. Peltonen (1991).
14. Rasila (1982), p. 15.
15. Schybergson (1964).
16. Hannikainen and Heikkinen (2006); Bergholm (2003).
17. See for example Myllyntaus (1990).
18. *Statistisk årsbok för Finland* (*Statistical Yearbook*), Statistics Finland (1928), Table 20.
19. Myllyntaus (1990).
20. Lilja and Tainio (1996).
21. Garcias-Iglesias and Kilponen (2006).
22. Herranen (2006).
23. Kuusterä (1990).
24. Pipping (1932), pp. 72–4.
25. Kuusterä (1990).
26. On labour market legislation and reactions to the ultra-liberalist policies see, for example, Kettunen (2006).
27. Rasila (1982).
28. Karonen (2004).
29. Kalela (1989), pp. 23–4.
30. Peltonen (2004); Haapala (1995).
31. Pekkarinen and Vartiainen (1993).
32. Ojala and Nummela (2006).
33. Hjerppe and Lamberg (2000); Ojala and Karonen (2006).
34. Krantz (2001).
35. Hjerppe and Jalava (2006).
36. Suvanto (1982).
37. Kuisma (1993).
38. Herranen (2006).
39. Kuusterä (1990).

40. Kuisma (2004).
41. Herranen (2006).
42. Herranen (2006).
43. Kuisma (1993), pp. 403–5.
44. Ahvenainen and Vartiainen (1982).
45. Kallioinen (2006).
46. *Suomen Taloushistoria*, 3, pp. 306–12; Kuisma (1993).
47. Bergholm (2003), p. 17.
48. Hannikainen and Heikkinen (2006).
49. Hannikainen and Heikkinen (2006).
50. Bergholm (2003), p. 24.
51. Bergholm (2003), p. 18.
52. Kettunen (2006).
53. Kettunen (2006).
54. *Statistical Yearbook* (1941), Statistics Finland, Table 20.
55. *Statistical Yearbook* (1961), Statistics Finland, Table 19.
56. Kuisma (1993), pp. 399–402.
57. Ahvenainen and Vartiainen (1982).
58. Ojala and Nummela (2006); Peltonen (2004).
59. Ahvenainen and Vartiainen (1982).
60. Kuisma (1993).
61. Pihkala (1982).
62. Pihkala (1982).
63. Bergholm (2003), pp. 30–5.
64. Auer (1963).
65. Pihkala (1982).
66. Pekkarinen and Vartiainen (1993).
67. Bergholm (2003), pp. 32–3.
68. Pekkarinen and Vartiainen (1993).
69. I am indebted to Professor Kari Lilja for this concept, in which he has outlined the Finnish business system of this period; Lilja (2006).
70. Hjerppe (1989).
71. *Teollisuustilastot* (*Industrial Statistics*), 1960–85.
72. Isacson and Fellman (2007).
73. Pekkarinen (1988).
74. Pekkarinen and Vartiainen (1993).
75. Tarkka (1988); Pekkarinen and Vartiainen (1993).
76. Aunesluoma and Fellman (2006).
77. Kuusterä (1990).
78. Kuisma (2004), pp. 204–5.
79. On the banks 'entrepreneurial activities' in big business, see Hjerppe (1979); Fellman (2000); Kuisma (2004).
80. Kuusterä (1994); Herranen (2006).
81. Tarkka (1988).
82. Kuusterä (1990).
83. Pohjola (1996).
84. Komiteanmietintö A (1952):33.
85. Kilpailutoimikunnan mietintö, 1982: B:52, p. 66 (1982).
86. Hannikainen and Heikkinen (2006).
87. Bergholm (2003), pp. 61–3.
88. Lilja and Tainio (1996).
89. Pekkarinen and Vartiainen (1993), p. 319.
90. Bergholm (2003), pp. 55–64.
91. Kettunen (2006).
92. *Statistical Yearbook*, various years.
93. Hannikainen and Heikkinen (2006).
94. Kettunen (2006).
95. Fellman and Lindholm (1996), pp. 164–5.

96. Fellman and Lindholm (1996), p. 167; *Statistical Yearbook*, various years.
97. Ojala and Nummela (2006).
98. Kettunen (2006).
99. Pekkarinen and Vartiainen (1993).
100. Ojala and Karonen (2006).
101. For excellent analyses of the Finnish crises of the 1990s, see Kalela *et al.* (2001).
102. Honkapohja and Koskela (2001).
103. See Mannio *et al.* (2003).
104. Kettunen (2006); Lehtonen *et al.* (2001).
105. Kettunen (2006).
106. Concept adapted from Lilja (2006).
107. See further Asplund and Maliranta (2006).
108. Asplund and Maliranta (2006).
109. Aunesluoma and Fellman (2003).
110. Hyytinen *et al.* (2003).
111. Ojala and Karonen (2006).
112. Isacson and Fellman (2007).
113. Moen and Lilja (2005).
114. Häikiö (2001).
115. Ojala and Karonen (2006); Moen and Lilja (2005).
116. Moen and Lilja (2005).
117. Kuisma (2004), p. 565.
118. Hyytinen *et al.* (2003).
119. Herranen (2006); Hyytinen and Pajarinen (2003).
120. Hyytinen *et al.* (2003).
121. Asplund and Maliranta (2006).
122. Asplund and Maliranta (2006).
123. *Statistical Yearbook* (2005), Statistics Finland.
124. Bergholm (2003), p. 85.
125. Hannikainen and Heikkinen (2006).
126. Lilja (2006).
127. For a discussion on institutional complementarities, see, e.g., Deeg (2005).
128. Moen and Lilja (2005).
129. Moen and Lilja (2005).
130. Kettunen (2006).
131. Fellman (2007).
132. Kettunen (2006).
133. Pekkarinen and Vartiainen (1993).
134. For a discussion on this in a Nordic context, see Isacson and Fellman (2007).
135. Gerschenkron (1996).
136. Teichova *et al.* (2001).
137. Moen and Lilja (2005).

References

Groningen Growth and Development, Total Economy database, available at http//www.ggdc.net./dseries/totecon.html.
Industrial Statistics, Statistics Finland, various years.
Statistical Yearbook, Statistics Finland, various years.
Ahvenainen, J. and Vartiainen, H. J., *Itsenäisen Suomen talouspolitiikka. In Suomen Taloushistoria 2* (Helsinki: Tammi, 1982), pp. 175–91.
Asplund, R. and Maliranta, M., 'Productivity Growth: The Role of Human Capital and Technology', in Ojala, J., Eloranta, J. and Jalava, J. (eds), *The Road to Prosperity: An Economic History of Finland* (Helsinki: Suomen Kirjallisuuden Seura, 2006) pp. 263–85.
Auer, J., 'Finland's War Reparations Deliveries to the Soviet Union', *Finnish Foreign Policy* (1963) pp. 66–83.

Aunesluoma, J. and Fellman, S. (eds), *Från olika till jämlika: Finlands och Sveriges ekonomier på 1900-talet* (Helsingfors: Svenska Litteratursällskapet, 2006).

Bergholm, T., *The History of SAK* (Helsinki: SAK, 2003).

Deeg, R., 'Path Dependence, Institutional Complementarity, and Change in National Business Systems', in Morgan, G., Whitely, R. and Moen, E. (eds), *Changing Capitalisms? Internationalization, Institutional Change, and Systems of Economic Organization* (Oxford: Oxford University Press, 2005).

Elorant, J., Garcia-Iglesias, C., Ojala, J. and Jalava, J. 'On the Road to Prosperity: An Introduction', in Ojala, J., Eloranta, J. and Jalava, J. (eds), *The Road to Prosperity: An Economic History of Finland* (Helsinki: Suomen Kirjallisuuden Seura, 2006) pp. 15–32.

Fellman, S., 'From Consolidation to Competition – The Development of Modern Management Education in Finland, 1958–2000', *Nordiske Organisasjonsstudier*, 3, (2007).

Fellman, S., *Uppkomsten av en direktörsprofession – Industriledarnas utbildning och karriär i Finland 1900–1975*, Bidrag till kännedom av Finlands natur och folk, 155, Finska (Helsinki: Vetenskaps–Societeten, 2000).

Fellman, S. and Lindholm, C., *Tilläxt, omvandling och kris: Finlands ekonomi efter 1945* (Helsingfors: Söderströms & Co. Förlagsaktiebolag, 1996).

Garcias-Iglesias, C. and Kilponen, J., 'Monetary Aspects of a Changing Economy', in Ojala, J., Eloranta, J. and Jalava, J. (eds), *The Road to Prosperity: An Economic History of Finland* (Helsinki: Suomen Kirjallisuuden Seura, 2006) pp. 187–216.

Gerschenkron, A., *Economic Backwardness in Historical Perspective, 1996* (Cambridge, MA: Harvard University Press, 1996).

Haapala, P., *Kun yhteiskunta hajosi: Suomi 1914–1920* (Helsinki: Valtion painatuskeskus, 1995).

Hannikainen, M. and Heikkinen, S., 'The Labour Market 1850–2000', in Ojala, J., Eloranta, J. and Jalava, J. (eds), *The Road to Prosperity: An Economic History of Finland* (Helsinki: Suomen Kirjallisuuden Seura, 2006) pp. 165–86.

Herranen, R., 'Rahoitussektorin merkitys Suomen kansantaloudelle', in Jalava, J., Eloranta, J. and Ojala, J. (eds), *Muutoksen merkit: Kvantitatiivisia perspektiivejä Suomen taloushistoriaan* (Helsinki: Statistics Finland, 2006) pp. 247–63.

Hjerppe, R., *Suurimmat yritykset Suomen teollisuudessa* (Helsinki: Finska Vetenskaps-Societeten, 1979).

Hjerppe, R., *The Finnish Economy 1860–1975: Growth and Structural Changes, Studies on Finland's Economic Growth XIII* (Helsinki: Bank of Finland, 1989).

Hjerppe R. and Lamberg, J., 'The Change of the Structure and Organization of Foreign Trade in Finland after the Russian Rule', in Teichova, A., Matis, H. and Patek, J. (eds), *Economic Change and the National Question in Twentieth-Century Europe* (Cambridge: Cambridge University Press, 2000).

Hjerppe R. and Jalava, J., 'Economic Growth Structural Change – A Century and a Half of Catching-up', in Ojala, J. *et al.* (eds) *The Road to Prosperity- An Economic History of Finland* (Helsinki: Suomen Kirjallisuuden Seura, 2006).

Häikiö, M., *Nokia Oyj:n historia: osa 3* (Helsinki: Edita, 2001).

Honkapohja, S. and Koskela, Erkki, 'The Economic Crisis in Finlannd in the 1990s', in Kalela J. et al. (eds), *Down from heaven up from the ashes: the Finnish economic crisis of the 1990s in light of economic and social research* (Helsinki: Government's Institute for Economic Research VATT, 2001).

Hyytinen, A. and Pajarinen, M., 'Financial Systems and Venture Capital in Nordic Countries: A Comparative Study', in Hyytinen, A. and Pajarinen, M. (eds), *Financial Systems and Firms' Performance: Theoretical and Empirical Perspectives* (Helsinki: ETLA B: 200, 2003) pp. 19–63.

Hyytinen, A. Kuosa, I. and Takalo, T. 'Investor Protection and FInancial Development in Finland', in Hyytinen A. and Pajarinen, M. (eds), *Financial Systems and Firms' Performance: Theoretical and Empirical Perspectives* (Helsinki: ETLA B: 200, 2003) pp. 65–96.

Isacson, M. and Fellman, S., 'The Nordic and Baltic Countries – Economy and Society in the Highly-Industrial Period', in Anja Kervanto Nevanlinna (ed.), *Industry and Modernism – Companies, Architecture and Identities During the High-Industrial Period* (Helsinki: SKS, 2007).

Kalela, Jorma, *Työttömyys suomalaisessa yhteiskunnassa* (Helsinki: Valtion Painatuskeskus, 1989).

Kalela J. *et al.* (eds), *Down from Heaven Up from the Ashes: The Finnish Economic Crisis of the 1990s in Light of Economic and Social Research* (Helsinki: Government's Institute for Economic Research, VATT, 2001).

Kallioinen, M., *Kesytetty kilpailu: yhteistyö ja kartellisoitumista Suomen puuvillateollisuudessa 1900–1939.* Turun Yliopiston historian laitoksen julk. 65. Turku, 2006.

Karonen, P., *Patruunat ja poliitikot: Yritysjohtajat taloudellisena ja poliittisina toimijoina Suomessa 1600–1920* (Helsinki: SKS, 2004).

Kartellitoimikunnan mietintö, Komiteanmietintö A 1952:33 (Helsinki, 1952).

Kekkonen, U., *Onko maallamme malttia vaurastua?* (Helsinki: Otava, 1952).

Kettunen, P., 'The Power of International Comparison – A Perspective on the Making and Challenging of the Nordic Welfare State', in Christensen, N.F., Petersen, K., Edling, N. and Haave, P. *The Nordic Model of Welfare: A Historical Appraisal* (University of Copenhagen, 2006; Museum Tusculanum Press, 2006a).

Kettunen, P., 'The Tension between the Social and the Economic – a Historical Perspective on the Welfare State', in Ojala, J., Eloranta, J. and Jalava, J. (eds), *The Road to Prosperity: An Economic History of Finland* (Helsinki: Suomen Kirjallisuuden Seura, 2006b) pp. 285–313.

Kilpailutoimikunnan mietintö, 1982: B:52. (Helsinki, 1982).

Krantz, O., 'Industrialization in Three Countries: A Comparative View', in Kryger Larsen, H. (ed.), *Economic Convergence? Industrialization in Denmark, Finland and Sweden* (Helsinki: Finnish Society of Science and Letters, 2001), pp. 23–63.

Kuisma, M., 'Government Actions, Cartels and National Corporations: The Development Strategy of a Small Peripheral Nation during the Period of Crisis and Economic Disintegration in Europe', *Scandinavian Economic History Review*, 41(3), (1993).

Kuisma, M., *Metsäteollisuuden maa. Suomi, metsät ja kansainvälinen järjestelmä 1620–1920* (Helsinki: Suomen Historiallinen Seura, 1993).

Kuisma, M., *Kahlittu raha: Kansallinen kapitalismi. Kansallis-Osake-Pankki 1940–1993* (Helsinki: SKS, 2004).

Kuusterä, A., 'The Finnish Banking System in Broad Outline From the 1860s to the Mid-1980s', in *Handbook on the History of European Banks*, European Association for Banking History EV (Edward Elgar, Cheltenham: 1990), pp. 135–81.

Kuusterä, Antti, 'Taloudellisesta vallasta Suomessa: Historia – käsitteitä – empiria', *TTT Katsaus*, 4, (1990), pp. 31–9.

Lehtonen, H. *et al.*, 'Did the Crisis Change the Welfare State in Finland?', in Kalela J. *et al.* (eds), *Down from Heaven up from the Ashes: The Finnish Economic Crisis of the 1990s in Light of Economic and Social Research* (Helsinki: Government's Institute for Economic Research, VATT, 2001).

Lilja, K., 'Presentation on the Finnish Business Systems', University of Helsinki, 21 Novmeber 2005.

Lilja, K. (ed.), *The National Business System in Finland: Structure, Actors and Change* (Helsinki: Helsinki School of Economics, 2006).

Lilja, K. and Tainio, R., 'The Nature of the Typical Finnish Firm', in Whitley, R. and Kristensen, P. H. (eds), *The Changing European Firm: Limits to Convergence* (London: Routledge, 1996).

Maddison, A. (1991), Groningen Growth and Development, Total Economy database.

Mannio, P., Vaara, E. and Ylä-Anttila, P. (eds), *Our Path Abroad: Exploring Post-War Internationalization of Finnish Corporations.* (Helsinki: Taloustieto Oy, 2003).

Moen, E. and Lilja, K., Change in Co-ordinated Market Economies: The Case of Nokia and Finland (in) Morgan, Glenn, Whitely, Richard and Moen, Eli (eds), *Changing Capitalisms? Internationalization, Institutional Change, and Systems of Economic Organization* (Oxford: Oxford University Press, 2005).

Murto, R. and Fellman, S., 'Miksi tarvitsemme valtionyhtiöitä?,' Manuscript, 2007.

Myllyntaus, T., *Education in the Making of Modern Finland*, ETLA Discussion Papers, 312 (1990).

Ojala, J., Eloranta, J. and Jalava, J. (eds), *The Road to Prosperity: An Economic History of Finland* (Helsinki: Suomen Kirjallisuuden Seura, 2006).

Ojala, J. and Karonen, P., 'Business: Rooted in Social Capital over the Centuries', in Ojala, J., Eloranta, J. and Jalava, J. (eds), The Road to Prosperity: An Economic History of Finland (Helsinki: Suomen Kirjallisuuden Seura, 2006) pp. 93–126.

Ojala, J. and Nummela, I., 'Feeding Economic Growth: Agriculture', in Ojala, J., Eloranta, J. and Jalava, J. (eds), The Road to Prosperity: An Economic History of Finland (Helsinki: Suomen Kirjallisuuden Seura, 2006) pp. 65–92.

Pekkarinen, J., Keynesianism and the Scandinavian Models for Economic Policy', in Hall, P. A. (ed.) The Political Power of Economic Ideas. Keynesianism Across Nations (Princeton: Princeton University Press, 1988).

Pekkarinen, J. and Vartiainen, J., Suomen Talouspolitiikan pitkä linja (Helsinki: WSOY, 1993).

Peltonen M., 'Alkoholi ja uusi maalaisjulkisuus: Alkoholikysymyksen syntyminen Suomessa kotipolton kiellon jälkeen', Alkoholipolitiikka, 55 (1991).

Peltonen, M. (ed.), Suomen Maatalouden Historia II: Kasvun ja kriisien aika 1870-luvulta – 1950-luvulle (Helsinki: SKS, 2004).

Pipping, H. E., Jean Cronstedt 1832–1932 (Helsingfors: Nordistia Föreningsbanken 1932).

Pihkala, E., 'Sotatalous', Suomen Taloushistoria 2 (Helsinki: Tammi 1982).

Pohjola, M., Tehoton pääoma: Uusi näkökulma talouteemme (Porvoo: WSOY, 1996).

Rasila, V., 'Liberalismin aika', Suomen Taloushistoria 2 (Helsinki, 1982), pp. 13–21.

Schybergson, P., Aktiebolagsformens genombrott i Finland: utvecklingen före 1895 års lag (Helsingfors: Finska Vetenskaps-Societeten, 1964).

Schybergson, P., Hantverk och Fabriker: Konsumtionsvaruindustrin i Finland 1815–1870, I–III (Helsingfors: Finska Vetenskaps-Societeten, 1973–74).

Suomen Taloushistoria 3 (Helsinki, 1982).

Suvanto, A., Raha-ja luottomarkkinat. In Suomen Taloushistoria 2 (Helsinki: Tammi, 1982), pp. 294–307.

Tarkka, J., 'Kahlitun rahan aika,' in Honkapohja, S. and Suvanto, A. (eds), Raha, inflaatio, talouspolitiikka (Helsinki: Valtion Painatuskeskus, 1988).

Teichova, A., Matis, H. and Patek, J. (eds), Economic Change and the National Question in Twentieth-Century Europe (Cambridge: Cambridge University , 2001).

appendix: the transformation of the Finnish business system

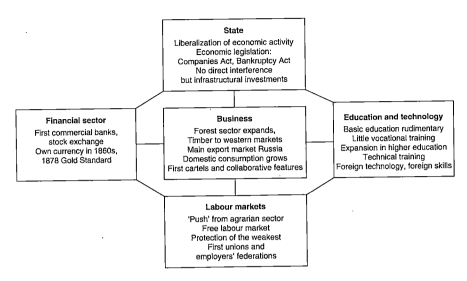

Figure 5A.1   *Finnish capitalism, 1850–1918: a liberal market economy*

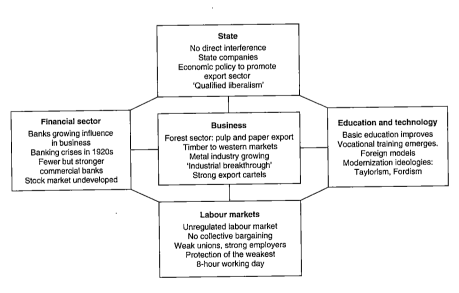

Figure 5A.2   *Finnish capitalism, 1919–39: an era of 'qualified liberalism'*

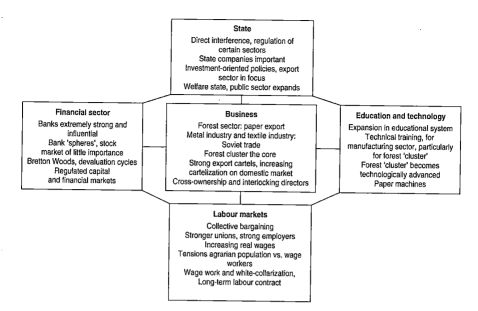

Figure 5A.3   *Finnish capitalism, 1945–81: a highly co-ordinated market economy*

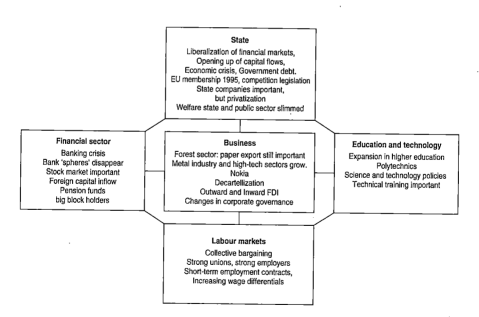

Figure 5A.4   *Finnish capitalism, 1982–2005: an inward and outward open, collaborative market economy*

WELFARE CAPITALISM: THE SWEDISH ECONOMY 1850–2005 • ENTREPRENEURSHIP AND OWNERSHIP: THE
TERM VIABILITY OF THE SWEDISH BONNIER AND WALLENBERG FAMILY BUSINESS GROUPS • FROM
STATE OWNERSHIP TO MULTINATIONAL CORPORATION: THE PATH OF ENSO-GUTZEIT TO STORA-ENSO • JH FINNISH
CAPITALISM, 1850S–2015 • FROM STATE OWNERSHIP TO MULTINATIONAL CORPORATION: THE PATH OF
ENSO-GUTZEIT TO STORA-ENSO • STRATEGIC
PATHS OF NOKIA AND TAMPELLA IN THE LIBERALIZING FINNISH ECONOMY AFTER THE SECOND WORLD
WAR • CO-OPERATIVE LIBERALISM: DENMARK FROM 1857 TO 2007 • ARLA: FROM DECENTRALIZED INDUSTRY
TO MULTINATIONAL ENTERPRISE • CARLSBERG AND THE SELF-REGULATION OF THE DANISH BEER MARKET
• NORWAY: A RESOURCE-BASED AND DEMOCRATIC CAPITALISM • CONSTRUCTIVE POWER
• FINANCE AND THE DEVELOPMENT OF NORWEGIAN CAPITALISM – THE CASE OF CHRISTIANIA BANK

⑥ from state ownership to MNC: the path of Enso-Gutzeit to Stora-Enso[1]

Jari Ojala, Juha-Antti Lamberg and Anders Melander

State ownership is an important part of Nordic business history. In 2007, for
example, the Finnish state had a considerable stake in five out of the ten largest
Finnish firms. In Denmark there has been a rising trend in the state ownership
from the 1970s to the third millennium, while in both Norway and Sweden
the state has played an important role as an owner of industries.[2] The share of
state ownership increased during the post-war period, when industries grew in
the Nordic countries. State intervention was seen as necessary due to the lack
of private capital and in order to secure national control of natural resources.
Furthermore, there was a clear ideological rationale for state ownership, as in
the Nordic welfare model the state was (and still is) an important player in
the markets. The state was seen as a safeguard for societal responsibility. This
was particularly apparent in the labour market, as the motive for state-owned
companies was not only to create profits but also to give employment. State
ownership created both possibilities and challenges for companies. On the
whole, the state is usually an active owner, with a long-term commitment,
so state ownership has made possible certain structural changes that would
have been impossible in privately owned companies. In Finland, Sweden and
Norway, for example, the state played an important role in restructuring the
shipbuilding industries during the 1970s and 1980s. On the other hand, state
ownership can also create challenges, as state-owned companies are generally
expected to follow political rather than private objectives.

In this chapter we will analyse a Finnish forestry industry company Enso
(-Gutzeit), with a special attention to state ownership. In 1998, a merger
between Swedish Stora and Finnish Enso-Gutzeit created the world's second
largest forestry company, Stora-Enso. The merger was among the largest in
Nordic history, and the companies it included were among the most notable

ones in their home countries. Stora, with roots in the thirteenth century, was among the flagship companies of Wallenberg group. Enso-Gutzeit was founded in 1872 with Norwegian capital, 'nationalized' in 1918 and continued as a state-owned firm up to the end of the millennium. Even after the merger the Finnish state had an important share in Stora-Enso. Therefore, Stora-Enso is a combination of Finnish state ownership, Norwegian nineteenth century FDI and Swedish Wallenbergian business systems.

Enso is also a typical case of early industrialization in the Nordic countries, namely, a company advancing from Nordic comparative advantages in terms of natural resources (timber) and cheap labour. Similarly, in Sweden and in Norway forest industries gained an important position in the industrial structure. In Finland the forest industry was the dominating sector in big business up to the 1980s, when first the metal industry and then electronic engineering started to challenge its position.

From the business system point of view, we argue that (Stora-) Enso can be seen as a company that has evolved from resource based 'catch-up' to technology- and innovation-driven growth, and from the 1980s onwards the growth has been created mostly through M&As. Managerial failures have been especially dramatic in the case of Enso (-Gutzeit) in several phases of its history – most notably during the 1970s, when state ownership caused challenges to the company.[3]

Today, Stora-Enso is not merely a Finnish company, since not only the main markets of the company are abroad but also large part of production takes place outside the home country. The purchase of Consolidated Paper in 2000 strengthened the company's role as a global player in forest industries. Also the ownership structure of the company is today more global; though the headquarters of the company is still in Helsinki, the share of foreign ownership in 1999 was already 70 per cent.[4]

This chapter falls into five parts. First, we shall outline the formative phases of Enso, then we will briefly analyse the ownership structure of the company over time. The growth of the company will then be described, followed by a strategy analysis and some concluding remarks.

Formative eras of Enso-Gutzeit

There are four distinctive formative eras in the development of Enso-Gutzeit. The first occurred in the 1860s and 1870s as a consequence of liberalization of the Finnish economy and the rise in international demand for forest industry products (sawn timber, pulp and paper). These features led to the inflow of investments to the country. Norwegians were especially eager to invest to Finland – Gutzeit (later known as Enso-Gutzeit) was among the companies established with Norwegian capital. This first era was also when industrial capitalism emerged in Finland.

The second can be traced to the first years of Finnish independence at the beginning of the 1920s, when the Finnish state took a major stake in Gutzeit after the withdrawal of the Norwegians. At the same time, a number of businesses were also otherwise restructured in Finland as the vital Russian markets were lost and substitute markets were sought in western Europe. Gutzeit, however, was not in as much trouble as many other firms, as western Europe was already a major market for the products of its sawmills. During this period, financial institutions also gained a more important role in Finland. That was, however, not the case with Gutzeit. As a number of other companies were driven under the umbrellas of different financial spheres, the state-owned companies slowly created their own 'sphere', in which Enso-Gutzeit was among the most influential industrial companies up to the late 1980s.

The third formative era occurred after the Second World War when the company suffered as a number of its industrial units (including the headquarters of the company) and a notable amount of land area and important energy supplies were lost to the Soviet Union. Again, the external shock forced the company to restructure.

The fourth, and so far the last, formative era started in the 1980s and continued up to the first years of the third millennium when global capitalism emerged. This time, the changes that took place were a consequence of a combination of internal and external pressures. The abolition of state ownership (at least partly) took place; the consolidation of the Finnish forest industry occurred in the 1980s and 1990s and continued with international rationalization. This development led to the merger between Finnish Enso and Swedish Stora in 1998.[']

Due to the adequate raw material resources, forest industries have long been among the most important lines of business in Finland. Timber remained as the most important export item from the 1830s up to the 1980s. Gutzeit was an example of the new companies that were created during the expansion period of Finnish sawmilling in the 1870s. The Norwegian Hans Gutzeit founded the company and opened its first sawmill in Kotka in

Table 6.1 **Percentage share of forest industry in the value of industrial exports: Finland, 1875–1999**

Year	Combined forest industry	Paper industry
1875	64	9
1890	68	15
1920	87	37
1950	69	42
1980	45	30
1999	28	23

Sources: Jääskeläinen (2001), p. 34; Hjerppe (1988); Statistics Finland.

1872. In the background was the technological shift from water-powered to steam-powered sawmills that occurred in Finland and Norway in the 1860s due to legislative changes, and in Sweden a couple of decades earlier. These legislative changes allowed owners to establish steam-powered mills as they had been forbidden earlier for fear of losing forest resources when using this efficient technology. Around the same time the invention of making paper from conifer trees became familiar and spread rapidly to the Nordic countries. A number of paper-producing firms started to operate in Finland and in Sweden during the latter part of the nineteenth century. Stora, for example, opened its first paper factory in 1894 and Gutzeit started in 1909 after it bought the Pankakoski factory. In Finland, pulp production expanded, and for a short period in the mid-twentieth century it was the most important export item in terms of value of sales. By the turn of the 1970s, however, pulp had been replaced by paper as the most important export product and paper remained in this position up to the 1990s. Enso's path follows the general trend of the development of Finnish forest industry: the start and early growth within sawmilling, then integration forwards in the production chain to pulp production, and lastly the concentration on paper production.

As Table 6.1 clearly shows, the forestry industry played a significant role in Finnish exports from the mid-nineteenth century up to the 1980s. At the turn of the millennium, the forest industry was still among the most important lines of businesses in both its share of export and as an employer. The forest industry and forestry sector as whole have also been key issues in domestic (economic) policies. Without any exaggeration one can demonstrate a co-evolutionary development of the forestry sector and society in Finland. These co-evolutionary paths can also explain the development of individual firms – as, in this particular case, the development of Enso.

The owner

The concept of 'co-evolution' is used to describe the long-term development of industries in different societies. In order to understand the 'paths' – either of success or of failure – of certain industries in certain countries, the role played by society, and the governmental role in particular, have to be taken into the analysis. Firms and industries are related to the society where they emerge and develop and, in turn, the society is dependent on the evolution of the industries and other branches of the economy.[5] As a state-owned company from 1918, (Enso)-Gutzeit is a good example by which to study business and government relations, as there was a direct collaborative link between the government and the company.

The founder of the company was a Norwegian businessman, Hans Gutzeit. His father, Wilhelm Gutzeit, operated in Norway within the timber trade in the mid-nineteenth century and founded a company called Wilh. Gutzeit & Co., which started to produce sawn timber with a steam-powered sawmill in 1860 in Glemmen, Norway. In Finland and Norway steam-powered sawmills were allowed only from the 1850s and 1860s, thus this mill was among the first in Norway using the modern technology. Hans Gutzeit inherited the businesses in the late 1860s. He became interested in Finland, where raw material resources were available. While Finland provided the raw materials, Gutzeit brought his business networks and export channels. In 1873, the company's first sawmill, at the time the largest in the country, was installed in Kotka and W. Gutzeit & Comp. was founded a year earlier. The first years of the company were not successful: the long depression from the mid-1870s onwards harmed the markets for sawn timber and the price of the raw material was not as low as Gutzeit had hoped for. Hans Gutzeit and the other Norwegians he persuaded to join the enterprise lost substantial amounts of money, and the company had gone through a number of changes in ownership even before the First World War.[6]

Finnish independence, followed by the short but violent civil war; thus, together with legislative changes in Finland (including a land acquisition Act of 1915 that prohibited companies to acquire forest land) scared the Norwegian owners of the company. The political turbulence together with uncertain economic development led to a situation in which the Norwegians decided to gave up their ownership in Gutzeit. This was not only the case with Gutzeit; also other Finnish companies previously owned by the Norwegians were sold to Finns, as with the Salvesen and Halla companies. As major national interests were involved, most notably in terms of the large forest areas the company owned, the Finnish state became interested in buying the shares in the company. By the end of 1918 the Finnish state had bought the company. At the same time it had also bought a company called Tornator from its Finnish owner – again, because of the large forest areas this company owned. Later in the 1930s Tornator was merged with Enso-Gutzeit.[7]

The reason why Gutzeit became a state-owned company was, thus, mostly related to political and economical turbulence in 1918 and to national interest in domestic forest resources. From the beginning, state ownership in an industry that also had private competitors was hard to justify – especially at a time when socialism was doomed in the aftermath of the Civil War. The initial idea was that the state would only own a part of the company (around 61 per cent), but due to the problems the company suffered in the 1920s the state was forced to increase its ownership share (to 87 per cent).[8] As whole, Enso-Gutzeit was never totally state-owned (or 'socialized'), as its shares were also available on the stock exchange.

In the inter-war period, Gutzeit functioned mainly according to the same conditions as other wood-refiners. The biggest difference was the possibility of government authorities and politicians participating in the management through the administrative board. Finnish historian Markku Kuisma (1993) has argued that the government-owned companies were a way to the top in economic life for Finnish-speaking top officials. As an example, Kuisma uses A.K. Cajander, who was the chairman of Enso-Gutzeit's administrative board in 1931–43. Representing Finland's small social elite, Cajander was also a politician and several times the Prime Minister of Finland during the 1920s and 1930s. Since the administrative board in the inter-war period consisted also of presidents P. E. Svinhufvud, Lauri Relander and Kyösti Kallio, as well as leading social democrat politician Väinö Tanner, it is no wonder that the administrative board became the organ that decided the company's strategy.[9]

Later in the twentieth century the Finnish state started to produce a number of intermediate products, such as chemicals and energy, that were needed in industries – thus, the state provided public goods for the companies.[10] But as a producer of similar products as their private competitors Enso-Gutzeit and a couple of other state-owned companies, most notably Valmet, were different cases. The competitors feared (and sometimes even accused these companies of using) their special position and direct contacts to state authorities to gain unfair profits.[11] For the government, the ownership of Enso-Gutzeit was a high-rank issue; for example, the decision on the CEO of the company was repeatedly dealt with at the highest political level.[12]

State ownership created certain peculiarities to the activities of Enso-Gutzeit. Though the state can be seen as a shareholder like any other, it was also able to make other demands on its companies. In the 1970s, government ownership and the massive balance sheet of Enso-Gutzeit provided an ample reason for referring to the government-owned company syndrome, where the owners have other interests to look after besides the success or failure of the company. This makes it difficult to make unpleasant decisions. These other interests can even prevent the management from taking actions which might have a positive influence on the functioning of the company. Social responsibility, for example, was pronounced in the activities of the state-owned firms.

It is a typical feature of the government-owned company that profitability and other basic functions of the company are defined imprecisely. Thus, the owner accepts a low level of performance as a starting point.[13] However, when comparing Enso-Gutzeit to other Finnish forest industry companies at the time, the results were not necessarily all bad. On the contrary, almost all forest industry companies were heavily indebted, provided poor returns on investment and had a balance sheet overburdened with landed property that reduced capital turnover.[14]

The state's special position as an owner can be seen in the way the company has been presented with profitability demands that deviate from shareholder thinking. For example, in the 1970s the company was expected to bring in a reasonable return as well as function in a socially responsible fashion. Ahvenainen (1992b) perceives that the fundamental function of Enso-Gutzeit was in fact not the maximization of dividends, but rather the development of the company in such a way that it would not become a financial burden on the state. Furthermore, he concludes, in the 1970s the company was, in a questionable sense, a tool for politics, and during this period nothing of strategic importance was accomplished.

According to Ahvenainen (1992b) the company became politicized in the 1970s when Olavi J. Mattila was nominated as the CEO. His nomination was more or less based on political grounds; as a personal friend of president Urho Kekkonen, Mattila was seen as someone who would emphasize the role of the state-owned firms and trade to Soviet Union.[15] The government-owned company syndrome, in which the additional interests of the owners hamper the management of a company, is almost an exact description of the administrative situation in Enso-Gutzeit in 1972–83, when Olavi J. Mattila was, as a representative of the state, the company's chairman of the board of directors.[16]

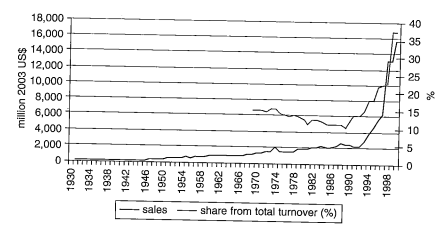

Figure 6.1 *Turnover of (Stora-) Enso (-Gutzeit), 1930–2000 (left axis) and its share of total turnover of twenty-three Finnish forest industry companies, 1969–2000 (right axis, %)*

Note: The twenty-three companies include: UPM (Yhtyneet Paperitehtaat), Kymmene, Metsäliitto, Rosenlew, Serlachius, Myllykoski, Schauman, Nokia, Ahlström, Rauma-Repola, Tampella, Oulu, Stockfors, Sunila, Tervakoski, Veitsiluoto, Wärtsilä, Haarla, Joutseno, Kyrö, Lohja and Metsä-Botnia. The data is not available accurately from all companies from all years; thus, the figure is not exact.

Sources: Annual reports; Ahvenainen (1992a); Lamberg (2006) and the database compiled by the authors.

The growth

In 1974, Enso-Gutzeit was the 32nd largest paper producer in the world by turnover. In 1999, Stora-Enso was the second largest in the world, after International Paper, which has been the industry leader from the beginning of the twentieth century. By 2005, Stora-Enso had over 45,000 employees in more than forty countries on five continents and company shares were listed in Helsinki, Stockholm and New York.

The company expanded rapidly after its creation in 1873: while in the 1870s Gutzeit produced around 30,000 m³ of sawn timber a year, the amount by 1901 was already over 300,000 m³. In the years 1924–38, sales of the company almost tripled. After the Second World War the growth accelerated: in 1948–61 the company's sales grew by 158 per cent, in 1962–81 by 107 per cent and in 1982–2000 by almost 800 per cent. This growth trend was similar to other Finnish forest industry companies, with M&As the common cause for growth in the last period.[17] (Figure 6.1)

The Second World War hit Enso hard. A number of the production units were situated in the Karelia region that was annexed to the Soviet Union after the war – including Enso, the village that gave its name to the whole company and where the headquarters of the company were situated before the war. Enso-Gutzeit lost 30 per cent of its forests and 60 per cent of its production

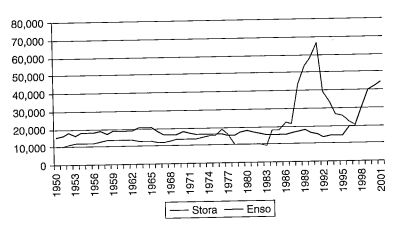

Figure 6.2 **The labour force in Stora and Enso, 1950–2001**
Sources: Annual reports.

capacity, although reconstruction after the war was rapid and successful. In 1965 Enso-Gutzeit was still the largest forest industry company in Finland, according to balance sheet totals, followed by Yhtyneet Paperitehtaat (later UPM), Tampella, Ahlström and Kymi (Kymmene)(Figure 6.2).[18]

Enso's share of the total turnover of twelve Finnish forest industry companies was around 10–15 per cent from the beginning of the 1970s (from which we have accurate data) up to the early 1990s, when the company's share rose first to 20 per cent and thereafter over 30 per cent (Figure 6.1). The rapid growth of Enso to become international player in three decades was achieved mainly through the M&As during the last decades of the twentieth century. However, organic growth, namely, building up new production facilities, also played a significant role. Furthermore, related and unrelated diversification during the first decades after the Second World War, and concentration on core competencies (mainly paper production) from the 1980s onwards played an important role. The internationalization of production started during the 1960s, but it was not until the 1980s and 1990s that production facilities outside Finland became really important for the company – though, at the same time, one should keep in mind that for Enso's markets, as for other forestry companies, have always been mainly abroad. During the inter-war period, Enso-Gutzeit was the biggest sawmilling company, and the largest company in Finland.

Though Enso has grown in terms of turnover and production, the number of employees remained moderate up to the beginning of the 1990s, when merging operations also increased the number of personnel. The same occurred also in Stora, whose labour force is also presented in Figure 6.2 for a comparative perspective. The rapid increase in the number of Stora's employ-ees in the late 1980s and early 1990s can be explained by acquisitions.[19] While Enso's sales and production rose, the size of the labour force remained moderate, illustrating a significant increase in productivity. However, though labour productivity increased, the same cannot be said for capital productiv-ity. As in other Finnish forest industry companies during the post-war era, investments reduced profits and diminished the return on investment. The capital turnover in months[20] in the case of Enso-Gutzeit during the 1970s and 1980s was around 20 months, which is poor compared to a capital turnover of less than half a year in efficient companies. The reason for the low capital turnover was not only investments, but also the company's expensive produc-tion facilities and large forest areas. In response to the low capital turnover, Stora-Enso and other Finnish forest industry companies sold large areas of properties during recent years. The return on investment was in Enso's case around 5–10 per cent throughout the 1970s, 1980s and 1990s.[21]

The strategy: organic growth, vertical integration and the rise and fall of diversification

The growth strategies of Enso-Gutzeit followed general trends within the Finnish and even the global forest industry. As in other Nordic forest industry companies, organic growth through building up new production facilities was the most important way to achieve growth up to the 1980s. The nineteenth-century and early twentieth-century growth was mainly achieved through building up new capacity. Right after the Second World War the energy question was acute, as important hydro-power plants were lost when parts of eastern Finland were ceded to the Soviet Union. The company had emerged as an important pulp producer during the inter-war period and this line of business was emphasized further after the Second World War as the company invested in pulp production. The strategy to integrate production forwards continued as the company invested also in paper and board production: in 1946–53 alone Enso-Gutzeit ordered five paper machines.[22] In fact, Enso-Gutzeit together with Yhtyneet Paperitehtaat (UPM) was among the few Finnish forest industry companies at the turn of the 1950s that actually made large investments in production facilities.[23]

As can be seen from the Figure 6.3, Enso-Gutzeit's investments followed the general trends within the Finnish forest industry, with the exception of the last peaks in the 1980s and 1990s. Furthermore, the investments followed a 'sprints and pauses' strategy – namely, after certain peak years in investments

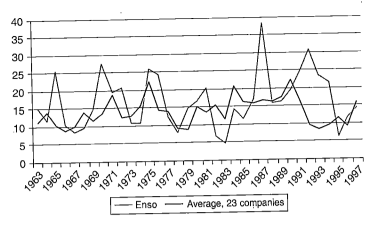

Figure 6.3 *Investments from turnover (per cent), Enso-Gutzeit and a sample of twenty-three Finnish companies (averages), 1963–97*
Note: The twenty-three companies include, besides Enso-Gutzeit, also UPM (Yhtyneet Paperitehtaat), Kymmene, Metsäliitto, Rosenlew, Serlachius, Myllykoski, Schauman, Nokia, Ahlström, Rauma-Repola, Tampella, Oulu, Stockfors, Sunila, Tervakoski, Veitsiluoto, Wärtsilä, Haarla, Joutseno, Kyrö, Lohja and Metsä-Botnia.
Sources: Annual reports and database compiled by the authors.

a number of years with a more modest amount of investment followed.[24] The peak in 1987 is related to purchase of Ahlström's Varkaus units in the previous year, whereas the peak in 1992 is related to building a new pulp factory.

Enso-Gutzeit was in the 1980s a diversified conglomerate, with activities in several industrial branches. Already before the Second World War Enso-Gutzeit had diversified into various forestry-related businesses (besides timber, pulp and board), such as bobbins, but also into the chemical industry and energy production. Before the war the company had also started metal industries, first as a machine shop but by the end of the 1930s also to produce machinery for pulp plants. Shipping had started in the nineteenth century, mainly to float timber through lake routes to factories. In the mid-twentieth century the company owned nine freight ships to carry exports, and later also passenger ships.[25]

Diversification occurred partly accidentally, partly intentionally. Vertical integration backwards in the production chain and thereafter forwards was a characteristic of the first decades of the company's history. At the turn of the twentieth century, among major achievements was active land acquisition – just before the Land Acquisition Law (1915) prohibited this for industrial companies. By the year 1915 Gutzeit was the largest private landowner in the country, with 434,000 ha of forest land. By that time the company had

Photograph 6.1 *During the inter-war period, the Finnish paper industry was already based on large-scale industry, which can be seen from this picture, taken in 1933, of paper machine no. 5 (PM V) in Mänttä paper mill. Mänttä was the main local company of the paper industry firm G. A. Serlachius Ab. This family-owned company was particularly renowned for its tissue papers and its production of cooking and baking paper, so-called greaseproof. Although the family sold out in 1986, the SERLA brand is still famous both on the Finnish market and abroad.*
Source: The Central Archives for Finnish Business Records (Elka), Mikkeli, Finland.

four large sawmills in Kotka and subsidiaries in Pankakoski (from 1909) and Enso (from 1911). Furthermore, the company had also diversified to wood pulp and board production – though in 1913 still almost 70 per cent of sales came from sawmills. Before the First World War Gutzeit was the second largest sawmilling company in Finland, after Ahlström.[26] By the 1920s the company was already the largest manufacturer of sawn timber in Finland. During the 1930s the centre of gravity of the company was, however, changing. The majority of the investments were allocated to wood and chemical pulp and even the small paper- and board-producing units received almost as much investment as the sawmills. By the end of the 1930s, Enso-Gutzeit was the largest producer of pulp in Finland, the second largest in Scandinavia and the third largest in Europe.[27]

The integration forwards within the production chain – namely, from sawmills to pulp production – was originally related to the question of adequate use of sawing waste. In the early 1920s, the sawmills produced around 40 per cent of the company's sales, but this figure had diminished to around

25–30 per cent by the end of the 1930s. At the same time the share of pulp (sulphite and sulphate) rose from 33 per cent to 51 per cent. The share of wood pulp and boards fell somewhat (from around 16 to 11 per cent) but there was no notable change in the share of paper production, which was only around 2–6 per cent of sales during the inter-war period.

During the first decades after the Second World War integration forwards in the production chain continued and the company emerged as primarily a board but also a paper producer. In 1950 pulp produced 39 per cent of sales, and sawn goods 24 per cent. The shares in 1962 were 8 per cent for pulp and 7 per cent for sawn goods. At the same time the share of sales of board production rose from 7 to 44 per cent and different paper grades from 4 to 13 per cent. During the 1960s the integration forwards was continued as paper-based packaging became a larger part of the company's portfolio; by 1972 it accounted for 20 per cent of sales.[28] It was not, however, until the 1980s when paper production took over as the most important line of production.

The share of unrelated diversification of sales was still rather insignificant after the Second World War, accounting for only a tiny fraction of sales. However, by the 1970s around 15 per cent of all the sales of the company were created within the branches of unrelated diversification, mainly from the engineering works and shipping. Diversification was supported in strategic planning and by the outside consultants and experts used by Enso at the time.

Like a number of other Finnish forest industry firms, Enso-Gutzeit also turned round its diversification strategy during the 1980s. Over a short period the company sold most of its ships, a large proportion of its power production capacity and even tens of thousands of hectares of forests. The company concentrated on core competencies, increased the level of refinement of wood-based resources (for example, from pulp to paper production, and in paper production to high-value added products) and sold units that were not part of these activities. The acquisition of Ahlström's Varkaus units in 1986 was a major step in Enso's concentration on paper production – as part of the same deal, Enso sold its metal industries to Ahlström. After the acquisition of Ahlström's facilities, paper production made up 70 per cent of the company's sales and the share of engineering works diminished.[29] Enso gave up shipping in the same year, while board and construction companies, together with several power plants, were sold in the early 1990s. The share of the shipping industry in the company's sales had already fallen: in the early 1970s shipping produced around 11 per cent of sales; the share was only 5 per cent a decade later.[30]

Photograph 6.2 **The resource-based economic development of Finland in a nut-shell, or rather in a wood truck. Timber is here transported from the forests to the Enso mills in the 1950s.**
Source: The Central Archives for Finnish Business Records (Elka), Mikkeli, Finland.

Mergers, acquisitions and internationalization

The majority of the twentieth-century growth of Enso was achieved during the 1980s and 1990s, as a consequence of M&As. Besides the acquisition of the Varkaus forest industry units from Ahlström, Enso also acquired Tampella's forestry industries from the Bank of Finland in 1993.[31] In 1995 Enso-Gutzeit and another state-owned forest industry company, Veitsiluoto, were merged to create a company that now bore only the name Enso.

Acquisitions were familiar in the case of Enso-Gutzeit: in 1986 it had bought the Tervakoski paper company from the Bank of Finland, while in 1931 another state-owned sawmill, Tornator, was merged with Enso-Gutzeit. The subsidiary companies Enso and Pankakoski were merged with Gutzeit during the 1920s – the name Enso-Gutzeit was used after these mergers in 1927. The common characteristics of all these deals (besides Ahlström) was that they all occurred within state ownership – thus, the state reorganized its ownership in various industrial enterprises leaving Enso as the 'winner'.

Internationalization of production was in fact a part of the consolidation process. There had, however, been more or less successful attempts to internationalise production already. For Enso-Gutzeit internationalization started in the mid-1960s when the company bought a share of a small Dutch paper-producing firm. The driving force in the deal was to get into the common European markets. Enso-Gutzeit built new machinery for the Dutch company but it never turned out to be a profitable investment and the plant was sold in 1971.[32]

According to Ahvenainen (2006), the CEO of the company at the time, Pentti Halle, put forward in the 1960s a proposal to expand production to North America, more precisely to Louisiana in the US and to British Columbia in Canada. There were a number of reasons to begin internationalization during the 1960s. First, the profitability of certain products produced in Finland was at the time weak – especially sackpaper and craftliner. This was related to the rising production costs in Finland, mainly due to the increased price of timber. Therefore, the 'virgin' Canadian forests were seen as an opportunity. Secondly, the markets in North America were expanding and Finnish firms had had only limited success in exporting products directly to the US. Thus, own production facilities in the US were seen as necessary to conquer these markets – as has been argued several times afterwards as well. Thirdly, in order to invest abroad a wide consortium, including a number of Finnish forest industry companies, was created. This was seen as an opportunity to strengthen industry links, especially between privately owned and state-owned companies. Fourthly, at the time there was a growing fear that North American companies would conquer European markets in the near future. Thus, internationalization can be seen as kind of advanced counter-attack. Fifthly, as a number of forestry companies also produced machinery for these industries, internationalization was also seen as an opportunity to achieve new markets for these products.[33]

The first case of internationalization in Louisiana, US, was a joint venture with two Finnish companies, Enso and Tampella, and US-based Bodcaw Co. The latter company sought Finnish partners to expand its sawmilling production to pulp and paper. The company, 'Pineville Kraft Corporation', started to produce board in 1968. The company was never as successful as had been hoped, and it was sold in 1973 to a subsidiary of International Paper.[34] The next step in internationalization was even worse, namely, the joint effort of four Finnish companies to build a new pulp and paper plant in Kitimati in British Columbia, Canada. In Finnish economic history this project is often viewed as an example of miscalculation and overly optimistic expectations. This project started in the mid-1960s with the combined forces of Enso-Gutzeit, Kymmene, Myllykoski and Tampella, together with a small share owned by Canadian investors. Enso-Gutzeit had the leading role in the project, and a new company 'Eurocan Pulp & Paper Co. Ltd' was founded. In this case, the presumed raw material resources were the major reason for the Finnish companies' interest. The ownership structure of the company altered over time so that finally Enso-Gutzeit was the only Finnish partner in the company. A number of issues went wrong right from the beginning; above all, the initial calculations on raw material prices and building costs proved to be too optimistic. Production in the company started in 1971, but it was not until the turn of the 1980s that it produced a profit for the owners. Actually, in twenty-one years (1971–92), when Enso was the major shareholder of the Eurocan company, only seven years were profitable.[35]

The Eurocan project is also an example how internationalization was carried out at the turn of the 1970s. The required capital was not available from Finnish or Canadian sources; thus, the majority of capital was acquired from US capital markets. Furthermore, a number of issues intervened in the project, including the previously mentioned co-operation between the state and privately owned companies, but also the need to get references for the domestic metal industries from abroad. Tampella produced the paper machinery for the company, whereas Enso-Gutzeit's engineering works in Savonlinna provided pulp machinery.[36]

The domestic consolidation of the 1980s and 1990s was soon followed with international moves as Stora and Enso were merged in 1998 and a couple of years later US-based Consolidated Paper was acquired by Stora-Enso.

Conclusions

The path of Enso-Gutzeit followed the general trends not only of Finnish but also of the global forestry industry during the twentieth century. As did the other Finnish forestry companies, Enso sought also growth first through large-scale investments in new production and technology and thereafter through consolidation. Diversification into related and unrelated lines of businesses was also a typical feature in Finnish business during the post-war era, as was the rapid dissolution of diversification in the 1980s and 1990s. The only notable exception in comparison to other Finnish forest industry firms was Enso's expansion to shipping business during the 1940s and 1950s.

Enso is, however, also different in other ways. Most notably its ownership structure has been different in comparison with other Finnish forestry companies throughout its history, starting with the Norwegian investments in the 1870s, the state ownership from the early years of independence to the end of this century and, lastly, the Nordic merger and globalization of ownership structure. The state-owned company syndrome described in the analysis above was especially archetypical for Enso in the 1970s. State ownership was necessary to begin with to secure vital natural resources, as the forest ownership of the company was important at the beginning of the twentieth century. However, during the latter part of the twentieth century social responsibility was often emphasized.

Enso's formative phases are closely related to the changes in Finnish business systems and capitalistic models; the last formative period, global capitalism, was still in its emergent phase at the beginning of this century. Though the company was already by then international, it was hardly yet global. Globalization in the forestry industry as whole has been a rather slow process as the companies have mainly operated in rather constrained geographical domains.

QUESTIONS
1. The state emerged as important owners of industrial enterprises in all Nordic countries during the twentieth century. What was the role played by the state as the owner of big business in different Nordic countries? Why did this emerge?
2. Forest industry was the key sector in Finnish industry from the nineteenth century up to the last decades of the twentieth century. Why was forest industry so pronounced in the Finnish economy from the mid-nineteenth century up to the 1990s? What explanatory factors can be found from, e.g., the company structure, raw material acquisitions, or economic policy?

Notes

1. The name of the company has changed over time: 1872–91, it was W. Gutzeit & Comp; 1891–6, W. Gutzeit & Comp. limeteret; 1896–1927, Aktiebolaget W. Gutzeit & Co.; 1928–81, Enso-Gutzeit Osakeyhtiö; 1981–95, Enso-Gutzeit Oy; 1996–7, Enso; 1998–Stora-Enso.

2. Kuisma (1993a); Sjögren (1999); Aanstad and Orstavik (2002); Henrekson and Jakobson (2003); Binda and Iversen (2007).
3. This chapter is based on our previous studies on the forest industry in general and on Nordic forest industry companies in particular. Furthermore, we have utilized the data sets compiled within our ongoing research project 'Strategic Management in the Forestry Sector: Retrospect and Prospect', in which we compare the global forest (mainly paper) industry. See especially Melander (1997); Lamberg (2005); Ojala, Lamberg *et al.* (2006).
4. Lammi (2000).
5. Murmann (2003).
6. Ahvenainen (1992b).
7. Detailed analysis of the selling of Gutzeit to the Finnish state can be found from Ahvenainen (1992b), pp. 225–34.
8. Ahvenainen (1992a), pp. 310–11.
9. Kuisma (1993b); Lamberg (2006).
10. Kuisma (1997).
11. This can be seen from number of company histories and memoirs from the time. See, for example, Hakkarainen (1993).
12. Ahvenainen (1992a), p. 446.
13. Veranen (1988, 1996); Lamberg (2006).
14. For more detailed accounts with international comparisons, see especially Artto (2001).
15. Ahvenainen (1992a), pp. 607–12: an analysis of Olavi J. Mattila as the CEO of Enso can be found from Lamberg (2005).
16. Veranen (1988); Lamberg (2006).
17. Ahvenainen (1992a), p. 416; Artto (2001); Lamberg (2006).
18. Ahvenainen (1992a, 2006).
19. Stora acquired Swedish Match in 1988 and Feldmuhle in 1990. In both cases large parts of the unrelated operations were sold shortly after their acquisition (1990–1).
20. The sum of assets in balance sheet/turnover * 12.
21. Lamberg (2006), p. 57, esp. Figure 3.6.
22. Ahvenainen (1992a), p. 457.
23. Nordberg (1998); Jensen-Eriksen (2007).
24. On a 'sprints and pauses' strategy, see Mintzberg and Waters (1982), pp. 492–3.
25. On Enso's activities in shipping business, see especially Karonen (1992).
26. Ahvenainen (1992b).
27. Ahvenainen (1992a), pp. 315, 320. The largest producer of pulp in Europe at the time was the German Zellstoffabrik Wadhof and the second Swedish Svenska Cellulosa Aktiebolag (SCA).
28. Ahvenainen (1992a), pp. 416, 503, 598.
29. Ojala and Pajunen (2006).
30. Lamberg (2006).
31. See also Skippari and Ojala, Chapter 7 in this volume.
32. Ahvenainen (1992a), pp. 551–3.
33. The most recent study on the 'Eurocan' and the other internationalization projects of Enso and other Finnish paper companies is Ahvenainen (2006).
34. Ahvenainen (2006).
35. A positive net result was achieved only in 1979, 1980 and 1985–9. Ahvenainen (2006).
36. Ahvenainen (2006).

References

Aanstad, S. and Orstavik, F., *State Ownership and Innovation in the Norwegian Governance Debate* (Oslo: STEP, 2002).
Ahvenainen, J., *Enso-Gutzeit Oy 1872–1992, 2: 1924–1992* (Jyväskylä: Gummerus, 1992a).
Ahvenainen, J., *Enso-Gutzeit Oy 1872–1992, 1: 1872–1923* (Jyväskylä: Gummerus, 1992b).
Ahvenainen, J., *Suomalainen metsäteollisuus Pohjois-Amerikassa 1960–2000. Finnish Paper Companies in North America 1960–2000* (Mikkeli: Suomen Elinkeinoelämän Keskusark-isto, 2006).

Artto, E., *Performance and International Competitiveness of Listed Paper Industry Groups 1992–2000: Finland vs Sweden, Canada and US* (Helsinki: Helsinki School of Economics and Business Administration, 2001).

Binda, V. and Iversen, M. J., 'Towards a "Managerial Revolution" in European Business? The Transformation of Danish and Spanish Big Business, 1973–2003', *Business History* 49 (2007).

Cantwell, J., 'The Changing Form of Multinational Enterprise Expansion in the Twentieth Century', in Teichova, A., Lévy-Leboyer, M. and Nussbaum, H. (eds), *Historical Studies in International Corporate Business* (Cambridge: Cambridge University Press, 1989) pp. 15–28.

Hakkarainen, N., *Oravanpyörässä* (Juva: WSOY, 1993).

Henrekson, M. and Jakobson, U., 'The Transformation of Ownership Policy and Structure in Sweden: Convergence towards the Anglo-Saxon Model?', *New Political Economy*, 8 (2003), pp. 73–102.

Hjerppe, R., *Suomen talous 1860–1985: Kasvu ja rakennemuutos* (Helsinki: Suomen Pankki, 1988).

Jensen-Eriksen, N.L., *Metsäteollisuus kasvun, integraation ja kylmän sodan Euroopassa 1950–1973, Metsäteollisuuden Maa4.* (Helsinki: SKS, 2007).

Jääskeläinen, J., *Klusteri tieteen ja politiikan välissä: Teollisuuspolitiikasta yhteiskuntapolitiikkaan.* (Helsinki: Taloustieto Oy, 2001).

Karonen, P., *Enso-Gutzeit Oy laivanvarustajana: Oy Finnlines Ltd ja Merivienti Oy vuosina 1947–1982* (Imatra: Enso-Gutzeit, 1992).

Kuisma, M., 'Government Action, Cartels and National Corporations – The Development Strategy of a Small Peripheral Nation during the period of Crisis and Economic Disintegration in Europe (Finland 1918–1938)', *Scandinavian Economic History Review*, 41 (1993a).

Kuisma, M., *Metsäteollisuuden maa: Suomi, metsät ja kansainvälinen järjestelmä 1620–1920* (Helsinki: SKS, 1993b).

Kuisma, M., *Kylmä sota, kuuma öljy: Neste, Suomi ja kaksi Eurooppaa* (Helsinki: WSOY, 1997).

Kuisma, M., *Kahlittu raha, kansallinen kapitalismi: Kansallis-Osake-Pankki 1940–1995* (Helsinki: Suomalaisen Kirjallisuuden Seura, 2004).

Lamberg, J.-A., *Strategic Action and Path Dependence: in Profiles and Archetypes of Competitive Behaviour Global Industry* (Espoo; Helsinki University of Technology, 2005).

Lamberg, J.-A., 'A Company and The State: Enso-Gutzeit', in Lamberg, J.-A., Ojala, J., Näsi J. and Sajasalo, P. (eds), *The Evolution of Competitive Strategies in Global Forestry Industries: Comparative Perspectives* (Dordrecht: Springer, 2006) pp. 45–63.

Lammi, M., *Metsäklusteri Suomen taloudessa/The Forest Cluster in the Finnish Economy* (Helsinki: Taloustieto Oy, 2000).

Melander, A., *Industrial Wisdom and Strategic Change: The Swedish Pulp and Paper Industry 1945–1990* (Jonköping: Jonköping International Business School, 1997).

Mintzberg, H. and Waters, J. A., 'Tracking Strategy in an Entrepreneurial Firm', *Academy of Management Journal*, 25 (1982), pp. 465–99.

Murmann, J. P., *Knowledge and Competitive Advantage: The Coevolution of Firms, Technology, and National Institutions* (Cambridge, MA: Cambridge University Press, 2003).

Nordberg, T., *Vuosisata paperiteollisuutta III: Yhtyneet paperitehtaat Osakeyhtiö 1952–1969: Juuso Waldenin aikaan* (Valkeakoski: UPM-Kymmene Oyj, 1998).

Ojala, J. and Karonen, P., 'Business: Rooted in Social Capital over the Centuries', in Ojala, J., Eloranta, J. and Jalava, J. (eds), *The Road to Prosperity: An Economic History of Finland* (Helsinki: SKS, 2006) pp. 92–125.

Ojala, J. and Lamberg, J.-A., *et al.*, 'The Ephemera of Success: Strategy, Structure and Performance in the Forestry Industries', in Lamberg, J.-A., Näsi, J., Ojala, J. and Sajasalo, P. (eds), *The Evolution of Competitive Strategies in Global Forestry Industries: Comparative Perspectives* (Dordrecht: Springer, 2006) pp. 257–86.

Ojala, J. and Pajunen, K., 'Two Finnish Family Firms in Comparison: Ahlström and Schauman during the 20th Century', in Lamberg, J.-A., Ojala, J., Näsi, J. and Sajasalo, P. (eds), *The Ephemera of Success: Strategy, Structure and Performance in the Forestry Industries* (Dordrecht: Springer, 2006) pp. 167–89.

Sjögren, H., 'Financial Contracts of Large Firms: A Longitudal Study of Swedish Firms and Commercial Banks, 1919–47', *Scandinavian Economic History Review,* 39 (1991), pp. 72–94.

Sjögren, H., *Spelet i Saléninvest. Staten, bankerna, ägarna och ledningen 1973–97* (Stockholm: SNS förlag, 1999).

Veranen, J., *Omistajat yrityksen menestystekijänä* (Espoo: Weilin & Göös, 1988).

Veranen, J., *Tuottoa vaativat omistajat: Menestykseen omistajalähtöisellä johtamisella* (Helsinki: WSOY, 1996).

Åström, S.-E., *From Tar to Timber: Studies in Northeast European Forest Exploitation and Foreign Trade 1660–1860* (Helsinki: Societas Scientiarum Fennica, 1988).

WELFARE CAPITALISM: THE SWEDISH ECONOMY 1850–2005 • ENTREPRENEURSHIP AND OWNERSHIP: THE FIRM VIABILITY OF THE SWEDISH DONNIER AND WALLENBERG FAMILY BUSINESS GROUPS • FROM CAPITALISM, 18 S–2005 • FROM STATE OWNERSHIP TO MULTINATIONAL CORPORATION: THE PATH OF ENSO-GUTZEI PATHS OF NO AND TAMPE A IN THE LIBERALI G FINNISH ECONOMY FTER THE SECOND WORLD WAR : CO-OPERA IVE L BERALISM: DENMARK FROM 185 TO 2007 • AKLA M DECENTRALIZED INDUSTRY TO MULTINATIONAL ENTERPRISE RKET • NORWAY: A RESOURCE-BASED AND DEMOCRATIC CAPITALISM • CONSTRUCTIVE POWER: ELKEM 1904–2004 • FINANCE AND THE DEVELOPMENT OF NORWEGIAN

7 The success and failure of a conglomerate firm: the strategic paths of Nokia and Tampella in the liberalizing Finnish economy after the Second World War

Mika Skippari and Jari Ojala

Introduction: conglomerate firms in the changing business environment

The rise and fall of the conglomerate corporation is among the most interesting chapters of twentieth-century business history. The conglomerate corporation that was diversified to a number of lines of business became the dominant form of the industrial firm in the US in the early part of the twentieth century and later also in Europe.[1] In Finland, diversification was seen as one of the best strategies for big business, especially during the 1960s and 1970s. The strategic logic was highly practical: when one branch of the industry was failing in terms of profitability, the corporation could still survive on the profits from other lines of business.

Although in the early 1980s there was still a clear goal of diversification among Finnish companies, by the end of the decade diversification was seen as problematic. That was due to number of reasons; the most obvious being that as firms grew in size, managing a conglomerate firm became difficult. Another reason was the fact that diversified firms were taken over and their parts sold off at a good profit. Third, increasing economic liberalization (in both financing and foreign trade) provided more opportunities for firms to find economies of scale in one or few business areas. Finally, the virtues of diversified firms were emphasized in the management literature up to the 1980s, when the deinstitutionalization of this organization form began. By the 1980s the tables had been turned and concentration on core competences was being emphasized both in management literature and among business managers.

Two large-scale Finnish conglomerates, Nokia and Tampella, were up to the late 1980s typical examples of companies that had for several decades followed an unrelated diversification strategy. After facing a deep financial crisis at the turn of the 1990s, however, the strategic paths of the companies diverged: Tampella's story as an independent company ended, as the Bank of Finland took over the company in order to avoid its bankruptcy. Nokia's economic position was also in a critical condition, but the new management team was able to make a successful turnaround, sold diversified lines of businesses and made a strategic decision to concentrate on mobile technology. By the end of the 1990s, Nokia had become the biggest success story in Finnish industrial history so far.[2]

In this chapter we examine the strategic paths of Nokia and Tampella in the liberalizing Finnish regulatory environment after the Second World War. In particular, we analyse how these both firms succeeded and failed to adapt their strategies to the changing regulatory environment. In this chapter, we will focus only on the post-war period, although we also briefly describe the key events in the companies' histories before the Second World War. We focus on two questions. First, we explore why Nokia and Tampella remained highly diversified companies up to the early 1990s. We argue that due to the stable nature of the Finnish business system during the 1940s and 1980s, labelled as 'co-operative capitalism' and characterized by high government intervention and close business–government relations, firms had relatively little room for strategic manoeuvring, and thus the strategic decisions made in both companies were rather similar. The second key question is why Nokia survived and Tampella failed. In this, we stress the importance of strategic capabilities: when the semi-closed economy was liberalized the companies with their path-dependent structures faced difficulties in making strategic decisions to survive. Our conclusion is that Nokia was in a more favourable position and, thus, was more capable than Tampella to respond to a changed business environment in the 1980s.

Nokia and Tampella in comparison: a brief history[3]

By the end of the 1980s the historical paths of Nokia and Tampella had a lot in common. They experienced a similar growth rate until the late 1970s (see Figures 7.1 and 7.2) and they were among the largest privatively owned industrial enterprises in Finland. Both firms were established around the same time and in the same geographical area. The first industrial conglomerate in Finnish business history, Tampella was founded in 1856, when two separate

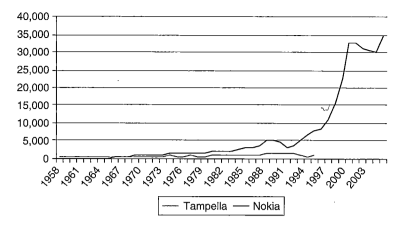

Figure 7.1 **Annual sales of Tampella and Nokia, 1958–2005 (2006 million Euros)**
Note: In the case of Nokia before the merger in 1966, only the turnover of the forest industry division is counted.
Sources: Annual reports.

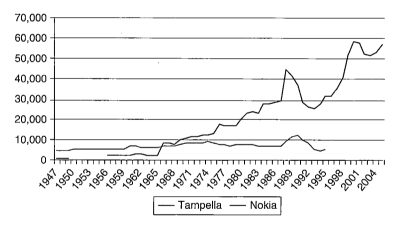

Figure 7.2 **Number in the labour force, Tampella and Nokia, 1947–2005**
Note: In the case of Nokia before the merger in 1966, only the labour force of the forest industry division is counted.
Sources: Annual reports.

factories, a blast furnace and a linen factory, were established in the city of Tampere.[4] Nokia's first industrial company, a wood pulp factory, was established in 1865 in a village called Nokia, about 15 km from Tampere. At first, Nokia produced wood pulp, but soon expanded to produce paper (1880) and chemical pulp (1886). As Tampella was among the forerunners of new technology in textile and iron industries, Nokia was the first wood pulp factory in Finland. Both companies were established with 'old money', namely, with the capital of old trading houses.[5]

Photograph 7.1 Tampella's Inkeroinen mills in the 1920s. The large investments of Inkeroinen worsened the financial crisis of the company in the 1980s
Source: Alka Central Business Archive.

During the 1870s and 1880s Tampella furthered its diversification by entering the wood-processing industry. Tampella started by producing mechanical wood pulp, but expanded to cardboard production by the end of the century.[6] Another substantial extension in Tampella's portfolio took place in the 1890s, when the engineering workshop started to manufacture steam locomotives. The initiative for locomotive production was encouraged by Finnish government, which offered direct subsidies for the initial phase of production. Moreover, all the locomotives were ordered by the state railways, which made the success of this business area highly dependent on government purchases.

Tampella's product portfolio remained practically unchanged up to the 1930s. As a result of increased tension in international politics and the consequent emergence of rearmament in Finland, Tampella started the production of mortars and cannons. In 1934 Tampella took over a cotton factory, and four years later it founded a paper mill.[7]

At the end of the Second World War Tampella had established its position in three branches of industry: wood-processing, engineering and textiles. Its resource base was abundant, especially in raw materials and energy: it owned large areas of forest land and several power plants.[8] The wood-processing industry was the main line of production, whereas the size of the engineering and textile industries was almost equal. The engineering division, however, started to grow rapidly right after the war, whereas the growth rate of the textile division gradually deteriorated and lagged behind the other businesses.

The diversification of Nokia occurred a bit later, during the late nineteenth and early twentieth century. Nokia diversified into three unrelated sectors. At first, each sector acted as an independent company: Nokia Forest and Power (1865–6) in the forestry industry (basically the manufacture of pulp and paper, but also power production); Finnish Rubber Works (1898–1966) in the rubber industry (especially shoes and car tyres); and Finnish Cable Works (1912–66) in cables.[9] All three companies were *de facto* owned from the turn of the 1920s by the Cable Works. In 1966, the rubber and cable company were officially merged with the forest industry company and the conglomerate was created, though these units had already been under the same ownership and leadership from the early twentieth century.[10] During the 1960s, electronics gained in importance as Nokia started to integrate cable manufacturing forwards in the production chain, into machinery.

In the mid-1970s Nokia was the fifth largest industrial enterprise in Finland with turnover of 1.3 million Euros (def. 2006 value) and around 13,000 employees. During the 1980s it became the largest privatively owned enterprise in Finland[11] (see also Figures 7.1 and 7.2). At the same time, it was a market leader in Europe in several products (televisions, computer monitors and rubber boots), and was the fifth largest producer of cables in Europe. In Scandinavia it was the largest producer of computers. Furthermore, it was involved in an alliance of tissue paper producers that had the largest capacity in Europe.

In the emerging mobile phone business, Nokia was already the largest manufacturer in the world by the end of the 1980s, though this line of business was among the smallest in the company, as mass markets for this product had not yet been developed. After shedding other lines of business, the role played by telecommunications grew rapidly within the company: in 1988 mobile phones accounted for only 5 per cent of Nokia's sales, but in 2000 the share had increased to 72 per cent. At the same time, the share of mobile networks rose from 5 to 25 per cent of the total turnover.

The history of both companies is a story of fluctuating periods of prosperity and decline, and both faced a number of financial difficulties, most notably

Photograph 7.2 **The roots of the mobile phone of today: Nokia 'portable' phone in the early 1970s**
Source: Alka Central Business Archive.

at the end of the 1980s. The first decades of Tampella were characterized by serious financial problems. During the 1880s, however, the new owners managed to stabilize the company.[12] The forest industry sector of Nokia suffered after Finland gained independence, as the company lost the vital Russian markets.[13] After a decade-long prosperity, the financial status of Tampella deteriorated in the 1970s, as the debt burden increased rapidly due to the investments in several industrial branches and unsuccessful international operations. By the end of the 1980s, Nokia was also in crisis. Investments in the production of consumer electronics, especially television production, turned out to be disastrous, the cable exports ceased when the Soviet Union collapsed and the company was lagging also behind in the traditional forestry industry.

In the following, we describe in more detail the strategic paths of Nokia and Tampella after the Second World War. We highlight various characteristics of Finnish market conditions in explaining the similarities – and eventually the divergence – in the companies' strategies.

Strategic rigidity and government regulation: 1940s–50s

The business environment of Tampella and Nokia from the mid-1940s to the late 1950s was characterized by strict governmental regulation. Foreign trade was regulated by a licencing system and protectionist tariffs. Accordingly, both companies became heavily dependent on government actions, because the supply and prices of several business resources were under government control. For example, export and import licences had to be applied for from the Licence Commission (*Lisenssitoimikunta*), the supply of energy was controlled by a state agency and the changes in product prices had to be confirmed by the Ministry of Social Affairs (*Kansanhuoltoministeriö*). Raw material acquisitions also were under governmental control; this was especially a problem in Nokia's rubber industries in which the government regulated when the raw materials were to be bought. Thus, the company was sometimes forced to buy raw materials even when market prices were exceptionally high.[14]

This high-level economic regulation resulted in an increasingly politicized business environment. Several business matters that had typically been related to business and production problems became political issues.[15] Under these conditions, sending petitions to various government agencies and applying for licences became a central strategic tool and a potential source of competitive advantage. In this, Tampella had two main objectives: first, to maintain the real prices of its products under rapid inflation and, second, to secure quotas in foreign trade negotiations for the raw materials that were the most crucial for its operations.

Another factor that shaped and restricted both companies' business environment was the war indemnities that Finland had to pay to the Soviet Union after the Second World War. The war indemnities were paid in 1944–52, the vehicle of payment being industrial products, most of which consisted of metal industry products. Nokia and Tampella were among the major deliverers of these products.

The effects of war indemnities were contradictory. On the one hand, a considerable share of production capacity potential for generating export incomes was engaged in these deliveries. In addition, Tampella, for example, had to invest heavily to expand their capacity in order to meet the new requirements of war indemnities. The continuity of sales after the war indemnities was uncertain, which worried Tampella's managers. Accordingly, they insisted that the Finnish government secure the continuity of sales after the payments of war indemnities. On the other hand, the war indemnities helped both companies to recover and adjust to the post-war market situation, when the export market was practically closed until mid-1945. Moreover, the war indemnities provided Nokia and Tampella with long-term export contracts with Soviet Union without economic risk. As for Tampella, the war indemnities were a bridge to (re-)start textile exports to the east; for Nokia they were especially important for cable production as 5.7 per cent of the indemnities were to be delivered as cable products.[16] During the following decades, cable exports to the Soviet Union rose to be among the most profitable lines of business in Nokia.

From the companies' point of view, the war indemnities were just like regular government contracts. Moreover, Tampella and Nokia had good possibilities to influence the process. The top managers of Tampella, Arno Solin and Åke Kihlman, possessed key positions in the central industry associations that negotiated the prices and allocation of deliveries among companies with the government agency Soteva. Similarly, the CEO of Finnish Cable Works (Suomen Kaapelitehdas Oy), Verner Weckman, possessed good relationships with the Finnish government actors, and was also a fluent speaker of Russian. Therefore, he was able to gain the company a good position in Soviet trade during the period of indemnities and even afterwards.[17]

This regulated and politicized business environment led to a strategic rigidity in companies' competitive strategy. Because of tight government control, there were only a few possibilities for large-scale strategic manoeuvres in the competitive market. Accordingly, the competitive strategy of all Finnish companies at the time was relatively inactive: for example, Tampella did not make any major investments in new plants during the late 1940s and 1950s. Instead, the main emphasis in investment activity was on modernizing the existing production equipment. The only significant strategic move was to start producing paper machines in the early 1950s. Before that, Tampella had produced paper machines under foreign licence.[18] Soon paper machines became one of the key products of Tampella's engineering division.

Strategic responses to deregulation: 1960s–70s

Emerging internationalization

The emerging trade liberalization of the late 1950s created a whole new business environment for Finnish companies. Although the Finnish economy still remained essentially closed, more competitive elements emerged. Import competition increased significantly, which imposed threats especially to Tampella's engineering and textile divisions, which had operated almost entirely on a protected domestic market for three decades. However, trade liberalization also provided opportunities for export expansion, as the multilateral reductions in import tariffs lowered entry barriers to foreign markets. In accordance with the emerging trade liberalization process, the Finnish government increased support for Finnish industry by creating public financing systems, such as public subsidies for export promotion and for R&D. The purpose of these systems was to enhance and facilitate the internationalization of Finnish industrial firms. These changes in government policies significantly altered market conditions, which had a clear impact on Nokia's and Tampella's strategies.

Trade liberalization had differing effect on various business divisions of the two companies. New opportunities for export expansion favoured especially the Finnish wood-processing industry, which had established a sound position in its main export markets. In the engineering division of Tampella, the effects were two-fold. On the one hand, the division had started to expand internationally during the late 1950s, exporting especially to the Soviet Union but also to some extent to western markets. Therefore, the emerging deregulation of foreign trade provided an incentive for further expansion in foreign markets. The beginning of drilling machine production in the 1950s was an example of how Tampella's engineering division responded to increased business opportunities abroad. On the other hand, increased import competition posed a threat to engineering division's favourable position in the domestic market which still played an important role for the division's performance. For example, some business sectors, such as armaments and turbine production, were highly dependent on government purchases.

Under these new market conditions, Tampella started to aggressively expand into foreign markets by acquiring foreign units. During the 1960s Tampella's investments increased significantly compared with the investments made in the 1950s. The internationalization of the company's operations (other than exports) was initiated in the engineering industry. Tampella started by establishing marketing offices in Sweden and Italy in 1961; a few years later operations were expanded to Latin America and finally in the mid-1960s to North America. All of these early sales offices were joint ventures. In the wood-processing industry, Tampella became involved in establishing two board mills in Spain, one of which ended up in Tampella's full ownership by the end of the 1960s. Moreover, Tampella initiated two joint ventures with local and other Finnish companies in North America.[19] As a consequence, an increasing share of Tampella's exports went to western European countries from the early 1960s.

In the textile industry, Tampella's situation was much more problematic. The competitiveness of the textile division was far more dependent on government interventions (government subsidies and purchases) than the engineering and wood-processing divisions. In fact, increased import competition threatened the very existence of the whole industry in Finland. Accordingly, the textile division had to defend its position *vis-à-vis* increased import competition on the domestic markets. Tampella temporarily adopted a more challenging approach to the government, appealing for compensation to secure and protect the competitiveness and continuity of the textile industry.

However, Tampella realized quite soon that the government would no longer provide significant protection for the textile industry. Thus, the textile division decided to adjust to the new market requirements and started to develop its market operations. It started to expand its business operations abroad by establishing foreign sales offices. In addition, the strategic goals shifted from producing mass market products towards focusing on special niche products and finding new markets for them abroad.

For Nokia, and especially for its cable production, the 1950s was the era of emerging Soviet exports. As the company had succeeded in war indemnity deliveries it gained a good reputation in the Soviet Union. This trade was tightly controlled by the Finnish state, thus, government relations gained more importance in the company's strategy. During the 1950s and 1960s around one-quarter of the production of the cable company was sold to the Soviet Union. The long-term contracts with the Soviet Union also made this line of business safe, though not always especially profitable. Towards the end of the 1970s, for example, cable production was the most profitable line of business in Nokia with almost 40 per cent returns in the best years.[20]

The idea of integrating cable production forwards in the production chain, namely, to the machinery, was created in the late 1950s under the leadership of Björn Westerlund. Thus, the seeds of the Nokia we know today were planted as the company invested in R&D and started to produce electrical equipment. This branch, however, was still a minor player in the conglomerate structure and was known by contemporaries as the 'cancer unit' of Nokia. Governmental orders were important for the production of electronic equipment, especially those from the defence forces. The company now started to produce, among other things, computers and different products to the army (e.g. radiophones).[21]

After the merger of Finnish Cable Works (*Suomen Kaapelitehdas*), Finnish Rubber Works (*Suomen Kumitehdas Oy*) and Nokia Forest and Power in 1966, the leadership of Nokia was also renewed. At that time, the cable company was the largest unit and owned the major shares of both the rubber company and the forestry industry company. Therefore, the CEO of the cable company, Björn Westerlund, was nominated as the CEO of the merged corporation. This was among the most important decisions in the history of the company, as Westerlund was the forerunner of electrical engineering in the company and, thus, among the 'founding fathers' of the contemporary Nokia. Remarkably both larger units (cable and rubber) were merged to the smallest one, to the forestry industry company. This was due to the legislation at the time that made the merging of forest industry to other branches of industries difficult. In 1966 combined forestry and power production accounted for 22 per cent of the combined sales of Nokia, while the share of cables was 49, rubber 26 and electronics 2.5 per cent, respectively.[22]

Transition to co-ordinated management systems

A major factor causing managerial problems to both companies was the lack of co-ordination and centralized planning of business operations. Tampella in particular was run in an authoritarian way and very little attention was paid to proper budgeting and long-range planning. In the early 1960s, Tampella underwent a series of radical changes in its management structure and practices that were clearly related to the changes in regulatory environment. As a response to more competitive environment, the management structure was decentralized by delegating the managing director's power to lower-level management. Operational units were restructured into four relatively independent divisions (forest, engineering, textile and power) and each division was assigned a responsible manager. In addition, Tampella recognized the need for a modern strategic planning system in the late 1960s, including, for example, a more goal-oriented attitude in each factory and the narrowing of product portfolios within the divisions. The implementation of these new practices, however, was very slow. In the early 1970s the company still lacked co-ordinated planning. Moreover, financial reporting and the co-ordination of investment plans among business divisions were considered inefficient and insufficient.

Tampella was, however, not the only Finnish corporation in the late 1960s that started to implement strategic planning. Similar decisions were made in number of forestry industry companies around the same time. The topic was discussed in Tampella in the late autumn of 1968, and Nokia had its long-term strategic planning already in use by the early spring in the same year. The rationale for doing so was the same as in the case of Tampella, namely, to respond to the competitive environment. Moreover, Nokia had undergone the merger of three units only couple of years earlier, and so there was an urgent need to reformulate corporate-level strategies.[23]

The transition to the new, co-ordinated management system was not easy. This was clearly seen in the case of Tampella, which was struggling with poor performance in the mid-1970s and faced a serious liquidity crisis. Consequently, Tampella's top management implemented a cost management project that included severe rationalization measures, such as closures of mills, restrictions in raw material acquisitions, denial of employment and lay-offs.[24] As a consequence of the critical financial situation, the top management of Tampella became aware of the need to change the management style of the company. The management of the company had for decades concentrated on expanding the volume of production. Now, CEO Grotenfelt argued for more emphasis on controlling costs and improving profitability. This clearly describes the management culture in the closed economy of Finland. In the regulated business environment, the main vehicle of competition was volume of production, not profitability.

Government relations

As a response to the changed regulatory environment, both companies put more emphasis on the management of government relations. Emerging economic liberalization required a more systematic monitoring and influencing of trade policy issues. During the 1940s and 1950s the management of government relations had been unsystematic and heavily dependent on the managing director's personal ability and willingness to devote managerial resources to political issues. In the early 1960s, however, the need for specialization in the area of business–government relations – and, more broadly, business–society relations – was recognized. The co-ordination of management practices was also extended to government relations in both companies. The recognition of the interests of various external stakeholders was determined to be one of the crucial tasks in the improvement of public relations.

In Tampella, another strategic move related to the changed business environment was the appointment of Johan Nykopp as the new managing director in 1962. Nykopp was an unusual choice because he had no prior experience of managing a business firm. Instead, he had decades-long experience as a ministry officer and as a high-ranking diplomat.[25] Thus, he possessed an extensive network of political connections. Most importantly, due to his background in the state administration, he had established confidential networks in Tampella's two major market areas, namely the Soviet Union and the US. In the role of state official, Nykopp participated in several trade agreement negotiations with the Soviet Union during the 1950s. As the Ambassador of Finland to the United States, Nykopp arranged US credits for Finland during the early 1950s, and thus created confidential relations with the major US banks. Therefore he was able to utilize these relationships as he consolidated Tampella's foreign loans in the early 1960s.[26]

Nokia put especial emphasis from the late 1960s onwards on energy policies and the building of the first nuclear power plants in Finland. CEO Björn Westerlund was especially active; his role in the process made him among the most notable industrial leaders in Finland, and consequently, in 1976 he was nominated as the chairman of the Federation of Finnish Industries, the central trade association of Finnish industry. For Nokia, the nuclear power plants also offered possibilities to develop and deliver equipment, which in turn appeared to be an important portent for in the future. Other managers in Nokia were also involved in government relations; Harry Mildh was a key figure in the management of government affairs especially during the 1970s and 1980s.[27]

In the early 1970s, tightened standards and regulations for air and water pollution and the increasing importance of trade policy issues urged Tampella to sharpen its government relations. At that time, Tampella had significant interests in foreign trade, since almost half of its production was sold in export markets. One-third was sold to the western European market (EEC and EFTA), whereas the shares of Eastern Europe (the Soviet Union and SEV countries) and North America were 12 and 5 per cent, respectively. Nokia was not as dependent on the export trade as Tampella, since the company had also wide domestic markets. The Soviet trade, however, was more pronounced in the case of Nokia as Soviet exports in the 1970s constituted, for example, about 50 per cent of the company's total exports.[28]

In the mid-1970s, world-wide oil crises and deepening economic problems increased Tampella's involvement in political issues. The top management team recommended that every business division pay particular attention to developing personal connections to the officials making the decisions about various state subsidies. Thus, it seems that Tampella's reaction to its poor economic performance was to put more emphasis on its government relations by increasing the level of political involvement.

Nokia was active in its governmental relations especially in the electronic engineering sector. The Finnish Defence Forces were a major buyer of Nokia's products. However, the co-operation with governmental actors was deepened in the 1970s when Nokia started to produce telephone exchanges together with the government-owned Televa. This decision was a major one on the path of the contemporary Nokia Networks. Another co-operative agreement, though at the time with less significance, with Televa and another private company, Salora, was made in 1975 to start to produce radiophones. In the following year these partners founded a joint venture to start the production of mobile phones. In the early 1980s Nokia acquired Televa and deepened the co-operation with Salora within mobile phones, finally acquiring the entire business. The share of electronics from Nokia's sales increased significantly: while in 1971 it produced only less than 8 per cent from the sales, in 1976 its share was already 15 per cent.[29]

Business and politics in Soviet trade

One of the specific sectors where political connections played a significant role at that time was the trade with the Soviet Union, which was especially important both for Nokia and Tampella throughout the post war era.[30] The trade that succeeded the war indemnities was based on the idea of bilateralism and long-range planning. The trade had a strong political flavour, as the Soviet Union was keen to demonstrate that it had close commercial relations to a western country. From the viewpoint of Finnish companies, the trade with the Soviet Union was beneficial because, for political reasons, the Soviet Union paid prices that exceeded world market prices. In the long term, the Soviet Union offered a buffer market for the Finns as exports to the east increased in periods when the demand in the west was falling, as was the case after the oil crisis in the 1970s. Finland imported gas and crude oil from the Soviet Union: from the early 1950s to the turn of the 1990s, around 50–70 per cent of imported crude oil came from the Soviet Union, and gas imports started in the mid-1970s.[31]

Therefore, it was essential for Finnish firms to build close and confidential relationships with the political establishment of the Soviet Union in order to secure their shares of the trade quotas. Partly, the politicized trade with the Soviet Union enhanced corporatism in Finnish society as business representatives achieved a strong position in trade agreement negotiations as well as in the various governmental committees established to co-ordinate the Soviet trade.[32]

For Nokia, cable manufacturing was undoubtedly the company's most important line of business in the 1970s, and its markets were mainly in the Soviet Union. Not only were cables sold to the Soviet Union from Nokia, but it was also among the rare Finnish paper producers for which the Soviet Union was a vital market. This was due to the fact that Nokia produced tissue papers that had good markets in the Soviet Union.[33] Another significant business area for Nokia was the sales of electronic equipment to the Soviet Union.

The role of Soviet trade was also important for various product lines in Tampella's engineering and textile divisions. In order to improve the company's business interests in the Soviet Union and other East European countries, CEO Grotenfelt hired a Bulgarian, Atanas Tilev, as secretary of commercial policy. Tilev's main task was to advance and co-ordinate Tampella's trade with the Soviet Union and the SEV countries, especially in the products of the engineering division. Due to his background and personal capabilities,[34] Tilev was able to build up a wide network of personal relations, in both Finland and abroad.

This large-scale investment of managerial resources on political connections was partly a response to the emerging change in the terms of Finnish–Soviet trade. The amount of trade had increased at an extremely fast pace after the Second World War, and had almost constantly shown a deficit for the Soviet Union. The Soviet Union started to pressure Finland by stating that if Finland did not increase its imports from the Soviet market, the Soviet Union would decrease its purchases from Finland. This posed a serious threat, especially to companies like Tampella and Nokia. Thus, the greater number of contacts with Soviet politicians and officials can be seen as a response to secure the company's favourable position in the Soviet trade.

Persistence in diversified business structure

Towards the end of the 1970s, worsening economic conditions made both companies reconsider their business structures. One of the main guidelines of both Tampella's and Nokia's top management during the post-war period had been a persistent belief in diversification. A generally accepted view was that a diversified structure would protect the company from the negative effects of unanticipated business fluctuations. This, in fact, was stressed when cable, rubber and forest industry companies were merged as Nokia in 1966. Nokia considered diversification as the foundation of their long-term success during the 1970s.[35]

In the case of Tampella, the economic trends of its business areas typically followed divergent patterns in the Finnish economy. The cyclical depression was aimed first at the wood-processing industry and after a few months at the textile industry. The engineering industry was affected much later, because the long-term deliveries gave the industry time to adapt to the changes in economic trends. In the case of cyclical recovery, the industries were affected in reverse order. Several positive experiences of the diversified business structure during the 1960s and the 1970s further strengthened the opinions of top management about the benefits of diversification.

However, the benefits in Tampella turned out to be highly debatable in the mid-1970s, when the financial situation of the company began to deteriorate. Although top management realized that the company had diversified into too many business areas and the issue was discussed several times by the board of directors, attempts to reorganize the business structure constantly failed. In fact, it seems that efficiency was not the main driving force behind the idea of a diversified business structure. Instead, the wish to maintain historical roots and the concerns about social responsibility were the more obvious factors increasing organizational rigidity and restraining the readiness for change.

The persistent adherence of Tampella to the textile industry was an example of the forces of social responsibility. Since the Second World War the profitability and competitiveness of the textile industry were heavily dependent on government interventions (price regulation, import tariffs and direct subsidies). Due to the trade liberalization initiated in the late 1950s, import competition intensified, causing further threats to profitability and increasing dependence on government actions. Top management was aware of the poor prospects of the industry and some tentative discussions on downsizing or merger with Finlayson took place in the late 1970s. However, top management was not willing to sell or close down the factories, fearing that the consequent unemployment would damage the company's reputation in society. CEO Grotenfelt defended the decision by pronouncing that 'the most important task of Finnish companies is to provide jobs for Finnish workers'.[36] Therefore, preferring social issues over economic efficiency was not only characteristic of state-owned companies in Finland,[37] but privately owned companies seemed to have a similar managerial mindset.

Towards the bankruptcy and turnaround: 1980s–90s

Deregulation of the financial sector
A dramatic change in the regulative environment of Finnish firms emerged in the early 1980s, as the Bank of Finland started to deregulate capital markets. Throughout the post-war period until the early 1980s, the government had regulated the financial markets by controlling interest rates, currency exchange and the issue of bonds. The main objective was to support domestic industrial investments and exports. For this purpose, the Bank of Finland, together with government, had regularly devalued the Finnish currency.[38] High regulation significantly restricted the accumulation of capital in Finland. Foreign ownership was prohibited by law and the supply of foreign loans was controlled by the government. Low interest rates together with relatively high inflation resulted in negative real interest rates. This kind of incentive structure, in turn, motivated firms to finance their growth primarily by loans, and moreover to take excessive risks.

As a consequence of deregulation, opportunities for obtaining foreign capital were improved. This increased the room for strategic manoeuvres in Finnish business. Partly due to this improvement, partly as a result of changes in international competition, several branches of industry started to consolidate through merging operations. As industrial enterprises, as well as banks, were given the right to freely seek foreign funding for their investments, companies expanded rapidly and were merged into bigger units to meet the requirements of open markets. At the same time, the old wisdom of diversified structure of business organizations lost its popularity and several firms started to focus on only a few key areas of business.

Under these conditions, both Tampella and Nokia faced a complicated business environment. One of the key strategic issues was to decide to what extent the firms should maintain their diversified business structure. In the case of Tampella, which had struggled with enormous financial problems since the mid-1960s, the high level of debt had not been a critical factor for firm performance under the regulated financial system that maintained a negative real interest rate. Due to deregulation, however, rapidly increasing interest charges threatened the very existence of the company. It was only then, in the middle of a crisis, that Tampella began to divest itself of businesses that had been unprofitable for a long time. Tampella sold its businesses in the textile and chemical industries and in electricity production in the mid-1980s.

However, an even bigger strategic question for both Tampella and Nokia was to determine what to do with their forestry industry businesses. Alongside the energy crises, the forestry industries also suffered in the 1970s with poor profits and tightening competition. In order to survive, the companies were forced to make significant investments or withdraw from the business: for example, Tampella had not invested in a new paper machine for forty years. Although both companies were considered as big businesses in Finland, both were still minor players in the forestry industry. Their competitive strategy had been based on close co-operation through sales cartels with other Finnish forestry companies. Throughout the 1970s and 1980s, the strategic discussions in both companies involved the major question: whether to exit from the forestry industry or make the necessary investments.[39] The problem was that both exit and investment were expensive.

In this matter, Nokia and Tampella followed different strategies. Although there were serious plans at one point to acquire United Paper Mills, Nokia never started to invest heavily in its own forestry division. Rather, it deepened the co-operation with other Finnish forest industry companies and took part in the establishment of Metsä-Botnia, which was a joint venture to create a company to produce pulp for paper factories. In addition, Nokia divested its own pulp production in the early 1980s and later also its share in Metsä-Botnia.[40] Though this production was already rather insignificant in the company's portfolio, the decision was still historically significant as the company had originally started as a pulp producer.

Conversely, Tampella made huge investments in the forestry industry in the 1980s by establishing a new paper mill in Anjalankoski. This was probably among the most important strategic differences between the companies and among the most important reasons why Tampella did not survive while Nokia did. The deep-rooted path dependence in Finnish business in the 1970s and 1980s stressed the importance of the forestry industry as the only possible long-term line of business in the country. Nokia was able to dismantle this path dependence, while Tampella was not.

This difference in strategic visions can be traced to different managerial approaches. CEO of Nokia Björn Westerlund was among the rare industrial leaders in Finland in the 1970s who was not really fascinated with the forest industry. On the contrary, he tended to be away when the forestry-related decisions were made. Tampella's CEO, Nils Grotenfelt, by contrast, had had a career rich in forest industry associations.[41]

Both Nokia and Tampella sought growth during the 1980s at the expense of profitability. This pattern was typical of a number of other Finnish industrial companies at the time. At least for contemporary observers, Nokia's situation in the 1980s was not as alarming as the case of Tampella. Nokia was still viewed in the business press as a dynamic and innovative forerunner of Finnish economy, with big plans waiting to be realized. For Tampella, however, there were already more critical voices: the company was bound up with old-fashioned textile and forestry industries, though with promising openings in the engineering sector.

Tampella was not able to solve its economic problems during the 1980s. The financial performance of the company was constantly poor; the major investments in engineering and wood-processing in the early 1980s turned out to be disappointments. Several reorganizations were made to find an efficient structure and product portfolio. The financial situation of the company deteriorated, and the main owner of the company, SYP bank, gradually lost its interest in developing the company.

In 1987 Tampella became a part of the restructuring of Finnish industry, as the SKOP bank acquired the majority of Tampella's shares from the SYP bank. The new owner implemented an intensive turnaround process in the company. The first priority was to grow as fast as possible, because the prospects in the deregulated financial markets were considered almost infinite. The new CEO, Pekka Salo, tried to rebuild the whole business culture of the company.

The basic problem of Tampella was related to the multidivisional structure of the company. Contrary to the general development in Finland, Tampella did not divest unrelated business areas from its portfolio. As a consequence, by the late 1980s Tampella was one of the few large-scale Finnish companies to remain diversified. Even the new owner, SKOP bank, continued the old tradition of diversification. The reason for this, however, was more likely the inexperience of SKOP bank in managing an industrial enterprise. As SKOP bank did not exactly know what to do with Tampella, they decided to maintain the old main business areas.[42]

The expansive strategy of Tampella boosted by the new owner seemed to work well for the first few years. However, as the economic boom in Finland turned into recession at the end of the 1990s, the company's major investments became unprofitable. The high-risk, expansionist strategy increased the debt burden of the company. At the same time, the economic position of the SKOP bank started to deteriorate. Accordingly, the Bank of Finland was forced to take over the SKOP bank and Tampella in 1991 in order to avoid bankruptcies of both organizations.

Nokia's strategic intent was somewhat clearer. Although the leading vision of Nokia's CEO, Kari Kairamo, in the mid-1980s was still to create a Japanese-type of conglomerate with tens or even hundreds of different lines of businesses, there were clear trends in investment decisions towards the development of the electronic division. Also the role played by the competing banking spheres SYP and KOP became acute by the end of the 1980s. Unlike most of the large Finnish industrial corporations, Nokia was not dominated by one banking sphere. On the contrary, both SYP and KOP had a large stake in the company. That meant that neither of the banks could dominate Nokia's decision-making. As the competition between the banks tightened and even the personal relations of their top management became worse, the operation of the board also became problematic.[43]

The crisis was deepened further through managerial failure after the CEO of the company, Kari Kairamo, committed suicide in 1988. Against this background, it is quite amazing how the company succeeded in getting back on its feet in only a couple of years in the early 1990s. During 1991 and 2001, under the new top management led by CEO Jorma Ollila, the number of

Photograph 7.3 **Representatives of Nokia's subcontractors demonstrated outside the company's annual general meeting in 2006. About one hundred workers reminded Nokia of the tightened subcontractor policies and its effects in Finland.**
Source: Lehtikuva Photographers: Ismo Pekkarinen and Riikka Hurri.

employees doubled, turnover grew over ten-fold profits grew a hundred-fold-, and the market value grew 312-fold, although at the same time all other lines of business except telecommunications were shed by the company. The rapid growth of Nokia was related to the rise of mass markets for mobile phones in the 1990s. The main reasons for Nokia's success in the 1990s and early third millennium have been considered to be the deregulation and digitalization of international telecommunications and the breakthrough of GSM technology. Nokia was able to exploit these changes in terms of both technology and business, and it also exerted its own influence on coming changes.

Conclusions

The stories of Nokia and Tampella do have lot in common. But the end was different: Tampella was taken over by the Bank of Finland and its units were sold in the 1990s, whilst Nokia's real take-off as a global player in mobile phone business started around the same time. How, then, can we explain why one conglomerate firm succeeded and the other failed?

As stated in the analysis, despite the multi-level crises, Nokia was still, by the end of the 1990s, in a more favourable position than Tampella as the company had diversified to emerging lines of businesses. Conversely, Tampella was bound up with mature industries with high capital costs. The focus in the diversified lines of businesses is, we argue, the most important explanation for both success and failure. Though both companies had sought possibilities to divest the unprofitable lines of businesses from the mid-1980s, Nokia was still more successful in implementing this change.

Two distinctive characteristics emerge from the business environment of Tampella and Nokia: relatively high and long-lasting economic regulation and close connections between business and government. Both of these environmental characteristics conditioned, and even to some extent dictated, the companies' strategic choices. The economic regulation restricted the autonomy of the firm to develop its business operations. In a small corporatist country like Finland, the personal connections between business and government were essential and, thus, the importance of non-market strategies was emphasized at the expense of market strategies.

The importance of personal relationships was closely connected to the special characteristics of Finland and the Finnish economy. First, Finland was (and still is) a small country, in which members of the political and economic elite knew each other. Second, the regulated economy and corporatist system facilitated the creation of personal relationships between business and politics. The confidential personal relations with politicians were especially essential to the firms deeply involved in the Soviet trade.

Our analysis also demonstrates the possible outcomes that high dependence on government interventions can have for firm performance in the long run. The high dependence of Tampella's engineering division and Nokia's cable division on the Soviet trade indicates that successful non-market strategy may lead to market power but not necessarily to economic efficiency. The large-scale orders were overpriced, which provided excessive profit margins. More-over, the stable flow of orders based on predetermined annual quotas ensured some predictability for the business environment. However, these extraordi-nary business conditions did not encourage innovation and the development of efficient business systems, mostly because of the lack of competition.

To conclude, one could point out several phases in history when Nokia seemed to have made 'smart' choices and Tampella had not. Though this kind of deterministic exercise can be fascinating, it is hardly justified, as at the same time one can also point out a number of obvious mistakes on Nokia's part and success stories on Tampella's side. Though conscious strategies can be found, success and failure is also related to pure good and bad luck. On Nokia's part one can, however, find a clear strategy from the late 1960s to emphasise electric engineering; for example, the share of R&D funding and even investments in this division were remarkable even during a period when its share of the company's turnover was still modest. Also, when the restructuring of the company from the mid-1980s emerged, the divestment of the mobile phone and network units were never at the top of the list, though also discussed. The take-off in the 1990s was, thus, largely based on these previous decisions, though the expansion of the markets in mobile communications was clearly more rapid than Nokia's top management could have ever dreamed about.

QUESTIONS
1. What was the role of Soviet trade to the strategic decision-making in Nokia and Tampella?
2. Describe the main differences and similarities in Nokia's and Tampella's strategic paths.

Notes

1. More precisely on the discussion in the United States, see especially Chandler (1962); Davis *et al.* (1994). For Nordic experiences see, for example, Moen and Lilja (2001).

2. See also Fellman (2008) in this volume.
3. In this chapter, the Tampella case is based on Skippari (2005) and the Nokia case on Häikiö (2002), if not otherwise noted.
4. Bonsdorff (1956a); Urbans (1956), pp. 23–33.
5. Häikiö (2001a) pp. 30, 53; 2002, p. 4; Bonsdorff (1956b, 1956c); Annual Report of Nokia (1964), pp. 3–6.
6. Urbans (1956), pp. 48–50.
7. Urbans (1956), pp. 138–48.
8. Urbans (1956), pp. 166-8; Hjerppe (1979), pp. 176–8.
9. In this article 'Nokia' is used anachronistically as the company name even for the period before the merger to avoid misunderstanding.
10. Annual Report of Nokia (1966), p. 5; Häikiö (2001a), pp. 101–9.
11. Ojala and Karonen (2006), pp. 118–21.
12. Urbans (1956), pp. 36–44.
13. Häikiö (2001a), p. 47.
14. Heikkinen (1994). Aunesluoma (2001b), p. 64.
15. Tainio *et al.* (1989).
16. Aunesluoma (2001b), p. 75.
17. Auer (1956), pp. 25–34; Aunesluoma (2001b), pp. 75–6; Skippari (2005).
18. Seppälä (1981), pp. 15–16.
19. See also Ojala *et al.* (2008) in this volume.
20. Häikiö (2001a), pp. 119, 182–4.
21. Aunesluoma (2001b), pp. 77–79; Häikiö (2001a), pp. 86–8, 97–8.
22. Annual Report of Nokia (1966); Häikiö (2001a), pp. 101–9.
23. Häikiö (2001a), p. 113. On strategic planning in Finnish corporations at the time, see also Fellman, (2000).
24. Skippari (2005).
25. During the 1930s, Nykopp worked at the Embassy of Finland in the Soviet Union and during the 1940s he served as a department head in the Ministry of Foreign Affairs. During the Second World War he worked as a personal secretary to Prime Minister Paasikivi. In 1951–8 he was Ambassador of Finland in the US. Then he worked three years as the managing director of the Central Association of Finnish Employers (Suomen Työnantajien Keskusliitto).
26. Nykopp (1985); Keskinen (1987), p. 49; Skippari (2005).
27. Häikiö (2001a), pp. 125–40; Ruostetsaari (1989), pp. 134, 141, 167, 186; Michelsen and Särkikoski (2005).
28. See, for example, Annual Report of Nokia (1975), p. 6, and (1977), p. 5.
29. Häikiö (2001a), pp. 162–71, 203.
30. For Finnish–Soviet trade, see also Fellman (2008) in this volume.
31. Kuisma (1997), p. 563; Eloranta and Ojala (2005).
32. Lamberg and Skippari (2001); Keskinen (1987), pp. 293–9.
33. Häikiö (2001b), p. 53; Aunesluoma (2001a), p. 105; Talouselämä (2/1979), p. 32.
34. Tilev was married to a daughter of Ahti Karjalainen, who was a close colleague of President Kekkonen and one of the most influential politicians in Finland during the 1970s. Grotenfelt was also a close friend of Karjalainen. Karjalainen was a crucial target of influence, because he was the chairman in the Finnish–Soviet Co-operation Commission (Suomalais-neuvostoliittolainen yhteistyökomissio). See Skippari (2005).
35. Häikiö (2001a), p. 104.
36. Skippari (2005).
37. See, Ojala *et al.* (2008) in this volume.
38. Pekkarinen and Vartiainen (1993), pp. 245–6.
39. For example, there was much speculation in the media about Tampella's desire to sell its forest industry to either Kymin Oy or Rauma-Repola in the late 1970s; see, for example, *Helsingin Sanomat*, 3 May 1977. On Nokia's plans for forest industry divestment, see Häikiö (2001a), p. 150. On co-operation see Skippari *et al.* (2005).
40. Häikiö (2001a), pp. 239–40; Annual Report of Nokia (1973), p. 11.
41. Häikiö (2001a), pp. 141–2. After graduating as a senior lawyer in 1951, Grotenfelt acted as a procurator in the sales association of Finnish paper producers (Finnpap) (Suomen Paperitehtaitten Yhdistys). From 1958 to 1972, Grotenfelt worked as the deputy manager and the chairman of the board of executives of Finnpap. See Skippari (2005).
42. Skippari (2005).
43. Häikiö (2001b), p. 36, pp. 70–1, 239, 145–6.

References

Ahvenainen, J., *Suomalainen metsäteollisuus Pohjois-Amerikassa 1960–2000 – Finnish Paper Companies in North America 1960–2000* (Mikkeli: Suomen Elinkeinoelämän Keskusarkisto, 2006).

Auer, J., *Suomen sotakorvaustoimituksen Neuvostoliitolle: Tutkimus tavaroiden luovutusohjelmista, niiden toteuttamisesta ja hyvityshinnoista* (Helsinki: Helsingin yliopisto, 1956).

Aunesluoma, J., 'Kaapelin idänkauppa kannattaa, mutta länteen pitäisi päästä', in Häikiö, M. (ed.), *Nokia Oyj:n historia 2: Sturm und Drang. Suurkaupoilla eurooppalaiseksi elektroniikkayritykseksi 1983–1991* (Helsinki: Edita, 2001a), pp. 100–11.

Aunesluoma, J., 'Sähköistämisen alkuvuosista sodanjälkeiseen idänkauppaan – kaapeli 1922–1966', in Häikiö, M. (ed.), *Nokia Oyj:n historia 1: Fuusio. Yhdistymisten kautta suomalaiseksi monialayritykseksi 1865–1982* (Helsinki: Edita, 2001b), pp. 69–81.

Bonsdorff, L. G. v., *Linne och jern 1: Textil- och metallindustrierna i Finland intill 1880-talet* (Helsingfors: Söderström, 1956a).

Bonsdorff, L. G. v., *Linne och jern 2: Adolf Törngren d.ä.* (Helsingfors: Söderström, 1956b).

Bonsdorff, L. G. v., *Linne och jern 3: Gustaf August Wasastjerna* (Helsingfors: Söderström, 1956c).

Chandler, A. D. J., *Strategy and Structure: Chapters in the History of the Industrial Enterprise* (Cambridge, MA: MIT Press, 1962).

Chandler, A. D. J., *Scale and Scope. The Dynamics of Industrial Capitalism* (Cambridge, MA: Belknap Press of Harvard University, 1990).

Davis, G. F., Diekmann, K. A. and Tinsley, C. H., 'The Decline and Fall of the Conglomerate Firm in the 1980s: The Deinstitutionalization of an Organizational Form', *American Sociological Review*, 59 (1994), pp. 547–70.

DiMaggio, P. and Powell, W. W. (eds), *The New Institutionalism in Organizational Analysis* (Chicago: University of Chicago Press, 1991).

Eloranta, J. and Ojala, J. 'Converta: A Finnish Conduit in the East-West Trade', in Eloranta, J. and Ojala, J. (eds), *East–West Trade and Cold War* (Jyväskylä: Studies in Humanities, University of Jyväskylä, 2005).

Fellman, S., *Uppkomsten av en direktrösprofession: Industriledarnas utbildning och karriär i Finland 1900–1975* (Helsingfors: Finska Vetenskaps-societen, 2000).

Heikkinen, S., *Suomeen ja maailmalle: Tullilaitoksen historia* (Helsinki: Tullilaitos, 1994).

Hjerppe, R., *Suurimmat yritykset Suomen teollisuudessa* (Helsinki: Finska vetenskapssocieteten, 1979).

Häikiö, M., *Nokia Oyj:n historia 1: Fuusio. Yhdistymisen kautta suomalaiseksi monialayritykseksi 1865–1982.* (Helsinki: Edita, 2001a).

Häikiö, M., *Nokia Oyj:n historia 2: Sturm und Drang. Suurkaupoilla eurooppalaiseksi elektroniikkayritykseksi 1983–1991* (Helsinki: Edita, 2001b).

Häikiö, M., *Nokia: The Inside Story* (Helsinki: Edita, 2002).

Keskinen, T., *Idänkauppa 1944–1987* (Porvoo: Kauppalehti, 1987).

Kuisma, M., *Kylmä sota, kuuma öljy: Neste, Suomi ja kaksi Eurooppaa* (Helsinki: WSOY, 1997).

Lamberg, J.-A. and Skippari, M., 'Endogenous and Exogenous Variables in Trade Agreement Policy: Finnish Trade Agreement Policy in the 1930–1960s', *Scandinavian Economic History Review*, 3 (2001).

Lilja, K., Räsänen, K. and Tainio, R., 'A Dominant Business Recipe: The Forest Sector in Finland', in Whit, R. (ed.), *European Business Systems* (London: Sage, 1992).

Manninen, A. T., *Elaboration of NMT and GSM standards. From idea to market* (Jyväskylä: University of Jyväskylä, 2002).

Michelsen, K.-E. and Särkikoski, T., *Suomalainen ydinvoimalaitos* (Helsinki: Edita, 2005).

Moen, E. and Lilja, K., 'Constructing Global Corporations: Contrasting National Legacies in the Nordic Forest Industry', in Morgan, G., Kristensen, P. H., and Whitley, R. (eds), *The Multinational Firm Organizing Across Insitutional and National Divides* (Oxford: Oxford University Press, 2001) pp. 97–121.

Nykopp, J., *Kauppaa ja diplomatiaa* (Helsinki: Kirjayhtymä, 1985).

Ojala, J. and Karonen, P., 'Business: Rooted in Social Capital over the Centuries', in Ojala, J., Eloranta, J. and Jalava, J., (eds), *The Road to Prosperity: An Economic History of Finland* (Helsinki: SKS, 2006) pp. 92–125.

Pekkarinen, J. and Vartiainen, J., *Suomen talouspolitiikan pitkä linja.* (Helsinki and Juva: WSOY, 1993).

Ruostetsaari, I., *Energiapolitiikan määräytyminen* (Tampere: Tampereen yliopisto, 1989).

Seppälä, R., *Koskesta syntynyt* (Tampere: Tampella, 1981).

Skippari, M., *Evolutionary Patterns in Corporate Political Activity: Insights from a Historical Single Case Study* (Tampere: Tampere University of Technology, 2005).

Skippari, M., Ojala, J. and Lamberg, J.-A., 'Long-Run Consequences of a Radical Change in Business Environment: Dualistic Corporate Co-operation in Finnish Wood-Processing Industry during the twentieth Century', *Scandinavian Economic History Review,* 53 (2005), pp. 44–65.

Tainio, R., Korhonen, M. and Ollonqvist, P., 'In Search of Institutional Management: The Finnish Forest Sector Case', *International Journal of Sociology and Social Policy,* 9 (1989), pp. 88–119.

Urbans, R., *Tampereen Pellava- ja rautateollisuus osake-yhtiö 1856–1956* (Helsinki: Söderström, 1956).

WELFARE CAPITALISM: THE SWEDISH ECONOMY 1850–2005 • ENTREPRENEURSHIP AND OWNERSHIP: THE
.ERM VIABILITY OF THE SWEDISH BONNIER AND WALLENBERG FAMILY BUSINESS GROUPS • FROM
ABB **prologue to the Danish chapter** VESTMENT: FINNISH
CAPITALISM, 1850S–2005 • FROM STATE OWNERSHIP TO MULTINATIONAL CORPORATION: THE PATH OF
ENSO-GUTZEIT TO STORA-ENSO • SUCCESS AND FAILURE OF A CONGLOMERATE FIRM: THE STRATEGIC
PATHS OF NOKIA AND TAMPELLA IN THE LIBERALIZING FINNISH ECONOMY AFTER THE SECOND WORLD
WAR • CO-OPERATIVE LIBERALISM: DENMARK FROM 1857 TO 2007 • ARLA – FROM DECENTRALIZED INDUSTRY
TO MULTINATIONAL ENTERPRISE • CARLSBERG AND THE SELF-REGULATION OF THE DANISH BEER MARKET
• NORWAY: A RESOURCE-BASED AND DEMOCRATIC CAPITALISM • CONSTRUCTIVE POWER: ELKEM 1904–2004
• FINANCE AND THE DEVELOPMENT OF NORWEGIAN CAPITALISM – THE CASE OF CHRISTIANIA BANK

Our focus will now change from the north eastern to the south western
part of the Nordic region. As the Finnish version of capitalism has been
marked by an influence from Russia and Sweden, Danish capitalism is an
odd combination of British-influenced liberalism, German-inspired organization methods and Nordic egalitarian co-operatism. We have labelled this
'Co-operative Liberalism'. The apparently paradoxical label reflects two
important aspects of the story of Danish capitalism:

First, the agricultural sector was the most important sector until the mid-
twentieth century. In contrast to the other Nordic countries Danish farmers –
their leaders, associations and political parties – were very influential in the
development of capitalism. Danish agriculture built upon substantial export,
particularly of butter and bacon to England and Germany, and its farmers
were thus dependent on free access to the large early industrialized markets
which surrounded Denmark. The Danish farmers thus dominated the liberal
Danish party, Venstre, which combined a liberal trade policy with opposition to a strong state and heavy tax burdens on individuals. Agricultural
Denmark, thus, seemed obviously liberal but in fact the core of the early
agrarian modernization consisted of co-operative dairies, slaughter houses
and savings banks. To make the liberal picture even more complex the standardization of agricultural export products such as Lurbrand butter built
upon state co-ordinated research as described in Chapter 9 on Arla Foods.

The second important aspect of the paradoxical label, is that, seen in a long
time perspective, Danish capitalism seems to have moved like a pendulum
between liberal and co-operative dominance. The chapter is divided in five
time periods and despite all the differences between them, which almost makes
it meaningless to talk about *one* national business system, all five periods have
one thing in common, namely the transition between liberal and co-operative
characteristics.

Early Danish capitalism was marked by the liberal political constitution from 1849 while in the beginning of the second period from 1899 to 1933 economic interests became increasingly organized and the state began to play a role as mediator between these interests. The pendulum moved further towards the co-operative side in the following period, from 1933 to 1956, when the Danish economy was marked by protectionism and a focus on labour-intensive production for the home market. After 1957 industrial export became a still more important target of the Danish state, which began to focus on the competitiveness and productivity of Danish manufacturing industry. Still it was the public sector and its service functions which was the truly revolutionary aspect of Danish development from 1957 to 1981 when the extensive welfare state was built. After 1982 the liberal focus became increasingly important as the Danish economy became still more engaged in the global division of labour. As Chapter 10 on Carlsberg describes, Danish corporations changed from being export-focused towards becoming part of a transnational division of labour. Already this short *tour de force* through Danish development shows the large difference between early and late capitalism, one aspect seem to have been constant. When Danish society was most, liberal or co-operative in its nature there always seem to have been economic, political and social forces present trying to pull the society in the opposite direction.

WELFARE CAPITALISM: THE SWEDISH ECONOMY 1850–2005 ● ENTREPRENEURSHIP AND OWNERSHIP: THE

⊗ ABB LONG-TERM VIABILITY OF THE SWEDISH BONNIER AND WALLENBERG FAMILY BUSINESS GROUPS ● FROM

ABB TO MNE **co-operative liberalism: Denmark**MANAGEMENT: FINNISH

CAPITALISM, 1850–2005 ● FROM STATE OWNERSHIP TO MULTINATIONAL CORPORATION: THE PATH OF

ENSO-GUTZEIT **from 1857 to 2007**SUCCESS AND FAILURE OF A CONGLOMERATE FIRM: THE STRATEGIC

PATHS OF NOKIA AND TAMPELLA IN THE LIBERALIZING FINNISH ECONOMY AFTER THE SECOND WORLD

WAR ● CO-OPERATIVE LIBERALISM: DENMARK FROM 1857 TO 2007 ● ARLA – FROM DECENTRALIZED INDUSTRY

TO MULTINATIONAL ENTERPRISE ● CARL **Martin Jes Iversen and Steen Andersen**

● NORWAY: A RESOURCE-BASED AND DEMOCRATIC CAPITALISM ● CONSTRUCTIVE POWER: ELKEM 1904–2004

● FINANCE AND THE DEVELOPMENT OF NORWEGIAN CAPITALISM – THE CASE OF CHRISTIANIA BANK

Introduction

This chapter concerns the 150 years from the mid-nineteenth century to the early twenty-first century, in which Denmark may be regarded as a capitalist country. In some periods the economy was highly regulated, in others more liberal. Still, during this period the Danish economy was based on capitalism's three basic principles: market-based economic co-ordination, private property rights and labour as a commodity with wages paid in money. Geographically, Denmark links the European continent with the Scandinavian peninsula. This geographic position reflects a peculiar economic system that contains elements from the extended Nordic welfare states, German corporate governance systems and British liberalism. Consequently it is a very difficult task to label the Danish business system with one defining headline. Some scholars have focused on the importance of a culturally homogeneous population that has been able to adapt to economic pressures and crisis through popular movements such as the agricultural co-operative system in the late nineteenth century and the trade unions in the early twentieth century.[1] In contrast, other political economists have labelled Danish capitalism as a 'fragmented' system in which the agricultural population, the industrial centre in Copenhagen and the craftsmen of small railways towns continuously struggled for very different economic priorities and political ideologies.[2] Finally, traditional economic historians have given up the task of finding a single heading for Danish capitalism and instead have described the development chronologically by empirical events and statistical evidence.[3]

An important feature of Danish capitalism is the historic importance of the agricultural sector in general, and of agricultural exports in particular. Since the 1880s, the Danish agricultural sector was organized on co-operative principles. On the other hand, the essential export was dependent on liberal trade principles such as free access to international markets. In the words of the American economic historian Joel Mokyr, 'Denmark makes an appearance as a free-trade country that stuck with agriculture'.[4] In this book we characterize Danish capitalism as Co-operative Liberalism. That is an odd, but consistent, combination of basic co-operative principles such as help for self-help and solidarity, combined with liberal principles, that is market power, individual rights and a strong reliance on access to the surrounding markets.

The chapter is structured chronologically, but it also intends to identify some particular characteristics of the 150 years of Danish capitalism. Characteristics regarded as essential for understanding the extensive capitalist 'journey' – from the mid-nineteenth century's agrarian, underdeveloped society with high mortality and low technological standards, towards the urbanized, rich and technologically developed society of the early twenty-first century. This journey has been highly complex. The route was often unpredictable – both to us as later observers and in particular also to contemporary decision-makers, entrepreneurs and citizens. A consistent road map is needed and this country chapter is therefore divided in five different phases of capitalistic development:

- The early liberal society, 1857–98
- Regulation and internationalization, 1899–1932
- Industrial growth under protective restrictions, 1933–56
- Export orientation and the expanding welfare state, 1957–81
- The global division of labour, 1982–2007.

This chapter is particularly focused on important economic actors such as associations, corporations and entrepreneurs including their respective strategies and structures. Still the formation and impact of these economic actors can be understood only in relation to their context: the state, the educational system, the labour market and the financial system. In Denmark – as in most other dynamic societies – the content and role of each of these factors has changed dramatically over time. In early Danish capitalism the state was weak and most economic changes were locally initiated, while in the mid-twentieth century the welfare state came to play an important role in almost every aspect of Danish society. Even within each phase some time periods have been marked by stability and others by crucial changes and important long-reaching decisions. We have labelled these transitional time periods 'formative periods' – that is, time periods often marked by struggles between different political and economic interests, and by crucial decisions that constituted the succeeding direction. The phenomenon can be illustrated by the following example. In the 'formative period' of the early 1930s, the Danish economy was intensively regulated and import regulations were imposed. Danish industrial enterprises became more domestically orientated and less efficient. This orientation and economic regulation had long-term consequences – at least for the following three decades.

The early liberal society, 1857–98

On Saturday evening, 27 August 1857, a large group of Copenhageners had gathered at the royal riding ground in front of Christiansborg Castle. Tickets were sold at the entrance to the castle yard and at 8.30pm the astonished audience saw Superior War Commissioner Høegh-Guldberg turn on an illuminated electrical fountain driven by a wet battery.[5] Modern times had come to Denmark, and in 1857 three other – apparently unrelated – events showed that a new époque was emerging. The abolition of the more than 400-year-old Sound Dues, the new Freedom of Trade Act and, finally, the founding of the first private bank in Copenhagen, Privatbanken, managed by perhaps the most influential business tycoon in Danish history – C.F. Tietgen.

The Sound Dues had been introduced in 1429 as a shipping tax on all traffic entering the Baltic Sea via the Danish Sound – the passage between Denmark and Sweden. The dues symbolized Denmark's international position in medieval Europe as a main power in the south Baltic region. In 1800, the Danish king still ruled over Denmark, Norway, Iceland, the Faeroe Islands, the German Duchies of Schleswig and Holstein plus the colonies of Greenland, the Danish West Indies, Tranquebar and Guinea. In short the Danish kingdom was a multinational state, of the kind known from the larger, but contemporary, Austro-Hungarian Empire. The Danish kingdom was both a fragile and decentralized state – culturally, geographically and linguistically heterogeneous as it was. In the aftermath of the Napoleonic Wars the Danish state had gone bankrupt and in 1814 Norway was separated from Denmark and joined a dual union with Sweden. The proportion of German-speaking people within the Danish kingdom thus increased from 20 per cent to 35 per cent.[6] The language question in particular became sensitive and following a national liberal German movement in the Duchies, a civil war broke out in 1848. The Royal Danish Army won the war in 1850 and the Danish king consequently introduced an unpopular Danish national economic and linguistic policy. This policy only lasted fourteen years, until 1864, when the Prussian chancellor Otto von Bismarck decided to support his fellow nationalists in the north German areas. The Danish army was defeated, but the national liberal government in Copenhagen continued an almost suicidal policy in the peace negotiations with Prussia and the great powers Russia and Great Britain. The end result was that the Danish monarchy by the end of 1864 was reduced by two-fifths of its land area and lost approximately 800,000 of its citizens.

The result of the lost lands in 1814 and 1864 was a transition from a multinational Danish monarchy to an extremely culturally and linguistically homogeneous population after 1864. The new Danish–German border along the tiny river Kongeåen constituted a great political and economic barrier and consequently the Danish agrarian export-oriented economy changed its focus from the German markets towards the British markets. A second important consequence of the defeat in 1864 was a Danish national movement eager to improve the economic situation – for instance by damming new agricultural land. The motto was: 'Winning inwards what has been lost to the outside' (*hvad udad tabt, skal indad vindes*). The abolishment of the Sound Dues in 1857 thus symbolized a period when the primacy of the old multinational Danish kingdom was lost, but the free passage to the Baltic Sea also symbolized the breakthrough of a new era with more liberal trade conditions.

The most important event in this respect was the comprehensive Trade Act of 29 December 1857 – asserting free trade as the leading economic principle. Due to this Act, which was enforced in 1862, the royal municipal charters of the towns were abolished and the guilds lost their monopolist position, even though they often continued as purely voluntary institutions. The Trade Act was the economic dimension of the Danish Free Constitution of 5 June 1849, when Denmark moved from the rule of monarchy towards a liberal democracy with restricted suffrage. Already in the aftermath of Adam Smith's liberal thoughts in *The Wealth of Nations* (1776), a new political–economical movement had emerged in Copenhagen. This movement was particularly strong among civil servants, such as the influential Jonas Collin, Deputy in the Royal Finance Department from 1816 to 1848, President of the Royal Danish Agricultural Society (Det Kgl. Danske Landhusholdningsselskab) from 1809 to 1855 and famous for being a patron of the author Hans Christian Andersen. Plans had been made to abolish the guilds in 1800, and it was stipulated that any journeyman who had worked steadily for four years might become a free master. These early liberal initiatives, which still took place under the monarchy, were blocked following the bankruptcy of the Danish state in 1813. In 1822, the provisions for the liberation of journeymen were withdrawn, and other reactionary regulations were introduced. Still, the liberal movement continued its activities and in 1849 the new constitution – which introduced freedom of speech and religion – was well prepared and received broad intellectual and public support. In 1922, the political scientist Harald Westergaard described the constitution in the following words:[7]

> These laws are evidently based on the view generally prevalent at the time that the chief aim must be to organize the community with reference to the free development of the powers of the individual. The individualist community was thus the great goal. The task of the state was to be limited so far as possible to the protection of rights and the maintenance of order.

The liberal political atmosphere obviously influenced the relatively small Danish business community of the 1850s. In the epoch-making year of 1857, a group of leading businessmen, bankers and merchants in Copenhagen, among them the later national liberal politician and grandfather of the famous physicist Niels Bohr, David B. Adler, initiated the founding of Privatbanken, the first private bank in Copenhagen. Adler had established his own banking firm, D.B.A. & Co., in 1850, when he returned from London, and like other businessmen in Copenhagen he was lacking a private deposit and lending bank. Adler and the fellow founders of Privatbanken appointed the just 28-year-old C.F. Tietgen as managing director. In its initial years, Privatbanken functioned as a traditional cautious deposit bank. But already by 1863 Tietgen had become involved in a Dutch initiative for the possible founding of a Scandinavian *Credit Mobilier* bank which would participate in the founding and management of industrial corporations. The Dutch initiators became reluctant to continue in 1864 when Denmark entered the war against Prussia. The plans were withdrawn, but Tietgen and the important chairman of the Board in Privatbanken, C.A. Broberg, were inspired by the high profitability of similar Dutch and French banks and in 1865 Privatbanken engaged in the founding, ownership and management of the new tram company Kjøbenhavns Sporveis-Selskab.[8] In the following years, Privatbanken aimed to develop a very close relationship to businesses, including manufacturing enterprises. Privatbanken thus followed a continental Universal Bank, mixed banking system, in which the bank both facilitated the actual creation of the enterprises, through the bank's activities in assembling equity capital and the general working credits, and participated in management of companies through board positions.

The financial sector

The financial sector in Denmark from 1857 to 1898 reflects two important aspects of early Danish capitalism. The first aspect is the liberal nature of the system – the Danish private banks existed without any special legal frameworks until 1919. Another important feature is that the capitalist economy did not conquer the Danish economy in a simple and unambiguous manner. Rather, the early capitalist period was marked by two separate financial economies. On the one hand there was the capitalist profit-oriented economy with industries, limited liability corporations and private banks, and on the other a co-operative economy that aimed to produce for national and international markets, but which at the same time was focused on facilitating certain economic and productive functions. The savings banks, credit associations and co-operative dairies and factories belonged to this primarily agricultural part of the economy.

The early fiscal policy and banking system was a product of the liberal age in Danish economic history.[9] In order to establish a bank, permission was required from the central bank, Nationalbanken. This permission did provide some regulation of initial functions and procedures, but once established the banks acted without any banking laws. The main aim of the state in these free conditions was to facilitate the founding of new independent banks. This effort succeeded and the number of banks increased from 18 in 1870 to 135 in 1910.[10] Still, the impact of the growing private bank sector should not be overestimated. As illustrated in Table 8.1 it was rather the small savings banks and the credit associations that dominated the picture until the early twentieth century.

The first Danish savings bank had been established in 1810 in Holsteinsborg and gradually these financial institutions were established in rural areas,

Table 8.1 **Structure of the Danish capital market, 1857–1914 (million DKR, current prices)**

	1857	1870	1877	1883	1891	1896	1899	1914
Private bank deposits	4	27	67	117	155	234	284	957
Saving banks deposits	47	113	208	316	466	578	586	910
Credit associations	28	68	131	248	435	569	700	1682
Assets of life insurance companies	9	24	35	51	77	98	109	284

Source: Dansk Pengehistorie I (1968).

resulting in twenty-one savings banks by 1840. In the following decades the savings banks changed their policy from pure saving towards saving and lending. The main role of the savings banks was to finance property, and their purpose was not to earn money but rather to facilitate saving and help to capitalise small investments that did not carry a high risk. The savings banks were thus part of the co-operative economy and central to agricultural modernization after 1880. The private banks consisted of two main spheres: a Copenhagen sphere and the provincial banks. The Copenhagen sphere consisted of the already mentioned Privatbanken founded in 1857, the Landmandsbanken from 1871 and the Handelsbanken from 1873. These three banks were all founded in Copenhagen and the management and the board of directors consisted of businessmen and bankers with strong connections to influential industrialists. A prime example was Isak Glückstadt, the Jewish director of Landmandsbanken for thirty-eight years from 1872 to 1910. Glückstadt was the leading force in the establishment of Københavns Frihavnsaktieselskab (Copenhagen Free Port Ltd) in 1892, established against the will of C.F. Tietgen, and in 1897 he participated in H.N. Andersens in founding the Østasiatisk Kompagni (the East Asian Company, EAC). Tietgen and thus Privatbanken rejected Andersen's ideas but EAC became the largest Danish enterprise throughout most of the twentieth century, combining shipping, trade and manufacturing interests. In the provinces, the controlling function of the private banks was more limited. It has been estimated that the provincial banks were represented in the management of only 6 per cent of the industrial firms, while the Copenhagen banks were represented in 11–12 per cent.[11]

Danish monetary policy was basically designed to ease access to credit. One of its main features was a continuous use of foreign capital resources. An important precondition for this policy was the grain export, which provided a Danish payment surplus until the mid-1850s. Another important factor was that the Danish government in 1857 received DKK 63.3 million (twice the annual state revenue) in compensation for the loss of the Sound Dues and in 1864 DKK 45.6 million from Germany as compensation for the losses in Schleswig-Holstein. With a basis in these remarkable extraordinary incomes, Denmark in 1873 joined a monetary union with Sweden (and Norway from 1875), which pegged the currency to the gold standard.

As a result of the compensations and the grain export, Denmark in the early 1870s gained a position as net creditor (Table 8.2). In the following decades there was thus room for combining a fixed currency with a permanent

Table 8.2 **Danish export, liabilities and assets in relation to foreign countries, 1870–1910 (million DKK)**[1]

	1870	1880	1890	1900	1910
Export agriculture	103	152	172	250	438
Export industry	8	8	10	14	25
Export other	2	12	14	18	27
Export total	113	152	195	282	490
National debt.	24[2]	n.a.	50[3]	204[4]	448
Bonds and shares sold abroad	6[2]	n.a.	50[3]	101[4]	445
Assets (funds in nat. bank, etc.)	187[2]	n.a.	100	117[4]	120
Net balance	157[2]	n.a.	0[3]	−198[4]	−843

Notes: 1. The large assets in 1872 can be explained by the compensation from the Sound Dues and the loss of Schleswig-Holstein, 2. 1872, 3. 1891, 4. 1899. n.a. = Not available.
Sources: Hansen (1970), p. 61; Fink (2005), pp. 40, 68.

consumption of foreign capital which helped the state to keep a low long-term interest rate – in the late nineteenth century below 3.6–3.7 per cent. The losses of the former multinational state and its political status thus not only created a culturally and linguistic homogeneous population; Denmark had also 'stabilized its *financial* position by liquidating certain of its former positions of *political* power' in the words of the Danish economic historian Svend Aage Hansen.[12]

The industrial sphere: from Tietgen's network to the industrial breakthrough of the 1890s

C.F. Tietgen was the most influential and important figure in the Danish business community of the 1860s and 1870s. He was the centre of a sophisticated business network which consisted of large companies, within both the service and manufacturing industries. In 1866 Tietgen took the initiative to found DFDS, Det forenede Dampskibs-Selskab (The United Steamship Company), which soon controlled the steamship lines between the Danish islands – the backbone of the Danish infrastructural system until the 1890s. At the turn of the century DFDS had acquired most of the important export shipping lines from Denmark and the shipping company was the most stable and in the long term most profitable of the Tietgen corporations. It was no coincidence that the Danish mogul pointed at DFDS when he recommended investments to the Danish King Christian IX. Nevertheless Tietgen's real pride was Det Store Nordiske Telegrafselskab (The Great Northern Telegraph Company), established in 1869. This company reflected his ambition of strengthening the

Danish position of neutrality after the defeat in 1864. Around 1870, Tietgen cleverly used diplomatic connections between the Danish royal family and the Russian Czar in order to gain an important Russian concession on international telegraphy and the company succeeded in connecting Northern Europe with East Asia via Siberia in 1872. On the basis of this important connection Great Northern became the most wealthy and successful Danish enterprise until around 1930 when the company was affected by the world depression, new wireless technologies and more state interference. In the 1860s and 1870s telegraphy and telephony were, together with railways, the most important new infrastructural technologies. The young modern entrepreneur Tietgen was at the centre of both new technologies – as Professor Ole Lange has stated: 'a contemporary Tietgen would properly be engaged in the internet, IP telephony or nanotechnology.'[13]

Within the industrial sphere Tietgen used Privatbanken as mediator in three large mergers in 1872 alone: De Danske Sukkerfabrikker (The Danish Sugar Factories), the shipyard Burmeister & Wain and De danske Cikoriefabrikker (The Danish Chicory Factories). Tietgen's and Privatbanken's ambitious plans continued and the brewery, glass and fertilizer factory Tuborg's Fabrikker was established in 1873, the De danske Spritfabrikker (The Danish Distilleries) in 1881 and Faxe Kalkbrud (Faxe Limestone Quarries) in 1883. Tietgen's accomplishments astonished contemporary observers as well as historians. In 1952, the economic historian Willerslev wrote that 'important parts of our industry [were given] a trust-like character, before trusts and cartels played any important role in the economic structure of other countries'.[14]

Tietgen was a key factor in the modernization of Danish society – in particular due to his engagement in modern infrastructure such as telegraphy, telephone and railways. Still, the core of the Danish economy was the agricultural sector, which was modernized through new industrial production methods. An industrial breakthrough came only at the turn of the century in Denmark and as late as the early 1890s a contemporary observer described the immature Danish industrialization in following words:[15]

> If we focus our attention upon true factories, ignoring those industrial establishments, such as tanneries, dyeworks, printing works, breweries etc., that are intermediate in size between factories and craft enterprises, we find almost everywhere that they stand in isolation: nowhere in Denmark are there any agglomerates of factories of the sort found in other countries.

Table 8.3 **Distribution of GDP, at factor cost, by principal industrial categories, 1855–1930 (million DKK, current prices) and manufacturing industries' export ratio (percentage)**

Sector	1855	1870	1890	1900	1930
Primary sector	261	335	365	399	1202
Secondary sector	93	134	215	346	1578
Tertiary sector	115	200	385	577	2925
Total GDP at factor cost	469	669	965	1322	5705
Man. industries export ratio, (%)	14	14	16	7	n.a.

Note: n.a. = Not available.
Source: Hansen (1970), p. 11.

As Table 8.3 indicates, manufacturing industries grew only at a very low output level from the 1860s to the 1880s and the stagnating – and even falling – export ratio indicates that industry was mainly orientated towards the home market. This home market orientation was still apparent in the 1890s when the secondary industrial sector grew substantially faster than the primary agricultural sector. The number of industrial workers grew substantially, from 42,526 in 1890 to 78,206 in 1900, while the number of companies grew from 1949 in 1890 to 3652 in 1900.[16] The growing Danish industry was characterized by many small workshops and factories which facilitated the Danish agricultural sector, which during these years went through a transition from crop to animal production. The average size of the Danish industrial companies in the 1890s was approximately 21–22 workers. In contrast to Sweden the Danish industrial environment was thus based on SMEs from the very outset. Most of these new SMEs were established outside Copenhagen and thus outside the large banks' spheres of interest. In Copenhagen the number of employees grew from 14,555 in 1890 to 22,904 in 1900 while in Jutland the number of industrial employees more than doubled in the 1890s from 9586 in 1890 to 23,085 in 1900.[17] This growth was related to the rise of new small towns alongside the railways (stationsbyer) from 1880 to 1920. These towns facilitated the needs of the local agricultural regions and typically housed the station, a hotel, the co-operative dairy, shops and small mechanical machine industries.

The decades after 1880 are regarded as the core of the second industrial revolution. During this time, new technologies made it possible to establish factories based on mass production and economies of scale. In Denmark, industrial production methods changed dramatically as well – particularly in the 1890s when the level of mechanization in factories rose from 19,475 hp 1890 to 51,591 hp in 1900, of which steam still accounted for 42,984 hp and the new efficient electricity still only 991 horsepower.[18] Despite this limited electrification, new technologies within electricity and metalworking provided the background for the establishment of some of most successful and fast-growing Danish corporations: the refrigerator companies Atlas and Vølund were established in 1897 and 1898, respectively; electric equipment producer Titan was established in 1897; Nordisk Kabel og Traadfabrikker (Nordic Cable and Wire Factories) was founded by N.P. Prior in 1891; and finally, the Thriges factories after 1894. The latter corporation was established by Thomas B. Thrige in the third largest Danish town, Odense. Thrige was an almost archetypical example of a late nineteenth-century Danish entrepreneur.

This career began with an qualification in machinery skills from one of the Danish technical schools, of which the first had been established in 1862. The system of these technical and craft-specific schools was established in 1876–7 when a national system of technical educations was established in the Society of Technical Schools (Det Tekniske Selskabs Skoler).[19] The number of technical schools peaked in 1930 with around 350 local schools, of which a majority were in provincial and small towns. In 1998 there were still about 60 of these technical schools with about 83,000 pupils in Denmark. Like most other contemporary entrepreneurs, Thrige began his professional career by gathering international experience. From 1888 to 1893 he was employed at Thomas A. Edison's laboratories in General Electric's large factories in the US. Following his return to Denmark Thrige established a small back-yard bicycle workshop in 1894, and in the following years he focused on the development and production of electrical motors. The successful and pioneering corporation introduced the production of elevators in 1896, cars in 1909, ship equipment in 1920 and finally trains in 1929.[20]

The innovation of this early Danish industrialization was most often based on organizational or technological entrepreneurs such as J.C. Jacobsen from Carlsberg, Tietgen, N.P. Prior and Thrige, all of whom went on educational journeys to the more advanced industrial societies in Germany, Great Britain or the US. When these young entrepreneurs returned to Denmark they intro-duced new technological and organizational methods they saw and in this way developed the market and established their own entrepreneurial success. In contrast to Sweden, it was only in rare cases that the Danish industrial cor-porations of the 1880s and 1890s were based on unique inventions. One

Table 8.4

Table 8.4 *Important Danish mergers within the paper and forest, food and beverages and chemicals industries 1889–1901*

Year	Company
1889	United Paper Mills (De Forenede Papirfabrikker)
1890	United Breweries (De Forenede Bryggerier)
1895	The Copenhagen Timber Company (Trækompagniet i København)
1895	United Malt Factories (De Forenede Maltfabrikker)
1896	United Soap Factories (De Forenede Sæbefabrikker)
1896	The Soda Factories (Sodafabrikkerne)
1897	United Constructional Joineries (De Forenede Bygningssnedkerier A/S)
1897	United Coffee Roasters (De Forenede Kaffebrænderier A/S)
1897	The Danish Steam Mills (De danske Dampmøller A/S)
1897/1902	Danish Sulphur and Phosphates Producers (Dansk Svovlsyre- og Superphosphat-fabrik)
1899	Silvan
1901	United Canneries (De Forenede Conservesfabrikker A/S)

of the few examples of an industrial inventor was Wilhelm Hellesen, who in 1887 invented the dry battery. The same year Hellesen and his partner Valdemar Ludvigsen founded a company later known as Hellesens Enke og V. Ludvigsen, and following an immediate success, the company was in the 1890s exporting dry batteries to more than sixty countries and had established licensed production in Vienna, London and Berlin.

The expanding industrialization of the 1890s was further strengthened by a wave of mergers. These mergers had two main purposes – both well known from economic theory: exploitation of new technologies through economies of scale and the limitation of competition. With inspiration from Tietgen's Danish mergers in 1872–3 and from the contemporary world-famous wave of mergers in the US, many of these Danish competition-limiting mergers of the 1890s were prefixed with the word 'United'. The most important example was the merger of the great majority of Danish paper and pulp factories which in 1889 formed De Forenede Papirfabrikker A/S (United Paper Mills). The de facto monopoly on paper production, which also made an extensive exploitation of economies of scale possible, provided an important inspiration for a number of Danish mergers in the following decade – mostly within three important industries: forestry and woodworking, food and beverages, and chemicals (Table 8.4).

As was the case with private banking, Danish industrial corporate law was extremely liberal. The initial Company Laws (Firmalovene) in 1862 and

1889 demanded only a registration of the new corporations – including names of the responsible persons and, for the latter law, the size of the share capital and a description of the articles of association. A real corporate law (Aktieselskabslovgivning) was introduced in Denmark only in 1917. This extreme liberal institutional corporate framework was exceptional in an international context.[21] In most countries there had been a tradition for a corporate approval rather than registration of the limited liability companies from the late nineteenth century. The merger wave in the 1890s also reflected a growing criticism or reaction against the extremely liberal Danish business environment. It was somehow paradoxical situation. A monopolistic merger such as the foundation of De Forenede Papirfabrikker in 1889 was possible because of the liberal lack of regulations. On the other hand the 'United' merger wave of the 1890s was an attempt to control and limit the devastating consequences of free competition – the central element of the liberal ideology. In 1892 A. Fraenkel – the first official Carlsberg biographer – criticized the lager beer marketed in Copenhagen in the late 1880s and early 1890s for being anarchistic and 'Manchester-like'.[22] Order was needed, and in the case of the beverage market this was far-reaching cartel which included a price agreement that lasted from 1899 to 1988. At the turn of the century the liberal Danish spirit of 1857 was thus under pressure, even from key actors within the manufacturing industry, the sector in Denmark, which traditionally was most capitalist in its nature.

The agricultural sector and the co-operative economy

Early Danish capitalist development was marked by a dramatic transition in the agricultural sector in terms of production, organization and technology. In terms of production, the development of the agricultural sector can be divided in two phases: the grain sale period (kornsalgsperioden) from the 1830s to the mid-1870s and the livestock-based period from the mid-1880s onwards. In the grain sale period, prices and production increased and the total value of Danish production measured in fixed prices grew from DKK 266 million in 1835 to DKK 479 million in 1879.[23] This growth can be explained by a combination of increasing prices – in 1860 the price of grain was about 55 per cent higher than in 1835 – and new more efficient machinery such as the iron swing plough.[24]

The explanation for the rising prices of this successful grain sale period are to be found outside Denmark. The European population grew by around 40 per cent from 1830 to 1880, and with industrialization came an increasing demand for food and a new balance of power between the expanding

Table 8.5 **Danish population, divided on culture–geography lines, 1860–1901 (1,000 inhabitants)**

	1860	1870	1880	1890	1901
Copenhagen	163	198	261	360	455
Provincial towns	214	246	291	362	482
Countryside districts	1.119	1.231	1.341	1.450	1.513
Total population	1.608	1.785	1.969	2.172	2.450

Source: Fink (2005).

urbanized people and the shrinking agrarian societies (Table 8.5). From 1838 the British Anti-Corn Law League worked intensively to abolish the Corn Laws, which since 1815 had protected British agriculture from lower prices of imported wheat. With support from the industrial classes and parts of the working classes, the League succeeded in 1846 in abolishing protection. Grain prices rose, and Danish agricultural export to Great Britain prospered in the 1850s and 1860s.

It was particularly the wealthier landowning classes in the countryside who gained from rising prices in the 1850s and 1860s. As a consequence of the high earnings real estate prices rose dramatically in the mid-nineteenth century – in the early 1870s the price of farms was two or three times the price in the mid-1840s.[25] But the high prices of real estate had severe social consequences. Table 8.5 shows that despite a growing urbanization, the number of inhabitants in countryside districts rose from 1.1 million in 1860 to 1.5 million in 1901. As a consequence a large group of poor agricultural day-labourers emerged – in sharp contrast to the still wealthier landowners.

With the democratic reforms, in particular the tenure law of 1861 initiated by the liberal Minister of Internal Affairs and former chief architect behind the 1849 Free Constitution, Ditlev Gothard Monrad, came a decrease in the number of copyhold farms from 70,000 out of 130,000 farms in 1835 to 45,000 out of 206,000 farms in 1873.[26] The structure of Danish agriculture thus moved towards fewer copyholders, more small farms and a new large group of poor day-labourer. In 1876 the prices of grain fell dramatically: from an index of 100 in 1870, the prices fell continuously to an index of 60 in 1900. This plummeting price had severe consequences for the agrarian, export-oriented Danish economy. The primary background for the falling prices was new transport technologies. At the end of the 1870s new railways made it possible to transport large amounts of grain from the American prairies and eastern European – particularly the Ukrainian – steppes to the large modernized harbours with their new regular, fast steamships. Some west

European countries reacted by increasing protective duties, but as new duties were in contrast to the liberal Danish policy and as the country still was a net exporter of grain, such a protection would only partly help.

Instead, Danish agriculture underwent a remarkably fast and efficient transition from the production of crops to livestock-based production. As with most large economic transitions it was a complex development in which both technological, organizational and financial aspects were important.[27] From 1876 to 1882 there were still doubts among agricultural experts and farmers about whether the low grain prices were permanent or temporary. At this stage, most advice was aimed at the individual farmer. From 1883, the low grain prices were considered permanent and primarily among the large group of land-owing medium-sized farmers, the re-adjustment of production accelerated. This proved extremely successful. In 1870 the value of the Danish grain export was DKK 38 million and already in the early 1880s Denmark imported as much grain as she exported, while in 1900 Denmark was becoming a net importer of the still relatively cheap grain to the value of approximately DKK 50 million.[28] This grain was used as feedstuff for livestock-based production, which now constituted the main agricultural exports. At the end of the 1860s animal export amounted to about 5,000 tonnes, while at the beginning of the twentieth century it was around 70,000 tonnes. It was an adjustment which was impossible to be undertaken by the individual farmer: new production and organizational functions were needed.

The most important element was co-operative ownership. In 1882 – when the grain-price crisis had lasted for almost five years – a group of farmers in the small town of Hjedding formed the first co-operative dairy. The articles of association for the Hjedding dairy were to become a key model for the co-operative dairies which rapidly spread around the country. By 1909 there were 1157 local co-operative dairies. The transition of the agricultural sector was endangered in the 1890s when the prices of milk, butter and meat fell dramatically. Danish farmers – who had invested intensively in co-operative dairies and new production methods – were in a perilous situation. It was impossible to return to producing the still very cheap grain, but a possible way out of the difficulties was to improve butter quality and sell to the lucrative British consumer market. To this end the common Lur brand was established in 1906 – first as a private initiative but from 1911 to 1991 as the property of the Danish state. It was quite a challenge to improve the quality of co-operative butter as the milk was delivered by approximately 200,000 farmers and the butter produced at more than 1100 local dairies around

1910. The transformation of the agricultural sector in the 1880s and 1890s was economically the most important event in early Danish capitalism. In Danish popular history, the co-operative movement has since been regarded as a unique Danish national development. Denmark was in fact also the country in the world in which the co-operative principles had the largest impact on the economy. In the early twenty-first Century three of the ten largest Danish corporations are still co-operatives. On the other hand, it should not be forgotten that the co-operative movement was dependent on Swedish technological innovations, new British organizational methods and liberal access to export markets. The rest of the world was crucial in the transition of the Danish agricultural sector – but one key institution was surprisingly absent in the modernization of the co-operatives as well as in the industrial Denmark, namely the Danish state.

The Danish state: liberal ideology and political deadlocks

The division of economic life in Denmark between the urban and the rural spheres in the second part of the nineteenth century was also present in the political life in which the liberal peasant movement (Venstre) was in opposition to the conservative politicians. J.B.S. Estrup was prime minister from 1875 to 1894 and in the difficult provisional period from 1877–94 his conservative government accomplished provisional financial state budgets against the will of the liberal majority of the parliament but with the support of the king who, according to par. 25 of the Free Constitution could enforce laws in 'extreme circumstances'. The most spectacular political conflict in this period between the liberals and the conservatives concerned the defence of Denmark and in particular the expensive but prestigious fortress of Copenhagen. The fundamental liberal principles behind economic policy were less questioned. It was the combination of a broadly accepted liberal ideology and the political deadlock that lead to the limited role of the state in the modernization of Denmark. Around 1900, Danish state gradually began to play a more important role – but still it was private rather than public initiatives that changed Danish society. The following three examples can help to illustrate this nineteenth-century phenomenon: infrastructure, labour market regulation and health insurance policy.

The telephone was introduced in Copenhagen in 1879. It was one of the most important new infrastructural technologies but still decades from its real breakthrough. Estrup's government worked for the establishment of a state monopoly – as known from domestic telegraphy – but the deadlocked political situation hampered these attempts. The telephone operation

Table 8.6 **Transport of shipping goods and railway goods, 1895–1914 (1,000 tonnes)**

Goods	1895	1900	1905	1910	1914
Shipping goods[1]	3.831	5.110	5.760	6.785	7.676
Railway goods	2.436	4.157	5.748	6.919	9.306

Note: 1. Including goods transported to Danish harbours and from Danish harbours.
Source: Fink (2006), p. 78.

network was thus established on the basis of a large number of small local companies. Already in 1881 – only four years after L.M. Ericsson's invention of the telephone exchange – Tietgen initiated a merger of the operators in Copenhagen resulting in the company Københavns Telefon Aktieselskab (KTAS) (Copenhagen Telephone Company Ltd). In 1895, a number of telephone operators in Jutland merged to form Jydsk Telefon Aktieselskab (JTAS). Finally, in 1897, it was decided that telephone operation should be handled as a state monopoly with private companies on the basis of long-term concessions.

Until 1905, the private shipping lines constituted the most important means of transport for goods between Danish towns and between Danish towns and export market (Table 8.6). This crucial infrastructure was controlled by the large monopolistic-like company DFDS initiated by Tietgen in 1866. In the 1890s and 1900s, DFDS lost its dominant status to a number of new steam shipping companies, including A.P. Møller's two shipping companies: Dampskibsselskabet Svendborg of 1904 and Dampskibsselskabet of 1912, later to become the largest, most globalized Danish enterprise – A.P. Møller-Mærsk A/S. Traditionally, infrastructure belongs to the interest sphere of the state. In the case of the railways, the Danish state did in fact play an active role, particularly in the operation of the primary route that connected Copenhagen with the main provincial towns. These connections were finished in the mid-1870s – from Copenhagen it was possible to reach Frederikshavn in the north and the new export harbour town of Esbjerg (aimed for export to the British market following the loss of Schleswig-Holstein in 1864) in the west. Still, the initiatives were taken by private investors and the siting of the railway was designed to promote local industries, unlike other countries such as Prussian Germany where the interests of the military–political state played a larger role.

In Jutland it was the British construction company Peto, Brassey & Betts which built the primary railways. For the first couple of years the British company also owned Det Danske Jernbane-Drifts-Selskab (The Danish

Railway Service Company), which operated the west Danish primary railways. This company was taken over by the Danish state in 1867 and a real national state railway company (DSB) was established in 1885 to service the primary railway network. The important secondary railways – which connected the export-oriented agrarian societies and new small towns with the main system – were managed by so-called 'private railways' (*privatbaner*). The public authorities – the state, but to a larger extent the local communities – invested in the founding and service of these networks, together with local private investors.

The regulation of the Danish labour market in the nineteenth century reflected the liberal conditions in the Danish business system. In the 1860s, a new debate emerged concerning the still hard and inhumane conditions of industrial workers. This debate led to a rather limited company law in 1873 after which it was illegal to employ children below the age of ten. Still, there was no unemployment relief and particularly during the winters the growing towns were marked by severe poverty and suffering. In the winter of 1885–6 one-third of the workforce in Copenhagen was unemployed. Private philanthropic associations provided food to approximately 5,000 people on a daily basis that winter. In these deep depressions, emigration to America proved to be an important hope. From 1868 to 1900 more than 38,000 people from Copenhagen immigrated, but the Danish immigration rate was still substantially lower than from Sweden and Norway, where the suffering was even worse.

Criticism of the consequences of liberalistic industrialization grew. In the 1870s, a social democratic movement was established, inspired by the new intellectual socialism that was particularly strong in Germany. In November 1881, the German chancellor Bismarck anticipated socialist discontent by issuing a deep-seated national social policy: reforms of sick funds, accident compensation and, in 1889, a complicated old age and health insurance. These pioneering German social reforms were based on contributions from employees, the state and, most importantly, the employer, who contributed one-third of the sick funds and half of the old age and invalid insurance. Inspired by the German reforms the Danish government in 1891 decided upon an Old Age Pension Act (*alderdomsforsørgelse*). This act was based on three fundamental principles: it was universal (all Danish citizens could apply for the pension), it was tax- and state-financed and finally the distribution and decisions on who should receive the pensions was decentralized to the local municipality.

In 1885 an accident and sickness social insurance commission was appointed and following seven years of preparatory work the Social Insurance Act of 1892 was agreed. This early Danish social policy was based on the existing local sick benefit association (*sygekasser*) (voluntary health insurance associations) whose structure can be traced back to the medieval guild system. Before the liberal Corporate Act in 1857, the guilds included a health insurance system for critical situations and in the 1860s this local system continued as a popular movement of sick benefit associations. The principle was 'help for self-help', meaning that members with good health and in work would pay in order to get access to help in case of illness or accident. As there was no alternative source of social support, the number of sick benefit association members rose rapidly along with urbanization: from around 20,000 in 1866 to 87,000 in 1874 to 120,000 members in 1885.[29] With the Act of 1892 the Danish state decided to support this widespread movement. If the Danish state recognized the local sick benefit associations, it would receive state subsidies to help the members. The minimum help was defined by the state, but the actual decision-making and daily administration of the system was extremely decentralized. The importance of this movement can be illustrated by the number of members, which in 1915 amounted to 892,000, or almost half of the adult Danish population. The health insurance system reflects two important characteristics of early Danish capitalism. Firstly, the state supported existing initiatives rather than initiating social reforms. And when the state did engage itself in social policy the administration was marked by a large degree of decentralization – as was also the case with the regional telephone operators and the private railways. Another important aspect was that, in contrast to the influential German system, Danish health insurance was based on contributions from the employees (the old guild-inspired help for self-help principles) and from the state. The third traditional contributor – the employer – was left out. One hundred years later, the principle that the state rather than employers should contribute to social and health insurance proved a cornerstone in the so-called Danish Flexicurity labour market model.

Regulation and internationalization, 1899–1932

The epoch-making moment in Danish labour market policy was September 1899, when the rules of the game in the Danish labour market were agreed upon. This agreement was the culmination of a still stronger division of interests between employers (*mestre*) and journeymen (*svende*). The division became still more apparent in the 1880s and as a result the employees began to organise their own labour movement. First, local craft-based unions were established and in 1886 the unions in Copenhagen formed De samvirkende Fagforeninger (The joined trade unions), which in 1896 was succeeded by the national union, De samvirkende Fagforbund (LO). The organizational development of employers came later, but fundamentally the structure mirrored their counterpart's. The employers were organized in terms of industries – a prime example was the Brewers' Association (Bryggeri-foreningen) established in 1899. As described in Chapter 10 on Carlsberg, the Brewers' Association had three main purposes: first and foremost it co-ordinated the relations with the trade unions. Second, the association organized a cartel with fixed prices and division of the market. Third, the association represented the industry's interests in relation to the state. Above these industrially defined associations an umbrella organization of employers (Arbejdsgiverforeningen af 1896) was established in 1896.

As a culmination of the still-stronger conflict between the interests of these as yet immature labour market organizations, the deepest and most serious labour conflict in Danish history broke out in May 1899. In four months more than half of the organized workers were striking or hit by lock-outs, but finally in September 1899 an agreement was reached. The agreement was important as it clarified that strikes and lock-outs were not to begin without due notice. Second, the right of the employer to conduct and distribute work was acknowledged and finally any violation of this agreement was to be dealt with in a court of arbitration.[30] Nine years later a new labour market conflict emerged between the newspapers and the typographers. For the first time the Danish state intervened in the conflict and in 1910 a permanent Court of Arbitration (den faste Voldgiftsret) was established. The court, which was paid for by the state, had the final word in labour market conflicts and was obliged to levy penalties on associations that did not follow its decisions.

The mid-1890s was the point of departure for almost two decades of strong economic growth in Denmark. The agricultural sector had succeeded in its transition from crop production towards high-quality export butter thanks to the co-operative organizational methods introduced from 1882 and new technological inventions, primarily Laval's cream-centrifuge after 1878. The industries grew substantially faster from 1900 to 1914 when mechanization had its real breakthrough – from a total of 131,124 hp in 1906 to 314,479 in 1914. In this *Belle Époque*, Danish society was gradually moving from the liberal spirit of 1857 towards a new type of capitalism marked by systematic co-operation between various organizations: the labour market systems was organized with the 1899 September agreement, the deadlock in political life was finally solved with the shift of political system (Systemskiftet) in 1901 after which the decision-takers reflected the majority of the population and the industrial interests were organized in employers' associations and industrial cartels. In short, the Danish economy from 1899 to 1932 became more organized and the Danish state began to play a more active role, as both a regulating and an initiating force. Still, the liberal spirit was strong. Influential decision-makers, particularly within industry and the agricultural sector, were sceptical about state initiatives at the expense of private initiatives. According to Professor Geoffrey Jones, Denmark, The Netherlands and Great Britain in 1914 were the last countries that still promoted a liberal, open-trade policy.[31] The question for the future was which of the two fundamentally different directions should be followed – the liberal path of weak state and loose regulation or organized capitalism, with detailed regulation of market conditions and an influential state?

Regulation and the after-effects of the crisis, 1914–18

The outbreak of war in Europe had immediate economic consequences in the neutral state of Denmark. In August 1914, the population began to panic and the banks had to reduce people's ability to make withdrawals from their accounts, as well as suspend the right to convert their bank deposits into gold. The unrest led to price rises and a shortage of goods. Among other things, the price of rye bread rose by one-third and the price of potatoes doubled during the first days of August. The Danish Social-Liberal Party, which was in government at the time, quickly responded to the supply shortage in an attempt to protect the population's living conditions against the influence of the war through several interventions in the market economy. Already on 7 August 1914, the Danish Rigsdag (Parliament) passed the so-called 'August Law', which authorized the Minister of the Interior, Ove Rode, to fix the prices of goods and conduct expropriations. In Parliament Ove Rode said: 'the authorization is very comprehensive and must hence be implemented with great caution. If necessary it must be applied with great force.' The law was applied to carry out an extensive regulation of the Danish national economy and provided the necessary authorization to circumvent Parliament. The actual instrument which regulated the economy was the so-called

Den Overordentlige Kommission (DOK), (the Commission for Extraordinary Measures).[32] The establishment of DOK was a practical solution, partly because the Danish state apparatus was not geared towards handling such a task and partly because it relieved Parliament of the regulation policy. At the same time, DOK's authority was secure because its members represented the interests of the major parties and organizations, linking them to the development of the regulation. The leader of DOK was the former Social-Liberal minister Christopher Hage (replaced by M. P. Friis in 1916) and its prominent members, who laid out the agenda, were Alexander Foss, chairman of the Federation of Danish Industries and a prominent member of the Conservative Party; P. Th. Nielsen, chairman of the Danish Farmers' Union and a Danish Liberal Party MP; Professor L. V. Birk, a Conservative MP; and Jens Jensen, the Social Democrat mayor of Copenhagen. With the establishment of DOK, corporatism was, so to speak, formally institutionalized in Denmark and the organizations of the corporate world became part of the state.

The work of the DOK featured several major controversies in relation to the establishment of the regulation policy and exhibited a lack of corporate co-operation. The political division became apparent in 1914–15 during the price setting of rye. The contrast between the representatives of the strong agricultural establishment and the other members made it impossible to reach an agreement.[33] Only in 1915, when Ove Rode recommended the introduction of a maximum price, did it become possible to secure a supply of bread at a reasonable price. In the following years this price regulation was followed by maximum prices on a number of goods. The agricultural community's resistance and encountered defeat this led to a change of strategy and subsequently it chose to enter into actual negotiations.[34] Voluntary implementation of the regulations in the shipping industry also turned out to be difficult. Only when the issue was elevated to the parliamentary level did the shipowners realize that intervention would prove much more expensive than an agreement between the shipping business and the state. Because the regulation was unpopular in wide circles, and hence much more difficult to implement than anticipated, Parliament was increasingly consulted: the government did not wish to carry the responsibility for the regulation alone (Table 8.7).

With the industrial chairman Alexander Foss at the helm, DOK made its influence felt beyond the war years 1914–18. In the process of formulating trade policy the commercial organizations attained a central position by making trade agreements. Initially they entered into contracts with the British government and later with a number of other countries – including Germany.

Table 8.7 **Danish export, 1910–18 (per cent)**

	Great Britain	Germany	Norway and Sweden	Other countries
1910–14	60	28	4	8
1915–18	27	49	14	10

Source: Johansen (1985), p. 65.

During the negotiations with Germany in the autumn of 1917, Alexander Foss showed his abilities as an outstanding negotiator by securing the interests of industry at the expense of the farming community.[35] For the government, and especially Ove Rode, it was of the utmost importance that the state had the upper hand in any co-operation initiated with the business community. While the government, and Rode in particular, were very satisfied with the regulation and control measures, the Danish Liberal Party, the Conservative Party in the opposition and the trade organizations naturally did not share this satisfaction. Rode's strong position of power, and his tendency to want things his own way, inspired the opposition to describe the regulation as 'Rode's Regime'. In a quasi-religious speech on 26 October 1916, Rode described his policies as 'the road to Gimle' (in Norse mythology, Gimle is the paradise where the survivors of Ragnarok would live), a new era where future governments should also be a strong factor in the regulation of the economy.[36] The August Law was not only designed to protect the country against the perils of war; one should also learn from the experiences it provided in terms of the regulation of prices and supplies after the war. The public sector should be in charge of the citizens' well-being. In this way, Rode used the war regulations to formulate a social-liberal/social democratic vision of a future welfare society opposed to the liberal wish to return to completely free and unregulated conditions.

The co-operation made it easier for the government to get large sectors of the business community to accept the control measures, when they were not carried out solely by the state. Although the state did its best to secure its position of power, the trade organizations attained a privileged position and the regulation policy did not just affect trade in negative ways. State interventions could in some cases be an advantage to parts of the business community. A case in point was DOK's intervention against the coal importers, which was caused by their refusal to comply with the instructions of the Federation of Danish Industries. The conflict was not just between trades and state, but also between the individual trades. Confronted by a sanction against a trade, there was a demand that the other trades should also carry their share of the burden. The state attempted to establish a corporate interaction between the trades; however, in the final analysis the trades did not consider corporate interaction an advantage. The trades entered into co-operation in order to secure their own interests in the best possible way. Alexander Foss entered DOK in order to secure the industry's conditions, not out of sympathy for a corporate vision, primarily designed to secure supplies for industrial production. In 1918, when Foss left DOK, it was precisely because the trades had to a large extent taken over supply policy themselves. DOK primarily concentrated on regulating the business community in order to safeguard consumers against profiteering generated by the war.

In March 1919, just after the end of the First World War, the Danish Liberal Party promoted a return to liberalism. During the government loan crisis, created by the large expenses associated with the extraordinary wartime measures, the Danish Liberal Party and the Conservative Party put pressure on the government to abolish the August Law and close down DOK. In 1920, the swift deregulation, which took place all over Europe, led to a profound crisis and throughout the 1920s economic liberalism was incapable of delivering sustainable solutions to national economic problems. This situation paved the road for the social democratic/social liberal constellation, which was in government from 1929 to 1940.

No turning back

In the wake of the First World War and the fundamental regulation of the entire national economy, the relationship between the state and the private market underwent a permanent change.[37] In spite of the Danish Liberal Party's efforts to save on the budgets, the liberal government led by Niels Neergaard did not succeed in returning public expenditures to a pre-war level. The close co-operation between the state and the business sector continued after the war, a fact that resulted in a recommendation by the Commission of Foreign Affairs to conduct a more business-oriented foreign policy. The state eventually played a larger and more active role, promoted politically by the Danish Social Democratic Party and the Danish Social-Liberal Party – despite the fact that the Danish Liberal Party in the post-war years attempted to turn the clock back to the *laissez-faire* era before the First World War. The post-war crisis was partly associated with the major changes brought by the First World War, partly with the neutral role the Danish business community had played on the international scene, a role that had now ended. Internationally, the major changes found their clearest manifestation in revolutionary uprisings, which in Tsarist Russia became an actual revolution: the revolutionary rebellions in Germany and other Central European countries were crushed. In October 1917, the Bolsheviks seized power, an act that in a long-term perspective closed the entire Russian market to capitalist business, assigning it to the plan economy. As a consequence, the Danish business community was excluded from its hitherto largest single market.

In the short term, the crashes in the financial sector that followed in the wake of the overheated wartime economy became significant factors in the difficulties facing the Danish business community. During the war the farming community, profiteers and speculation consortiums, specialising in shipping shares, competed for the big money. After the war, the bubble burst with a bang. One of the biggest was the crash of the Landmandsbanken in 1922; the largest bank in Scandinavia was, however, saved by the state, which thereby limited the damage. The closest Denmark came to political unrest was the Easter crisis of 1920, when King Christian X dismissed the Zahle ministry and appointed his own Liebe ministry. The reaction was direct and marked by demonstrations and the labour movement issued threats of a general strike, prompting the king to swiftly withdraw. In 1927, the incipient change in the relationship between state and market were shown when for the first time an actual trade policy was introduced with a document from the Industrial Committee of the Ministry of Trade and Industry. The project was begun in the years 1924–6 during the first Social Democratic government with Thorvald Stauning at the helm. It was now presented by the ultra-liberal government, headed by the Danish Liberal Party and Madsen-Mygdal as Prime Minister. In spite of the Danish Liberal Party government's endeavours to turn the development back to pre-1914 liberalism, the policy document broke away from the idea that the state should not regulate and support the economy for certain substantial purposes. This also influenced policies in the technological arena – and thereby the framework of the activities carried out by the Danish Institute of Technology. The ever-rising unemployment and industry's considerable difficulties in selling its goods in the export market were also factors in the new development. Concerned with the stability of the currency, Danmark's Nationalbank (The Danish National Bank) had since 1924 conducted a policy that prompted the rate of exchange of the Danish crown to rise. This made it difficult for the export trades to sell their goods – and the situation was reflected in the unemployment figures.[38]

Against this background an Industrial Committee under the Ministry of Trade and Industry recommended 'to give direct economic support where this, in accordance with one's best judgment, was needed in order to achieve significant, permanent progress'. This was an attempt to regulate the market in a number of places, where the market, in stark contrast to the liberal conception, turned out not to function.[39]

The economic crisis had hit the SMEs especially hard. For this reason the policy document pointed directly to the fact that there was a lack of 'funds for individual efficient research into and processing of all the difficulties generated by the task ... It is impossible for small and medium sized companies to make their mark in competition with other countries, which are subsidized with greater funds.'[40] In actual fact this meant that the state, among other things, suggested that the Danish Institute of Technology should have increased allocation of funds for R&D, which could support the competitive position of small- and medium-sized businesses.[41]

With this new trade policy focus, which broke away from the economic liberalism and the *laissez-faire* policy – the state – or perhaps rather the Social Democratic Party – opened up the possibility that the Danish Institute of Technology could play a more active part in the development of the Danish business community. Concern for the national economy prompted the state to take partial responsibility for the economy; among other things, this entailed giving relevant and competent institutions the possibility to influence the modes of business production.

Continued internationalization despite crisis

After the German defeat and the Russian revolution, two major European great powers had been seriously weakened. Great Britain, with its world-wide empire, was now Europe's leading great power. This was a gigantic market with great importance for Danish companies like the East Asia Company and Great Northern Telegraph Company. The situation led to a new Danish trade policy recommended by the Foreign Policy Commission in 1921. This commission was very focused on the new opportunities for Danish business on the global markets, in contrast to the previous focus only on the German and English markets.[42]

The economic boom followed by the peace in 1918 led to a Danish expansion on eastern European markets. The euphoria ended in the autumn of 1920 when the international markets were hit by a slump and although it proved an advantage for Denmark's competitive power in the short run, it influenced earning power in agriculture and industry in the medium term. At the same time Danish financial circles had been engaged in speculative business in eastern Europe and in Russia; when the downswing came it led to a disaster in 1922 when the Landmandsbanken collapsed.

Despite the ambitions of the Foreign Policy Commission to influence Danish foreign policy by a new 'commercial policy spirit' it became clear that this new global strategy was difficult to implement. Entering new markets became hard during the slump and Denmark was still dependent on its traditional markets; agricultural export increased in the early part of the 1920s and reached a peak of DKK 1.5 billion, which was reached again only after the Second World War. Industrial exports totalled only one-third of agricultural export and declined at the beginning of the 1920s. Danish industrial exports first recovered in the middle of the 1930s when they again totalled one-third of agricultural exports. In 1937, industrial exports reached the same level as they had in 1920 and the major breakthrough came after the Second World War. It is therefore obvious to conclude, as did the Danish business historian Per Boje, that the 1920s and 1930s resulted in a general setback for Danish internationally-oriented business.[43] But in fact several export companies were able to get a solid foothold on international markets. One important example was the large multinational F.L. Smidth & Co., founded in 1882, which exploited the German defeat to become a major exporter of both cement and industrial equipment for cement production.[44] Machine producers like Thomas B. Thrige, Titan, Atlas and Thomas Ths. Sabroe & Co. all increased their direct investments on overseas markets in the 1920s.

The Danish construction industry in particular had a unique position on the world market. After the First World War, a number of Danish construction companies were founded. Compared to the construction industry in the other Nordic countries the Danish industry was characterized by a high degree of internationalization. Only one Swedish construction company, Sentab, was working internationally and no Norwegian firms were working outside its country's borders. The Norwegian construction industry had plenty of business opportunities on the domestic market after the First World War and was therefore not forced to compete on the more uncertain international market. In addition, the Norwegian construction industry was also suffering from a lack of trained and experienced engineers who could take on international operations. Norway's Technical High School was founded in 1910–12 and until then engineer students had been forced to get their fundamental technical education in Norway and thereafter continue their training abroad. Very few could get their studies funded and those who graduated from European technical high schools were very often recruited by foreign companies. A large

Photograph 8.1   *The 1000 km-long Trans-Iranian Railway from the Caspian Sea to the Persian Gulf was constructed by the Danish company Kampsax between 1933 and 1938. Danish engineering and construction companies held a remarkable position on the international market in the inter-war period. Following the First World War, the construction companies experienced a considerable demand both on the domestic and international market. Danish companies had succeeded in gaining solid positions on the Iranian and Latin American market, in close competition with the largest German, British and French entrepreneurial companies.*
Source: Steen Andersen Private Archive.

number of Norwegian engineers were employed by Danish companies like Christiani & Nielsen, Kampsax and Wright and Thomsen & Kier. A common feature was that they were established engineers who had been working for the large Danish contractor Christiani & Nielsen and had been studying the use of reinforced concrete at the Technological University (Polyteknisk Læreanstalt) in Copenhagen. The newly founded companies were helped by close co-operation with the Technological University, who assisted in making reinforced concrete more efficient and commercially viable. Those conditions helped the Danish companies to force their way into the international construction market. Christiani & Nielsen in particular were able to get a solid foothold on the German, French, British, South African, Thai, Brazilian and Mexican markets where it built harbours with reinforced concrete, quarry walls and concrete roads, and pioneered the construction of a submerged, reinforced concrete tunnel in Rotterdam. In the 1920s and 1930s, Christiani & Nielsen was the largest multinational contractor on the Brazilian market and the company has been described by Marc Linder in his analysis of the development of the international construction industry as 'one of the more remarkable phenomena of pre-World War II international construction'.[45] Geoffrey Jones likewise emphasises the international expansion of the Danish entrepreneurial companies, pointing to their significance in the construction of a global economy after First World War, when cross-border entrepreneurial activity experienced considerable growth.[46]

The world depression came to Denmark in the summer and autumn of 1930 when the prices of butter and bacon fell by some 35 per cent and 50 per cent, respectively. During similar falls in agricultural prices ten years earlier, the liberal leader Thomas Madsen-Mygdal had reacted firmly by stating: 'Decrease production costs, decrease standards of living and decrease the demands to others, but increase the demands to ourselves.'[47] This time, increased production led only to decreasing prices. Under pressure from the agricultural associations Madsen-Mygdal found it necessary to co-operate with the Social Democratic government and on 29 January 1932 a far-reaching import restriction was introduced. All imports to Denmark had consequently to be approved by the new state agency 'Valutacentral', which ensured that precious foreign currency was used only for the import of goods absolutely necessary for the production facilities in Danish society.

The import regulation of 1932 was the most radical economic state regulation in Denmark since the First World War. It is symptomatic that Madsen-Mygdal in January 1932 regarded it as a contemporary necessity – it was agreed with the government that the Valutacentral should last only for two months. In fact, the existence of Valutacentral was prolonged, not once but several times. It existed until 1960, when it was succeeded by the highest Danish import tariffs since the year 1797.[48]

Industrial growth and protective restrictions, 1933–56

On Sunday 29 January 1933, at 10 a.m., nine leading politicians met in the Social Democratic Prime Minister Thorvald Stauning's private apartment in Kanslergade in the centre of Copenhagen. The meeting proved to be one of the most important events in modern Danish history. On the agenda were negotiations of a social-economic reform that could meet the serious situation in Danish society: a general labour market conflict imminent, agricultural export to Great Britain and Germany was under pressure and unemployment had peaked at 38 per cent in 1932. The negotiations were difficult

Photograph 8.2 *Election poster of Thorvald Stauning, the first Social Democrat Prime Minister. In 1935, the Social Democrats won the election through the famous slogan 'Stauning eller Kaos'. Stauning was at the time regarded as 'the father of the nation' and the Social Democrats received votes from a great majority of the Danish population.*
Source: Arbejderbevægelsens Bibliotek og Arkiv.

and according to social-liberal minister of the interior Bertel Dahlgaard, the liberal participants were about to leave around three o'clock in the morning when prime minister Stauning suggested a nightcap.[49] The negotiations then went on and in the early morning a compromise between the liberal and social democratic politicians were reached. The compromise known as the 'Kanslergadeforliget' (Kanslergade compromise) consisted of three main parts:

- The agricultural sector obtained special dispensations through a devaluation of the Danish currency which would ease the export to Britain, a reduction of the property tax, conversion of debts, bulk purchasing of beef and a prolongation of contemporary crisis settlements.
- On the labour market the employers' demand of a 20 per cent salary reduction and a possible lockout was averted by legal force (in the following years, real wages did fall due to the devaluation). Winter subsidies were introduced for the unemployed and support given to house building and new public building projects
- Finally the Liberal Party (Venstre) confirmed that it would not oppose the implementation of the social reform prepared by the social democratic social minister K.K. Steincke. It was signed 20 May 1933 by the Danish king and it consisted of four parts: an accident insurance (which the

employer should pay); a new social insurance (with increased grant-in-aids for medical treatment); and, as the most important, a new general public assistance that succeeded the poor law of 1891 under which recipients lost their civil liberties. The fourth part, on unemployment insurances, had already been agreed upon in 1932.

The notion of the Kanslergade compromise as *the* fundamental building brick of the Danish welfare society has been questioned in recent literature, as many important initiatives had already been prepared previous to January 1933.[50] On the other hand, the compromise is a forceful symbol of the consensus culture shared by the Danish politicians, businessmen and associations in an age of turmoil and threats to democracy. 30 January 1933, the day the Kanslergade agreement was announced, was also the day when Adolf Hitler took over in Berlin, less than 400 km south of Copenhagen.

The British economist W. Arthur Lewis has rightly stated that the economists of the 1920s almost regarded the economic climate similarly to the way meteorologists looked upon the weather while the economists of the 1930s regarded it as a natural task to interrupt and direct economic development.[51] In 1936 J.M. Keynes published his famous book *The General Theory of Employment, Interest and Money*, in which the British economist provided a coherent theory on why a liberal market-based society risked stagnating, with continued unemployment as a result. Since the late 1920s Swedish economists and politicians such as Erik Lindahl, Gunnar Myrdal and Bertil Ohlin had worked on the theoretical foundations for the expansive financial policy which was introduced in order to increase employment. Danish economists such as Jens Whamming, (who worked with Keynes in Cambridge) and Bent Hansen (who worked at the universities of Uppsala and Stockholm from 1947 to 1967) participated in this theoretical development and the leading Danish social democratic politicians co-operated actively with their fellow party members in Sweden and Norway. Regulation and the demand-driven economy were no longer economic emergency measures, but rather a calculated policy based upon an expanding theoretical literature.

It was a complicated matter to administer the new socio-economic demand-oriented laws and the protective currency policy from 1932. In fact, the administration had to consider any request on import and assess the importance of the good to the Danish economy. From the outset the authorities therefore co-operated with representatives from business organizations – a well-known procedure which had been widely used in 1914–18. This procedure was institutionalized in 1935 when the so-called Valutaråd (currency council) was established. The council consisted of twenty-two members, most of them appointed by industrial interest groups, and if possible the relevant interest group was always asked for advice when specific currency permissions were given. There was a mutual interest in this co-operation for three reasons. First, the administration lacked the specific knowledge on the interest spheres; second, the politicians could reject criticism due to the joint responsibility; and, finally, the organizations could enforce power within their interest spheres. In the following decades several such private–public commissions or councils were appointed for economic, social and cultural issues – such as the demographic commission (befolkningskommissionen) or the pregnancy commission (svangerskabskommissionen), which functioned from 1932 to 1936.[52] The commissions and councils should be regarded as a fundamental cornerstone of the so-called 'negotiated economy', in which procedures to reach compromises between different economic and political interests were institutionalized. According to Professor Ove Kay Pedersen, the ability to negotiate between the private and public interests is one of the most important competences in the Danish society.[53] The small and large committees reflected that Danish society had become complex. After 1933, regulation went far beyond the currency question – indeed, the state came to play a much more active role in almost all aspects of Danish society. Three important areas – the labour market, the financial sector and agricultural matters – reflect the new empowered role of the Danish state from 1933–56.

State control over the labour market system

With the Kanslergade compromise in 1933, the Danish state showed that it possessed the means and the will to stop a far-reaching conflict in the Danish labour market in an extremely difficult situation marked by an exploding unemployment rate, rising production costs and falling prices. Already in the following year the centralization of power in the Danish labour market was institutionalized by the Official Conciliator's Act (forligsmandsloven) of 1934. The conciliator could now combine proposals regarding all trades in one decision-making process and, secondly, the power of the large trade unions was enforced in relation to ballots among the members. Despite this centralization of power, then, a remarkable practice developed in the 1930s as the state several times interfered in serious labour disputes. As already mentioned, this happened in January 1933 with the Kanslergadeforliget and then again in 1934, 1936 and 1937.[54] In an article of 1937, the economist

H. Widding Pedersen analysed the motives behind these interventions, pointing at the importance of the export industries for the national economy and,
perhaps more typical for the age – the interest of 'third parties' (*trediemand*).[55]
Conflicts in the labour market were no longer only something that regarded
the involved partners – from the mid-1930s these negotiations concerned the
universal function and progress of the *nation*. This approach was empowered
during the German occupation from 1940 to 1945, when most strikes were
aimed at the occupying forces rather than against the employers.

Following the Second World War, the atmosphere among the Danish population was marked by a general frustration with the established politicians,
and at the general election in 1945 the support of the communist party culminated in 18 seats in the Danish parliament. Wild-cat strikes followed in
1946 and 1947, but a general election in October 1947 bought the Social
Democrats back to power and ten peaceful years followed on the labour
market. Two-year agreements were signed between employers and workers in
1950, 1952 and 1954 and these secured a peaceful labour market and index-
regulated modest wage increases for the workers. In 1956, the situation was
more difficult – the communist party members were active in different unions
and a debate for a shorter working week had been going on for several years.
On 17 March 1956, general strikes began and paralyzed some of the most
crucial parts of the society – distribution of oil and gas, ferry traffic between
the islands, all non-socialist newspapers, etc. The social democratic prime
minister, H.C. Hansen, was in a very difficult situation, but he persuaded the
partners to continue the negotiations. This lead to a compromise on 12 April
1956, but this was rejected by 53 per cent of the striking workers. The strike
in 1956 had caused approximately 1 million lost working days and already
by 13 April Parliament had decided to enforce the proposed settlement and
prohibit strikes and lockouts for two years. The Danish state had once again
showed its will to use its power in the labour market and the legislation
in 1956 was even followed by social democratic restrictions on employers'
control of prices and profits, including an enforced mandate to the public
Registrar of Restrictive Trade Practices.

From universal banks to cautious banks

The Danish financial sector was relatively stable from 1933 to 1956 as the
sector was dominated by the key institutions established in the later part
of the twentieth century: savings banks, private banks and credit associations. An important change was that by 1915 deposits in private banks had

exceeded deposits in savings banks. The private banks had continued to be most important throughout the rest of the twentieth century, but it is worth noting that even in 1935 the deposits in these two types of institutions were almost equal. An important reason for the sustainable importance of the savings banks was a loss of confidence in the Danish private banks in the 1920s. In 1922, the largest bank in Scandinavia, the Landmandsbanken, went bankrupt due to speculation and extended investments particularly in the trading company Transatlantisk Kompagni in which Landmandsbanken in 1919 had an outstanding interest of DKK 112.6 million – more than the share capital of the bank itself. The bankruptcy was part of a general Danish banking crisis in the 1920s in which thirty-six small and large Danish banks closed down.[56] The crisis had consequences for the Banking Law of 1930, which sharpened the existing rules from 1919 and introduced new regulations. The two main considerations behind the law were, on the one hand, protection of customers' deposits through demands on available funds and, on the other, a separation of banking from other kinds of corporate activities. As a consequence of the crisis the universal banking principle drawn from Germany was replaced by a more simple banking structure. In the new Bank Law of 1956, it finally became illegal for Danish bank managers to participate on the boards of directors of non-financial enterprises. 'Security' and 'solidity' were the key words of the financial sector from 1933 to 1957 – perhaps at the expense of competition and growth.

The lost primacy of the agricultural sector

The general economic crisis of 1932–3 was particularly hard on the Danish farmers as the falling prices of agricultural products was combined with difficulties in getting access to the crucial British and German export markets. In order to solve the crises the government initiated a number of regulatory initiatives in 1932 and 1933. An important initial step was the devaluation of the Danish currency, as decided in the Kanslergadeforliget in January 1933, which eased the export to Great Britain. A large Danish trade delegation went to Great Britain, which was highly sceptical about the devaluation, and in 1933 Denmark and Great Britain entered a bilateral agreement in which Denmark was obliged to import more British industrial goods and raw materials so that the large Danish trade surplus was lowered. Agricultural export was thus regulated but domestic production also followed suit. In 1932 the sugar arrangement (*sukkerordningen*) was introduced, and it secured a higher price for sugar beet producers through regulation of domestic production and

Table 8.8 Size of farms (small: 0.55–9.9 ha, medium: 10–59.9 ha, large: 60–>120 ha), gross income at factor cost*, 1933–2002 (million DKK, 1929 prices)

Size	1933	1937	1946	1955	1966	1970	2002
Small	105.677	106.225	101.573	93.128	61.881	44.038	8.100
Medium	93.758	96.827	102.044	101.597	99.871	90.686	22.900
Large	4.796	4.771	4.530	4.058	4.554	5.473	17.400
Total	204.231	207.823	208.147	198.783	166.306	140.197	48.400
Gross inc.	1372	1316	1342	1645	1817	1647	

Source: Fink (2005), various tables.

import. In 1933 a number of regulative policies followed: bacon regulation (*svinereguleringen*), a corn arrangement (*kornordningen*), a meat regulation (*kødordningen*) and a butter arrangement (*smørordningen*). Consequently, by the mid-1930s, the Danish agricultural sector could only sell products by special permission from the state which, on the other hand, secured minimum prices and eased the financial situation through loan subsidies, low rents, etc.

The years of regulation and crisis were followed by an interesting – and perhaps surprising – tendency, namely an increasing *de-centralization* of agrarian Denmark. The number of very small farms – the so-called *familielandbrug* or family farms – increased from 105,677 in 1933 to a peak of 106,225 in 1937. From the mid-1950s these small farms lost their leading position: at the end of the 1960s there were fewer than 45,000 small farms left and in the year 2002 only 8,100. In the long term, the very small family farms proved unsustainable in a Danish context (Table 8.8).

The Danish state actively supported the precariously late decentralization of the agricultural sector from the 1930s to the 1950s by providing specific loan opportunities and regulations for the small farmers in the so-called Husmandsbevægelse, a popular movement for smallholders, and by prohibiting amalgamations of smaller farms until the large land reform prepared in 1960. This phenomenon can perhaps be explained by ideological reasons as the social-liberal government coalition from 1929 to 1942 actively supported the growth of small farms. At the same time, the decentralized structure was regarded as economically efficient in the 1920s and 1930s; finally, the social perspective is also important, as these small farms provided employment for many people. In the agricultural production sector – the dairies and slaughterhouses – the decentralized structure continued until the early 1960s. In the 1960s the number of dairies fell from around 1400 in 1957 to only 348 in 1972. The ownership structure was continuously co-operative and in 1962 it was suggested that a common co-operative dairy company 'Mejeriselskabet Danmark' be established. It took eight years of negotiations before the new company began its operations in 1970. It was not an easy task to change the decentralized Danish farming structure which had peaked as late as the mid-1930s.

Home-market-oriented manufacturing industries

Danish trade and industries went through a sound expansion in the aftermath of the First World War – every year from 1921 to 1930 the GDP of the industries grew, from DKK 765 million in 1921 to DKK 1324 million in 1930. This expansion can be regarded as an effect of the breakthrough of new electro-chemical technologies. In the chemicals and basic metal industries the number of companies expanded from 620 chemical enterprises in 1919 to 1351 enterprises in 1935 and from 10,755 basic metal industries in 1914 to 17,619 enterprises in 1935. In contrast, the number of enterprises in the textile industry fell from 1388 in 1914 to 980 in 1935. Most of these enterprises were very small – the 1351 chemical enterprises in 1935 employed in total 12,000 workers, or fewer than ten workers per unit. The archetypal Danish company was still a small family-run corporation with around twenty employees producing machines or goods – often related to the agricultural sector.

These SMEs experienced falling prices for manufactured goods after 1931 and due to the world depression Danish industrial export decreased almost 33 per cent from 1929 to 1931 while unemployment rose to more than 30 per cent in 1932. In order to solve the crisis the government in 1933 introduced three sets of laws which in many respects formed the later strategic and structural development of Danish industry:

- First, a new monetary policy resulted in lower interest rates – down to a record 2.5 per cent from 1933 to 1935 – causing increased investment, which helped boost employment.
- Second, public investment increased with an expansive financial policy. The government decided in 1933 to invest DKK 75 million in new public projects such as road infrastructure, new bridges and houses. The money was raised through foreign loans and increased taxes on income, a capital tax and special taxes on goods such as coffee and sugar.
- Third, and perhaps most important, was that the government restricted imports through the previously mentioned Valutacentral. The aim was primarily to secure a stable currency balance and that aim was stressed

to foreign trade partners. In fact, the import regulation functioned as a very efficient protection of Danish industry, which could now expand on the home market in areas that had previously been dominated by foreign competitors. Danish manufacturing enterprises expanded their share of the home market from 56 per cent in 1930 to some 70 per cent after 1933.[57]

An illustrative example is the light electrical equipment producer Laur. Knudsen mekaniske establissement A/S (LK). The company was founded by Lauritz Knudsen (1863–1917) in 1893, and in the beginning produced watches. Soon, Knudsen was specialising in the expanding area of electrical installations – first lighting installations in trains and, from the late 1890s, large high-tension systems and domestic electrical installations. In the late 1920s the number of employees rose from approximately 380 in 1925 to 950 and to 150 white-collar workers in 1930, when LK participated in the extension of the large power station H. C. Ørstedsværket in Copenhagen. The world crisis in 1931 lead to a halt in building and construction activities and LK's workforce fell dramatically to 520 workers in 1932. LK survived, and expanded by exploiting the protected home market through new products such as electrical cookers and ovens in 1939 the number of workers had reached 1150. The following quotation from LK's 75-year anniversary volume is an almost archetypal example of the recovery of Danish industries in the 1930s – fewer activities abroad, but expansion through diversification on the protected home market:[58]

Around New Year 1932 LK's revenue was reduced to an alarmingly low level and it was announced that all white collar workers with seniority less than two years must consider themselves as dismissed with one month's notice. All countries affected by the crisis aimed to limit their import towards the most necessary... under these conditions LK's export to Sweden and Norway was obviously difficult... Then finally in the spring of 1933 the prospects were getting brighter; the construction work expanded following a long quiet period and LK became busy... Due to the devaluation of the Danish currency the prices rose, and it stimulated the will to acquire and invest in real estate. While there were only 7,000 apartments built in Copenhagen in 1932, 14,000 new apartments were initiated in 1933, and a similar development took place in other parts of the country... In 1933 we began the preparation of manufacturing electrical cookers... with the help of the Swedish engineer Hans von Kantzow's (1887–1979) 'Kanthal' filament. 1934 was a busy year with growing employment at LK, and again it was necessary to work on two shifts in several departments... Our sales in Sweden had in the latter years been

Table 8.9 **Danish industrial development, 1897–1970**

	1897	1914	1925	1935	1948	1958	1970
Corporations	77.204	82.346	88.821	101.772	102.303	78.010	97.860
Employees	175.819	230.665	265.919	313.788	442.175	468.111	472.200
Horsepower	47.958	228.978	434.455	684.046	1,266.032	–	–

Source: Statistical Yearbook.

Table 8.10 **Productivity: Danish industry, 1947–57 (1955 = 100)**

	1947	1949	1951	1953	1955	1957
Production index	69	81	92	91	100	108

Source: Statistical Yearbook.

 obstructed because – as in our country – import was limited due to the trade balance. We had considered the option to establish a sister factory in Sweden, and in the fall of 1934 we acquired a suitable site in Malmö. For different reasons the project was later relinquished.

The LK story does not explain why the greenfield investment in the south Swedish town of Malmö in 1934 was abandoned, but the reason could have been a possible cartel agreement between LK, which dominated the Danish electrical installation market, and its Swedish competitors. Such agreements were widespread in the 1920s and 1930s – often within the new capital-intensive industries dominated by a few very large corporations such as electrical machinery, chemicals and transport equipment. In general, Danish companies were not predominant in these large international cartels – most Danish enterprises were still small and the average size was only around thirty-five employees from 1930 to the mid-1950s. Still, the protected home market provided a strong demand for these SMEs and from 1932 to 1939, employ-ment within manufacturing industries rose by almost 72,000 new jobs – an increase of around 60 per cent (Table 8.9).

Protectionism had proved its validity in terms of employment, but the remaining problem was falling productivity (Table 8.10). The combination of home-market orientation and increased labour force caused decreasing productivity and the problem accelerated during the German occupation from 1940 to 1945, when production and export was thoroughly regulated and thus outside ordinary market mechanisms. In 1946, the Federation of Danish Industries (Industrirådet) established a new department for rational-ization (*rationalitetsrådet*) which in 1947 published a report pointing at a lack of concrete political and economic initiatives on institutional grounds such as the tax system, regulation of prices, import restrictions and the scarcity of goods.[59] The European Recovery Programme presented by US foreign minister George Marshall on 5 June 1947 (the 'Marshall Plan'), aimed at a 'help to self-help' principle that supported investments in more efficient machinery and production facilities. In 1949, the Marshall Plan representation in Copenhagen made the Social Democrat government aware of the need for substantial new initiatives that could improve industrial productivity. At the end of 1949, a National Productivity Council (Produktivitetsudvalget) was appointed and again the well-known Danish collaborative model of state–industry–labour co-operation was used. The council consisted of four industry representatives, four labour union members and four state officials. At the initial meeting, the direction of Danish industrial policy was decided upon: productivity within specific industries should be investigated and study trips to the US planned under the so-called 'Technical Assistance' programme. Despite these initiatives, it was not an easy task to improve the productivity of the home-market-oriented Danish industry and the industrial policy was not an unequivocal success. From 1951 to 1958, productivity only rose from 92 to 112 (with 1955 as index 100). The limited industrial post-war improvement in the 1950s was reflected in a macroeconomic perspective: in general Danish economy did not perform as well as other west European states from 1950 to 1957.

Export orientation and the expanding welfare state, 1957–82

The year 1957 marked a sharp turning-point in Danish economic development: from being one of the slowest-growing western economies towards becoming one of the best-performing economies from 1957 to 1970 (Table 8.11). The background for the upswing is complex, but it is possible to identify two fundamental foundations: the growth of export-oriented industries able to exploit new international trade agreements, and an almost explosive expansion of domestic service industries, particularly within the public sector. Still, the period from 1957 to 1982 should not be regarded as a sustained upswing. In the early 1970s the upswing turned into the most severe economic crisis since the 1930s as both foundations were eroded: the dynamic of international trade organizations was halted and the continued expansion of the public sector was faced by serious economic and human imbalances.

Country	1950–7	1957–65	1965–70	1957–70
Denmark	2.7	5.3	4.4	5.0
Norway	3.5	4.3	4.6	4.4
Sweden	3.3	4.6	3.9	4.3
Germany	8.2	5.4	4.7	5.2
UK	2.7	3.3	2.3	2.9
Netherlands	5.0	4.9	5.2	5.1
US	3.6	4.0	3.2	3.7

Source: Hansen (1974), pp. 148, 177.

International trade agreements and export-oriented industries

During the early post-war years the American-influenced trade policy was an important counter-force against continued national protectionism. In 1948, as we have seen, the US decided to support the re-building of western Europe through the so-called 'Marshall Plan'. The plan was a result of the slow pace of reconstruction due to currency problems, protectionism and a constant lack of dollars in western countries. The political division between the communist countries in the east and the capitalist countries in the west of Europe was a reality in 1946, when Churchill described the situation with his famous metaphor of the 'Iron Curtain'.

The Marshall Plan consisted of donations and cheap dollar loans and the aid to Denmark amounted to USD 278 million. These funds were important for the reconstruction of the country in two ways. First, it helped to stabilize the currency situation and, second, the new machines, raw materials, instruments, etc. increased productivity in both the agricultural sector – in which tractors replaced horses in these years – and in industry, which had suffered from lowered productivity during the Second World War.

The Marshall funds were distributed through the Organization for European Economic Co-operation (OEEC) founded in 1948. Surprisingly for Danish politicians, the OEEC in the autumn of 1949 required the receiving countries to eliminate 50 per cent of their quantitative import restrictions on trade with other member states before 15 December of the same year. The OEEC's aim was to enforce trade and thus prosperity between the member states. Import restrictions and bilateral trade agreements were particularly considered a hindrance to such a development. In 1950, the OEEC enforced its policy against protectionism through the establishment of the European Payment Union (EPU). The balance of currency payments between the seventeen west European members was co-ordinated through a quota system, which meant that it was no longer the balance between two individual countries that counted, but rather the balance between one country and all the others. The next step was gradually to remove all import regulations. Gradually, Denmark removed its regulation – mostly on goods that were already imported and thus not in competition with Danish products. The agricultural sector was a particular problem for Denmark in this liberalization process. It was only in 1961 that the Danish industrial exports exceeded agricultural exports and in most countries liberalization of agricultural products was slower than for industrial products as states were eager to protect domestic, often labour-intensive, farms. If Denmark opened her borders completely it would have meant open competition for the industrial sector both at home and abroad, combined with restrictions on high-earning agricultural exports. This problem was strengthened further in the 1960s due to European market agreements. In 1957, six western European countries, including West Germany, Italy and France, agreed to the Treaty of Rome and thus a European Economic Community (EEC). The EEC was a customs union, meaning that internal customs were abolished while common customs for countries outside the community were retained. It was particularly serious for Denmark that West Germany, which again had become an important trade partner and receiver of Danish agricultural exports, was inside this union. Great Britain was still the most important market and in 1958 Great Britain took the initiative to form the European Free Trade Association, (EFTA), which included Great Britain, Denmark, Norway, Sweden, Switzerland, Austria and Portugal. EFTA was also a free-trade association, but in contrast to the EEC, it did not include the agricultural sector. Denmark's two most important trade partners West Germany and Great Britain were now in two different trade zones. As a result the German market fell from 31 per cent of agricultural export in 1961 to only 16 per cent in 1970. These market access problems only accelerated a broader development and by the 1960s agriculture had lost its primacy in Danish trade – it was no longer the largest export sector, no longer the largest employer and from the late 1950s on agrarian production was based on subsidies from the forceful and regulating Danish state (Table 8.12).

In the late 1950s, the general perception was that economic growth in Denmark must be based on increased industrial efficiency combined with an expanding service sector, rather than the old backbone of agricultural export. Following decades of home-market protection and stable income from the exporting agricultural sector, the atmosphere among politicians and

Table 8.12 GDP at factor cost Agriculture Trade & Industry Commerce (all million DKK, 1929 prices) and Industrial, Agricultural export (in percentages), 1857–1975

	Agriculture	Trade & ind.	Commerce		Ind.exp. (%)	Agr. exp. (%)
1857	383	115.5	70.1	1850–9	10	80
1867	441	147.7	98.6	1860–96	11	88
1877	446	205.0	164.5	1875–9	5	87
1887	515	288.7	266.8	1880–9	6	86
1897	549	429.2	439.7	1890–7	6	86
1907	720	579.0	659.0	1900–9	5	90
1917	813	649.0	723.0	1915–18	13	78
1927	1060	1086	1198	1921–31	16	80
1937	1316	1713	1501	1936–9	23	72
1947	1234	2122	1717	1946–9	25	64
1958	1786	3134	2416	1954–9	36	53
1966	1817	5411	3730	1965–9	57	29
1975	1783	8070	5183	1975–9	68	21

Sources: Hansen (1974), Tables 3 and 4; Fink (2005).

businessmen was not marked by self-confidence. Rather, opening markets and subsequent competition were met by fear and anxiety. In 1958, the Danish government published a White Paper on the effects of open competition on the industrial sector. The paper was renamed the 'Shock Report', and it predicted that lower production was likely within 40 per cent of the Danish industrial sector should Denmark join the EEC. In fact, the development proved to be much more beneficial than predicted. The value of exports from manufacturing industries rose from DKK 2.8 billion in 1957 to DKK 14.6 billion in 1970, or from less than 35 per cent of total exports to almost 60 per cent. Industry succeeded in exploiting new market opportunities and thus reinforcing their exports, particularly to the expanding markets in West Germany, Sweden and the US. To understand this expansion, it is worth pointing out three different factors:

■ First, the export-oriented growth obviously built upon the new west European market agreements with the EEC, EFTA and OECD. Export-based expansion would have been almost impossible in market circumstances based on bilateral agreements, such as in the 1930s and 1940s. The increasing export was based, and relied, upon the international upswing and particularly the increasing demand from the three neighbouring countries, West Germany, Sweden and Norway, which experienced the *Wirtschaftswunder* and the fast rise of Scandinavian welfare societies.

The importance of the German market rose from 4 per cent of total exports in 1946–9 to 19 per cent ten years later in 1955–8. The importance of the Norwegian and Swedish markets simultaneously grew from 13 per cent in 1946–9 to 21 per cent in the late 1960s. Denmark's geographical position, close to three of the most expanding and demanding northern European economies, was thus an important explanation for increasing industrial exports after 1957.

- The second explanation was domestic Danish institutional factors. On 28 May 1957, the Social Democrat's chairman, H.C. Hansen, established one of the few majority-based governments in Danish political history. The government initiated a business-friendly policy in terms of new depreciation principles in order to strengthen industrial investment. The next couple of years saw a modification of corporate taxes and more a flexible price regulation policy initiated by the Monopolies and Mergers Commission. Perhaps even more important, access to the necessary capital for industrial expansion was eased around 1958 when a new credit association (Finansieringsinstituttet for Industri og Håndværk) was established by the National Bank in co-operation with the Federation of Danish Industries and a number of private banks. The aims were to provide SMEs with advantageous cash loans – mainly for investment in new production facilities. In 1960 and 1961 similar institutions followed for the agricultural sector and the shipping industry. At the same time, the government began for the first time to formulate specific programmes aimed at attracting FDI to Denmark. In 1960, the Royal Danish Consulate in New York published a 34-page brochure, *Investment of Foreign Capital in Denmark*, with convincing arguments for future American investments in Denmark:

> – Many American firms have already established branches in Denmark because foreign direct investments in Denmark are governed by very liberal legislative and administrative rules; direct investments made by American citizens are accorded the same treatment in every respect as investments made by Danish citizens.
> – Danish workers are well trained. A good atmosphere has, through the years, prevailed in the labour market. Since the war, wages and working conditions have been regulated by two-year agreements. Thus far, Denmark is one of the European countries that has had the lowest number of working days lost as a result of work stoppages. Industry is in an advanced stage of technical development

- The aim to attract foreign investments was only partial successful. Until the mid-1980s, the Danish economy was in fact marked by a relatively low level of foreign ownership – it has been estimated that in the early 1970s only 8 per cent of the output was controlled by foreigners.[60] On the other hand, several Danish companies had international minority shareholders and it is important to note that commercial banks arranged substantial international loans for Danish firms, particularly in the mid-1960s and early 1970s. The educational level was another important aspect of the domestic institutional factors behind expanding industrial export after 1957. From 1958 to 1970 Danish industrial expansion was particularly strong within the chemical industries and the manufacturing of light electrical equipment and heavy machines. These industries were based on complicated production processes that required skilled labour forces. In general, the educational level in Denmark rose: in 1955, only 5.1 per cent of the relevant age group took the General Certificate (Studentereksamen), while in 1969 it was 12.6 per cent. At the university level the expansion was even more impressive: the number of graduates rose from 1442 in 1956–7 to 5348 in 1966–7. The number of new students at the Technical University of Denmark rose from 330 in 1947–8 to 528 in 1966–7.[61] These new engineers and university graduates were needed for the expanding exporting industries.

The combination of increased international demand and more pro-business financial, educational and legal institutions thus constituted the foundation of the crucial industrial export which succeeded the agricultural sector as the prime engine of the Danish economy after 1957. The economic historian Hans Chr. Johansen has stated that from 1959 to 1970 structural changes were marked by two main tendencies – concentration and regionalization.[62]

The opening of foreign markets caused greater concentration. It was characteristic that export came from larger firms. The ten largest corporations controlled about one-sixth of total industrial production. This phenomenon was particularly evident in capital-intensive industries with a large potential for economies of scale, such as the dairy sector. Three-quarters of all dairies were closed between 1958 and 1972 and as illustrated in Chapter 10 on Carlsberg, the number of Danish breweries fell from twenty-four in 1959 to twelve in 1990 while production increased from 2.8 to 3.8 million hl. The export from the two dominating Danish breweries,

Carlsberg and Tuborg, which merged in 1970, more than trebled from 1958 to 1972.

Regionalization was another important tendency in Danish post-war industrialization. From 1880 to 1960 in Copenhagen and the provincial towns approximately 40 per cent of the population was employed within trades and industries. These figures were remarkably stable, but in the rural districts an important change took place from 1930 to 1960, when the percentage employed within trades and industries rose from 20 to 30, while the importance of agriculture declined from 51 per cent in 1930 to 34 per cent in 1960.[63]

In isolated areas of Jutland, large export-oriented companies such as Lego, Danfoss, Grundfos and Ecco Shoes expanded rapidly in the 1950s and 1960s. These companies were family-owned and family-managed, building upon the founders' specific technical, commercial and organizational competences.[64] One of the world's leading toy producers, Lego, was founded by the local carpenter Ole Kirk Kristiansen in 1932 in the small town of Billund in Jutland, less than 100 km from the German border. Due to the economic crisis and a lack of work, Kirk Kristiansen began to produce wooden toys and with the technical assistance of the state-funded Technological Institute Lego acquired the first plastic-needling machine in Denmark in 1947. In 1955, the company initiated its crucial export to West Germany and the details of this story illustrate how difficult it was to cross national borders economically ten years after the end of the Second World War. In 1955, Lego's annual revenue was approximately DKK 3 million, there were only around 120 employees and the enterprise wanted to invest around 20.000 German Marks in order to establish sales in Hamburg through an agent. Such investments required permission from the National Bank, and the procedure might take several weeks or even months. In a late biography, Lego's second-generation owner, Godtfred Kirk Christiansen, explained that he was afraid that the prolonged procedure with the National Bank would endanger the whole export plan; instead, he contacted the manager of the local bank (Veile Bank), Frede Sunesen:[65]

 'Frede, you need to help us, otherwise we will not get started in Germany.' Frede Suensen made a fast decision. The next day we met in Rendsburg, in Northern Germany and he provided a cheque of 20,000 German Marks, guaranteed by Veile Bank. I don't know if Sunesen had confirmed this transaction with the National Bank, and I did not ask. Frede Sunesen took a big risk, as he surely did not follow the common practice. But those were the conditions back then. You simply could not lend money in foreign currencies. Nothing. If I had taken 100,000 DKK with me in a suitcase and changed them to German Marks in a Bank in Hamburg, it would have been illegal, and I would have been penalized.

Lego's real breakthrough on the export market came in 1958 when the Lego brick system was patented. In the late 1980s Lego entered the Danish top 40 list of large corporations and had almost 6000 employees, including production facilities in several countries.

In the second half of the twentieth century Denmark was no longer an agricultural country and the number of workers in the agricultural sector fell from 409,000 in 1957 to 228,000 in 1974. Despite the success of companies such as Lego, Danfoss and Grundfos, it was not the expanding exporting industries that absorbed these almost 200,000 employees – the number within industries only rose from 251,000 in 1958 to 308,000 in 1970. The most important economic sector in terms of growing employment was the service sector. As illustrated in Table 8.13, the combined importance of commerce, transport, administration the liberal professions and 'Other' (people provided for) grew from 41 per cent in 1950 to 66 per cent in 1986. These figures reflect an almost revolutionary change in Danish society and it was the private and public service sectors that proved to be the dynamic engines from 1957 to 1982.

In 1940, around 13 per cent of the Danish workforce was employed within the commercial sector. This figure was rather stable for the remainder of the twentieth century but this stability should not be mistaken for a structural stability. In fact, the number of grocers fell from 14,750 in 1948 to 12,290 in 1968 and 6497 in 1988. In the late 1960s a new Danish word was introduced – 'butiksdøden' ('shop death') – and described a painful process in which thousands of small, local grocers disappeared in the face of the advance of large supermarkets.

Supermarkets were introduced in Denmark in the 1950s, but the real breakthrough came around 1970. Until then, the typical Danish retailing shop was a local and independent grocer's shop like the one on Enevold Sørensengade in Kolding acquired by the 26-year-old tradesman Møller H. Merrild in May 1956. This shop was only 62 m^2, its annual revenue less than DKK 200,000 and its customers were to be found mainly in the local residential district. In 1960, Merrild sold his shop and focused his efforts on the production, distribution and marketing of coffee and during the 1960s

Table 8.13 *Grocery stores: Denmark, 1925–88*

	1925	1948	1958	1968[1]	1978	1988
Number of shops	15,364	14,750	12,424	12,290	8,185	6,497
Total revenue (billion DKK)	1.6	1.8	2.3	8.8	39.3	66.5
Average revenue per shop (K DKK)	96	120	185	700	4,800	10,200

Note: 1. From 1968, the figures include supermarkets. Grocery and supermarkets were registered in total from 1978.
Source: Statistical Yearbook, various editions.

and 1970s he established one of the leading Danish coffee brands – Merrild Kaffe – acquired by the Dutch–American giant Douwe Egberts in 1979. This success was only possible due to the fact that Møller Merrild from the early 1970s had sold his coffee through the expanding large chains of supermarkets rather than through small independent shops. On 7 October 1970 the doors were opened at the first large Danish discount mega-supermarket (*lavprisvarehus*), the 16,000 m² Bilka in Tilst just outside Århus, the second largest town in Denmark. At the beginning of 1977 the German discount supermarket chain, Aldi, opened its first two shops and these events demonstrated that the Danish retailing sector in the following years would be concentrated within the hands of a few very large chains – large supermarkets and shopping centres became the growth engines of the sector.

These structural changes from the 1960s were based on a 'motorization' of Danish infrastructure. Oil was the core input in the expanding Danish economy after 1957 – not only in relation to transport but also in heating and industrial production. In the early 1970s, oil accounted for more than 90 per cent of Danish gross energy consumption – a higher percentage than in any other west European country.[66] In January 1956, the first Danish motorway was opened in Jægersborg, north of Copenhagen, and in the following decade railways and domestic shipping lost its leading role to cars and trucks. The length of the railway system fell from 4740 km in 1953 to 2493 km in 1973, while the length of the main roads (*hovedlandeveje*) more than doubled from 2220 km in 1957 to 4619 km in 1973. The number of cars quadrupled from 280,000 in 1957 to 1.3 million in 1973, and along with this expansion a whole new industry developed with service stations and road construction.[67] The landscape changed through expanding suburbs in the periphery of the large cities. Still the fast – almost revolutionary – changes were not unproblematic. In 1971, a record of 1213 people were killed in car accidents in

Denmark – four times the number in 2006 – and some of the new sub-urbs attracted social problems and increasing levels of crime – the number of annual robberies in Denmark rose continuously from less than 50 in the mid-1950s to around 150 in the early 1970s to more than 300 at the end of the 1970s.

Social challenges such as crime, poverty and health problems were met by a wide range of public state initiatives after 1957. In the 1960s alone the personnel in administration expanded from 267,000 to 475,000 and the growth continued from 1973 to 1982 when 330,000 *new* public jobs were established in Denmark. The welfare state was born and from the mid-1950s to the end of the 1960s, health and welfare costs rose from 6 per cent of GDP in 1952–3 to 16 per cent of GDP in 1972–3. It is possible to identify two fundamental reasons behind these rising costs. First, the number of senior citizens and young people under education rose in the period and second – and even more importantly – a whole series of new social laws were introduced which succeeded the Social Reform of 1933. The first important step was taken in 1957, when the national old age pension (*folkepensionen*) was introduced. It built upon the universal principle that the pension should be financed via taxes and that every citizen above a specific age should receive the same amount of money. In the rest of Europe, the principle was that pensions should be based on savings paid by employers and employees during a working life. As a result of demographic changes and the reform, the number of pensioners increased from 55,000 in 1956 to 129,000 in 1972. The labour market policy focused on three interrelated issues: more state responsibility, which meant that in 1970 the state paid about 70 per cent of the unemployment relief; a new employment exchange service, established in 1968, that could mobilise the available manpower; and the rate of the relief, increased to a maximum of 90 per cent of ordinary wages by the end of the 1960s. In the long term, these initiatives from the late 1960s proved the cornerstones in the so-called 'Flexicurity' labour market model, which consisted of a combination of flexible hire-and-fire options for the employers (a system which can be traced back to the September Agreement of 1899), an active re-employment and re-education policy and high rates of relief – mainly paid by the state and not the employers as in most other countries. It is important to mention that the number of kindergartens more than tripled from 550 in 1956 to 1727 in 1972, reaching 2346 in 1981. It became normal that both parents had full-time jobs and it was the public sector which organized, and to a large extent financed, the daily care of Danish children.

The crisis from 1973 to 1981

The large upswing of the Danish economy from 1957 to 1972 was based on an effective triangle consisting of an expanding manufacturing sector that successfully exploited new export opportunities, combined with an almost explosive growth in public welfare systems and a new technological paradigm in terms of an oil-based motorization of infrastructure and production facilities.

In the early 1970s this triangle broke apart. First of all, the growth of the welfare state had proved still more difficult to finance from the end of the 1960s and the tax issue had become the core of a heated political and economic debate. Taxes on personal income proved to be insufficient, and in 1962 a new 9 per cent general tax on all commodities was introduced. A 10 per cent value added tax (VAT) was introduced in 1967 to make EEC membership possible. VAT and, from 1970, the direct pay-as-you-earn (PAYE) tax system became important items in the toolbox of instruments which could increase tax revenue to the state and decrease possible inflation. The new economists – known as 'social engineers' – actively developed and used these tools and in the early 1970s the tax burden had reached a level that created growing dissatisfaction among the population. As illustrated above, the country had altered very fast – crime was growing, the role of the family had changed, suburbs appeared and old shops closed down. Dissatisfaction appeared with the economic downswing in 1973–4 and in December 1973 Danish political life was shaken when three new parties entered Parliament, among them a new rightist tax-refusal party called the Progressive Party (Fremskridtspartiet), which gained 16 per cent of the votes. In the following years, a minority Liberal government attempted to control the economic crisis by tight fiscal policy, including higher indirect taxes and a curtailing of public expenditures. This policy led to increased unemployment and negative growth. A Social Democrat government tried the opposite cure in 1975, with tax reductions and a series of measures aimed at combating unemployment. This policy caused severe currency deficits and unemployment stayed at a high level. The public sector continued to grow: 330,000 new jobs from 1973 to 1982, but still unemployment increased ten-fold from, 25,000 in 1973 to 263,000 in 1982. One reason was that 270,000 new employees entered the labour market – many of them women and young people born in the late 1940s and educated at the universities.

Contemporary analysts compared the oil crisis with the depression of the 1930s – but in contrast to the old crisis real wages did not fall in the 1970s.

The Danish people in broad terms continued their economic habits and private consumption rose 12 per cent from 1972 to 1976. In these four years, approximately 5,000 new summer houses were built annually in Denmark and the number of cars grew from 1,076,876 in 1970 to 1,389,547 cars in 1980.[68] Following the second oil crisis in 1979, Danish national finances were in a terrible state, with high unemployment, growing state deficits and a permanent deficit on the currency balance. The situation was described by the Social Democrat Minister of Finance, Knud Heinesen, as 'the road to the precipice'. Still, it is worth noting that for many Danes this journey took place in business class.

Denmark and the global division of labour, 1982–

Since the large waves of migrants to the US in the 1880s and 1890s, migration and immigration had not played an important role in Danish development. That changed after 1980. The number of immigrants to Denmark and their descendants tripled in only twenty-seven years from 153,000 in 1980 to 463,000 in 2007 or from 3 per cent to 9 per cent of the population. In 1980 more than two-thirds of these 153,000 people came from other European countries (often Sweden and Norway) or North America, while in 2007 less than one-third originated from the western world. It was particularly the African and Middle Eastern groups that expanded, and consequently a Muslim–Danish minority increased. This rapid change from a homogeneous population – actually without any substantial minorities before 1980 – towards a real multicultural population in less than thirty years has not been without problems. The religious minorities were often concentrated in particular areas of the cities and it proved difficult for many immigrants to get job. Uncertainty and fear of these new Danes grew in the Danish population and from around 1995 to 2007 the migrant-opposing 'Dansk Folkeparti' constantly had around 10 per cent popular support. In the winter of 2006, Denmark hit the headlines of the world media with the so-called 'Mohammad cartoon crisis'. To test the country's freedom of speech, a Danish newspaper asked a group of cartoonists to draw the Prophet Mohammed. Following a diplomatic crisis, offended governments and religious groups, particularly in Lebanon, Syria, Egypt, Iran and Saudi Arabia, reacted very strongly, culminating with a wide-reaching boycott of Danish goods and companies and an arson attack on the Danish embassy in Damascus by furious demonstrators on 4 February 2006. It has been estimated that the cost of the boycott amounted to more than DKK 2 billion.

The 'cartoon crisis' illustrated three important aspects of both Danish and western societies in an age of globalization. The crisis showed to the rest of the world – and to the Danish population – that there are serious differences in the understanding of important ethical concepts such as religion, honour and the rights of freedom within multicultural western populations – differences which politicians, populations and indeed also companies will have to deal with in the future. The crisis also illuminated a stirring sense of *national* loyalty – despite a small group of religious leaders, the Muslim minority in Denmark stayed calm and it was striking that no large demonstrations or riots took place in Denmark itself in the suddenly-heated winter months of 2006. Finally, the crisis showed that large multinational enterprises (MNEs) have strong and valuable experience and knowledge concerning cultural differences. The world's largest shipping company, A.P. Møller-Mærsk, avoided any boycotts through a firm and opportunistic diplomatic reaction, while the giant Danish–Swedish dairy group, Arla Foods (see Chapter 9) used its substantial resources to re-establish strong credibility among ordinary Muslim customers. In that sense the 'Mohammad cartoon crisis' confirmed what was already apparent in Denmark following the popular rejection of the Maastricht Treaty in 1992: a substantial gap between a political–economic globally-oriented elite and a more sceptical population. In 2007, Denmark was still in an age of transition between a national homogeneous (near) past and a global heterogeneous future.

The Danish state and European integration

Traditionally, Danish historians have pinpointed the year 1973 as the epoch-making year in modern history.[69] In January 1973 Denmark became a member of the EEC, in November the first oil crisis accelerated and finally on 4 December the so-called 'landslide election' (*jordskredsvalget*) turned Danish politics upside down. Despite these important political and economic occurrences in 1973, it makes sense to consider the early- and mid-1980s as the actual 'formative phase' in contemporary Danish history, for three reasons: the introduction of a new political regime, changing economic development and a radical internationalization of the Danish business environment.

On 10 September 1982 the Conservative Poul Schlüter became Prime Minister in Denmark, starting a period of Conservative–Liberal governments that continued until 1993. It was the longest governmental regime in Denmark since the 1930s and it marked the end of the post-war dominance of the Social

Democrats. Already in his opening speech the new Prime Minister announced a radical shift in Danish economic policy based on a restrictive incomes policy and substantial public budget cuts. In November and December 1982, Schlüter used the opportunity to visit Prime Minister Margaret Thatcher in London and President Ronald Reagan in Washington. These visits symbolized a new Danish policy inspired by the liberal movement of 'Reaganomics', which stated that growth should be based on private initiatives and that the state should secure low inflation through restrictive income, a fixed currency policy and an active trade policy.

The aim of the trade policy was to compensate for the absence of large industrial powerhouses by dividing companies into so-called 'clusters' that would generate internal networks. Therefore, around the middle of the 1980s, trade policy was focused on solving the structural problems within the Danish business community, as well as on breaking down the barriers hindering socio-economic growth. A further aim of the trade policy was to pinpoint future growth area and identify well-grounded companies that would originate from the interaction between service establishments and business enterprises. This trade policy venture stemmed from the structural problems pointed out by the Danish Economic Council. A report published in the spring of 1984 established that Denmark had fallen behind other countries in the areas of R&D. As a result, the percentage of technology in Danish exports was lower than that of competitors on export markets. The report indicated that, in general, companies, but also society as a whole, did not invest sufficient resources in R&D.[70]

One specific proposal to solve the structural problems was by providing more grants for R&D work. In 1986, the Ministry of Finance followed up on this report by pointing out that Danish exports were dominated by goods with poor development potential and, finally, that efforts were being concentrated on export markets with low economic growth. As a result of the identification of these structural problems, a group of government ministers joined forces in May 1986 and released a Discussion Paper on growth and change.[71] The Discussion Paper indicated that Denmark's lack of competitive strength could be attributed to the poor technological standard of her companies combined with the fact that the business community was made up of many small companies lacking the ability to switch to high-technology production methods. Danish companies' lack of ability to accept new technology was defined as a resource problem, but was also attributed to the lack of qualifications of business leaders. Similar to the trade policy of the 1950s, individual companies were sharply criticized in the 1980s for failing to act rationally to benefit the economy, and the incentive system was still seen as the best means of inspiring companies to act more logically, thus benefiting the country's competitiveness. Specifically, the proposal indicated that Denmark had a significant R&D backlog and a lack of ability and willingness to take risks in new areas of growth. The Danish business community could almost be considered 'a sick, old man', ruled by old routines, and the remedy being recommended was 'a radical injection of technology into every corner of the Danish business community'. This should help to increase the ability of Danish businesses to win market shares in high-technology sectors. At the same time, this injection of technology should contribute to the reduction of the harmful effects of an industrial structure consisting of many small companies with limited background in the area of development and research.

To achieve results in this field, the government required the Danish business community to increase their ability to change, at both management level and in relation to development of workers' skills. One solution to the structural problems was to communicate clearly that, if competitive strength was to improve, Danish businesses would have to co-operate more closely with R&D establishments, which would inform the business community of new technological developments abroad. Again, a clear parallel can be drawn to the late 1950s when the government launched new initiatives to help businesses acquire knowledge of new products and production methods.[72]

Schlüter's rehabilitation strategy in the 1980s thus relied on reducing unemployment through increased activities in the private sector – and this worked, as Denmark, for the first time since 1970, experienced a rise in private employment from 1983 to 1987. The problem, however, was that rising economic growth was sparked by borrowed money, resulting in a dramatic growth in the balance of payments deficit in the mid-1980s. From 1987 to 1992, the Danish economy stabilized with lower deficits, while unemployment still soared, reaching new heights in the early 1990s when over 300,000 people were without a job. In 1993, the much-awaited economic upswing finally arrived. To begin with, the upswing did not affect job creation, but from the middle of the 1990s unemployment fell and by 2007 the unemployment total had fallen to less than 100,000. In contrast to the situation in 1986–7, the rising employment in the mid-2000s was combined with a surplus on the currency balance and low inflation. To understand this strong development, it is necessary to focus on Denmark's position within – and its exploitation of – the new global division of labour that accelerated from the mid-1980s onwards. The globalization process affected all parts of the Danish business system: the state, the corporations, the financial system, the educational system and the labour market.

Denmark's entrance in to the EEC was followed by ten years of stagnation in the integration process in which member states initiated unco-ordinated national crisis policies through devaluations and even state-funded 'buy-national' campaigns. This so-called 'Euro sclerosis' lasted until January 1985 when Jacques Delors was appointed as the new chairman of the European Commission. His accession marked the beginning of a more dynamic European development, enforced by three important factors. In France, François Mitterrand had experienced a failed attempt to introduce a new socialist policy on a national level; after several years of negotiations, Spain and Portugal were about to enter the Community; and finally, the long-lasting British budget problems were about to be solved. In January 1986, the European leaders agreed upon the Single European Act (SEA) which involved new institutional changes, such as a stronger role for the Parliament and more majority voting at the expense of the former unanimity rules, and new con-crete political economic initiatives – most importantly the preparation for the internal market in 1992, which included 'abolishing of barriers of all kinds, approximation of legislation and tax structures, strengthening of monetary co-operation and the necessary flanking measures to encourage European firms to work together'.[73] In Denmark, there was broad consensus behind this European policy until around 1986. The economic perspectives in European co-operation gained support, while the Danish government – and particu-larly the socialist opposition – was sceptical about institutional changes that could mean surrender of sovereignty. The consensus broke in 1986 when the opposition – the Social Democrats and the Social Liberals – rejected the institutional changes of the SEA which was then dependent on a popular referendum. On 27 February 1987, 56.2 per cent of the Danish popula-tion supported the Act and Danish policy was seen to be changing in a more pro-European direction. The Liberal foreign minister, Uffe Ellemann-Jensen, personified this change. In a speech to the Danish Parliament in November 1988 he stated that, 'We do not have the opportunity to be a small country, which floats independently in the air and do what ever we want to, and at the same time keep our welfare and wealth.'[74] The Social Democrat party was still sceptical about political integration, but as in many other instances a series of events outside the Danish borders changed their position. The breakdown of the communist regimes in 1989 and 1990 encouraged the need for a co-ordinated political project in Europe. In a speech in Berlin in February 1990, the chairman of the Danish Social Democrats, Svend Auken, stated that he was particularly anxious that the socialists had for too long left the European initiative to the conservative politicians. One month later Foreign Minister Ellemann-Jensen stated that the European development was of particular importance for Denmark for two reasons: first, because German re-unification would have consequences for a small neighbouring country and, secondly, because Denmark's position would change from the periphery to the centre of the community due to the new East and Central European regimes.[75]

This new political consensus was jolted in June 1992 when a majority of the Danish voters rejected the Maastricht Treaty in a popular referendum. The changing political direction from 1987 to 1992 had apparently been too fast for the Danish population. Denmark continued its membership but with certain exceptions: the common defence policy, the common currency and matters of law. It is worth noting that the economic internal market policy was unaffected by these exceptions; in fact, Denmark proved to be one of the most eager to follow the new legislative guidelines. Even when Denmark's rejection of the common currency union was confirmed in a referendum in 1998, the Danish currency was tightly linked to the Euro system.

From the 1990s onwards, Danish domestic policy became a part of European policy, and vice versa. In particular, the relation between the state and corporations was affected. Economic policy was co-ordinated with European legislation – restrictive limits to income policy, currency policy and budgetary policy were introduced. The state also changed competition policy in the early 1990s and simultaneously a privatization and deregulation programme lead to multinational ownership of former Danish state-owned enterprises (SOEs) within infrastructural key sectors. In 1998, the American enterprise Ameritech acquired 42 per cent of the national Danish telecommunication company, TeleDanmark, and in 2005 five international capital venture funds acquired almost 90 per cent of the enterprise. In 2005, the British capital fund CVC Capital Partners acquired 22 per cent of the Danish P&T and finally, in 2006, the Swedish multinational energy giant Vattenfall A/S acquired a large share of the national Danish energy production facilities and distribution networks.

Table 8.14 Outward FDI, by Denmark; EEC, in total, EEC % of total,
1982–92 (million DKK, annual prices)

Denmark out. FDI	1982	1987	1992	1997	2002
FDI out. EEC	124	2.395	11.402	18.300	24.420
FDI out. total	596	4.227	13.502	27.800	37.378
EEC % of total FDI	20.81	56.66	84.45	65.83	65.33

Note: The EEC included the following countries: Belgium–Luxembourg,
France, Germany, Greece, Ireland, Italy, the Netherlands, Portugal, Spain
and the UK.
Source: Danish Statistical Department, for 1982–1990.

Danish corporations and the global division of labour

Following membership of the European Economic Community in 1973,
Danish trade with European countries rose from DKK 24.4 billion in 1973
to DKK 42.1 billion in 1978, or from 65 to 69.5 per cent of total exports.
But, remarkably, the share of Danish export to the other member countries
stagnated and even fell in the early 1980s, from 63.5 per cent in 1982 to
58.7 per cent at the lowest point in 1984. This stagnation – which indicates
that Danish membership was not followed by any immediate 'Europeanization' of the economy – went on until the mid-1980s. The picture changed in
the latter part of the 1980s in line with the rising dynamics of the European
integration process. From 1985 to 1991, the share of exports to the other
Community members rose from 58.7 per cent in 1984 to 68 per cent in 1991.
Exports to other member countries were stable around 65 per cent throughout the 1990s and early 2000s. The high share of EU exports within total
Danish exports indicates that the European market gradually became more
important for Danish companies, particularly in the late 1980s and early
1990s when the institutional framework of the SEA and the Single Market
was implemented.

Danish companies went through a substantial transition in a very short
time, from a relatively low level of outward FDI in the early 1980s to a
very high level of outward FDI in the 1990s and early 2000s. The total rose
from DKK 596 million (or only 0.3 per cent of GDP) in 1982 to 10.3 and
3.6 per cent, respectively, of in GDP 2000 and 2001. In other words Danish
companies – and, indeed, the Danish economy – became more open and
international from the mid-1980s onwards (Table 8.14).

In terms of employment, the development from 1982 to 2006 was marked
by a short intense upswing from 1983 to 1987 when the total number of jobs
in Denmark increased; but from 1987 to 1994 unemployment rose dramatically, from 220,000 to 349,000, followed by a remarkable period of falling

Table 8.15 **Total revenue of the top 40 corporations in relation to national GDP: Denmark, 1973–2003 (per cent)**

	1973	1983	1993	2003
Denmark	42	46	48	68

Source: Binda and Iversen (2007).

unemployment. From 1994 to 2006, 200,000 new jobs were established in Denmark and total employment rose from 2.6 million to 2.8 million. The service sector in particular powered this growth. It is worth noting that from 2003 to 2006, 59,700 new jobs were established in the private sector, but the industrial sector lost 19,200 jobs and the service sector gained 58,800 new jobs. Only within the IT service sector did the number of employed rise, from 27,658 in 1999 to 36,173 in 2004. In the period after 1982, a whole new industrial sector with relevant jobs was created, and the IT sector had consequences for organizational and production methods in many other sectors as well. Business historians such as Chris Freeman and Francisca Louçã have equated the IT revolution with the breakthrough of the railways at the end of the 19th century because it, in the same way, created a new sector while changing infrastructure and organizational methods in the rest of society.

The largest Danish export-oriented enterprises experienced extraordinary growth after 1993. The total revenue of the largest 40 corporations grew substantially faster than total GDP – and the growth of the very largest companies led to a re-interpretation of the Danish economy as consisting primarily of SMEs. Indeed, a more subtle interpretation would suggest that the dynamics of the Danish economy entailed a complex interplay, where the behaviour and international success of the few very large companies acted as engines driving the behaviour, performance and strategic orientation of the smaller companies.

One could be tempted to believe that the world's largest shipping, company – and the largest corporation in Denmark – AP Møller-Mærsk – carried the biggest weight of this centralization but the reasons for the growing influence of the largest Danish companies in the 1980s and 1990s was rather to be found lower down the ranks, where global companies such as Arla Food (see Chapter 9), Coloplast, Danish Crown, Danske Bank, ISS, Lundbeck, Novo Nordisk and others expanded intensively. Over these two decades many medium-sized dairy companies as well as slaughterhouses merged to make two large companies, Arla Foods and Danish Crown. In 1970, there were no fewer than seventeen slaughterhouses and meat exporters among

Photograph 8.3   The Emma Maersk is the biggest container ship in the world and is owned by the A.P. Moeller Maersk Group. The ship is named after Maersk McKinney Moeller's wife Emma, who died in December 2005. The Emma Maersk was labelled 'Santa's big helper' after it arrived, in 2006, in a Suffolk port, in Britain, to unload tonnes of Christmas gifts shipped from China.
Source: Maersk Archives.

the 100 biggest Danish companies. By the year 2007 there was only one, Danish Crown.

The financial sector went through a similar structural transition, in three important phases. In the first phase, the Danish banks prepared themselves for enhanced international competition through a number of large mergers: in 1990, Provinsbanken, Handelsbanken and Den Danske Bank were brought together creating the new Danske Bank, while Andelsbanken, Privatbanken and the savings bank SDS became Unibank. In the second phase, in the 1990s, the Danish banks diversified through the acquisition of national insurance companies, real estate agents and mortgage-credit institutions – the aim being to create so-called 'financial supermarkets' that could offer almost all financial needs for private and corporate customers. Finally, in the third phase, the now substantially larger banks went international. Internationalization of the banking industry had taken place since the early 1970s, but it was only with the deregulation of the national banking laws in Europe in the late 1980s that large-scale international operations became both possible and attractive. Before the 1990s, Danish banks followed their Danish customers to important international markets, but from the 1990s internationalization became an independent growth strategy for the financial sector in its own right. The large Nordic Nordea bank merger – which involved Unibank – took place in 2001. In 1997, Danske Bank launched a new growth strategy – the Nordic region as home market – acquiring Östgöta Enskilda Bank and establishing branches in Oslo, Stockholm and Helsinki. The acquisition of the Norwegian Focus Bank followed in 1999, and in 2005 banks from Ireland and Northern Ireland became part of the Danish banking group. Finally, Danske Bank acquired the third largest Finnish bank, Sampo Bank, including a wide network of local branches in the three Baltic States and Russia in November 2006. Danske Bank was now among the 500 largest corporations in the world and at the same time closely related to the largest Danish corporation A.P. Møller-Mærsk which owned 22 per cent of the bank.

The European political–economic institutions thus seemed to have played a key role for the transition of the Danish industries after the mid-1980s. Interestingly, it was primarily the large Danish enterprises that were export-oriented and thus able to exploit the new international institutional opportunities (for example, within the Single European Market). Among Danish enterprises with more than 100 employees (within the Danish statistical category of 'large enterprises'), approximately 60 per cent of revenue was generated through exports, while among Danish enterprises with 50–99 employees, only about 40 per cent of the revenue was generated through exports.[76] Large corporations were thus at the centre of the growing Danish export.

How do we explain the Danish success?

Danish GDP *per capita* rose dramatically from USD 35,865 in 1990 to USD 47,234 in 2005, while Danish unemployment decreased from a record high 11 per cent in 1993 to only 4.3 per cent in 2006.[77] From 1983 to 1986, Denmark also experienced a limited upturn marked by rising private consumption, growing GDP *per capita* – from USD 15,966 in 1983 to USD 17,993 in 1986 – and particularly growing employment. At this stage Denmark already had a Flexicurity labour market system (based on the hire–fire principle), a homogeneous population and a negotiated economy, but there were few globalized corporate giants and no single European market.[78] Still, due to the lack of a growing export the economic upturn of the mid-1980s caused rising deficits on the current account balance – from – DKK 12.78 billion in 1983 to – DKK 34.66 billion in 1986.[79] Consequently, the Danish government decided to halt the upturn in 1987 by an economic reform (*Kartoffelkuren*), which limited private consumption and thus improved the current account balance, but also caused rising Danish unemployment which, as we have already seen, peaked in 1993. If we focus on the upswing from the mid-1990s to the mid-2000s, exports and increasing inward FDI meant that the upswing was followed by a surplus on the Danish current account balance (USD 7.753 billion in 2005).[80] Factors such as North Sea oil production, global shipping activities, medical exports and European banking activities were crucial to this surplus, and these were facilitated by some of the very largest Danish multinationals – A.P. Møller-Mærsk, Novo Nordisk and Danske Bank – huge corporations able to exploit the new open-market opportunities.

We have earlier argued that the remarkable upswing from 1957 to 1972 was based on a forceful triangle between the rise of the export-oriented industry, a new oil-based motorization of society and finally the explosive growth of the public sector. Analogically, we will argue that the upswing from 1994 to 2007 was based on a forceful triangle with three new components:

- First, the 'old' national institutional factors – in particular, the Flexicurity labour market (system based on the right to hire and fire employees, high social security payments and an active employment programme), the negotiated economy including a high level of trust between public and private sectors and a low degree of corruption.
- Second, the new IT systems not only constituted a whole new industry with thousands of jobs, but also changed infrastructure, organizational systems and production methods.
- Third, the 'new' international institutional factors, in particular the internal European market from 1993, made it possible for Danish enterprises not only to export (as in the upswing from 1957 to 1972), but truly to participate in the global division of labour. Different functions were outsourced to new areas and some of the largest Danish enterprises were able to exploit new market opportunities and thus grow towards the global or European elite, for instance within banking, shipping, wind turbines, hearing aids and office services.

Growing exports and increasing inward and outward FDI were the substantial ingredient and the essential factor for the sustainability of the Danish economic upturn after 1994. But who facilitated and caused this growing export and FDI? While political economists tend to focus on *national* Danish institutions (the negotiated economy) there seems to be evidence for the increasing importance of the large MNCs and the *international* institutions. The integrating European institutions – particularly the SEA of 1987 and the internal market of 1993 – combined with the GATT/WTO global agreements, seemed to have played a key role for growing exports and inward–outward FDI. These *non-Danish* institutions in combination with historically constituted national factors thus provided the real foundation for a sustainable economic upturn in Denmark after 1994.

The forceful triangle of the upswing in the 1960s fell apart in 1973 when oil prices rose and the Danish population rejected the expanding public sector. The new upswing seems consistent, but the referendum in 1992 and the 'Mohammad cartoon crisis' in 2006 indicated that it is difficult to build a national welfare on a combination of global liberal and national co-operative principles. European referendums, public riots and the success of anti-global national parties have revealed how many Danish – and European – people do not feel familiar with the increasing Europeanization, the new information technologies and the enforced role of the largest MNEs. They may have good reasons for their scepticism, but it is the same three main components in the upswing whose benefits they enjoy.

Conclusion

In a detailed analysis, the Danish political economist Peer Hull Kristensen has characterized Danish capitalism as a 'Fragmented system'. In this chapter we have suggested that one can specify this fragmentation by using the label 'Co-operative Liberalism'. Co-operative liberalism contains two apparently opposite currents. On the one hand, Denmark was continuously marked by liberal characteristics in terms of market economic principles, individual rights and high reliance on intense knowledge-sharing with other societies. On the other hand, co-operative aspects have been a feature of Danish society since the mid-nineteenth century: 'help to self-help', solidarity, traditions from many civil organizations and an intense negotiation tradition between private and public interests.

In the period of early liberal capitalism from 1857 to 1899, the combination of co-operative and liberal aspects was straightforward. The political constitution of 1849 and the Freedom of Trade Act of 1857 were both based on the dominant ideology of the time: liberalism. The Danish state was weak and important initiatives came from below: the new telecommunication infrastructure was organized in a decentralized manner, social policies were based on the old guild systems and the most important economic group, the peasants, were in favour of liberal trade principles and a weak concentration of power in the Copenhagen-based state. The peasants, however, also organized the important dairies and slaughterhouses through very non-liberal co-operative principles. In the 1880s and 1890s, Danish labour became organized and even on the commercial markets – such as the beer market – free competition was gradually confined by industrial agreements, trusts and cartels. The regulation and internationalization period from 1899 to 1933 was an interesting interval in which both co-operative and liberals dominated. Together with the Netherlands and Great Britain, Denmark was the last country to insist on free trade and in the 1920s the Danish peasant-dominated Venstre government insisted on an extremely liberal policy base. The growing Danish industrial firms used these years to expand their activities – domestically through new, more efficient production methods and abroad through export and licence agreements. Still, the co-operative aspects were important to Danish capitalism from 1899 to 1932. During the First World War the Overordentlige Kommission institutionalized an extremely close relationship between corporate and public interests. The fundamental principles of the Danish labour market system can be traced back to this period. The September Agreement of 1899 gave the employers the right to hire and fire employees, who were in turn ensured their right to organize. In the early 1930s, Danish capitalism entered a period that was clearly marked by co-operative principles: imports were regulated, the old liberal 'combatant', the agricultural sector, came under strict state control and during the Second World War a strong triangle of state, unions and employers' associations controlled the labour market and economic policy. The industrial sector became more important as an employer of the Danish workforce, but at the same time the sector became more focused on the home market and less efficient in its production methods. The inefficiency caused many problems in the following period. From 1957 to 1982 Danish companies took a more active part in the rising international trade. The Danish activities, carried out by large new companies such as Velux, Lego, Danfoss and Grundfos, were most often based on export rather than greenfield investment or acquisitions. Liberal-based trade agreements in the 1960s were still essential to rising Danish industrial production, and indeed for the Danish upswing. Another important aspect was the fast-growing public service sector.

The welfare state expanded in the 1960s and 1970s based on a widely accepted social vision of national equality. Solidarity between different classes in terms of equal access to health care, education and pensions demanded considerable resources and thus caused rising taxes and growing imports. In the 1970s, the Danish economy went into a stage of imbalance – the trade deficit, unemployment and inflation rose at the same time. Keynes' well-known solution of increased public spending proved unable to solve these challenges. In the last period – after 1982 – Danish businesses entered a new and more liberal age. International institutions such as the EU, the GATT/WTO and the OECD are important in understanding how Danish business changed from export-based growth in the 1960s, 1970s and 1980s towards participation in the global division of labour. From the mid-1980s Danish outward and inward FDI sky-rocketed. The creation of a real European market, with common standards, competition policy and currency made it possible for Danish corporations to grow from being large companies to becoming corporate giants that could efficiently focus on global niche markets such as hearing aids, wind turbines and insulin. The infrastructural sectors such as telecommunications, energy and aviation were particularly affected by deregulation and intensified competition. These enterprises used to be state-owned and driven on the basis of national monopolies. From the early 1990s they became part of an intensive international competition between still larger global competitors. Behind these liberal characteristics, it is important to keep in mind that the Danish state continued to be important and that the welfare system kept its social vision of equal access to education and health care. Danish ownership structures continued to be marked by historical–national-dependent peculiarities such as co-operatives within the agricultural sector and family foundations within the non-financial sectors. After 1982, Danish capitalism still had a foot in both the liberal and co-operative camps. The dual references and experiences that we have labelled 'Co-operative Liberalism' may help to understand the recent success of Danish capitalism, as the Danish economic actors had historic roots in both co-operation and competition.

QUESTIONS   1. In this chapter, Danish capitalism is characterized under the heading 'Co-operative liberalism'. Which periods of the Danish business system could be regarded as mainly dominated by liberal economic principles and which were mainly dominated by co-operative economic principles? Discuss why the Danish business system seems to have moved between liberal and

co-operative principles and to what extent this dialectic movement is a principle common to all Nordic economies.

2. The Danish economy experienced fast growth from 1993 to 2007.
What were the main reasons for this upswing and to which extent
should the fundamental background of the upswing be identified
inside or outside the Danish business system?

Notes

1. Innovationsrådet: Danmark i det globale videnssamfund (2004).
2. Kristensen (1995).
3. Hansen (1978); Fink (2005).
4. Mokyr (2006), p. 8.
5. Thorndal (2007).
6. Østergaard, in Hall *et al.* (2006), p. 68.
7. Westergaard (1922), p. 18.
8. Ole Lange (2006), pp. 165–76.
9. Hansen (1970), p. 40.
10. Hansen (1970), p. 40, emphasis in the orginal.
11. *Ibid.*
12. Hansen (1970), p. 60.
13. Interview with Ole Lange (2006).
14. Willerslev (1952), p. 233 and interview with Ole Lange.
15. Will. Scharling, *Berlingske Aftenavis*, 8 June 1892.
16. Westergaard (1922), p. 34.
17. Fink (2005), p. 43.
18. Hansen (1970), p. 21.
19. Andersen and Federspiel (2006), p. 24.
20. Boje (1997), p. 85.
21. Boje (1997), p. 37
22. Fraenkel (1897).
23. Olsen (1974?), p. 50.
24. Hansen (1974), p. 145
25. Westergaard (1922), p. 22
26. Fink (2006), p. 9.
27. Fink (2006), p. 33.
28. Westergaard (1922), p. 68.
29. Westergaard (1922), pp. 33–34.
30. Westergaard (1922), p. 28.
31. Jones (1996).
32. Christiansen *et al.* (1988), pp. 89ff.
33. Forhandlingsprotokol for Den Overordentlige Kommission, den 9., 10., 19. 20 og 24. august 1914; De overordentlige Foranstaltninger (1914), p. 23.
34. Jørgensen (2005), pp. 86ff.
35. Dansk Industriberetning (1918) p. 79; Foss (1972) pp. 146ff.; Hansgaard (1976), p. 113.
36. Kaarsted (1989), p. 143; Rasmussen (1965), p. 88; Boje and Kallestrup (2004), p. 43.
37. Thomsen (1991), p. 226; Fink (2000), p. 212
38. Hansen (1996), pp. 87ff.
39. *Erhvervsministeriets Industriudvalgs IIIdie Betænkning* (1926), p. 10.
40. *Ibid.*
41. Andersen and Federspiel (2006), p. 74f.
42. Lidegaard (1996, pp. 45ff.; 2003, pp. 215ff).
43. Boje (2000), pp. 163ff.

44. Ellemose (2005), pp. 64ff.
45. Linder (1994), p. 85.
46. Jones (2005), p. 119
47. Hansen (1977), p. 43.
48. Valutacentral was renamed Direktoratet for Vareforsyning in 1940.
49. Tage Kaarsted: Gyldedal og Politikens Danmarkshistorie, 1925–50.
50. Arzourini (2006).
51. Lewis (1957).
52. Mørch (1983), p. 172.
53. Ove Kay Petersen (2006), pp. 456–7.
54. Hansen (1977), p. 51.
55. Pedersen (1937), pp. 290–317.
56. Hansen (1996), pp. 407–12.
57. Hansen (1977), p. 66.
58. Hansen (1968).
59. Andersen and Federspiel (2006).
60. Johansen (1987), p. 122.
61. Statistisk Årbog (various years).
62. Johansen (1987), p. 141.
63. Johansen (1985), p. 35.
64. Danfoss was not managed on a daily basis by the family after the death of the founder in 1966 but the family still controlled the board of directors and thus the overall management. In the three other cases, the family both controlled the board of directors and the daily management until the early 2000s.
65. Cortzen (1996), p. 77.
66. Note, Johansen (1987).
67. Statistisk Årbog (various years).
68. Statistisk Årbog (various years).
69. See, for instance, *Dansk Industri Historie, 1870–1973* (1995–2004), or the debate in *Jyske Historiker* (2003).
70. Danish Economic Council (1984).
71. The Ministry of Labour, the Ministry of Finance, the Ministry of Trade and Industry and the Ministry of Education: *Discussion Paper on Growth and Change* (Copenhagen, 1986).
72. The Ministry of Trade and Industry, *Review of Industrial Policy*, (Copenhagen 1986), p. 55.
73. European Commission (1985).
74. Petersen (1994), p. 226.
75. Petersen (1994), p. 222.
76. Danmarks Statistik, *Statistisk Efterretning 2005*, p. 16.
77. http://www.ggdc.net/index.html.
78. http://www.ggdc.net/index.html.
79. *Danmarks Statistik*, Statistisk Årbog (1989).
80. https://www.cia.gov/cia/publications/factbook/geos/da.html.

References

Andersen, S. and Federspiel, S., *Nytænkning gennem 100 år: Teknologisk Instituts Historie 1906–2006* (Copenhagen: Lindhardt & Ringhof, 2006).
Binda, V. and Iversen, M.J., 'Towards a "Managerial Revolution" in European Business? The Transformation of Danish and Spanish Big Business, 1973–2003,' *Business History*, (4) (July 2007), pp. 506–30.
Boje, P., *Ledere, ledelse og organization 1870–1972, Dansk industri efter 1870, bind 5* (Odense, Odense Universitetforlag, 1997).
Boje, P., *Memorier fra I. Verdenskrig*, (Syddansk Universitetsforlag, Odense, 2000).
Boje, P. and Kallestrup, M., *Marked, erhvervsliv og stat, danskkonkurrencelovgivning og det store erhvervsliv* (Aarhus: Aarhus Universitetsforlag, 2004).
Christiansen, N.F., Lammers, K.C. and Nissen, H.S., *Danmarks historie. 1914–45. Vol. 7.* (Copenhagen: Gyldendal, 1988).

Cortzen, J., *Legomanden, Historien om Godtfred Kirk Christiansen* (Copenhagen, Børsens forlag, 1996).

Danmarks Statistik, *Statistical Yearbook* (Copenhagen: Denmarks Statistik, 1895–2006).

Danish Economic Council, *Danish Economy* (Copenhagen, 1984).

Elmquist Jørgensen, K. *Studier i samspillet mellem stat og erhvervsliv i Danmark under 1. Verdenskrig*, (Copenhagen: CBS, 2005).

European Commission, *Completing the Internal Market: White Paper from the Commission to the European Council*, COM (85) 310 final (1985).

Fink, J., *Storindustri eller middelstand – Det ideologiske opgør i Det konservative Folkeparti 1918–1920.* (Aarhus: Aarhus Universitets förlag, 2000).

Fink, J., (unpublished manuscript) *Dansk Ervervshistorie 1850–2000* (Aarhus: Århus University, 2005).

Fligstein, N. and Merand, F., 'Globalization or Europeanization: Changes in the European Economy, 1980–2000', *Acta Sociologica*, 55, (2002) pp. 7–22.

Foss, A. *Memorier fra I. Verdenskrig*, (Copenhagen: Gyldendal, 1972).

Fraenkel, A., *Gamle Carlsberg : et bidrag til dansk industrihistorie og industriel udviklingshistorie* (Copenhagen, H. Hagerups Boghandel, 1897).

Freeman, C. and Louçã, F. *As Time Goes by: From the Industrial Revolution to the Information Revolution* (New York: Oxford University Press, 2001).

Hall, P. and Soskice, D., *Varieties of Capitalism: The Institutional Foundations of Comparative Advantage* (New York: Oxford University Press, 2001).

Hansen, H. I., *Firmaet Laur. Knudsen's historie* (København: LK, 1968).

Hansen, P. H., *På glidebanen til den bitre ende: Dansk bankvæsen i krise, 1920–1933, disputats.* (Odense: Odense Universitetsforlag 1996), p. 496.

Hansen, S. Å., *The Early Industrialization of Denmark* (Copenhagen, 1970).

Hansen, S. Å., *Økonomisk Vækst i Danmark* (Copenhagen: Akademisk förlag, 1974).

Hansgaard, T., *Landbrugsrådets tilblivelse* (Copenhagen, 1976).

Hyldtoft, O., *Danmarks økonomiske historie 1840–1910* (Århus: Forlaget Systime, 1999).

Innovationsrådet, *Den Danske Strategi – Danmarks muligheder i det globale videnssamfund* (2004).

Iversen, M. J., *Kaffetræ i vækst . . .* (Kolding: Merrild Kaffe A/S, 1999).

Johansen, H. C., *Dansk Økonomisk Statistik, 1814–1980*, 9 (Copenhagen: Gyldendal, 1985).

Johansen, H. C., *The Danish Economy in the Twentieth Century, The Croom Helm Series on the Contemporary Economic History of Europe*, (London: Croom Helm, 1987) p. 221.

Johansen, H. C. and Møller, A. M., *Foundations as Owners of Danish Manufacturing Companies* (Odense: Syddansk Universitetsforslag, 2004).

Jones, G. *The Evoultion of International Business* (London: Routledge, 1996).

Kaarsted, T., *Ove Rode som indenrigsminister* (Odense: University Press of Southern Denmark, 1989).

Kaarup Jensen, J., *Farvel til den sidste bonde* (Copenhagen: DR, 2006).

Kristensen, P.H., 'Strategies against Structure: Institutions and Economies Organization in Denmark', in R. Whitley (ed.), *European Business Systems: Firms and Markets in their National Context* (London: Sage, 1992) pp. 117–36.

Lange, O., *Stormogulen, C.F. Tietgen – en finansmand, hans imperium og hans tid 1829–1901* (Copenhagen: Gyldendal, 2006).

Laursen, J., *et al.* (eds), *Danmark i Europa, 1945–93* (Copenhagen: Munksgaard, 1994).

Lewis, W.A., *Economic Survey 1919–1939* (London, 1957).

Lidegaard, B., *I Kongens Navn – Henrik Kaufmann i dansk diplomati 1919–58*, (Copenhagen: Gyldendal, 1996).

Mokyr, J., *Successful Small Open Economies and the Importance of Good Institutions* in Ojala, J., Eloranta, J. and Jalava, J., *The Road to Prosperity: An Economic History of Finland* (Helsinki: SKS, 2006), pp. 8–14.

Mørch, S., *Den ny Danmarkshistorie 1880–1960* (Copenhagen: Gyldendal, 1983).

Olsen, Erling., *Danmarks økonomiske historie siden 1750.* Studier fra Køobenhavns universitets økonomiske institut, nr. 3. (Copenhagen: Gad, 1967).

Olsen, E. and Hoffmeyer, E., *Dansk Pengehistorie 1914–1960*, 2 (Copenhagen: Danmarks Nationalbanken, 1968).

Pedersen, H.W., Tidsskrift (1937), Arbejdsstandsningernes økonomiske virkninger', *Nationaløkonomisk* pp. 290–317.

Pedersen, N., *Vejen til den europæiske union, 1980–93*, in J. Laursen, *et al.* (eds), *Danmark i Europa, 1945–93* (Copenhagen: Munksgaard, 1994).

Pedersen, P. J., 'Postwar growth of the Danish economy', in Crafts, N. and Toniolo, G., *Economic Growth in Europe since 1945*, (Cambridge: Cambridge University Press, 1996).

Rasmussen, E., *Velfærdsstaten på vej. Politikens Danmarkshistorie* (Copenhagen: Politikens forlag, 1965).

Rasmussens, E. B., 'Notes from the years at FLS', (unpublished, private manuscript).

Sorge, A., *Changing Capitalisms?: Internationalization, Institutional Change, and Systems of Economic Organization* (New York: Oxford University Press, 2005) p. 110.

Svenden, Knud Erik and Hansen, Svend Aage, *Dansk Pengehistorie, bind 1* (Copenhagen: Danmarks Nationalbank, 1968).

Thomsen, N., *Industri, stat og samfund. 1870–1939* (Odense: University Press of Southern Denmark, 1991).

Thorndahl, J., 'Energi på dåse – et dansk industrieventyr – der endte i det fjerne – om firmaet W. Hellesen's og Alkaline Batteries', *Elmuseets Skrifter*, Horsens, 2007.

Westergaard, Harald, *Economic Development in Denmark before and during the World War*, (Oxford: The Clarendon Press, 1922).

Willerslev, R., *Studier i dansk industrihistorie: 1850–1880* (Copenhagen: E. Harck, 1952) p. 233.

Interview with Ole Lange, *Politiken*, November 2006.

appendix: the transformation of the Danish business system

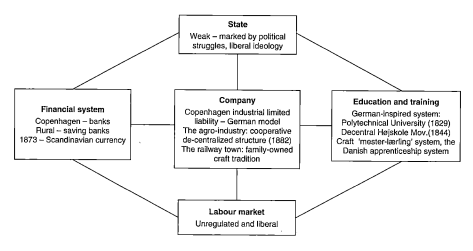

Figure 8A.1   *The Danish business system, 1857–98*

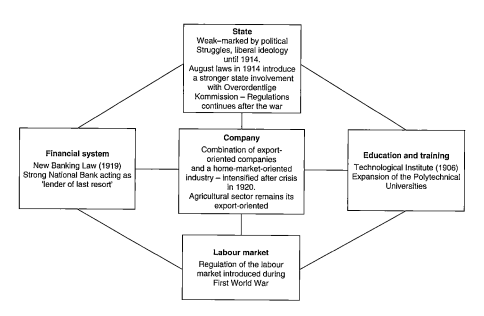

Figùre 8A.2   *The Danish business system, 1899–1932*

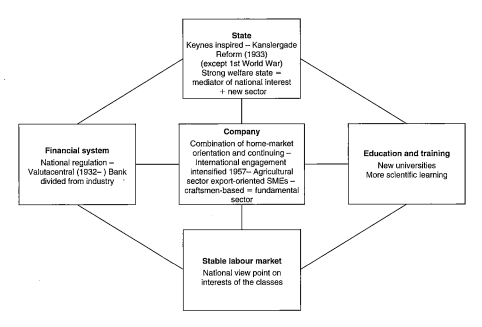

Figure 8A.3   **The Danish business system, 1933–56**

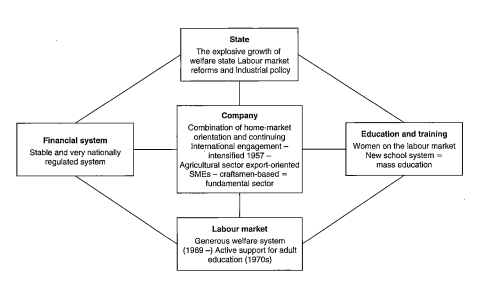

Figure 8A.4   **The Danish business system, 1957–82**

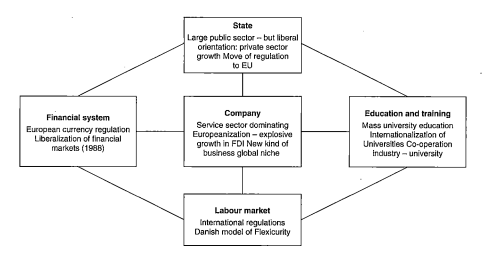

Figure 8A.5   The Danish business system, 1982–

WELFARE CAPITALISM: THE SWEDISH ECONOMY 1850–2005 ▪ ENTREPRENEURSHIP AND OWNERSHIP: THE
⟨9⟩ ABB LONG-TERM VIABILITY OF THE SWEDISH BONNIER AND WALLENBERG FAMILY BUSINESS GROUPS ▪ FROM
CAPITALISM, 1850S–2005 ▪ FROM STATE OWNERSHIP TO MULTINATIONAL CORPORATION: THE PATH OF
ENSO-GUTZEIT ... GROWTH AND INVESTMENT, FINNISH ... FROM ... TO ... FUTURE OF A ... CONGLOMERATE FIRM: THE STRATEGIC
PATHS OF NOKIA AND TAMPELLA IN THE LIBERALIZING FINNISH ECONOMY AFTER THE SECOND WORLD
WAR ▪ CO-OPERATIVE LIBERALISM: DENMARK FROM 1857 TO 2007 ▪ ARLA – FROM DECENTRALIZED INDUSTRY
TO MULTINATIONAL ENTERPRISE ▪ CARLSBERG AND THE SELF-REGULATION OF THE DANISH BEER MARKET
▪ NORWAY: A RESOURCE-BASED AND DEMOCRATIC CAPITALISM ▪ CONSTRUCTIVE POWER: ELKEM 1904–2004
▪ FINANCE AND THE DEVELOPMENT OF NORWEGIAN CAPITALISM – THE CASE OF CHRISTIANIA BANK

Arla: from a decentralized co-operation to an MNE

Mads Mordhorst

Introduction

Unlike the other Scandinavian countries, where agriculture has lost its position in the process of industrialization, the Danish economy is characterized by the dominant position of agriculture and the food industries.[1] With a population of only 5.4 million, Denmark is No. eight on the list of global food and beverage exporters. More than a third of Danish export income comes from the food industry, and agriculture was the largest sector until the 1960s.[2] Danish agriculture is highly industrialized, and among the most efficient in the world, involving the use of a wide range of computer technologies: for example, most Danish cows are monitored by implanted chips to optimize their milk production.

This raises important questions. What is capitalism, and what is industrialization? Is the traditional contrast between agriculture and industry valid in the Danish case? In this chapter, we examine developments in the Danish agricultural sector in the late 1800s as an important part of Denmark's ongoing industrialization. We focus on dairy production which, together with bacon production, has dominated the Danish food industry since the late nineteenth century. At that time, more than 1400 dairies were founded in less than two decades. The dairies were in fact small industrial plants and they brought Denmark into the global economy, where division of labour was a prime source of competitive advantage.

On the other hand, agricultural production in Denmark has some characteristics that distinguish it from the traditional 'industrial' industries. First, it has a history of decentralized structure with low concentrations of labour and capital. Second, ownership has traditionally been organized as co-operative associations and not as joint stock companies. Third, at the cultural and discursive level, the Danish agricultural sector and the industrial sector have positioned themselves as antithetical to each other.[3] So, even today, when the dairy sector is concentrated around a single multinational and highly effective enterprise, Arla, many Danes still see the business as rooted in traditional agrarian ideals.

The chapter focuses on three periods in the history of Danish agriculture and what would become Arla Foods. The first is from 1875 to 1900, when the agricultural sector shifted its focus from grain products to livestock products. Export and production was focused on the British market, as a result of British industrial revolution and urbanization. As a part of this transition, a huge number of dairies were founded to manufacture products suitable for export. We discuss how this decentralized system was counterbalanced in a highly co-ordinated business system involving the Danish state at several levels.

From the late 1950s, the dairy sector faced a structural crisis. Fundamental changes had to be made if the agricultural sector was to keep its position as a major exporter. The answer was found in a process of concentration. Internationally, Denmark was still linked to the British market, at least until England and Denmark became members of the EEC in 1973.

The last period we focus on begins in the year 2000. At the end of the millennium, structural development had come to an end in Denmark. By 2007, a single company, Arla Foods, had almost completely replaced the small dairies. With about 90 per cent of the milk production in Denmark, it controls the market. However, the trend to structural development has continued but now on an international level. Today, Arla is an MNE with dairies in twelve countries.[4] On the national market, this development has been problematic, and the enterprise has faced several crises and consumer boycotts.

The breakthrough of the butter industry

In the last two decades of the nineteenth century, the Danish butter industry enjoyed a global breakthrough. More than 1400 dairies were established in less than three decades, nearly all producing butter for the British market. Output of the industry grew rapidly. In terms of weight, average yearly exports increased from 11,760 tonnes in 1870–9, through 19,960 in 1880–9, to 53,810 in 1890–9, and in the last four years before the outbreak of the First World War, they averaged 89,920 tonnes.[5]

In the late nineteenth century Britain was still at the centre of the international economy. One of the key features of this position was that Britain became highly dependent on imports of raw materials and foodstuffs either for consumption within Britain or for processing and re-export. This dependence meant that countries supplying the British market had considerable opportunities for export-led growth and economic development. A telling example of this symbiotic relationship is provided by the importance of the British market to Danish butter producers. Between 1865–9 and 1895–9, the average proportion of total Danish export butter (by weight) sent to Britain increased from 69.1 per cent to 97.2 per cent. Around the year 1900, butter to Britain made up more than 40 per cent of total Danish exports. In other words, butter integrated the Danish economy in the international market, while at the same time making Denmark dependent on the export of a single product to the British market.

Denmark and the global challenge at the end of the nineteenth century

At the end of the nineteenth century, Denmark faced a number of crises. In 1864, Denmark suffered a defeat in the war against Prussia, resulting in the withdrawal from the duchy of Schleswig Holstein. Aside from re-establishing Denmark's position as a small state, the defeat also resulted in the loss of the most productive and technologically advanced area of the country.[6] Shortly after the defeat, the most important export of the Danish economy by far was threatened. Grain production, which had assured stable growth for thirty years, was now in foreign hands.[7]

The actual cause was the flooding of the international market with cheap grain from Russia and the US, among other countries. Seen in a broader perspective, this was the result of the international breakthrough of industrialism and capitalism, which clearly created a significantly more global and work-divided economy.

In this situation, there was nothing for Denmark to do but reorganize its agricultural production and adapt itself to the new global economy. This might have been for the better in any case, since the farming soil in Denmark had become exhausted due to the rapid increase in corn production between 1770 and 1840, a period often referred to as the 'great period of corn selling'.[8]

In an important sense, Danish butter production emerged from the particular way Danish farmers handled their adaptation to the new global economy. The needs of grain production had increased the demand for manure, which drove an increase in stockbreeding to produce it.[9] A by-product of manure production was milk, establishing a ready supply of raw material for butter production on an industrial scale.

The lack of structure in dairy production, however, meant that most butter produced on the average Danish farm was of such poor quality that it was unsuitable for anything other than making lubricants.[10] Only the manors had the skills and stocks to produce high-quality butter. However, the early shift of focus from grain to animal products, motivated by the perception that this was the only way to maintain agriculture as an export-based sector, helped establish a competitive advantage for Danish agriculture over other European countries.

A number of forward-looking Danish business people operating in London realised how industrialization was creating new markets for these products. Along with a growing middle class in the more industrialized countries, like England and Germany, new patterns of nutritional standards and food preferences were emerging. The wealthier segment of the growing working class in the industrial areas in England could afford food with high calorific value, which increased demand accordingly. In other words, the market for grain was shrinking while the market for livestock production was enjoying significant growth.

The shift from grain to animal products, however, required the development of a manufacturing process shaped by the constraints of slaughterhouses and dairy plants. Since the end of the eighteenth century, Danish agricultural structure has been decentralized. Medium-sized farms, where each farmer possessed a limited number of cows, constituted the most important production unit. As a result, the concentration of capital needed to invest in production apparatus for manufacturing the milk was absent. The co-operative movement emerged from this need.

The co-operative method as an organizational solution

In 1882, Danish farmers in Hjedding, a village in one of the poorer areas of west Denmark, discussed how they could improve the quality of their butter production. None of the known solutions seemed attractive. Home production on the farms had been the traditional solution, but this suffered from several problems. Most of the farmers lacked skills to produce butter of an acceptable quality, and it could take months to derive enough butter from existing processes for sale. Without any means of cooling the butter, the quality quickly suffered. Another solution was to establish a small privately owned dairy. These had emerged around the country in the previous decades, but were normally too small and poor to process the milk in a manner that would yield high-quality butter, comparable to that of the larger landowners.

Moreover, the farmers lacked both the capital and the interest to establish their own dairies.

Instead, the farmers decided to try to found a dairy on a co-operative basis. The idea was that all paid an equal share, so that they owned and ran the dairy in common. By doing this they created the first co-operative production unit in the world.[11] The idea of a co-operative itself was not entirely new, of course, nor was it Danish in origin. It had started the 1840s in Rochdale, near Manchester, where workers joined together in a co-operative association to buy foodstuffs like sugar, flour and butter. In 1872, it became a nationwide chain under the name the Co-operative Wholesale Society (CWS). What was new in the Danish case was that the principles were used in production instead of purchase.

This was, in other words, an instance of forward integration, bringing the producers of raw materials into the process of manufacturing. With their membership of a co-operative dairy, the farmers gained the right to have their milk processed, and were paid in accordance with the amount of milk they delivered, after an allotment for maintenance and development had been deducted. This contrasted with the joint stock companies, where the profit went to the shareholders of a company, who may not have been its customers. This innovative form of organising business suited the decentralized agricultural structure in Denmark perfectly. It both solved the problem of capital to build the dairies and strengthened the local networks among the farmers.

The co-operative approach spread throughout the country with remarkable speed. In 1890, eight years after the founding of the first co-operative dairy it is estimated that there were around 800 such dairies round in Denmark.[12] Likewise, the co-operative approach to organising business spread to other industries. In 1887, the first co-operative slaughterhouse opened, in Horsens. A feed co-operative opened in 1885.[13] In this way, the co-operative approach fostered path dependency, where co-operatives became the way of organizing business in the agricultural sector.

It is a significant Danish characteristic that co-operatives are concentrated in the agricultural sector and rural areas. In most countries, co-operation was connected to the workers' movement and gained influence in the urbanized and industrialized areas. Thus, on a linguistic level, the word 'co-operative movement' in Denmark does not indicate all sorts of co-operation but only those connected with the agricultural sector. In Danish, the word '*koorporation*' is used in reference to undertakings that have historically been linked to the workers' movement, whereas 'andelsbevægelsen' is associated with the rural community.[14] In this chapter, co-operative movement will be used in the latter sense. Another characteristic is that the co-operatives in Denmark did not include a social programme; it was a strictly economic community.[15] The members were farmers not wage-earners; they owned their land, and were typically associated with a liberal ideology and the Liberal Party (Venstre). However, we cannot conclude that the co-operative movement did not experience any ideological and cultural evolution in Denmark. In fact, the co-operative idea had a huge impact on not only economic development but also on the shaping of modern Danish identity. The *Danish Encyclopaedia* explains that:

> an understanding of co-operation [in Denmark] cannot be based on its particular legal, financial or organizational characteristics alone, but must also include the historical and cultural community, which has its roots in the structure of the rural community in the late nineteenth century. In the minds of the public, the co-operative movement is viewed as a unique cultural/democratic Danish tradition, which has played an important role in the rise of modern Denmark.[16]

This means that the co-operatives have been viewed as a uniquely Danish paradigm in the establishment of a modern society.[17] According to this narrative, the model has ensured that Denmark has not only developed into a rich society but also became capable of navigating through both the industrial era's political and social deformations and the tendencies toward planning and the rejection of individuality as pursued by socialism.[18] In other words, the model was built up around certain liberal virtues of self-organization, the market, freedom, small-scale operations, democracy and respect for the individual. Thus, the co-operative organization and the co-operative movement in Denmark play a much more interesting role than simply a way of doing business.

However, the main problem with the focus on the co-operative organizational form is that it creates a tendency to neglect a range of other factors that were just as important for the development of the dairy industry in Denmark. One of these was the invention of the continuous milk centrifuge.

The centrifuge as a technological solution
Fundamentally, the process of butter production was unaltered for centuries until around 1870. It was a slow and craft-based process that was traditionally

carried out by women at the farms and manors. As the demand for butter at the world market grew, it became clear that is was important to industrialize and rationalize this process.

The first step in the process of butter manufacturing is to separate the cream from the skimmed milk. This is done by placing the milk in vessels. Then the cream then slowly concentrates at the top of the vessel, where it can be skimmed. Apart from being a slow and time-demanding process, the problem was that milk that had been mixed by being transported on the bumpy roads was unusable in this process. In other words, the milk produced on an average farm was unsuitable for this kind of production.[19]

Experiments by German engineers had shown that centrifuging milk speeded up the process. A race to develop a centrifuge that could separate the cream on an industrial level started among engineers in Germany, Italy, Sweden and Denmark. On 6 November 1878, the Danish engineer Rasmus Nielsen from the small Maglekilde engine works, won a patent for the first continuous milk centrifuge in the world. He was the first, but only slightly ahead of Swedish engineers and the Alfa Laval centrifuge was patented shortly after.[20] In the following years, the two methods were in competition to dominate the market, a competition that Alfa Laval won. Nevertheless, the Danish centrifuge gave the Danish farmers a first-mover advantage.

The centrifuge created a revolution in the dairy industry and especially in butter production (Photograph 9.1). With the continuous milk centrifuge it was suddenly possible to separate the cream from the skimmed milk much faster and much more effectively than ever before. More importantly, it made it economically possible to collect milk from small farmers for use in dairies.

The demand for the centrifuge in Denmark was huge. The first centrifuge was placed in the centre of Copenhagen in 1878.[21] Within a year, 98 centrifuges had been established around Denmark, and by 1888 2500 were working. Each dairy had to invest in a range of other machines and equipment: buildings, carriages to collect the milk, milk cans, pasteurization machines, cooling systems, churns and butter workers, scales and, of course, powerful engines to make it all work.[22]

All this demanded a machine industry, and initiated a large Danish agro-machine industry that is an important export industry to this day.[23] On a financial level, the co-operative system was a perfect solution to the problem of finding sufficient sources of investment. In other words, the new dairies were not based on the patterns of the traditional agricultural production, but on the patterns of industry.

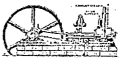

Burmeister & Wain's danske Mejericentrifuge,

tilkjendt

Ærespræmier, Guld- og Sølv-Medailler

i alle Lande.

over 4000 store og smaa i Brug,

hvilket svarer til mindst 0,500 af den mindste Konstruktion.

Blandt de særlige Fortrin, som denne Centrifuge har, skal nævnes

Stigrør, Sikkerhedsforlagstoj, Kontrolcentrifuge,

Emulsion, forøget Skumningsevne,

moderat Hastighed, ringe Kraftforbrug, Skumning af kold Mælk.

Fuldstændige Dampmejerianlæg

udføres under Garanti til billige Priser

efter forud givet

Overslag

og paa gunstige

Betalingsvilkaar.

Mejerikyndig Assistance staar til vore ærede Kunders Raadighed.

Photograph 9.1 **The manufacturing plant: B & W could sell 'total' solutions to the dairies, combining centrifuges and steam engines.**
Source: Advertisement from 1888.

Governmental support

The development of milk centrifuges and the spread of dairies led to a range of practical problems that were impossible for a small dairy to solve by itself. One set of problems was connected with quality. Today butter is a standardized product that does not differ much in quality. This was different in the late nineteenth century. Most butter produced on the manors had a high quality and good reputation, in contrast to the butter produced in the small private and co-operative dairies. In the 1870s, typical Danish farm butter had such a poor reputation that it was mostly exported to Britain as a machine lubricant and as an ointment to protect sheep from parasites. In Germany, the reputation of Danish butter was not any better. In Hamburg, for example, it was practically impossible to sell because it was often mixed with potatoes.[24] If butter production was to have success as an export industry, it needed to improve its quality dramatically and change its reputation.

It was recognized by the Danish government that these problems could not be solved by the dairies alone. The state therefore supported butter producers by a range of initiatives. One of them was the establishment of the Agricultural Research Laboratory, in 1883. The aim of the laboratory was to support the agricultural sector with research and practical solutions – in other words to act as the sectors' R& D department.[25] One important innovation was a control apparatus for measuring the fat level in the milk, which kept farmers from diluting the milk with water.[26] Controlled attempts with better feed types also resulted in increasing milk production and the discovery of new applications. For example, experiments showed that the residual skimmed milk, left over from butter production, could be used as feed for pigs. The dairies could now deliver the skimmed milk back to the farmers. This, however, resulted in a danger of epidemics that could be spread through milk infected with diseases like cow tuberculosis.

In fact, the first co-operative dairy in Hjedding was the centre of an epidemic only a few months after it opened, where several people died, among them employees at the dairy. Analyses made by government-funded research showed that the bacteria could be eliminated by pasteurization, which led to pasteurizers developed especially for dairies. In 1898, Denmark was the first country to make it compulsory to pasteurize milk[27] and, as a side benefit, it was soon realised that butter produced from the pasteurized milk was more homogeneous in taste. Subsequently, another breakthrough in the laboratory's work with bacteriology turned out to be even more important to the development of a consistent butter quality. In 1890, the Danish chemist Wilhelm Storch succeed in isolating the different lactic acid bacteria in the milk and on this basis optimized the bacterial culture best suited to butter.[28] The year after Storch published his research, dairies began to use bacterial cultures produced in laboratories to sour cream. This brief history shows a repeating pattern of close co-operation between laboratory practice and dairy applications. Two other institutions that were established and financed by the government contributed to this: an advisory service established in 1885 and dairy schools established from 1887.

The advisory service consisted of five persons who visited the dairies and delivered lectures to the dairymen in all parts of the country.[29] The fast spread of dairies created a demand for skilled dairymen, which was met by establishing the dairy schools in Ladelund (1887), and Dallum (1889).[30] Along with these educational programmes, three journals were published on a weekly basis: the *Co-operative Journal* (from 1900), which was distributed to the farmers and dairymen; the *Dairy Journal* (from 1888), which dealt with the newest innovations in dairy techniques; and the *Butter Trade Journal* (from 1889), of which nearly half was written in English to ensure communication between Britain and Denmark. In this way, the decentralized Danish dairy sector developed as a highly co-ordinated business system.[31]

The success was outstanding. The reputation of Danish butter changed, and from around 1885 Danish butter was recognized as a brand that was synonymous with butter of high quality, and received a price premium compared to the butter from other countries on the butter market.[32]

Denmark as a European butter trade centre

Denmark was not the only country to expand its butter production in the late nineteenth century, however. Countries like Russia, Finland and Sweden also had a rising butter export. This changed the patterns of international butter production. Eastern and northern Europe emerged as the centres for butter production and Copenhagen became the new centre for the butter trade. It was the evolution of Danish butter production itself and Denmark's geographical position that gave Denmark its competitive advantage.

The rise of the Danish butter industry created the need for skilled butter merchants and trade companies who had knowledge of the international butter market and skills to examine the quality of the butter. The butter merchants could easily adapt these skills to butter production in other countries, and Danish butter merchants expanded into Russia, Finland and Sweden.[33] Located at the mouth of the Baltic Sea and with harbours in Copenhagen, Esbjerg and Aarhus, Denmark was a natural junction between northern and eastern Europe and Britain and central Europe. In the 1890s, 20 million 1b of butter produced outside Denmark were re-exported through Danish ports.[34] By 1890 the price of butter in Copenhagen began to be seen as the leading and determining price for the world market. The combination of geographical position and technical expertise thus placed Denmark at the centre of the international butter trade.[35]

While this was a benefit to trade and shipping, along with the Danish national income, it created problems for the national butter export. One problem was that a shipment of butter originating from a Danish harbour did not imply that the butter was of Danish origin or quality. In the case of Russian butter this was not a problem because it was clearly of lower quality and had a different taste. After transportation from Siberia in wagons without cooling, the butter was often in an obviously miserable condition.[36] But there was the problem of making sure that there had been no adulteration of the butter by, for example, mixing Danish and Russian butter or by repackaging the butter and disguising it as Danish.

'The margarine war'

In 1883, the Danish merchant Otto Mønsted founded the Aarhus Butterine Company.[37] This sent out shock waves in the Danish butter sector. The dairies had seen how Dutch butter had lost its reputation for quality with the advent of the Dutch margarine industry. In several cases, Dutch margarine had been sold directly as butter, or mixed with butter and sold as pure butter. This had sent the price of Dutch butter plummeting, though it had been highly regarded in the 1870s. Faced with this risk, the Danish butter producers hoped to prohibit margarine production in Denmark. Under the simple headline 'Butter' on the front page of the Danish newspaper, a leading Danish politician, Viggo Hørup, proclaimed, 'If we want to advertise for Danish butter in England, then we have to say: Denmark is a cleanly country, there is no butterine in Denmark . . . It is the British market that is at stake, let the authorities make sure that the state does not suffer.'[38]

The conflict between the margarine industry and the butter producers resulted in two laws intended to establish a clear distinction between margarine and butter, especially in export matters. The first law, from 1885, ordered margarine exporters to use packaging that clearly showed that it did not contain butter and to declare the contents with the name 'Margarine'. This was followed up by another law in 1888 that placed a number of further restrictions on margarine production and export, the most important being that it became illegal to add colour to the export margarine so it looked like butter. This was, in fact, a technical export embargo. No other countries had a law like this, so the consequence was that the Danish margarine was unsaleable on the international market. A consequence of the margarine laws was the development of a system to ensure the laws were obeyed. This was institutionalized with the Margarine and Butter Control, who collected samples of butter and analysed them.

The British market

As the above-mentioned quotation from Viggo Hørup indicates, the butter export was a matter of national interest. There was a clear understanding that if Denmark was to maintain its lead, it was not enough to produce high-quality butter. Its reputation had to be protected, marketed and branded in Britain. To this end, the office of the Danish Agricultural Commissioner in London was established in 1888, with Harald Faber as its first commissioner. Under the terms of his appointment, his primary job was specified as the protection and expansion of the reputation of Danish butter and the facilitation of communication between the butter industry in Denmark and the British market.[39]

Faber, who held the post until 1932, carried out his job with great success. He established a wide network among butter agents and the administration, and gained insight into the market and the British consumers.[40] His work on the reputation of Danish butter bears comparison with modern marketing strategies and branding.[41] In Denmark, his work was acknowledged by all parts of the sector and his frequent reports concerning the British market were taken very seriously. He saw that if Danish butter was to maintain its reputation as superior in quality, new initiatives were necessary. As it was concluded in a report on the protection of Danish butter on the British market from 1899, 'there was a time when Danish butter was the only good butter sold in Middle and Northern England. At this time, Danish butter established the reputation that Danish butter was identical with excellent butter. But today butter of high quality is also produced in Sweden, Netherlands, Finland, Canada and Australia.'[42] It was the firm reputation of Danish butter, not its absolute superiority, that kept it selling at higher prices in Britain. As a Swedish newspaper wrote with ill-concealed envy: 'It is about time that an expert presents the myth of "excellent Danish butter" in its proper proportions. For all Danes, without exception, this is just an irrefutable dogma, much like the impression that all humanity is green with envy over the wonders of Tivoli. We will not deny that Danish butter is good, but there is not any reason to claim that Danish butter is any better than butter from other countries.'[43]

Transit butter and the adulteration of Danish butter constituted the main challenges for protecting the reputation of Danish butter in England. That they could be dealt with through a national trademark was recognized early on in the rise of the Danish butter industry. From 1885, Danish butter was marked 'Danish Produced'. Confidence, however, was very low both in Britain and in Denmark.[44] A significant amount of butter produced outside of Denmark was fraudulently marked.

The fundamental problem was that the Danish state lacked any authority to demand the use of the 'Danish Produced' mark. In Britain only an organization that had actual production could be registered as the holder of a trademark. As a solution to these problems, a plan was formed by Faber and the butter producers. The butter producers had to make an association themselves and then the state would help them in protecting it in both Denmark and Britain. To carry out the plan, the dairies founded the Danish Dairies Buttermark Association, with the aim to make a trademark exclusively for

Photograph 9.2 **In 1954 the 'Lurbrand' changed its name to 'Lurpak'. Since 1901 it has been one of the few Danish megabrands. In 2007, Lurpak was the most sold butter product in UK and on the list of the twenty largest brands in the UK.**
Source: Arla Foods.

butter produced in Denmark and from Danish milk. At the first general meeting, in September 1900, 400 dairies had already joined. Two years later, 1155 of the 1235 registered dairies were members of the association. In 1901, the 'Lurbrand' was registered as a trademark in Britain and Denmark and soon became a commercial success. After a few months, British retailers and butter grocers demanded that all the butter they bought was Lurbrand. And after a few years the situation, as one butter importer described it, was that 'it is hardly possible to find any British importer or retailer selling Danish butter if it not marked with the Lurbrand (Photograph 9.2). If the Lurbrand is missing, it will undoubtedly result in a lower price. The Lurbrand is obviously also important for the separation between Danish butter and butter produced in other countries.'[45]

The government's help in protecting the brand, along with Faber's advocacy, was important in its success. At the first sign of fraud, they tracked it down and brought the case to court. Besides protecting the brand, this had the effect that the British market regarded the brand as 'officially Danish' even though it was legally a privately owned brand. However, this was changed in 1906 when the Lurmark, at the request of the Buttermark Association, became protected by a law, which declared that all export butter had to be produced from pasteurized cream and marked 'Lurbrand.' After the adoption of the law, the management of the brand was delegated back to the Buttermark Association, and later to the Danish Dairy Board.

In 1907, the law was expanded so Lurbrand also had to be used on bacon, the other huge Danish agriculture export article. Consequently Lurbrand had become much more than just a trademark intended to protect Danish butter from adulteration. It had become a co-operative national brand signifying high quality. Even today, it is an important brand for Denmark. A huge poll made by the trade ministry concerning other countries' views on Denmark in 2006 shows that bacon and butter, together with the fairytales written by Hans Christian Andersen, are the main things foreigners associate with Denmark.

1910–60: overview

While the world had undergone global depression, been ravaged by two world wars and been divided between East and West, the Danish dairy sector had been remarkably stable. The main product was still butter and the main market was still Britain. It is worth noting that the global butter industry had more or less permanently suffered from crises which resulted from the shifting international political and economic situation. Danish butter, however, had been able to deal more effectively with the crisis.

The First World War had pitted the two main markets for Danish food export, namely, Germany and Britain, against each other. At the beginning of the war, Denmark tried to protect its markets through a policy of neutrality. However, during the war it became clear that the winner would be the alliance that had the largest amount of resources and food supply and not necessarily the most efficient war machine. In this situation, Germany threatened to attack the Danish ships loaded with butter for Britain. The result was a suspension of the export connection between Denmark and Britain. In order to ensure a minimum level of goods to the Danish citizens during the war, the Danish economy was regulated in a degree not seen before. After the war, the regulations on the agricultural sector had not been lifted before the stock market crashed in 1929. This led to a further regulation of the Danish agricultural export. From 1932, all Danish agricultural export was co-ordinated and regulated through the state export boards. These boards were administered in a close co-operation between the agricultural organizations and the state.[46] During the Second World War and German occupation, Danish butter production faced new problems. Production fell dramatically, not so much because of the barrier to the British market (the butter was simply supplied to German troops instead), but rather because of a lack of import of fodder for the cows. In the aftermath of the Second World War, the Danish dairy system was still competitive. Many of the other butter-exporting countries' production systems lay in ruins, while the Danish system was still intact. In the post-war period, regulation continued at both national level and at the international level.[47] The strategy of the Danish butter producers was to rebuild the British market. Bilateral negotiations with the British authorities resulted in a trade agreement stating that Britain from 1949 to 1955 would import 75 per cent of Danish butter at fixed prices. In the beginning, the Danish butter producers were satisfied with this agreement, but when Britain in 1949 devalued the pound sterling by 30 per cent the agreement proved less attractive.[48] The British market provided stability but the trade agreement clearly showed the problems in being dependent on one market, with one specialized product.

In the 1950s it became evident that the decentralized Danish dairy system was outdated. The world market had fully recovered from the war and during the post-war period new, more concentrated and efficient dairies were established in a number of countries. This led to an international overproduction with a sharp drop in the international butter price. This coincided with the expiry of the trade agreement with Britain in 1955. The result was that the value of the Danish export butter market dropped by 50 per cent from 1955 to 1958 and the crisis in the Danish dairy system was a reality.[49] The situation had parallels to the 1870s when the international grain market had been flooded with grain and the response had had a similar depth. However, this time it was impossible to switch from one product to another. Instead, changes had to be made within the dairy industry itself.

Problems and conflicts in the dairy sector

The dairy industry was not as homogeneous as at the end of the nineteenth century, when all dairies had a common goal to produce the maximum amount of butter for the British market.

The fundamental fragmentation was between the export-based butter dairies and the dairies who supplied the domestic market with milk products. The domestic market was, in contrast to the international market, relatively stable. So when the global market was struck by crisis after crisis, the domestic market became increasingly important for the dairies. By the 1930s every local dairy placed one or more dairy shops in the nearby town where they sold milk. With 1740 dairies in Denmark this resulted in quite a number of shops. In Copenhagen alone there were more than 2500 milk shops in 1937.[50] This was not a rational process, expensive as it was both for consumers and producers. To regulate this chaotic situation a law was adopted in 1940 specifying that only a few, larger, dairies were allowed to sell milk in the towns. As a direct consequence 160 dairies closed down. Even more important, the law divided the dairy sector in two parts: the stable and richer dairies who supplied the domestic market, and the poorer export-based dairies.

Another latent conflict was between the private and the co-operative dairies. More than 80 per cent of the dairies were run by co-operatives. But concurrently with the development of the co-operative dairy, a niche of privately owned dairies had developed. Instead of butter, the private dairies produced mainly cheese which, in contrast to butter, offered a developing market.

These conflicts were broadened by regional differences between eastern and western Denmark.[51] The poor, decentralized butter exporting co-operative dairies were concentrated in rural western Denmark while in the more urbanized areas around Copenhagen, dairies were centralized, producing for a stable domestic market and with a more diversified production of milk and cheese.

The legal changes of the co-operative system

When Danish butter exports faced a structural crisis in the late 1950s, it was a national problem. Denmark was dependent on its agricultural exports. It was not so much a question whether the authorities should take and steps to help the dairy industry, but rather what steps should be taken. Much of the Danish national and foreign policy in the twentieth century was closely connected with the protection of the interests of the agricultural sector. Following the path from the 1930s, state export boards co-ordinated and discussed solutions with the agricultural organizations. This resulted in two laws in 1961.

The first law had the aim of regulating and centralizing export activities in one unit to prevent price competition among the Danish producers.[52] The second law regulated the home market by a setting a minimum price for dairy products that was considerably higher than the world market price. It was the Danish consumers who had to pay for the problems on the export market.[53]

The administration of the laws, and the decision concerning the use of the funds, was placed in the hands of the sector itself and especially the Danish Dairy Board. In this, the authorities followed a tradition going back to Lurbrand, where the political system made laws and regulations on behalf of recommendations from the agricultural sector. After the laws had been adopted, the administration of the law was delegated back to the industry itself. As a part of this, the dairy sector became strongly organized. The Danish Dairy Board (1912), the Danish Agricultural Council (1919) and the Co-operative Council (1899) saw significant growth. Through the different crises, they got more powerful and integrated in working out the laws and taking part in administering them. The Danish state was dependent on a strong export-based sector, and the butter industry had become dependent on the state's involvement during the crises. The system of a close co-operation between state and business community had developed. From the highly co-ordinated business system characterized by corporations, the system became economically and legally integrated. As a part of this, the agricultural sector became dependent on a state subsidy,[54] and later an EU subsidy.

The laws of 1961 made the Danish Dairy Board the most powerful organization in the dairy industry. The law on regulation of the home market was administered by the Dairy Board. They were given the power to distribute the flow of money from the overprice the consumers paid. As a part of the law, the Dairy Board was allowed to save some of the funds and invest them in rationalization and development of the dairy sector.[55] It is not too much to say that the Dairy Board was at the same time police, politician, administrator and judge in the dairy business.

At the beginning of the 1960s, production was still decentralized, with more than 1000 independent productions units, but in matters of sale and distribution many of the key elements were centralized in the hands of the Danish Dairy Board. This contrast became important in the forthcoming transformation of the industry.

The EC as a part of the solution

Just as important as the laws and the development in the dairy sector was the evolution of the EC. From 1961, it became clear that the Danish state and the dairy sector thought that the future for Denmark, if it wanted to maintain its export-based agricultural sector, was to become a member of the EC.[56] The background was that Britain in 1961 had applied for membership. As Britain still by far was the most important Danish export market for agriculture, Danish foreign and international trade policy was determined by Britain's acts and policies. Thus, when Britain applied for membership of the EC, Denmark followed and applied for membership together with Britain.

It was questionable whether the rest of Danish industry would benefit from membership and the application is a clear sign of how important the agricultural sector was regarded in the Danish economy. However, the benefits of EC membership for the dairies would be considerable. It would create access to a much larger market than just the British market; the EC subsidies to agriculture would reduce the pressure on the Danish state; and, perhaps the most important, the EC price system would guarantee the sale of Danish products at a minimum price in times when the market could not absorb production. With this future scenario, the Danish government started to supply the dairy business with subsidies to make it competitive for entry to the EC. Unfortunately for the Danish dairies and the government, the negotiations between EEC and Britain collapsed when France rejected Britain's application for membership in 1963. At that time the Danish government had already started on the path of subsidising and could not stop the process. By the end of the 1960s different subsidies contributed to more than 40 per cent of the milk and dairy sector's income.[57] Denmark had to wait and hope for a better climate between EC and Britain. This came at last, and with a delay of ten years, Denmark could together with Britain at last join the EC in 1973.

MD Foods

In the following section, we focus on the process behind the structural development that led to the transformation of the decentralized dairy sector from more than 1000 small dairies to one dominant dairy company. This company was MD Foods (The Danish Dairy Company), which controlled more than 90 per cent of the dairy production in Denmark after 1993.

From an international perspective the structural development in the Danish dairy sector was as 'a late-comer'. The Swedish dairy industry had gone through a structural development process between 1933 and 1945 that had halved the number of dairies from 1672 to 817.[58] However when the process of structural development started in Denmark it was fast and deep. It was not only a horizontal integration but also a forward integration, with the aim of controlling and planning the process from the farmer to sales. This structural development was partly a result of an internal process in the dairy sector and partly of an external impetus for change by the still more regulated markets, first at a national level and later on at a European level.

Despite the internal conflicts in the dairy sector, the primary problem was the decentralized Danish dairy system. When it was developed in the late nineteenth century it fitted quite well the financial resources of the farmers, the rural village-based structure and the badly-paved roads. With new roads and tankers, it was no longer necessary to have a dairy in each village. However, the villages and the farmers were reluctant to give up their own dairy. With the lack of internal competition in the dairy sector, this decentralized system had been able to sustain itself, even though several initiatives had been taken to start a process of structural development.

However, faced with the crisis in the 1950s, the Dairy Board had started in 1958 to examine the structure and plan to reduce the numbers of independent dairies.

This resulted in a pilot process, in which 10–30 small dairies merged into a single financial business – although still with several production units. As a consequence, from 1958 to 1964 the number of dairies was reduced from 1422 to 1051.[59] However, the crisis made it clear that this was too late and the process was too slow to meet the problems. According to the Dairy Board more radical amalgamations were needed: sustaining the decentralized system would not only lead to giving up the local dairies, but also to the end of the agricultural business itself. In 1963, the Dairy Board's CEO, T. Mathiassen, said: 'The conclusion is that the whole Danish dairy business has to be amalgamated into one common unit at all levels: financial, production and sale. Only this way will the dairy sector be able to gain the necessary force and power if milk and dairy production is to have any future at all in Denmark.'[60]

This was the first time the idea of creating one nationwide dairy enterprise had been aired in public. To stress that this was not unrealistic, belonging to a remote future, the new strategy of the Dairy Board caused it to be named 'The Danish Dairy Company' (Mejeriselskabet Danmark) (MD), and a set of rules and regulations for the new company was adopted. The idea was to create MD on a voluntary basis, by focusing production at the largest and most developed dairies and giving a compensation to the rest of the dairies and dairy tenants.

Even though this form of economic perspective seemed rational, it was in conflict with the ideology of the dairy sector and the public mind-set. The co-operative movement had created a myth about themselves as a specific Danish way of becoming a modern country, which was based on the local community and in opposition to large-scale industry. Shortly after the launch of the idea, T. Mathiassen was asked in an interview whether this would contradict the spirit of the co-operative movement, and he responded:

> You use the term co-operative movement. I don't like that expression even though I unfortunately cannot find anything better. Co-operation, which has found its greatest and earliest expansion, is not a 'movement' in a late practical and present sense. It is a term to describe an economic form of co-operation influenced by business-like principles.[61]

While the discourse about the co-operative movement as a socially and locally based movement had a positive function in relation to the building up of an institutional apparatus, it became a problem in the process of creation of a large-scale business. Despite the crisis, farmers and Danish citizens saw MD as a betrayal of the Danish co-operative model. At the structural level, the co-operative system was also a problem for the Dairy Board's plan. In each dairy, a majority of the farmers who owned the dairy had to be in favour of the idea. In the years following the launch of the plan, the Dairy Board used a lot of energy to persuade the farmers of the benefits of the idea, but in vain.

Even though the Dairy Board had economic and organizational power, indirect governmental support, and was motivated by an idea that seemed capable of saving the dairies from most of their problems, they lacked the decisive element of having the means to back up their words. It was a fundamental problem that the conflict between the eastern and western dairies was met with silence. Local patriotism combined with the co-operative ideology made the farmers and local communities reluctant to give up their dairies.

Instead of following the Dairy Board's plan, many dairies started to consolidate on a regional basis. From the initiation of the Dairy Board's plan in 1963 to 1970, the number of dairies halved, to about 500. The plan prepared the way for the realization of a MD from below. However, it became realised through a process very different from the voluntary model proposed by the Dairy Board.

MD created on a bottom-up model
In 1969, six years after the launch of the Dairy Board idea, the value of dairy exports fell to their lowest level in the post-war period. Despite state subsidies and heavy investment in the primary agricultural sector, the amount of milk produced in Denmark fell for the first time in twenty-five years. EC membership was still on stand-by, but it was taken for granted that it was just a matter of time before it was resolved and Denmark could become a member. This would demand significant changes to the dairy system.

The time had run out for the Dairy Board's model. Despite all the efforts, only four of the larger merged dairy companies and sixteen independent co-operative dairies had declared that they were willing to join the voluntary MD project. All dairies were settled in Jutland and together they controlled less than 7 per cent of the milk in Denmark. The situation was far from satisfactory, especially for the four larger dairy companies who had accepted the Dairy Board's plan. If nothing happened it was doubtful whether they could survive. Either the plan had to be rejected, or a new strategy made. The four dairy companies took matters into their own hands; they did not have the time to wait for a common solution that included most of the dairy sector. At a secret meeting they decided to create their own company, adopting the name MD from the former project. This new MD was founded in the summer 1970.[62]

Their vision was to create a huge company based on export-based dairies in the western part of Denmark. In contrast to the plan of the Dairy Board, they would allow only the profitable dairies to join them, the rest had to be broken by competition and then the milk farmers who had no alternative could become members of the company. Production had to be rationalized and concentrated in large specialized units that produced either milk, butter, cheese, or condensed milk. The aim was not only to rationalize and gain economies of scale; the new MD wanted to dominate the Danish dairy sector at all levels. At a basic level, this meant that they had to control a considerable amount of the Danish-produced milk. Just as important was the ability to get a dominant influence in the organs that controlled the political environment and the markets – that is, the Danish Dairy board, the export boards and so on.

When the plan began to be carried out, it changed the dairy sector fundamentally. MD's strategy was a declaration of war in an industry where co-operation, local commitment and internal unity had been keywords. The rest of the sector responded to MD's plan by speeding up the process of regional concentration. After a few years the competition became oligopolistic in its form; it became just as important to damage the other dairy companies as to serve one's own (Figure 9.1).[63]

Export strategy: from butter to cheese

The dependency on one product (butter) and one market (Britain) had long been a problem for the Danish dairy export. One of the aims of the new MD was to break this path. Concentration should not only rationalize butter production, it was also the key to a more diversified production. The focus in production should change from butter to cheese. This was both a more diversified and refined product than butter, and it was expected that it would be possible to gain or win market shares in markets outside Britain. The expected membership of the EC also played a role, as cheese subsidies were much higher than butter subsidies.

The problem was that MD lacked know-how, finance and time to build the necessary production units, sales network and market share. All these factors

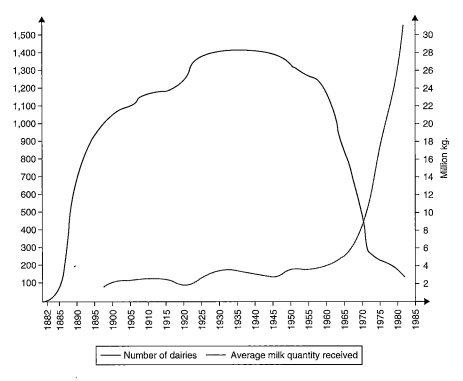

*Figure 9.1 **Development in numbers of co-operative Danish dairy factories 1882–1981, and average quantity milk received by each unit or company***

except finance were found in the largest Danish cheese dairy Høng. Høng was the flagship of the private dairies. It was innovative and had developed a range of successful different cheese brands. However, a few unsuccessful investments and bacterial pollution at their largest dairy had brought Høng close to bankruptcy.[64] The problems were kept secret from the public so when MD, a few months after its start, could announce the purchase of the dairy it came as a shock. With this takeover MD got all it lacked to execute its strategic change towards cheese products. As Høng was in the eastern part of Denmark, it could thus be used as a spearhead to break down the resistance against MD among dairies in this part of the country.

Two questions remained. How did MD know about the problems at Høng, and where did the financing to acquire it come from? The answer to both questions can be found in the Dairy Board and Mathiassen. He was the only person outside the board of directors in Høng who knew about the problems, and he made the plan. Likewise it was the Dairy Board who lent MD the money to buy Høng, although this was kept secret for many years. Even though the new MD was officially just one of the Dairy Board's members, in reality it had the support of the powerful organization. The takeover was a success, and in the coming years MD systematically bought up private cheese dairies, making it the main product.

The more diversified production had an impact on internal organization in MD. At the beginning the structure was regional, and based on the four larger dairies who had founded MD. This structure worked well as long as the main aim was concentration and rationalization within the existing decentralized dairy structure. This was changed in 1974 when a model based on different product groups such as milk, cheese and butter was accepted.[65] This divisional structure was useful to make specific strategies for different markets: cheese went to new markets and EC, butter still concentrated on the British market and milk went to the domestic market. The domestic market was the main problem for MD, and it was on the domestic market that the final battle took place.[66]

The domestic market: the 'milk war' and MD's victory

Membership of the EEC in 1973 provided a welcome stability for the export-based part of the dairy sector. From 1970–1 to 1973–4 the overall value of dairy exports rose by 250 per cent. For MD, however, investments in new production and takeovers had pressed its finances to the limit. When the American market was closed by an import embargo against the EC, the dairy ran into serious problems. Instead of being the turning point that ended the state of permanent crisis, the very survival of MD was now at stake. It was the milk farmers who had to pay, and they demanded a plan that would increase their income fast.

In this situation, MD decided to go for the home market. The domestic market was stable and lucrative and was still seen as the key to success for MD and the other dairy companies. As part of the preparations to join the EC, the 1940 laws concerning regulation of the market in the towns had been revoked in 1971. However, prices in the domestic market were still kept higher than the world market with subsidies. Dairies which supplied the lucrative urban markets had reacted to MD's expansion by organizing themselves into cartel-like systems, with the aim of ensuring that MD only got a smaller part of the domestic market. When MD, after years of fruitless negotiations, decided to drop out and instead try to let the market rule they started what the media soon called the 'milk war'. The 'milk war' enhanced the ongoing concentration. In reality, it soon became a duopolistic competition between MD and Kløver Milk (based in the urbanized east Denmark dairy community). This duopolistic battle was highly influenced by the structural development of the retail sector which was completely altered in the 1970s and 1980s. By the 1970s the market situation was different from the 1940s, when the law to rationalize the urban domestic markets had been introduced. In the 1940s, milk was sold from small milk shops or delivered directly to the consumers by milkmen. Meanwhile the supermarket chains had emerged, and when they were allowed to sell milk products in 1971 the number of milk shops fell by 50 per cent in one year. It soon became clear that competition would be concentrated on agreements with the supermarket chains. In order to be attractive to a supermarket chain it was important to guarantee the necessary amounts of a diversified range of products. Here MD's size in the long run turned out to be the difference that made them the winner of the 'milk war'. The war ended when MD and Kløver Milk formed a partnership in 1992. This was in reality the first step in a takeover that became a reality in 1999. MD then controlled more than 90 per cent of milk production in Denmark.[67] This had been done through nearly 200 mergers and takeovers. Dairying in Denmark was no longer a decentralized trade connected to the local agricultural society; it had become a modern industrial business based on economies of scale and scope.

Arla Foods: from national dairy to MNE

In the late 1980s, MD changed its focus from the domestic market and back to the international market. In 1988, it officially changed name from the Danish Mejeriselskabet Danmark (MD) to the more international 'MD Foods'. The following year, MD Foods International A/S was formed for the purpose of acquiring dairies abroad, and in 1990 they made their first acquisition, Associated Fresh Foods, the fifth largest dairy company in Britain. Another breakthrough came five years later when MD and the largest Swedish co-operative dairy, Arla, joined in a strategic co-operation. With the final merger between the two in year 2000, the name was changed to 'Arla Foods'. However, the majority of the milk was produced in Denmark and the headquarters and leadership of Arla was located in Denmark. With this merger, an important milestone was reached. Arla was now a leading multinational business ready to meet the challenges of a still more globalized food market. The 'home market' was now Sweden, Britain and Denmark.

Three factors were essential to this multinational transition of the Danish dairy sector. The first factor was is the membership of EEC (later, the EU). In central areas of legislation, planning, subsidies and trade, Brussels has become more important than Copenhagen. The second important factor was that agriculture and dairy production has gradually lost its importance. By the 1970s Denmark was no longer dependent on agriculture, and dairy production became just one among other export industries. This has loosened the connection between the Danish state and the agricultural sector. As the final factor, the position between business and organization had changed. Power was now in the hands of the centralized MD Foods – later Arla – and not in the hands of the co-ordinating Dairy Board.

The very existence of Arla, and the fact that dairy production is still a profitable industry in a highly developed country such as Denmark, must be seen a successful deployment of the ability to adapt to different patterns and transform a national, decentralized highly regulated industry in to a multinational competitive corporation. However, the changes have not been without failures and problems. In recent years, Arla has suffered from a more or less permanently bad reputation in Denmark. This is closely connected to the idea of the co-operative movement as a special Danish and local way of doing business. Even though Arla is still structured as a co-operative, it has become everything to which the narrative of the co-operative was opposed: an industrial multinational and capitalistic business. In the following section we will focus on three crises which Arla has recently been through, related to this discrepancy between the old 'co-operative' narrative and the contemporary multinational reality.

Between national identity and global strategy

The first crisis started in December 2003, when the small Hirtshals Dairy, located in Northern Jutland, accused Arla Foods of exploiting its size to keep their products off the shelves of the major supermarket chains. Hirtshals Dairy was one of only fourteen smaller independent co-operative dairies that had survived the 'milk war'. The Danish Competition Authority took up the case and charges were filed against Arla based on Hirtshal's claims. On 10 February 2006, Arla was found guilty of engaging in unfair business practices on the national market and was penalized with the largest fine of its kind in Denmark.[68]

The case came as a shock to Arla. In reality, Arla had just continued to use the same methods that had been used during the 'milk war'. However, they had not been aware that times had changed. Arla, with a share of 90 per cent, totally dominated the market. It was not only the Competition Authorities that found Arla's actions unacceptable; the media, consumers and the politicians were not willing to accept Arla's methods. The accusation from Hirtshals in December 2003 caused a snowball effect and in the months that followed, Arla faced fresh accusations in the media on a weekly basis. Arla was presented as a near-monopoly that exploited the dairy farmers, bullied the smaller dairies and made the consumers pay too much for their products. The Danish consumers started to boycott Arla's products. Arla responded with apologies and promised to change. As Åke Modig, the CEO of Arla, said in an interview in 2004: 'Arla is a fantastic company, and we have good prospects to win next year's battle for survival against the large dairy plants of Europe. But we also need to win the battle in Denmark. We have to teach the Danish population to love Arla.'[69] However, Arla did not succeed. The consumer boycott was apparently permanent and Arla lost market share in Denmark.

More serious than the loss of domestic market share was the problems that Arla's tarnished national image posed for the realization of its strategy to be a dominant player in the global market. In December 2004, Arla declared that it would initiate 'the largest business fusion in Danish history, that would create the largest dairy enterprise in the world' by amalgamating with the Dutch dairy plant Campina. However, the idea never became a reality, and the project had been abandoned by the spring of 2005.[70] One of the main reasons was that Arla's troubles in Denmark created doubts in Campina's management.

Also, on the international stage, Arla had to deal with problems of reputation. In 2006 through a series of misfortunes Arla became a central part of what came to be known as the 'Danish cartoon crisis'. The conflict had started with the publication of twelve cartoons of the prophet Mohammed in the Danish newspaper *Jyllands-Posten* in September 2005. This action was regarded as blasphemy and was denounced by Muslims both in Denmark and abroad. In January 2006, religious and political leaders in Saudi Arabia called for a boycott of all Danish products. As Arla was by far the most important Danish business in the Middle East, the boycott became synonymous with boycotting Arla. The boycott was efficient and at its peak the company lost EUR 4 million in daily revenues.

In Denmark, the boycott in the Middle East started a wave of sympathy for Arla. Danish consumers started to buy Arla products in amounts not seen since the problems with Hirtshals. The week after the boycott began, the dairy increased its sales by 15 per cent on the Danish market, and opinion polls showed a significant rise in Arla's popularity.[71] The media and consumers viewed Arla as an innocent victim in a global political and cultural conflict between the Danish government and Muslim society, the former insisting on the freedom of speech, the latter condemning the publication of the cartoons as an act of blasphemy. Paradoxically, this support drew Arla more directly into the conflict. Arla went from being a mere business to being a symbol of Danish nationalism, carrying positive connotations in Denmark and negative ones in Muslim societies.

These positive and negative connotations were inverted after a couple of weeks. Arla's management feared that its market share would permanently collapse in the Middle East, which was a key area in the company's global strategy that had been pursued over the last forty years. Arla's CEO, Peter Tuborgh, addressed the crisis directly, the following month by saying, 'I feel it is necessary that Arla stress its sympathy and respect towards the millions of Muslim consumers we have, and take exception to the humiliations they have gone through'.[72] This was the beginning of a campaign in which Arla tried to repair the damage their brand and image had suffered in the Middle East, by distancing itself from Danish politics and Danish symbols.

In Denmark, the reactions against Arla were harsh. Jens Rode, a member of the ruling Liberal Party, called Arla's campaign a 'pathetic genuflection to filthy lucre' and elaborated the point by saying, 'Arla is willing to sell its own grandmother in order to do business in dictator states. I do not understand how they can take principles so lightly. My freedoms are not for sale for two litres of milk.' He concluded by suggesting that 'if Arla is so dissatisfied with Denmark, let it move to Teheran'.[73] In addition, several organizations like Women for Freedom and the Danish Free Press Association called on Danish consumers to boycott Arla.

Though the crises of Hirtshals, Campina and the 'Mohammed cartoons' have different backgrounds, they were all involved in the tension between national and global concerns. The crises resulted in problems on the national market and had a negative effect on Arla's global strategy. The boycott caused by the Hirtshals case contributed to the collapse of the proposed merger with Campina. The consumer support Arla received at the beginning of the 'cartoon' controversy implicated Arla in nationalistic branding that belied the global brand they had been trying to build up. When Arla distanced themselves from this surge of nationalistic support, it resulted in accusations of unpatriotic and avaricious behaviour.

Therefore, even if the Danish dairy today is a part of an MNE, it is deeply connected to Danish development and identity: an identity that today is troublesome for Arla but also one that they have had a huge part in creating.

QUESTIONS 1. At the end of nineteenth century century the Danish butter indus-try experienced a real breakthrough on the British market. What specific circumstances were particularly important to this break-through, and why did these reasons prove to be so important for the position of the Danish butter in Great Britain?

2. The case of Arla Food is focused on three specific time peri-ods: 1875–1900, 1950–73 and 1973–2007. To what extent was the relationship to the Danish government and the international political institutions important in all three time periods? Which role did these institutions play in the rise of the industry and the growth of Arla Foods in each of these three periods?

Notes

1. Christensen (2007).
2. Johansen (1985), pp. 189–93.
3. Mordhorst (2005).
4. http://www.arlafoods.com.
5. Calculated from *Annual Statement of Trade and Navigation of United Kingdom with Foreign Countries and British Possessions* (various issues).
6. Skovgaard-Petersen (1985), p. 68.
7. From 1830 to 1857 the export value of grain more than quadrupled. See Hansen (1974), p. 137.
8. See e.g Hyldtoft (1999), p. 39.
9. See e.g:Hyldtoft (1999), p. 48.
10. Bøggild (1900) p. 5.
11. See, e.g., Bjørn (1982), p. 49.
12. Bjørn (1982), p. 121.
13. Drejer (1952).
14. Lund (2004), p. 381.
15. Nielsen (1910), p. 14.
16. Lund (2004), p. 381.
17. See, e.g., Bjørn, (1998).
18. Smitt (1977).
19. Drejer (1933).
20. Bøggild (1916), p. 396.
21. Bøggild (1916), p. 398.
22. Bøggild (1916).
23. Christensen (2003).
24. Bøgild (1910), p. 5.
25. Nielsen (2003a).
26. Bøggild (1916), p. 224.
27. Nielsen (2003b).

28. Nielsen (2003a).
29. Bjørn (1982), p. 79.
30. Hertel (1917).
31. This development was in contrast to the development in other countries like the Netherlands, the former main butter exporter to Britain.
32. Higgens (2007).
33. Larsen (2001).
34. *Tidsskrift for landøkonomi* (Denmark, 1899), p. 210.
35. Larsen (2001).
36. Larsen (2001).
37. Strandskov (1998).
38. Hørup, *Politiken* (21/11–1887).
39. Bjørn (1982), p. 185.
40. The Danish National Archives, 'Statskonsulentet i London kopibøger'.
41. Higgens (2007).
42. *Tidsskrift for landøkonomi* (1899), p. 208.
43. *Butter Trade Journal* (3/10–1891).
44. *Butter Trade Journal* (9/8–1889).
45. Nielsen (1906), p. 58.
46. Just (1992).
47. Immediately after the war, the Allies appointed a 'Food Surplus Committee', and gave it the right to allocate the Danish export butter.
48. Rasmussen (1982), p. 213.
49. Bjørn (1982), p. 311; Kristensen (1986), p. 18.
50. Lando (1937), p. 32.
51. Kristensen (1986), p. 9.
52. *Lov om afsættelse af landbrugsvarer* fra 2. *juni 1958*, Bjørn (1982), p. 324.
53. *Lov om hjemmemarketspriser på mejeriprodukter*, 21. maj 1959; Bjørn (1982), p. 335.
54. In 1969, the total subsidy from seven different funds was 1.025 million DDK (Bjørn, 1982).
55. The growing power of the Dairy Board can be illustrated by the growth in numbers employed in the organization. In 1940 there were 43, in 1960, 200 and in 1971, 450.
56. Buksti (1982), p. 405.
57. Buksti (1982), p. 311.
58. Rasmussen (1982), p. 235.
59. Kristensen (1986), p. 23.
60. *Andelsbladet* (1963), p. 263.
61. *Andelsbladet* (1963), p. 563.
62. *Kristensen* (1986); Vedholm (1995).
63. Søgaard (1990).
64. Vedholm (1995), pp. 37–45; Kirstensen (1986), p. 92.
65. *Kristensen* (1986), pp. 140–8.
66. Søgaard (1990), p. 230; Kristensen (1986); Buksti (1982), p. 455.
67. http://www.arlafoods.dk/C1256D8F0044D6CB/O/4CD8F003805C8CBAC1256D6A00275C4F.
68. *Politiken* (November 2006).
69. Interview: 'Arlas nye profil', *Jyllands-Posten* (January 2004).
70. See e.g., 'Spildt mælk' *Jyllands-Posten* (April 2005).
71. 'Arlas salg stiger i Danmark', *Jyllands-Posten* (September 2005).
72. *Politikken* (February 2006).
73. *Berlingske* (February 2006).

References

Bjørn, C., *Dansk mejeribrug 1882–2000* (Århus: Danske Mejeriers Fælleorganisation, 1982).
Bjørn, C., *Dengang Danmark blev moderen – eller historien om den virkelige danske utopi* (Copenhagen: Fremad, 1998).

Buksti, J. A., 'Dansk mejeribrug 1995–82', in Bjørn, C. (ed.) *Dansk mejeribrug 1882–2000* (Århus: Danske Mejeriers Fælleorganisation, 1982).

Bøggild, B., *Andelsmælkerierne* (Copenhagen, 1910).

Bøggild, B., *Mælkeribruget i Danmark* (Copenhagen: Gyldendal, 1916).

Christensen, J., *Forretning og teknologi: landbrugsmaskinindustrier midt I verden 19. til 21 århundrede* (Århus: Århus Universitetsforlag, 2003).

Christensen, J., (ed.) *Agriculture in Denmark: Facts and Figures 2007* (Varde: Danish Agriculture and Danish Agricultural Council, 2007).

Degerbøl, S., *Andelsbevægelsen* (Copenhagen: Gyldendal, 1931).

Drejer, A. A., *Mejeribrugets Historie* (Copenhagen: Gads förlag, 1933).

Drejer, A. A., *Den Danske Andelsbevægelse.* (Copenhagen: Det Danske förlag, 1952).

Hansen, S. Å., *Økonomisk Vækst i Danmark* (Copenhagen: Akademisk Forlag, 1974).

Hertel, H., *Andelsbevægelsen* (Copenhagen: Gyldendalske boghandel, 1917).

Higgens, D. and Mordhorst M., 'Reputation and Export Performance: Danish Butter Exports and the British Market c. 1880–1914' (unpublished paper, 2007).

Hyldtoft, O., *Teknologiske forandringer i dansk industri 1870–1896* (Odense: Odense Universitetsforlag, 1996).

Hyldtoft, O., *Danmarks økonomiske historie* (Denmark: Systime, 1999).

Johansen, H. C., 'Dansk økonomisk statistik 1814–1990/Danish Historical Statistics 1814–1990', in Clausen H. P., Ellehøj S., and Mørch S., (eds), *Danmarks historie*, 9 (Copenhagen: Gyldendal, 1985).

Just, F., *Landbruget staten og eksporten 1930–1950* (Esbjerg: Syddanske Universitetsforlag, 1992).

Kristensen, S. W., *Kampen om mælken* (Odense: Landbohistorisk Selskab, 1986).

Lando, Z. D. 'Københavns konsummælk og deres handelsveje' *Handelsvidenskabeligt tidsskrift* (1937).

Larsen, I. M., *Kampen og det sibirske smør 1895–1905* (Denmark: Odense 2001).

Lund, J. (ed.), *Den Store Danske Encyklopædi*, 1 (Copenhagen: Gyldendal, 2004).

Mordhorst, M. 'Andelsbevægelsen – Mellem national identitet og erindring', *Den jyske historiker*, 109 (Århus Werks Forlagsdistribution, 2005).

Nielsen, A., *Uddrag af DMS forhistorie* (Aarhus, 1906).

Nielsen, A., *Andelsbevægelsen* (Aarhus: De forenede bogtrykkerier, 1910).

Nielsen, A. K., 'En videnskabshistorisk vinkel på den danske smøreksport', *Den jyske historiker*, 102–3 (Århus: Werks Forlagsdistribution, 2003a).

Nielsen, A. K., 'Mikrobiologi og lurmærket smør', *Aktuel naturvidenskab*, 5 (Copenhagen, 2003b).

Rasmussen, J. D., 'Dansk Mejeribrug 1914–55' in Bjørn, C. (ed.), *Dansk mejeribrug 1882–2000* (Århus: Danske Mejeriers Fælleorganisation, 1982).

Smitt, O., *Den tredje mulighed* (Andelsudvalget, 1977).

Strandskov, S. and Pedersen O. M. (Århus: Systime, 1998).

Søgaard, *Spildt mælk* (Odense: Sydjysk Universitetsforlag, 1990).

Vedholm, H., *Kernen i mejeribruget* (Århus: MD Foods, 1995).

Hørup, V., *Politikken*, 21/11–1887.

WELFARE CAPITALISM: THE SWEDISH ECONOMY 1850–2005 ◦ ENTREPRENEURSHIP AND OWNERSHIP: THE
FIRM VIABILITY OF THE SWEDISH BONNIER AND WALLENBERG FAMILY BUSINESS GROUPS ◦ FROM
[...] AGE [...] MENT: FINNISH
CAPITALISM, 1850s–2001 ◦ FROM STATE OWNERSHIP TO MULTINATIONAL CORPORATION: THE PATH OF
ENSO-GUTZEIT [...] STRATEGIC
PATHS OF NOKIA AND TAMPELLA IN THE LIBERALIZING FINNISH ECONOMY AFTER THE SECOND WORLD
WAR ◦ CO-OPERATIVE LIBERALISM: DENMARK [...]
TO MULTINATIONAL ENTERPRISE ◦ CARLSBERG AND THE SELF-REGULATION OF THE DANISH BEER MARKET
◦ NORWAY: A RESOURCE-BASED AND DEMOCRATIC CAPITALISM ◦ CONSTRUCTIVE POWER: ELKEM 1904–2004
◦ FINANCE AND THE DEVELOPMENT OF NORWEGIAN CAPITALISM – THE CASE OF CHRISTIANIA BANK

10 Carlsberg: regulation of the home market and international expansion

Martin Jes Iversen and Andrew Arnold

Introduction

On 1 June 2000, Carlsberg hosted a well-attended press conference in the converted maltings at its headquarters. The CEO of the Norwegian conglomerate Orkla, Jens Heyerdahl d.y. and Carlsberg CEO Flemming Lindeløv presented one of the largest Nordic mergers ever, joining the 157-year-old Danish brewery and the 119-year-old Norwegian conglomerate. The new company, Carlsberg Breweries, was owned 60 per cent by Carlsberg and 40 per cent by Orkla. It had 27,000 employees producing and marketing approximately 54 million hl of beer – enough to place it as the sixth largest brewery in the world. Perhaps even more importantly, the new Carlsberg Breweries was the dominant market leader in the three Scandinavian countries and several Eastern European countries, including the Baltic States and Russia. The merger announcement in June 2000 was a milestone in Carlsberg's history. From 2000, the Nordic region rather than the Danish market became its home market and the merger was a crucial stage in Carlsberg's transition from an international exporter to a focused enterprise taking part in the global division of labour.

This chapter concerns two crucial aspects in Carlsberg's development from a local brewer in Copenhagen in 1847 to a global giant in 2007. It focuses partly on almost 100 years of severe competition regulation of the Danish home market, from the 1890s to the 1980s, and partly on the internationalization process, with an emphasis on developments after 1970.

The Danish beer market has been dominated by Carlsberg/Tuborg[1] a privately owned player that succeeded in sustaining a national market share above 75 per cent from the 1880s to the 1980s. Carlsberg's market share was extremely stable despite fundamentally different competition conditions at each end of the period. In the late nineteenth century, competition in the Danish beer market was firmly self-regulated, while at the end of the twentieth century international public authorities defined the competition rules. Carlsberg played a leading role in private competition regulation in the Danish beer market that survived the upheavals of the twentieth century.

The regulation of the Danish market has fluctuated between highly regulated non-competitive markets and more competitive periods. In broad terms, competition development in Denmark can be divided in four phases: the uncompetitive guild system from the sixteenth century to the 1850s, the competitive markets of early capitalism from the 1850s until around 1900, the nationally and privately regulated market from around 1900 to the 1980s and finally the internationalized competitive markets after the 1980s.

In medieval, pre-capitalistic, Danish society trade and commerce was regulated by the state through geographical and functional privileges. Alongside this centralized regulation the economy was characterized by the local guilds, which protected craftsmen's competences and markets. The democratic Constitution of 1849 foreshadowed a full freedom of trade. The promise was kept in 1857, but only came into effect after 1862 when all guilds and geographical privileges were abandoned. Early Danish industrialization occurred during a liberal period with weak public regulation and growing international commerce. The First World War represented an exceptional period when public interests overshadowed private self-regulation and after 1918 in particular the workers and small businessmen demanded a new public regulation of private trusts and market agreements. Competition regulation constituted an important battlefield between liberal and socialist ideologies. The political negotiations continued throughout the 1920s and Denmark's first real Competition Law was passed in 1937, more than ten years after the neighbouring countries, Sweden and Norway.[2] Price agreements were allowed as long as they did not cause 'unnaturally' high prices and disadvantages for customers. In 1949, a large public investigation into private trusts was started, but the basic principles behind the competition law were left unaltered in the following decades. It was only following the Single European Agreement (SEA) in 1987 that Danish competition law gradually changed in accordance with European standards. Even so, in 1993 the OECD criticized the Danish legal system for its inability to control private trusts and price regulation. From the 1990s Danish competition law could be regarded as being just as strict and consistent as in most other west European countries.

These different stages provide an essential background for Carlsberg's self-regulation of the Danish beer market from 1899 to the mid-1980s. How did this self-regulation prove so strong and long-lasting? And when it finally came to an end in 1988, was it due to pressure from the Danish or international authorities, the result of structural changes in the Danish and international beer market, or a combination of the two?[3]

The four phases of competition regulation mirror the level of international activity in the Danish business system. In the home-market-oriented period that peaked in the mid-twentieth century, competition was often regulated both by public and private interests, while in periods marked by severe international competition, such as in the mid-nineteenth century and after the mid-1980s, the economic system was marked by more liberal, intense competition on both the national and the international level.

Competition and internationalization are thus related factors in capitalist economic systems and this chapter covers both aspects in relation to Carlsberg.

The term 'internationalization' refers to both the actual carrying out of activities abroad and particular learning processes and experiences.[4] Johanson and Wiedersheim-Paul from the so-called 'Uppsala School' of international studies have combined these two aspects and analysed how companies experience a learning process through concrete stages of internationalization. Often internationalization of companies from small relatively open economies, such as the Nordic ones, is not a matter of large impressive foreign investments but rather a modest process of relatively small and gradually expanding operations abroad. Johanson and Wiedersheim-Paul have identified four general stages in this development:[5]

- No regular export activities
- Export via independent representatives (agents)
- Sales subsidiaries
- Trans-national production/manufacturing.

These four phases are important because they reflect the degree of involvement in international activities. Internationalization is often a complicated process that is met by several 'distance obstacles'. These obstacles can be geographic, political, cultural, social and economic distances between the well-known home market and the new markets. To meet these 'distance obstacles', corporations need a certain level of experience and resource. Often companies begin the internationalization process by entering geographically close markets with low 'distance obstacles'. Later follow more distant, often larger markets, with potential for substantial growth but also a higher need for high levels of experience and resource. Carlsberg was an early 'internationalizer', but a late 'globalizer'. Initial exports went to Sweden in the 1860s as a test market but, as we shall see, Carlsberg moved slowly through the above-mentioned phases. Only around 2000 did Carlsberg change its nature from a large, decentralized exporter present, but marginalized, on many markets to become a globalized corporation which co-ordinated its production, management and marketing functions globally.

Carlsberg and 'anarchistic competition'

In 1823 the Danish physicist and discoverer of electromagnetism, H.C. Ørsted visited the industrial and scientific centre of London. Ørsted was inspired by the British 'Societies' that connected scientists, industrialists and merchants and the following year he made a great plan for a Danish Society for the Diffusion of Physics (Selskabet for Naturlærens Udbredelse). One of its first members was Chresten Jacobsen, the owner of a small but expanding brew-house in the centre of Copenhagen.[6] In 1828 Chresten Jacobsen encouraged his only son to join the society, and the seventeen-year-old J.C. Jacobsen was immediately attracted to Ørsted's lectures. The world-famous physicist had a particular interest in the fermentation industries, including the brewery processes, as he had in 1806 become a member of a royal commission for the improvement of breweries in Copenhagen.

The young Jacobsen was at this stage about to finish his education in a small private school in Copenhagen and he was particularly interested in mathematics, ancient history and German literature. His plan was to continue studies in chemistry but these plans collided with the illness of his father. In 1835 Chresten Jacobsen died and at twenty-four J.C. Jacobsen took over responsibility for the family brewery. On a spring day in 1836 the young brewer invited his friend Frants Djørup to a small old wine merchant in the medieval centre of Copenhagen. Jacobsen was not interested in the wine, but rather the special imported Bavarian beer, which the German staff of the Danish Foreign Ministry preferred to drink. The Bavarian brew methods were characterized by bottom fermentation under cold conditions and a slow secondary fermentation which lasted several months in cold cellars – this lead to a carbonated, vinous, bright beer. In the following months Jacobsen established a small experimental arrangement in the cellar of his brewery and on 17 April 1838 he was able to offer a small 'Bavarian' brew to the local customers. The market was present and Jacobsen realized that the imported German Bavarian beer was about to clear the way for a changing beer demand in Copenhagen. But a precondition for exploiting this development was further knowledge of Bavarian brew methods and in the early summer of 1844 Jacobsen visited Munich for the first time. Following his return to Copenhagen the dynamic young brewer received official permission to construct two large storage cellars in Hahns Bastion at the rampart around the medieval centre of Copenhagen. Jacobsen's second – and most famous – visit to Munich took place in the autumn of 1845. This time Jacobsen acquired a share of the important bottom yeast from the German brewer Gabriel Sedlmayr; the yeast was kept in a small tin and several times he had to leave the stagecoach or train in order to find a water pump and chill his precious cargo. The yeast survived the long and difficult journey and in the winter of 1845–6 Jacobsen made a very successful brew of Bavarian beer. Jacobsen was gaining a good name among his Danish customers and with the capital from an inheritance following his mother's death in 1844 he decided to establish a modern brewery outside Copenhagen. Most important, he needed access to large quantities of fresh, cold water and with help from friends from the Danish Society for the Diffusion of Physics Jacobsen identified a site 5 km west of the city, in Valby, along the first Danish railway line from Copenhagen to Roskilde (some 30 km). Here Jacobsen found space for further expansion, access to fresh water and facilities for the all-important storing of beer. On 10 November 1847 Jacobsen presented the first Danish 'Bavarian' brew (a dark lager) from the Carlsberg Brewery – named after Jacobsen's only child, Carl Jacobsen. The public in Copenhagen praised the new beer and until the late 1870s the demand for Carlsberg beer was much higher than the presented output despite continuous extension of the production facilities. In the initial twenty-five years beer production at Carlsberg rose from 3548 hl in 1847–8 to 52,950 hl in 1872–3; the number of employees rose from ten to fifty-one.[7] In contrast to the existing Danish breweries Jacobsen established a truly industrialized brewery based on modern factory principles. In 1856 he introduced a shift worker system, which made two daily brews possible, and the following year he acquired a 10 hp steam engine and a newly developed 'Belgian' closed boiler. As a result in the winter of 1859–60 it was possible to make four daily brews.

The new industrialized lager beer production process was imitated by a number of local competitors: first in 1852 by the Svanholm brewery, followed

Photograph 10.1 *J.C. Jacobsen (1811–87) founded Carlsberg on 10 November 1847. Jacobsen introduced industrialized brewing methods to Denmark, emphasized high quality and modernized production methods.*
Source: Carlsberg Corporate Archive.

in 1860 by the Aldersro brewery. In 1871, Jacobsen created competition for himself by giving his son, Carl Jacobsen, the so-called Annexe Brewery (or Ny Carlsberg) next door to the old Carlsberg, renamed 'Gamle Carlsberg'.[8] The relationship between the two generations of brewers became increasingly difficult at the end of the 1870s when Carl Jacobsen felt that his father was about to subsume his brewery 'Ny Carlsberg' (New Carlsberg) into the Carlsberg Foundation, established by J.C. Jacobsen in 1876. The conflict between the two generations was very intense – Carl Jacobsen, for instance, blocked the easiest way from his father's brewery to the centre of Copenhagen and they also fought over the right to use the 'Carlsberg' name. In January 1882 the two generations signed a compromise: Carl Jacobsen got his paternal inheritance immediately – one-third of J.C. Jacobsen's fortune – and one year later Carl Jacobsen opened a brand new very modern brewery (again called Ny Carlsberg) next to his father's old site.

The Danish beer market was not only dominated by the two 'Carlsbergs' (Table 10.1). In the 1880s an increasing number of new breweries entered the production of Bavarian beer and by the 1880s fifteen such breweries in

Table 10.1 *Gamle Carlsberg's share of the Danish production of Bavarian beer, 1872–96*

Year	App. share (%)
1872	41
1881	23
1886	29
1892	30
1893	31
1894	31
1895	30
1896	27

Source: Fraenkel (1897).

Copenhagen. According to the economic historian, Kristof Glamann, there was not open competition on prices and quality:[9]

> The competition in the 1880s was not an open competition on price, but an indirect competition in terms of over measure, discounts, cash loans – in reality free gifts to the middlemen, lending of equipment . . . Following the foreign model the competition threatened to develop further into acquisitions of restaurants and shops.

The first official Carlsberg biographer, A. Fraenkel, described the Danish lager beer market in 1880s as a 'Manchester-like' and anarchistic market. This might have sounded promising for a liberal, but to Fraenkel it was of the utmost importance to avoid this destructive competition and establish an efficient cartel.[10] In 1881, 1883 and 1890 attempts were made to establish self-regulation of the market, but in vain. However, the prospects of the introduction of beer taxes in 1891 seems to have had a decisive impact. The tax caused stagnation in the demand for lager beer and consequently the breweries felt motivated to regulate the competition. In the early 1890s the incentives for self-regulation were particularly strong for the largest Danish breweries – Old and New Carlsberg – as they were faced by intensified competition from new products. In 1881, Tuborg Breweries introduced pilsner beer to the Danish market. The new beer was, unlike other beers, bottled at the brewery and Tuborg established an alternative distribution network outside the traditional local distributors. The lighter pilsner completely changed the market. In 1893 traditional 'Bavarian' lager still amounted to 95 per cent of beer production, but by 1912 its market share had fallen to 36 per cent as pilsner became the most important type of beer. Carlsberg's incentive to regulate the competition was further strengthened in 1891 when the important business tycoon, C.F. Tietgen, succeeded in uniting eleven small lager and 'hvidtøl' (a Danish type of household beer) breweries in Copenhagen to the new company De forenede Bryggerier (DfB). In September 1894 Tuborg joined the new Tietgen company and the chairman Harald Fritsche left no doubt about the intention of the merger: 'DfB will attain a completely different position from the one we have now, and this position will cause a more equal co-operation with the two large lager beer breweries [Old and New Carlsberg], which perhaps can contribute to homogeneous rules for sale and credit.'[11]

The result of Fritsch's invitation to further corporation with Carlsberg was realized in February 1895 when DfB and Carlsberg signed a ten-year market agreement. The two Carlsberg breweries abstained from producing 'hvidtøl' and the three breweries' future production was fixed on the basis of production in the previous four years. The beer market in Copenhagen was thus regulated, but all the provincial towns were still open to 'anarchistic' competition. In the autumn of 1898, several meetings were held between the brewers in the different regions of Denmark and a countrywide price and competition agreement was signed in September 1899.[12] The three large Copenhagen breweries committed themselves to take higher prices outside Copenhagen and it was forbidden to lend money to customers and to use other types of alternative competition methods. At the end of the negotiations Tuborg's manager, Benny Dessau, enquired after the future of the 1895 agreement. Carlsberg's manager, Aa van der Kühle, replied that in 1904 – when the agreement ended – it would be impossible to get a cartel agreement unless the profit was shared. The next step after a cartel was a real trust.[13]

The Carlsberg–Tuborg 1903 agreement

Carlsberg's willingness to enter such a trust was enhanced in 1902 when Carl Jacobsen transferred the ownership of Ny Carlsberg to the Carlsberg Foundation as his father had already done with Old Carlsberg. Both Carlsberg breweries faced substantial investment in bottling equipment for the new Carlsberg Pilsner beer introduced in 1904. The cautious owners in the Carlsberg Foundation – led by scientists without specific knowledge of the brewery industry – were therefore eager to continue the 1895 co-operation in some form, and on the initiative of Carlsberg's manager, van der Kühle, Carlsberg and Tuborg initiated negotiations in the autumn of 1902 concerning a new agreement. The basic principle of the agreement, signed in

May 1903, was equality: the partners were equally represented in the common management, the profit was shared equally every year and new investments were financed equally by the partners. The 1903 trust has been described as the most peculiar agreement in Danish business history. When it was signed it had an exceptional lifetime, namely ninety-seven years until 30 September 2000 and, even more remarkably, it operated with one idea – common profitability and shared investment – simultaneously with two independent companies in terms of production and sale.[14] This odd dualism proved to be problematic from the very beginning. Due to its success with bottled pilsner beer, Tuborg had by 1909 already paid DKK 3.35 million directly to Carlsberg and so Tuborg demanded a new agreement for profit-sharing.[15] By the end of 1909 a compromise was agreed upon and in the following six years Carlsberg paid DKK 900,000 extra to Tuborg. But this compromise endangered the whole idea of profit-sharing. In 1916 and 1921 attempts were made to merge the companies, but at the first attempt Vagn Jacobsen (grandson of J.C. Jacobsen) prevented the merger by raising a public debate about the future of the Carlsberg Foundation. In 1921, Tuborg's dynamic manager, Benny Dessau, planned a new nationwide trust including all the large Danish breweries, but this far-reaching plan was opposed by the chairman of the Carlsberg Foundation, Professor Kristian Erslev. The end result was an accepted – but not passionate – partnership between Carlsberg and Tuborg from 1921 to 1970.[16]

The national 1899 cartel on the Danish beer market

Besides the sharing of all investments and profits, Carlsberg and Tuborg had the right to appoint the chairman of the national Brewers' Association (Bryggeriforeningen), which hosted the national price and market agreement after 1899. This agreement existed until 1988 and besides price regulation it also limited marketing methods and defined the rules for distribution. In 1899, the Brewers' Association consisted of thirty-one breweries, but market conditions were difficult. In 1911, a new political proposal for higher beer taxes were made, but the Brewers' Association warned about the consequences particularly for the small breweries:

 In the last 12–15 years most of the breweries in this country have fought hard for their life. Of the countries' 37 lager beer breweries, five have gone bankrupt. Attempts have once more been made to reconstruct these, but it has succeeded for one of them.

Beer production fell from 917,000 hl in 1899 to 905,000 hl in 1914 and the small breweries in particular felt the effects of a declining market, higher prices for raw materials and more efficient large competitors. In the 1920s, Tuborg's share of the Danish market was around 30–33 per cent and Carlsberg's was around 42–44 per cent, or together more than 73 per cent.[17] Particularly in the early 1920s the market share rose for both companies at the expense of the small provincial breweries. The two large breweries in Copenhagen further strengthened their position after the Second World War, and by 1950 they had around 81 per cent of the total market. Perhaps even more importantly, the Danish beer market grew dramatically, from around 1.5 million hl in 1945 to 2.8 million hl in 1959.

Pressure on the Carlsberg–Tuborg 1903 agreement

The steady progress in market shares and total production combined with stable profits probably suppressed potential conflict between Carlsberg and Tuborg, which still operated and regarded themselves as two independent companies. But gradually, in the 1950s and 1960s, the 1903 agreement came under severe pressure for three reasons: unreasonable profit-sharing, growing exports and the authorities' growing interest in price agreements.

As stated earlier, the equal sharing of all profit was a source of tension between the two partners from 1909 onwards. A compromise was reached in 1912 and until 1938–9 the difference was not significant. But gap opened after 1932 because of Carlsberg's growing sales. From 1902–14, Tuborg paid DKK 5.5 million extra to Carlsberg, while between 1915 and 1948 Carlsberg paid DKK 29.8 million to Tuborg.[18] By the end of the 1940s both partners agreed that the situation was not tenable. Tuborg argued that the partners should increase their marketing budget as Carlsberg had strong advantages as a national institution that supported scientific and cultural purposes. Carlsberg, on the other hand, pointed out the need for an investigation of the causes of higher production expenses at the Tuborg brewery in Hellerup compared with the Carlsberg brewery in Valby. Tuborg rejected the need for such an investigation and demanded the matter referred to arbitration. Here it was confirmed that the 1903 agreement did not include any guarantee for balance in profitability. The issue was about to become a real crisis for the partners as Carlsberg was suddenly hit by unexpected production problems caused by so-called 'wild yeast', which disrupted fermentation. From 1950 to 1955, Carlsberg's market share fell from 55.2 per cent to 34.3 per cent while Tuborg's

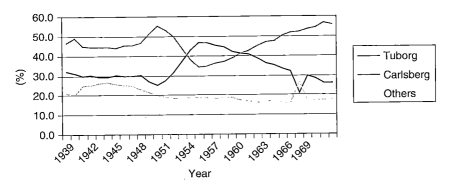

Figure 10.1 *Carlsberg v. Tuborg, 1939–72 (per cent of total market)*
Source: Nüchel Thomsen (1973).

rose from 25 to 46.8 per cent.[19] Tuborg again supported Carlsberg and the conflict evaporated. In 1955 Carlsberg's technicians found the cause for the problems and at the same time a new and strong manager, A.W. Nielsen, was appointed. Carlsberg's market share rose again, from 48.7 per cent in 1957 to 54.4 per cent in 1969.[20] In other words, the situation had returned to that seen in the late 1940s – and it was still not tenable (Figure 10.1). The agreement of 1903 was based on the assumption that the partners' profit would contribute approximately equally and it included no regulating mechanisms in the case of unequal profitability.

Perhaps even more aggravating, the 1903 agreement included no statements about exports. Tuborg's exports grew from around 25,000 hl in 1945–6 to 250,000 hl in 1956–7, while Carlsberg's grew from 83,000 hl in 1946–7 to around 341,000 hl in 1956–7 and it then expanded further to 845,000 hl in 1968–9.[21] In the 1960s some of the large international breweries went through structural changes, followed by investments in foreign facilities. The Dutch family-owned brewery Heineken invested in its own production facilities in England. Carlsberg wished to make a similar investment but Tuborg opposed the idea, arguing that it would hamper the important export to England and thus weaken the Danish breweries. According to the former chairman of DfB, Bernt Hjejle, Carlsberg lost around ten important years on the British market due to the limiting 1903 agreement.[22]

In the 1950s and 1960s the public authorities also investigated the 1903 agreement, to see whether it caused any unreasonable disadvantages to customers. The authorities were particularly interested in the way Carlsberg and Tuborg shared production expenses and profit: the question was whether the fixed market prices were based on Tuborg's high production costs or Carlsberg's lower ones.

The so-called 'Trust Commission' was appointed in March 1949 by the Danish government to investigate to what extent the Danish business environment was marked by restriction of free competition and to assess whether a new Competition Law was needed.[23] The investigation of the breweries began in 1950 along with a few other industries that were regarded as being regulated by private companies. After several years of work the authorities submitted a draft of its conclusions to Carlsberg, Tuborg and the Brewers' Association in November 1956. The conclusions were very critical of the 1903 agreement and its consequences for the brewing industry as a whole. In a letter to the authorities, the partners defended the agreement strongly,[24] the partnership was – and always had been – marked by strong internal competition in terms of both production and sales. According to the letter, the agreement's lifetime (until September 2000) was an essential explanation for this competition – in other words, each of the partners were aware of the need for a strong position forty-four years later. The unique feature in the 1903 agreement was that, according the letter, it had retained a specific kind of competition that eliminated the usual disadvantages of competition – namely, unreasonably high sales and marketing costs.[25] In the final report on competition in the Danish beer market, the Trust Commission loyally referred to Carlsberg/DfB's objections, but the final conclusion left no doubt about the consequences of the industry's self-regulation:[26]

> According to the information the commission has received from the breweries, the stable mutual market shares are not caused by any allocation of the customers or any other similar transfer of businesses from one partner to the other, and the commission has no reasons to doubt the Breweries' comments regarding a sharp competition in the daily sales promotion ... On the other hand it should also be emphasized that competition has been limited due the 1903 agreement, additional clauses, the shared managements' decisions, and the two breweries participation in Brewers' Association's agreements [the 1899 agreement]. Price competition has been abolished, advertising expenses have been jointly decided upon, and ... the different competitive devices have been restricted.

The unequivocal conclusions meant the Trust Commission's report had no immediate consequences for the 1903 agreement. But the problem caused by Tuborg's inefficiency and the unequal shared profit was still present. In a book about the 1970 merger, the chairman of DfB, Bernt Hjejle, regarded the monopoly authorities as a volcano under the 1903 agreement, which included a number of elements, 'quite inconsistent with the lines that the Monopoly authorities gradually draw out as principal viewpoints for their work'.[27]

The national 'beer wedding': 1970

In August 1969, the Brewers' Association applied to the Danish Monopoly Council for permission to raise Danish beer prices. The authorities rejected the application because the breweries' calculations showed that Tuborg had substantially higher production costs than Carlsberg. The former chairman of the Carlsberg Foundation has described the succeeding events in following words:[28]

> With this background, the Monopoly Council found that the 1903 agreement had developed into a pretext for doing nothing and that the time had come for a structural change within the brewery industry. The most efficient company's results should form the basis for decisions concerning higher prices, and not an average cost calculation that blurred the picture. The refusal started negotiations between the partners.

Three months earlier, in May 1969, the council of the Carlsberg/Tuborg trust held a meeting with three items on the agenda, which reflected the acute problems of the 1903 agreement:[29]

1. Discussion about the Monopoly authorities' attitude towards the trust
2. Carlsberg and Tuborg's need for capital in the following years
3. Carlsberg and Tuborg's activities abroad.

The Chairman of the Carlsberg Foundation, Stig Iuul (who had written the answer to Monopoly authorities in 1956), opened the meeting with a long and important speech in which he stated that the EC and the following economic integration, plus the unequal profitability, created an urgent need to merge Carlsberg and Tuborg. As negotiations began, the most difficult issues proved to be the questions of whether the head of the new company should take detailed decisions about both companies, and whether the new company should be managed by Carlsberg's manager, A.W. Nielsen, or Tuborg's manager, Viggo Rasmussen. After several months of secret negotiations and a temporary interruption at the turn of 1969–70, the merger was signed on 25 May 1970. Carlsberg and Tuborg continued as independent production facilities, but within the framework of one private limited company with a share capital of DKK 171 million, of which the Carlsberg Foundation received the largest block of shares (DKK 85.5 million) as payment for the brewery.

In November 1974, Carlsberg opened its first brewery in Northampton, a move that signified a new stage in Carlsberg's development. Sales abroad rose from 1.6 million hl in 1970 to 16.1 million hl in 1990, while sales in Denmark only grew from 4.1 million hl in 1969 to 5.3 million hl in 1990. Carlsberg's future expansion lay outside Denmark – and, indeed, outside the restrictive 1903 agreement. But the 1970 merger did not bring an end to the self-regulation of the Danish beer market. The Brewers' Association continued to be dominated by Carlsberg and the national price and marketing agreement continued until 1988. According to the contemporary Danish competition law it was legal to arrange prices as long as they were reported to the authorities, justified by the actual production expenses and did not cause limits to competition. In May 1987 the monopoly authorities published a detailed investigation of the brewery industry and concluded that the price agreements and the distribution system limited competition and caused a high degree of concentration in the market. Negotiations with the breweries went on during the autumn of 1987 and the cartel partners decided to dissolve the market agreements with effect from 15 February 1988.

Several years before the dissolution in February 1988 some small Danish breweries had already left the price agreement (and thus the Brewers' Association) in order to serve the new and expanding discount beer market. At the General Assembly of the Brewers' Association in 1988, the chairman of the association and managing director of Carlsberg, Poul Svanholm, stated that it was the authorities who had forced the dissolution of the market agreements, but 'it ought not to be forgotten that more than ten years of discount brands and cheap beer made the competition situation indefensible'.[30]

The history of Carlsberg and the cartel agreements in the Danish beer market follow closely the general pattern of Danish competition regulation. First there was the highly regulated local beer market that built upon guilds until around year 1850. This was followed by a gradual liberalization and stronger competition. The breweries reacted to these 'anarchistic' conditions by self-regulation in terms of national price and marketing agreements, plus an odd partnership between the market's two most important players, Carlsberg and Tuborg. Then followed some interference from the public authorities that supervised and investigated self-regulation after 1949, and finally by the end of the twentieth century national self-regulation was dissolved.

The core of this story is obviously the self-regulation from around 1900 to the end of the 1980s. And in the case of Carlsberg the *continuity* and *validity* of self-regulation is extremely important. The 1903 agreement lasted until 1970 when it was opposed by the Danish authorities' regulation of justifiable price-setting. At this stage the 1903 agreement was also a dangerous drag on Carlsberg's international expansion. A drag that, according to a former chairman of DfB, Bernt Hjejle, caused Carlsberg a ten-year delay on the British market.[31] The Brewers' Association's national marketing and price agreement lasted from 1899 to 1988. Again, the authorities rejected the fundamental parts of the cartel agreement, but it survived until the breweries no longer could continue due to new competition in the market in terms of the expanding discount beer sector.

According to the Danish historian, Per Boje, Denmark has fundamentally been marked by a capitalistic liberal market economy and the private sector was forced to accept a Competition Law it strongly opposed.[32] The lesson from the brewing industry is that self-regulation could continue right until it no longer made sense for the industry itself – either because of international competition or because of new market conditions. Carlsberg's managers probably disliked the public investigation of the private competition regulation – but the trusts and cartels could still continue for decades. The remarkable aspect of the 1903 agreement between Carlsberg and Tuborg is not that it was cancelled in 1970, but rather that it could survive for sixty-seven years. In this case a public counterbalance to private self-regulation seemed limited – if not harmless.

From exporter to global company

The 1960s were a time of unrivalled growth as an increase in purchasing power across Europe helped push Carlsberg/Tuborg's sales to new heights.

Between 1959 and 1973 domestic sales more than tripled, to reach 5.7 million hl. Exports more than doubled, reaching 2 million hl in 1970 from 591,000 hl in 1957.[33] By 1967, Denmark was the largest exporter of beer in Europe.

Carlsberg and Tuborg both had historically strong links to the export market. Carlsberg began experimenting with exports in the 1860s, but really began to look at opportunities after 1869 when it sent its first modest exports to the UK and test exports to Rangoon, Singapore, Calcutta and Hong Kong. Tuborg was founded in 1873, specifically as an export brewery, although exporting did not begin until the 1880s when Tuborg's director used the many foreign contacts he had cultivated through his butter export company to place the company firmly on the world map. However, at this stage, the companies had little direct involvement with exports and Carlsberg and Tuborg sold their beers to Asia and the Middle East through trading companies such as the East Asiatic Company and various merchants operating out of Hamburg.

Carlsberg, driven by the quality obsession of its founder J.C. Jacobsen, enjoyed the better sales of the two and immediately before the First World War

Photograph 10.2 **Already in 1869 Carlsberg had commenced its exporting activities to England – in previous years it had exported beer to Sweden and Iceland. These early exports were rather symbolic and did not have any direct impact on the turnover of the brewery. The long-term effect was perhaps more important, namely that Carlsberg established its name very early on in important markets around Denmark.**
Source: Carlsberg Corporate Archive.

Carlsberg alone exported 42,322 hl of beer.[34] This fell away to nothing during the war years but the Carlsberg name and reputation for quality recovered slowly throughout the 1920s, helped by the formation of Carlsberg Distributors Ltd in Bond Street to serve the lucrative trade in London. Carlsberg was acknowledged as a quality beer and was by 1931 advertising itself as 'The World's Best'. The Second World War brought expansion to a halt once again and shortages of raw materials at home limited exports. After 1945, Carlsberg's sales during this period were dominated by the UK, which accounted for a growing percentage of all exports. The basis for this growth was returning British servicemen who had developed a taste for 'lager' (as pilsner beer is called in the UK). Carlsberg, desperate for foreign currency after the war, was quick to sell its beers to the NAAFI canteens and shops that the servicemen used and developed into loyal customers who took their new drinking habits home. However, the international market was still of limited financial importance and represented only a fraction of total sales.

Licensing and investment

While the terms of the 1903 agreement gave a framework for co-operation within Denmark, there was no agreement about co-operation in international markets.

The two competed with each other already in Belgium and the UK, and to avoid a worsening of the competition they agreed that investment in new breweries could take place as long as it was outside their main markets. This gave rise to brewery projects in Turkey and Iran for Tuborg (1967), and Cyprus (1967), Malawi (1968), Brazil (1970) and Malaysia (1972) for Carlsberg.

According to the former chairman of the Carlsberg Foundation, Kristof Glamann, 'The two breweries almost blocked each on the international market. The German breweries had started to merge and we feared that the Dutch would make acquisitions in Denmark. With the merger with Tuborg we gathered our strength and started our expansion seriously'.[35]

In the years after the merger it was no longer just exports that counted towards sales in foreign markets. Licensing deals became more important as a source of both income and volume. In 1970, exports made up only around 24 per cent of total sales and sales from licence agreements were negligible. However, during the 1970s and 1980s sales outside Denmark, from exports, licence deals and investments, rose rapidly as a percentage of total sales. Sales of Carlsberg and Tuborg produced outside Denmark surpassed sales in the

Photograph 10.3   *Carlsberg's famous hand-drawn logo was designed in 1904 by the Danish artist Thorvald Bindesbøll for the launch of Carlsberg pilsner. Bindesbøll was Carlsberg's favoured graphic designer from the 1880s. He was also involved in the design of exhibition catalogues, anniversary books, a bottle tray and beer labels for old and New Carlsberg. As this photo illustrates the logo was used for decoration of trucks, beer crates and bottles. In 2007 the logo was awarded a design prize by the Danish Design Centre.*
Source: Carlsberg Corporate Archive.

home market for the first time in 1976[36] and continued to grow. From 24 per cent in 1970, they climbed to 60 per cent in 1980–1 and 90 per cent in 1999–2000. At that time Carlsberg and Tuborg products were available in more than 140 countries.

Exports as a percentage of overseas sales fell throughout this period. The move towards licence agreements was driven by the need to cut costs after the oil shock of 1973 As fuel costs increased, so too did the cost of exporting beer. It was cheaper to export know-how in the form of licensing agreements, while a licensing agreement together with a minority stake allowed greater access to the partner's distribution network. Increasing unrest among Danish labour unions also meant that supply from Denmark had become unreliable.

Although the merger solved immediate problems, there were still differences that needed to be resolved between the two former competitors. Throughout his time at the company CEO Poul Svanholm kept two offices – one at Carlsberg in Valby and one at Tuborg in Hellerup – to ensure that both organizations felt themselves equally treated. His rationale for keeping the two organizations separate was to maintain 'power and vitality', although it was also necessary to ensure visible proof to the authorities of the competition that existed in the Danish market. However, it also helped prevent the development of a single head office capable of rational and strategic decisions at home and abroad. Marketing was a particular challenge. Carlsberg and Tuborg were often available on the same markets, competing for similar customers and often with different licence brewers for the two brands.

The lack of clarity in marketing internationally was also a result of an organizational structure that was far more suited for an export and licensing company than it was to a global brewer. Just as DfB had separate sales organizations for Carlsberg and Tuborg in Denmark, the United Breweries (a literal translation of DfB) also had separate organizations for its overseas business. Carlsberg International looked after export sales and licensing agreements for Carlsberg, while Tuborg International did the same job for Tuborg. A third organization, United Breweries International, looked after foreign breweries in which United Breweries had a shareholding.

Expansion abroad throughout the 1970s and 1980s was still driven by the idea that Carlsberg and Tuborg were high-quality, high-priced products that didn't take market share from established, domestic breweries. This policy was described by Carlsberg's managing director, Poul Svanholm, in an interview in 1983:

> We would like to enter those markets where we see an opportunity for a growth in beer sales so we can get a share of that growth. We are not so interested in gaining sales by taking market share from other breweries. That's not our way. We have, by the way, a policy of going to the local brewers and telling them that we intend to establish ourselves in the country.[37]

The choice of partners and investment type was governed by a mixture of traditional attachments, chance and some conscious strategic choices. Investment in the breweries in Hong Kong and Malaysia was undertaken with its old export partner the East Asiatic Company, while other investments were a development of existing strong export markets such as the UK. However, many of the partnerships in this period were a result of interested breweries contacting Carlsberg enquiring about the possibilities of licensing the beer.[38] This policy of taking a small stake was dubbed a 'business card' strategy as it allowed Carlsberg to quickly gain a foothold in a market with limited investment. However, it also meant that Carlsberg rarely had a majority in the companies concerned, and therefore little management control.

In the period up until 1997 it was rare for Carlsberg to take a majority stake in a brewery. When it did invest in a brewery, it generally did so as part of a licensing agreement and the total share rarely rose above 30 per cent and was more typically under 20 per cent.[39] In 1996, the company held a majority in only eight of the twenty-seven foreign breweries in which it had a stake.

Carlsberg's technical organization was one of the few common elements. Licensing agreements included access to Carlsberg's laboratory research and quality control, which gave its partners an advantage on their home markets as the technology was transferred to local beers.[40] But it also underlined the company's focus on the ability to produce a 'quality' product rather than sell it.

Technical know-how was formalized with the creation of Danbrew, a 100 per cent-owned subsidiary that took the knowledge gained from building breweries in Northampton in the UK and Fredericia in Denmark, and used it to build breweries abroad – often in connection with a licensing deal.

The end of the 'business card' strategy

The year 1997 marked several important events in Carlsberg's history as a company. It was the year that it celebrated 150 years as a brewer, it was the year that Poul Svanholm retired, and it was the year that marked the end of the 'business card' strategy. In the years since the merger, the policy of expanding through licensing and minority partnerships had resulted in a patchwork of holdings across the world, but with little strength outside the top five markets for both the Carlsberg and Tuborg brands. The situation was worsened by the fact, that in many of these markets, Carlsberg was a minority shareholder. Where it did have the majority, profitability was poor. Added to this was an international organization that was little more than an export sales function with virtually no control over partners or their production. Despite the fact that international sales had outstripped domestic sales since 1976, the international organization was still subordinate to a Danish-dominated administration that spent a proportionately large amount of time on managing domestic issues.

Carlsberg's weakness was underlined in 1999 when the Dutch brewer Heineken bought Cruzcampo in Spain from under its nose, despite Carlsberg's existing 11 per cent share in the brewery acquired in connection with a licensing agreement. In effect, Carlsberg was thrown out of Spain – one of its top 10 profitable breweries – and the 'business card' strategy was shown to be ineffective in the face of growing worldwide consolidation in the brewing industry.

Flemming Lindeløv's 'Ten Principles'

The arrival of Flemming Lindeløv as CEO in 1997 marked a change in Carlsberg's domestic and international strategies. His strategy, developed with outside management consultants (itself an innovation in Carlsberg) was the 'Ten Principles'. It laid out the ten characteristics of the brewing industry, and how Carlsberg was to react. The principles committed Carlsberg to focusing on the beer industry (heralding the start of a sell-off of non-core business), investing in focus markets to achieve leading positions with a complete distribution apparatus and investing in branding with Carlsberg as the leading international brand, among other things.

The problem of too many minority shareholdings was not directly mentioned in the Principles, but it soon became clear that this was an important part of the new strategy. In the years 1997–9, Carlsberg increased shareholdings or bought majority shares in breweries in the UK, Finland, Sweden, Italy and Poland. To free up capital to finance this and other activities, Carlsberg sold its shareholdings in the Royal Copenhagen porcelain business and the Tivoli amusement park in Copenhagen. This activity culminated in the merging of Carlsberg's beer activities with that of Orkla, the Norwegian conglomerate, in June 2000.

The birth of a global brewer

The Ten Principles aimed to set the basic premises for the company, but in the face of growing global competition and consolidation among competitors, Carlsberg needed to answer one more question: was it going to remain on the global stage or retreat and create a northern European brewing group?

To solve the lack of focus on beer, the company was organized along new lines, with separate divisions for Beer, Finance and Soft Drink (which looked after the Coca Cola Nordic Beverages (CCNB) joint venture). However, domestic issues still dominated, witness the splitting of the Beer Division into just two sections: Denmark and International.

'Division Danmark' represented only around 10 per cent of sales but as a home market consumed a proportionately large amount of management time. However, with the split it became a separate profit centre with its own corporate functions.

The Carlsberg Foundation really opened the way for international expansion in 1999 by relinquishing the requirement that it hold a minimum of

51 per cent of the Carlsberg brewery in return for holding a 'significant interest' in subsidiaries owned by Carlsberg A/S (in 2007, this was further reduced to 25 per cent). The requirement to hold a minimum of 51 per cent had been criticized by stock market analysts as it limited Carlsberg's ability to attract capital for expansion. This was underlined in March 2000 when Carlsberg missed out on acquiring the Kronenbourg brewery because its owners, the French conglomerate Danone, wanted part-payment in shares. Carlsberg's ownership structure made this sort of deal impossible.

The deciding step in the brewery's future came in June 2000, when Carlsberg and Orkla announced the creation of a new brewing group – Carlsberg Breweries – made possible by the Foundation's decision. In one move, Carlsberg secured its Nordic market by acquiring the leaders in Norway and Sweden, and gained access to the booming Central and Eastern European markets through a 50 per cent share in Baltic Beverage Holding (BBH).

Orkla and Carlsberg

Orkla's impact on Carlsberg was to be more than a simple securing of Carlsberg's Nordic backyard. The Norwegian conglomerate accelerated the process of internationalism by providing the management capacity that Carlsberg lacked in depth and bringing tools that would help Carlsberg manage its existing breweries and make it easier to take on more. In the first two years, the new organization began the job of integrating IT, accounting, marketing, production and logistics, starting with the Nordic region. Brewery acquisition continued, driven by the merger, and in the years 2000–2 Carlsberg Breweries increased its share or bought outright eleven breweries and entered a major joint venture in Asia.

Additional managers brought in by the merger allowed Carlsberg to take on ambitious tasks such as the turnaround of the Swiss brewery Feldschlösschen and spending time on the Polish and Turkish businesses.[41] A major restructuring of Carlsberg's head office took place in November 2001, which removed the remaining 'export sales' characteristics, was realized by one of the new vice-presidents recruited from Orkla.

However, the new co-operation was not without its teething troubles. An unfortunate comment from Orkla's CEO, Jens P. Heyerdahl, that suggested that the deal was merely the first step towards an acquisition of Carlsberg was not popular with the Carlsberg Foundation and began the process that led first to the dismissal of Flemming Lindeløv, who was seen to be pro-Orkla, and finally to the decision to buy Orkla's 40 per cent share of Carlsberg Breweries.

Carlsberg: the global brewer

Lindeløv's successor as CEO, Nils Smedegaard Andersen, took the opportunities offered by the creation of Carlsberg Breweries to form it into a truly global enterprise and can rightly be called the architect of the modern Carlsberg.

In the spring of 2002, Carlsberg Breweries' new international focus was underlined with the holding of its first international management meeting outside Denmark, bringing together managers to discuss the recent past and the future of the Group. This was followed by a strategy that resulted in the creation of six 'Must-Win Battles' that were seen as vital for the success of the Group:[42] Carlsberg's response to the changing conditions was a global strategy in terms of marketing, corporate culture and production/logistics.

In 1987 the official company name was changed from The United Breweries to Carlsberg. This was followed by a growing tendency to promote Carlsberg as the main international brand, with Tuborg as a regional player apart from several of its strong markets in Eastern Europe.[43] However, it was not until after the 'Ten Principles' strategy in 1997–8 that Carlsberg finally became the focus of branding activity for the company.

Increasing focus on marketing led in 2001 to a project called 'Brand Spirit' to rejuvenate the Carlsberg brand and ensure global consistency in the way the brand was positioned and marketed. This project now took off under the 'Must-Win Battles' programme and reflected the brand strategy of a broad portfolio of local brands supported by an international premium brand, Carlsberg Beer. It marked a change of policy over earlier years when Carlsberg had existed in a vacuum, with few or no connections to local beers. Now, Carlsberg and Tuborg were part of a portfolio that could be managed in terms of cost and sales efforts.

This new approach was only possible with tighter management control over Carlsberg's majority-owned subsidiaries, especially within production and distribution. From now on it would be marketing and sales that would drive production, rather than vice versa.

'Operational Excellence' was the name given to a programme of improvements to reduce the cost base and improve efficiency that was born out of an international benchmarking study in 2001. Carlsberg described it as a move from 'Probably the Best Beer' to 'Probably the Best Beer Company'. The 'Excellence' programme covering production, administration, commercial skills and procurement was the first of its kind in the company and represented a clean break with Carlsberg's previous 'hands-off' management style. It was one of several projects, such as joint IT systems and financial service centres, that began to be run across Carlsberg's businesses, rather than out from the head office. Where previously new breweries would be more or less untouched by head office, it became more common to change their names to Carlsberg and receive an injection of managerial capital.

It is perhaps in Carlsberg's rapid advance in China – especially western China where it now has control of six brewery groups and 290 breweries – that we can see the results of Carlsberg's transformation from exporter to global player. Carlsberg had been present on the Chinese market since the 1890s, largely distributed by ØK (the East Asiatic Company). In 1982, the two companies formed a joint venture to build Carlsberg Brewery Hong Kong. In 1995, the industrial conglomerate the Swire Group was brought into the partnership and the three partners took over the Huizhou Brewing Company in Guangdong, on the Chinese mainland. Carlsberg and Swire bought out ØK, leaving the partners with 51 per cent and 49 per cent, respectively, in the brewery in Hong Kong and Guangdong. In 1998, Carlsberg opened a state-of-the-art brewery in Shanghai, eastern China, only to have their growth ambitions frustrated by Chinese drinkers' preference for cheaper local brands. Production capacity was massively under utilized and Carlsberg sold 75 per cent of the brewery to local Chinese market leader, Tsingtao, at a loss.

It returned to the Chinese market in 2003 with a strategy of building up a network of local breweries focusing on the mainstream beer market. The idea of introducing Carlsberg as a niche brand survived, but only within a broader, owned portfolio.

Since the large merger in 1970, Carlsberg thus underwent a tremendous transition from a small exporter to a global player with majority-owned and controlled breweries in most parts of the world. Carlsberg's 'business cards' were converted to bricks and mortar while further major acquisitions in the Nordic region (Ringnes, Pripps, Sinebrychoff), Eastern Europe (BBH), Germany (Holsten) and China have helped make Carlsberg the fastest-growing international beer brand by the early 2000s.

Conclusion

The business history of Carlsberg includes at least· two important characteristics of Danish capitalism – the widespread national self-regulation of competition throughout most of the twentieth century and changes in corporate growth strategies after the 1980s from export-oriented multinationals towards a transnational focus on globally consistent brand, production and management systems. In the first respect Carlsberg and the Danish beer market illustrates how the Danish business system has moved from liberal market conditions in the mid-nineteenth century via a high degree of self-regulation of the competition in the early and mid-twentieth century towards a renaissance of liberal principles after the 1980s. It is worth analysing the reasons for the abolition of the competition agreements on the Danish beer market in February 1988. The background consisted of a combination of three factors: pressure from the Danish state, new European legislation on competition and, perhaps most important, an increasing competition on the market which caused a decrease in corporate loyalty to the internal agreements. In Carlsberg's case developments in the 1990s implied an increased focus on establishing a global consistent strategy of branding, management, production and distribution. In the twenty-first century Carlsberg was still a Danish company but the importance of the Danish home market had deceased substantially and it would even make sense to suggest that Carlsberg now considered all Nordic countries as their 'home markets' – that is, beer markets dominated by Carlsberg. It was the combination of the dominant position on a number of foreign market and the new consistent globalized business which created the platform for Carlsberg's growth after the merger with Orkla in 2000.

QUESTIONS
1. One of the important characteristics of Danish capitalism in the first half of the twentieth century was the widespread self-regulation of competition. Identify the different methods which Carlsberg used in order to control competition on the Danish beer market, and discuss the reasons why the market moved from a protected co-operative market toward a competitive liberal market in the 1980s.

2. In recent years, Carlsberg has changed its nature from being an export-oriented multinational towards becoming a transnational company with a globally co-ordinated policy on branding, management, production methods, R&D, etc. What changes lead to this transition of Carlsberg, and in comparison with other large breweries could we then regard Carlsberg as a first-mover or a late-mover in this transition?

Notes

1. The two Carlsberg breweries (Gamle Carlsberg and Ny Carlsberg) and DfB (Tuborg and several small breweries) became partners in 1903 and are thus referred to as 'Carlsberg' in this chapter.
2. The first Trust Law was passed in 1931 but according to Boje it did not have any consequences for business life.
3. Boje (2004).

4. Johanson and Wiedersheim-Paul (1975).
5. Johanson and Wiedersheim-Paul (1975).
6. Glamann (1990), pp. 36–40.
7. Fraenkel (1897), pp. 132–67.
8. Glamann (1976), p. 35.
9. Glamann (1976), pp. 49–50.
10. Boje (2004), p. 29.
11. Glamann (1976), p. 50.
12. Dahlberg *et al.* (1999), pp. 41–2.
13. Glamann (1976), p. 53.
14. Nüchel Thomsen (1973), p. 61.
15. Hjejle (1982), p. 51.
16. *Ibid.*, pp. 52–3.
17. Glamann (1976), p. 86.
18. Glamann (1976), p. 87; in the single year 1918–19 Tuborg, also paid money to Carlsberg.
19. Glamann (1976), p. 89.
20. Glamann (1976), p. 97.
21. Hjejle (1982), p. 87.
22. Hjejle (1982), pp. 87–8.
23. Trustkommissionen (1960).
24. Hjejle (1982), p. 81.
25. Hjejle (1982), p. 81, citation of the letter from the partners to the Danish authorities, 6 November 1956.
26. Trustkommissionen (1960), pp. 91–2.
27. Hjejle (1982), p. 87, Hjejle thought that the bomb would explode if Tuborg provided practically no profit to the partnership and the entire profit came from Carlsberg.
28. Glamann (1997), p. 24.
29. Hjejle (1982), p. 109.
30. Dahlberg *et al.* (1999), p. 140.
31. Hjejle (1982), p. 89.
32. Boje (2004), p. 292.
33. Vores Øl, Kristof Glaman (1997).
34. Glamann (1976).
35. Interview with Kristof Glamann, Børsen (1993).
36. Carlsberg, *Annual Report* (1977).
37. Interview with Poul Svanholm, Måneds Børsen (August 1983).
38. Interview with Poul Svanhlom .
39. Figures from Carlsberg Annual Reports.
40. Danish newspaper article (26 January 1973).
41. Interview with Nils Smedegaard Andersen, *The Brew* (Carlsberg Breweries' Internal magazine Spring 2003).
42. *The Brew* (Spring 2003).
43. Vores Øl, Kristof Glamann.

References

Boje, P., *Marked, erhvervsliv og stat* (Aarhus: Aarhus Universitersforlag, 2004).
Dahlberg, R., Iversen, M. and Linden, T., *Bryggerne og de tre store udfordringer* (Copenhagen, 1999).
Fleet, D. and Wren, D., 'Teaching History in Business Schools, 1982–2003', *Academy of Management Learning and Education*, 4(1), (2005).
Fraenkel, A., *Gamle Carlsberg* (Copenhagen: Hegeneps Boghandel 1897).
Glamann, K., *Bryggeriets historie i Danmark indtil slutningen af det 19. århunderede* (Copenhagen: Gyldendal, 1962).
Glamann, K., *Carlsbergfondet* (Copenhagen: Gyldendal, 1976).
Glamann, K., *Bryggeren, J.C. Jacobsen på Carlsberg* (Copenhagen: Gyldendal, 1990).

Glamann, K., *Vores ØL – og hele verdens*, (Copenhagen: Gyldendal, 1997).

Hjejle, B., *Hof eller Tuborg, konkurrence og fusion, 1895–1970* (Copenhagen: Arnold Bust, 1982).

Johanson, J. and Wiedersheim–Paul, F., 'The Internationalization of the Firm, Four Swedish Cases', *Journal of Management Studies*, 12(3) October 1975, pp. 305–22.

'Konkurrencebegrænsninger i dansk erhvervsliv', *Trustkommissionens Betænkning* 8 (1960).

McCraw, T. K. 'Regulation in America: A Review Article' (1990).

McCraw, T. K. *Creating Modern Capitalism* (Cambridge, MA: Harvard University Press, 1995).

Nüchel Thomsen, B., *Tuborg's Bryggerier A/S 1873–1973,* (Copenhagen: Gyldendal, 1973).

Trustkommissionen, *Konkurrencebegrænsningen i dansk erhvervsliv*, Trustkommissionens betænkninger, 8 (1960).

World Economic Forum, *Global Competitiveness Report.*

WELFARE CAPITALISM: THE SWEDISH ECONOMY 1850–2005 ◦ ENTREPRENEURSHIP AND OWNERSHIP: THE
FIRM VIABILITY OF THE SWEDISH BONNIER AND WALLENBERG FAMILY BUSINESS GROUPS ◦ FROM

prologue to the Norwegian chapter

ABB ... FINNISH
CAPITALISM, 1850S–2005 ◦ FROM STATE OWNERSHIP TO MULTINATIONAL CORPORATION: THE PATH OF
ENSO-GUTZEIT TO STORA-ENSO ◦ SUCCESS AND FAILURE OF A CONGLOMERATE FIRM: THE STRATEGIC
PATHS OF NOKIA AND TAMPELLA IN THE LIBERALIZING FINNISH ECONOMY AFTER THE SECOND WORLD
WAR ◦ CO-OPERATIVE LIBERALISM: DENMARK FROM 1857 TO 2007 ◦ ARLA – FROM DECENTRALIZED INDUSTRY
TO MULTINATIONAL ENTERPRISE ◦ CARLSBERG AND THE SELF-REGULATION OF THE DANISH BEER MARKET
◦ NORWAY: A RESOURCE-BASED AND DEMOCRATIC CAPITALISM ◦ CONSTRUCTIVE POWER: ELKEM 1904–2004
◦ FINANCE AND THE DEVELOPMENT OF NORWEGIAN CAPITALISM – THE CASE OF CHRISTIANIA BANK

According to the National Geographic's *Traveller* magazine, in 2004 the
'Norwegian fjord' was the highest rated of ninety-four destinations from
UNESCO's list of World Heritage Destinations. In 2006, the same panel of
experts gave one of these fjords, the Geirangerfjord, the highest rating. The
panel wrote:

> To float into the Geirangerfjord is an astonishingly complete natural
> experience–steep, lush and rocky canyon walls, endless waterfalls,
> a snow-capped backdrop and inconceivably deep, emerald green
> water. There are a wealth of farms, now largely abandoned (Skagefla,
> Knivsfla and Blomberg) along Geirangerfjord's banks, one of which
> is only accessed by climbing a flimsy rope ladder which spans
> hundreds of metres from the water, along the cliff face, to the farm
> plateau . . . The presence of the 'shelf farms' and human population
> scattered along this dramatic coastline is unique and wondrous.[1]

The fjords are parts of the growing 'experience economy', making profit
from both magnificent nature and exotic historical remnants. There are,
however, other ways of observing the mountainous nature and scattered
farms. The Norwegian sociologist, Gudmund Hernes, takes a long historical
perspective:

> Norway is a country more suited for pack saddle than for cavalry.
> Feudalism never took root in the barren Norwegian soil as it did on
> the flat ground on the continent. The Norwegian rural communities
> were located in valleys confined by mountains, and the farms were
> scattered around in the landscape. It was these impossible natural
> conditions in itself that made the Norwegian peasants . . . freeholders
> to a larger degree than in European countries. They were much more
> masters on their own farms, and got callus in their own hands, not
> as subordinates.[2]

This historical background of a freeholder society has contributed to the development of a Norwegian model of capitalism, what we in the country chapter (Chapter 11) call 'Democratic Capitalism'. The chapter will show how this capitalism, and its public and private entrepreneurs, benefited from and learned to exploit what once seemed only to be 'the barren Norwegian soil', its natural resources, like minerals, forests, waterfalls and fish – and petroleum. We will discuss how this resource-based economy has developed through different stages. Each stage is identified by a certain interaction between nature, new technological paradigms and institutional changes. Inside the broad framework of 'Democratic Capitalism', these institutional changes represent the formation and stabilization of different stages in the development of Norwegian business systems.

Both the case chapters (Chapters 12 and 13) explore important aspects of Norwegian capitalism. The study of Elkem tells the story of a firm established early in the twentieth century to exploit the country's natural resources, especially its favourable waterfalls. The narrative demonstrates how the resource-based industry has also been heavily knowledge based and internationally market-oriented. Elkem's success (Chapter 12) was grounded on daring entrepreneurship and sustained by innovation, the Söderberg electrode being the most important. Elkem, and other resource-based firms such as Hydro and Statoil, has been working inside a rather large-scale, internationally-oriented framework, not unlike many Swedish firms–but in contrast to the most representative Norwegian firms.

The second case (Chapter 13) discusses the history of Christiania Bank in relation to the development of Norway's financial system and macroeconomic trends and fluctuations. Comparatively, the small-scale and locally and regionally-based savings and commercial banks have been more important in Norway than in the other Nordic countries. Christiania Bank for a long time confined its market to the capital city, Oslo. During the last decades of the twentieth century, Christiania Bank became more expansive and internationally-oriented. As a consequence of the banking crises of the late 1980s, Christiania Bank was taken over by the state, and in 2000 the bank was sold to the Swedish-dominated MeritaNordbanken – later called Nordea.

Notes

1. *National Geographic Traveler*, (November–December 2006).
2. Hernes (1977), p. 11.

WELFARE CAPITALISM: THE SWEDISH ECONOMY 1850-2005 ≈ ENTREPRENEURSHIP AND OWNERSHIP: THE
ERM VIABILITY OF THE SWEDISH BONNIER AND WALLENBERG FAMILY BUSINESS GROUPS ≈ FROM
ABB ... Norway: a resource-based and INVESTMENT: FINNISH
CAPITALISM, 1850-2005 ≈ FROM STATE OWNERSHIP TO MULTINATIONAL CORPORATION: THE PATH OF
ENSO-GUTZEIT democratic capitalism CONGLOMERATE FIRM: THE STRATEGIC
PATHS OF NOKIA AND TAMPELLA IN THE LIBERALIZING FINNISH ECONOMY AFTER THE SECOND WORLD
WAR ≈ CO-OPERATIVE LIBERALISM: DENMARK FROM 1857 TO 2007 ≈ ARLA Lars Thue FROM DECENTRALIZED INDUSTRY
TO MULTINATIONAL ENTERPRISE ≈ CARLSBERG AND THE SELF-REGULATION OF THE DANISH BEER MARKET
≈ NORWAY: A RESOURCE-BASED AND DEMOCRATIC CAPITALISM ≈ CONSTRUCTIVE POWER: ELKEM 1904-2004
≈ FINANCE AND THE DEVELOPMENT OF NORWEGIAN CAPITALISM – THE CASE OF CHRISTIANIA BANK

In 2007, the US Central Intelligence Agency (CIA) characterized the Norwegian economy as follows:

> The Norwegian economy is a prosperous bastion of welfare capital-
> ism, featuring a combination of free market activity and government
> intervention. The government controls key areas such as the vital
> petroleum sector (through large-scale state enterprises). The country
> is richly endowed with natural resources – petroleum, hydro power,
> fish, forests, and minerals – and is highly dependent on its oil pro-
> duction and international oil prices, with oil and gas accounting for
> one-third of exports. Only Saudi Arabia and Russia export more oil
> than Norway.[1]

The agency's short account of the Norwegian economy is to the point. For centuries the Norwegian economy has been based on the exploitation of natural resources. In 2007 the petroleum sector was responsible for one-quarter of all value creation and one-quarter of the state's revenue.

Most parts of Norway are geographically located in the European periphery; Norway is Europe's northernmost country. But the country is a privileged periphery. In addition to its many natural resources, Norway has one of the longest coastlines in the world, a coastline that shortened the distance to both Britain and the continent, and that was decisive for the development of a very profitable maritime economic cluster. The sea also served as an internal transport infrastructure, compensating for the troublesome inland communication caused by a mountainous topography intersected with fjords and valleys. Not least, the warm Gulf Stream heats the water along the coast. That has been a necessary condition not only for the rich fisheries, but also for a habitable climate in large parts of the country.

The importance of natural resources has contributed to three institutional characteristics of the Norwegian business system. First, significant local and regional variations in the business system have emerged because people have adapted their economic activities, their local institutions and ways of organizing to the differences in resource endowment. Second, the wide distribution of natural resources combined with topographic limits to strong centralized political and economic governance have promoted relatively autonomous and economically active local communities. Third, the often high resource rent and high value of the natural resources have prompted the state to intervene in the economy, through regulations, economic support or ownership.

The co-operation and the conflicts between an ambitious state and strong local communities have had several consequences for the structure of the Norwegian economy. Decisions favouring local and regional development have sometimes conflicted with what has been perceived as national interests. Mostly, however, there has been a synergy effect. The state has supported the initiatives and ambitions of local communities. Such local initiatives have contributed to national prosperity. On the other hand, strong municipalities and local communities have been instrumental for implementing economic initiatives from the central government.

The state has also been responsive to locally- and regionally-based organizations related to the exploitation of national resources, like the co-operatives of farmers, fishermen and forest owners. Co-operative structures often function as an alternative to hierarchic organizations for taking care of economies of scale. In this way a relatively dispersed ownership of important natural resources has been maintained without too much loss of efficiency.

The broad public involvement in the economy, the decentralized structure of economic activity and strong intermediary organizations are some of the arguments for classifying the Norwegian economy as 'Democratic Capitalism'.[2] There are, however, additional arguments for such a label: Relative to many other industrialized countries, the Norwegian economy has been dominated by SMEs with limited economic power. As a consequence, the bourgeoisie's influence in the Norwegian society has been restricted. Many firms have been tightly embedded in their local communities – marked by a strong 'stakeholder' orientation. In most of the twentieth century the labour unions have had a fairly large influence both inside firms and in the economy as a whole.

Nature gives nothing for free! Accumulated knowledge, competencies and technological diffusion and innovations have been preconditions for the increasingly efficient exploitation and processing of most natural resources. The technological paradigms connected to the three industrial revolutions have all opened up new opportunities for value added refining and new forms of distribution of resource-based products. We divide this chapter into five periods, reflecting the interaction of the business system's institutional fabric on the one hand and the changing technological paradigms, with its succeeding three industrial revolutions, on the other. The periods are:

1. Merchant capitalism and the creation of a national business system, up to 1840
2. A classical liberal market economy facilitating the first industrial revolution, 1840–90
3. A contested liberal market economy striving with the second industrial revolution, 1890–1935
4. A co-ordinated market economy completing the second industrial revolution, 1935–70
5. Neo-liberal politics during a petroleum-fuelled, third industrial revolution, 1970–2007

All these periods gave some more or less lasting cultural, institutional and technological contribution to the evolving Norwegian democratic capitalism.

In addition to the business system theory of Richard Whitley mentioned in Chapter 1, this country chapter will draw on a parallel research tradition called 'varieties of capitalism'.[3] This tradition operates with only two main classes of business systems, 'liberal market economies' and 'co-ordinated market economies'. Co-ordinated market economies are characterized by co-operation between the different economic actors and a more active state. Market co-ordination is more extensive and the state is less interventionist in the liberal market economies. In this simple classification scheme, both Whitley's co-ordinated industrial district, the state-organized, collaborative and highly co-ordinated business systems are best classified as 'co-ordinated market economies'. What Whitley calls the compartmentalized and the fragmented business system are best classified as 'liberal market economies'.

As a way to underline the close relation between the main political ideologies and the business systems, the concept of 'political economic orders' is also used in this chapter. This concept designates the politically created parts of the business system – like laws, regulations and public organizations and authorities. Liberalism, social liberalism and social democracy have been three dominating ideologies, representing three 'hegemonic' orders, in Norway after 1840. A classical liberalist order dominated the period 1840–90. In this period it was a broad consensus within the dominant political strata that state intervention in the market should be very restricted. Markets should be created and extended, not restrained. A social liberal order, with some more focus on social welfare and the necessity to regulate markets, dominated from the early twentieth century until about 1920. The social democratic order, taking the welfare state and a rather extensive state and municipal participation in the economy for granted, had its culmination in the post-war years and until the 1980s. Thereafter, a neo-liberalist order gained prominence, underlining the virtues of deregulation, privatization and individualism. Between the periods with hegemonic order there have been years of instability and hard ideological struggle. For instance, during the 1930s communism, more hard-core socialism, fascism and religious conservatism were among the ideologies trying with more or less success to influence the political–economic order.

Up to 1840: merchant capitalism and the construction of a national business system

On 28 May 1767, the two Norwegian brothers Peter and Carsten Anker, eighteen and fifteen years old, and their tutor, the Norwegian student Andreas Holt, visited Professor Adam Smith in Glasgow. After a stimulating conversation, Smith wrote a greeting in the boys' diary: 'I shall always be happy to hear of the welfare & prosperity of three Gentlemen in whose conversation I have had so much pleasure, as in that of the two Messrs. Anchor & of their worthy Tutor Mr. Holt.'[4] After being in Glasgow, Carsten and Peter met their cousins from Oslo, Bernt (twenty-one) and Peder Anker (eighteen) in London. A 'grand tour' around Europe, often lasting several years, was at this time a regular part of the education of young men from the higher bourgeoisie – as the Anker brothers were.

In 1776, nine years after this meeting, Adam Smith published his book *An Inquiry into the Nature and Causes of the Wealth of Nations*, probably the most influential book on economics, but also on economic liberalism, ever written. Adam Smith and his writings contributed significantly to the turn from a mercantilist period of active state intervention to a long period of economic liberalism in Britain. In the Danish–Norwegian state, a network of businessmen and public officials, including the Anker brothers and their tutor Andreas Holt, was instrumental in establishing a more liberal political–economic regime.[5] Even more important for us, this upper-class network was decisive for the emergence of a Norwegian national business system: First, their extensive commercial activity contributed significantly to the development of a market economy and a market- and profit-oriented mentality in different regions of Norway. A critical mass of business activity was created, conducive for self-sustained economic growth. Secondly, they helped establish a set of nationally grounded organizations and institutions, making it valid to characterize the institutional configuration a *national* or *Norwegian* business system.

The Napoleonic Wars, the subsequent economic crisis and national conflicts, made the formative years of a liberal Norwegian business system last from the late seventeenth century until the early 1840s. As its creators, however, this liberal business system had deep roots in the mercantilist past.

The shifting balance of three economic layers
The French historian, Fernand Braudel, identifies three layers of economic activity in his account of the international economy, 1400–1800.[6] From the fourteenth century onwards Norwegian cities like Oslo (from 1814 the Norwegian capital and until 1924 called Christiania/Kristiania), Bergen and Trondheim became nodes in what Braudel called the upper, or third, layer of the international economy. This layer contained the expanding, profit-oriented and genuinely capitalist activity and transactions headed by wealthy merchants. Members of the Anker family located in Oslo and surrounding districts, were prominent participants in this layer, with timber trade and shipping as their main businesses. The British Navigation Act of 1651 had given incentives for Norwegian shipping by reserving the lumber export for British and Norwegian ships. The Norwegian progenitor of the family was the merchant Erik Olufsen Anker who came to Oslo from Sweden in the late seventeenth century. His grandson Christian Anker, the father of Bernt and Peder, was in the 1760s the biggest timber exporter in Oslo.

From the time of the Hansa in the thirteenth century, the merchants in Bergen were the main exporters of Norwegian fish – to a large extent delivered by fishermen from Northern Norway. The merchant families in Trondheim, most of them descending from the city of Flensburg, developed a more varied economic base, with fish, timber and but also products from copper and iron works as export items.

The resource base for export during these formative years of the market economy – timber, fish and minerals – have continued to be of importance up until today. The same goes for hydro power, being used by the timber exporting merchants' sawmills – with their waterwheels and single-bladed saws. There are also some institutional legacies from the establishment of the absolute monarchy, in 1660, not only the existence of a relatively strong state *per se*, but also what is called a *developmental* state. Depending on the customs duty from trade and on the economic and political support of the merchant aristocracy, the state actively tried to further trade and industry. From the 1730s, the commerce department (Kommersekollegiet) headed a mercantilist offensive, liberalizing internal trade and giving financial support, protective tariffs and privileges to selected industries and companies, like mining, glass, iron and copper works and shipping. Danish merchants and companies were granted most of the privileges, but iron, glass and salt were among the Norwegian products holding advantages on the Danish market. Members of the Anker family were engaged in both glass works and iron works.

During the second half of the eighteenth century the capitalist 'first layer' of the market economy expanded heavily. This strong growth in international trade stimulated the activity in Braudel's 'second layer' of local and regional markets. The money economy as a whole expanded strongly at the expense of the more self-sufficient 'third layer' of material life. The fisheries and timber export experienced a substantial increase in sales, benefiting from expansion in Great Britain. In the early nineteenth century, Bernt Anker was the richest man in Norway, at the peak, probably more than 20,000 people were in his service. The voluntary and compulsory work that the peasants did on the mercantilist glass, iron and copper works was another way the money and market economy found its way into agricultural society.[7] The Norwegian production of grain nearly doubled in the period 1723–1809. Until the middle of the century, most of the taxes and rents from the peasants had been delivered in agricultural products. From then on, there was a gradual change to money rents.

From Danish–Norwegian mercantilism to liberalism and Norwegian patriotism

The tutor of the Anker brothers, Andreas Holt, advanced to be the head of the Danish–Norwegian commerce department. One of his colleagues in this department, Franz Dræbye, had also been the tutor of two Norwegian brothers, Peter Collett and John (Johan) Collett, the sons of a rich relative of the Anker family, the merchant James Collett. Dræbye translated Adam Smith's *An Inquiry into the Nature and Causes of the Wealth of Nations* into Danish.[8] The translation and publication of Smith's book in 1779 seems to have been a joint project by Holt, Dræbye, the two Anker brothers Peter and Carsten and the Collett family. This event was only one sign of a broad change in the political–economic order, or the general and hegemonic conception of how the economy should be organized, a change from mercantilism to liberalism. The change was certainly inspired by the British example, but also by the problems mercantilist regulations had in coping with economic expansion. The Norwegian glassworks exemplify how the economic expansion nurtured by mercantilism was hampered by the same system. From 1741 several glassworks were established in Norway, supported and partly owned by the state, but regulated because it was given monopoly. As the demand for different types of glass increased, the price and quality regulations became obsolete and the works experienced big losses. In 1788 the monopoly and regulations ended, the import restrictions were withdrawn and it was decided to sell off the state's part in the works.[9]

The liberal momentum was somewhat slowed by the Napoleonic Wars (1799–1815) and by the crisis in Norway more than a decade after the wars. On the other hand, the war strengthened Norwegian patriotism. Christian and Bernt Anker went public with a strong support for a Norwegian university and an autonomous Norwegian bank. The university became operative in 1813, the bank had to wait to 1816. As a loser in the Napoleonic wars, Denmark had to surrender Norway to Sweden in 1814. After a short war, Norway accepted a personal union with Sweden under one king. It was at Carsten Anker's residence at Eidsvoll ironworks north of Oslo that a national assembly adopted a constitution and on 17 May 1814 declared independence; later, it was here that the Norwegian Parliament, the Storting, elected Karl XIII of Sweden as King of Norway, creating a union without an independent foreign office and with a governor (Stadtholder) in Norway appointed by the king. Bernt Anker's brother, Peder Anker became in 1814 the first Norwegian Prime Minister in Stockholm, and remained so until 1822.

The constitution of 1814 became the institutional backbone of the Norwegian business system, and was the most liberal and democratic constitution in Europe: no new and permanent restrictions on the freedom of commerce and industry would be tolerated. Compensation should be given in cases of expropriation and the freedom of expression was affirmed.

Photograph 11.1 **Peder Anker together with his wife and daughter. Anker was the Norwegian prime minister in Stockholm 1814–22.**
Source: Bogstad Manor.
Painter: Jens Juel.

Farmers, burghers and state officials had right to participate in the elections to the Storting – stimulating a participative civic society. One important clause in the Constitution, with a paradoxical effect in the long run, required that two-thirds of the members of the Storting were to be elected from rural counties, and one-third from the cities. This so-called 'peasant paragraph' was meant to ensure an appropriate representation for the relatively small urban population. With urbanization, it had the effect of overrepresenting the periphery and rural districts at the expense of the urban centres, partly explaining the long-standing political power of the Norwegian periphery.

One of the most prominent members of the small Norwegian nobility, Herman Wedel Jarlsberg, was appointed Minister of Finance in 1814. He was part of the Anker network, married to Prime Minister Peder Anker's daughter. Wedel Jarlsberg fronted the establishment of an autonomous and stable monetary and financial system. The Bank of Norway was decided upon by the Storting in 1816, and after a hard deflationary period until 1842 the Norwegian speciedaler was pegged to silver at par. Creating a stable currency was a tough job, but decisive for Norway being accepted as an independent state and a trustworthy trade partner in the long run.

Catching-up the lost years, altering the social formation

The Anker network only represented a spearhead in the creation of an independent Norwegian business system. The whole country was mobilized for the new nation, if for nothing else, at least by financing the necessary institutions and bearing the economic consequences of a long period of deflation. Decisive for the consolidation of the new state was the gradual restoration of the economy after the Napoleonic Wars. This catching-up with lost years also implied changes in the country's social structure, having lasting consequences for the structure of the business system.

The Anker family and the merchant aristocracy suffered serious losses, first because of the British blockade during the Napoleonic Wars and later due to the prohibitive import duties on Norwegian timber and the international recession after the wars. Most of the old merchant aristocracy collapsed and their properties were appropriated, thereby strengthening the egalitarian social structure. In 1823 even Carsten Anker at Eidsvoll went bankrupt. Peder Anker was one of the few merchants that only just avoided a catastrophe. The revival of international trade in the 1840s and the British reduction of customs duties from 1842 benefited a more modest layer of merchants and capitalists. The hierarchies and established international networks of the merchant houses were to some extent replaced by more market-based economic relations.

In 1836 Herman Wedel Jarlsberg was appointed as governor, but he died in 1840. His death symbolized the end of an era, of the influence both of the Anker network and the already marginal nobility. Creation of new noble titles was forbidden by the constitution of 1814, and the last legal privileges were dissolved by the parliament in 1821, to expire upon the deaths of their then holders.

Alongside the dissolution of the top economic and social positions, parts of the lower strata in society experienced an improvement in their position. The fisheries were the most vital part of the economy during the first decades of the nineteenth century and the most important earner of foreign currency, stimulated by a growing European population. About 80 per cent of the catches, mostly cod and herring, were exported. The livelihood of that large part of the coastal population who combined mostly subsistence farming with fishing, increased. The main resource base, the coastal fisheries made possible by the warm Gulf Stream, had a 'democratic' character: small investments were needed to participate both in the main season fisheries and the day-to-day fishing close to home. Boats and equipment were often owned and used by a boat team, several boat teams making up a rural hamlet. Traditionally, the fishermen in northern and western Norway depended on the big exporters in Bergen to have their catch distributed to the European market, and to some extent on the local 'væreier' who owned the local stores and the shacks that the fishermen had to use during the seasonal fisheries. But the exporter and the væreier also depended on the fishermen, offering them the necessary credit for buying boats and equipment and providing commodities such as grain, spices, tobacco and spirits. The local co-operation among the coastal peasant fishermen produced a social capital that was useful in many economic contexts, but also in politics and other organizational efforts.

The capability for local co-operation among the peasants had roots back to the peasant communalism of the middle ages. Aspects of the property structure and ways of farming created both individualism and collectiveness. In many locations, the open field system and strip farming made co-operation between the peasants necessary. At the same time, in comparison with most of Europe, Denmark, Sweden and Norway had a high proportion of freeholders, and moderate economic and personal demands on the tenants. From the late sixteenth and most of the seventeenth century, the Norwegian aristocracy barely exceeded 100 people out of a population of 440,000. In Denmark, the aristocracy constituted ten times that proportion in the mid-seventeenth century – still a modest share compared with many other European regions. At this time, about 8 per cent of the land rent was in the hands of the Norwegian aristocracy, in Denmark the aristocracy took 44 per cent of the rent.[10] The selling out of crown lands after 1660 resulted in a first wave of transition to peasant proprietorship until 1750. During the absolute monarchy after 1660, the nobility of Denmark–Norway was also substantially diminished, while the Swedish nobility maintained their strength through the eighteenth century. The market economy was both stimulated by and stimulated the increase in freeholds. Around 1800 about 75 per cent of the farmers were freeholders. A Land Act of 1821, strongly supported by the peasant members of the Storting, resulted in the sale of most of the remaining church and crown land to the peasants. In the 1840s, the percentage of freeholders had increased to about 80. The average freehold was very small, but there were often alternative means of income from fisheries, forests, shipping and the mining industry. These alternatives forced the peasants to take strategic decisions on how to distribute their labour, an important part of making autonomous citizens.

A law from 1754, renewed in 1816, placed some restrictions on the freedom of the lower classes to migrate. Adult males were required to seek annual employment or risked being prosecuted as vagabonds or beggars. The law was repealed in 1854, but had for long been of limited practical importance.

Democracy was strengthened significantly by the introduction of local democracy in 1837, a democratic reform far ahead of both the continental and the other Nordic countries. The new municipal assemblies developed as instruments for political, economic and administrative local co-operation. Initiatives to establish savings banks and mutual insurance societies were also expressions of the capabilities for local co-operation, often interacting with activities in the municipal assemblies.

The decades from the last part of the eighteenth century up until the 1840s were the formative years of a Norwegian national business system. The institutional configuration of this business system was liberal in character. From the 1840s, the liberal ideal of government was broadly accepted, and this ideological hegemony paved the way for further liberal reforms in the following decades. This liberal system represented the first phase in the development of Norwegian 'Democratic Capitalism'.

One of the main achievements of the first half of the nineteenth century was the building up of a state administration with competent state officials, or *embetsmenn*. During the 1830s a new generation of public officials, educated professionals and artists emerged, ready to take over the leading role of the national modernization project that the Ankers and Wedel Jarlsberg had left. A developmental state with an ongoing modernization project was a lasting inheritance from the mercantilist era, and the establishing of the Interior Department in 1842 represented the main modernizing ambition of what is called the '*embetsmannsstaten*'.

A classical liberal market economy facilitating the first industrial revolution, 1840–90

In 1844 two young Norwegians accidentally met in Manchester. Both the twenty-eight-year-old shopkeeper Adam Hiorth and the one-year-younger shop assistant Knud Graah visited this British centre of modern textile industry to learn about prices, functions, quality and operations of textile machinery. Two years later, Hiorth was the factory manager of Nydalen Mill and Graah was the factory manager of Vøien Mill, both newly established and located by the Aker River close to Oslo. In the following years, the waterfalls of the Aker River were heavily utilized as power sources for modern textile factories, mechanical workshops and other industrial undertakings. The main ingredients of the British industrial revolution were introduced to a new corner of Europe.

The emerging liberal business system made it easier for entrepreneurs such as Hiorth and Graah to achieve economic success. They could import and export with gradually lower tariffs. The overland trade with Sweden was duty-free from 1827, while goods transported by sea paid half the normal duties. By the early 1870s, Norway had adopted completely free trade. A liberal Industry Act of 1839 opened a more competitive market for all sorts of crafts, being further strengthened by amendments in 1866 and 1874. This made it easier for the new industry to get the skilled services they needed. The gradual liberalization of retail trade started in 1842 and was completed by 1868, followed by liberalization of the wholesale trade in 1882. This made it easier to for industry to have its products sold all over the country. In the first decades of industrialization there were few regulations on work conditions, and no labour unions seeking shorter working hours at higher wages. It was a golden era for business in general.

Appropriating the technology of the first industrial revolution

The Anker brothers had actively promoted British liberalist ideas about politics and institutions. People like Hiorth and Graah became promoters of the British technology of the first industrial revolution. Like the Anker brothers, they were part of a broader network actively communicating technological knowledge and the gospel of industrial modernization. Hiorth and Graah were members of the Technical Society founded in 1847 and the Polytechnic Society founded in 1852. Both organizations were expressions of an emerging civil society, a vital element in the broader mobilization of social and human capital for economic growth. Industrialists, craftsmen, merchants, but also high-ranking civil servants, participated in these organizations. The separation of private business and public affairs had been more clearly drawn within the new liberal 'Rechtsstaat', but important ingredients of mercantilism survived. Leading state officials saw it as their duty actively to support economic growth and modernization.

The initiatives of the industrial entrepreneurs symbolized the coming of a new technological, economic and social era. Technologically, it brought the *machine* into the world of production. The early spinning and weaving machines were powered by steam engines and water turbines. This change from manual to mechanized production brought productive work from families to factories. The factory was the most significant social invention of the first industrial revolution. The assembly of many workers in one place, having more or less the same hard working and living conditions, disciplined by the rhythm of the machines and the command of the capitalist, created the social foundation for a new social force: the industrial working class. The factory became a standard of reference for many social organizations, be it schools, prisons, or hospitals.

These early industrial initiatives had their prerequisites not only in the British industrial revolution but also in the general growth of the Norwegian economy. Working in shops in Christiania, Adam Hiorth and Knud Graah had first-hand knowledge of the main urban market in Norway. Intimately following the fast-growing textile market certainly gave incentives for initiatives and investment decisions. People connected to internal commerce and trade was among the most important entrepreneurs in the new textile industry. Table 11.1 shows the increasing import of cotton and wool manufactures between 1830 and 1845. As in many other consumer markets, there was an opening for substituting import by domestic production.

Some less advanced and smaller textile factories had already been established in the late eighteenth century. 'Enigheten' ('Unity') was one example, established with mercantilist support in the 1780s in Stor-Elvdal. It soon went bankrupt. Haldens Bomuldspinderi og Væveri established in 1815 close to the town of Halden had severe problems in the early years, but managed from the 1840s, when the market for textiles was more developed, to be profitable. The Solberg Spinning Mill, established in 1818 close to the city of Drammen, also survived after some difficulties. The Solberg Mill was

Table 11.1 **Imports of cotton and wool manufactures to Norway '1830–45' (tons)**

Year	Cotton	Wool
1830	90	93
1835	136	138
1840	187	151
1845	375	229

Source: Central Bureau of Statistics, 'Historical Statistics', Oslo (1978), pp. 276–7.

founded by Hans Nilsen Hauge, an influential revivalist and a controversial lay preacher, imprisoned several times. Hauge founded numerous factories and mills on his travels around the country, preaching modesty, honesty and hard work. Even more important, several of his followers and people from communities heavily influenced by his preaching later became industrial entrepreneurs. Like the glass and iron works and mining industries established during the mercantilist period, these early initiatives, close to what have been called proto-industrialization, created some sort of preparedness facilitating the 'take-off' from the 1840s.

The increasing importance of textiles and other commodities reflected an increasing population, economic growth and a slow but ongoing urbanization. From the end of the 1830s, the country experienced more stable economic growth. The growing size and purchasing power of the home market also invigorated a lot of small-scale, often manually driven factories or manufacture. Fritz Heinrich Frølich founded the bank Christiania Creditkasse in 1848; he also fabricated hairpins, Eau de Cologne, walking sticks, wallpaper, toys, suspenders, belts, matches, etc. His building was known as Noah's Ark.

The continued industrialization in the period 1840–90 was both stimulated by and contributed to high economic growth. GDP *per capita* increased by 118 per cent, the population expanded from 1.2 to 2.0 million, of which 24 per cent lived in towns or cities. This strong population growth came despite extensive emigration. In 1895, Nydalen Compagnie was Norway's largest factory, with about 1000 employees. The canvas producer Christiania Sailcloth factory had 558 and Halden Bomuldspinderi og Væveri 376 employees. The textile industry produced consumer goods for the domestic markets. Among the companies ranking high on this list were also producers of capital goods, mechanical works like machine shops and shipyards. Among them were Nyland Verksted (822 employees), Bergen Mek. Verksted (490), Trondhiem Mek. Verksted (434), Aker Mek. Verksted (464) and Myren Mek. Verksted (365). The first mechanical workshops of any significance started in the 1840s, but they were only gradually becoming a decisive tool for Norwegian industrialization.

The birth of mechanical engineering

It was the British, not the domestic machine shops that supplied the early textile industries with machinery for spinning and weaving. In 1843 the prohibition on the export of machinery from Britain was repealed. This was a new opportunity for Norwegian entrepreneurs to import, but also a

Photograph 11.2 **Nydalen Compagnie was established in 1845. This picture is from the early 1960s.**
Source: Oslo Municipal City Archive.

favourable chance for British firms to market their own products and competence in other countries. The historian Christine Bruland considers the early Norwegian textile industrialization to be 'not so much an imitation as an *extension* of British developments'.[11] The Norwegian entrepreneurs imported 'technological packages'. The British engineering firms provided machinery, technical information, ancillary equipment and construction expertise, and they recruited some skilled British operative workers and supervisors.

Despite this, there was some obvious need for mechanical expertise and workshops close to the new textile industries, for repairs, adjustments and smaller deliveries. When Adam Hiorth and his investors started the production of textiles at Nydalen Compagnie in 1847, they used water turbines as their source of power. As a power reserve, however, Aker's Mechanical Works delivered a steam engine.

Aker's mechanical workshop later became one of the main engineering enterprises and shipyards in Norway. The company had some interesting historical roots. Even if the mercantilist ambition to establish manufacturing enterprises did not create any conspicuous results, some trajectories of experience and competence turned out to be useful. The main entrepreneur behind Aker's foundation in 1841 was the thirty-two-year-old marine officer, Peter Severin Steenstrup. His father, Paul Steenstrup, had been educated at the Norske Berg-Seminarium in the city of Kongsberg. The seminary was one of the first mining schools in Europe, established in 1747, and provided the first higher technical education in Norway. The seminary was closely connected to the silver mines at Kongsberg. These mines had a history back to 1624 and were owned by the state from 1683. In 1770 close to 4000 people were engaged in this mining industry and Kongsberg was the second largest city in Norway, after Bergen. Paul Steenstrup was instrumental in building up the state-owned Kongsberg Weapons Factory in 1814 (later one of Norway's main technology firms, today Kongsberg Gruppen). His son, Peter Severin Steenstrup, had no formal technical education, but grew up in Norway's most technology-oriented environment. Steenstrup's co-founder, Stephanus Bronn, had been chief engineer on the ship *Constitutionen* when Steenstrup was the ship's captain. Bronn was the son of the first technical manager at the Kongsberg Weapons Factory.

Another important mechanical works, also situated by the Aker River, was Myren's mechanical workshop. The workshop was founded by the brothers and mechanics Andreas and Jens Jacob Jensen in 1848 as a blacksmith's workshop. The two brothers also had their background in Kongsberg, where their father was a millwright. Shortly after they had established their workshop they started to construct turbines. From the mid-century turbines replaced the waterwheels as a power technology, and this made the exploitation of Norway's hydro power resources more efficient. Norway lacked one main core input of the industrial revolution: coal. Even if coal could be imported from Britain and transported relatively cheap as return freight and ballast on Norwegian ships, which made the efficient use of hydro power even more important.

In constructing their first turbines, the Jensen brothers co-operated with Oluf N. Roll, the first Norwegian civil engineer, who had graduated from the technical college of Hannover in Germany. During the second half of nineteenth century the German technical colleges became the main supplier of higher education for Norwegian civil engineers. A Norwegian polytechnic college was not established until 1910 in Trondheim. A more practical-oriented engineering education was, however, begun in 1855 in connection with the naval yard at Horten. In the 1870s, schools that gave elementary technical education were established in Trondheim (1870), Oslo (1873) and Bergen (1875).

The forest-based industry: from sawmills to pulp and paper

The Myren workshop gradually developed into a competent engineering firm, especially good at producing water turbines. From the 1860s, the fast-expanding wood processing industry needed turbines, but they also needed other sorts of machines, making up an attractive market for the newly formed domestic machine shops. The sawmill industry was boosted from 1842 after the British Parliament reduced the customs duty on foreign timber, and continued to reduce it until it was removed in 1860. In general, a substantial part of Europe developed in these years into a low-tariff area.

The boom put pressure on one of the last relics of mercantilism, the sawmill privileges of 1688. In 1818 farmers had been given right to saw and export timber from their own forest, and by 1849 there were 2831 sawmills without privileges, but there were still 712 privileged sawmills left. In 1860 these last privileges were removed. In 1838, Norway exported 894,000 m^2 of sawn timber to England: in 1873, the export to Britain peaked at 2,230,000 m^2 of timber.

During the second half of the eighteenth century, several value added processes redefined the forest industry. The change from waterwheels to water turbines had importance for sawmills; but the closeness to timber resources and to harbours was even more decisive for the sawmills' economy than cheap waterpower. The steam engine made it possible to locate sawmills independent of waterfalls: it could use waste from the mills as fuel, and it made possible the use of the most modern sawing and planing machinery. The introduction of planing machinery and the thin, circular blade during the second half of the nineteenth century together helped making sawmills and planing mills the most important industry. From 1860 to 1890 the employment in the sawmills and planing mills increased from 4,090 to 13,720 workers. In the districts west and southwest of Oslo fjord, the resources of big timber were being exhausted. The centre of gravity of the sawmills moved to the towns of Fredrikstad, Halden and Sarpsborg. The sawmills and planing mills in this area could handle timber floated down Glomma, Norway's largest and longest river with widespread forests nearby.

The removal of the sawmills' privileges and the 'steam revolution' also made it feasible to exploit the rich forest resources in Namdalen, the valley region in the northern part of Mid-Norway, in the county of North Trøndelag. A growing number of sawmills were established from the 1850s in and around the town of Namsos.

The mechanical works and engineering firms like Myren, Kværner Brug, Nyland Værksted and the Thune mechanical works made good business by supplying machinery to the wood-processing industries. Myren supplied most of the machinery and equipment that the pioneering entrepreneur

J. N. Jacobsen needed when first setting up his steam mill outside Fredrikstad in 1860 and his planing mill in 1863. J.N. Jacobsen was one of the many businessmen connected to the forest industry migrating from the Drammen district to the Fredrikstad area.

The new capital-intensive sawmills and planing mills moved the resource-based industry away from being a simple and mere raw material-producing activity. After some mistakes in the 1860s, manufacturing mechanical pulp became a new way of adding value to the forest resources in the following two decades. Mechanical pulp was input for the European paper factories, serving a fast-expanding market for newspapers. In the 1870s twenty-five pulp mills were established, among them companies that have dominated the wood-processing industry into our own millennium, like Union Co. in Skien and Follum Co. Ltd near Hønefoss, north of Oslo. Another twenty-five factories were started in the next decade, many of the on the Drammen and Skien rivers, utilizing the smaller dimension of timber not useful for sawmills and the waterpower and turbines to operate the heavy machinery. The Norwegian mechanical works and engineering firms were not only able to supply the export-oriented Norwegian factories with necessary machines; firms like Kværner Brug and Myren themselves developed into advanced exporters of machinery for the wood-processing industry.

The communication revolution

The forest-based industry did not only stimulate the machine-producing engineering industry. The second half of the nineteenth century experienced a communication revolution with some obvious and strong connection to the needs for the transport of timber, boards and pulp.

Floating down the rivers was a traditional way of transporting timber and was still important until the late 1950s when motor vehicles gradually took over. During the nineteenth century the state took several measures to make rivers more suitable for the floating of timbers. Through its canal administration the state also opened some rivers for smaller steamships. The administration of the rivers, and the financing of these different undertakings, was carried out in close co-operation with local organizations like the floating-associations and associations of the industrial users of waterfalls (brukseierforeninger). The floating associations were co-operatives of forest owners organizing the floating of timber down the rivers.

More ambitious plans for canals were overtaken by the coming of the railways. The first public railway in Norway, the 68 km long 'Hovedbanen' between Oslo and Eidsvoll, opened in 1854. The main purpose of the railway was to freight lumber over lake Mjøsa to the capital. The railway was constructed by British engineers, and the financing was divided between British investors and the Norwegian government. The transport of lumber made the railway highly profitable, and the transport of lumber was also used as one of the main justification for the opening of other railway lines. The state gradually took full control over the administration of the railways. Local communities lobbied strongly for new tracks, and normally municipalities and local interest groups also had to contribute some of the capital for new railway investments. The same principle of central and local co-operation was implemented in the building of other infrastructure, like the building and maintenance of roads. The gradual development of roads, harbours and lighthouses began in the first half of the century.

The railway operated its own telegraph, but in 1855, the first public telegraph lines, built and operated by the governmental Telegraph Administration, opened between Oslo and Drammen. In the most industrialized, eastern part of Norway, the interests of the wood-processing industry gave one of the main arguments for a further extension of the telegraph network. From the start, however, the national telegraph stations were connected to the fast-expanding international network. The international connection made the telegraph an excellent tool for all export and import firms, but especially for the growing, internationally-oriented shipping industry. During most of the nineteenth century, shipping contributed even more to Norwegian export than the timber trade and wood-processing industry. From the start, the timber trade also formed the basis for the expansion of the shipping industry. As part of the kingdom, Norwegian sailing vessels could transport a substantial part of the timber exported from Sweden.

From the 1840s, the general liberalization of international trade, and especially the abolition of the British Navigation Act in 1849, allowed Norwegian ships to engage in international trade, no longer being solely dependent upon Norwegian export and import. A major source of earning was the transportation of timber between other countries – for instance, between Canada and Britain. In 1850 the Norwegian merchant fleet was the world's fourth largest, in 1890, the third largest, surpassed only by Britain and US. International trade was stimulated by the introduction of the monetary Gold Standard system in the economically advanced countries. Norway and the other Nordic countries joined the Gold Standard in 1875.

The southern part of Norway played a dominant role in the shipping industry. The ownership and financing of the vessels reflected both the modest investments necessary to build and equip a ship, but also the capabilities for local co-operation. The vessels were often owned by a partnership consisting of local merchants, the future captain of the vessel and the peasants who provided timber for building the ship. In 1841 about 14,000 workers were employed in the merchant fleet. In 1890 the number was 58,200. In 1841 all the 2509 vessels were sailing vessels, except for 11 paddle steamers. In 1890 the fleet had grown to 7432 vessels, 672 of them steam vessels. The transition from sail and tree to steam and iron went slowly in Norway compared to the other leading shipping nations. The tonnage of sailing vessels reached its peak only in 1890; the cheap transport offered by cheap, often old sailing vessels, still had an economic rationality in some freights.

The fisheries

After the forest industry and shipping, the fisheries were the third largest export sector. About 80 per cent of the catch was exported. From 1866 to 1890 the export value of fish products doubled in absolute figures, even if its share of total commodity export went down from 47 to 36 per cent. The seasonal cod and herring fisheries at the coast from Lindesnes in the far south to Finnmark in the far north were the most important. Between 12 and 15 per cent of the total workforce were engaged in these seasonal fisheries. The fisheries east of Lindesnes, at the eastern part of southern Norway, only took a very small part of the total catches.

The traditional cod products – the klippfisk (split, salted and dried cod) and the dried stockfish – remained important throughout the period. The takings of herring fluctuated more between the years. In the late 1870s the herring temporary disappeared from part of the west coast, resulting in an increased emigration to the US from some fishing districts. The seasonal character of the fisheries made it hard to be a full-time fisherman, and fisheries were most often combined with farming.

Until 1890, there were only a few significant technological changes in the fisheries. The Telegraph Administration's early introduction of the 'fishing telegraph' made it possible to quickly inform the fishermen where the fish was located. As part of the liberalization efforts, in 1857 the cod fisheries in Lofoten were opened to all sorts of equipment, but until the 1870s the traditional coastal fisheries were totally dominant. Bigger sailing vessels with decks, and then even some steam vessels, made it possible first to fish on the nearby banks, and gradually on the open ocean. This movement was facilitated by the government-financed surveys of the coastal waters and the publishing of new nautical maps, but also the considerable investments in lighthouses along the coast. In the 1880s, some steamers from the towns like Haugesund, Bergen and Ålesund, using efficient trawl-nets, challenged the traditional use of sailing vessels and hand lines.

The canning industry evolved first in the west coast city of Stavanger in the late 1870s. The pioneer was the 'canning king' Christian Bjelland who made an excellent profit by exporting smoked sprat and other small herring varieties. Norwegian sardines became and international brand name. The pharmacist Peter Møller from Oslo was another entrepreneur, inventing a new way of distilling cod liver oil from cod liver in the 1850s. The oil was rich in vitamins A and D and export rose from 10 million l in 1866 to 236 million l in 1890.

Agriculture: the most important but not fastest-growing
Agriculture maintained its position as the most important sector during the whole nineteenth century. Employment in agriculture increased until the 1850s, and then decreased. In the fifteen years from 1875 to 1890 it fell from 421,000 to 389,000. Of all 828,000 'gainfully employed' in 1890, 47 per cent were employed in agriculture; the next largest group, industry and crafts, employed 22 per cent.

Agriculture was, however, not the main contributor to economic growth. In 1845 it contributed to 27 per cent of GDP, in 1910, the share had fallen to 13 per cent. In contrast especially to Denmark, but also to several other European countries, the export of products from farming was negligible. Nor did the quality of the arable land give any capital gains that could be transferred to and invested in other industries. Only the transfer of people, as both labour in the expanding sectors and as emigrants, was substantial.

Even so, productivity in agriculture increased. The total production of grains and peas increased from 166 tons in 1835 to 328 tons in 1890, almost a doubling of production. The production of potatoes increased even more. Horse-driven machinery, like the mowing machine, better ploughs, harrows and rakes, replaced human labour. Most machinery was imported, but some engineering and blacksmiths' workshops started copying foreign products. In 1879, Ole Gabriel Kverneland built a small forge to manufacture scythes in the village of Kvernaland near Stavanger. By way of mass production, he managed to produce 7000–8000 scythes annually. Later he expanded production to small ploughs and other equipment. Today, Kverneland ASA is one of the world's leading producers of farming machinery.[12] Other industrial linkages to agriculture were the commercial flour mills being established from the 1860s. Vaksdal Mill, established in 1873 by the patrician Gjerdt Meyer from Bergen, was one example. The mill took advantage of cheap energy from a local waterfall, and became later the largest flour mill in Scandinavia.

Central to the modernization and transformation of agriculture from the mid-century, was a new focus on animal husbandry. From the late 1870s, Norwegian farmers strongly felt the competition from low-priced Russian, East European and American grain. Between 1850 and 1890, the import of grain increased five times, from meeting 30 per cent to covering two-thirds of the demand. The railways and steamships made the transport of grain cheaper. At the same time, the railway and better inland and coastal transportation also made it easier for peasants to transport dairy products to urban areas. The new attention to animal husbandry did not primarily mean more cows, but more milk yield per cow. From 1865 to 1890 the annual yield per cow rose from 981 kg to 1210 kg. Another expression of the new priority of dairy farming was the breakthrough of dairies. In 1860 only six dairies were registered; in 1890 the number was 308.

In accordance with the general pattern of modernization, the progress of agriculture was the result of a multilevel co-operation. Economic sectors had their own 'modernization regimes', reflecting both features of the national business system and its specific institutional and technological characteristics. Most Norwegian economic enterprises were small scale compared with the economic units of other European nations, and this was especially true in agriculture. In his account of the Norwegian farm, Fritz Hodne sums up: 'The size of holdings in Norway was ridiculously small by European and American standards.'[13] The same was true when compared with Sweden and Denmark. In 1865 about 58 per cent of all farms were only 5 ha or less, while 25 per cent were less than 2 ha.[14] During the next decades the share of small farms even increased somewhat. The Norwegian 'odel' or allodial institution protected family ownership of farms. It was supported by the constitution and prevented arable land from being a commercial commodity. It also created barriers to prevent the merger of farms into larger units.

Part of the diseconomies of small scale could be compensated by co-operation. Different forms of common ownership had in many districts made co-operation and collective working a necessity. An enclosure movement during the eighteenth and early nineteenth century was pushed forward by an Enclosure Act in 1857. By 1900 most cultivated land had been re-apportioned and collected into individual units. In 1840 the value of the freehold farms was 81 per cent of the total farm value, increasing to 91 per cent in 1890. The mixture of collectivism and individualism arising from the traditional organization of production became an important resource in the operation of local institutions such as municipal administration, savings banks, mutual insurance associations and dairies. Larger distilleries were also mostly organized as co-operatives. All these local institutions became instruments for furthering local entrepreneurship and modernization.

The local ambitions were supported by the government. A state-owned mortgage bank, Norges Hypotekbank, was established to supply farmers with credit in 1851. In 1854 the Storting decided to establish an agricultural institute and school at Ås, south-east of Oslo. In 1877 a directorate of agriculture was established under the dynamic director-general Jonas Smitt, educated at the school at Ås.

An uneven development

During the period 1840–90 Norway, together with many other nations, took advantage of the technology and the new organizational forms connected to what we in Chapter 1 call the first and second 'Kondratiev waves'. Norway, however, was among the fastest-growing nations. For instance, according to new estimates, the Norwegian GDP *per capita* increased significantly more than the Swedish from the 1830s to the 1870s.[15] A proposed explanation for this has been the differences in natural resources:

> During the first period from the 1830s to the 1870s, Norway exploited fish resources far better than in earlier centuries. In addition, the export of timber and the utilization of the closeness to the coast by the merchant fleet increased significantly ... On the other hand, Sweden had timber, but not fish. Not being an equal maritime power to Norway also made them lag behind in this service industry, taking advantage of the plentiful Scandinavian, and in particular Norwegian resource, the ocean.[16]

Differences in natural resources are, however, probably only part of the explanation. The differences in social capital and the capability of local participation and co-operation might, however, also be of importance. Sweden was a society of more large-scale and hierarchical social units – a form of social capital more fit to meet the challenges of the third and fourth 'Kondratiev wave', or the second industrial revolution.

Most industrializing countries experienced a structural crisis of adjustment from the early 1870s and into the 1890s. Established technologies and ways of doing things were outstripped by newer innovations. Some of these innovations represented the emerging second industrial revolution. Enterprises established during the first industrial revolution gradually met harder competition and falling prices, because of the ongoing liberalization, the improvement of infrastructure and the international standardization of measures: weight, length and time.

A contested liberal market economy striving with the second industrial revolution, 1890–1935

'The big accomplishments in the field of electricity that scientific research in the later years has achieved, seem definitely to point to that our land with her innumerable waterfalls, of which barely a fraction is exploited, has the conditions for an industrial development, where mechanical work is required, as no other nation in Europe.'[17] This quote is taken from a letter the young member of the Storting, Gunnar Knudsen, formally sent to the Storting in 1892. Knudsen proposed that the state should actively engage itself in the hydro power business. He wanted the government to buy attractive waterfalls partly for electrifying the state-owned railways and partly to have them sold to industrial enterprises at reasonable prices. Knudsen feared that the waterfalls would be objects of speculation, resulting in high prices and reducing the utilization of hydro power for industrial and economic development.

Educated as an engineer, Gunnar Knudsen was a dynamic private and public entrepreneur, active in many businesses, from agriculture to shipping and industry. He represented the Liberal Party and was Prime Minister from 1908 to 1910 and from 1913 to 1920. On the private as well as the municipal and the governmental level he pioneered the use of hydro power for producing electricity. In 1885 he built a small hydro power station in his wood-processing factory, Laugstol Brug. This station became the first public utility in Norway, supplying electricity for lighting to the people on the outskirts of the town of Skien. In 1912 he was the initiator of the inter-municipal utility, Skienfjordens Kommunale Kraftselskap, owned by three municipalities in the county of Telemark. First of all, he wanted the state to ensure that the hydro power resources benefited the whole of society. In addition, to promote the appropriate laws and regulations, Knudsen, as we shall see, took initiatives to have the state directly engage in electricity production. But first, let us consider the years 1890–1935 more broadly.

Growth and crisis within a contested business system

The period 1890–1935 is close to what we in Chapter 1 called the time of the 'third technological paradigm' or the third 'Kondratiev wave'. It also represents the formative years of the second industrial revolution. Electrification was the main new technology introduced and implemented in this period, but other science-based products and processes in, for instance, chemicals and metallurgy, also had a decisive influence. Steel was the revolutionary material of the period. Electricity networks, steel railways, steel ships and the new telephone networks were innovations in infrastructure.

Internationally, the years from 1890 to 1918 represented an upswing based on investment in these technologies, while the two following decades saw severe economic problems and turbulence – because of speculative investment and overinvestment in the new businesses and failure for many of the traditional sectors. Norway remained neutral during the First World War (1914–18), but the war stimulated speculation, especially in shipping investments. It also increased the regulatory ambitions of the government.

From the 1890s, the Liberal Party had the political initiative in Norwegian politics. The party represented the majority of the peasants and parts of the radical urban middle class, while the Conservative Party mainly represented the powerful group of civil servants and some vested economic interests. The Liberal Party was both anti-unionist and socially radical, and during the period until 1920 the party challenged the business system of classical liberalism. The first tampering with liberalist principles was some moderate tariff protection implemented in 1897 and 1905. After an impressive growth of private telephone companies in the cities, the state granted itself formal monopoly of all electric communication in 1899; private telephone associations and companies had to get a concession from the state to operate. Laws on labour protection were decided upon in 1892, 1909 and 1915. Accident insurance for factory workers was implemented from 1895. The most far-reaching regulations were, as we shall see, related to the exploitation of natural resources, regulations that had a definite national stamp. The nationalism of the time was strengthened by the struggle for full independence from Sweden, and the tension between the two nations increased during the 1890s. On 7 June 1905, the union was dissolved by what Swedish newspapers called a *coup d'état*. In November the same year, after a majority had voted for a monarchy instead of a republic, the Danish prince Carl became the king of Norway, taking Haakon VII as his new name.

Both the state and the municipalities actively engaged in initiatives that supported economic growth. A primary school law from 1889 and a law on secondary schools in 1896 extended and modernized education. A national agricultural college was established in 1897, and at last, a higher technical college opened in Trondheim in 1910. Among the main modernizing contributions by the municipalities were the expansion of savings banks and investment in local infrastructures, such as ports, roads, primary schools and electrification. In 1891, the world's most northern city, Hammerfest, established the first municipal-owned electricity utility in the country and an impressive mostly municipally-based electrification followed in the next three decades. Democracy was extended when women got the right to vote at the municipal elections in 1910 and universal suffrage in 1913.

The period 1890–20 was a formative period of a social liberal political–economic order, or what might be seen as the politically created parts of the business system. The social aspects of this order were also due to the growing support for the Labour Party, founded in 1887. It was represented at the Storting in 1912: the Labour Party got 26 per cent of the vote and became a radical challenge to the established order. The combination of high growth rates and sharp price increases during the First World War radicalized the Labour Party, which became one of the most left-wing labour parties in Europe.

1920–35 were years of political and economic turbulence, with the newly established order being contested both from right and left. The case chapter on Christiania Bank (Chapter 13) gives the main lines of the dramatic bank and financial crisis after 1920. The financial situation of the central government was near to a catastrophe because of the unhealthy spending of Gunnar Knudsen and his government – among other things, the purchase of a large power station in Glomfjord in the county of Nordland, which experienced heavy losses during the inter-war years. The economic downturn made it impossible for many municipalities to gain sufficiently income from their heavy investments in electrical utilities, which burdened them with large debts.

In the 1920s, the central bank's effort to restore the Gold Standard that had been abolished at the beginning of the war created a deflation that worsened the situation for many firms. Unemployment rose, and strikes and lock-outs damaged the relation between employers and workers. The international turmoil after the Wall Street Crash in October 1929 worsened the situation. Despite all these problems, GDP *per capita* rose by 38 per cent from 1920 to 1935. This was less than the 45 per cent growth from 1905 to 1920, but still a substantial increase. It is time to look at the realities behind these figures.

The dual character of Norwegian hydro power

With an average elevation of a little less than 500 m combined with an abundance of precipitation in critical areas, the theoretical energy potential of Norway's 4000 river systems is about 600 TWh/year. Two-thirds of the country is mountainous and large areas are suited for storing water by damming to moderate heights. In 2007, about 205 TWh/year of the hydro power potential was calculated as being technically and financially available (of which 119 TWh/year was already developed).[18]

The physical structure of the hydro power resources set the conditions for its utilization. Much of western Norway has a mean annual precipitation of 3000–3500 mm and many high mountain plateaux with steep slopes towards the ocean. Developing the big waterfalls in areas like this demands high investments, centralized organization and complex engineering work on large-scale power stations.

On the other hand, the generally short distance from watershed to sea leaves a large number of smaller watercourses, many of them short and steep. As a consequence, there are waterfalls favourable for more modest, small-scale development with standardized technological solutions near most population centres.

Technologies for electric power production and transmission were among the main science-based innovations of the third 'Kondratiev wave', or the first part of the second industrial revolution. The dual structure of the waterfalls were reflected in the dual character of the economic sectors taking advantage of this new energy carrier – placed within two different types of economic circuits of knowledge. One was mainly based on the established configurations of the business system; the other challenged and changed some of these structures. Let us start with looking at the last and more transforming group, what contemporaries named 'the big industry', representing a cluster of characteristic representatives of the second industrial revolution.

The large-scale economic circuits of the second industrial revolution

The history of 'The Norwegian Company for Electrochemical Industry', or Elkem, demonstrate some important aspects of the new electricity-based industry (Chapter 12). Sam Eyde, the main entrepreneur behind both Elkem and the fertilizer producer Norsk Hydro, was not a 'local' initiator, he was educated in Berlin, had worked as an engineer in Hamburg and other German cities and established his own engineering firm with offices in both Oslo and Stockholm. His education was more advanced than any of the Norwegian technical schools could offer. Neither the Norwegian savings banks nor the domestic commercial banks or rich Norwegians could provide his projects with sufficient capital; he had to trust foreign loans and foreign co-owners. Real, science-based innovation contrasted with other industries' widespread use of standardized or imitated technology. Core parts of the machinery used by Elkem and Hydro exceeded the competence of the national engineering workshops and had to be imported. The main markets for most the companies Eyde established were outside Norway. At the same time, however, enterprises such as Elkem and Norsk Hydro had local and national interfaces creating important experiences and learning for Norwegian engineers, lawyers, managers and workers – and, not least, local and national politicians.

In hindsight, Eyde's main entrepreneurial achievement was not Elkem, but Norsk Hydro. In many of the years after it was incorporated in 1905, Hydro ranked as Norway's largest enterprise – in 2007, it was second, after Statoil.[19] The total share capital at the start was 7.5 million kroner. The Swedish bank Enskildabanken of Stockholm controlled half, Banque de Paris et des Pays-Bas nearly half, and only 8 per cent of the shares were held by Norwegians. By exploiting the energy-demanding Birkeland–Eyde process of converting the nitrogen in air into nitric oxide, Hydro became one of the world's largest producers of synthetic fertilizers. In 1927, Hydro went into a partnership with the German company I.G. Farben. The Birkeland-Eyde process was no longer competitive, and Hydro's plants at Rjukan started using I.G. Farben's ammonia or Haber–Bosch method.

Even if some of the most experienced construction workers in this period were Swedes, most of the workers, and the natural resources were Norwegian. Norsk Hydro used the natural resources primarily of hydro power, air and some chalk. Other new, large-scale and power-hungry enterprises represented value added and transforming developments of established resource-based industries. The wood-processing industries saw the coming of cellulose and modern paper factories. In 1889, the English industrialist Edward Partington founded the Kellner–Partington Paper Pulp Company Ltd and built up a leading international corporation in the expanding pulp and paper industry.[20] In 1892 a Norwegian division was established, the cellulose-producing Borregaard Fabrikker at the town of Sarpsborg in the south-east county of

Østfold. The national foundations of this enterprise were even more limited than Hydro's. Borregaard was from the start a part of an integrated, multinational wood-processing corporation. The innovations used in the processes were developed by Partington and his partner, the German–Austrian cellulose expert, Dr Karl Kellner. The chemical engineer Oscar Pedersen represented the most important Norwegian contributor to the success of Borregaard. Educated in Dresden, he was an expert on sulphite pulp and played the role of 'skilled partner, resident expert and capable implementer of Partington's plan'.[21]

In 1909, more than 2000 workers were employed at Borregaard; at that time it was the country's largest workplace. For several decades, Borregaard challenged Hydro for the title as the largest enterprise in Norway. After Partington's involvement in Norway, several other English paper manufacturers followed. From the 1890s, wood-processing and pulp-producing companies like Hønefoss Brug, Vittingfoss Brug and Bøndsdalen Mills and Follum Fabrikker were taken over by English paper-producing firms, many of whom had been earlier customers of the Norwegian pulp factories. In this way, the wood-processing industry exemplified another change in the business system following the second industrial revolution – the growth of vertically integrated companies: The 'visible hand' of organizational hierarchies replaced the 'invisible hand' of markets.

Mining for profits
Mining was one of Norway's oldest industries. The silver mines of Kongsberg Sølvverk had a history lasting from 1623 to 1958. The history of the copper mines of Røros Kobberverk started in 1644 and ended in 1977. However, the mining industry had an important revival connected to the second industrial revolution. Innovations within chemistry and electricity made possible the commercial use of previously non-exploitable minerals in low-grade iron and pyrite fields. The new high-cost and high-risk mining industry, mostly located in the northern parts of the country, also relied heavily on foreign capital and foreign expertise and technology. The Swedish industrialist, Nils Persson, was a pioneer in the Norwegian mining industry. Persson needed supplies of phosphorus material for his fertilizer-producing company Skånska superfosfat- och svavelesyrefabriks AB in Helsingborg, in the south of Sweden. After hearing about the deposits of pyrite ore rich in copper and sulphur in Sulitjelma, Persson secured the rights, and started regular mining in 1887. After four years of experimental operation the company

Sulitjelma Aktiebolag was founded in 1891. Shortly after the turn of the century Sulitjelma had become the largest mine in Norway, and one of the largest industry business in the country. Just before the First World War, Sulitjelma Aktiebolag had 1700 employees, a part of Persson's vertically integrated enterprise. He also founded a copper factory in Helsingborg, based on the Sulitjelma pyrite.

Christian A. Anker, a part of the Anker family, we met earlier in this chapter, was a well-educated Norwegian engineer and entrepreneur industrially active in the neighbourhood of the town of Halden in south-eastern Norway. His most ambitious project was, however, located far north, in Sydvaranger near Kirkenes. In 1906 he established the company AS Sydvaranger to exploit promising iron ore in the district. AS Sydvaranger was financed by a Swedish consortium that included the Wallenberg family. The original capital stock was 5 million kroner, of which Anker held 36.4 per cent. In 1907, however, it was raised to 10 million, and the Swedish group purchased Anker's share.[22] Some of the new methods of separating, either by flotation or by magnetism, depended on electricity. After having relied on a steam power station from 1910, the building of a hydro power station was started in 1919. The huge open cast Syd-Varanger mine the world's most northerly iron mine, and for many years the most productive in Norway, was finally closed down in 1996.

Most impressive in its early use of electricity in mining was the Dunderland Iron Ore Company Ltd, established in London in 1902 as the largest English enterprise for the import of foreign iron ore. The Dunderland iron ore deposits were located in Nord-Rana, in the county of Nordland. In the 1890s, Nils Persson had prospected the deposits, claming the rights to most of the resources, building barracks and buying waterfalls and the grounds for the necessary ports and railways. In 1899 he sold it all to Edison Ore Milling Syndicate for £182,000. The Edison company was set up to exploit Thomas A. Edison's patent for magnetic separation. In 1902 the Dunderland Iron Ore Company Ltd bought the properties and the right to use the Edison patent for £2 million. The company's board consisted of many high-ranking British capitalists together with Thomas A. Edison himself and the famous British scientist, Lord Kelvin. Despite an impressive, costly, technically advanced and large-scale effort, the project was not profitable, and in 1908, the capital stock had gone. A couple of later attempts to operate the mines also failed.

We need to mention one more mining company – Orkla – if only for its position as one of the largest Norwegian corporations today, also having full ownership of what is left of Elkem and Borregaard. Orkla was established in

1654. That year, mining started at the Løkken field near the river Orkla in the county of Sør-Trøndelag, one of the biggest deposits of chalcopyrite in the world.[23] Traditionally copper was extracted from the ore, but in 1904 the local entrepreneur Christian M. Thams decided to use the pyrite to get sulphur. Sulphur was essential to a lot of other processes within the new chemical industries, like the production of cellulose, fertilizers and explosives. In 1904 Thams established the Orkla-Grube-Aktiebolag. In 1905 the Wallenberg family provided new capital to the firm, and in 1913, after some serious start-up problems, the Wallenbergs took over control of the company. By the 1930s, Orkla had developed into one of Norway's large industrial enterprises.

Big, ugly and alien?

The entrepreneurial stories above show a pattern that is representative of most of the new industries based on Norwegian minerals, forests and waterfalls. The new energy-intensive companies within aluminium, carbide and ferro-alloys had also a high proportion of foreign ownership, were mostly part of a vertically integrated MNC, and were relatively large-scale. Norwegian engineers were often in charge of the entrepreneurial functions. The engineer Knud Bryn was decisive in establishing the Hafslund company in 1898, constructing an electrical power facility with capital and equipment from the German electrotechnical Schuckert Company. Hafslund started by producing calcium carbide. During the first two decades of the twentieth century, Norway became one of the world's largest producers of primary aluminium, six smelters coming into operation between 1908 and 1927. All but one of these companies were controlled by foreign enterprises, primarily The British Aluminium Company and the French aluminium company Pechiney. The one Norwegian-owned company, A/S Høyangfaldene Norsk Aluminium Company, was founded 1915 by the engineer Sigurd Klouman. In 1923 the company was forced to form a 50–50 partnership with the American ALCOA to salvage the Norwegian operation.

The effects of all these new initiatives and investment on the national business system were partly a result of decisions inside these companies, concerning their internal organizational structures, their corporate governance and finance, market relations, cartel agreements and so on. These were the internal, business-generated parts of the business system. Both the growing trade unions and the trade organization of the industrial companies were part of these structures. The first local trade unions were established in the 1880s, and in 1899 the National Federation of Labour was founded with

5000 members. The Norwegian Employers' Confederation was established the year after. Both organizations had the larger companies as their most important source of recruitment.

Other parts of the business system were created in the political system, by the Parliament, the state bureaucrats and even the municipalities, as a reaction or as an anticipation of the actions of business men and the business community. During the first part of the twentieth century, the political reactions, debates and creativity related to the industries of the second industrial revolution were astonishing. They resulted in a radically changed institutional environment and new rules of the game for the businesses working inside resource-based industry. A substantial part of the political community looked at the new industries as big, ugly and alien. The new industry threatened not only the established way of doing business, but the also the established way of life. It represented a boom in industrialization and industrialized life, the coming of an industrial proletariat and thereby antagonism and class struggle in society. National control of the management of natural resources and the distribution of the resource rent become particularly important issues. The hard struggle for national independence from Sweden, won in 1905, strengthened the national feelings in general and the resentment against powerful Swedes such as the influential Wallenberg family.

Political support for small-scale economic circuits

The legislation on the acquisition and use of waterfalls, mines and forests between 1906 and 1917 represented a divide between a classical liberal and a more regulatory state.[24] A long political process, led by the Liberal Party and its Prime Minister Gunnar Knudsen and his Minister of Justice Johan Castberg, ended with three important concession laws. The Forest Concession Act for the acquisition of forests of 1909 was in 1917 followed by the Watercourse Regulation Act and the Act relating to acquisition of waterfalls, mines and other real estate, called the Industrial Concession Act.

The legislation on natural resources was inspired by the 'Georgists', an international movement named after the American economist and social philosopher Henry George. George's main idea was that everyone deserved and should own the values that they created with their own work, but that the values supplied by nature belonged to all humanity, to society. Johan Castberg was a member of the Norwegian 'Henry George Society'.

The laws on waterfalls and forests made it very difficult for commercial private and foreign interest to acquire ownership of these resources. The Forest

Photograph 11.3 **Johan Castberg was a radical politician who strongly influenced the rules of the game for the resource-based industries.**
Source: The National Library of Norway.

Concession Act protected the farmers, the municipalities and community ownership. The state already held substantial forest property. The laws related to waterfalls gave strong priority and preferences to municipal ownership of hydro power and to the supply of electricity to agriculture, craft and small industry and household consumption. Private and foreign companies that got a concession to buy and develop waterfalls and mines had to comply with many regulations and clauses securing workers' welfare, the local community and the use of national suppliers. Clauses of reversion said that private waterfalls and power stations had to be handed over free to the state not later than sixty years after the concession was given. The mines reverted to the state after fifty years.

Most of the power-hungry industries and larger mining companies that we have mentioned so far had got hold of their resources either before the concession laws were implemented, or had got concessions before the strict legislation of 1917. They represented a breakthrough in the industrialization of the Norwegian economy, and many of them continued to be among the largest companies during most of the twentieth century – and, for some, even further. These industries certainly contributed to the high economic growth especially in the period 1906–20. In the troubled years to come, however, small-scale industry and economic circuits became of greater importance for growth. Through its legislation and other forms of support, the state supported modernization within traditional institutional and organizational forms. Let us go back to 1890 and the battle of the Trollfjorden to exemplify this modernization strategy.

Industrial divides: alternatives of modernization and growth

During the winter cod-fishing season in Lofoten in the county of Nordland in 1890, local fishermen using traditional handlines clashed with the crew of steamers using trawl-net and modern tackle in the narrow Trollfjorden. Apparently, it was a battle between the past and the future. At this time, the fisheries still represented about 36 per cent of the value of Norwegian total commodity export. About 90 per cent of the catches were exported. Could the fisheries be sustained as one of the most important export trades without a transition to large-scale, capital-intensive iron-made steamers with efficient trawls?

  After the battle, the hand-liners sent a telegram to the Storting and demanded all purse nets be made illegal. Unwilling to wait for a law to be implemented, the Storting accepted an immediate ban on the use of trawls in the traditional fishing grounds in Lofoten, finally codified by the Lofoten Act in 1897. The protection against industrialized cod fisheries became an established line of policy until the Second World War with new restrictive laws being enacted by the Storting in 1908 and in 1925.[25] The fishing communities were given extensive responsibility for controlling and administering the regulations.

  Despite pressure from commercial interests in the towns, some technocrats and public officials, on the whole fisheries continued to be coastal and small-scale with some protective measures from the state. Substantial parts of the technological modernization took place within the traditional institutional and organizational structures. The choice of technology represented a choice of lifestyle. The traditional fishing boat was small, made of wood, with oars or sails – built by craftsmen and affordable for the fishermen.[26] Especially in Britain, it was the engine of development for an industrialized fishery with a more centralized ownership of the means of production. Bigger, more expensive steamships made of steel were produced by specialized shipyards and operated by a fishing proletariat often living in the cities.

The alternative small-scale technology was wooden boats with decks that were equipped with internal combustion engines. These boats were largely adaptable to the traditional social structures. In 1920, most of the fishing fleet was motorized. Interestingly, the rate of change was higher along the western coast than in Northern Norway. One explanation for this difference was the easier access to farmland in the north. In western Norway fishing became the sole occupation for many people.

During the 1920s fisheries expanded rapidly. Norway increased its export of salt fish from 37,000 to 49,000 tonnes. This made it possible for the fishermen to further develop their boats and gear. In 1920 Norway's share of the total fish catch in Europe was 20 per cent. Ten years later it was 29 per cent.[27] However, other European nations expanded their fisheries during the same period, not least Iceland, and problems of overproduction led to a fall in prices. Despite the market problems in the 1930s, the number of fishermen expanded greatly, with 23 per cent in 1929–39. Unemployment in other parts of the economy, and continued easy access to both the fish resources and to boats and gear, was one reason for this. The other was the many measures taken in co-operation between the fishermen and the state. Norway's Association of Fishermen was founded as a general national interest organization in 1926. From the late 1920s, many other organizations saw the light of day, such as the Association of Norwegian Klipfisk Exporters, the Association of Finnmark's Stockfish Producers, the Norwegian Stockfish Exporters' Association and the Association of Salted Herring Exporters. Some of these organizations became efficient cartels supported by the government. For example, the Storting decided on a Herring Act in 1930 that required all exporters to be members of the Association of Salted Herring Exporters. In parallel, the government strictly regulated the use of trawlers and supported the small-scale fishermen by favourable loans from a loan office for fishers (Lånekassen for fiskere) established in 1932. The local municipalities and the savings and commercial banks were also supportive of the fishermen. By transferring the first-hand sales to the fishermen's sales organizations, and by giving these sales organizations regulatory authority, the government contributed to the continuation of the overall small-scale structure of the fisheries. A strong regulation of the canning industry was part of the same policy.

Aspects of both the same development and policy evolved within agriculture. After some hard years of adjustment in the last part of the nineteenth century, especially from grain-growing to animal husbandry, the years from 1900 until the early 1920s were prosperous. Fertilizers from Norsk Hydro were slowly taken more into use, but other factors were even more important for increased productivity, like the rotation of crops, the continued priority of ditching and the refinements of breeds of livestock and crops.[28] Electricity brought light into both farmhouses and barns. Electric motors and the diffusion of the horse-driven mowing machine were examples of mechanization that reduced the need for labour. Gradually most farms developed into businesses run by the nuclear family, maybe with some close relatives. Still, in 1920 more than half the population lived in the countryside, and in the two decades that followed that proportion was only slowly reduced because of the tough times in the manufacturing industry. New land was cultivated in many locations.

Until the 1920s, the price of milk increased somewhat more than the consumer price index. During the next decade, milk production increased and in 1930 milk accounted for more than 40 per cent of total agricultural production. Better transportation made it easier for more farmers to deliver fresh milk to the city dwellers. Fresh milk paid better than industrial milk. More competition among the milk producers meant lower prices, and a circular movement of lower prices followed by efforts to compensate for falling prices by more production occurred. As agricultural prices fell, farmers' debt increased. The parity policy followed by the central bank during the 1920s made things even worse. The aim of this policy was to have the value of the Norwegian krone back to its former gold parity. It implied highly deflationary measures.

Like the fishermen, the farmers used organizing both to cope with the market and to gain political influence. The Farmers' Union was already set up in 1896, and the Smallholders' Union was established in 1913 in both competition and co-operation with their forerunner. In 1920, the majority of the members in the Farmers' Union founded their own Farmers' Party. The co-operative movement, inspired by the Danish pioneers, were also growing during the first decades of the century. The Norwegian Milk Producers' Association was established in 1881, but was more efficiently reorganized in 1921. Slaughtering co-operatives also thrived. In 1917 there were 800 local purchasing pools with 26,650 members, and a farmers' co-operative bank was established in 1918. In parallel, the municipal and the savings banks constituted a local buffer and support for the farmers, even if debt burdens in many places put restrictions on the municipal banks' opportunities for action.

Already in 1897 and in 1905 the farmers achieved some modest duties on import of animal products. Shortly after the outbreak of the First World War, a duty was also charged on imported grain. One important further contribution to stabilising the market for grain was achieved by the setting up of the state grain monopoly in 1929, in effect until 1995. Private grain buyers and mills became enrolled into the monopoly system, and the farmers could sell their grain to the new organization at prices above the world market price.[29] But the main problem was the threat of collapsing prices of milk. In 1930 the Storting passed a Marketing Act giving the milk producers' co-operative legal authority to decide on a variable marketing fee for all milk products. A council representing producer, sales and consumer interests was set up to fix the marketing fee and to supervise the operation of the regulations. To get rid of all the produced milk, the Storting decided in 1931 that the producers of margarine should mixed their products with butter. The success of these measures led producers in other part of the sector to organise co-operatives. Pork was brought under the arrangement in 1931, sheep in 1934 and beef and veal in 1940.

As in the fisheries, the market regulations contributed to conserve the small-scale structure in agriculture. The number of farms increased from 186,290 in 1929 to 197,260 in 1939, but the average size of the farm stayed almost the same. Within this small-scale economic structure, significant modernization took place.

'Organization is the solution of the time!'

The claim that 'organization was the solution of the time' was put forward by the chairman Christian Platou of the Federation of Norwegian Industries at the federation's general meeting in 1922. It was the same as what was being expressed among fishermen and farmers. But the way of organising across sectors also had some differences. The fisheries and agriculture were sectors with relatively small units and small class differences. It was otherwise in parts of the manufacturing industry. The number of workers in secondary industries increased from 242,642 in 1900 to 309,525 in 1920. As we have seen, a substantial part of that expansion took place in 'big industry'. This stimulated the growth of another kind of industrial organization, the labour unions. In 1900 the Norwegian Federation of Labour had 3930 members. Two decades later, just after the Federation had succeeded in achieving the 8-hour day and 7 days' summer holiday, the number was 142,642. During the boom of 1905–20 it was easy for the confederation's leader, Ole O. Lian, and his shop stewards to convince the workers to organise, and there was a fair chance of having their demands met by the employers. Organization among the employers was also progressing. In 1919 the Norwegian Employers' Confederation had 853 member firms from manufacturing.[30] In 1919, the Federation of Norwegian Industries was established, with 375 member firms. The first national wage agreement in 1907 was in the metal industry.

During the economic hard times to come, the relations between the workers' and the employers' organizations were mainly one of conflict. In 1921 about 150,000 workers struck, leading to a severe defeat for the labour unions, and membership decreased to 84,000. Labour disputes and strikes followed during the 1920s, peaking in 1931 with a extensive lock-out involving 60,000 workers and lasting about five months.

The co-operation between employers and firms involved several objectives beyond coping with the workers and their unions. The international management trend of the time, well adapted to the problems of organising manual workers within mass producing industry, was called 'scientific management'. These management principles were based on the work on industrial rationalization done by the American engineer Fredrick Winslow Taylor. Already the first year after its foundation, in 1920, the Federation of Norwegian Industries invited a former collaborator of Taylor, Dr R. Roesler, to talk about 'The Taylor system. Scientific, rational management'. The same year, the Norwegian engineer Joakim Lehmkuhl published an introduction to scientific management, 'Rational Management. An Overview.' Lehmkuhl had studied engineering in the US at MIT outside Boston. The concepts of rationalization and 'technocracy' achieved a high standing in some circles, especially among engineers, and the Federation of Norwegian Industries established its Rationalization Office in 1927. However, the more practical lessons of scientific management were at this time of limited use in the Norwegian context. It was only after 1945 that industrial rationalization really took off. However, a somewhat more systematic and rational approach to industrial problems also had some favourable effects, not least through the extensive work on product standardization.

In most parts of the business community, there were efforts to influence prices and competition, through both formal and informal cartels. The critical attitudes towards big and foreign industry among social liberals during the first decades of the century actualized the so called 'trust problem' that had been formulated in the US as a result of the industrial concentration and centralization in the latter part of the nineteenth century. In 1920 a provisional Prices Act introduced compulsory notifications and registration of restrictive business arrangements and dominant enterprises.[31] In 1926 the Storting passed a Trust Act that was intended to strengthen the control of prices and cartels and the misuse of market power even further. Because of the economic crises, the new Trust Control Office, with its Director General Wilhelm Thagaard, took another direction than what was originally intended – and feared in the business community. Thagaard saw the necessity for Norwegian companies to co-operate, not only to avoid ruinous competition, as in fishing and agriculture, but also as a protection against big foreign firms trying to conquer the Norwegian market. In some industries market-sharing became a means to secure some economies of scale among the producers. Instead of being hampered, co-operative agreements and cartels were more often stimulated.

In manufacturing, market regulation and co-operation supported the established industrial structure. The concession laws of 1917 made it difficult to establish a new electrochemical or electrometallurgical industry based on cheap hydro power. The whole business community worked hard to have the concessions laws changed, but without success. The crisis for power-demanding industries during most of the inter-war years increased the element of foreign ownership. Foreign capital also took hold on companies in other industries. In some sectors, as the electrotechnical industry, this had long-term consequences for the development path of the companies.

But behind the very visible expansion of electricity-based big industry, the ambitious electrification efforts of the municipals started to have positive economic effects. The electric motor opened small-scale efficient production, very much according to the intention of the Concession Law's supporters. The share of electricity in industry used for motors (instead of electrochemical and electrometallurgical processes) was 10 per cent in 1910. It increased sharply to 40 per cent during the 1920s and reached 43 per cent in 1939. Between 1910 and 1920 the number of electric motors increased from about 4000 to 18,000. In 1930 the number was 32,500. Almost all industry took advantage of the new technology; the effects were the most pronounced in printing and the manufactures of foodstuff, textiles, clothing, wood and metal products.[32] The more protectionist trade regime in both Norway and the rest of Europe also gave small firms working for the home market a better chance to thrive.

A growth industry at sea: shipping

Shipping, sometimes combined with whaling, was the important growth industry during the inter-war years. The period from 1875 until the First World War was a tough period of restructuring for the Norwegian merchant fleet. The transfer from sail to steam progressed slowly. The shipping industry along the southern coast was very much embedded in their local economy. Shipowners often had investments in both the shipyards and in the forests that provided the shipyards with wood. The distributed joint partnership system made radical decisions on restructuring hard to take. In addition, for some time after the steam ships were introduced, sailing vessels were able to compete in bulk and long distance trade. However, improved steam ships made it increasingly difficult for sailing vessels to compete on all markets. In 1884, the city of Arendal had the largest merchant fleet in the country, with about 500 ships. From then on, the city and its surrounding districts went into a long period of economic stagnation. The problems also hit several other towns along the southern cost, and Stavanger on the western coast. Oslo and Bergen now became the two main shipping towns. In Bergen, the need to have fast and regular delivery of fish gave incentives to invest in steam ships. The steam ships also opened up for passenger liners, demanding speed and precision.[33]

In 1914, steamers made up 77 per cent of the fleet, sailing vessels 23 per cent. The next technological step was the introduction of motorized ships, a transformation led by Norwegian shipowners. The First World War boosted the restructuring. More than 2000 sailors lost their lives but the freights were exceptionally high and the shipowners' insurance claims in Britain after the war amounted to about 1 billion kroner.[34] With money and self-confidence, the shipowners increased their fleet from 1.9 million gross tons in 1919 to 4.8 million gross tons in 1939. The ocean-going fleet employed 23,600 men in 1919, growing to 32,000 in 1939; about 90 per cent of these sailors were Norwegian. In 1939 60 per cent of the gross tonnage was equipped with diesel engines, saving fuels, space and men to operate the machines. The shipowners also moved into the growing oil market. In 1939 had Norway the third-largest fleet of tankers, behind only the US and Great Britain.

The position of the shipowners in Norwegian society is hard to measure, but the economic historian, Fritz Hodne, has made a good point by correctly arguing that during seventeen of the first thirty-five years of the century, a shipowner was Prime Minister. These were Christian Michelsen from Bergen (1905–7), Gunnar Knudsen from Skien (1908–10 and 1913–20) and Johan Ludwig Mowinckel from Bergen, Prime Minister three times between 1924 and 1935. The first two of these men were also the first presidents of the Norwegian Shipowners' Association, founded in 1909.[35]

From competition to co-operation
All in all, the whole trend toward co-operation and organization during the 1920s and 1930s was formative for the co-ordinated market economy that finally succeed the liberal market economy after the Second World War. It also gradually stabilized the operation of the business system. Within the traditional small-scale structure of the economy, motorization, electrification and other technologies made possible a considerable growth in productivity. The small-scale structure also contributed to preserving the democratic character of Norwegian capitalism. Even big industry, established to exploit the cheap hydro power, had to adjust to the strict regulations of the Storting. This industry itself had some democratic aspects; in 1907 a German representative from the German chemical company Bayer called Duisberg visited the sites of Norsk Hydro at Notodden and Rjukan. He was impressed by Hydro's engineers and the Norwegians' confidence in handling the big challenges on their own. 'One thinks and feels democratically in a way probably not found among any other people', Duisburg wrote to his German board.[36]

A co-ordinated market economy completing the second industrial revolution, 1935–70

On 15 March 1935, a son of a smallholder, the sawmill and construction worker Johan Nygaardsvold, became the Prime Minister of Norway. Nygaardsvold and his Labour Party government contributed to the formation of a new political–economic order in Norway. The hard times of the early 1930s had strengthened Labour Party's more pragmatic and moderate wing. The party and the unions evolved into a broad, reform-oriented labour movement. Practical steps to lower unemployment, recreate stable economic growth and develop a national welfare society became more important than the principles of revolutionary internationalism.

The party's moderate profile became further strengthened by the social compromize behind the government's formation. The Agrarian Party's support of Nygaardsvold and his ministers was based on an agreement to use government expenditures to meet the severe crises that beset the rural areas. The Labour Party held the government from 1935 to 1965, with the exception of a one-month non-socialist interregnum in 1963. There was, however, one major break in the Labour Party's *de facto* governance of Norwegian territory. Even if the government had declared Norway neutral after the outbreak of the war in September 1939, a surprise attack during the early hours of 9 April 1940, brought all the main Norwegian harbours under German control. King Haakon and the government managed to escape from Oslo, and the Storting gave the government authority to fight the Germans. The German control of the harbours, the confusion after the sudden attack and military defences in bad shape, made the battle hopeless. Norway formally surrendered on 10 June, but the terms of the agreement applied only to the forces within the country. During the occupation of 1940–5 the Nygaardsvold government was in exile in London, joining its forces, most prominently the Norwegian merchant fleet, with the Allies.[37]

The non-socialist coalition government in 1965–71 hardly challenged the social democratic order. A proactive state willing to regulate the economy was broadly accepted. With some nuances, this political–economic order was not seriously challenged until the late 1970s, when neo-liberalism emerged in Norway as in most of the industrialized world. The social democratic order represented a distillation, cultivation and extension of tendencies already visible during the social-liberal order, as a more interventionist state, a more co-operative economy and the increasing confidence in the use of science in most fields of society developed. At the level of the business system, the period 1935–45 represented the definitive transition from a liberal to a co-ordinated market economy. To take it one step further: among the different categories of co-ordinated market economies, a collaborative business system, as defined by Richard Whitley, developed in Norway.

Social stability, economic growth, motorization – and war

Internationally, the period discussed in this section represented the upswing part of the fourth 'Kondratiev wave'. It was also the last part of the second industrial revolution. The upswing was influenced by a new technological paradigm, the motorization of transport: the introduction of automobiles, trucks, tractors, aircrafts and motorized ships. In consequence, oil turned out to be a natural resource in demand, and refineries became important production units. Modern roads and motorways, with an adequate number of petrol stations and airports, evolved as the corresponding infrastructure.

As with all technological paradigms, its effects differed between nations. The US and some European countries, among them Sweden, became large producers of cars, airplanes and motorized military equipment. The best-known Norwegian effort to engage in car production was located in Lunde in Telemark. Started in 1956, the firm produced five cars with the brand-name 'Troll' before it went bankrupt. But Norwegian shipyards, however, built both motorized ships and diesel engines for sale. Aker Mek. Verksted started building motors under licence from the Danish Burmeister og Wain in the inter-war years. After the war, more shipyards started production of diesel motors. More simple motors for the fishing boats were produced in several locations along the coast from early in the century. The increased demand for oil created an opportunity for the shipping industry and its tankers that the Norwegian shipowners knew how to exploit.

It was, however, primarily the *use* of motorized vehicles that affected the Norwegian economy. In 1935, about 63,000 cars were driving on Norwegian roads, and 60 per cent were passenger cars. In 1970 the number was 903,000 cars, and about 80 per cent of them were passenger cars. Restrictions on the import of cars were removed in 1960. The length of public roads increased from 39,600 km in 1935 to 72,300 in 1970 but, compared to the other Nordic countries, the quality of the roads was poor. As a coastal nation, the use of the combustion engine in boats and ships was of special importance. The number of motor vessels increased from 2081 in 1935 to 6128 in 1970, but the tonnage of motorized boats increased more than eight times. Not before the mid-1990s did national freight transportation on the roads surpass that on the sea. The use of railways stagnated. In agriculture, nearly 240,000 horses after the war decreased to less than 40,000 in 1970. In the same period, the number of tractors increased from about 10,000 to 110,000. In the fisheries, the number of open motor vessels doubled. In addition to motorization, a revitalized effort to take advantage of Norwegian hydro power and the systematic use of R&D characterized the technological regime after the war.

Undoubtedly it was a period of economic upswing – both internationally and nationally. From 1933, the economic indicators in western Europe started to point upwards, two years before Nygaardsvold's government came to power. A much-debated question is to what extent the strong growth in the last half of the 1930s also was dependent on the more expansive policy of the new government. Many factors contributed to the positive turn. International war preparations on a large scale increased the demand for Norwegian shipping and export industries. The suspension of Gold Standard in 1931 and the subsequent depreciation of the krone made Norwegian products relatively cheaper both abroad and at home. The end of the restrictive monetary policy also made it possible for the central bank to lower rents and go for a more expansionary credit policy. A 'growth through the crisis' hypothesis focused on how the crises stimulated initiatives and entrepreneurship, especially among people from declining industries and among the increasing number of young people trying to find their way into the workforce. The resulting new firms most often made new products for the home market, such as the car and the motorboat, electric household appliances, sports articles, pharmaceuticals and cosmetics and manufactured foods.[38] The production of radios also experienced a breakthrough in the second half of the 1930s. The 'consumer society' was on its way.

There was a definite heritage of social welfare measures in the social liberal order, but from the mid-1930s a new more universalistic welfare state emerged. Nygaardsvold's government launched several new social reforms. The sickness insurance of 1909 was extended to new groups. In 1936, a law including benefits for the disabled were implemented, and two years later a compulsory scheme for unemployment insurance was put in place. New categories of workers were covered by a revision of the law on worker protection. In 1936 the old social liberal dream of establishing an old-age pension was made fact. For a short period, Norway became one of the leading nations in the social policy arena.[39] These new initiatives certainly had some expansionary effects on the economy, but since state expenditures were small in relation to the whole economy, the effects were limited.

The German occupying power had the ambition to integrate Norway into their European 'Grossraumwirtschaft'. Plans were prepared to take advantage of the power resources to produce heavy water and magnesium, but also to transmit Norwegian hydro power directly to Germany. The commander of the Luftwaffe, field marshal Hermann Göring, considered Norwegian aluminium critical to the production of war planes. The German firm Nordische Aluminium Aktiegesellschaft (Nordag) started construction work on several power stations and manufacturing plants for aluminium, and some were nearly finished by the end of the war. Other strategically important installations were destroyed by sabotage and Allied bombing. The Norwegian-led sabotage in 1943 against Hydro's production site for heavy water at Vemork in Telemark was one of the most successful act of sabotage during the Second World War; the Germans had planned to use the heavy water for making atomic bombs.

It is difficult to estimate the development of GDP during the war. In general, the economic welfare, nutrition and comfort of the people fell considerably. About 10,000 Norwegians lost their lives as victims of the war, but as a proportion of the population this was less than many other European countries. The Nordic people were regarded as representatives of the Aryan race and treated much less brutally than, for example, the Slavic-speaking people of eastern Europe. Some calculations indicate that GDP in 1945 was only two-thirds of the 1939 level.[40] A substantial proportion of production was consumed and confiscated by the occupying power, and the maintenance of real capital was sparse. However, the construction industry expanded during the occupation: the occupying army of some 400,000 soldiers had to be housed. Important Norwegian infrastructures were improved, extended and adapted to serve the German military efforts. Building of barracks and fortifications, together with works on railways, airports and roads, resulted in a quadrupling of the man-hours in construction. Many unemployed grabbed the opportunity to work on German fortifications and installations. Since trading relations with countries outside the territories controlled by Germany and its allies were cut off, the industry had a rather protected home market. Considerable parts of the business community co-operated more or less closely with the Germans. But after the war, it was difficult to have a fair and just settlement on such 'economic treachery'.

Norway's most significant contribution to the Allied war effort was to place the merchant fleet of the world's biggest shipping company, The Norwegian Shipping and Trade Mission (Nortraship), at the British, later at the Allied powers', disposal. Of special importance was the modern tanker fleet built up during the inter-war years. This fleet transported nearly half of the British oil import during the war and also financed the Norwegian administration abroad.

A state-guided collaborative economy

By in late 1946, national output and private consumption reached pre-war levels, indicating that the economic losses during the war had been limited. The year after, exports had the same share of GDP as before the war. Thereafter and until 1973, Norway enjoyed the longest period of stable growth since the birth of the market economy – reflecting an international economic upswing often called the 'Golden Age'. Growth in Norway was very much in line with that of most OECD countries. In most industrialized nations, growth was framed by more regulation and state involvement in the economy than before the crises of the 1930s. Not least in countries such as

Great Britain, Italy and France, but even in US, state regulation multiplied after the mid-1930s.

The failures of the market economy during the inter-war years created strong support in the Norwegian Labour Party for a more planned economy. The impressive results of many governments' war efforts seemed to have demonstrated the efficiency of centralized planning and organizing. A specific Norwegian background for strong planning aspirations, supplementing the general influence of the British economist John Maynard Keynes, was the teaching of Professor of Economics Ragnar Frisch at the University of Oslo. Frisch had a profound influence on a generation of students who ended up as high-ranking public officials and powerful politicians. Frisch, who was the first to receive the Nobel Prize in economics together with the Dutchman Jan Tinbergen in 1968, had a firm belief in the superiority of rational planning compared to the blind forces of the market. One of Frisch's acolytes, the economist Erik Brofoss, was a spearhead for the planned economy in government and state administration. First he worked as a Minister of Finance (1945–7), as a Minister of Trade (1947–54) and then as Central Bank Governor (1954–70). Brofoss eagerly recruited other economists to important positions in the state administration. Frisch and his students thought that the economy could be treated in much the same way as a firm or a household. In line with this conception, a national budget was presented by the government in 1947 and a four-year plan begun in 1948.

On 8 May 1945, the same day as the German troops in Norway surrendered, the government decided on a provisional law, later called the Lex Thagaard after its initiator, the Director General of the Price Directorate, Wilhelm Thagaard. The provision, later renewed, strengthened the quantitative restrictions, price and other regulations from the war and gave the Price Directorate and the government authority to regulate what had formerly been the exclusive rights of the managers and owners. These measures provoked a strong reaction, especially from the Conservative Party, liberalist intellectuals and many business leaders. With the support of many business associations the liberalist organization Libertas was established in secrecy to fight what seemed to be steps towards the introduction of socialism. The business associations also created the Research Institute for Industrial Economics, employing more liberalist economists than the Frisch students. The business journal *Farmand*, edited by the economist Trygve J.B. Hoff, also actively opposed the Labour Party's planning ambitions. Hoff was one of the founding members of the neo-liberal international organization, the

Mont Pelerin Society. Members of this society, like the later Nobel Prize winners in economics, Friedrich von Hayek, Milton Friedman and George Stigler, contributed articles to Hoff's *Farmand*. So the radical economic policy of the post-war years contributed to the establishment of neo-liberal organizations and discourse. This preserved, developed and kept neo-liberal ideas in a state of readiness till they were actualized during the economic downswing in the 1970s.

Certainly, the strong reactions from the business community made it more difficult to develop co-operative relations between industry, labour unions and the state. In 1947 a committee was appointed to propose a more permanent law of regulation. The political distance between the business representatives in the committee, on the one hand, and the radical social liberal Wilhelm Thagaard and the labour representatives, on the other, proved unbridgeable. This was one reason why the committee's proposal could not be presented until 1952. The radical majority in the committee proposed a price and rationalization law that rightly could be suspected as an opening for socialization – and socialism. It ended up with very much less. The proposed law on rationalization was wholly abandoned and the final Price Act of 1953 was a watered-down version of what the majority in the committee proposed.

Why did the Labour Party, with a majority in the Storting, suddenly turn away from what many saw as the road to socialism? A progressive dependence in the US and integration into an Atlantic community was one obvious reason. The communist assumption of power in Czechoslovakia in 1948 created a fear that Norway's independence could be in danger. In 1949 Norway abandoned its neutral status and became a member of the military alliance NATO. The Korean War of 1950–3 further increased the tension between the USSR and the US and their respective allies. In several European countries the communists had a strong position after the war, and in 1947, the US announced the European Recovery Plan (ERP), or the Marshall Plan, as described in Chapter 8. After some hesitation, the Labour government agreed to be one of the sixteen nations that participated in the programme. During the years 1948–52 Norway received about $350 million as gift aid and $49 million as loans, in total amounting to 2.8 billion kroner. The Marshall Aid was given on the condition that the European recipients began to liberalize their trade. The Organization for European Cooperation (OEEC) became a means to this end. Norway also took part in the emerging international trade and financial regime heavily influenced by the US. Norway had ratified the Bretton Woods Agreement of 1944, setting up fixed exchange rates between trading partners.

Two years later Norway subscribed to the plan for the International Monetary Fund (IMF) and the World Bank, and Norway participated actively in establishing the General Agreement on Trade and Tariffs (GATT) in 1947.

Participation in NATO, OEEC and the other international organizations implied both rights and duties – and gave members of the political and administrative elite an arena for communication and negotiation with colleagues from other western countries. The feedback from US officials on the Labour government's regulatory ambitions was reasonably clear, and the changing international context for Norwegian policy-making made it difficult to implement any form of socialism. There was neither a separate ministry nor a strong unit for planning within the state administration; the regulatory authority was placed within the different ministries. The Ministry of Finance was a sort of 'super-ministry', but primarily on the budget side. What evolved was a state-guided collaborative economy influenced by the norms, values and the relative strength of the Labour Party and its supporting social classes.

The co-operative part of the emerging governance structure had several elements and several levels, with roots in the pre-war era. Both the early efforts to cope with the crises and the war itself strengthened social and national solidarity and the quest for co-operation. The compromise between the farmers and the working class supporting the Nygaardsvold government was not the only collaborative event of consequence in 1935. The year also saw the establishment of the Basic Agreement between the Norwegian Employers' Confederation and the National Federation of Labour. This 'Industry Constitution' gave a general framework for how to solve the conflicts between the two parties. Basic regulations in agriculture and the fisheries, built on the co-operatives and organizations of farmers and fishermen, were mostly in place even before 1935.

Intended to be part of a comprehensive planning structure, the government tried to arrange a co-operative three-level industrial structure. A National Economic Co-ordination Committee was set up in 1945. This consultative body involved representatives from the government, the state administration and the most important national interest groups. In accordance with an agreement between the National Federation of Labour and the Norwegian Employers' Confederation in 1946, co-operating production committees were set up in individual firms. Finally, a law from 1947 established industry-by-industry committees for co-ordination and planning at the level of branches and sectors. The National Committee was dissolved in 1954, having experience continued conflicts of interests. The industry-by-industry bodies functioned more satisfactorily as consultative bodies. The co-operative aspects of the firm-based committees were pursued in legal form by the law on industrial democracy passed by the Storting with a broad majority in 1972. The law decided that companies with more than 200 employees must elect a corporate assembly with two-thirds of the representatives elected by shareholders and one-third by the employees. The assembly elected of the board of directors, and had some duties of supervision, issuing opinions and decision-making.

In 1950, the government agreed with the Farmers' Union and the Small-holders' Union on a Basic Agricultural Agreement involving negotiations on biennial agricultural agreements. The agreement's framework was divided between subsidies allocated via the national budget and changes in the market prices for agricultural products. In 1964 a similar Basic Agreement for the Fishing Industry was implemented between the state and the Norwegian Fishermen's Association.

What emerged was a corporative structure, also visible through broad interest representation in a large number of more or less permanent official committees, boards and councils. In 1970, national organizations had 1900 representatives in such bodies, often being delegated some important public authority within a sector.[41] On the one hand, this meant an extension of democracy. On the other, the strong interest organizations' influence on policy challenged the power of Parliament. The political scientist, Stein Rokkan, formulated it this way: 'Votes count but resources decide.' The historian Edvard Bull, Jr named the corporative governance structure a 'partnership of the elite'.

The entrepreneurial and industrial state

In the sections describing the periods up until 1935, we presented many private entrepreneurs, some of whom also played a role as public entrepreneurs, like Gunnar Knudsen. In the period 1935–70, we find fewer outstanding private entrepreneurs. At least three reasons account for this. First, since we usually focus on entrepreneurs establishing what become large and successful firms, most of the large and successful firms after 1945 had been established long ago (Table 11.2). Managers more than creative and risk-taking entrepreneurs occupied the commanding heights of private business.

Among the big companies in manufacturing and mining were well-established firms such as AS Sydvaranger (1906), Christiania Portland Cementfabrik (1892), Borregaard (1889–1892) and Elektrisk Bureau (1882). However, some of the most prominent managers in big firms had family

Table 11.2 **The 10 private companies with the greatest capital assets, 1960 (with founding year)**

Company name	Company type
1. Den norske Creditbank	Bank (1857)
2. Bergen Privatbank	Bank (1855)
3. Norske Folk	Insurance (1917)
4. Chr. Bank & Kreditkasse	Bank (1848)
5. Norsk Hydro	Manufacturing (1905)
6. Fellesbanken	Bank (1920)
7. Norsk Kollektiv Pensjonskasse	Insurance (1938)
8. Idun	Insurance (1861)
9. Gjensidige	Insurance (1816/1847)
10. Akers mek.Verksted	Manufacturing (1841)

relations to members of the pre-war industrial bourgeoisie of active owners and entrepreneurs.

Second, the financial situation and structure did not encourage business start-ups. The Labour government kept interest rates low, but credit was rationed and allocated according to political decision. The stock exchange the Oslo Børs, was of little importance for getting equity, and private venture capital was scarce. Financing of the investments within manufacturing after 1950 was primarily provided by loan capital, and the proportion of equity capital decreased in the following decades. This strengthened the position of the managers relative to the owners.

Third, in the post-war years, the state was the leading industrial entrepreneur. One indication of a more offensive policy was the establishment of several new ministries. In 1947 the Ministry of Industry and Craft was established, headed by Lars Evensen from the National Federation of Labour. The Ministry of Trade and Shipping was established in the same year with Erik Brofoss as minster. The Ministry of Fisheries was up and going in 1946, while the Ministry of Agriculture was inherited from the start of the century.

Reconstruction was the main priority of economic policy in the early post-war years. The Germans had used the 'scorched-earth' policy in the two northern counties of Finnmark and Troms, and large regions had to be completely rebuilt. Other parts of the country were also hard hit by the war. But in parallel with the reconstruction efforts, several initiatives were taken to secure long-term economic growth. Manufacturing industry was seen as the main productive source, and two lines of strategy for state entrepreneurship were of special importance for stimulating further industrialization. One was to make most of the nation's comparative advantages by revitalizing the large-scale exploitation of hydro power and other natural resources. This was an industrialization path that had been halted after the First World War. The other was to invest in institutions for R&D supporting industrial growth, inspired by how new science-based technology had contributed to warfare. We start with the first line of strategy.

In 1946, the Storting decided on building the steel and iron producing Norsk Jernverk and the aluminium factory Årdal Verk. With promises of support from the Marshall Plan, in 1951 the Storting also decided to let Årdal Verk go on building an aluminium factory in Sunndal, resulting in the new name, Årdal og Sunndal Verk. State entrepreneurship in aluminium was pushed forward by the war heritage. The aluminium works in Årdal and the related Tyin power plant was close to being finished by the Germans when it was confiscated by the Norwegian state. The Germans had also started constructing an aluminium plant in Sunndal and the Aura power plant. Norsk Jernverk represented the final realization of a broad national ambition going back to the 1920s. In the middle of the 1960s the state-owned Norsk Jernverk and Årdal og Sunndal Verk were Norway's third and fifth biggest manufacturing companies. Parts of the established business community acknowledged the lack of strong modernizing initiatives in the private sector during the inter-war years and co-operated with the new Labour government. In Chapter 12 on Elkem, we can see how this firm collaborated with and helped the Labour government in their industrial ambitions and at the same time secured a market for the Söderberg electrode at both Jernverket and Årdal og Sunndal Verk.

After the early 1920s, few new power plants were constructed. In 1947, the President of the Norwegian Technical College, the prominent Professor Fredrik Vogt, was recruited as Director General of the nearly defunct Norwegian Watercourse and Electricity Board (NVE). NVE was strengthened to build the huge power stations serving the new power-demanding industries. This state-owned institution developed into the largest supplier of hydro power to both private and state-owned power-intensive industry, also being responsible for the national grid.

Norsk Hydro was the private company most privileged by the supply of very cheap electricity from NVE. After the war, the state had taken possession of German property in Norway, and the German shares in Norsk Hydro. After the confiscation, the state owned 44 per cent of the company, extended to 51 per cent in 1970, one reason for the long-term relationship between the state and the company. Another reason for privileging Norsk Hydro was its substantial export of fertilizers, providing the nation with much-needed foreign currency. Elkem was another company favoured by the state with favourable tax concessions and cheap energy – for instance, when setting up its aluminium factory in Mosjøen in North Norway in 1956 in a joint venture with the Swiss AIAG (later Alusuisse). Such positive economic incentives were an integrated part of the social democratic governance system.

Foreign capital for the power-intensive industries was actively sought by Trygve Lie, who in 1959 was appointed as a 'travelling ambassador'. Lie was former Secretary-General of the United Nations (UN) and had participated in several Labour governments. Lie's ambassadorship contributed to the building of two oil refineries (Esso and Shell) and three aluminium works. The aluminium work Søral at Husnes (1965) had AIAG as the dominant owner, while Norsk Hydro and the American company Harvey Aluminium joined forces to build the Alnor aluminium factory at Karmøy (1963). This was Norsk Hydro's first foray into the aluminium industry (its only significant area of business in late 2007), and Harvey had to provide the competence in the initial phase. Hydro and Harvey had 51 and 49 per cent of the ownership, respectively. Finally, Elkem and American Alcoa owned equal shares in a new aluminium work at Lista (1971). In 1969 Aloca also took over AIAG's part in the Mosjøen aluminium plant.

How could a Labour government be so welcoming to big foreign firms? Among other possible reasons for scepticism, the foreigners were also carriers of unfamiliar management cultures. In talks with Norsk Hydro's director general, Johan B. Holte, a representative from Harvey commented: 'You act and think like a government. If you continue like this you must sooner or later go broke.'[42] However, the results for both economic growth and the realization of regional policy aims were positively evaluated in their own right. In addition, the aluminium industry was highly vertically integrated and until the 1970s dominated by the 'Big Six', among them Alcoa, Alcan and AIAG/Alusuisse. The Norwegian smelters were dependent on both supplies of raw material (alumina) and on being able to sell their semi-finished products to manufacturers of finished products. The foreign aluminium companies reduced the risks at both ends of the value chain. Such consideration also motivated the sale of 50 per cent of the shares in Årdal og Sunndal Verk to Canadadian Alcan in 1966. Several fabricating firms had been bought by foreign aluminium companies, and the management at Årdal og Sunndal feared that the sale of their products would be more difficult. Since Alcan

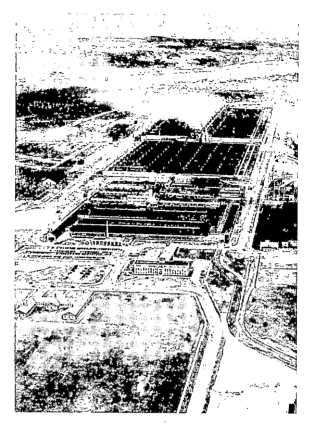

Photograph 11.4 **The Arvida aluminium plant, owned by the Aluminium Company of Canada.** *The picture is from the late 1940s, when Arvida was the largest aluminium factory in the world, producing approximately 400,000 tons per year.*
Source: Elkem.

had a substantial share in Norsk Aluminium Company (NACO), NACO was merged with Årdal og Sunndal Verk in 1969. However, the sale to Alcan provoked a lot of political noise, and in 1974 and 1979 the state bought back Alcan's shares in Årdal and Sunndal Verk.

Having entered aluminium, Norsk Hydro developed an ambition to be the main player in the Norwegian aluminium industry. It started both to establish and to buy firms upstream and downstream in the value chain. In 1986, the aluminium division of Norsk Hydro merged with Årdal og Sunndal Verk. The new company was called Hydro Aluminium and was owned 70 per cent by Norsk Hydro and 30 per cent by the state. In 1988, the state sold its shares to Norsk Hydro. In 2007, Hydro was the world's third largest vertically integrated aluminium company, and the state was still Hydro's largest owner.

With the Södeberg electrode as the main exception, the national contribution to innovation and knowledge creation within the aluminium industry was not a pioneering one. Co-operation with foreign firms was until the 1970s vital to the operation and modernization of Norwegian companies. Only from the mid-1960 did Årdal og Sunndal Verk start to develop a more fertile and permanent relation to the relevant Norwegian institutions for R&D. In 1977 Norsk Hydro established its own R&D centre at Karmøy with a focus on both metallurgical development and on value adding activities such as extrusion, casting and rolling.[43] From being dependent on high shares of imported competence and foreign capital, the aluminium industry was transformed into a national, well-integrated business centrally situated within a broader innovation and knowledge creation system.[44]

Public–private combines and the systems of knowledge and innovation

A forerunner within aluminium-related R&D was Kai Grjotheim from the Norwegian Institute of Technology. In 1956, he wrote his PhD thesis on aluminium electrolysis. He collaborated with people at Elkem's factory, Fiskaa verk, and as a professor at the Institute he initiated a long-term project on the 'theory of aluminium electrolysis'. Many of Grjotheim's students became valuable managers and employees in the industry.[45] What evolved at the Institute of Technology in Trondheim after the war was one of the main centres of technological R&D. In 1946, the Labour government doubled the budget allocation to the Institute. The same year, the Norwegian Council for Scientific and Industrial Research (NTNF) was set up. NTNF was one more example of the co-operative relationship between state and industry, partly financed by the state (income from a state-owned lottery) and partly by industry. Initiatives of NTNF created several industrially focused R&D institutes. NTNF's first executive director was the young geologist Robert Major (the man who recommended Kai Grjotheim to write his PhD thesis on aluminium electrolysis). The influential chairman of the board, Alf Ihlen, was one of the most well-respected industrialists and the CEO of Strømmens Verksted, a pioneer in using aluminium as a material for buses, trams and trains, and part of a public–private combine. The company cultivated strong and long-term co-operative relations first of all with the Norwegian State Railways, and also with Oslo Sporveier, the company responsible for the tramways and public transport in the capital city.

When the aluminium industry in the late 1960s started to search for research-based technological knowledge, it could draw on a knowledge-creation system developed over a couple of decades. People such as Major and Ihlen represented a proactive attitude towards the industrial need for systematic R&D. The supply of research resources sometimes and in some areas even seemed to exceed the demand. Public–private combines became the most productive arenas for interaction between R&D on the one side and industrial innovation and problem-solving on the other. Somewhat paradoxically Strømmens Verksted and its main customer the Norwegian State Railway never developed a strong R&D collaboration. Probably this was one reason for the company's failure to meet its main customer's requirement from the 1980s. It could also explain why the rump of the company in 2007 was only a repair shop, not a centre of excellence, inside Bomardier Transportation – the world's largest company for rail equipment manufacturing.

In 1950 NTNF established the Central Institute for Industrial Research in Oslo, close to the University of Oslo. The staff at the Norwegian Institute of Technology was disappointed at not having the new research centre to Trondheim. They established the Foundation for Scientific and Industrial Research at the Norwegian Institute of Technology (SINTEF) the same year. At least as important for industrial innovation and progress was the foundation of the Norwegian Defence Research Establishment (FFI), in 1946. It was organized as an administrative agency subordinate to the Ministry of Defence. The head of this ministry in 1945–53, the lawyer Jens Chr. Hauge, was the main entrepreneur behind both the establishment of FFI and the Institute for Nuclear Research (IFA) in 1951.

As a leader of the military resistance organization Milorg during the German occupation, Hauge had a high standing and personal connections in most political quarters. He was also in a favourable position to cultivate good relations to the many Norwegian engineers that had been in Great Britain during the war. Several of these had participated in the efforts to develop weapon and defence systems, especially related to electronics and microwave systems. These engineers were eager to bring their knowledge and experience into useful practice in Norway. A generation of nationally-oriented, well-educated engineers complemented the parallel generation of economists. Jens Chr. Hauge joined professions and politicians in building up a military–industrial complex of private–public combines. This complex also functioned as an innovations system, with some important results for civil companies.

One example of FFI's civil importance was its contribution to fostering Nera, for a long time the only wholly Norwegian telecoms firm of any significance. Among the confiscated German property were the electrotechnical subsidiaries of Siemens, AEG and Telefunken, and Nera was based on the remains of Telefunken. In 1947, the state made a deal with the owners of the private telephone company Bergen Telefonkompagni; the owners accepted 80 per cent of the shares in the confiscated companies as payment for letting the Norwegian Telegraph Administration take over the telephone system. The owner-group took the name Bergen Industri-Investering and became an important industrial actor. The microwave competence in FFI was then transferred to Nera and the company was commissioned to build the first microwave radio link systems for the armed forces' communication network. Later the telegraph administration also used Nera as their favoured supplier of radio links, and in building the extensive broadcasting network for television in the 1960s. Radio links became an important export product for Nera. Simrad was another company used and supported by FFI. The main entrepreneur behind Simrad, Willy Simonsen, was part of the network of engineers in Britain during the war. FFI contributed their competence in high-frequency radio technology and electronics to assist Simrad build maritime radiotelephones, echo sounders and sonars both for civil and military use. Simrad also became an important part of the Norwegian maritime cluster, with other companies located close to the Norwegian Navy's shipbuilding yard in Horten.

A more purely military arrangement was the connection between FFI, the Kongsberg Weapons Factory and Raufoss Ammunisjonsfabrikk. Both the Kongsberg Weapons Factory and Raufoss Ammunisjonsfabrikk were old, state-owned firms. The factory at Kongsberg had been established in 1814 producing swords, guns, pistols and later cannon, while the ammunition producer at Raufoss had been set up in 1896. Both factories had alternated between a focus on military and on civil production, dependent on changes in foreign politics and the perception of military threats. In 1947 FFI and Raufoss Ammunisjonsfabrikk started a long and troubled collaboration on the production of missiles based on British design. Later the Kongsberg Weapons Factory became the most important partner for FFI, especially in developing the advanced anti-submarine missile Terne from the mid-1950s and the anti-ship missile Penguin from the mid-1960s. The rocket motors were produced at Raufoss. The missile projects were part of NATO's weapons programme and were economically supported by the US Navy. The development work was carried out in close collaboration with the Norwegian Navy.

Until the 1960s, FFI dominated the partnership with the companies at Kongsberg. But the complexity of the missiles systems also brought the engineers at Kongsberg into contact with most of the other research institutes, like SINTEF, SI and the Christian Michelsen's Institute in Bergen. Competence in fields such as control engineering and cybernetics, electronics, automation, computing and especially system integration was gradually built up inside the weapons factory itself. From the start in 1955 until 1965, the development department increased from two to 150 staff members. The weapons factory became more autonomous. After leaving office as a minister in the mid-1950s, Jens Chr. Hauge carried on as the chairman of the board at both Kongsberg and Raufoss and did his best to secure political support for these core parts of the military–industrial complex. The advanced weapons factory was not able to create a profit on its own, so the authorities' benevolence was necessary. As we shall see in the next section, this mostly unprofitable building up of competence became a platform for advanced and profitable businesses from the late 1980s.

One main collaborator for Hauge was Finn Lied, another of the bright engineers from war-time Britain and also a member of the Labour Party. Lied started to work at FFI in 1946 and took over as the executive director of the Institute in 1957. In the 1970s FFI had a staff of 500 people and Lied became one of the most influential people in the Norwegian R&D sectors. Hauge and Lied had a special responsibility for Norway becoming the world's seventh largest exporter of weapons in the 1970s – for good or bad.

In accordance with the visions of Hauge and Lied, viable efforts to secure a long-term civil production at Kongsberg and Raufoss gradually emerged. In 1957, Raufoss Ammunisjonsfabrikk and the Kongsberg Weapons Factory made an agreement with Volvo for the production of car parts. In 1965, Raufoss made a new and much bigger deal with Volvo, starting with the supply of 500,000 aluminium bumpers. About the same time, Raufoss started substantial production of aluminium sections, creating a holding company with Årdal og Sunndal Verk called I/S Aluminiumprofiler. Raufoss critical competence was, in the same way as at Kongsberg, developed during the first couple of decades after the war. In the late 1990s, Raufoss Aluminiumsfabrikk was divested into several smaller niche producing and profitable companies, not unlike the Kongsberg Weapons Factory.

An atomic failure

Until the 1970s, FFI, Jens Chr. Hauge and the network of research engineers gave a strong and positive impetus to the modernization of Norwegian industry. Certainly, far from all initiatives were successful. Sometimes the gap between vision, input of economic resources and manpower, on the one hand, and industrial output on the other, was formidable – as in the attempt to industrialize nuclear energy in Norway.

In 1947 Hauge achieved political support for the construction of a nuclear research reactor at Kjeller. It was first planned to be integrated with FFI's activities, but scepticism about letting the military have a hand in the project led to the establishment of the Norwegian Institute for Atomic Energy in 1948. The first executive director of the Institute was one more of the talented young men doing war research in Britain, the astrophysicist Gunnar Randers. Filled with optimism for both nuclear power in general and for nuclear-powered ships in particular, the first reactor JEEP was started at Kjeller in 1951. At this time, only the US, Great Britain, France and Soviet Union were the countries with their own nuclear reactors. In 1959 a second reactor was started in Halden. From 1960 to 1971 Finn Lied was the chairman of the board at the Institute, underlining the strong connection with the Institute's neighbour at Kjeller, FFI.

The Nuclear Institute devoured a huge proportion of the public expenditure directed at scientific and technological research. The university scientists were not surprisingly among the most outspoken opponent of the large grants in the late 1960s. Abundance of water power, the discovery of oil, increased political scepticism about nuclear power, no feasible powering solutions for ships and the inability to compete on the international market all put the Institute under pressure. After strong political protests, the Storting in the early 1970s decided not to go on with the plans to build nuclear power plants in Norway, and the Institute had to strongly pull back its ambitions. Some commercial activity was carried out through NORATOM, organized as a private limited company in 1959. NORATOM was an engineering and consultant company interacting with Norwegian industry for commercialising nuclear technology. Both Norsk Hydro and the Kongsberg Weapons Factory were among the shareholders in NORATOM. Central on the board was, again Jens Chr. Hauge. The executive director from the start to 1971 was the earlier leader of FFI, Fredrik Møller. NORATOM was a failure and closed down in 1979. Its resources and competence were transferred to the Kongsberg Weapons Factory.

The economic and human resources channelled to nuclear research certainly could have been allocated more productively. But especially by serving the emerging petroleum sector, the Institute's competence in material technology, process control and mathematical modelling were productively utilized.

In 1980 the Institute was renamed the Institute for Energy Technology. The research activity connected to the nuclear reactor in Halden as part of the explanation for the city's becoming a vital technology city in the early 2000s.

Electricity as necessity, telephones as 'luxury'

When the state kept 20 per cent of the shares in the confiscated German electrotechnical firms, it was seen as an instrument to facilitate the build-up of a genuinely national electro-technical industry. This ambition was in line with the state's strong focus on hydro power development and electrification. A competitive national electrotechnical industry would strengthen the industrial foundations of a vulnerable open economy. The Minister of Industry, Lars Evensen, was eager to stimulate business serving the home market, not only the export-oriented industry.

To create national public–private combines in both the power supply and telecommunications industries was one main instrument in supporting national production. However, the largest equipment suppliers in both the 'high-current' and 'low-current' electro-technical industry located in Norway were still controlled by foreign firms. Among the most important firms in the high-current part, supplying generators, high-voltage circuit breakers and transformers to the utilities, NEBB was controlled by the Swiss Brown Boveri and Per Kure A/S by the Swedish ASEA. Among the main low-current producers of telephone sets, exchanges and cables, Standard Telefon og Kabelfabrikk and Elektrisk Bureau/Norsk Kabelfabrikk were controlled by the American ITT and the Swedish L.M. Ericsson, respectively. In 1960, the confiscated former Siemens subsidiary Proton was sold back to Siemens; Proton was in any case still very dependent on the competence and the licences of its former owner. After all, one main policy goal was to secure full employment. And to meet the policy-makers' expectations, the foreign subsidiaries produced most equipment on licence in Norway. The large foreign subsidiaries also had strong labour unions and vested local interests strongly interested in securing employment opportunities. There public utilities seemingly had difficulties in discriminating between the wholly Norwegian-owned companies and the foreign subsidiaries.

Until the late 1960s, electrification was seen as more important than the modernization and extension of the telephone network. Electricity was a necessity for all. Telephones in ordinary households were luxury. This understanding was reflected in both the Parliament's budgets and in the strongly regulated credit allocations. In 1970, only 1000 people in very remote areas were without electricity. In 1980, nearly 100,000 people were waiting in the 'telephone queue'.

The state's share of total electricity production increased mainly because NVE served much of the power-demanding industry. The municipal and county-owned utilities still supplied most of the general supply. The electricity supply was extremely decentralized, with more than 800 utilities in the early 1960s. Through a variety of support schemes, use of credit allocations and concessions, NVE tried to rationalize this structure, but in 1970, there still were 550 utilities, a modest result given NVE's ambitions and the size of the country. A large proportion of the centralization came as a result of mergers of municipals.

The decentralized structure was compensated by tight networking, at both the regional and the national level. The utilities' national trade organiza-tion was an arena for knowledge transfer, standardization and technological development. In 1952, the Norwegian Electric Power Research Institute was established, doing developmental work in close co-operation with the trade organization and the many utilities. Co-operation was facilitated by the monopoly in supply, transmission and distribution. The bigger utilities and NVE often took responsibility for more large-scale developmental projects.

The foreign ownership of the main electro-technical companies and the general small-scale character of the whole power supply industry created struc-tural barriers for developing a very productive national innovation system in the high-voltage industry. It was also a paradox that the power research institute in the country with the highest *per capita* consumption of electricity never had half the number of employees as the institute for atomic energy.

In telecommunications, the state at least had some success with its ration-alization of structure. During the period 1936–74 the Norwegian Telegraph Administration rationalized 233 local telephone companies, creating a state monopoly only a few years before it became contested. The long under invest-ment in this infrastructure created serious problems when the first indications of an information society started to emerge in the late 1960s. Large parts of the telephone system were still based on manual exchanges; most of the tech-nical staff in the state telegraph administration was home-educated and not in touch with what was going on in microelectronics and digital technology. After pressure from the engineering elite in NTNF and FFI, an R&D institute was established in 1968 as a department within the telegraph administration (from 1970 changing its name from Telegrafverket to Televerket, or from Norwegian Telegraph Administration to Norwegian Telecommunications

Administration). This ambitious institute, together with much more generous appropriations especially in the 1970s, resulted in an internal upgrading of Norwegian telecommunications being visible to most customers after 1980. But even if most of the telecoms equipment was bought from firms located in Norway and the new research department institutionalized propitious developmental contracts with industry, Norway did not develop viable telecom manufacturers as Sweden and Finland had done. We will return to this topic when discussing the period 1970–2007.

Industrial rationalization and the liberalization of trade

The efforts to centralize the telecoms and electricity system were placed under the label of 'rationalization'. The consequences of such rationalizing initiatives were sometimes doubtful. Both Finland and Denmark maintained a decentralized telecom structure without losing pace in modernization. Electricity prices in the decentralized Norwegian electricity supply were lower than in any other industrialized country. Together with the favourable hydro power, there were small-scale advantages, such as the local politicians' ability to exercise control over the utilities. The utilities still functioned as co-operatives embedded in and a part of the local communities.

In other sectors, large scale obviously represented an economically more efficient way of organizing. We have seen that the Labour government reneged on their ambition to have a separate rationalization law. But the ambition to increase productivity by the structural rationalization of sectors and by the rationalization of work processes continued to be an integrated part of the social democratic order. To some extent it implied a vitalization of the technocratic visions of the inter-war years. The young economists' hubris on behalf of economic planning was only one example of such a vision. Similar currents of technocracy and scientism mixed with social commitment were also evident in pedagogy, architecture, psychology and medicine.

In 1947 the Storting decided to set up a Directorate of Rationalization with special responsibility for the efficient organization of the state administration. With push from the US, with economic support from Marshall Aid, and with backing from both the Industrial Association and the National Federation of Labour, the Storting decided in 1953 to establish the Norwegian Institute of Productivity, which could be interpreted as compensating the lack of a rationalization law. Rationalization offices and departments were organized not only in private factories, but also in the large public utilities. In 1946 the government established a rationalization committee for agriculture, the year after, the fisheries got their own committee.

Norway's gradual integration into a more liberalized international economy increased the incentives for rationalization. In 1961 the OEEC was renamed the Organization for Economic Co-operation and Development (OECD), continuing to promote the use of market mechanism both between and inside national economies. In 1959, Norway joined the European Free Trade Association (EFTA), despite widespread scepticism among manufacturers. In 1967, most manufactured products were part of free trade.

Part of the rationalization effort was directed at the workplaces. Its practical implementation, like work measurement and reorganization, was done in co-operation between the employers and the unions. In 1952 the National Federation of Labour started an extensive programme of TWI (Training Within Industry) courses. The plan and structure of these courses was developed in the US during the war in order to make the manufacturing industry more efficient. The courses were partly financed by the federation itself, partly by American support. Within ten years, 4350 TWI courses had been arranged, with more than 42,000 participants. The Labour government, the strong national labour union and the collective bargaining gave the workers a security that the increased productivity would also benefit them. From 1945 to 1970 the number of members in the National Federation of Labour increased from 400,000 to 602,000, by the end of the period having 43 per cent of all employees as members. Including other wage-earner organizations, the union density in 1970 was 51 per cent. The positive attitude of the unions and the workforce towards rationalization probably contributed significantly to the high increase in productivity during the 1950s and 1960s.

The wood-processing industry was one of the sectors where the need for structural rationalization seemed most urgent. Until the 1920s, the Norwegian firms had been among the internationally leading producers of mechanical and chemical pulp. The natural comparative advantages deciding the location of the factories were the cheap hydro power used for mechanically driven machinery and the rivers for timber floating. After the war, these locations were less favourable. The possibility of transmitting electricity over large distances and the increasing use of trucks for transporting the timber, made locations near good harbours the most competitive. Most of the companies were small and not in a good position to invest in the new sulphate method for the production of pulp. The Ministry of Industry was rather unsuccessful during the 1960s in its effort to push for structural rationalization within the industry. In the mid-1960s, Norwegian firms were on average only one-third of the size of Finnish companies, and half of Swedish.[46] The export of pulp, paper and fibre boards became less important; its share of total export commodities fall from 23.2 per cent in 1950 to 11.9 per cent in 1970. In 1962 the forest owners established what ended up as the corporation Norske Skog. As we shall see later, through M&As this firm gradually managed to rationalize the industry.

Within other industries the rationalization was more profound. The engineering industry, and especially the shipyards, went through an extensive modernization and rationalization during the upswing in the 1950s and 1960s. The expansion of the shipyards was tightly connected to the parallel growth and modernization in shipping. As GDP tripled between 1946 and 1970, the merchant fleet increased from 3.4 to 20.1 gross tons, which was a six-fold increase: in 1968 Norway was the fourth biggest shipping nation. The demand for bigger and more complex ships was met with a transition from a 'British' to an 'American' style of production. Craft-oriented production was replaced by the use of production lines and sectioning of construction. Different part of the ship could be constructed at different yards. As a result of mergers, what became Akers Verft in the 1960s consisted of the former Akers Mek. Verksted, Nylands Verksted, Kampens Mek. Verksted, Stord, Tangen Verft, Trondjhems Mek. Verksted and Bergens Mek. Verksteder. Most of the merged companies had existed independently since the mid-nineteenth century. From next to nothing, the engineering industry was exporting about one-fifth of its production in 1970. In this year, ships accounted for 12 per cent of the total commodity export, and machinery 8.6 per cent, exemplifying a movement away from the one-sided natural resource-based industries. But 1970 was just the turning point for the coming of a new oil lubricated economy.

Making bigger units by M&As was one alternative for meeting the challenges of liberalized trade. In the 1960s there was a boom in mergers and co-operation agreements. In 1958, before EFTA was decided on, there existed only five co-operation agreements between 15 manufacturing firms. In 1960 and 1961, 44 co-operation agreements were made between 161 Norwegian manufacturing companies, 35 co-operation agreements between 76 Norwegian and foreign firms and 21 mergers between 42 Norwegian firms.[47] In 1968, 541 registered cartels covered a large proportion of products from agriculture, fishing, process industries, manufacturing and services.

Larger firms meant a need for larger amounts of capital and more sophisticated financial services. In 1954 there were 78 commercial banks, in 1970 the number had fallen to 40. Internationalization also meant that Norwegian firms started to establish subsidiaries abroad. In 1970 there were about 30 firms having such subsidiaries, among them banks.

The transformation and rationalization of agriculture after the war was more extensive than in any other period, without any threat of liberalization. To transfer labour from agriculture to the more productive manufacturing industry was considered necessary to reach satisfactory economic growth. The farmlands were decreased somewhat, the number of persons occupied in agriculture decreased dramatically (from 295,000 in 1946 to 124,000 in 1969), and the number of farms decreased from 196,000 in 1949 to 155,000 in 1969. The average size of farms increased by 24 per cent. In the same period, there was a strong growth in capital equipment, not only in the number of tractors. The number of milking machines went up from 6360 in 1949 to 51,540 in 1969; forage harvesters and motorized hay cutters became quite common. A substantial increase in production followed. About 70 per cent of production value came from animal husbandry, which increased 40 per cent from 1952 to 1960.

Compared to some other countries, the rationalization in Norwegian agriculture was not that impressive. In the period 1960–8, the use of labour in Swedish agriculture went down 6.9 per cent and in Denmark 6.2 per cent. The comparative decrease in Norway over 1959–68 was only 3.3 per cent. Agricultural development was seen as part of the prioritized district or regional policy.

As late as 1936, the Storting had banned the expansion of trawler fishing and denied Norwegian trawlers operating outside the territorial limit the right to deliver fresh fish in Norwegian harbours. At this time, there were only eleven Norwegian trawlers in operation.[48] The post-war years represented a radical shift in policy. The small-scale structure of the fisheries, upheld by the traditional combination of fishing and farming, was a main point of attack by the Labour government. The aim was to increase productivity through rationalization and mechanization and to transfer redundant labour to manufacturing industry. There were, however, opposing fractions within the Labour Party on how to restructure the industry. One fraction was led by the chairman of Norwegian Fishermen's Association, Jens Steffensen, who was also the chairman of the committee in the Storting that dealt with questions of fisheries. Steffensen ended up as a spokesperson for the minority in the rationalization committee appointed by the government in 1947. The majority wanted a substantial extension of the trawler fleet and to let the Directorate of the Fisheries have full control over the granting of concessions to new trawlers. Steffensen, all the representatives in the Storting from Northern Norway and the majority of the Labour Party representatives wanted the fishermen's organization to have more control with the granting of concessions. The Labour government's proposition was passed in the Storting only because of support from the non-socialist parties.

The production in the fisheries tripled from the late 1930s to 1970, representing an overfishing that seriously threatened the resource base of some fish. Even if about 80–90 per cent of the catches continued to be exported, the value of fish and fish products of total export decreased from 16.2 to 7.7 per cent from 1950 to 1970. As late as the 1950s, about 85 per cent of the catch volumes were taken at the coast and the nearest fishing grounds. After the extensive introduction of trawlers during the 1960s, more than half of the fish was caught in distant waters. Despite all the rationalization efforts, the fisheries maintained much of its traditional characteristics. In 1972, the Professor of Fishing Economics, Gerhard Meidell Gerhardsen, characterized the fisheries in this way: 'The Norwegian fisheries are strongly decentralized, both geographically and organizationally. In contrast to what is normal in several other countries, the settlement of the fishermen are scattered, and the catches are delivered in a large number of harbours.'[49]

Creating the welfare state

After the war, there were high ambitions to create extensive welfare arrangements and full employment in many countries. A main problem with such ambitions was the danger that an expansionary financial policy would create unwanted inflation. In explaining the early success of the welfare policy, especially in Sweden and Norway, the Danish sociologist Gøsta Esping-Andersen writes that within Scandinavia, 'as well as among all the capitalist democracies', it was 'only Norway and Sweden that were capable of translating the full-employment commitment into reality'.[50] The foundation for an active welfare and employment policy were similar in the two countries: 'strong universalist trade unions, and a labour party capable of dominating the political coalition of farmers and workers that, in the first place, permitted social democratic [ascendancy]'. In contrast to Denmark, the trade union movements in Sweden and Norway 'were far more unified and capable of central co-ordination of bargaining, while farmers were both politically and economically more marginal'.[51] It was possible for the trade unions to accept a solidaristic wage policy by guaranteeing continued high industrial investments. In Norway, this guarantee was secured by regulated credit allocations.

The gradual building up of the National Insurance Scheme (*Folketrygden*) was probably the most substantial welfare reform, implemented from 1967. It entitled members to pensions (e.g. old-age, survivors', and disability) as well as benefits in connection with industrial accident, accident and illness, pregnancy, birth, single-parent families and funerals. In 1964, the old law on poor relief was replaced by a law on social care giving the municipalities the duty to provide supplementary benefits to people in severe economic difficulties. A considerable extension of education on all levels had also important welfare aspects.

Larger scale: but not 'large scale'

The social democratic order gradually let economic policy serve more large-scale and centralized organizational forms within companies and branches. Economic co-ordination was brought more in accordance with the mainstream thinking on international Fordist orthodoxy. It was, however, not a one-dimensional and unilateral development. It was carried out most efficiently in the industries and economic sectors were the state had influence through direct ownership. In parts of the economy, the government's rationalization efforts met resistance. In an article from 1972, the economist Einar Hope summarized the structure of Norwegian industry in this way: 'Nevertheless, there is little doubt that the small firms put a stronger mark on the business structure in Norway than in any other country on the same level of industrial development and mostly the same sector structure.'[52]

1970–2007: neo-liberal politics during a petroleum-fuelled, third industrial revolution

In the spring of 1970, Philips Petroleum Co. discovered oil in the Norwegian part of the North Sea and an adventurous history of oil and gas started. To understand the specific changes in the Norwegian economy and business system after 1970, we must take the activity in the North Sea into account.

Internationally, the period 1970–2007 partly represents the downswing of the fourth 'Kondratiev wave'. Traditional industries like textiles, steel production and car manufacturing had to cope with overproduction, competition from new industrialized countries and the demand for more flexibility. But the early 1970s also saw the introduction of a new technological paradigm. Digital information and communication technology (ICT) started the fifth 'Kondratiev wave' and the third industrial revolution. The birth of the microprocessor in 1972 was a 'Big Bang' initiating this technological revolution.[53] The digital communication networks of cables, radio waves, fibre optics and satellites emerged as a core infrastructure of the new age. The interaction of the petroleum sector and the emerging ICT industries is of special relevance for understanding the specifics of the Norwegian economy from the 1970s.

The ICT and the petroleum economies also interacted with the neo-liberal political shift from the late 1970s. The new natural resource represented an incentive for more state involvement, while the complex and fast-evolving digital technology was mostly unsuited for political governance and created pressure for less state intervention, especially in the telecom sector. Neo-liberalism challenged some basic qualities of the social democratic order, of the collaborative business system and even of Democratic Capitalism. The clear outline of the new order was, however, not always easy to discover. Less co-operation and more competition was the neo-liberal credo, while the 'network society' is often used as a diagnosis of contemporary social structure. Networks meant co-operation, and digital technology such as the Internet made social networks easier to establish. Competition made it profitable to make extensive use of co-operation, but competition also set definite limits to such co-operation. Many established co-operative ties disintegrated. Globalization evolved as a response to the liberalization of trade – and generally resulted in more big firms. But the firms were often corporations, or group of firms, with a lot of decentralized decision-making. The Norwegian telecom incumbent, Telenor, consisted in the early 2000s of about 400 limited companies. De-merger and specialization based on the slogan 'back to basics', was a trend with less effect. Globalization implied the shutdown of some firms, but also the making of some local centres of excellence within the international firm. For example, the Norwegian unit ABB Marine at Billingstad outside Oslo became a centre of excellence for some oil-related activities within the global firm ABB.

The oil-rich Norway had more than satisfactory economic growth in the decades after 1970. The international oil crisis in 1973, when the actions from the Organization of the Petroleum Exporting Countries (OPEC) substantially increased oil prices, triggered a downturn in western economies. Obviously, increased oil prices were no big problem for an oil-producing nation: the real growth of GDP from 1970 to 2007 has been more than 160 per cent.

On the one hand, this made it easier to keep the welfare state going: when, for instance, the number of public employees in Sweden feel by 200,000 between 1980 and 1998, in Norway it rose by 50 per cent. A review of the European welfare states during the 1990s concluded that 'Norway has been in a Nordic World of its own'.[54] In the period 1970–2006 the number of employees in education doubled, and those in health and social services increased four-fold.[55]

On the other hand, the new source of income for both the state and the citizens demanded budgetary and financial discipline. The Petroleum Fund of Norway was established in 1990 to counter the effects of the coming decline in income from the sector, to secure the pension schemes of the future, to prevent overheating and inflation in the economy and to smooth out the effects of fluctuating oil prices. In 2006 the fund changed its name to the Government Pension Fund – Global – it is the largest pension fund in Europe and the second largest in the world. In April 2007 it was estimated to total 1908 trillion kroner (US$ 317 billion).

Still, structural economic problems were clearly visible in Norway and contributed to the neo-liberal shift. From the early 1970s to the economic downturn in 1982–3, the unemployment rate was stable at about 2 per cent of the labour force. Since then, the figure has generally been a lot higher. In the early 1990s it reached 6 per cent, so let us start with the most troubled parts of the economy.

Questioning the industrial policy regime

The aggregate employment in manufacturing decreased substantially, from a peak of 385,000 people in 1973 to 260,000 in 1992. Then it increased somewhat before going down to 259,658 in 2005. This de-industrialization took place in all the 'old' industrialized countries, having a parallel in the growth of the so-called newly industrialized countries such as South Korea, Singapore and Taiwan and, later, China, Malaysia and Thailand. The blame for the industrial problems in the 'old economies' was not surprisingly laid at the door of the Keynesian or social democratic-inspired ruling parties. The decline of the blue-collar workers and voters created additional problems for the continuation of the social democratic order.

The Norwegian Labour Party was closely identified with some of the state-owned enterprises that had already by the 1960s experienced huge economic problems, most notably in the Norwegian Iron Works and the Coke Works in Mo i Rana. Both were established to create economic growth and support the development in northern Norway by exploiting natural resources. By 1970, the total expenditures on the steel mill had mounted to 1 billion kroner, and it still gave no promise of profit. Different boards, managers, ministries of industry, socialist and non-socialist governments tried to find ways out of the mess – without success.

The non-socialist parties made the state enterprises in Mo i Rana a symbol of a failed industrial and economic policy. But they also had more apparent failures to choose from. During the 1970s, the state monopoly Norwegian Telecommunications Administration (NTA) had huge problems in meeting the demand for telephones. Nor did it succeed in providing trade and industry with the most advanced and digital private branch exchanges and equipment. As late as in 1980, nearly 100,000 people were in the 'telephone queue'. The awareness of a coming information society made this situation even more worrying.

The post-war economic concept of 'market failure' was an integral part of social democratic ideology. As a rule, economic problems were interpreted as market failures. Solutions to problems in state-owned and state-regulated industries were often even more government intervention. To cope with the economic problems after the oil crisis, even private industrial companies increasingly benefited from the attention of the state. The Labour government interpreted the crisis as cyclical and expected high future revenues from oil production. In addition, the early 1970s were also characterized by a short, radical shift in politics. The shift to the left reflected both the general radicalization of young people and parts of the working class, and the heated political debate on the membership in the EC before the referendum in 1972, which the 'No' vote won. As a consequence, the government started an extensive selective industrial policy especially directed at the home-market-oriented textile industry (including clothing and footwear) on the one hand, and the shipyards on the other. Shipbuilding was also one of the traditional industries confronting international overproduction and intense competition worsened by the oil crisis.

Confidence in the interventionist, selective industrial policy gradually crumbled. Among the failures important in this learning process was the unsuccessful effort to create 'cornerstone enterprises' in the electronic industry. This industry was closely related both to the telecom and the military–state–private combine. A public report concluded in 1976 that the electronic industry had considerable problems, despite all its government support. To meet these problems, central politicians in the Labour Party and the Ministry of Industry drew up a 'cornerstone plan'. Three 'cornerstone enterprises' were given government's support: Tandberg Radiofabrikk, the Kongsberg Weapons Factory and Elektrisk Bureau. By co-operation and state support, these cornerstone enterprises were supposed to meet the requirements of scale in R&D, manufacturing and marketing.

When the technologically advanced Tandberg Radiofabrikk went bankrupt only two years later, it was the straw that broke the camel's back. Technocrats and politicians within the Labour Party started to doubt their own policy. The earlier Labour Minister of Industry, Finn Lied, headed a commission whole report of 1979 argued for policy change. The commission argued for more general support to strengthen competitiveness and to a higher degree let the market pick the winners and losers.[56]

The coming of a neo-liberal order

In 1981, the Labour Party's vice chairman, Einar Førde, published the book *We Are All Social Democrats*. The self-confident title reflected some truth about the political situation during the social democratic order. But in the year of publication, the first majority Conservative government since 1928 took power. Prime Minister Kåre Willoch and his Conservative Party were riding on the tide of an international shift to the right, a turn in political opinion which had made Margaret Thatcher the Conservative British Prime Minister in 1979 and the Republican Ronald Reagan US President in 1981.

From this time on, sector after sector faced the challenges of market-based competition. On the Norwegian policy front, the Progress Party was pulling a somewhat more moderate Conservative Party towards a more liberalist position, and the other parties were following. In the case history on Christiania Bank (Chapter 13) you see the liberalization of the credit and financial market, starting in the late 1970s and initiated by the Labour government. In several respects, despite the rhetoric, ministers, political leaders and bureaucrats related to the Labour Party were instrumental in introducing market-based competition, internationalization and privatization in many sectors. The Labour Party became 'modernized'. During the 1980s an economic political shift from a social democratic to a neoliberal order took place. In the same way as market failure had been the most common social democratic diagnosis of economic problems, 'government failure' now became the popular slogan.

Liberalization was tightly connected to the challenge of competition following internationalization and globalization. Even if Norwegians voted against joining the EC in 1972 and the EU in 1994, Norway was one of the first signatories to the GATT, and among the founding members of the WTO. The EFTA Convention established a free-trade area among its member states in 1960. The convention was followed up with free-trade agreements (FTAs) with several other countries. In 1994, the Agreement on the European Economic Area (EEA) between the EFTA countries (now Liechtenstein, Iceland and Norway) and the EU entered into force. The EEA is based on the same four 'freedoms' as that of the EU: the free movement of goods, persons, services, and capital.

The liberalization had consequences for most sectors. Among the most economically significant were perhaps the unbundling of the infrastructural state–private combines and most resource-based industries.

The disintegration of the state–private combines

Some backing and subsidizing of specific industries lasted through the 1980s. Many of the troubled firms were located outside the central areas. The continued support of these firms relied on the efficient mix of regional, industrial and social policy arguments. But, the lessons from the selective industry policy continued to be disappointing. From 1975 to 1985 employment in the textile industry fell to 14,000 from 26,000, despite heavy support. However, the closing down of factories was delayed and people had some time to adjust to the new situation.

After years of technological upgrading and expansion, but also with severe losses, the second company in the 'cornerstone enterprises' plan, the Kongsberg Weapons Factory, went bankrupt in 1987. With the Ministry of Defence and the Norwegian Defence Research Establishment as close allies, the bankruptcy of the factory was also a hard blow for an industrial policy trying to combine R&D on the one hand and industrial production on the other. The third cornerstone company, Elektrisk Bureau had, together with Standard Telefon- og Kabelfabrik, been a protected and favoured supplier of telephone exchanges to the NTA. During the 1980s, a modernized and a more market-oriented NTA changed its procurement practice. In 1983 Elektrisk Bureau lost the bid for supplying NTA with new digital switches to Standard Telefon- og Kabelfabrik. In 1988, together with all ASEA's and Brown Boveri's electronic and electro-technical undertakings in Norway, the much-reduced Elektrisk Bureau became part of the Swedish–Swiss ABB industrial group.

Standard Telefon- og Kabelfabrik had won the one big contract for digital switches, but the tender had been hard-fought, and the delivery of the very advanced switches resulted in heavy losses. The expectation was that the first supplies should secure a profitable contract during the next bid in 1990. NTA chose the best offer without any national industrial policy consideration, and the Swedish Ericsson Telecom won the contract. As a result, both the main suppliers of telecoms equipment in Norway ended up reduced and partly fragmented.[57]

The national state–private combine between the State Power Board, on the one hand, and the electro-technical, mechanical and construction industry one the other, also disintegrated. From the 1980s, the investments in dams, power stations and transmission lines fell substantially. The demand for electric power flattened out somewhat, and the liberalization of the power market from 1991 made it difficult for the state-owned utility, now named Statkraft, to make industrial policy a part of the purchase of equipment and services. After 1994, the EEA made it illegal to give preference to Norwegian firms. In the late 1990s it was also made clear that one of the main supports to the power-hungry electro-metallurgical and electro-chemical industries, cheap power from Statkraft, broke the rules of EEA. This led to the closing down of some factories and gave corporations such as Hydro and Elkem new incentives to invest abroad. Hydro is building a huge metal plant in Qatar, expected to be ready in 2010. Elkem decided in 2006 to move its smelting plant in Ålvik to Iceland, where the corporation was offered a better power contract. The connection to the Nordic and European power market resulted in a substantial increase in Norwegian electricity prices. The resource rent of the low-cost hydro power was now taken by the utilities and its owners. In 2007, 35 per cent of the hydro power production capacity in Norway was owned by the fully state-owned Statkraft, about 12 per cent by private corporations such as Hydro, Elkem and Hafslund. The rest, more than half of the capacity, was located in utilities where municipalities and counties owned the majority of shares.

The dissolution of the traditional state–private combines was closely connected with the liberalization of infrastructure. In some sectors, like telecoms, new technology was an important driver for liberalization. Digitalization and the subsequent convergence between telecoms, IT, broadcasting and consumer electronics made it impossible for NTA to keep its monopoly on equipment connected to the network or services distributed in it. Less obvious was the liberalization of the physical network and its operation. In 1988, the distribution of all sort of terminals, like telephones, modems, telefax and equipment for data communication, were opened up to competition. Through the 1990s a gradual liberalization of the telecoms sector ended with full liberalization in 1998, following the timetable of the EU's directives. In parallel with liberalization, the regulatory and monitoring authority, the Norwegian Post and Telecommunications Authority, was established and expanded. In 2000, the old telecoms incumbent, renamed Telenor from 1995, was partly privatized and listed on the stock exchange.

As during the introduction of the earlier political economic orders, the neo-liberal order had its public and private entrepreneurs. The economist, Labour Party member and, in a critical period Secretary General for the Ministry of Finance, Tormod Hermansen, probably was the most important public entrepreneur. Also heading public commissions, he was central in introducing the New Public Management (NPM) into the public sector. The central message of this management ideology was that more market orientation in the public sector, like outsourcing and competition, would lead to greater cost efficiency. Hermansen had a critical role in initiating the pioneering liberalization in the electricity sector from 1990. In 1991 he became the CEO of NTA, and used his good relations with politicians, ministers and public officials to commercialize, internationalize and privatize what became Telenor.

Recycling, developing and restructuring competence

The concept 'creative destruction' of the economist Joseph Schumpeter fits well into the technological paradigm and 'Kondratiev wave' way of thinking. So far, we have mostly focused on the destruction part of the period 1970–2007. It is time to look into what was created in those years. Let us start with the petroleum adventure.

It could have gone wrong – several times. It could have gone wrong in the autumn of 1962; then the US Philips Petroleum Company promised to establish considerable industrial activity in Norway if Philips was given exclusive rights of exploration and exploitation of the natural resources on the Norwegian continental shelf. Exxon and Shell expressed their interest the same autumn. With much doubt whether there would be oil to find, the government luckily said 'no'! However, the requests triggered questions on how the government should meet inquiries of this kind. A fundamental move was taken in 1963 when the government declared Norwegian sovereignty over the continental shelf, but only in 1965 were the first permits for exploration granted.

After many unsuccessful trials, just before Christmas Eve 1969 it was confirmed that Philips had found a commercially sustainable oil field, soon after called Ekofisk. It was the largest oil and gas discovery in the history of the North Sea, exploited over several decades. To further secure these values, by an Act of 17 December 1976 Norway granted itself an economic zone extending 200 nautical miles from the so-called 'base line' with sovereign rights to explore, exploit and manage natural resources in these waters. The main public entrepreneur initiating, negotiating, arguing and finding solutions in relation to international and law of the sea was the lawyer Jens Evensen. During the 1970s he was first Minister of Trade and Shipping and later Minister for the Law of the Sea in the Labour governments. A set of concession laws, very much in line with the laws that were introduced for the acquisition of waterfalls during the early part of the twentieth century was put in place. A tax regime with due consideration of the potential resource rent was also established. The Norwegian Petroleum Directorate and the wholly state-owned company Statoil was established in 1972 in the 'oil city' of Stavanger. A Ministry of Oil and Energy was separated from the Ministry of Industry in 1979, and by then the architecture of the state-constructed petroleum regime was mostly in place. Fearing, however, that Statoil might be too powerful and hard to control, the non-socialist government in 1984 divided Statoil's ownership. Until then, Statoil had normally got ownership of about 50 per cent of all licences in the North Sea. The government now established the State's Direct Financial Interest (SDFI) as a separate legal entity. Statoil's ownership in new licences was divided in two, one part to Statoil itself (typically 20 per cent), and the rest to the state through SDFI. Statoil administered SDFI until Statoil was partly privatized in 2001. Then the wholly state-owned company Petoro was established to manage SDFI.

Foreign oil companies were gradually given licences for exploration and exploitation in the North Sea. To achieve a good evaluation in the government's 'beauty contest' – that is, to be assigned the most interesting licences – the foreign oil companies went a long way to meet expectations on the use of and co-operation with Norwegian suppliers and research institutions, co-operation with Statoil, and a reasonable transfer of technology. Statoil not only became the most important petroleum company; it soon evolved as Norway's largest company. The Statfjord oil field, partly located in the British sector, was declared commercial in 1974. Statfjord received 50 per cent of the licence, while Mobil became the operator. Statfjord became Statoil's main challenger in the 1970s with regard to building up its organization, its competence and positioning itself in its political, technological and business environment. In 1979, regular production of oil and gas began at the Statfjord A field.

In 1981 Statoil got responsibility for the Gullfaks oil field, and the company became the first Norwegian operator on the shelf. In 1987, Statoil took over as an operator of Statfjord. Statoil became a vertically integrated corporation engaged in the exploration, production, transportation, refining and marketing of petroleum and petroleum-based products. In 2007 it is the operator of more than twenty oil fields. An internationalization strategy was implemented during the 1990s, based on a long lasting co-operation with BP. In 2007 Statoil was represented in thirty-four countries and had exploration and production activities in fifteen of them. Production outside Norway represented about 15 per cent of all output in 2006. At the end of 2006 Statoil had a market capitalization of 358 billion kroner and 25,400 employees. Norsk Hydro was the next biggest company according to market capitalization, 248.9 billion kroner in 2006. Hydro employed 33,000 employees in nearly forty countries.

We already know that Norsk Hydro was traditionally a big producer of fertilizers and entered into aluminium production in 1963. It also developed as the main Norwegian oil company beside Statoil. Already in 1963 Hydro had entered exploration activity in the North Sea as part of the Petronord group, consisting of Hydro, Elf and six other French companies. New methods of fertilizer production implied a conversion from ammonia production to the use of oil as a raw material. Hydro wanted to secure a stable supply of this raw material. Some hoped that Hydro would be the government's instrument to secure national interests, including the non-socialist four-party government lead by Prime Minister Per Borten from 1965 to 1971. For this reason, the Borten government worked in secrecy to increase its ownership in Hydro from 48 per cent to 51 per cent of the shares, with the help of Hambros Bank in London. In January 1971, the Storting approved the transaction. As we have seen, after the Labour Party took over the government, only a fully state-owned company constructed by central party members, like the Minister of Industry Finn Lied, was trusted.

With Philips, Hydro succeeded in negotiating a smaller stake in Ekofisk field as a participant. As with Statoil, Hydro's direct and practical work in the North Sea was limited during the 1970s. In 1982 Hydro got its first responsibility as an operator at the Oseberg oil and gas field, followed by Brage, and the gas field Troll and Ormen Lange. In the 1990s Hydro also went international with its expertise. In 1999 Hydro's petroleum section was significantly strengthened by the acquisition of Saga Petroleum, a fully privately owned company started in 1972 with partial ownership in sixty oil field licences and an operator of eighteen. Saga had a strong international focus, including major operations in the British sector as well as minor operations in Angola, Indonesia, Libya and Namibia. Hydro bought Saga after a period of low oil prices and mediocre results for Hydro's petroleum business. The CEO, Egil Myklebust, felt that a takeover would increase Hydro's reserves by 40 per cent, production by 45 per cent and give highly profitable synergies.[58] Both Statoil and Hydro were already shareholders in Saga. Statoil was, however, bought out by getting some of Saga's field licences.

In 2006, with the consent of the 'red–green' government of Prime Minister Jens Stoltenberg's Labour Party, Statoil and Hydro decided to merge their petroleum activity within one corporation, provisionally called StatoilHydro in 2007. The Norwegian state still holds approximately 62.5 per cent – in a Norwegian context, a giant state. The merged company is meant to be a strong actor in the competitive international arena, and is one of many cases of restructuring that challenges the structure of SMEs characterizing Democratic Capitalism. There were, however, also examples of de-mergers. In 2004, through a sell out of its fertilizer production (given the new name Yara), Hydro primarily remains an significant aluminium producer, the fifth biggest in the world.

The petroleum sector meeting the ICT paradigm

Both the formal regulations and the practice of licensing guided the foreign oil companies towards using Norwegian suppliers. Three groups of firms were particularly engaged in serving the activities in the North Sea: shipping, the engineering industry and the catalyst of the new technological paradigm, the ICT industry. First, how did the petroleum economy affect the introduction of advanced ICT?

On the one hand, the development of a profitable petroleum 'cluster' created a demand for advanced and tailor-made ICT services and equipment inside it. High economic growth also stimulated the use of ICT in other industries and among the general public. Early international statistics showed Norway to have a very high distribution of mobile phones, PCs and access to the Internet. On the other hand, a high price and wage level and the predominant channelling of political focus, investments and qualified people into the petroleum cluster, made it harder for parts of the ICT industry to succeed.

The interaction between established ICT competence and the new oil industry started out promisingly. In the first years of exploration, the traditional coastal radio network sufficed. By the early 1970s, Philips' activities on the Ekofisk field demanded more advanced services than could be provided by coastal radio. In 1976, a satellite communications network between the installations in the North Sea and a satellite earth station in the county of Rogaland, was built by NTA in co-operation with Norwegian research institutes and industry. Within few years, an oilfield operator such as Philips had also become a telecoms operator, managing a system with thirteen connected electronic exchanges, about 1000 telephones and terminals for data communication. This system was then connected to the Norwegian shore by satellite communication.

The North Sea project contributed to the evolving competence in satellite communications in both NTA and in the electronic company Nera in Bergen. Nera was a privileged supplier of microwave equipment to the extensive Norwegian radio-relay system. NTA became a leading participant in the International Maritime Satellite Organization (INMARSAT) established in 1979, an organization (later a company) that offers mobile satellite services. Nera became an important supplier of an accompanying mobile satellite terminal. After becoming Telenor, this company evolved as a prominent supplier of satellite broadcasting networks, and later broadcasting services by satellite, cable and terrestrial networks in the Nordic countries through Canal Digital.

During the 1990s, Telenor mostly lost connection with continually more advanced demand for transmission capacity and services in the petroleum sector. Other companies provided the oil companies with optical fibre networks. The liberalization of the telecoms sector made it possible for the oil companies increasingly to take care of communication services themselves. The networks were joined to extensive ICT systems where land-based control centres managed a growing set of activities either on the platforms or in the emerging sub-sea installations.

Why does Norway not have a Nokia or an Ericsson producing fancy digital mobile phones? The question has been asked repeatedly, also because of the fact that the entrepreneur Willy Simonsen and his firm Simonsen Radio had had success with producing high-quality analogue mobile telephones during the 1980s. Even more importantly, Norwegian engineers and researchers had participated extensively in the development of the GSM (Global System for Mobile communications) standard for digital mobile telephony. Together with more accidental reasons, foreign ownership of the main telecoms firms, the loss of NTA as a secure purchaser, and the gravitation of competence, investments and political focus on the petroleum economy provides some explanation. On the other hand, when NTA/Telenor internationalized in the early 1990s, its competence was used to make mobile telephone investments in emerging economies a successful area. In 2007 Telenor participated in twelve mobile operators outside Norway, one in Denmark and Sweden, four in Eastern Europe and five in Asia. Already by 1999, the number of international subscribers surpassed the number of Norwegian subscribers. In 2007, Telenor as an international operator had 115 million subscriptions. In early 2007, Telenor was the company with the third largest market capitalization, after Statoil and Hydro, confirming the ICT paradigm's real importance in this period.

In the more specialized computer industry, Norsk Data was the Norwegian firm that for a couple of decades seemed to be a success. Norsk Data started in 1967, recruiting its core staff among the researchers connected to the development of digital computers at the Norwegian Defence Research Establishment. A first version of its operating system Sintran was developed in 1968 by the group led by engineering cybernetics professor Jens G. Balchen at the technical college in Trondheim. Norsk Data supplied minicomputers to international research institutions and to Norwegian universities, municipal administration data centres, newspapers and the educational and health institutions. Norsk Data was for a period a preferred supplier to the public administration. In 1987, Norsk Data was the second largest company by stock value in Norway, second to Norsk Hydro, employing more than 4500 people. The dissolution of Norsk Data in early 1990 had several causes, including the company's holding on to its operating system Sintran too long, and not understanding the challenges from the PC early enough. Norsk Data dissolved into several rather small niche firms, including Dolphin Interconnect Solutions, a manufacturer of high-speed data communication systems, parts of the staff moving to companies Telenor and Siemens Nixdorf.

The reorganization and redirection of competence was widespread throughout the period. Firms that were victims of the 'creative destruction' of new technology and new framework conditions, like Tandberg and the Kongsberg Weapons Factory, gave birth to new internationally oriented and specialized firms that sometimes drew on a well-known company name of the past. After Tandberg went bankrupt in 1979, the firm split into Tandberg, Tandberg Data and Tandberg Television. The new Tandberg in 2007 was a producer of advanced systems of videoconferencing, competing on an international market. Tandberg Data focuses on data storage products, its specialized character becoming even more obvious when the firm in 2003 split into Tandberg Data, focusing on storage by streamers, and Tandberg

Storage, specializing in magnetic tape. Tandberg Television is a manufacturer of digital television broadcast systems.

Both the production of videoconferencing systems and digital television broadcast systems were closely connected to work done at NTA's research centre at Kjeller outside Oslo, as Norsk Data was an offspring of work at the Norwegian Defence Research Establishment also located at Kjeller. On the whole, a substantial part of the advanced competence being commercialized in the ICT industry in this period was generated here and at the research organizations of the Norwegian Technical University. The two most prominent ICT successes from the 1990s were Opera Software and Fast Search & Transfer. Opera originated as a research project developing a Web browser at NTA's research centre in 1994. Two of the researchers on the project, Jon S. von Tetzchner and Geir Ivarsøy, left NTA and started up an independent company in 1995. Opera developed a multi-platform product for a wide range of platforms, operating systems and embedded internet products. Fast was set up in 1997, and had its background in research on the fundamental problem of searching and filtering large volumes of data by many users at the Norwegian School of Technology and Science (NTNU) at the beginning of the 1990s. The CEO in 2007, John Lervik, was only one of several people from NTNU co-operating to establish the company. Typical of this sort of firm, Fast has a highly qualified staff: half of the about 700 employees are engineers, 50 have a PhD.

In addition to these Norwegian ICT firms, the big international firms like Microsoft, Siemens, Alcatel, Motorola and IBM had their smaller or larger subsidiaries supplying hardware and software and setting up connections with their headquarters. Interestingly, an inquiry using data from 1998 found that consulting firms like Cap Gemini, Avenir and EDB had about 40 per cent of all employees in the ICT industry. They were responsible for at least 50 per cent of the value creation.[59] The extensive use of consultancy firms in this and other areas indicates the end of a dominant mass producing Fordism. Consultants were often used to customize and adapt the use of complex equipment and software.

From a policy of the past to a profit of the present

Many of the largest companies after 1970 like Telenor, Hydro and Statoil, had a full or a majority share of state ownership. But even during the neo-liberal era, the state held a prominent place within the Norwegian business system. At the end of 2006, the Norwegian state controlled 32 per cent of the total

Oslo stock market. The country's largest bank, with a dominating position in the financial sector, was DnBNOR. The main organizational element in this financial corporation was the former Den norske Bank (DnB), again the result of a merger between Den norske Creditbank (DnC) and Bergens Bank in 1990. The financial crises hit DnB hard. In 1994, after the state's rescue action, the state owned 87.5 per cent of DnB. DnB NOR in 2007 is the end-point of several mergers, including the Norwegian Postal Bank and the main savings banks in eastern Norway. The state still owns 34 per cent of the corporation.

The state also owns some extremely valuable firms outside the stock market, most prominently the power producer Statkraft. An analysis from 2006 estimates that Statkraft, if quoted on the stock exchange, would have had the third largest market capitalization among Norwegian firms. The neo-liberal aspects of state ownership were less its extent than its prudent and non-interventionist practice.

As we have seen, state-owned research institutions from the social democratic order, provided the necessary competence for several entrepreneurial initiatives in the ICT sector. Some of these research institutions had far lower growth, or even experienced decreases, after the neo-liberal shift, as with Telenor. To some extent, the new age surfed on investments done in the past. During the 1990s, Telenor's research department was substantially scaled down. In the electricity industry, what was criticized as uneconomically high investments, or 'gold-plating', made it possible for the utilities to reap profits almost without investment well into the 2000s. Even the much-criticized selective industrial policy had some positive consequences during the neo-liberal order. The shipyards in most of the world confronted huge problems after the oil crises in 1973. Probably the state's support was a prerequisite for their successful readjustment to meet the demands of the oil companies.[60] The Aker Group was one striking example of the ability to take advantage of the new market. The first Norwegian-built drilling rig 'Ocean Viking' was taken into use by Philips in 1967, and was the rig used during the first oil discovery in 1969. A more innovative semisubmersible rig, the Aker H-3, was then designed, and during the period 1972–9 alone it produced 28 H-3 rigs, eighteen, of them by the Aker Group's own yards. It was the rig type most in demand during the 1970s.

The size and complexity of construction in the North Sea demanded a close co-operation between both the Aker Group and the operators, but also between the different yards within the Aker Group and between the Aker

Group and other sub-contractors. Market-based relations between companies and hierarchical relations inside companies were increasingly supplemented or even replaced by more network-oriented, co-operative relations. In 1970, the building contractors Engineer Thor Furuholmen, Høyer-Ellefsen and Engineer F. Selmer established the joint venture Norwegian Contractors to build a huge concrete storage tank to be used by Philips. The storage tank was a success, and in 1973 Norwegian Contractors, supplemented by firms as Aker, Kværner and the Kongsberg Weapons Factory, started the development of a concrete gravity-base platform to replace the traditional steel structures. These platforms were given a base of concrete oil storage tanks from which the concrete shafts rise. It was possible to finish a larger part of the construction on these Condeep (*con*crete *deep* water structure) platforms inshore, making production cheaper. Besides combining the platform with a tank, it was better adapted to the weather conditions and the water depths in the North Sea. What seemed to be one of the most sensational Norwegian innovations met a hard blow when a one of these huge concrete structures sank during trials in 1991. It provoked several actions for damages, and after reorganizing in 1995, Norwegian Contractors was gradually dissolved. Aker Norwegian Contractors was established to follow up demands for new concrete platforms.

After several stages of platform development, the last stage in producing oil and gas is not from platforms, but from subsea installations. Subsea systems extract oil and gas at a lower price and from depths that rule out the use of rigs.[61] Here, the oil economy could draw on competence built up by the industrial policy regime of the social democratic order. After the breakup of the Kongsberg Weapons Factory in 1987, the civil parts of the corporation were separated from the military parts. While the military part was named Norsk Forsvarsteknologi (after being quoted on the Oslo Børs in 1996, the company was renamed Kongsberg Gruppen), the oil division, started in 1974, was called Kongsberg Offshore. The oil division started producing pre-designed wellheads for the American firm Cameron Iron Works, but developed into a leading company for designing and integrating subsea production systems. From 1994 it has been a part of the American FMC Technology. By 2007 FMC Kongsberg Subsea Systems was completing its mission in the Ormen Lange gas field on the Norwegian shelf. With Hydro as an operator, the development of this gas field off the coast of Møre and Romsdal county probably represents the biggest project in Norwegian industrial history. In finishing the project, more than 9000 people from fifty-seven countries worked together in the little municipality of Aukra. According to

Hydro, the Ormen Lange field will provide about 20 per cent of Britain's gas needs for up to forty years. The heavy and complex subsea installations have been located at 800–1000 m water depth, 100 km from the coast, and demand intricate remote control systems for transporting, processing and controlling information. The project illustrates well the transition from relatively homogeneous technological systems to more composite and heterogeneous technological complexes.

Another extremely successful product from the Kongsberg industry is the dynamic positioning system, first called Albatross, a system that could maintain the stable position of supply vessels, special ships and offshore installations in the North Sea during rough weather with propellers instead of anchors. The production of Albatross started within the Kongsberg Weapons Factory in the mid-1970s. Today's Kongsberg Maritime is the carrier of this heritage together with other products and control systems for the ships and other parts of the maritime industry. By M&A from the late 1990s, Kongsberg Maritime today consists of people and organizational parts from several advanced maritime electronic firms such as Norcontrol and Simrad, both part of a 'cluster' of firms close to the city of Horten. Norway's main naval yard was established in Horten in 1849, stimulating the development of maritime competence in the same way as the Kongsberg Weapons Factory had from 1814. The axis between Kongsberg and Horten is today seen as an innovations system in its own right. Kongsberg Maritime is one part of the Kongsberg Group, the other part being Kongsberg Defence & Aerospace. The Norwegian State owns 50 per cent of the Kongsberg Group. Two other firms in the Kongsberg industrial district are Volvo Aero Norge, manufacturing jet engine components, and Kongsberg Automotive, developing and manufacturing systems for gearshifts and other products for the automotive and commercial vehicles markets. The six biggest firms at Kongsberg together employed 8100 people in 2006 with a turnover of 15 billion kroner.

Kongsberg Maritime was only one example of the interface between the maritime and petroleum 'clusters' of advanced suppliers, demanding customers, research institutions, regulators and classification societies, characterized by both co-operation and competition. The maritime 'cluster' survived the shipping crises in the 1970s, but Norwegian fleet had the highest relative reduction of all major fleets in the period 1973–87. Even modern shipping had become one of the mature and standardized industries with reduced competitive advantage to the established maritime nations.[62] Asian shipowners above all challenged the traditional market structure, acquiring about

17 per cent of the Norwegian fleet in the period 1973–87. Norwegian shipping owners started to register their ships in countries offering Flag of Convenience facilities, and offering more convenient terms for the shipowners as, for instance, lower taxes and less strict regulations. In 1987 the Norwegian International Ship Register (NIS) was established to compete with the Flags of Convenience registers. NIS has been a successful institutional innovation, but has been criticized for having no restrictions on the nationality of the crew and having lower safety standards than the ordinary registers. From the late 1980s the Norwegian fleet expanded. In 2001 Norway was still the third largest shipping nation after Greece and Japan, ranked by dead weight tonnage (dwt). During the following years the tonnage decreased somewhat and Norway was passed by Germany and China. In late 2007, the Norwegian fleet consisted of 1793 ships.[63]

The shipping 'cluster' consists of competent actors and organizations, some with a long history. Det Norske Veritas was established in 1864 by Norwegian marine insurers to standardise technical standards for classifications of ships and to improve safety at sea. In 2007 Den Norske Veritas provides services for managing risk, certification, classification in the maritime and petroleum sector and diverse consultancy services in many other sectors. The corporation's 7000 employees are located in more than 100 countries. Vital shipbrokers are another part of the maritime cluster. The large Astrup Fearnley group dates their history back to 1869 when the founder Thomas Fearnley started a shipbroking and agency business in Oslo. When Fernley's cousin Johan Eger joined the firm in 1874, its name changed to Fearnley & Eger. During the first decades of the twentieth century Fearnley & Eger also developed as a shipowner, and later as a general transportation broker and a rig broker. The Astrup family came into the firm thorough the nephew of Thomas Fearnley. In 2007 the sole owner of the holding company Astrup Fearnley is Hans Rasmus Astrup, a member of a rather small group within the Norwegian bourgeoisie that also have some prominent ancestors. DnB NOR and Nordea today are among the leading shipping banks; they owe their success to the long relationship between Norwegian shipowners, on the one hand, and Den norske Creditbank (founded in 1857) and Christiania Bank (1848) (see the case study in Chapter 13), on the other.

A knowledge-intensive resource-based economy

Kongsberg has Norway's highest 'engineer-density', and a considerably higher percentage of people with higher education. Serving the resource-based petroleum industry in the North Sea demands a high level of knowledge and innovative capacity. In most other resource-based industries, it was the same. As we have seen, before becoming a part of the Kongsberg Group in 1996, Simrad was an independent company also manufacturing radio telephones for the fishing fleet. Co-operating within an innovation system consisting not only of the Norwegian Defence Research Establishment but also the Institute of Marine Research, and the fishermen themselves, Simrad produced advanced electronic products for the fisheries, like echo sounders and asdic. In 1972, the Norwegian College of Fishery Science was established as part of the new University of Tromsø, with about 600 students in 2007. Through the declaration of a 200 nautical mile economic zone in 1977, Norway administers a maritime zone that is six times larger than its land area. The Institute of Marine Research in Bergen, with a staff of almost 700 people, is the main adviser to the Ministry of Fisheries and Coastal Affairs on the management of the resources within the economic zone. The Norwegian Institute of Fisheries and Aquaculture Research in Tromsø is another institution mostly working with the more downstream parts of the value chain, after the catch.

One of the most conspicuous marine businesses after 1970 has been fish farming. From being a supplementary agricultural occupation without any real economic significance, it has evolved into a major export business making farmed fish one of the most important domestic products in Norway. The 'natural resource' here is the numerous, unpolluted fjords, protected from the tough condition on the open sea, and with an ideal water temperature for the production of salmon, trout, cod and halibut.

Norway is still Europe's largest supplier of fish and fish products. About 95 per cent of production is exported to around 150 countries. The export value was more than 30 billion kroner in 2006, a doubling from the mid-1990s when the fisheries were in a historical downturn. The industry employed in 2006 30,000 people, of whom 14,000 were in fishing, 6000 in fish farming, and 10,000 in processing, but amounting to only 0.7 per cent of GDP. More than half the people that have fishing as their main occupation live in three counties of northern Norway and much of the north Norwegian identity is rooted in the fisherman–farming community of the past. Given there are now far more teachers and researchers than farmers and fishermen in northern Norway, this might seem like a paradox.[64]

During the last two decades, there has also been a loosening of the strong national and often local connection between resources and processing. Catches by Norwegian fishermen in coastal waters or in waters near Norway were processed in Norway and exported by Norwegian companies. During the 1990s, the seafood industry was transformed into a much more global activity:

 By 2006 fish caught in Norwegian waters could be shipped to The People's Republic of China for processing and transported back again as frozen fillets for consumption in Scandinavia, packed and labelled with Norwegian looking brands. Likewise, pacific cod could be frozen on board a Russian trawler operating in the Bering Sea, transported to Norway for processing into salt fish and then marketed in the traditional markets in countries like Brazil or Portugal as Norwegian bacalhau.[65]

Interestingly, fish farming could make use of the extensive knowledge on breeding developed especially within cattle and pig breeding. With a history back to the 1950s, the breed 'Norwegian Red Cattle' was established based on several cattle breeds. In the same way, the fish farmers used different breeds of wild salmon to create suitable domesticated salmon. As with other farm animals, breeding stations for salmon and trout were established. Other parts of the long emphasis on R&D in the agriculture sector were also relevant for fish farming. In 2005, when the Norwegian Agricultural College was granted university status, it renamed itself the Norwegian University of Life Sciences, partly to tap into this broader scope of activity.

In agriculture itself, the long trends of scientification and technification continued. This led to a continual rationalization and a decline in the numbers of farms, from 154,977 in 1969 to 51,200 in 2006, without any decrease in agricultural area. It is mostly the small farms that have vanished, leading to an increase in the average size of farm of about 150 per cent during the last twenty-five years. Comparatively, Norway is still has a 'small-scale' agricultural structure compared with the other Nordic countries and the EU. In the EU, only in Italy and Portugal is the average farm size even smaller then in Norway.

Nearly three-quarters of agricultural output is from livestock production, the combined milk and meat production for which the Norwegian Red Cattle is so well suited being the most important. The production of meat has increased by more than 50 per cent and the production of milk has decreased with about 20 per cent in the last twenty-five years. The degree of self-sufficiency has been stable at about 50 per cent. How is it possible to reach this level of self-sufficiency in such a mountainous country, at a high latitude, with a harsh climate and with very little arable land and fertile soil? The productivity, for instance, of wheat and potatoes is 40 per cent less than in central Europe. The combination of agriculture with fishing and forestry has traditionally been crucial. Today, the agricultural regime created during the social democratic area is even more important. During recent years, the support from the government budget has been between 10 and 11 billion kroner, and the value of import protections 8–10 billion. The political support for the vested agricultural interests in the sector culminated after the mid-1970s, when the Storting decided that the farmer's income from one year's work should reach the same level as the industrial worker's within three years. For some years, even the decrease in number of farms slowed down.

As with industrial policy, agricultural policy showed some adverse effects. Overproduction and increasing dependency on subsidies put a strain on the established agricultural regime. The consequences of GATT/WTO decisions and the Norwegian membership of the EEA made it more difficult to use the old policy instruments. Despite a clear movement in a neo-liberal direction visible from the early 1990s, parts of the old regime are still in place and being fought for by the Norwegian Foreign Ministry in WTO negotiations. The support to farmers is still seen as a way of taking care of many policy considerations, regional policy being only one.

The small-scale character of Norwegian farms was also reinforced by the allodial law and a concession law stating that the owner of a farm had to live on it. Farmland was protected from the forces of the 'free market'. This wide distribution of ownership to farms was also closely connected to the ownership of forests. Forest ownership remained mostly as it had been when the forest concession law was pasted in 1909. The forests were part of the farms, and non-industrial private ownership dominated. Of 125,000 forest owners in 1989, more than 120,000 individuals owned 78.5 per cent of the forest. Municipalities, co-operatives and common forests owned most of the rest.

The decentralized ownership structure of upstream activities in fishing, agriculture and forestry was contrasted by increasingly centralized down-stream manufacturing, wholesale and retail sectors. The farmers' co-operative dairies and slaughterhouses centralized, developed into more manufactured and diversified branded products and created commercial industrial groups. The dairy co-operative Tine in 2007 was owned by 17,400 farmers, with 5,500 employees, with close to monopoly status on the first-hand sale of milk and a dominant market share of most other dairy products. The local and regional slaughterhouses integrated in to what became the corporation Gilde Norsk Kjøtt in 2004. In 2006 it merged with the white meat and egg processing company Prior and established Nortura, owned by 31,200 Norwegian farmers. Nortura's market share of the first-hand sale of eggs and most types of red and white meat was more than 70 per cent. The market shares to consumers were 50 per cent on red and 65 per cent on white meat.

The grocery business went through a parallel development of concentration and centralization from the mid-1980s. In 2007, the market share of NorgesGruppen was 37.9 per cent, Coop Norge 24.3, ICA Norge 18.9 and REMA 1000 16.9 per cent. These four chains had 98 per cent of the market, and Norway had probably the most concentrated structure of grocery business in Europe. Two entrepreneurs, the 'parvenus' Stein Erik Hangen (RIMI and Hakon Gruppen, in 2004 bought by ICA) and Odd Reitan (REMA), were instrumental in this dramatic restructuring.

One significant manufacturer of consumer goods was the conglomerate Orkla Group – evolving from the old mining company. In the 1970s Orkla experienced difficulties with its mining business because of a shrinking pyrite market and falling copper prices. The company started downsizing its activities at the Løkken Works and looked for alternative business areas. From the early 1940s, Orkla had invested some of its profits into a portfolio of Norwegian listed companies. These investments were of considerable value in the 1970s, and gave Orkla the freedom to try out different industrial projects. At the same time, the financial investment business was professionalized and able to profit from the revitalized stock market in the 1980s. The investment that really gave a new direction for Orkla's development was the merger with Borregaard. Borregaard had specialized in wood-based chemicals. In 1959 it had acquired the chemical company De-No-Fa and the producer of hygiene and the cleaning articles company Lilleborg Fabrikker from Unilever. The food producer Stabburet was also part of the Borregaard group. Lilleborg in particular had a strong history of brand development that became an important part of Orkla's strategy. When Orkla in 1991 merged with Nora Industrier, a main producer of beverages and food, the direction of Orkla's development into a main supplier of consumer goods in the Nordic grocery market seemed inevitable. At the end of 2006, Orkla was the fourth largest firm listed on the Oslo Børs, according to its market capitalization. Partly because of its strong financial department, Orkla developed into a corporation with a very broad scope, with consumer goods, chemicals and for a long time newspapers and media as its main business areas. True to its history of making unexpected moves, Orkla in 2005 took over Elkem, which in 2001 had acquired the Swedish aluminium company, Sapa. Metals once more became an important part of Orkla's portfolio. In 2006, Orkla sold its interests in Orkla Media.

If Orkla has been one of the main purchasers of products from farmers, Norske Skogindustrier (Norske Skog) has been the main purchaser of timber from the forest owners. As we have seen, the Norwegian pulp and paper industry was slow to consolidate and modernize, in contrast with what was going on in Sweden and Finland. From the late 1960s, initiatives from the Norwegian Forest Owners' Federation led to a thorough restructuring during the following decades. It was the forest owners in Central Norway that in 1962 started the Nordenfjelske Trefordeling, today Norske Skog Skogn, to have a stable market for its products. In 1966 the first newsprint machine started in Skogn in Nord-Trøndelag County. After a period of co-operation and gradual acquisitions, Norske Skog, the paper producer, Follum, and the wood pulp producer, Tofte Industrier, merged in 1989. Shortly after, the group took over another old paper producer, Saugbruksforeningen, and having been the main shareholder since 1985, Norske Skog acquired Union in 1999. At the same time, Norske Skog sold its lumber industry. The Norwegian paper industry was then consolidated. From the early 1990s, Norske Skog invested heavily in paper mills in other countries, and also in emerging markets like China. In 2007, Norske Skog is one of the world's leading paper producers of newsprint and magazine paper, having about 13 per cent and 8 per cent of the world market of these segments, respectively. Even having only a minority share of about 20 per cent, the 43,000 members of the Norwegian Forest Owners' Federation still have significant say in deciding the strategy of the company, and the chairman of the Board in 2007 is still a forest owner.

In the forest industry, as in fisheries and agriculture, the ownership of forests was highly regulated. Local and distributed ownership was for that reason to some extent preserved. On the other hand, the more market-oriented, resource-based processing industries became much more centralized. In what way did this dual development, and other trends during the neo-liberal order, affect the democratic character of Norwegian capitalism? It is time for some summarizing and concluding comments.

Conclusion: a contested Democratic Capitalism

Is 'Democratic Capitalism' still a proper designation for the Norwegian economy? Does Norway still have what Peter A. Hall and David Soskice call a 'co-ordinated market economy' and what Richard Whitley calls a 'collaborative business system'? Or has a convergence between capitalist countries redirected the Norwegian economy towards a liberal market economy and what Whitley calls a 'compartmentalized business system'? Has the Norwegian business system been 'Americanized'? These are questions we will discuss in this section. Since the coming pages also end the whole Norwegian chapter, we should also look for some general long-run stability and changes in the economy. We start with some relatively stable phenomena.

From the late nineteenth century to the early twenty-first, export and import has constituted a more significant part of the Norwegian market economy than in most other countries. Norway's exports and imports in 2006 represented 47 and 28 per cent of GDP, respectively. As a rule, the import value has been higher than the export; this changed when export of oil and gas took off in the late 1970s. Through more than two centuries, the same countries have been the main trading partners, even if their relative position has alternated somewhat: Sweden, Great Britain, Germany, Denmark and other European countries, and US became increasingly more important during the twentieth century. Today Sweden is Norway's most important trading partner. The open economy makes a small country such as Norway vulnerable to fluctuations in the international economy. This has been one impetus for the state to engage in the economy, to establish co-operative relations both between firms and between labour, capital and the state.[66] This kind of neo-corporatism has strengthened the collaborative aspects of the business system.

Natural resources have always played an important part in foreign trades like fish, forest products, minerals, hydro power-demanding products and then oil and gas. The value added by capital and human efforts in exploration, exploitation, manufacturing and transport has, however, increased. Researchers have tried to calculate the resource rent over time, the specific rate of return on natural resources, supplementing the rate of return from real capital, financial capital and human capital. A study of the natural resource rent in Norway 1930–95 concludes 'that the most important economic resource throughout the period was a highly qualified labour force, varying from 60 to 80 per cent of the total national wealth in most years'.[67] Further, 'apart from the petroleum sector, the resource rent for most natural resources was generally small or negative'. Being heavily subsidized, agriculture has had an increasingly negative resource rent. The resource rent in fishing has varied more, and has been most positive in periods of overfishing – that is, fishing

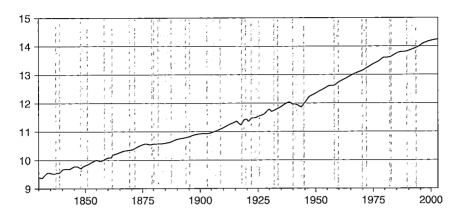

Figure 11.1   *Norway: GDP, 1830–2003 million NOK, 2000 prices*
Notes: Logarithmic scale. Shaded areas designate recession periods.[68]
Source: Eitrheim (2004), p. 14.

threatening to deplete fish stocks. The resource rent has as a rule been positive in forestry and logging. Surprisingly, it has mostly been negative in the hydro power-based electricity industry. The potential income from resource rents in the electricity sector has to a great extent has been used to reach non-economic objectives. Until liberalization, the utilities provided electricity at cost-based or subsidized prices to both households and power-hungry industries in an effort to secure welfare and a dispersed settlement, and to reduce unemployment. Since a large share of the resource-based industries produce for export, at times the need for foreign currency has been a motive for supporting these industries. The high resource rent from the petroleum sector has increased Norway's character of a being resource-based economy. An increase in human capital has been a precondition for the positive resource rent in this industry.

Despite all the focus on economic crisis and employment problems, economic growth has had a very stable trend for at least 170 years (Figure 11.1). There are few periods in the modern economic history of Norway with negative growth. Even the decade called the 'hard thirties' in total experienced substantial growth. Crisis and slowdowns have often been periods of 'creative destruction', when new technological paradigms and industries started to replace old ones.

The population has also steadily increased, even if growth rates have varied; 1 million people was reached by 1822, 2 million by 1890, 3 million by 1942 and 4 million by 1975. In 2007, Norway's population was 4.7 million.

The three main economic sectors have mostly shown stable development trends. The primary sector was an absolutely dominant sector in 1865,

Table 11.3 Employment shares, 1865–2006 (% of all employees), main sectors in Norway

Year	Primary sector	Secondary sector	Tertiary sector
1865	71	16	13
1890	50	22	28
1930	36	27	37
1950	25	35	40
1970	13	32	55
2006	4	22	75

Source: Statistical series, Statistics Norway.

employing 71 per cent of all employees, but represented only 4 per cent in 2006, when the sector's contribution to GDP was only 2 per cent. The secondary sector, like manufacturing, construction and crafts, increased from 16 per cent of the workforce in 1865 to 35 per cent during the 1950s. Thereafter, it declined to 22 per cent. Partly because the oil activities are classified as part of the secondary sector, it contributes close to 40 per cent of GDP. From being the smallest in 1866, the tertiary sector is today the largest. It consists of private and public services, like trade and commerce, shipping and other transport services, and not least the many people working in the public institutions (Table 11.3).

What about stability and change in Democratic Capitalism and the collaborative business system? Some of the development trends during the neo-liberal order weakened the characteristics of Democratic Capitalism described in the Introduction to this chapter. First, there are more big firms, as the new StatoilHydro corporation most visibly shows. On the other hand, many international oil companies are much bigger than StatoilHydro. The same goes for most of the larger firms in Norway; internationally they are comparatively small within their sector.

Another central aspect of Democratic Capitalism has been the public involvement in the economy. Public ownership and strong regulation make it possible to influence the economy through political processes. The relation we have postulated between the natural resource-based economy and the involvement of the state is still there. Even if the Norwegian Labour government party privatized Statoil in 2001, in the new StatoilHydro the state share will be about 62.5 per cent. The public ownership of hydro power has so far not changed after the neo-liberal shift, but Statkraft has increased its ownership at the expense of the counties and municipalities. In 2007, the red–green government had a case in the EFTA Court on the rules governing the reversion of the power stations to the state. The Norwegian government argues that it regards pubic ownership of hydro power as critical for securing national interests. The EEA agreement has positive economic consequences, but has also reduced the democratic character of the economy. Generally, Norway has to accept new directives without being a regular participant in decision processes within EU.

The extent and type of state ownership have many similarities with the other Nordic countries, being extensive within energy, air traffic, railways and telecoms. In this respect, Denmark is the most neo-liberal, having sold all its shares in telecoms and 25 per cent of its shares in Post Denmark, for instance. Still, in critical industries the share of public ownership has declined, and extensive political control of state-owned firms is an exception. The companies are primarily expected to make profit, implementing a shareholder rather then a stakeholder governance. However, state ownership is considered as a guarantee of the main office staying in Norway and to prevent the board and management from making decisions clearly against national interests.

Was the power of the trade unions reduced during the neo-liberal order? In many of the new ICT firms, consultancies, financial brokers and other knowledge-based industries emerging during the 1980s and 1990s, trade unionism has been weak or absent. Globalization has in some cases reduced the employees' chances of influencing the decisions of boards and managements often located in other countries. In 2005, at a time when the workforce consisted of 2.3 million people, or about 50 per cent of the population, the main national labour union (LO) still had 830,000 members, or 36 per cent of the workforce. The decrease in the secondary industries and the increase in services have reduced LO's share of organized labour, but from the 1970s other central federations have grown considerably. On the whole, it is fair to say that the trade unions are still strong. The corporative aspects are also still there, the employers and the employees co-operating to cope with their differing interests and taking some consideration of the economy as a whole – with the state as a supporter and provider of important institutional contexts.

Local co-operation and participation in economic development has been an important aspect of Democratic Capitalism. It is hard to evaluate the participatory aspects. In general, many of the traditional organizations and political parties have become more professionalized and bureaucratized, but lost members and active participation from the remaining members. The voter turnout in 1963 was the highest in local government elections after the war; 81 per cent voted. In 2003, only 59 per cent voted, increasing to 61 per cent in 2007. The centralization of the savings banks, of resource-based and food-processing industries and the vanishing of thousands of post offices and local offices of the main telecoms operator, of the state railway and other utilities, have had adverse effects on local economic circuits. On the other hand, there has been some strengthening at the regional level. For instance, in 1969 the three first regional colleges were opened. During the next decades, twenty-eight state university colleges were established, often involving a merger between earlier independent schools. The University of Tromsø was opened in 1972. After 2005, three of the regional colleges gained the status of universities, so that Norway now has seven universities.

In our comparative perspective, it is the relative differences that matter when we label economies and business systems. If we are forced to issue a conclusion, it could be that Norway has a 'contested Democratic Capitalism'. In absolute terms, the democratic character of the economy clearly seems to have been reduced. On the other hand, compared to many other economies, it might still have retained sufficiently democratic aspects to be called 'Democratic Capitalism'. The strong public involvement in the economy, the continued co-operation between labour and capital, and the strong protection of labour security are among the qualities that still make it meaningful to talk about a 'co-ordinated market economy' and a 'collaborative business system'. During the neo-liberal order, the economy certainly moved in the direction of more economic liberalism. On the other hand, many of the classical liberal market economies have moved even further in that direction. The Norwegian welfare state has even been extended during the last decades. In a statement by the Ministry of Finance of June 2007, it was said: 'The Government is committed to the Nordic model, with a well-functioning welfare system, close co-operation with and between social partners and a competitive business sector.'[68] This seems to be an appropriate account of the situation.

QUESTIONS   1. The concept of 'Democratic Capitalism', as used in this chapter, has been constructed and developed by historians. The concept represents an effort to catch some distinct and lasting features of the Norwegian economy – amid a complex and what often seems to be a messy reality. How do you think the concept fits Norwegian development? What are the arguments for and against? Discuss whether it could be used to characterize the other Nordic economies.

2. The business system emerging in the nineteenth and the late twentieth centuries, has been characterized as 'liberal'. What are the similarities and differences between the organizational and institutional structures of these periods?

Notes

1. CIA, *The World Factbook* (2007).
2. Sejersted (1993). Sejersted's book and perspectives have been a main inspiration for this chapter. Some other works have been used over and over again because of their rich content, both of facts and findings, first and formost: Bergh *et al.* (1980), Hodne (1977), Grytten and Hodne (2002) and Grytten and Hodne (2000). Many facts and figures have been taken from these books without further reference. That also goes for the many figures taken from the publications of Statistics Norway.
3. Hall and Soskice (2001).
4. Munthe, P. (2005).
5. Norway had been in union with Denmark since 1380, with Copenhagen as the common capital.
6. Braudel (1986).
7. Tranberg and Sprauten (1996).
8. Peter Kurrild-Klitgaard, 'Adam Smith og kredsen bag National-Velstands Natur', http://www.ideeromfrihet.no/1998-3-klitgaard.php, downloaded 16 April 2006.
9. Amdam *et al.* (1989).
10. Petersen (1998).
11. Bruland (1989), p. 6, emphasis in the original.
12. In 2007, the company operated in twenty-two countries, exported to more than sixty countries and employed approximately 2600 people throughout the world.
13. Hodne (1975), p. 136.
14. 1 he (or 1 hectare) is equal to 10 decares, and a decare equals 0.25 acres.
15. Grytten and Lindmark (2005).
16. *Ibid.*, p. 21.
17. Thue (1994), p. 21.
18. In 2007, 119 TWh/year of hydro power had already been developed. 44.2 TWh/year of the total hydro power potential was in protected watercourses, and therefore not available for development. Around 41.3 TWh/year was not protected, and was available for development. At this time, however, the harnessing of new river systems usually created political conflict.
19. By annual turnover.
20. The story of Kellner–Partington and Borregaard is taken from Lange (1994).
21. Lange (1994), p. 25.
22. Stonehill (1965), p. 39.
23. Bergh *et al.* (2004).
24. Slagstad (1998).
25. Wicken (1994), p. 8.
26. A classical description sympathetic to the small-scale fisheries in North Norway is Brox (1966).
27. Jonsson (2006) is an interesting comparison between the Norwegian and Icelandic fishing industries' development during the 1920s and 1930s.
28. Gjerdåker (2004), p. 274.
29. Almås (2004), pp. 311–12.
30. Espeli (2003), p. 200.
31. The discussion on cartels is based on Espeli (2003).
32. Venneslan (2006).
33. Bergh *et al.* (1980).
34. Hodne (1975), p. 418.
35. Hodne (1975), p. 423.
36. Andersen (2005), p. 18.

37. The London government also had some representatives from other parties. A coalition government from June to November 1945 was led by Prime Minister Einar Gerhardsen from the Labour Party.
38. Bergh *et al.* (1980), p. 113.
39. Danielsen (1995), pp. 342–4.
40. Stolz (1955), p. 70.
41. Danielsen (1995), p. 424.
42. Johannessen *et al.* (2005), p. 241.
43. Moen (2006).
44. Sandvik (2008), gives a short but informed overview of the history of the Norwegian aluminium industry.
45. Gulowsen (2000), p. 144.
46. Søilen (2002).
47. Wasberg and Svendsen (1969), p. 291.
48. Jonsson (2006).
49. Gerhardsen (1972), p. 299.
50. Esping-Andersen (1990).
51. *Ibid.*
52. Hope (1972), p. 214
53. Perez (2002), p. 14.
54. Kuhnle (2000), p. 48.
55. http://www.ssb.no/english/subjects/06/arbeid_en/ (downloaded 21 September 2007).
56. NOU (1979):35, Strukturproblemer og vekstmuligheter i norsk industri.
57. Christensen (2005).
58. Nore (2003).
59. Reve (2000), p. 225.
60. Mjelva (2005).
61. Bjørnstad (2005) has been useful source to the development at Kongsberg.
62. Tenold (2000) has informed the paragraph on shipping.
63. 'Støkurs. Regjeringens strategi for miljøvennlig vekst i de maritime næringer', Ministry of Trade and Industry (2007).
64. Tjelmeland (2000).
65. Rønning (2006).
66. Katzenstein (1985).
67. Lindholt (2000).
68. Information about the Kingdom of Norway and the Norwegian economy (June 2007), Norwegian Ministry of Finance, p. 13.

References

Almås, R., 'From State-Driven Modernization to Green Liberalism', in Almås, R. (ed.), *Norwegian Agricultural History* (Trondheim: Tapir Academic Press, 2004).

Amdam, R. P., Pharo, I. and Hanisch, T. J., *Vel blåst! : Christiania Glasmagasin og norsk glassindustri 1739–1989* (Oslo: Gyldendal, 1989).

Andersen, K. G., *Flaggskip i fremmed eie: Hydro 1905–45* (Oslo: Pax forlag A/S, 2005).

Bergh, T., Sogner, K., Espeli, H. and Orkla, *Brytningstider storselskapet Orkla 1654–2004* (Oslo: Orion forlag, 2004).

Bergh, T. *et al.*, *Growth and Development: The Norwegian Experience 1830–1980* (Oslo: Norwegian Institute of International Affairs, 1980).

Bjørnstad, S., *Daring Innovation and Dear Ignorance: Kongsberg 1960 to the Present* (Oslo: unpublished manuscript, 2005).

Braudel, F., *Kapitalismens dynamikk* (Oslo: Forlaget ARS, 1986).

Brox, O., *Hva skjer i Nord-Norge: en studie i norsk utkantpolitikk* (Oslo: Pax forlag, 1966).

Bruland, C., *British Technology and European Industrialization. The Norwegian textile industry in the mid-nineteenth century* (Cambridge: Cambridge University Press, 1989).

Christensen, S., *Switching Relations. The Rise and Fall of the Norwegian Telecom Industry* (Oslo, Norwegian School of Management, Phd thesis, 2006).

Danielsen, R. *et al.*, *Norway: A History from the Vikings to Our Own Times* (Oslo: Scandinavian University Press 1995).

Espeli, H., 'Perspectives on the Distinctiveness of Norwegian Price and Competition policy' in the XXth Century, *Journal of European Economic History 31*, (2003) pp. 621–60.

Espeli, H., 'Organiseringens makt', in Christensen, S., Espeli, H., Larsen, E. and Sogner, K. (eds), *Kapitalistisk demokrati? Norsk næringsliv gjennom 100 år* (Oslo: Gyldendal Akademisk, 2003).

Esping-Andersen, G., *The Three World of Welfare Capitalism* (Princeton, NJ: Princeton University Press, 1990).

Gerhardsen, G. M., 'Norges fiskerier', in Hope, E. (ed.), *Næringsøkonomiske oversikter. Bind. 1. Primærnæringene* (Oslo: Johan Grundt Tanum forlag, 1972).

Gjerdåker, B., 'Continuity and Modernity 1815–1920', in Almås, R. (ed.), *Norwegian Agricultural History* (Trondheim: Tapir Academic Press, 2004).

Grytten, O. H. and Hodne, F., *Norsk økonomi i det nittende århundre* (Bergen: Fagbokforlaget, 2000).

Grytten, O. H. and Hodne, F., *Norsk økonomi i det tyrende århundre* (Bergen: Fagbokforlaget, 2002).

Grytten, O. H. and Lindmark, M., *Natural Resources, Convergence and Divergence in Two Neighbouring Economies* (Bergen: unpublished manuscript, 2005).

Gulowsen, J., *Bro mellom vitenskap og teknologi. SINTEF 1950–2000* (Trondheim: Tapir, 2000).

Hall, P. A. and Soskice, D. (eds), *Varities of Capitalism: The Institutional Foundations of Comparative Advantage* (Oxford: Oxford University Press, 2001).

Hernes, Helga, Betraktninger om arbeidet med 'Kvinners levekår og livsløp'. I: Kvinneforskning. Oslo: sekretariatet, vol. 21, no. 3–4, s. 21–25(1997).

Hodne, F., *An Economic History of Norway 1815–1970* (Bergen: Tapir, 1975).

Hope, E., 'Norges Industri', in Hope, E. (ed.), *Næringsøkonomiske oversikter. Bind 2. Sekundærnæringene* (Oslo: Johan Grundt Tanum forlag, 1972).

Johannessen, F. E., Rønning, A. and Sandvik, P. T., *Nasjonal kontrol og industriell fornyelse: Hydro 1945–77* (Oslo: Pax forlag A/S, 2005).

Jonsson, G., 'Comparing the Icelandic and Norwegian Fishing Industries' Response to the Economic Crisis of the 1930s', 14 (*International Economic History Congress*, Helsinki, 2006).

Katzenstein, P. J., *Small States in World Markets: Industrial Policy in Europe* (Ithaca: NY: Cornell University Press, 1985).

Kuhnle, S. (ed.), *Survival of the European Welfare State* (London: Routledge, 2000).

Lange, E. (1994), 'The Rise and Fall of Borregaard: A Corporate History', in Amdam, R. and Lange, E. (eds), *Crossing the Borders: Studies in Norwegian Business History* (Oslo: Universitetsforlaget, 1994).

Lindholt, L., *On Natural Resource Rent and the Wealth of a Nation: A Study based on National Accounts in Norway 1930–95* (Oslo: Statistics Norway, 2000).

Mjelva, H. K., *Tre storverft i norsk industris finaste stund* (Bergen: University of Bergen, 2005).

Moen, S. E., *Innovation and Production in the Norwegian Aluminium Industry: A Case of Path Creation and Path Dependency* (Oslo: Centre for Technology, Innovation and culture, 2006).

Munthe, P. (2005). 'Adam Smith's norske ankerfeste', *Norges Banks skriftserie*, 37 (2005).

Nore, P., *Norsk Hydro's Takeover of Saga Petroleum in 1999*, Rapport 73 (Oslo, 2003).

Perez, C., *Technological Revolutions and Financial Capital: The Dynamics of Bubbles and Golden Ages* (Cheltenham: Edward Elgar, 2002).

Petersen, E. L., 'Adelsøkonomi i Norge fra reformasjonstiden og fram mot 1660', *Historisk tidsskrift*, 1 (1998), pp. 90–8.

Reve, T., *Et verdiskapende Norge: Fra kokurransedyktighet til verdiskaping* (unpublished manuscript, 2000).

Rønning, A., *From National Business to Global Value Chains: Changes in the Norwegian Whitefish Industry 1980–2006* (Oslo: unpublished manuscript, 2006).

Sandvik, P. T., 'European, Global or Norwegian? The Norwegian Aluminium Companies 1946–2005', in Schröter, H. (ed.), *The European Enterprise* (Berlin: Springer, 2008).

Sejersted, F., *Demokratisk kapitalisme* (Oslo: Universitetsforlaget, 1993).

Slagstad, R., *De nasjonale strateger* (Oslo: Pax forlag A/S, 1998).

Stolz, G., *Økonomisk utsyn 1900–50* (Oslo: Statistisk Sentralbyrå, 1955).

Stonehill, A., *Foreign Ownership in Norwegian Enterprises* (Oslo: Statistisk Sentralbyrå, 1965).

Søilen, E., *Hvorfor gikk det galt? Statens rolle i utviklingen av norsk næringsliv etter 1945* (Oslo: Gyldendal Akademisk, 2002).

Tenold, S., *Changes in the Distribution of the World Fleet, 1970–87* (Bergen: Centre for International Economics and Shipping, 2000).

Thue, L., *Statens kraft 1890–1947: Kraftutbygging og samfunnsutvikling* (Oslo: J. W. Cappelens forlag A.S., 1994).

Tjelmeland, H., The Making of a Sub-Arctic Region: Northern Norway, 1900–2000', *19th International Congress of Historical Sciences, 6–13 August 2000* (Oslo, 2000).

Tranberg, A. and Sprauten, K. (eds), *Norsk bondeøkonomi 1650–1850* (Oslo: Det Norske Samlaget, 1996).

Venneslan, C., 'Labour Markets and Recovery of the Great Depression in Norway', *XIV International Economic Congress* (Helsinki, 2006).

Wasberg, G. C. and Svendsen, A. S., *Industriens historie i Norge* (Oslo: Norges Industriforbund, 1969).

Whitley, R., *Divergent Capitalism: The Social Structuring and Change of Business Systems* (Oxford: Oxford University Press, 1999).

Wicken, O., *Norsk fiskeriteknologi – politiske mål i møte med regionale kulturer* (Oslo: Step-Group, 1994).

Øyvind Eitrheim, J. T. K. and Qvigstad, Jan F., *Historical Monetary Statistics for Norway 1819–2003* (Oslo: Norges Bank, 2004).

appendix: the transformation of the Norwegian business system

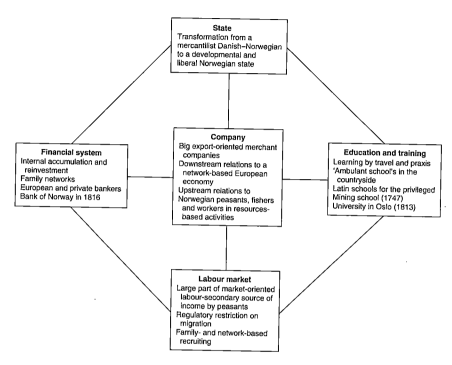

Figure 11.A.1   The formation of a national business system, 1770–1840

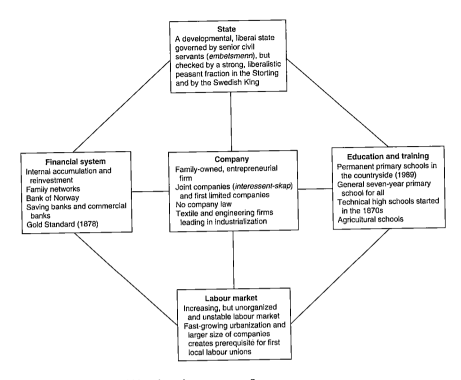

Figure 11.A.2 **A classical liberal market economy, 1840–90**

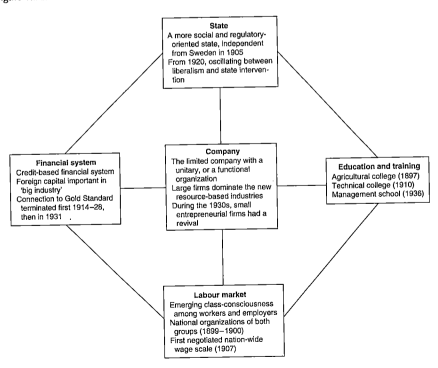

Figure 11.A.3 **A contested liberal market economy, 1890–1935**

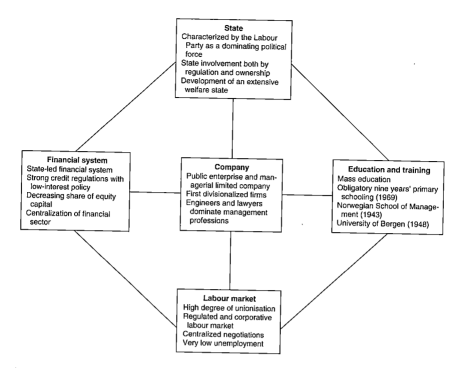

Figure 11.A.4 **A co-ordinated market economy, 1935–70**

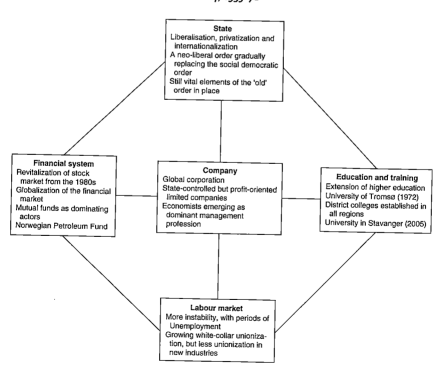

Figure 11.A.5 **A contested co-ordinated market economy, 1970–2005**

WELFARE CAPITALISM: THE SWEDISH ECONOMY 1850–2005 ° ENTREPRENEURSHIP AND OWNERSHIP: THE
ERM VIABILITY OF THE SWEDISH BONNIER AND WALLENBERG FAMILY BUSINESS GROUPS ° FROM
ABB ... VES ... V ... AND INVESTMENT: FINNISH
CAPITALISM, 1850–2005 ° FROM STATE OWNERSHIP TO MULTINATIONAL CORPORATION: THE PATH OF
ENSO-GUTZEIT ... ESS AND FAILURE OF A CONGLOMERATE FIRM: THE STRATEGIC
PATHS OF NOKIA AND TAMPELLA IN THE LIBERALIZING FINNISH ECONOMY AFTER THE SECOND WORLD
WAR ° CO-OPERATIVE LIBERALISM: DENMARK FROM 1857 TO 2007 ° ARLA- FROM DECENTRALISED INDUSTRY
TO MULTINATIONAL ENTERPRISE ° CARLSBERG AND THE SELF-REGULATION OF THE DANISH BEER MARKET
° NORWAY: A RESOURCE-BASED AND DEMOCRATIC CAPITALISM ° CONSTRUCTIVE POWER: ELKEM 1904–2004
° FINANCE AND THE DEVELOPMENT OF NORWEGIAN CAPITALISM – THE CASE OF CHRISTIANIA BANK

12 constructive power: Elkem 1904–2004

Knut Sogner

Ever since Elkem started, on 2 January 1904, it has been one of Norway's
most important industrial ventures, though for various reasons.[1] Elkem began
life as 'The Norwegian Company for the Electrochemical Industry', and it
took centre stage in many of the seminal developments in the Norwegian
economy: Norsk Hydro, the international producer of nitrogenous fertilizer,
was started in 1905 on the basis of Elkem's technology; Elkem's metallurgical
innovations have been used by other companies all over the globe, and by
around 1970 Elkem was one of Norway's largest enterprises in terms of both
value and of people employed.

Elkem is also representative of Norway. Elkem's specialties from the 1910s
onwards, electric smelting and aluminium production, are also Norwegian
industrial specialities, and Elkem's development is best understood as part
of the larger Norwegian development. Although Norway is a small country,
production of primary metals has become a national specialty, and Elkem
has been central in this development. Norway enjoyed many of the necessary
physical prerequisites. It had waterfalls that could produce huge amounts of
electricity. These were often located close to sheltered fjords where the sea
did not freeze in winter, with harbours that could easily export metals and
import raw materials. There were rich national deposits of minerals such as
iron, pyrites and quartzite, while commodities such as coal, bauxite, nickel,
chrome ores and manganese ores could be shipped in from around the world
by the Norwegian national fleet. Elkem was born in 1904 with the ambition
of becoming the major industrial player in this arena. Its trajectory was to
first embark on new ventures (the 1910s), then to develop and sell technology
(the 1920s to the 1950s), and finally to become a large producer (the 1950s
until today).

Elkem is at the time of writing undergoing important changes after being purchased by the Norwegian conglomerate Orkla in 2005. Several new developments that will radically change the company have been announced, and it is safe to say that it will be a very different company – or companies – in the future. It is still, however, a leading supplier of metals and materials, and one of Norway's biggest industrial enterprises. Elkem had about 10,000 employees at the end of 2003, with more than twenty wholly- or partly-owned companies and production plants in Europe, North America and South America, in addition to a wide-ranging network of sales offices and agents, Elkem has now acquired the Swedish aluminium-processing company Sapa with factories all over Europe. Elkem actually began in Stockholm, and the purchase of Sapa thereby closed a circle – for the time being, as Sapa is involved in the changes taking place at the time of writing.

Despite being a thoroughly Norwegian company, Elkem has had a strong attachment to other nations, in terms of operations, competence and ownership. Metals and metallurgy have for Elkem been both typically Norwegian and thoroughly international affairs, and this is the theme in the following chapter. But more than merely combining a national and international presence, Elkem – the private company – has played a role as the national organiser of technical advancement in typically Norwegian activities. This has contributed to the building of a strong Norwegian aluminium industry beyond Elkem. It contributed to a strong ferroalloy industry, and at the time of writing Elkem is in the middle of the building of a strong Norwegian industry for solar energy, another of the avenues that may change the company in the future.

The birth of a large company and the invention of the Söderberg electrode

On 2 January 1904, four men met in Stockholm, Sweden to found Elkem. Each was an important figure in his own right. The driving force – the entrepreneur, so to speak – was Sam Eyde, a Norwegian engineer and head of an enterprise that specialized in planning large infrastructure projects. Eyde was born into what had been, until the Great Depression of the 1870s, one of Norway's wealthiest shipowning families. The Wallenberg brothers, Knut Agathon and Marcus, provided capital for Elkem in 1904. Knut A. Wallenberg was head of one of Scandinavia's richest banks, Stockholms Enskilda Bank (SEB), a position that the younger Marcus eventually inherited. The fourth man was the Swedish politician and investor Knut Tillberg, Eyde's original partner and a friend of the Wallenbergs.

They met to form a company that could handle the single most important Scandinavian industrial venture at the time: the Birkeland–Eyde process to make synthetic fertilizers containing nitrogen. Elkem was founded in early 1904 as the vehicle for taking forward the invention of Professor Kristian Birkeland and testing it in a pilot plant. At the end of 1905, when Elkem's job was successfully done, Norsk Hydro was founded as the vehicle for starting production. But there was a second idea behind the creation of Elkem in 1904. This was apparent in the company's full name, Det Norske Aktieselskab for elektro-kemisk Industri (The Norwegian Joint Stock Company for Electrochemical Industry), 'Elektrokemisk' for short and Elkem since 1969. As well as making the Norsk Hydro venture viable, Elkem was to create new companies; it was to be a venture company in an era of industrial change.

Since 1814, Norway and Sweden had been twin kingdoms, and both the Wallenberg brothers and Knut Tillberg were very active in Norway at the time of Elkem's foundation. They financed a variety of ventures, purchased rights to waterfalls and sought to exploit the opportunities provided by the times. SEB and the Wallenberg brothers were the main financial players behind the industrial transformation in the Norwegian–Swedish area at the time. They were central in the establishment of large companies like ASEA (ABB), Orkla and Atlas Copco, not to mention Elkem and Norsk Hydro. The two decades on either side of 1900 are often called 'the second industrial revolution'. The period was characterized by the emergence of new technologies (telephones, cars, synthetic fertilizers, primary aluminium, etc.), by large science-based industrial enterprises, by economic growth and by social change (the organized Labour movement). In both Norway and Sweden, new technologies to exploit abundant natural resources became the main attraction. Several applications based on the understanding of electricity – for making artificial light, electric motors and creating chemical and metallurgical processes – received close attention from inventors, engineers and speculators. The creation of Elkem, drawing on the knowledge, wealth and personal contacts of its four resourceful founders, was one way to bring to fruition – and institutionalise – a multitude of electrical–industrial experimental activities in the Norwegian–Swedish kingdom.

Sam Eyde was the inspirational driving force behind Elkem. He was himself somewhat of a newcomer to Norwegian society, returning home in 1898

Photograph 12.1 **The German Emperor Wilhelm visiting Sam Eyde at the Norwegian valley Tyssedal, possibly in 1908. The picture illustrates Eyde's strong relations with Germany at a high political level.**
Source: Nasjonalbiblioteket.

after several years studying and working in Germany. Active, charming and sociable, Eyde had no problem building relations, and befriended several prominent figures in the upper echelons of German society, such as Werner von Siemens. After completing his engineering studies in 1891, he continued his work as a construction engineer – and entrepreneur – with increasing success. His return to Norway, at the height of an economic boom, was a triumph; he won several competitions for major construction contracts, notably railway stations. When crisis hit the Norwegian economy in 1899, Eyde, who had come back to Norway to work for others, began to buy out investors in difficulties, cherry-picking at bargain prices. In this, he came to team up with Tillberg, to buy waterfalls (Rjukan was the most important, and was later used by Norsk Hydro), to collaborate with Professor Kristian Birkeland about how to perfect an industrial process to use electricity to provide nitrogen fertilizer, and to start Elkem.

Elkem was an 'elite' company in several respects. First, its four founding shareholders represented the wealthiest industrialists of Norway and Sweden. Elkem's goal of developing industrial processes accentuated the expected role of the company, and reflected the growing innovative activities related to the new and industrial application of electricity. Electricity could be used to change and create processes to make chemicals as well as metals, not least the new metal, aluminium. In Sweden and Norway, these years were characterized by experiments, and the introduction of an electrically charged electrode on top of a traditional smelting bath increased the temperature and changed the properties of the smelting processes. Elkem was founded both to experiment and to enhance previous experiments to make industrially viable production processes. With its four partners and their combined networks of information it was ideally suited to pick up new developments. Little happened, however, as the four partners were involved in the huge task of getting Norsk Hydro off the ground. Tensions also developed between the partners, and in 1910 the Wallenbergs and Tillberg parted ways with Eyde both in Elkem and in some other companies.

As head of a group of investors, in 1910 Eyde bought Elkem from the Wallenberg brothers and Knut Tillberg. The transaction reflected the growing division between the former partners, and it was also a response to deep political changes in the period since Elkem's inception. The Swedish–Norwegian union had been abolished in 1905, and Norway became an independent country for the first time in more than 500 years. One of the new country's first acts was to create laws to utilize its rich natural resources. The 'Concession Laws' placed restrictions on the ownership of waterfalls and mineral deposits, making private transactions dependent on government concessions, and imposing strict rules on foreign ownership. The laws were a direct consequence of rapid industrialization. The establishment of Norsk Hydro in 1905, with Swedish capital and foreign shareholding, to utilise the Rjukan waterfall, was a controversial topic in the political process leading to the 'Concession Laws'.

For six intense years after 1911, Eyde vitalized Elkem and steered it towards very ambitious tasks. Elkem had lost momentum after Norsk Hydro had been established in 1905. It lost the rights to the Birkeland–Eyde process as well as two large waterfalls to Norsk Hydro. Apart from owning the rights to a medium-sized waterfall close to Arendal in southern Norway (Eyde's home town), Elkem was almost a shell company. During the 1910s, Elkem became involved in an increasing number of projects, and built a series of companies: Arendals Fossekompani was an electricity generator using the Arendal waterfall; Arendals Smelteverk produced silicon-carbide with German methods and capital (its current owner is Saint Gobain); DNN, also located in Arendal, produced aluminium with French methods and capital (both these Arendal companies purchased electricity from Arendals Fossekompani); Bjølvefossen produced calcium carbide, but was intended as a vehicle for a range of processes leading to the fertilizer ammonium sulphate; and Titan Co. manufactured a white pigment, titanium dioxide.

Titan Co. represented Elkem's second important technological achievement after the Birkeland–Eyde process. The process of isolating the titanium-white compound found in some iron ore deposits was later sold to National Lead (now N. L. Industries). It has been used worldwide, and has been the significant colouring agent in white paint ever since. Titan Co. was established in 1916, with Elkem as a major owner, and in 1920 Titan Co. and National Lead concluded an agreement to divide markets and share technology worldwide. Later, in the 1920s, National Lead bought Titan Co. outright, securing the superior process for itself and continuing the development of this Norwegian invention into a globally important technique.

Titan Co. and these other relatively successful companies were partly sold by Elkem to raise capital. Thus ended a broad expansion effort – also into international trade – that led the company to near-bankruptcy in 1921. In 1919 Elkem was one of the largest Norwegian companies in terms of share capital. Its head office employed around 200 people, and it had interests in fifty-one enterprises, ranging from the companies mentioned above to some very small properties. Elkem had overextended itself. Its efforts were spread over too many commercial ventures, and it was badly exposed to the severe cyclical downturn after the end of the First World War. Nevertheless, some of Elkem's activities had long-term viability, and Titan Co. represented a thorough, practical and deeply scientific venture into metallurgical processes. Elkem had done systematic research in a pilot plant from 1915, and in 1917 it had purchased BASF's old research factory in Kristiansand at the southern tip of Norway in order to conduct its own electrometallurgical research. In the Kristiansand plant Elkem achieved its third important technical breakthrough, the Söderberg electrode, which became the basis of the company over several decades.

Photograph 12.2 Important researchers gathered at the Fiskaa factory, 17 August 1919.
C. W. Söderberg is third from the left, Mathias Sem fourth from left. At this occasion a delegation
of international researchers investigated the importance of the so-called 'Söderberg electrode'.
Source: Elkem.

The Söderberg electrode was a new idea, and it soon came to be recognized as a generic approach to electric smelting. The idea came from Carl Wilhelm Söderberg, an engineer whose Swedish parents had settled in Norway when Carl was a small child because his father started what was to become an important Norwegian maker of telecommunications and electrical equipment, Elektrisk Bureau. C. W. Söderberg wanted to create a 'self-baking, continuous electrode', an approach that would decrease the costs of electrodes and would enable non-stop, continuous production. The electrode is the medium by which electricity is introduced to electro-thermic metallurgical processes. The traditional method of smelting metals and minerals involved baths of raw material and carbon-containing material (such as charcoal or coke); heat liberated the primary metals from raw materials, and the freed metals were purified when carbon reacted with the oxygen attached to the metals to form CO_2. Such processes are called 'reduction' processes and have CO_2 as a by-product. Introducing a carbon-rich electrode *above* such smelting baths created extra heat, because when electricity was introduced into the electrode, an electric arc was created between the end of the electrode and the smelting bath. This vastly increased the temperature and changed the atmosphere of the smelting process. These electrodes were made of carbon-rich material, and because of this were additional sources of carbon for the metal-purifying process. The electrode had to be pre-baked into a hard form in order to be able to conduct electricity.

Pre-baked electrodes, however, had a limited life in the furnaces, which had to be stopped and cooled every time a new electrode was needed. There was an obvious attraction in Söderberg's conception: an electrode that was continuous because you could fill in unbaked carbon material on the top of a casing, while the heat from the smelting process melted away the lower part and the middle part was being baked. Thus the electrode could be continuously lowered towards the smelting bath as its electricity-conducting end was eaten away by the release of carbons into the smelting process. This principle came to conquer the world from the 1920s and is the dominant method of electric smelting even today.

The idea was not unique, as Elkem subsequently discovered; other companies had tried in vain to achieve the same effect. But it was highly inspirational, an idea to reflect on while doing other kinds of research. This is part of the reason why Elkem succeeded. Söderberg first formulated the idea while working in a small, experimental iron-smelting plant in southern Norway, before he joined Elkem. There were several small electric-smelting ventures in Norway at the time, part of a broad national effort to marry the country's rich iron deposits with a potent new tool, electricity for smelting. Söderberg was hired because of Elkem's interest in finding methods for electric smelting of iron. During the 1910s the company's research went in several directions, but four branches were more important than others: electrical methods for iron-smelting; the titanium methods mentioned above; methods to make synthetic fertilizer; and new raw material for aluminium oxide. Söderberg's idea was not yet central in the official company strategy.

Elkem succeeded with the Söderberg electrode above all because of the company's high ambitions and its general high purpose. Elkem's research was conducted by a well-educated group of engineers, including some with doctoral qualifications; some of Elkem's research was done in collaboration with professors at the Universities. The scope of these efforts proved to be too large for every individual project to succeed, and this is not particularly surprising. Yet the overall success rate was, in retrospect, astonishing, reflecting the fact that Elkem was more than a company, and held a special position in national research networks. The Birkeland–Eyde breakthrough occurred outside Elkem and was the reason Elkem was created; the process for finding titanium-white was a focused long-term project (lasting around ten years) that started outside Elkem and became one of the sources of the company's revitalization in 1911. The Söderberg breakthrough was rooted in activities undertaken before Söderberg joined Elkem; for all that, it is best understood as the consequence of systematic and team-based research efforts which Elkem initiated and which gained momentum from 1915.

The Söderberg electrode breakthrough may be explained as follows. Söderberg had formulated the original idea, but his own experiments in the 1910s had not been successful. Another young engineer, Dr Mathias Sem, was inspired by Söderberg's idea and kept it alive through 1917, at a time when Söderberg himself had become disillusioned. Sem persuaded the research director, Dr Gustav Jebsen, to allow them to continue to pursue the effort alongside other research work. In 1918, in the course of experiments on a process for zinc, there were encouraging signs of a solution to the major problem of keeping the electrode in its casing (in a partly unbaked condition it was soft and tended to fall off the casing). A fourth engineer then entered the scene – one who allegedly did not believe in Söderberg's idea. Jens Westly, arguably Elkem's most experienced engineer, saw that the objective could be realized and he reconstructed the casing. From there onwards, the goal was clear: they had found a way to make Söderberg's idea work.

The Söderberg breakthrough happened because of Elkem and the Norwegian system of innovation in metallurgy. Several of Elkem's engineers had experience from other Norwegian companies and from different kinds of metallurgical processes. They were brought together by Elkem and introduced into a multitude of projects. Finding a solution to Söderberg's generic idea was the central component of this effort, but it was a generic by-product that was in no way accidental, given the team's large and varied efforts and expertise in metallurgy. Elkem undertook some tasks in collaboration with other companies; the zinc project that paid for much of the successful Söderberg effort was partly funded by one of these, Bremanger. It could be argued that Elkem's discovery of the Söderberg electrode was coincidental to other efforts; but this would misinterpret what actually happened. The efforts were on a large scale; they were connected to the wider *Norwegian* – and even Scandinavian, as there were important research links to Sweden – search for new electrometallurgical processes; and Elkem consciously adopted the role of (a national) co-ordinator. Given this context, the Söderberg success was the product of systematic research. Furthermore, it was an outcome of a social innovation. Elkem was a leading Norwegian example of an international trend towards research-based companies, with regular staff and permanent equipment, operating under commercial pressure to deliver results.

The art of innovation

Elkem's research effort took place in a fundamentally Norwegian–Scandinavian electro-metallurgical environment, and one which was very supportive. Yet the target was research results of international significance. Like its successor, Norsk Hydro, Elkem wanted to be a big international company, and the range of its activities reflected this ambition. Elkem duly became an international company, but it soon became clear that it did not have enough capital behind it to remain large, and certainly not to become a giant. In 1920 and the early part of 1921, until the axe of the general assembly fell in early summer, Elkem fought a losing battle to save a range of activities other than the Söderberg electrode. The value of Elkem's share capital was written down from 28.8 million Norwegian kroner to 5.8 million.

That Elkem successfully exploited the Söderberg electrode was partly because it operated as a big and internationally oriented company up to 1921. One of its three top directors, Gustav Jebsen, spent the best part of 1920 in the US trying to capitalise on Elkem's two inventions, the Söderberg process and the titanium-white process of its subsidiary Titan Co. Jebsen held a doctorate from Zürich and was of wealthy Norwegian stock, and operated confidently and capably in American industrial circles, possibly aided by a certain aristocratic European air. Jebsen concluded a deal with National Lead that shared technology between Titan Co. and the American company, while dividing the world market between them. He also turned down the opportunities to sell the US rights to the Söderberg electrode to companies like Union Carbide, who were able to see for themselves how well it worked when Elkem set it up at Southern Manganese in Alabama. Reflecting on the commercial possibilities of various metallurgical processes arising from the Söderberg principle – it worked in ferrosilicon, ferromanganese and pig iron – Jebsen thought it would be wrong to sell the rights until more work had been done on these and other processes. Jebsen was also focused on the possibility of applying the Söderberg principle to aluminium.

In his letters home, Jebsen argued that Elektrokemisk should not sell outright but should seek new collaborative ventures by licensing out the Söderberg techniques to other metallurgical companies: 'The question is very difficult and my attitude to it will depend very much on whether we can find a suitable arrangement to benefit from the income generated by future developments.'[2] Elkem wanted to accomplish such an arrangement through their contracts. They licensed out the right to use the Söderberg system, but established Elkem's right to any improvement the licensee made. At the same time they also gave the licensee the right to use the most up-to-date version of a continuously improving Söderberg system. Elektrokemisk actively sought 'systems of innovations', which through collaboration would encourage constant international technological exchange, as well as providing Elkem with income proportionate to the partners' Söderberg-based production.

Right from the start, in 1920, the Söderberg system for electric smelting sold well internationally. This reflected Elkem's accurate assessment of its international relevance, as well as its ability to make the invention known in the right circles. By 1926, sixty-six plants worldwide had installed 164 furnaces with Söderberg electrodes. The system's first commercial breakthrough came in 1920 with the carbide installation of Aktiengesellschaft für Stickstoffdünger in Knapsack, Cologne. Improvements by this company, particularly in the electricity supply to the electrode, proved very important for Elkem's continued sale of the system. Elkem sold all over the world, and dispatched engineers to build, start, operate and maintain furnaces. It thus gained access to the international metallurgical industry, and brought valuable inputs home to its headquarters in Oslo and its research plant in Kristiansand. Elkem's competence grew and the Söderberg electrode became able to offer even greater benefits to customers. Through a combination of major inputs from companies like Knapsack and numerous smaller inputs from around the world, Elkem was able to sell a Söderberg system that became the established means of electric smelting of carbide and most ferroalloys, and was a viable alternative in a number of other processes. Although it operated in a fairly small niche, Elkem proved it had a future as a knowledge-selling company. Nevertheless, income from international sales remained limited, both compared to the company's early ambitions and compared to its outstanding bank loans after the financial reorganization in 1921.

The future was in aluminium. In the 1910s, Elkem had already conducted research on Norwegian minerals in order to find an alternative raw material to bauxite, and as a consequence the idea of transferring the Söderberg principle to aluminium followed quickly on the original technical breakthrough. Aluminium was made with electrolytic processes using cathodes and anodes, not electrodes; the transfer of the Söderberg system to aluminium entailed a profound reconstruction. In 1926, after more than five years of experimentation, Elkem found new techniques that vastly improved its Söderberg system for aluminium, and as a result production facilities were built in France, Spain and the US. Alcoa, the world's largest maker of aluminium and the company Elkem expected the most from, met with little success, and Elkem was disappointed with the American company's lack of effort. It was no consolation that Alcoa in the early 1930s acknowledged that access to the Söderberg system helped improve its own techniques with pre-baked anodes.

The breakthrough in aluminium came in the early 1930s through the French company Pechiney (more correctly in the company Alais, Froges et Camargue which later became part of Pechiney). Pechiney constructed a new aluminium furnace with the use of the Söderberg principle, and it was left to Elkem to commercialise the anode part of the procedure. This was a requirement of Elkem's contract with its licensees, but nevertheless Pechiney's achievement was significant and its subsequent behaviour towards Elkem was very dignified. Pechiney and Elkem became promoters of the Söderberg system in aluminium from 1932, and the growth of the European aluminium industry from the mid-1930s was very much based on this technological platform. This expansion occurred to a large degree in Germany – and it turned out to be a preparation for the Second World War. Aluminium came into wider use, but one product that generated increasing demand was the aeroplane. The late 1930s were very good for Elkem. Aluminium capacity in Europe grew rapidly, and production was mostly based on the Söderberg system; in 1960 around 60 per cent of the global aluminium production used the system. A remarkable achievement, not least for the small company Elkem became. But it was an achievement that reflected Elkem's early ambitions and the tactic of placing itself in the middle of things (Table 12.1).

A company for Norway; the company as organiser

The achievement of Elkem could certainly not have been planned. But there was a serious and systematic attitude to the direction of Elkem right from the start that goes a long way to explain the ambitions behind what later became a success. Elkem was the 'baby' of the richest and most enterprising Swedish and Norwegian bourgeoisie of their time, and as such it was typical of its day and age – the large big business enterprise based on large capital and systematic R&D activities. In some ways, it must be said, it was more of a Swedish than a Norwegian enterprise, at least superficially.

Year	Income electrode,	Profits before taxes	Dividend
1923–4	371,000		
24–5	234,000		
25–6	247,000		
26–7	357,000		
27–8	352,000	149,000	
28–9	688,000	448,000	
1929–30	870,000[1]	496,000	
30–1	900,000[1]	419,000	256,000
31–2	832,000[1]	291,000	256,000
32–3	813,000[1]	344,000	256,000
33–4	840,000[1]	395,000	239,000
34–5	949,000[1]	520,000	250,000
35–6	1,840,000[1]	1,096,000	400,000
36–7	2,435,000[1]	1,380,000	429,000
37–8	2,641,000[1]	2,075,000	572,000
38–9	2,569,000[1]	974,000	572,000
1939–40	2,437,000[1]	691,000	572,000
40–1	2,726,000[1]	684,000	458,000

Note: 1. The number may include more than the electrode/anode.
Source: Elkem's yearly accounts.

Such big business enterprises were much more common in Sweden than in Norway. Norway, with strong shipping and fishing sectors, had a much smaller segment of exporting industrial enterprises than Sweden. Moreover, the making of big business in Sweden also involved the part-creators of Elkem, Norsk Hydro and Orkla, the Wallenbergs, indicating that a significant amount of the Norwegian big business-companies also had a Swedish heritage and should be understood as a cross-border phenomenon. The might of the Wallenbergs – their access to finance of various sorts, international contacts and industrial understanding – are often used to illustrate the difference between Norway and Sweden (see Chapter 3). And because the Wallenbergs were not alone in representing Swedish banking power, the difference between the role of Norwegian and Swedish banks in facilitating the second industrial revolution is accentuated. The Elkem case illustrated this very well.

First, Elkem filled that role of being a venture company in the 1910s. For a short period in the 1910s Elkem itself became a bank. General manager Sam Eyde was able to lobby for a change in Norwegian law to make industrial enterprises able to issue bonds and thereby finance industrial ventures.

In short, it might be said Eyde tried to copy his former allies, the Wallenbergs. The perceived need for this change in the law also illustrated that access to capital was deemed a problem for the creation of Norwegian industry. The availability of finance and the First World War and the ensuing crisis made this law ineffectual and Elkem hardly used this opportunity.

Second, when Elkem was hit very hard by the crisis and had to reorganise in 1921, the relationships with the banks was perceived by Elkem's management as very problematic and as a source of long-term uncertainty. Not only was the reorganization tough, Elkem's management saw the payback plan as destructive, which was why Elkem contacted Alcoa as a prospective new owner. When Gustav Jebsen visited the US in 1920 he discussed a number of proposals with Alcoa's legendary leader Arthur Vining Davis. In 1924 Elkem's leader Willy Eger (effective from 1921; Sam Eyde had left the company in 1916) forged a lasting relationship with Alcoa by inviting the American giant to take 55 per cent of Elkem's stock, while Elkem's debt was at the same time refinanced by a favourable loan from Alcoa. Alcoa had already invested in other Norwegian companies in order to get access to waterfalls for electricity production, and it was clearly interested in examining the potential of the Söderberg principle for aluminium production. The deal with Alcoa gave Elkem financial certainty for the steady development of the Söderberg systems and their gradual deployment in the international metallurgical industry.

The Alcoa solution was only temporary and in 1935 the company was once more mainly Norwegian-owned. As Elkem became more self-assured and developed a growing business, its relationship with Alcoa soured. Alcoa had been good for Elkem in the 1920s, when it provided financial stability. But Alcoa lost interest in the Söderberg system in the 1930s; its understanding of the system had been fixed prior to Pechiney's advance. The American market was effectively closed to Elkem; Alcoa through its monopoly was its only potential customer there in the inter-war period. Alcoa also changed its policy towards Europe after the company divided into an American (Alcoa) and Canadian (Alcan) component in 1928. The company's stake in Elkem was assigned to the new Canadian company, Alcan, and in early 1935 a Norwegian consortium, working closely with Elkem leader Willy Eger, acquired Alcan's shares in the company. As part of this deal, Elkem had to guarantee that the Söderberg system would be limited to the members of the Aluminium Alliance, the producers' international cartel. The Aluminium Alliance approved the transaction.

There were several cases of problems in the 1920s between Norwegian big business and its Norwegian banking connections. Orkla, who had a strong Wallenberg connection through the Wallenberg family's 20-odd per cent ownership, had two main banks. One of them was SEB, the Wallenberg bank, and the other was a Norwegian bank. During the problems of the 1920s, which were not that bad for Orkla, but which hit Orkla's Norwegian bank very hard, Orkla and SEB had great difficulty getting one of the sound Norwegian banks to take Orkla's business. The argument – given in a personal letter from the chairman of Christiania Bank og Kreditkasse, Hieronymous Heyerdahl, to Marcus Wallenberg – was that this solvent bank in this way protested against the Norwegian government's handling of the banking crisis at the time. It would not have anything to do with Orkla. Thus SEB had to increase its exposure to Orkla and a Norwegian bank took a much smaller part than Orkla had bargained for, a remarkable illustration of Norwegian banks not assuming national responsibility.

Was there a difference in attitude between Norwegian and Swedish banks? The Kiær and Solberg families certainly believed so at the time. They were major owners in Nordic industry at the time and were hard hit by the crisis after the First World War. Following their investments during the 1920s their perception was that Swedish paper and pulp companies – some of which they owned shares in – had much better relationships with their banks than their Norwegian counterparts. When companies were in trouble – and they invariably were – the Swedish companies had better access to investment money conducive to the long-term development of their business. The Norwegian paper and pulp companies – just like Elkem – had to pay back money even if they could make very good use of new investments.

There are two possible sources of the differences between Sweden and Norway. One, which is rather vague, but it needs mentioning, is that Sweden had the better developed industrial society and so the importance of industry's future was better taken care of by the banks. The other, which the history of Elkem helps to illuminate, has to do with the historic relationships between banks and industry. In Sweden, banks were traditionally more involved in industrial expansion. There is no better example of this than the Wallenbergs, who were personal investors in industrial companies, who used SEB to purchase shares, and who also financed these and other companies via the bank. The Norwegian banks were just a banking connection and did not participate in the so-called 'investment banking' done by the Swedes. While Swedish bankers were sometimes masters of industry, in Norway the bourgeoisie, the owners of industry, were masters of the banks. In a time of crisis like the 1920s the banks were left to take care of themselves, and their alleged masters, the owners of industry, were not in a financial position to exert influence on the banks.

Elkem in its original form may be seen as a reflection of these Norwegian traditions. The idea behind Elkem – to be an instrument for the creation of new industry – was a banking business in Sweden. In Norway this function was carried out from within a special company, Elkem. Elkem, owned after 1910 by prominent Norwegian bourgeoisie, tried to carve out a national role that was also reflected in the company name. There are other telling examples of the same phenomenon in Norway. The Kiær and Solberg families collected the family money in one company where four cousins of the family became directors, and through individual investments and this collective company they played an important role as investors in Norwegian, Swedish, Finnish and Russian industrial development. The increased need for large capital formation seems to have been met with different arrangements in Norway and Sweden, and in Norway collaboration of individuals and families – an 'associative capitalism', with banks as junior partners – was an important development in the decades around 1900. Both in and around Elkem, and with regard to the Kiær and Solberg families, there is a national ethos. This was about developing business and earning money, but national needs and pride in making a modern industry was also part of the process. Elkem – 'the Norwegian joint stock company for the electrochemical industry' – was such an instrument for the betterment of business, and for Norway. Elkem was more than a mere company; it was also very much an undertaking by the bourgeois, almost a reflection of citizenship.

Elkem's CEO from 1921 to 1951, Willy Eger, was very representative of this role. Born into one of Norway's richest families, he had the connections to reorganise the ownership of Elkem in 1935. He was a close relative to possibly the richest Norwegian of the time, Thomas Fearnley, Jr, a close friend of both Marcus Wallenberg (1864–1943) and the Crown Prince of Sweden. Elkem actually rented office space from Fearnley's shipping company Fearnley & Eger (the name came from an uncle of Willy Eger). Eger and Elkem's problems with Norwegian banks in the 1920s, and their solution with new Norwegian owners in the 1930s, seem to be very representative of the broader situation in Norwegian industry. The new and independent Elkem was very well positioned to take advantage of the outbreak of the Second World War and the global need for aluminium.

A new beginning: and an end in sight

When the Second World War broke out and Germany occupied Norway, Elkem was in very awkward position. Germany was a user of the Söderberg system, as was the rest of the aluminium-producing world with the exception of the US. However, due to strategic choices made by Elkem, and new developments outside Elkem's control, a new situation that finally created a global breakthrough for the Söderberg system emerged. One vital part of this process was that Elkem was able to run an office in New York all through the war and thus position the company within the changing landscape.

At the beginning of the Second World War, the US government challenged Alcoa's American production monopoly. This enabled Reynolds and other newcomers to begin aluminium production, and several of these new producers chose the Söderberg system. Alcoa did not. Elkem's new American business was taken care of by Georg Hagerup-Larssen, who later (in 1959) became CEO. Hagerup-Larssen was a colourful, outgoing engineer with a thorough understanding of the technical aspects of aluminium production. He was sent on a 'wild' mission to the US after Germany occupied Norway in 1940. With the explicit aim of raising new business in North America, he fled through Sweden and the Soviet Union into Japan. There he was given money that a licensee Mitsui owed Elkem: this was before Pearl Harbor. He finally landed in San Francisco after sixty-two days of travelling:

'I stood there without plan or programme, but with the authority to do what the hell I wanted and the money to do it with. An exciting, but not at all uninteresting situation for a not yet too old engineer! One could say that chance served me well. I sat in the hotel in San Francisco and read a newspaper when my eyes fell on a note stating that Reynolds Metal Corporation was starting production of aluminium. I was told that the company had offices in New York. I went there. In New York I learned that the company leadership was holding a meeting in Shoreham Hotel in Washington. I went there and checked in at Shoreham. This happened at the same time as the Reynolds board were still meeting and had just decided to start production of aluminium with pre-baked anodes. At this meeting was the leader of Reynolds' aluminium strategy, a Mr Horsfield. I sent a card to him that explained that I *had* to talk to him at once. He came out to meet me, I presented the drawings of our newest aluminium anode, and I was immediately summoned into the board meeting where I could explain our constructions personally. The matter was concluded by the company's president, old R.S. Reynolds himself, with the following line: 'I bet on you, young man!'[2]

Hagerup-Larssen's story is an account of how far initiative and charm can get you, and it underplays both the actual preparation for his trip and Elkem's use of good connections in New York. Elkem's CEO knew a number of important business people in New York, including Arthur Vining Davis and Elkem's old director Gustav Jebsen. Elkem's contract with Alcoa had to be renegotiated before Elkem and Reynolds could sign a contract. Little more was gained in the US during the war, as the American government put Arthur Vining Davis in charge of the new government-run aluminium plants raised to meet wartime requirements, and Davis preferred the pre-baked methods applied by Alcoa. But a large portion of the increased production in Canada was from Söderberg plants. All in all Elkem earned a healthy sum from licence fees in North America during the war, which proved a major breakthrough for the Söderberg system in aluminium, and post-war developments continued this success to a certain extent. New plants were built with the Söderberg system, and Pechiney again made improvements – they introduced vertical spikes to bring the electricity supply to the anode. Elkem conducted major research to develop Pechiney's ideas and to prove scientifically that it did indeed outperform the old system. From 1951, Elkem was able to sell a new and improved version of a globally competitive aluminium smelting system. This time round its own research department, vastly expanded since the late 1930s, was very much engaged in the system. Yet there was resistance to Elkem's technology. Alcoa did not believe in it. The American government considered that Elkem's patent system, which conferred on Elkem the rights to improvements made by licensees, violated the anti-trust law, since Elkem had a monopoly of the Söderberg system. In the aluminium industry people spoke of the 'continuous patent' for the 'continuous production system', implying that Elkem's practice was unfair. When Elkem's patent system was deemed illegal in the US in 1951 (in the aftermath of Alcoa losing its production monopoly), Elkem had to change its practices. European companies also became reluctant to continue with the old contracts. But all this concerned the long-term future. Meanwhile, Elkem had patented the improvements made after the Second World War and thereby extended patent-based income from the Söderberg system up to the late 1960s.

Overall, as Tables 12.2 and 12.3 show, Elkem's fortunes were improving. It gradually extended its technical competence and amassed greater financial resources. In the 1950s large-scale production based on the Söderberg anode gave solid revenues that opened many possibilities. One new path was obvious: immediately after the Second World War, an engineering division

Table 12.2 Elkem: key figures (Norwegian kroner), 1941–51 (year of account 1 April to 31 March)

Year	Income[1]	Pre-tax profit	Dividend
1941–2	2,647,000	910,000	572,000
42–3	2,725,000	814,000	572,000
43–4	2,485,000	633,000	572,000
44–5	2,030,000	600,000	572,000
45–6	2,415,000		
46–7	3,234,000	1,680,000	358,000
47–8	2,367,000	983,000	429,000
48–9	4,294,000	1,485,000	572,000
1949–50	2,641,000	998,000	572,000
50–1	4,147,000	3,315,000	715,000
51–2	9,617,000	7,686,000	715,000

Note: 1. Mostly from electrode/anode.
Source: Elkem's yearly accounts.

was established to sell furnaces for electric smelting. Unlike the aluminium system, the patents of smelting operations were not continuous, but Elkem had accumulated knowledge and expertise that could be used in order to sell furnaces – and, indeed, entire plants. From the mid-1950s this became a blossoming business. Yet questions remained about the future. Both the new engineering business and the aluminium patents derived from the invention and international exploitation of the Söderberg principle. In the mid-1950s Elkem had money to invest, and its response was to begin to produce metals itself. To understand why, we have return to the Second World War and to examine anew the wartime developments.

National production for the international market

During the inter-war period, Elkem's key assets were technical knowledge and the exploitation of the Söderberg principle. After the Second World War and up to the 1970s, Elkem's exceptional growth and development was based on its national position and its role in the reconstruction of the Norwegian industrial economy. One could argue that a sophisticated strategy to pursue international innovation was gradually replaced by one to utilise national networks.

Since 1921, Elkem's CEO was Willy Eger, who had joined the company as a director eleven years earlier, at the age of thirty. As the scion of a wealthy

Table 12.3   Elkem: income (Norwegian kroner) from the Söderberg system for aluminium, 1945–70

Year	Income
1945–6[1]	1,827,000
46–7	2,985,000
47–8	2,442,000
48–9	3,156,000
1949–50	2,799,000
50–1	3,028,000
51–2[1]	9,923,000[1]
1952[2]	9,055,000[2]
1953	7,281,000
1954[3]	12,521,000[3]
1955	9,820,000
1956	8,902,000
1957	7,387,000
1958	6,732,000
1959	8,606,000
1960	10,252,000
1961	9,786,000
1962	9,404,000
1963	9,031,000
1964	10,507,000
1965	11,837,000
1966	11,183,000
1967	13,020,000
1968	9,653,000
1969	9,500,000
1970	8,188,000

Notes: 1. Including adjustment of the new contract with Reynolds (January 1946 to September 1950); 2. Last three quarters of 1952 plus the payment for use in the US (1941–5); 3. Includes payment for use in Canada (1941–5).
Source: Elkem's Engineering Division's Yearly Report for 1970.

family, he represented the progressive bourgeoisie that sought to create a strong Norwegian industry in the 1910s. Elkem's effort was a national effort; Elkem's failure was the failure of the national bourgeoisie. It reflected how badly Norway's export-oriented economy had fared in the inter-war period. In Norway, fortunes have traditionally been accumulated through export activity rather than in the confines of the national economy, which had been very vulnerable to international crises. Had investment capital been readily available, Elkem's knowledge and the abundance of waterfalls suitable for hydroelectric power could have allowed Norway to become a leading international producer of aluminium in the inter-war period. Instead, the know-how and technology Elkem controlled were used abroad. Eger's actions towards Alcoa in this period reflected his national sentiments, and he was alive to the opportunities which R&D could provide for Elkem. In conversation with the leadership of Alcan just after the Second World War, he affirmed his belief that Elkem could succeed without a large research staff and without large plants: 'I said that we . . . did not need huge Research Works.'[3] Smartness prevailed.

Eger was a chief architect of the new political economy of Norway after the Second World War. He came from a rich family and often came across as distant and upper-class, but he was a genuine democrat who believed in pragmatic strategies for creating national wealth. Eger was a pioneer in the type of government–business collaboration that greatly influenced developments after 1945. During the First World War, national programmes were developed in order to counteract material shortages, and in the early 1920s Elkem took this idea forward when it persuaded the state to become involved in the production of pig iron. The state, Elkem and Christiania Spigerverk, an iron and steel company, collaborated to develop a new pig iron furnace that used the Söderberg approach. Christiania Spigerverk's furthering of the development work then led to the creation of the 'Tysland-Hole' pig iron furnace in the late 1930s. This was a solid and reliable furnace that grew out of national industrial planning. It used the Söderberg principle for electric smelting of iron ore and it fell to Elkem to market it internationally. Alongside the knowledge built on the Söderberg system patents, this furnace was the foundation of Elkem's new engineering division.

Eger took an active part in the Norwegian resistance during the Second World War and worked to encourage opposition to German occupation among the industrial bourgeoisie. With this background, Eger was able to play a key role in the development of better relations with the labour movement during and after the war. Former antagonists came to a common understanding and forged a new partnership for economic wealth; both believed in the importance of this kind of state industrial planning. This time round, war-planning activities had important ramifications. Eger became a key advisor to the Labour government that came to power in 1945. He took part as a consultant in the decision to create a new state-owned, Söderberg system aluminium plant and a new state-owned iron and steel works. Both enterprises used Elkem technology; both were Elkem customers.

Elkem prospered in the new post-war political economy. Its engineering division enjoyed remarkable success from the outset, and by the mid-1950s it was a major international operation, selling Norwegian technology worldwide. It was an expert organization for techniques for non-stop continuous smelting at high temperatures (above 2000°C). In the 1930s, it mainly sold pig iron furnaces. Mitsui & Co of Japan and Fiat of Italy were important customers for early versions; GVC Siderúrgica del Orinoco (Venezuela) and Rudnici I Zelezara Skopje (Yugoslavia) were major customers for the larger versions of the late 1950s and early 1960s. Elkem also sold furnaces for calcium carbide, but the company gradually became a specialist in ferroalloy furnaces. Elkem provided hundreds of furnaces for manganese alloys, ferrosilicon, ferronickel and chromium alloys to customers all over the world: India, South Africa, Brazil, Japan, Sweden, Spain, Egypt, Australia, Portugal, the Philippines, France, Iceland, West Germany, Indonesia, Iran, Colombia, Switzerland, Zimbabwe, New Caledonia, Norway and the US. Union Carbide was almost conspicuous by its absence from this extensive list of customers; it was a large producer of ferroalloys and calcium carbide and had as early as 1920 considered purchasing the US rights to the Söderberg principle. Between 1955 and 1975, Elkem's engineering division grew both in size and in turnover, and earned the company considerable profits.

Elkem's path to large-scale production was gradual and reflected its increasing profitability after 1945 (see Tables 12.2 and 12.3, pp. 512 and 513 and Table 12A.1, p. 528). The research plant in Kristiansand had always produced a small line of ferrosilicon, and this was expanded during the early 1950s, when Marshall Plan activities earmarked Norway as a provider of ferrosilicon to the British steel industry. Elkem owned pyrite deposits at Skorovas in central Norway. Pyrite is a complex mineral containing sulphur, copper, zinc, iron and minute quantities of other minerals. With the backing of the Marshall Plan Administration (ECA) and the Norwegian government, Elkem secured finance to develop Skorovas as well as a market for the product. Elkem originally purchased this property in 1913 in order to secure sulphur for making ammonium sulphate, a fertilizer, but nothing became of this plan. Elkem lacked the necessary resources to utilise these deposits until after 1945, when the reconstruction of western Europe got under way. The expansion of the ferrosilicon works and the construction of the pyrite mine involved extensive and innovative tax concessions on the behalf of the state. That these were forthcoming was an indication of Elkem's central role as a provider of ideas, methods and processes for the creation of a new industrial society in

Norway. A new partnership blossomed. The Social Democratic government provided electricity, loans, guarantees and tax concessions, while semi-state companies like Norsk Hydro and private companies like Elkem showed what could actually be done. The state's industrial planning relied heavily on the technological know-how of private industry, and on half a century of history which could be traced back to the establishment of Norsk Hydro and Elkem and the birth of the idea of a highly industrialized Norway.

By the mid-1950s Elkem was ready to progress to the next stage: the building of a large, state-of-the-art aluminium plant in Mosjøen in northern Norway, again with huge tax concessions. The necessary financial muscle was built up with the help of a healthy patent business in aluminium and a strong engineering business in electric furnaces. In addition, the Korean War boom enhanced the profitability of the pyrite mine and of the smaller ferrosilicon furnaces. Elkem needed a partner to get access to bauxite and to sell the produce, and the medium-sized Swiss company Alusuisse (then called AIAG) came on board, taking one-third of the stock. The necessary electricity was provided by the Norwegian state, through very favourable long-term contracts. When Willy Eger stepped down as chairman of the board of Elkem in 1959, after forty-nine years with the company, the new aluminium plant had been in production for a year. It was a major expression of his long-term efforts to create industrial wealth.

The 1960s became a decade of glorious industrial growth and wealth creation; in 1969 and 1970 Elkem was the biggest Norwegian company in terms of stock market valuation. Elkem was far from being the country's largest employer, but its workforce grew from a couple of hundred in 1945 to several thousand in 1970. In 1972, Elkem merged with the similar-sized Christiania Spigerverk, an iron and steel works with a ferrosilicon plant. The combined company was comparable in size to Norsk Hydro and Borregaard, hitherto the two biggest industrial employers with between 8,000 and 9,000 workers each. During the 1960s, Elkem had bought an old producer of ferroalloys and had built a new, modern ferrosilicon plant. In 1971, a large new plant for aluminium production was opened in Lista, southern Norway (near Kristiansand). Both this and the other aluminium plant were owned in partnership with Alcoa, who had replaced Alusuisse as Elkem's partner in aluminium.

The 1960s also became a growth period for the Norwegian aluminium industry, based on Elkem's Söderberg system. The growth of the 1960s was very much the result of industrial policy and involved a number of companies.

The Norwegian government facilitated growth by a number of measures, the most important of these being the building of new power plants and the advantageous long-term contracts for the delivery of electricity. This was a more offensive policy, with the government taking charge, and the time when a company like Elkem could expect to be in a special position among those that were privileged was gone. The government wanted co-operation with large foreign manufacturers. Through the ensuing political process of finding partners for Norway, the relationship between AIAG and Elkem soured because AIAG was able to build its own plant in Norway. Elkem, who needed a partner for access to bauxite and for selling the aluminium, teamed up with Alcoa as a replacement for AIAG. The team Elkem–Alcoa, who owned 50 percent each of their Norwegian collaboration, got its second plant, Lista. Norsk Hydro, who teamed up with American Harvey, got started with a plant. In addition there was the state's own company, called Årdal og Sunndal Verk. The expansion of the Norwegian aluminium industry of the 1960s – making Norway an important producer in a global context – was a logical development for an electricity-rich country, and it also followed from Elkem's important position as technology provider for aluminium production.

During the 1960s, Elkem also changed into a financially oriented company with a strong emphasis on managerial policies and responsibilities. Engineers were partly replaced by economists. Top management changed its focus from the Söderberg technologies and competences and on to financial matters and economic planning. This partly reflected the growth in the number of plants and the broadening of Elkem's activities. Engineers still had a place in Elkem's strategic thinking, but technological considerations gradually became less important. One important decision was to prevent the mighty engineering division from expanding, whether into aluminium in the 1960s (partly because of opposition from Alcoa), oil in the 1970s (with a huge national market), or new technology developments in its old fields of expertise. Elkem became a producer, and American management thinking about running large enterprises became dominant – as in many European companies at the time. Elkem's success in the 1960s reflected, and to some extent anticipated, general economic growth, and its markets – the steel industry, aluminium processors – were in the mainstream of economic activity. After the 1972 merger with Christiania Spigerverk, Elkem itself became a small-scale steel producer. In 1973 it built a mini-plant in Manchester, UK, for the production of steel, using scrap as input. It added another plant in Liverpool a few years later in order to benefit from economies of scale.

The post-Second World War growth period of Elkem was a remarkable achievement, in terms of growth, return on investment and as an example of the benefits of establishing strategies on the basis of organizational capabilities. Elkem went from being a small engineering company with a couple of hundred employees to become possibly Norway's largest industrial enterprise, at least for a short time. Elkem's growth also benefited from a good dose of political entrepreneurship, as the establishment of a common goal between industry and the social democrats in power – growth in energy-intensive industries – rested on reciprocal respect and trust. The common fight against the German occupation was one such reason, but the willingness of an elitist company – in the social meaning – like Elkem to collaborate with the Labour Party in governmental power, and thereby marking acceptance and social stability, was equally important. The ensuing growth no doubt benefited a lot from the favourable conditions created by the government: it was a rosy situation, and one that could not last.

Overstretch

In the mid-1970s Elkem was hit hard by the international economic downturn. This was a general economic crisis, but it reflected long-term factors. After the 1970s, times were never the same again, yet for Elkem the process of change that would create a viable platform for the future would be hard won, the result of Elkem's crisis around 1990.

Elkem, of course, did change somewhat during the 1970s. Its steel and ferrosilicon business were especially affected during the crises. Even though its steel operations were small and well run, the UK was arguably the worst place to start steel operations in the 1970s. Elkem had long believed that its specialized Norwegian steel business would be sheltered from competition, but the major steel crises changed every producer's strategy. Even small countries and small niches became attractive in the hunt for viable business. Elkem's steel business was dismantled in the 1980s. The British companies were sold to a branch of British Steel, while the Norwegian business was sold to Norway's state-owned, fully integrated steel company. In financial terms, Elkem came out of its steel ventures reasonably well, but this does not take into account the time and effort involved. The ferroalloy business mirrored developments in the steel industry to some extent, but it did much better. Elkem, after all, was a pioneer in the very large furnaces that it made available as the 1960s progressed, and that increased global capacity while providing much-needed rationalization in many areas. Aluminium also fared better than steel, but it was not without problems, especially after 1980 when the whole industry was in deep crisis.

The 1970s also heralded an end to Elkem's special status in Norwegian industrial planning. One problem was pollution. This was gradually taken care of during the next three decades, but the rebuilding of plants – especially the aluminium-producing ones – to create better working environments was particularly costly. A bigger problem was growing scepticism in society towards energy-consuming industry and the use of national energy resources for industrial purposes. Elkem could no longer expect ready access to cheap electricity for industrial expansion, so it directed its attention to foreign expansion. The British steel expansion in 1973 was partly due to this redirection. The establishment in 1979 of a new ferrosilicon plant in Iceland, in partnership with Icelandic interests, was even more significant. The purchase of Union Carbide's huge ferroalloy division in 1981 further expressed a completely new take on a problematic national situation.

The 1981 purchase made Elkem the world's largest producer of ferroalloys. By adding most of Union Carbide's plants to its own, it built a portfolio that within a decade extended to sixteen plants in the US, Canada, Iceland and Norway, mainly producing ferrosilicon, pure silicon and ferromanganese. This was a huge financial commitment, and it brought Elkem close to bankruptcy. There were severe problems in 1987 and 1992. Elkem's CEO at the time, Kaspar Kielland, lost his job in 1987; he proved to be the last of the line of CEOs that came up through the company's own ranks. His successor did not fare much better; he left in 1992 in the midst of Elkem's deepest crisis since 1921. The thinking behind the Union Carbide purchase was that, in ferroalloys, greater size meant cheaper production and the possibility of achieving higher prices through the role of the largest provider.

A globally active Elkem faced a new and difficult market and huge and complex organizational challenges. Union Carbide's range of furnaces was old and cumbersome; some of the biggest of the American furnaces were not originally made by Elkem and did not even use the Söderberg system. International competition increased throughout the 1980s, notably from Russia and China but also from other Norwegian producers and from other parts of the world. This proved hard to live with. In no way did Elkem control the prices of ferroalloys. Ironically, Elkem had helped establish this competition by selling furnaces worldwide; as a consequence Elkem's engineering division came to lose importance as the company no longer wanted to sell to its competitors. The 1980s was characterized by a dual dilemma: neither metals production nor sale of furnaces did well. The wheel had turned full circle from the 1950s and 1960s, when both sides of the business prospered.

In the early 1950s, Elkem began to produce for the international market, and this new strategy exposed it to new problems. OPEC's decision to raise oil prices led a cyclical change in the global economy in the mid-1970s. Elkem felt the effects keenly, as the entire European and North American steel industry experienced structural problems that profoundly changed the whole sector. As a producer of ferroalloys Elkem operated on the margins of the West's established steel industry. It sought opportunities in the emerging steel industry of the newly industrialising countries, and this partly accounts for its relative success up to the early 1980s. But the company's fortunes were in continual decline. Each economic downturn – 1982, 1987 and 1992 – brought Elkem greater problems. The sale of assets was a viable solution during the 1980s, but in 1992 there was little left to sell. There was no quick fix for the company's problems.

The rise of the new Elkem

Elkem transformed itself in the years up to 2005, and became a very different company. Through reorganization and rationalization, Elkem increased the profitability of its metal production. It modernized its ferrosilicon and pure silicon production, and with its partner Alcoa expanded and modernized their two Norwegian aluminium plants. Reorganization created a company that was less hierarchical and more successful. Increased profits and the sale of its manganese alloy business financed Elkem's 2002 acquisition of 72 per cent of Sapa, the Swedish aluminium processing company. The transaction roughly doubled both Elkem's turnover and its workforce. In 2005 the remaining 28 per cent of Sapa was purchased at the same time as Orkla purchased Elkem.

The large Norwegian company Orkla played a crucial role in Elkem's transformation after 1992. Orkla bought 30 per cent of Elkem in 1989, wrongly believing that it was a sound financial investment. Orkla is unusual among Norwegian companies in that it frequently buys into other Norwegian enterprises, best understood by reference to its own history. Orkla was originally a huge mining and industrial company exploiting one of the world's largest pyrite mines. In order to prepare for a future after the mine was exhausted,

Orkla began to invest surplus income in the 1940s by buying shares in other Norwegian companies, including Elkem. Some of Orkla's owners also bought on their own account shares in Elkem and other part-owned companies; this facilitated the 1972 merger of Elkem and Christiania Spigerverk. When the crisis of 1992 struck, Orkla was the largest shareholder in Elkem, and Orkla's actions proved decisive for Elkem's future.

Orkla wanted Elkem to continue and to make the most of its position as a metal producer. While Orkla had not been responsible for the decision to buy Union Carbide's ferroalloy business, it had tacitly supported the deal as the owner of around 8 per cent of Elkem's stocks. In 1986, Orkla sold its Norwegian ferroalloy plant to Elkem along with the controlling rights in another one (Bjølvefossen, which Elkem had had to give up in the inter-war-period) in the belief that the Norwegian and global ferroalloy business needed restructuring. Much of 1992 was taken up with the effort to refinance Elkem and to persuade sceptical banks to renegotiate Elkem's loans. At the same time, Elkem's administration did all it could to cut costs and to keep the ship afloat. Ole Enger – who came from Norsk Hydro as second in command in 1991 – was appointed CEO of Elkem in 1992. This was one of the first steps taken by the new chairman of the board, Orkla director Finn Jebsen, to change Elkem administratively.

In the short term, the chief focus was a ruthless effort to cut costs. What was done structurally profoundly affected Elkem's public image. Elkem had been one of Norway's proudest companies. It was active in industrial circles and was a feature in the physical landscape of central Oslo. Elkem's expensive and specially commissioned headquarters in central Oslo had been sold to raise money in 1988. Instead, the head office moved to the old premises of Christiania Spigerverk, a large industrial site with several huge buildings. This property increased rapidly in value as the city of Oslo needed new office space. Elkem knew that the timing was bad – the property market in Oslo hit an all-time low in 1992 – but the old site was sold in order to keep Elkem afloat. Other assets were also sold, and Elkem found new and cheaper offices for a reduced head office staff.

Over the next few years Elkem's attitude to its various plants gradually changed. The aluminium plants were sizeable units and production was developed in close co-operation with Alcoa. Both plants were extensively modernized during the late 1980s and 1990s, in order to improve efficiency and reduce emissions. Elkem's ferroalloy operations were much more diverse than its aluminium business. Production ranged from manganese alloys, ferrosilicon and pure silicon, and was spread among many countries, plants and furnaces. As Elkem grew after 1960, it strove to use modern equipment where it would be efficient, and the push for lower costs led to rationalization of the workforce. But some plants were old. Some of the former Union Carbide plants in America were huge and impractical, while the older Norwegian plants had small and inefficient furnaces. The response in the early 1990s was a strong focus on the technical operation of the furnaces, with a view to identifying best practices. This process revealed a wide variety of practices among its many plants, despite the fact that much of Elkem's research effort since the 1950s had been devoted to optimising the operation of furnaces. The effort in the 1990s to ensure uninterrupted running of furnaces – with minimum inputs – brought substantial increases in cost efficiency, and Elkem broadened its capabilities by adding expertise in the running of furnaces to its well-established expertise in their construction.

The effort to improve the production process in general, and the operation of furnaces in particular, has continued up to the present. But there is a limit to where this will lead. Elkem will continue to face rising salaries and energy prices and must come to terms with the high costs of operating in rich countries. The greatest improvement in the company's cost structure has been achieved by a major reorientation in the way Elkem operates as a company. On one level this reflects Ole Enger's personality and his effort to create a down-to-earth, cost-conscious corporate culture; this almost felt natural after years of serious trouble. On another level it reflects a deliberate move to profoundly change the company, from the American-style company created in the 1960s into a Japanese-influenced, decentralized company that does not need as many employees.

Since the mid-1990s Elkem has been rebuilding the company from the ground floor. More and more responsibility has been given to the operators. This creates more efficient operators, and in the process several layers of management have been cut out. Following the model of the best Japanese production facilities, Elkem's workers have greater responsibility and influence over the work process. Leadership is no longer synonymous with management and instruction, but is a link in the chain driving production forward. More and more, Elkem's production is run without leaders in the workplace, with responsibility in the hands of the workforce. Elkem's ideal is to balance centralization of competence and the development of a scientific understanding of how to optimise production with decentralization of responsibility. The effort to make plants work according to the same practices in a sense takes individual choice away from the workers and the plants, which is balanced with according the workers a key role in identifying what the best practices are. The distance between top and bottom in Elkem has become much shorter than before. Plant management, local engineers and foremen – very numerous in a company with almost twenty plants – have partly been replaced as those performing the actual work directly apply the key competences distilled by the company. Elkem has changed profoundly; productivity and profitability have increased as a result of the reorganization of work and attendant staff reductions.

Alcoa deserves much of the credit for inspiring Elkem. Alcoa adopted Toyota's ideals and made them work in an American metallurgical context. Elkem then studied Alcoa's success and adapted it to Norway, beginning with the aluminium plants and then extending it. But in some ways Elkem has gone further towards decentralization than Alcoa, and there is some evidence that increased responsibility suits the Norwegian worker. It could be argued that Norway has a national advantage as a country that prides itself on egalitarian ideals. The long cyclical upturn of the global economy must also be granted some credit for Elkem's success in the 1990s, as must the strategic operations to change Elkem's competitive position.

Elkem actively sought to make more out of its manganese business, and to either integrate backward into manganese mining or to sell off its smelters. This accounts for the 1999 sale of three large plants to the French mining company, Eramet. Its silicon operations are increasingly being steered away from the steel industry and towards the computer and solar industries (pure metal) and the foundry business (which also takes alloys, some custom-made); the margins are usually higher in these niches. The combined income from these changes, the sale of the manganese business and the constant improvement of general operations, ultimately led to a new orientation of the company in 2001 when it secured the 72 per cent stake in Sapa. For the first time since starting production of primary aluminium in 1958, Elkem had genuinely integrated downstream. In the 1960s, it ventured into aluminium processing in two collaborative ventures with Alcoa, but for several reasons this did not turn out especially well. The move for Sapa was the realization of long-term ambitions and seemingly opened up a number of future opportunities.

With an annual turnover of around NOK 20 billion, Elkem again became a large company. Its future holds great possibilities, albeit with some uncertainties. For several years after 2000 Alcoa tried to buy Elkem, and for a while Orkla and other Norwegian shareholders chose to preserve its independence.

Then, out of the blue in 2005, Orkla purchased Elkem. An important reason for this is Elkem's position in the solar energy business, both because of its decades-long research in making very pure silicon metal (building on competence in ferrosilicon) and its strong ownership position in a vertically integrated solar energy company that had its technological roots in Elkem. In 2006, it was announced that Elkem was to start building new plants for pure silicon particularly made for solar cell production, a venture that may – if Elkem succeeds technically – radically reduce prices for solar energy and possibly create a new foundation for the company.

Elkem completes a century

Elkem began as a venture company in the electro-metallurgical field with the purpose of creating knowledge and enterprises for others to buy. For a long time Elkem sold knowledge and technology – in Norway and around the world – to other companies to enable them to start production. Paradoxically, Elkem gradually developed into an important producer. The company has travelled a long way, and in the last few years has started R&D projects that signal an ambition to return to its innovative roots. Creative, highly explorative research and development projects are again part of Elkem. There was a lot of excitement about its solar energy projects on the Oslo stock exchange in 2006.

Two different lines of reasoning offer broad explanations for Elkem's development. On the one hand, one could say that the national setting forged Elkem. The national context – Norway was particularly good in electro-metallurgy – was crucial in Elkem's early years as an innovative company. The national context also contributed to Elkem's rise as a producer after the Second World War, as government policies facilitated investment opportunpities. On the other hand, one could highlight Elkem's deliberate choice to locate its core knowledge in an international setting. This was how it exploited the Söderberg system for electric smelting and for aluminium. The sale of the rights to the system accompanied the creation of partnerships with international actors, some of whom in turn helped to further improve the systems themselves. In the 1990s the relationship with Alcoa inspired Elkem to reorganise its production, and opened up the possibility of long-term viability in the business of producing metals. Elkem has now reached a hundred years of activity. Along the way it has picked up both competence and companies on the national stage, while it has diffused and appropriated knowledge to and from its international connections.

Some things have changed profoundly. Elkem was an elitist company from the outset, run by Norway's richest and best-educated. It was dedicated to creating superior knowledge, and for a long time this may have perpetuated the social divide between top and bottom in the company. The past ten–fifteen years have seen this change markedly. This reflects deeper changes in Norwegian society, and may prove to have significant implications for the continuation of industrial society. Elkem now manages to earn money even during cyclical downturns, and had made visible the value that was inherent in the large and sclerotic company of 1992. But the company has been part of a turnaround that is fundamentally changing the way industry is run, both in Norway and elsewhere. Through its seemingly successful industrial relations and its metallurgical competences, not least in solar energy, Elkem – or what has come out of Elkem – should have a bright future.

QUESTIONS 1. Elkem has been active in sectors that are typical of Norway, but would it be right to call Elkem a 'typical Norwegian company'?
2. How did Elkem achieve international importance in the inter-war years?

Notes

1. This chapter is based on my book: *Skaperkraft: Elkem gjennom 100 år 1904–2004* (Oslo: Messel forlag 2004).
2. Elkem's archive in Rjukan (Industriarbeidermuseet), series 0001, G009, 'Elektrodesak. Korresp . . .': Jebsen to Elektrokemisk (30 November 1920).
3. Elkem's archive, Smerstad, confidential correspondence, E, Eger: PM, 'Notater fra reise I U.S.A. og Canada', C.W. Eger (19 July 1946).

References

Adamson, O. J. (ed.), *Industries of Norway. Technical and Commercial Achievements* (Oslo: Dreyer, 1952).
Amdam, R. P. and Kvålshaugen, R., 'Etablering og utvikling av ledelseskulturer: norsk kenningisme', *Nordiske organisasjonsstudier*, 1 (2000).
Andersen, K. G. and Yttri G., *Et forsøk verdt: Forskning og utvikling i Norsk Hydro gjennom 90 år* (Oslo: Universitetsforlaget, 1997).
Byrkjeland, M., *A/S Bjølvefossen 1905–1931: Ein analyse av eit foretaks etablering, upublisert hovedoppgave i historie* (Bergen: UiB, 1985).
Børtnes, K. F., *Lista Aluminiumsverk, veien frem 1960–1971: Bakgrunnen for opprettelsen av Lista Aluminiumsverk* upublisert hovedoppgave i historie (UiO, 1999).
Chandler, A. D., Jr, *The Visible Hand: The Managerial Revolution in American Business* (Cambridge, MA: The Belknap Press, 1977).

Chandler, A. D., Jr, *Scale and Scope: The Dynamics of Industrial Capitalism*, (Cambridge, MA and London: The Belknap Press, 1990).

Christensen, S. A., *Statens forhold til Norsk Hydro 1945–1952*, upublisert hovedoppgave i historie (UiO, 1997).

Collett, J. P., *Videnskap og politikk. Samarbeide og konflikt om forskning for industriformål 1917–1930*, upublisert hovedoppgave i historie (UiO, 1983).

Dannevig, B., *Aktieselskabet Arendals Fossekompani 1896–1911–1961* (Arendal: Arendals Fossekompani, 1960).

Didriksen, J., *Industrien under hakekorset* (Oslo: Universitetsforlaget, 1987).

Dybesland, S. B., *Elkems engasjement innen stålindustrien i England – Manchester Steel Ltd*, upublisert notat våren (2003a).

Dybesland, S. B., 'Icelandic Alloys 1976–', upublisert notat våren (2003b).

Dybesland, S. B., 'Utviklingen til Elkem Metals Company 1981–1985', notat våren (2003c).

Dybesland, S. B., 'Søken etter det tredje benet i Elkem 1984–1986' upublisert notat våren (2003d).

Dybesland, S. B., 'Forsøkene på samling av norsk ferrolegeringsindustri fra 1982–', upublisert notat våren (2003e).

Eyde, S., *Mitt liv og mitt livsverk* (Oslo: Gyldendal, 1939).

Fasting, K., *Norsk aluminium gjennom 50 år* (Oslo: Naco, 1965).

Fløgstad, K., *Arbeidets Lys: Tungindustrien i Sauda gjennom 75 år* (Oslo: Det NorskeSamlaget, 1990).

Gammelsæter, H., *Organisasjonsendring gjennom generasjoner av ledere* (Molde: Møreforskning, 1991).

Gasslander, O., *Bank och industriellt genombrott: Stockholms Enskilda Bank kring sekelskiftet 1900, I–II* (Stockholm: Centraltryckeriet/Esselte Aktiebolag, 1956–9).

Goold, M. and Luchs K., 'Why Diversify? Four Decades of Management Thinking', *Academy of Management Executive* 7(3) (1993).

Grimnes, O. K., *Sam Eyde – den grenseløse gründer* (Oslo: Aschehoug, 2001).

Grønlie, T., *Statsdrift: Staten som industrieier i Norge 1945–1963* (Oslo: Tano 1989, Fagbokforlaget, 2003).

Gundersen, H., *Sam Eyde og Jernsaken 1902–1913: En anledning til å se ham alene*, Upublisert hovedoppgave i historie (UiO, 1998).

Gøthe, O. C., *Norsk Jernverk 1946–1988: Fra tro til fall* (Oslo: Schibsted, 1994).

Gøthe, O. C., *Det lette metall, Aluminiumindustrien i Norge* (Oslo: Schibsted, 2001).

Hoffstad, E., *Merkantilt leksikon: Hvem er hvem i næringslivet* (Oslo: Yrkesforlaget 1935).

Hynne, P., *Elkem A/S PEA gjennom 75 år, 1913–1988* (Porsgrunn: Elkem 1988).

Knutsen, S., *Bank, samfunn og økonomisk vekst: En analyse av norske forretningsbankers rolle i den industrielle utviklingen til 1920, med hovedvekt på perioden ca. 1890–1913*, hovedoppgave i historie (UiO, 1990).

Kocka, J., 'The European Pattern and the German Case', in Kocka J., and Mitchell A. R.I. (eds), *Bourgeois Society in Nineteenth-Century Europe*, (Providence, and Oxford: Berg, 1993).

Kollenborg, E., *Det norske Nitridaktieselskap 1912–1962* (Oslo: DNN, 1962).

Milward, A. S., *The Fascist Economy in Norway* (Oxford: Clarendon Press, 1972).

Nerheim, G., *Elektrisitet, vannkraft og industrialisering: Utbyggingen av Svelgen 1917–1928, Volund 1979* (Oslo: Teknisk Museum, 1979).

Nerheim, G., *Elektroingeniørene og det industrielle gjennombrudd, 1890–1920, Volund 1997–98* (Oslo: Teknisk Museum, 1998).

Olsen, K. A., *Norsk Hydro gjennom 50 år: Et eventyr fra realitetenes verden* (Oslo: Norsk Hydro, 1955).

Pedersen, R., *Til Verket: Elkem Aluminium Mosjøens historie gjennom 40 år* (Mosjøen: Elkem, 1997).

Petersen, E. (ed.), *Elektrokemisk A/S 1904–1954* (Oslo: Elektrokemisk, 1953).

Raaum, T., *Elkem Salten 25 år* (Bodø: Elkem Salten 1992). Rinde, Harald, 'Utenlandske interesser i norsk aluminiumsindustri', arbeidsnotat; 1996/10, (Handelshøyskolen BI, 1996).

Rinde, H., *Den lange ventetida, i: Rolv Petter Amdam, Dag Gjestland og Andreas Hompland, Verket og bygda 1947–1997* (Oslo: Det Norske Samlaget, 1997a).

Rinde, H., 'Alcan tur-retur', in Amdam, Gjestland, and Hompland, (1997b).

Rinde, H., Asdal K. and Sogner K., *Producing Innovation through Environmental Regulation: The Case of the Aluminium Industry and the Söderberg Anode*, unpublished paper presented to the Society for the History of Technology's Conference in Atlanta, Georgia (October 2003).

Schartum, D., *Hvordan NOCO ble til . . .* (Oslo: Norwegian Oil Consortium A/S & Co. 1990).

Schei, A., Tuset J. K. and Tveit H., *Production of High Silicon Alloys* (Trondheim: Tapir forlag, 1998).

Schieldrop, E. B., *Christiania Spigerverk: 1853–1961*, (Oslo: Spigerverket, 1961).

Sejersted, F., *Sør-Norge Aluminium A/S*, in Sejersted, Francis (ed.), *En storbank i blandingsøkonomien: Den norske Creditbank 1957–1982* (Oslo: Gyldendal, 1982).

Sejersted, F., *Demokratisk kapitalisme* (Oslo: Universitetsforlaget, 1993).

Smil, V., *Enriching the Earth. Fritz Haber, Carl Bosch and the Transformation of World Food Production* (Cambridge, MA: MIT Press, 2001).

Smith, G. D., *From Monopoly to Competition: The Transformation of Alcoa, 1888–1986* (Cambridge: Cambridge University Press, 1988).

Sogner, K. (med bidrag av Sverre A. Christensen), *Plankeadel: Kiær- og Solbergfamilien under den 2. industrielle revolusjon* (Oslo: Andresen & Butenschøn/Handelshøyskolen BI, 2001).

Sogner, K., 'Makt over beslutningene: Norske storbedrifter gjennom 100 år', in Christensen S. A., Espeli H., and Larsen E., *Kapitalistisk demokrati?* (Oslo: Gyldendal Akademisk 2003).

Spear, S. and Kent Bowen, H. 'Decoding the DNA of the Toyota Production System', *Harvard Business Review* (September–October 1999).

Stocking, G. W. and Watkins Myron W. *Cartels in Action: Case Studies in International Business Diplomacy* (New York: The Twentieth Century Fund, 1946).

Thue, L., *Statens kraft 1890–1947. Kraftutbygging og samfunnsutvikling* (Oslo: Cappelen Fakta, 1994).

appendix

Table 12.A.1 Key figures (in Elkem: Mulhon Norwegian kroner), 1953–2002, data from yearly accounts

Year	Sales	Profits (before tax)	Total assets	Equity nominal	Loans	% (interest)	Number of employees
1953	n.a.	12.6	79.7	28.6	36	18.6	717
1954	n.a.	16.6	94.2	39.7	42	17.7	796
1955	n.a.	19.4	109.4	48.6	44	16.9	810
1956	n.a.	23.3	165.4	60.2	36	16.0	858
1957	n.a.	20.9	282.7	84.3	30	15.0	894
1958	n.a.	25.9	246.6	73.7	30	44.4	1,257
1959	160	26.5	290.7	96.6	33	67.3	1,270
1960	169	24.9	328.3	101.8	31	92.6	1,465
1961	235	25.7	382.1	110.8	29	126.3	1,496
1962	208	21.6	391.2	116.3	30	116.0	1,502
1963	198	31.9	268.8	111.0	41	79.2	1,533
1964	207	47.3	310.0	135.9	44	79.5	1,600
1965	271	60.1	409.0	169.6	41	111.0	2,500
1966	338	69.8	525.2	210.8	40	112.8	3,000
1967	337	62.7	532.9	222.8	42	141.6	3,240
1968	412	75.7	568.0	240.6	42	148.0	3,250
1969	509	91.9	670.5	272.7	41	164.4	3,500
1970	571	109.7	835.2	330.8	40	218.6	3,770
1971	528	34.9	947.2	336.3	36	361.3	3,810
1972	1,219	3.2	1,750.6	546.3	31	745.9	8,276
1973	1,502	58.0	1,763.8	553.0	31	795.1	8,466
1974	2,124	213.3	2,196.3	618.0	28	884.4	8,861
1975	2,061	106.3	2,434.8	732.6	30	962.3	8,517
1976	2,600	40.2	2,842.0	824.9	29	1,267.1	9,324
1977	2,665	27.7	2,918.6	904.6	31	1,333.0	9,108
1978	3,063	34.4	3,019.9	884.3	29	1,402.3	9,030
1979	3,570	262.4	3,388.5	995.5	29	1,542.2	9,577
1980	3,961	177.7	3,842.4	1,105.8	29	1,668.7	9,905
1981	4,874	(152.5)	5,141.1	1,026.8	20	2,859.9	13,244
1982	5,364	(308.2)	4,924.6	740.1	15	3,113.7	11,154
1983	6,117	235.6	5,307.7	882.4	17	2,969.1	9,943
1984	7,876	658.0	8,254.0	1,788.0	22	4,211.0	10,403
1985	8,156	273.0	7,690.0	1,823.0	24	3,765.0	8,738
1986	7,198	(296.0)	9,027.0	1,606.0	18	5,437.0	8,550
1987	7,594	(123.0)	9,119.0	1,530.0	17	5,577.0	8,516
1988	9,754	908.0	9,177.0	2,266.0	25	4,257.0	7,805

(Continued)

Table 12.A.1 **(Continued)**

Year	Sales	Profits (before tax)	Total assets	Equity nominal	Loans	% (interest)	Number of employees
1989	10,178	1,049.0	9,642.0	2,956.0	31	3,989.0	7,582
1990	8,008	(659.0)	9,284.0	2,188.0	24	4,870	7,454
1991	7,814	(528)	8,818	1,685	19	4,756	6,724
1992	7,300	(673)	8,807	2,233	25	4,919	6,045
1993	7,829	166	8,364	2,592	31	3,695	5,721
1994	8,719	308	8,070	2,771	34	3,150	5,352
1995	9,320	1,079	8,170	3,291	40	2,363	5,301
1996	9,334	945	8,277	3,782	46	1,900	5,048
1997	9,594	983	9,229	4,602	50	1,805	5,203
1998	9,957	764	10,321	4,912	48	2,650	5,254
1999	9,583	1,163	9,671	5,330	55	1,729	4,030
2000	9,703	874	10,342	5,419	52	2,141	4,065
2001	9,259	368	11,632	5,315	46	3,829	3,800
2002	10,872	1,300	17,416	6,911	40	5,954	10,194

Note: n.a. Not available.
Source: Banks' annual reports.

WELFARE CAPITALISM: THE SWEDISH ECONOMY 1850-2005 & ENTREPRENEURSHIP AND OWNERSHIP: THE
FIRM VIABILITY OF THE SWEDISH BONNIER AND WALLENBERG FAMILY BUSINESS GROUPS & FROM
ABS... ...STMENT: FINNISH
CAPITALISM, 1895-2005 & FROM STATE OWNERSHIP TO MULTINATIONAL CORPORATION: THE PATH OF
ENSO-GUTZEIT ... ...HE STRATEGIC
PATHS OF NOR... ...ND ...LLA IN THE ...BERALIZING FINNISH ECONOMY AFTER THE SECOND WORLD
WAR & CO-OPERATIVE LIBERALISM: DENMARK FROM 1857 TO 2007 & ARLA - FROM DECENTRALIZED INDUSTRY
TO MULTINATIONAL ENTERPRISE & CARLSBERG AND THE SELF-REGULATION OF THE DANISH BEER MARKET
& NORWAY: A RESOURCE-BASED AND DEMOCRATIC CAPITALISM & CONSTRUCTIVE POWER: ELKEM 1904-2004
& FINANCE AND THE DEVELOPMENT OF NORWEGIAN CAPITALISM - THE CASE OF CHRISTIANIA BANK

13 Finance and the development of Norwegian capitalism: the case of Christiania Bank

Sverre Knutsen

Introduction

This chapter presents the development of a Norwegian commercial bank, from its start in 1848, through different stages of its expansion, until it was acquired by the mainly Swedish-owned, pan-Nordic Nordea bank in 2000. The Christiania Bank – later called the Christiania Bank & Kreditkasse (CBK) – was named after Norway's capital city Christiania. However, when the city reverted to its old name Oslo in 1923, the bank kept its original name.

The development of Christiania Bank is analysed from the perspective of dynamic financial systems and their role in evolving business systems. Hence, we go beyond a simplistic debt–equity dichotomy, applying a more nuanced and historical approach to the understanding of the configuration of financial systems and their impact on business systems, and their role in the economy.

This chapter focuses the following problems. First, the study addresses the problem of banks and economic performance:

- What was CBK's credit policy, and how was it carried out?
- Who were the bank's customers?
- Did the activities of CBK enhance entrepreneurship and value creating enterprises?

Secondly:

- How was the bank organized and managed?
- How were the relations between management and owners?

Thirdly, how was the banking system, and consequently CBK, regulated and supervised? Fourthly, how did the CBK cope with turmoil and crises in the banking sector?

To deal with those questions we will present a chronological narrative of CBK and its relations to owners, customers, institutional arrangements and changing business cycles.

Business and economic growth, 1850–1920

As already mentioned in Chapter 11, the 1840s marked a watershed in the economic modernization of Norway, as the country took the first steps leading to industrialization, three-quarters of a century after Britain. The traditional businesses in Christiania, comprising mainly import and export of merchandise and staple goods, also expanded after the 1840s. Exports of timber were the major trade of the city. Shipping, connected to the timber trade, and to the imports of grain and different kinds of consumer goods, was also important. When CBK was established in 1848 the majority of the directors were merchants, with F.H. Frølich in the head. Some of the merchants engaged in CBK's board of directors and board of representatives at the outset were also involved as entrepreneurs in Christiania's and the surrounding area's evolving manufacturing industry.

Another important part of Norwegian economic growth was industrialization, of which the first wave took place during the 1840s and 1850s. Then followed a phase (1860–75), characterized by both export-led growth along with the growth of export-substituting industries, especially in cotton spinning and the textile industry, but also in a growing mechanical engineering industry. While the export-led industry was dominated by sawmills along the largest rivers in the eastern parts of Norway, the import-substituting firms were mainly located in and around the capital city of Christiania. Two-thirds of the workers engaged in the Norwegian manufacturing industry in 1900 were occupied in factories in and around the city. From the late 1860s, but particularly after 1870, a relatively large paper and pulp industry evolved in Norway. In connection with this industry, a capital equipment industry that produced machinery for the paper and pulp industry evolved. During the period 1875–1900, which can be termed the years of industrial breakthrough, a growing manufacturing industry, making use of hydroelectric power also expanded rapidly. So did the construction of hydroelectric power plants, and a large-scale electrochemical and electrometallurgical industry emerged in 1900–20. Big business firms like Norsk Hydro and Elkem came forward and expanded substantially during this fourth phase of Norwegian industrial growth.

One decisive prerequisite for economic modernization and industrialization during the nineteenth century was the development of modern infrastructures such as the telegraph and later the telephone, road construction, railway lines and steam ship lines along the long Norwegian coast, to mention just a few of the most important new communication systems. From the 1880s, even networks for distribution of electricity were built.

Financing of modernization and economic growth, 1850–1920

How was industrialization financed? How did the Norwegian financial system contribute to economic growth? Industrial ventures were very risky, and particularly during the first two-mentioned phases of industrialization long-term investments in business firms were typically financed by the founders' own savings or by partnership networks. Banks played a minor role in providing long-term capital. Savings banks first of all provided farmers with credit, while the few commercial banks chiefly financed commerce by advancing short-term credits to trading firms. Throughout the 1880s, the commercial banks were to an increasing extent providing credit to industrial firms, essentially to meet their need for working capital. From this time on, commercial banks like the CBK and savings banks provided more long-term loans for industry. In a study of the regional development in the south-western county of Rogaland, the economic historian Helge Nordvik found that savings banks played a crucial role in financing economic modernization at a county level during the phase of industrial breakthrough:

 A well-functioning local and regional credit market based largely on savings banks provided vital assistance not only to agricultural growth, but also to investment in local industry, the development of a modern fishing industry, important infrastructure investment such as electricity supply, as well as to investment in modern steam shipping in the period after 1880 to the first world war.[1]

The business cycle and the development of bank assets

From a macroeconomic perspective, the period 1850–75 was characterized by almost steady long-term economic growth, interrupted by only minor recessions. After 1875, however, growth stagnated. It is important, though, to stress that Norway experienced modern economic growth when we judge the whole period 1850–1920. But the relative growth rates between 1875 and 1905 were weak compared to those of neighbouring countries. There were two main factors causing this development. First, traditional Norwegian export

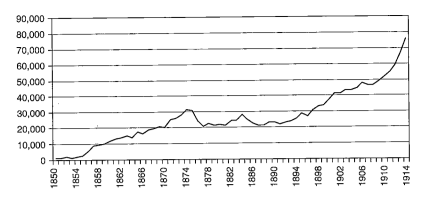

Figure 13.1   CBK: growth in assets, 1850–1914 (nominal values, NOK 1000 by end of year)
Source: Engebretsen (1948).

trades of fish, timber and minerals and the shipping industry failed, because of the collapse of the herring fisheries and declining export markets caused by the 'Great Depression'. Secondly, poorly developed securities markets slowed down investments in new industrial ventures to a certain extent. The worst period was the 1880s, characterized by reduced growth. This development was reflected in an increased emigration to the US, peaking in the early 1880s. The development is also reflected in stagnating activities in the banking sector, as demonstrated in Figure 13.1, showing the long-term development of CBK's total assets.

Figure 13.1 reveals that the turning point in growth of assets was reached in 1874, followed by a long stagnation period until 1894, when a new growth period started, with the brief intermission of the 1899–1905 recession.

Growth and banking, 1905–20

During the period 1905–20, Norway experienced its hitherto largest economic growth, particularly up until 1916. The contribution of the large energy-intensive enterprises based on the utilization of hydroelectric power was vital for this growth, but even sectors like paper and pulp, canned food and textile production proliferated. Norway was a part of international capital markets, since it was on the Gold Standard. Most of the large-scale industries like Hydro were financed by inward direct investments and foreign loan capital. However, Norwegian banks like DnC, Christiania Bank and The Central Bank of Norway (established in 1900 as a commercial bank, not to be confused with the National bank, (the Bank of Norway) contributed, and syndicated the current account credit financing of Norsk Hydro's working capital. Norwegian banks, both commercial and savings banks, provided credit to finance expansion in the other growing industries. The expansion of the Akers shipyard in Christiania was, for example, financed by Christiania Savings Bank, which was Norway's largest savings bank.

In co-operation with the state, foreign as well as Norwegian capitalists invested in modern infrastructure, with the participation of the banks. The first railway trunk line from Christiania to Eidsvold, which opened in 1854, was financed in this way. The railway line was built to increase the efficiency of timber transport to Christiania's port; later, most of railway construction in Norway was financed by the state, by floating bonds on foreign bond markets. CBK participated in the financing of several railway projects, by both buying stocks and providing loans. The bank participated in the construction of the railway connection to Sweden, via Kongsvinger, for example. Another project in which the bank participated was the construction of the railway line between Christiania and Drammen, an important commercial city southwest of Christiania. The bank invested in railway shares and also provided a NOK 1.2 million loan (NOK 60 million in 2005 currency). In 1873, CBK participated in the financing of the Swedish line from Gothenburg to Falun – the so-called 'Bergslagernas Järnväger.'

Two 'formative phases' of banking

By 1850 there were ninety savings banks with total assets of 4,625,000 speciedaler equivalent to NOK 18.5 million. The Norwegian currency, the speciedaler, was fixed to silver in 1842 after a long period of deflation. The silver standard was replaced by the Gold Standard in 1873 and effective from 1874. From 1875, Norway joined the Scandinavian Currency Union. Total advances by the organized banking system at this juncture were NOK 51.4 million. In addition, the largest merchants also acted as private bankers, engaging in discount business, trading of foreign currency, etc. The period between the end of the 1840s and 1860 can be termed the first 'formative phase' of the Norwegian banking system. The savings banks, numbering 181 independent units in 1860, were complemented with commercial banking during this period. Simultaneously, an increasing number of the savings banks developed into ordinary credit institutions providing credit to various types of business enterprises and agriculture. In 1870, the commercial banks' assets were equal to the total assets of both CBK and all the savings banks in 1850, while total assets in the whole private banking system had almost tripled. This growth was the result of a gradual expansion during the 1850s and 1860s.

Christiania Bank in the first 'formative phase' of Norwegian commercial banking

A few years after CBK was set up, two other commercial banks were established – the Bergen Privat Bank in 1855 and the Norwegian Credit Bank (DnC) in 1857. The latter developed into the largest Norwegian bank during the second part of the nineteenth century. The CBK was already from the outset organized as a joint stock bank with limited liability. It started with an equity capital of NOK 160,000, which was raised to NOK 320,000 in 1855, NOK 640,000 in 1856 and NOK 3.2 million in 1857, each time by issuing new shares. This was the bank's equity capital until 1911, when it was expanded to NOK 4 million.

CBK took up deposit banking from the start in 1848. Funding by deposits was an innovation that allowed the bank increased room for expansion, and deposit funding gradually increased.[2] From July 1848 to March 1849, CBK reached a deposit surplus (deposits–withdrawals) of NOK 104,168 NOK 6,162,158 in 2005 value. Even though CBK took up deposit banking, the bank acted primarily as a discount house during the first years of its operation, although it early on developed a range of commercial banking activities. According to an advertisement in the daily paper *Morgenbladet* in January 1862, the bank offered the following services: acceptance of deposits; provision of advances against securities or merchandise as collateral; discounting of bills of commerce, transfer of payments, trading of stocks and bonds; and trading of foreign currency. Thus, although CBK was primarily engaged in commercial banking, the bank also showed some traits of universal banking.

The second 'formative phase' of banking

A second 'formative phase' of the banking system occurred between 1895 and 1900. Table 13.1 demonstrates that commercial banking expanded substantially in these years, doubling in both numbers of banks as well as assets. During this period the commercial banks' deposits for the first time exceeded those of the savings banks (Figure 13.1). All the banks depicted in Table 13.1 were independent units, with no branches outside their local areas. During this 'formative phase', the structure of the Norwegian banking system was consolidated and continued almost unchanged for fifty–sixty years. Thus, Norway developed a de-centralized and locally-based unit bank system, with almost no branch banking. As late as 1950, Norwegian banks had fewer than forty branches outside their head office

Table 13.1 **Norwegian banks: total assets and number of banks, 1870–1920 (assets in million NOK)**

	Commercial banks		Savings banks		Total, all banks	
	Total assets	No. banks	Total assets	No. banks	Total assets	No. banks
1870	51	8	91	252	142	260
1880	110	15	157	311	267	326
1890	170	33	221	350	391	383
1895	213	36	257	373	470	409
1900	427	76	344	413	771	489
1905	477	85	422	446	899	531
1910	669	102	570	487	1,239	589
1913	910	116	684	519	1,594	635
1914	979	119	724	525	1,703	644
1918	4,721	193	1,711	549	6,432	742
1920	5,461	192	1,697	562	7,158	754

Source: Imset Matre (1992); Statistiske oversikter 1948, Statistisk sentralbyrå, Oslo 1949.

municipality. Until 1957, it was the strategy of CBK to confine its organ-ization to the capital city of Oslo. During the 1870s, CBK had built up branches in the cities of Bergen and Hamar, but this endeavour met with fierce local resistance, so the bank decided to sell these branches to local interests.

Modern political parties were established during the second half of the nineteenth century. The Liberal Party (Venstre) developed from the 1860s, well before parliamentary rule was adopted in 1884. Venstre, which was a broad coalition of farmers, the petty bourgeoisie of small towns and the social liberals of the cities, became the dominant party in Norway, and maintained this position until the inter-war years after 1918. The 1814 Constitution gave the cities one-third and the peripheral and rural areas two-thirds of the seats in the parliament – the Storting. This distribution of power was fixed by an amendment to the Constitution in 1859, the so-called 'Farmers' Paragraph'. This legislation endorsed the strong political representation of the rural and peripheral areas, and safeguarded them against the consequences of diminishing political representation; hence the strong Norwegian periphery built an institutional bulwark against deteriorating political power caused by industrialization and urbanization.

The majority of MPs were strongly in favour of local savings banks, in which they were in command. The parliamentary representatives of the evolving Venstre were thus to a large extent also local savings banks administrators (Sparebank Venstre). The savings banks became tools in the hands of local

Table 13.2 Norway: Largest banks, by assets 1870–1910 (million NOK)

Bank	1870	1880	1890	1900	1910
CBK	19.9	22.0	23.1	38.1	51.3
DnC	10.3	24.6	30.5	46.8	82.2
BP	10,8	17.5	25.1	38.5	54.2
CBfN	–	–	–	23.8	95.8

Note: CBK: Christiana Bank og a Kreditkasse; BP: Bergens Privatbank.
Source: Banks' Annual Reports.

farmers as well as of local commerce and industry, and developed very much as substitutes for commercial banking. The savings banks had a solid and large lobby on the Storting, used to defend their own interests and position. For instance, when a proposal to create a centralized state-owned postal bank was put forward in the early 1880s, a majority defending the interests of local savings banks turned down the scheme. Their main argument was that a postal bank would drain capital from the local capital markets, into the country's capital city.[3] This was the salient political and institutional foundation for the configuration of the Norwegian banking system, and the major source of the system's decentralized make-up.

A very important feature of the Norwegian banking system was not only the strong positions of the savings banks, but also the way they operated. From the 1840s and 1850s, the savings banks increasingly worked as ordinary credit institutions. This distinguishes Norwegian savings banks from savings banks operating in, for example, Denmark. According to the Danish savings bank legislation passed in 1919 (Sparkasseloven av 4. October 1919), section 1 stated, 'savings banks are prohibited to engage in banking business'. This meant that Danish savings bank had to steer clear of advances to commercial businesses, and to confine their activities to more safe investments in government bonds, lending against mortgages, etc. Even today, savings banks take a strong position in Norwegian banking, in both the market for business credit as well as in retail banking (Table 13.2).

In all the Nordic countries commercial banking featured some sort of universal banking (Figure 13.2). We have seen that this involved CBK during its early years. Moreover, the Norwegian banking system at the turn of the nineteenth century was a locally-based and decentralized unit bank system, and branches hardly existed, a situation until well after 1945. The banking systems in the neighbouring Scandinavian countries were also originally unit bank systems. Unlike Norway, however, an increasing degree of consolidation

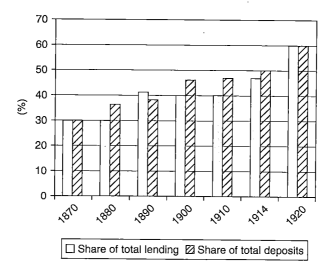

Figure 13.2 **Commercial banks' share of total deposits and lending, 1870–1920**
Source: Imset Matre (1992).

leading to more branch banking ensued in both Sweden and Denmark shortly after the turn of the nineteenth century. In Sweden, for example, an important structural change took place in commercial banking after approximately 1910, and a system of branch banking developed. Until 1920, the number of Swedish commercial banks halved, while the number of bank offices more than doubled. Even in Denmark, commercial banks experienced a similar consolidation movement and growth in branch banking.

Another difference is reflected in the fact that bank groups evolved both in Denmark and Sweden. Such 'banking spheres' with a dominant bank controlling industrial firms, investment companies, etc., such as the Wallenberg group, did not develop in Norway.

Institutional framework

Two important institutional features regarding the regulation of banking should be emphasized here. Firstly, commercial banks as such were not regulated until a preliminary law in 1919 and a permanent law on commercial banking was enacted by the Parliament only in 1924. Furthermore, all commercial banks were organized as joint stock banks with limited liability, except private bankers, who also engaged in some aspects of commercial banking during the nineteenth century. Secondly, the National Bank (the Bank of Norway) had a currency monopoly, just like Denmark but unlike Sweden.

The first Norwegian Savings Banks Law was passed in 1824, but had a very limited aim. Its main objective was to secure a sound basis for the management of a savings bank. When a bank registered with the Ministry of Finance, it were obliged to follow a management plan written by the Ministry. In return, the bank had some privileges, among them permission to take a 1 percentage point higher interest rate on loans against collateral in real estate than allowed by the Usury Laws. The banks were, however, free to register or not. Until 1888, a 4 per cent interest rate ceiling, due to the regulations against usury, regulated interest rates on mortgage loans. To gain these privileges, the bank had to adopt a set of minimum rules for its investments and send its financial statements to the Ministry of Finance once a year.

The government started the preparations for modern savings banks legislation. In 1887 new legislation on savings banks was enacted by Parliament. This regulatory change was mainly caused by the failure of several savings banks during the spring of that year. The new Savings Banks Law confirmed the way the savings banks were managed, but introduced procedures for a system of strengthened internal control. However, the proposal of a centralized regulatory authority was rejected, and not established until 1900. Commercial banks like CBK were not regulated by separate banking laws until 1924, nor were they supervised by a public agency until 1925.

CBK's position in the banking system, 1870–1920

As demonstrated in Table 13.2, CBK had become the largest Norwegian bank in terms of assets by 1870. By 1880, however, DnC had grown slightly larger. By 1910, The Central Bank of Norway (Centralbanken for Norge) had become the largest, while CBK now was the fourth-largest commercial bank in Norway Bank in terms of total assets.

Table 13.3 also reveals that CBK at the turn of the century was rather a small bank with sixty-four employees in 1900, while DnC had forty-seven employees. These figures imply that Norwegian banks in general at the turn of the century were rather small organizations.

Table 13.3   CBK: Number of staff, 1848–1939

	1848	1872	1875	1900	1913	1918	1923	1939
Number of employees	5	35	52	64	86	116	308	517

Source: CBK's Annual Reports.

Financial distress from the 1880s to the early 20th century

In 1887, no dividends on shares were paid out to CBK's stockholders. This was the first time since the establishment of the bank that this had happened, reflecting the sharp economic downswing of the business cycle during the mid-1880s; 1886 had been a bad year, and numerous bankruptcies in the non-financial sector had led to substantial loan losses for the banks. Not only CBK, but also several banks and numerous private bankers, had to write off considerable credit losses. The overall banking system experienced a deficit, and several banks, both commercial and savings banks, had to close their doors. It is thus reasonable to see this as the first systemic banking crisis in the Norwegian banking system. This was caused by a combination of a preceding boom and increased risk taking rooted in the growing transition from private to joint stock banking. Another institutional feature contributing to the financial distress was the lack of regulation and absence of any supervision.

For CBK, the losses were a signal to start a consolidation process. The starting point for this was the appointment of P.H. Castberg as the bank's new CEO in September 1886. Castberg developed a new, more cautious strategy, particularly concerning the bank's credit policy.

The Kristiania crash

The upswing during the 1890s developed into a boom after 1895. A striking aspect of the boom was a steep price increase in asset markets, which after a while developed into an asset price inflation. The speculation was driven by the increased supply of credit provided by the banking system. In the real estate market, the development was stimulated by a substantial increase in Kristiania's population (the city's name was increasingly written with a 'K' from the late 1870s). From 1889 to 1898, the population grew by 63,000 inhabitants. But this development was transformed into speculation in the market for dwellings as well as commercial buildings in Kristiania, causing steep rising prices in these segments.

In 1897, after a decision in 1895, the Swedish government abandoned the legislation that had created a common Swedish–Norwegian market for industrial goods. This was an institutional impetus to the start of a great many new industrial ventures in Norway, several of them import-substituting enterprises. A lot of these new enterprises were financed by a combination of easy credit provided by newly established banks as well as equities from a booming stock market. The shares of these companies soon became speculation objects, resulting in a stock market financial bubble. Six new commercial banks were established in Kristiania during 1897, and these were the main source for financing speculations in the asset markets. These new banks all held a high-risk profile and poor decision-making meant that they acquired a relatively large share of bad credit risks. The existing commercial banks' in particular CBK, carried out a more conscious and conservative strategy during the boom.

The bubble burst in 1899, starting with the sudden bankruptcy in a large holding company, owning companies within the production and export of pulp and paper. The holding company was controlled by the well-known Norwegian businessman, Chr. Christophersen, and had a very high gearing. From the spring of 1898 the Bank of Norway started to raise the discount rate (the central bank rate) several times. This contraction policy dried up the credit market, making it increasingly difficult to re-finance mature loans. The bank with the largest engagements with Chr. Christophersen's firm (Den norske Discontobank) did not have the strength to carry the burden of losses inflicted on it by Christophersen's bankruptcy. Because of the commitments made in the interbank market, the problems reverberated through the banking system. The Bank of Norway decided to act as a lender of last resort, but requested at the same time that private banks should put up a guarantee to underpin the central bank's commitments. Several private bankers and commercial banks, including DnC, joined the guarantee. However, CBK and the largest Norwegian private banker and discount house, Tho. Joh. Heftye & Søn, refused to back the guarantee. Primarily, the ground for this was discontent with the central bank's plan to liquidate the failed Den norske Discontobank over a long period of time. CBK wanted to apply 'surgery' – a quick and comprehensive liquidation.

The real estate market also crashed in 1899, and the prices of housing dropped 50 per cent during five subsequent years. Rents decreased between 20 and 33 per cent, and by around 1905 10 per cent of housing was empty. Even the number of inhabitants dropped substantially between 1900 and 1905, falling by 2 per cent of the total population, largely because of emigration to the US.

Several factors caused the boom–bust sequence ending in the asset markets' crash and the subsequent banking crisis. An international boom stimulated the Norwegian upswing of the mid-1890s. But fundamentally, institutional changes altered the rules of the game and reinforced the boom in such a way that credit-driven financial bubbles evolved in asset markets and the financial system was filled with systemic risk. The number of firms with limited liability grew substantially from the early 1890s. From 1891 to 1900, the number of companies with limited liability grew by more than 130 per cent, from 1497 to 3460.[4] Secondly, the dismantling of the legislation of the Swedish–Norwegian free trade zone stimulated expansion in the industrial sector, even more than can be explained by the upswing. Easy capital markets stimulated by the Bank of Norway's expansive monetary policy also contributed to increased credit risk in the banking system and rising financial fragility in the non-financial sector of the economy.

CBK and its customers, 1890–1914

Despite of the boom and the subsequent Kristiania crash, CBK grew steadily in assets, as demonstrated in Figure 13.1 (p. 536). This expansion continued even after the banking crisis and the following recession (1899–1905). From 1910–14 CBK increased deposits by 58 per cent compared with 30 per cent for DnC and 34 per cent for Centralbanken for Norge, founded in 1900. During the same period, the three banks' lending increased 78, 54 and 56 per cent, respectively. The remarkable fact is that this expansion in credit volume occurred in parallel with a cautious lending policy.

CBK provided loans to a wide spectrum of businesses, in both trade and manufacturing industry, during this period. Loans to businesses in the paper and pulp industry took a large share of total advances. The bank also made sizeable advances to the textile, printing, chemical, engineering and electrochemical industries. Loans in the latter sector comprised companies like Hafslund, Tyssefaldene and Norsk Hydro. Norsk Hydro, established in December 1905, required a huge amount of capital. At the outset, the enterprise needed a NOK 12 million current account credit. French banks committed themselves for half of the loan, and the rest was provided by a banking syndicate consisting of CBK and Centralbanken for Norge from Norway, SEB from Sweden and Den Danske Landmandsbank and Privatbanken i København from Denmark.

In Norway, the Kristiania Stock Exchange was not established until 1881 at the Kristiania Bourse, which had operated as an organized market for trade of staple goods and the trading in bills of commerce. Outside the organized securities market, a brokers' list was published from 1889 by a stockbrokers' firm in Kristiania. From 1897 this list was published by all brokers in common, and included 162 quoted papers, increasing to 202 at the start of 1905. The stock market thus developed substantially during the period 1890–1914. CBK took advantage of this development and expanded its securities business. To handle the growing volume in the securities trade, CBK in 1910 organized this business in a new securities department. The stock market crash of 1899, however, reduced the trade substantially, until a new surge upwards in stock prices started during the First World War.

The First World War and the banking crisis of the 1920s

The outbreak the First World War suddenly changed the economy's rules of the game, with the abrupt ending of the Gold Standard. This removed most constraints on credit expansion, gave a strong impetus to increasingly reckless lending, and boosted the banks' credit risk. At the same time the wartime economy was characterized by blockades and submarine warfare, limited supply of goods, increased import-substituting and surrogate production, which reinforced the credit risk. Rapidly increased debt dramatically enhanced financial fragility in the non-financial sector. A restricted supply of goods contributed to inflation, as did large political loans to the belligerent parties provided under pressure in order to retain neutrality. The large Norwegian merchant fleet experienced a steep rise in income, and hence increased inflow of gold, which facilitated an increase in the circulating money stock, further reinforcing inflation. The banks' uncontrolled credit expansion financed unsound speculation in asset markets, particularly in the stock market. Shares in shipping companies became the preferred object of speculation. Freight income increased substantially, but share prices rose even more, resulting in asset price inflation. The stock market mania was fuelled by easy bank credit, and the shares were used as collateral.

The total assets of the commercial banks rose six-fold to NOK 5461 million during the period 1914–20, and their total loans to the public soared correspondingly. Even when we take inflation into consideration, the real growth in lending was tremendous, and total assets doubled in real value. In comparison, the savings banks' total assets and loans grew more modestly. But behind these average growth figures we find a substantial variation. Some banks expanded almost uncontrollably, while others revealed a more balanced and controlled growth. CBK was among the latter, and reduced its share of the commercial banks' total assets from 7.4 per cent in 1913 to 5 per cent in 1920.

The government attempted to re-establish the Gold Standard shortly after the armistice of November 1918. During the aftermath of the war, a new post-war boom surged in Norway, fuelling inflation further, so in the spring the Gold Standard was once more suspended to prevent the outflow of gold.

At the same time, however, the international post-war recession, which started in the US in early 1920, spread to Europe and to Norway. From the early autumn of 1920, prices fell dramatically and a serious deflation emerged. The deflation was not a result of an active Norwegian monetary policy; actually, the Bank of Norway's actions were characterized by *ex post* adjustment to international developments. The central bank raised the discount rate very late in 1920 to curb an inflation that had been in place for more than a year. Thus, the deflation was imported from the international economy. At the same time Norwegian export was hit very hard by the post-war crisis, and fell almost 50 per cent in one year, and did not start to recover until late 1922. Investments also fell dramatically and were almost halved from 1920 to 1925, even in real value. Unemployment among organized workers increased from 2 per cent in 1920 to 18 per cent in 1921.

With deflation, the real interest rates rose substantially, contributing to falling investments and financial distress in the business sector. A large number of Norwegian firms were not able to handle the huge debt burden acquired during the wartime boom. The number of bankruptcies increased and an increasing number of firms defaulted on their loans and left the banks with a large stock of non-performing loans as well as a swelling amount of loan losses.

The result was a shocking banking crisis between the autumn of 1920 and 1924. The goal to restore the Norwegian currency to its pre-war parity and hence again fixed to gold was postponed by the Bank of Norway. Instead the central bank started to carry out a policy of supplying liquidity to distressed commercial banks, while attempting simultaneously to reconstruct failed banks with the assistance of better-performing private banks. The large loan losses also instigated depositor runs on several banks: three out of the five largest commercial banks failed. (Norway's largest commercial bank Centralbanken for Norge), the Norwegian trade bank (Den norske Handelsbank) and the Union Bank (Foreningsbanken) were all forced to close, only to be liquidated later on.

The result of the banking crisis was disastrous; the commercial banks' assets were halved. Altogether 127 banks failed and disappeared as a consequence of bankruptcy, acquisition by a more solid bank, or by the way of managed liquidation by the authorities. While the banking sector provided 86 per cent of total credits in 1920, this share had shrunk to 56 per cent in 1935. The commercial banks' share of the total organized credit market was reduced from 60 to 25 per cent during these years, whereas their advances to the industrial sector decreased substantially.

CBK's development during the banking crisis diverged from the path followed by most of the banks. As already mentioned, CBK chose a more balanced and cautious strategy during the post-war boom and was hence less exposed to risky engagements than the rest of the banks. This strategy led to fewer loan losses for CBK, which strengthened its position during the inter-war years.[5]

In spite of CBK's cautious lending policy during the war and the post-war boom, it was of course impossible for it to totally avoid harmful effects from the crisis. During the period 1919–32, CBK wrote off loan losses amounting to NOK 50.5 million. Failing bank debtors inflicted almost 20 per cent of the losses suffered by the banks. Losses on ordinary credits provided to business clients within industry, trade and shipping represented roughly 50 per cent. The rest related to debtors in the primary sector as well as a substantial number of private borrowers, most likely speculative investors who had bought shares during the stock exchange boom financed by borrowing against the shares as collateral.

During the crisis, CBK increased its assets as well as its lending considerably, when we adjust for the strong increase in value of the currency in 1925–7, when the Norwegian krone reached its pre-war parity and the country experienced 'the gold-parity depression'. From 1920 to 1932 the real value of lending actually tripled. Simultaneously, CBK reinforced its cautious credit policy and placed a larger share of the bank's assets in low risk and liquid bearer bonds instead of direct loans to business clients. This was a safeguard against a potential depositor-run in an era where no deposit insurance schemes existed in Norway.

Normally, such a change in the composition of assets entails a reduced return on assets. But the circumstances were not normal during the 1920s, characterized by decreasing nominal interest rates and declining prices. As a result, CBK earned an outstanding profit on the bank's large bearer bonds portfolio during the second part of the 1920s.[6] From 1920 to 1932 CBK increased its securities portfolio from 6 to 20 per cent of total assets. In 1920, CBK's portfolio of bonds and stocks constituted 5 per cent of all securities held by commercial banks. In 1932, however, the bank's share of such assets comprised 26 per cent of the total, while CBK's share of total assets held by commercial banks at the same time amounted to 20 per cent.

Another feature of CBK's strategy during the 1920s was an extensive diversification of its lending practices. While CBK's main competitors Bergens Privatbank (BP) and DnC had a large share of their lending concentrated on a few sectors, CBK's loans were spread over a much wider spectrum of sectors. Moreover, the bank had avoided engaging strongly in paper and pulp, and shipping, both troubled sectors during the 1920s. By 1932, CBK had become the largest commercial bank in terms of assets, followed by BP and DnC.

The crisis had obvious institutional and macroeconomic causes, but CBK's performance during the war and the post-war boom and the subsequent banking crisis demonstrate that strategy matters. CBK's strengthened position was even reflected in a substantial growth in the number of employees, from 116 in 1918 to 308 in 1923 and 517 in 1939. But still, CBK limited its organization to Oslo.

The bank and customers during the era of strategic capitalism, 1945–80

The period 1945–80 featured a profound change in the financial sector's regulatory environment. During the late 1940s a new regulatory regime emerged under the social democratic order. The Social Democrats won the elections in the early autumn of 1945 and remained in power for twenty years, and then for most of the 1970s. This led to increased state intervention in the financial system and to enlarged government control of financial institutions and the flows of capital and credit. Paradoxically, the liberal-conservative government 1965 to 1971 didn't change this principal line.

Credit policy and credit budgeting

First, a corporative system for managing and monitoring financial institutions and monetary policies, under the operative control of Norges Bank (the Bank of Norway) was set up. Representatives from commercial banks, savings banks and insurance companies participated in a so-called 'Co-operation Council' under the patronage of the Bank of Norway and its governor. Here the institutions had to accept binding agreements on interest rates, investments in government bonds and lending quotas. The government forced the participants to accept the guidelines on credit policy with a barely hidden threat to introduce extensive legislation regulating all the activities of financial institutions and markets by law.

This corporative system was supplemented by some temporary laws (which were renewed several times) giving the government the right to administer interest rates and to impose strict capital market controls. Furthermore, state banks and state funds with a special purpose, like financing regional policy

Photograph 13.1 **Manager of the Norwegian central bank, The Bank of Norway, Erik Brofoss,** **visiting the Mosjøen. Brofoss was one of the main driving forces behind the important role of the** **state in the development of Norwegian industry after 1945.**
Source: Erik Brofoss.

or selected industrial enterprises, became an important tool in carrying out credit policy. National capital markets were also heavily regulated and protected against foreign influence. The purpose of this regulatory regime was to utilize the financial system as a tool for credit targeting in order to funnel funds to politically prioritized enterprises and sectors. In the mid-1960s, the regulatory regime was based on a new, radical and comprehensive law on money, which was passed in 1965. This regulatory regime based on public credit rationing and administered interest rates has been termed 'strategic capitalism'.[7]

CBK during the era of managed credit
The banks, including CBK, had to adjust to the system of capital controls, administered interest rates and lending quotas. On the other hand, the banks

were allowed to form a price cartel on all kind of fees, interest rates on deposits, etc. Banking strategy was in reality lifted out of the banking sector up to the government level, and banks were turned into rationing offices. The post-war regulatory regime did not give room for competition on price in financial markets. However, there was room for manoeuvring, particularly in two fields. One was customer services; the other was to grow by M&As.

Structural development

But growth by M&As was relatively costly because of the government's structural policy. The doctrines of this policy were that that the three largest commercial banks should not be given a concession to acquire local banks outside Oslo and Bergen, the two largest Norwegian cities. These banks were DnC, CBK and BP, all established between 1848 and 1857. Furthermore, the regulatory authorities should restrict the same three largest banks when setting up branches outside Oslo and Bergen. The argument for these regulatory measures was regional politics and to secure a local supply of credit to local businesses 'in all districts'. During the 1960s, this policy was also linked to the goal to uphold the geographic spread of population 'as it is', regardless of costs.

In 1957, the CBK board of directors decided to expand organization outside Oslo. Between 1960 and 1980, CBK acquired eighteen banks, including Andresens Bank in 1980. At that time this was Norway's fifth-largest commercial bank, and the merger deal was the largest acquisition in Norwegian banking until then. Notwithstanding 'structural policy', a movement of bank consolidation did thus evolve in Norway from 1960 to 1980. During this period forty-four local unit banks disappeared, while the number of branches grew from 161 to almost 600. Thus commercial banks experienced substantial concentration during this period. In the savings banks sector, however, the situation was different. It was not until the late 1970s and early 1980s that the savings banks system saw centralization and consolidation to a certain extent. The number of savings banks was reduced from 509 in 1969 to 322 in 1980, and a further reduction continued to 142 in 1990. This development gave birth to the development of regional savings bank groups, as well as a large savings bank group at national level.

The reason why structural policy inflicted additional costs on the banks' acquisition activities is primarily the fact that it entailed a great deal of lobbying and an extra price on shares in banks that other banks wanted to acquire. Moreover, the policy entailed a long, drawn-out process in order to acquire another bank.

Lending policy

In 1965 the CBK leadership developed a document containing major goals for the bank's activities. Because of substantial increase in income among wage-earners during the late 1950s and early 1960s, the bank wanted to expand in the growing retail market, by boosting its share of the deposit market and increasing lending to households. To achieve these goals, CBK planned to build an extensive network of branches. The large number of acquisitions carried out by CBK between 1960 and 1980 has to be seen in this context. Loans to households increased considerably as part of the commercial banks' lending during the period 1960–80. In 1960, 3 per cent of CBK's total lending were such loans; this share had grown to 33 per cent in 1975. Deposits from households grew at the same rate.

But business firms in manufacturing industries were still an important group among the borrowers until the middle of the 1970s. In 1965 industrial firms held nearly one-third of CBK's outstanding loans, while trading companies held 28 per cent. The latter group of enterprises kept the same share of CBK's loans during the 1970s. Contrary to this, the bank reduced its share of lending to shipping from 7 per cent of total lending in 1964 to around 2 per cent during the 1970s. This was a consequence of a strategic choice because of the turbulent situation in the shipping industry caused by the Opec I crisis in October 1973. On the other hand, CBK's major competitor, DnC, continued its heavy engagement in shipping. Among the manufacturing industries, CBK was especially engaged in paper and pulp enterprises, textile industry firms and companies within the sectors of electro-mechanical and electronic equipment. CBK was also the leading bank for the largest enterprises of the building and construction industry.

Internationalization

A bank's international operations can assume several organizational forms: correspondence networks, representation offices, consortium banks, independent subsidiaries and branches. The internationalization of CBK can be divided into five distinct phases. Until the middle of the 1960s, the banks international activities were organized through correspondence relations.

During the first phase, from the middle of the 1960s until 1973, CBK took the first careful steps towards multinational operations. First, the bank participated in consortium banks with shares from 5 to 10–12 per cent, particularly in banks set up to finance shipping. Consortium banks were creatures of the evolving Euromarkets during the early 1960s and expanded during the 1970s. They were engaged in Eurocurrency syndicated lending, and some were also Eurobond lead managers.

As a consortium bank partner, CBK could, for example, provide their shipping customers with finance for international shipping business. However, this type of co-operation had several limitations and there were considerable tensions inherent in the joint venture approach to business development. Consequently, consortium bank managements and shareholders faced a number of strategic dilemmas. The consortium bank had to balance interests between all the participants; as a result it was difficult for a single partner bank of the consortium to gain priority for its own customers. The dominant partner banks were, on the other hand, inclined to maximize their own interests, so consortium banks were highly exposed to opportunism. Finally, consortium banks were reliant upon the heavy national credit policy regulations existing in most industrialized countries during the post-war era. Partner banks did not represent a competitive threat to each other in their domestic markets provided that the national regulations creating huge barriers to entry for foreign banks were in existence. Once these barriers to entry were removed, however, the heyday of consortium banks was over.

CBK therefore set up a subsidiary in Luxembourg in 1973. Luxembourg was an emerging financial centre in Europe, and the costs for setting up a subsidiary here was far less than in London. The reason why CBK chose to establish a subsidiary and not a branch was primarily a consequence of Norwegian credit policy regulations. The Norwegian authorities only accepted subsidiaries, because this organizational form did not have any impact on the Norwegian credit market. A branch could use Norwegian funds for advances outside Norway. The major task of CBK Luxembourg was to provide loans in foreign currency to Norwegian companies to finance their international operations.

The second phase, from 1973 to 1981, was characterized by efforts to start building a network outside Europe with representative offices in New York and Singapore. CBK focused particularly on expansion in new markets during the third phase of internationalization, which roughly took place between 1981 and 1986. To carry out this strategy, CBK formed a strategic alliance with the Swedish state-owned PK-banken to establish 50–50-owned subsidiaries in Hong Kong, Singapore and London. In 1985 CBK and PK-banken established the fourth joint venture bank in New York, named PK Christiania [US] Banking Corporation.

The results did not match the expectations, and the strategic alliance was dissolved in the spring of 1986. From this point, the Norwegian authorities no longer required that Norwegian banks' international business outside Norway be subjugated to local equity requirements and local supervision. From now on, CBK could carry out such business by setting up branches. However, Christiania Bank s.a., Luxembourg continued as a wholly-owned subsidiary. At the same time CBK bought out PK-banken and took over the operation in London and turned it into a branch from 1 January 1987. The same deal was done in New York, and the joint venture there continued as a wholly-owned subsidiary under the name Christiania Banking [US] Corporation, New York. In Singapore, CBK established Christiania Bank, Singapore Branch. In addition, CBK set up representative offices in Houston, San Francisco, Copenhagen, Rio de Janeiro, Sydney, Tokyo and Beijing.

A fourth phase of internationalization can be identified in 1986–91. In this period, CBK adopted a global niche strategy. Instead of taking up local business in the different markets where CBK was located, the bank concentrated on energy, shipping/transport and fish in global markets. All these were strong Norwegian industries in which the bank possessed considerable competence. From 1984, CBK even re-engaged in shipping finance, and recruited very competent people to handle this business area. The strategy worked, and in 1991 these three global business areas made up almost 50 per cent of the income earned by CBK's international network of branches and subsidiaries. From 1986 to 1990, international lending increased from NOK 13 to NOK 20 billion, and loan losses were small. This strategy distinguished CBK from the other major Norwegian banks, who put their faith in conducting local business in local markets in several countries. DnC and BP, who merged to form Norway's largest commercial bank (Den norske Bank) in 1989, followed that strategy and suffered considerable losses.

CBK and the IT revolution

During the early 1960s, the CBK top management started to realise that the bank ought to move into electronic data processing. Computers were purchased to handle accounting work. At the same time, CBK went into co-operation with its two major competitors to form a joint venture company to handle large data processing jobs, and the company IDA (Integrated Data Processing) was established in 1963. This company was operative from January 1967 with the three major banks as the main owners, but open to all Norwegian commercial banks. IDA handled several large routine tasks like cheque clearing, bank account transactions, etc. In 1972, another co-operative enterprise (BBS) was established to operate the payment network. Investments in electronic data processing were expensive and demanding, and these investments were undertaken by co-operative solutions among the Norwegian banks.

However, productivity did not improve in CBK between 1960 and 1980. Total assets relative to staff fell from NOK 1.8 million in 1960 to NOK 1.4 million in 1980. During the 1980s, however, this ratio doubled to NOK 3.2 million (in 1960 krone) in 1988.[8] This was due to the advent and spread of PCs in the bank. Moreover, during the 1980s ATMs had been installed in every CBK branch.

Financing innovations

CBK was not only financing mature, ongoing business, but also innovation and growth in new ventures. Examples are financing of the development and subsequent large-scale production of plasterboard for the construction industry (NORGIPS); new methods in house building (Selvaag); development and production of electronic equipment (EB, Standard/ITT-Norway, G.A. Ring Systems); and pioneering in Norwegian fish farming, to mention only a few. The bank was also among the first to establish venture capital firms and funds in Norway, like K-Venture.

CBK and the Norwegian banking crisis, 1987–92

During the years 1987–93 Norwegian banks had to write off NOK 73 billion because of loan losses. This extensive banking crisis reached its height in the autumn of 1991. The losses suffered by the three largest Norwegian commercial banks on non-performing loans were so vast that they lost all their equity and had to be bailed out by the government. CBK wrote off an unbelievable NOK 17 billion on loan losses during this period; it lost its equity and was rescued and taken over by the state during the autumn of 1991. A banking crisis of similar character and magnitude occurred in Sweden and Finland, while Danish banks, despite increasing loan losses, escaped a systemic financial crisis.

The neo-liberal shift in the financial sector
To explain why CBK and the other major banks failed during the banking crisis, we will first address the neo-liberal shift in the financial sector. During

the years 1977–84, a profound and extensive sequence of regulatory changes took place in Norway. The core of this process was the liberalization of the financial markets and institutions. This neo-liberal shift was primarily caused by globalization of financial markets and a growing mismatch between the needs of the non-financial sector and the national protected and administered financial system. The banks, supported by the Bank of Norway, put an increasing pressure on the government to abandon the system of administratively fixed interest rates, aimed at the maintenance of a 'low-lever' interest rate policy. In 1985, the authorities also permitted foreign banks to set up subsidiaries or branches in Norway.

The first move to alter the system was undertaken during the autumn of 1977 and the spring of 1978. At the same time the government lifted most of the exchange controls, with the result that banks could acquire funding in international capital markets. From January 1984, direct controls on lending were lifted for banks and insurance companies. But, at the same time, the government tried to manage the interest rate level downwards, below the market price. Consequently, the supply of credit expanded rapidly, causing a credit-fuelled boom to develop. Furthermore, the system of taxation was designed in such a way that taxpayers could deduct all interest rate expenses from their income. Consequently, with rising inflation, the real interest rate after tax gave a strong incentive to borrow.[9] So did an expansive fiscal policy carried out by the centre-right government that came to office in 1983.

The huge credit expansion created asset-price inflation in the real estate market, and a similar development occurred in the stock market. A financial bubble occurred in the asset markets during the boom of 1983–6, and the non-financial sector's steep increase in debt boosted financial fragility, among both firms and households. Concurrently, credit risk increased substantially in the banking sector. But the severe falls in oil prices during the winter of 1985–6 punctured the bubble in the asset markets, first in the stock market, in October 1987; then a dramatic fall in prices took place in the real estate market during the autumn of 1988.

CBK's road to disaster, 1980–92

CBK expanded considerably, even more than the other commercial banks during the years 1980–87. CBK's outstanding loans increased from NOK 11.5 billion to NOK 67 billion during this period, representing an average yearly growth rate of 34 per cent, compared with an average of 28 per cent for the commercial banks in total. CBK's market share in the credit market swelled from 20 per cent in 1983 to 31 per cent in 1989. Its most significant growth period was 1984–6, when the credit market was deregulated most extensively.[10]

This expansion was part of an explicit growth strategy developed by the bank's top management. The staff were 786 in 1960, and increased almost seven-fold to 5512 in 1990. In parallel with the credit expansion, the bank was reorganized and divisionalized according to both product markets and geography. Both the decision structure and bank operations were strongly decentralized. Before 1980, CBK had a functioning and tight system of credit decisions and a system for internal control. The merger with Andresens Bank in 1980 and the following reorganization of the bank – in parallel with the huge expansion in lending – caused the total dissolution of these systems. The result was a complete loss of control. The unlimited credit authorization, which was held by the chief credit officer (CCO) alone until 1980, spread to the bank's middle management. When the business cycle turned downward, CBK held an increasingly number of non-performing loans. For the first time in a hundred years, the bank had to report a deficit in 1987. The situation deteriorated further, and in the year of catastrophe, 1991, CBK had to write off NOK 7 billion in loan losses. This meant that all the equity had gone, and the bank had to be rescued and re-capitalized by the state.

It is interesting to observe that the board of directors had little impact on the CEO's and the top-management's strategy choices. Nor was any owner or group of owners strong enough to exert its influence on the administration. Actually, the ownership structure in CBK was dispersed and, like other major Norwegian banks, to a very high degree management-led. There was thus a principal–agent problem, reinforced during the post-war period, and particularly during the 1980s. One consequence was that the bank became very vulnerable to empire-building, which inflicted extra costs on the shareholders. The reckless expansion during the 1980s featured significant traits of empire-building.

Reconstruction and consolidation

CBK got a new CEO during the summer 1991, and the new top management started to sort out most parts of the organization and to strengthen the bank's capital base. The new CEO – Borger Lenth – actually concentrated on three major tasks leader during his period as from the summer of 1991 to the spring of 1997. The first task was to re-capitalize the bank, which was done by a series of stock market offers through 1991 and 1992. The bank got a lot of new shareowners, although the state continued to retain a controlling position. The second task was to normalize the bank's business operations and regain and consolidate CBK's position as a leading financial institution in Norway. The third task was to develop CBK as head of an integrated financial group, including banking, insurance, investment banking and operations in the securities market. A regulatory change in 1991 permitted it to form financial conglomerates headed by either a bank or an insurance company. In 1993 CBK acquired Norske Liv, a Norwegian life insurance company; in 1994 it acquired a leading mortgage bank, Norgeskreditt.[11]

During the spring of 1993, a new economic upswing started. Nominal interest rates fell substantially, and so did the real interest rate because of falling prices. CBK strengthened its position considerably; it increased its operational profit continuously, carried out a new stock market offer in December 1993 and was again quoted at Oslo Stock Exchange.

The political authorities blocked CBK's initiative to acquire Norway's third largest bank, the Fokus Bank. The motive was regional policy. Since Fokus Bank had its headquarters in Trondheim, local MPs, supported by a strong regional policy lobby in Parliament, put forward a plan to develop Trondheim into 'a national financial centre', built around Fokus Bank. But instead of leading the development of Trondheim to become a financial centre, Fokus Bank was acquired by Den Danske Bank to become this bank's subsidiary in Norway. In 2000 the government accepted an offer put forward by the Swedish-dominated MeritaNordbanken to buy CBK. The Swedish state had a 60 per cent stake in MeritaNordbanken, and this bank's strategy was to develop a large pan-Nordic bank. Later it changed its name to Nordea, of which the former CBK become the Norwegian part.

Conclusion

In conclusion, we will return to the questions posed at the start of this chapter. Let us first address the question of banks and economic performance. Our narrative shows that CBK has contributed to the financing of innovative businesses and has thus played a part in economic growth from 1848 until the present day. Most of the time, CBK has been controlled by its management, while the owners have been dispersed, with limited influence. This have sometimes brought about principal–agent problems.

Another important trait in the bank's long-term development is a trend towards an increasing degree of universality. More and more financial services and products have been integrated into CBK's activities.

The CBK case also demonstrates that banks are very vulnerable to financial instability. But our narrative also tells the story that strategy matters. Despite downswings and recessions, the bank had the opportunity to choose its course. In particular, policy choices during a boom have always turned out to be decisive. During the banking crisis at the turn of the century and that of the 1920s, CBK followed a strategy that enabled the bank to stay clear of collapse. Furthermore, CBK strengthened its position throughout the aftermath of the crises. But during the boom – sequence of the 1980s and the subsequent financial crisis, CBK manoeuvred towards disaster.

The CBK story also makes it evident that the quality of regulations and institutional arrangements are vital to the performance of the banking system, both for their capacity to enhance growth and for financial stability.

This chapter has also demonstrated variation in financial systems over time and space. Norwegian commercial banks like CBK have not been as large and powerful as the major Danish and Swedish banks. Norwegian banks like CBK have never been the leading force in 'financial spheres' as, for instance, SEB in the Wallenberg group. Nor have interlocking directorships been widespread in Norwegian finance. But the Norwegian banking system with its mix of a large number of local savings banks and commercial banks like CBK, has managed to meet demand from innovative and growth-oriented enterprises.

QUESTIONS   1. To what extent do you consider modern banking to be important to long-term economic growth?
2. Dicuss CBK's internationalization strategy in the second period of globalization. Compare with what you know about banking in other countries (for instance your own country, if that is other than Norway). Can you observe any major differences? Can they be related to the configuration of the business system?

Notes

1. Nordvik *et al.* (1989); Nordvik (1990), p. 18.
2. Engebretsen (1948), p. 63.
3. Bergh (1975); Knutsen (1995).
4. Central Bureau of Statistics, NOS V 169, Table 12.
5. Knutsen *et al.* (1998), p. 33.
6. Knutsen *et al.* (1998), p. 35.
7. Knutsen *et al.* (1998), pp. 106–27.

8. Knutsen *et al.* (1998), p. 239.
9. Knutsen and Lie (2002), pp. 88–111.
10. Knutsen and Lie (2002), p. 101.
11. Knutsen *et al.* (1998), p. 450.

References

Bergh, T., *Fra fædrelandssag til storbank: Norges Postsparebank 1950–75* (Oslo, 1975).

Engebretsen, E. *Christiania Bank og Kreditkasse 1848–1948* (Oslo: Aschehoug & Co., 1948).

Knutsen, S., *Etterkrigstidens Strateqiske Kapitalisme og Styringen av Kapitalmarkedet som Industripolitisk Virkemiddel 1950–70, Arbeidsnotat 50* (Oslo: Handelshøyskolen BI, 1995).

Knutsen, S., Lange, E. and Nordvik, H. W., *Mellom Næringsliv og Politikk: Kreditkassen i Vekst og Kriser 1918–98.* (Oslo: Universitetsforlaget, 1998).

Knutsen, S., 'Phases in the Development of the Norwegian Banking System 1880–1980', in Cassis, Feldman and Olsson (eds), *The Evolution of Financial Institutions and Markets in Twentieth-Century Europe* (Aldershot: Scolar Press, 2006a).

Knutsen, S., 'Post-War Strategic Capitalism in Norway: A Theoretical and Analytical Framework', *Business History*, 39(4) (2006b), pp. 106–27.

Knutsen, S. and Lie, E., 'Financial Fragility, Growth Strategies and Banking Failures: The Major Norwegian Banks and the Banking Crisis, 1987–92', *Business History*, 44(2) (2002) pp. 88–111.

Matre, Hege Imset, *Norske forretningsbanker 1984–90. En tilbakeføring av forretningsbanksta-tistikken. KS Rapport. 1992: Det nye pengesamfunnet nr. 41* (Oslo: Forskningsrådet, 1992).

Nordvik, H.W., Nerheim, G. and Brandal, T., *Penger spart, penger tjent: Sparebanker og økonomisk utvikling på Sør-Vestlandet fra 1839 til 1989* (Stavanger: SR-Ban, 1989).

Nordvik, H.W., 'Industrialization and Economic Growth in Norway, 1850–1914: The Role of the Banking Sector', in Nordvik, H.W. and Knutsen, S., *Bankenes rolle i norsk industriell utvikling 1850–1914,* Den nye pengesamfunnet, rapport 10 (1990).

WELFARE CAPITALISM: THE SWEDISH ECONOMY 1850-2005 ● ENTREPRENEURSHIP AND OWNERSHIP: THE

ERM VIABILITY OF THE SWEDISH BONNIER AND WALLENBERG FAMILY BUSINESS GROUPS ● FROM

ABB BUSINESS THE SWEDISH WAY ● GROWTH AND INVESTMENT: FINNISH

CAPITALISM, 1850S-2005 ● FROM STATE OWNERSHIP TO MULTINATIONAL CORPORATION: THE PATH OF

ENSO-GUTZEIT TO STORA-ENSO ● SUCCESS AND FAILURE OF A CONGLOMERATE FIRM: THE STRATEGIC

PATHS OF NOKIA AND TAMPELLA IN THE LIBERALIZING FINNISH ECONOMY AFTER THE SECOND WORLD

WAR ● CO-OPERATIVE LIBERALISM: DENMARK FROM 1857 TO 2007 ● ARLA – FROM DECENTRALIZED INDUSTRY

TO MULTINATIONAL ENTERPRISE ● CARLSBERG AND THE SELF-REGULATION OF THE DANISH BEER MARKET

● NORWAY: A RESOURCE-BASED AND DEMOCRATIC CAPITALISM ● CONSTRUCTIVE POWER: ELKEM 1904-2004

● FINANCE AND THE DEVELOPMENT OF NORWEGIAN CAPITALISM – THE CASE OF CHRISTIANIA BANK

14 conclusion

Susanna Fellman and Hans Sjögren

Where are we now?

In this book, we have been studying four Nordic models of capitalism over a long period of time. As Chapter 1 pointed out, one of the main aims was to deal with the question whether there has been a common Nordic model of capitalism, or if there has been four of them. We have drawn up the development path in the individual country chapters and tracked down their historical roots. A related issue was to find the main factors behind the transformation in each country, when substantial changes occurred, and what dynamic effects these changes had on individual companies and their strategies. The problem of change was approached by means of using so-called 'formative phases', while the development was divided into periods.

By using case studies on firms and branches, we have been able to investigate how individual companies and/or branches have acted within, and adapted to, the current institutional and economic settings. The company cases illuminate how the models of capitalism and business systems operated in practice and what actions and strategies the institutional context created at the company level. The company cases also provide detailed insights into problems and readjustments at company level which the institutional transformations stimulated. At the same time, the cases show individual companies' significance in the transformation process, as key players in innovation, skill formation and the reshaping of the business systems.

In this Conclusion, we will summarize and discuss the empirical findings arising from a reading of the country chapters and the cases. We will make comparisons and draw some conclusions about our main question – i.e. about a 'Nordic model'. Furthermore, we will put our findings in a larger historical and geographical context, although here the findings are only tentative and further research is called for. Finally, we will try to evaluate our methodological basis and our theoretical and conceptual tools for addressing these research questions. Have we been able to track down the key factors in the evolving 'Nordic model(s)' of capitalism and to answer our research questions in a convincing way by means of the analytical tools we have used?

One, two or four 'Nordic models'?

As pointed out at the outset, for outsiders, the Nordic countries have during recent decades been seen as dynamic, flexible and adaptable societies, but also countries with a large public sector, generous welfare systems and a high level of taxation, This can be regarded as something of a paradox not fitting the 'textbook case' of a modern efficient, capitalist economy well prepared for the challenges of globalization and the swiftly growing economies in new regions. The 'Nordic model' has, however, also brought about other positive institutional commonalities, like successful state-owned firms, high levels of human capital development, low corruption levels, a high degree of consensus and gender equality, and these factors are usually recognized as having had positive effects on economic development. From the country chapters it becomes evident that such reforms have often had strong economic motivations: these small, late-coming open economies have mobilized and made efficient use of their scarce resources in order to enhance growth. For example, the promotion of a high labour participation rate and a high rate of investment in human and fixed capital has been an important measure for the 'virtuous circles' of these countries. Such measures have, however, also gone hand in hand with egalitarian policies consisting of equal opportunities to free education, low income differentials and policies supporting labour supply by means of income-based transfers and publicly subsidized welfare services – for example old-age care, day care centres for children, generous parental leave, etc.

According to the Finnish political historian, Pauli Kettunen, the histories of the Nordic welfare states have been based on an intertwining of an idealized heritage of the free independent peasant, the spirit of capitalism and the utopia of socialism.[1] In the mid-1930s, this pragmatic balance between capitalism and socialism was named 'the middle way', a label that was also spread internationally by Michael Childs in his book about how Sweden handled contemporary problems.[2] The 'middle way' carries a tradition of compromise thinking that goes back a long way in the history of Scandinavia, and has survived even in times of strong internationalization. To maintain relations with the opposition and obtain mutual advantages has been a common objective in the behaviour of Parliament, trade unions and industrial leaders since the Second World War. This could be interpreted as a type of corporatism where the state is centralized but still open, the bureaucracy professional but not authoritarian, and where the policies are differentiated but have a central co-ordination. This has also enabled the building of strong elements of trust between various interest groups and parties, a phenomenon often put forward of being one of the strengths of the Nordic societies. These four countries certainly show that policies that enhance growth do not necessarily conflict with policies that enhance social equality.

The Nordic countries also have been fairly stable societies in a global perspective, with little tension and conflict, which has contributed to a 'virtuous circle'. Active consensual policies aiming to bridge conflicts and create, or strengthen, the elements of trust have been a particularly prominent goal of the post-war period. However, there have probably been more both open and underlying tensions in these societies than is commonly assumed. By a closer reading of the chapters we can discern traces of tensions and conflicting forces in all four countries. In the case of Finland, such tensions are particularly evident, where open conflict has occurred from time to time. The most striking example is the Civil War, but strikes and other conflicts on the labour market also occurred frequently in the post-war consensus society: in the 1950s and 1960s, Finland lost proportionally more working days to strikes than any other Nordic country. But in Denmark discontent on the labour market was also not uncommon during the decades after the war and Denmark experienced a general strike in 1956. In Sweden, there were bitter protests against private capitalists in the 1960s and 1970s. The idea of *folkhemmet* (the peoples' home) was questioned, while the owners of big business, particularly the influential Wallenberg family, were shocked to observe that their role in the building of the Swedish welfare state was being questioned.[3]

There have, thus, been features of both collectivism and individualism, of both a social orientation and liberal forces and of a strong nationalism and aims of openness and multiculturalism. A striving for consensus was challenged and opposing forces existed. It might actually be the case that these partly conflicting forces, opposite trends and competing opinions have been beneficial, particularly by contributing to the success and adaptability of the countries. However, this is an interesting, but difficult question that needs further investigation.

Similarities and differences

So, by reading these chapters, can we talk about one, or two, or four models of capitalism? If we particularly focus on the business system and the model of capitalism, some similarities are evident. First, on a broad level, it is evident that all four countries, although going through extensive transformations, have been marked by clear continuities, as a result of path dependencies and co-existing historical layers. On the other hand, development has also occasionally taken a rapid turn and deviation from the path previously followed. It would, thus, be dangerous to see the development as pre-determined or as a sequence of steps logically following each other. Occasionally rapid and unexpected changes, or even ruptures, have occurred, turning the path in a new direction. Such turns have sometimes been a result of a conscious active policy change, sometimes the result of outside shocks and pressures, and most commonly a mix of these.

When we look more closely at both paths and periods, we can see clear similarities between the countries. We may talk about a 'Nordic model' of capitalism, although we are aware of variations. This is largely a result of the similar economic structures: the countries have all been small open economies, which at the beginning of industrialization exploited natural resources, the advantages of a growing demand for such products on foreign markets and the international division of labour. In spite of some divergences in the stage and pace of industrial and economic development, the late nineteenth century saw a period of rapid economic progress in all four countries. This occurred in connection with the introduction of a liberalistic period. The transition from mercantilism to economic liberalism was part of an international phenomenon, but also a response to the progressing industrialization in all four countries. It was also a period of infrastructural investment, institutional modernization and commercialization of agrarian production, followed by profound societal transformations and the emergence of what is best described as an 'industrial society' (Chapter 2 in this volume).

In Sweden, Norway and Denmark, the inter-war period saw the evolution of Nordic welfare capitalism. An attempt to smooth out conflicts by introducing new labour market practices and by actively promoting equal opportunities and a decent living standard for all citizens through welfare reforms was prominent. This model took its most pronounced form in the construction of the Swedish *folkhemmet*, but can be found in some shape in all four countries, although in Finland it actually evolved only in the post-war period.

In general, the inter-war period in all four countries was marked by increasing state involvement and the emergence of a more pronounced co-operative environment. The social democratic and labour movement grew stronger both internationally and in the Nordic countries, which brought with it changing perceptions on labour market, social welfare and political reforms. At the same time this was also the era of modernization, motorization, rationalization and large-scale mass production – or, as is stressed in the Norwegian country chapter (Chapter 11), 'organization is the solution of the time'. Such a model of thinking extended to all aspects of society.

In the post-war period, all four countries adopted models of so called 'mixed economies', with fairly strong state intervention through direct regulation, an increase in the number of state companies and public utility enterprises, and policies supporting co-operation across and within sectors. The public sector grew, while the redistribution of income and welfare services became extensive. During this 'Golden Age' with favourable growth figures in the industrialized countries, these models of mixed economy worked fairly well and led to higher living standards for whole populations.

However, in the long run these models also created structural problems, lock-in effects and in the end staggering growth or even acute economic crises, particularly after the oil shocks and the global recession of the 1970s. All four countries experienced some sort of economic and structural crisis. Denmark had one in the early 1980s, its famous economic crisis policy called the 'potato cure'; in Norway, a severe banking crisis and a slump in asset prices and on the housing market struck in the late 1980s, while Sweden and Finland went through deep financial and real economic crises in the early 1990s. Sweden had, however, experienced staggering growth since the 1970s; although a severe recession occurred in Norway and Finland in the 1970s, the lower long-run average growth rate in Sweden enabled Norway to by-pass and Finland to catch-up with Sweden economically.

These economic problems springing from imbalances and structural problems led in all four countries to a debate about the 'Nordic model' of welfare: it was claimed it had come to an end. The ideological turn internationally supported the criticism of the model. There was an ideological challenge to welfare capitalism, to regulation of the economy and to state intervention. Liberalization of the economy, re-regulation of the financial and capital markets, privatization of state companies, increasing competition and cuts in the public sector and in welfare services became a common trend in all the Nordic countries, although with some variations with respect to both timing and extent. The pressures from globalization and deepening European integration also forced a shift in the regime. In Denmark, the re-regulation and adjustment to European economic integration started earlier as they became members of EEC in 1973. The Danish economy was also much more open than the Finnish and Swedish in the post-war era with respect to foreign capital and FDI.

A factor often forgotten, but stressed by Sjögren in the Swedish country chapter (Chapter 2) – namely, the increasing multiculturalism and a general diversification or fragmentation of the Nordic societies – also made the implementation of models set centrally by the state difficult. The corporative growth model, promoting 'big business' and large-scale solutions, had demanded a certain amount of 'top-down' steering, but this was challenged by the increasing openness and multiculturalism and the influence of global developments. On the other hand, institutional regime shifts also made way for extensive changes in the basis of economic industrial activity although, as Fellman points out (Chapter 5), such adaptability in Finland was built in to previous institutional settings and traditions deeply rooted in former periods. Thus, in spite of extensive transformations in all four Nordic countries, the chapters show how the models of today have been built upon divergent institutional layers.

When studying the individual countries and their institutional models in more detail, some differences are discernable as well. It appears that Swedish and Finnish capitalism are more similar, as are Denmark and Norway. Thus, we might sometimes talk about a 'West-Nordic' and an 'East-Nordic' model. This Sweden–Finland and Denmark–Norway division arises primarily from two factors: similarity in economic structure and a common heritage in these pairs of countries. For example, in Sweden and in Finland large-scale manufacturing firms within primarily the forest, metal and electronic industries have been core sectors within the whole economy, and the institutional models have been influenced to support these key export sectors. As a contrast, the economic models and business systems in Norway and Denmark have been influenced by the strong position of small-scale entrepreneurship. In Denmark the key agrarian sector has put a distinctive mark on the business system, while the maritime 'cluster' and some energy-based industries have had the same impact on the institutional setting in Norway. In both countries the primary sector saw much of the early industrialization: in Denmark it was agricultural production, in Norway the exploitation of fishing and forest resources.

Denmark and Norway were, on the other hand, also dual economies, with small-scale entrepreneurship but at the same time hosts of large corporations. In Norway this was in particularly in the energy sector and the mining sector, where MNCs were common, but also within the traditional maritime and fishing industries. Norway has the world's largest sea-carriers and the world's largest merchant fleet, at the same time as it is one of the world's largest oil exporters. The country is also one of the two largest fish exporters and one of the largest aluminium exporters in the world. In Denmark both within the food industry, closely related to the agrarian 'cluster', and within other sectors, there were a prominent group of large firms based on innovation and exploitation of skills and entrepreneurship, such as the medical multinational Novo Nordisk, Coloplast and the world's largest windmill producer, Vestas.

The differences in these models have also been influenced by divergent political and social development paths. In spite of similar economic structures and similar institutional settings, the early international orientation of Swedish big business, the country's strong MNCs and their ability to exploit innovations made the Finnish and Swedish economies appear different, particularly during early industrialization. Finland clearly remained an exploiter of some (one) key resources for much longer, although the forest 'cluster' developed into a high-tech sector in the postwar period. The institutional model supported this sector until the early 1980s.

The differences between the countries also influence the structure of this book and its chapters. The country chapters are somewhat different, and this does not entirely depend on the authors and their personal focus, but also on the divergent development paths. For example, the strong stress on wars in the Finnish chapter is motivated by the fact that they have heavily influenced the institutional and economic development.

The Danish and Norwegian economies and their business systems have been more fragmented and more decentralized than the Finnish and Swedish ones. The business system has also been based more on a small scale and the policies moulded to support small-scale entrepreneurship. Although there are obvious regional variations in Sweden and Finland already by being geographically large, the Danish and Norwegian economies were more clearly divided into local and regional spheres. In Denmark there was a clear division between the large-scale Copenhagen-based industry and the Jutland area, based on small-scale entrepreneurship. Likewise, the economic activity in Norway has been decentralized and regionally dispersed. For example, the financial system was based on primarily local (savings) banks operating locally. Not even bigger banks like Christiania Bank, dealt with in the case chapter (Chapter 13), developed an extensive branch network.

In Sweden and Finland the commercial banks were more concentrated, although also in the beginning more fragmented. A few very big banks had a significant role in the business system. At an early stage Swedish universal banks became key financiers of 'big business', exercising extensive influence in the manufacturing sector. This was partly a result of the strong Wallenberg family, extending its activities at an early stage into manufacturing companies and including them into their 'sphere'. In Finland the close relations between banks and industry evolved more slowly, although becoming very strong in the post-war period, as a result of the economic model of the time.

In Sweden and Denmark, societies and labour markets have long had a large number of immigrants and, thus, a dependence on a foreign labour force earlier than Norway and Finland, where the societies were very homogeneous until recent decades. In general, Denmark has also been much more 'open' than the other economies and participated much earlier in the European integration process; Norway is today still outside the EU. On the other hand, formal membership is not everything. Economically, Norway is highly integrated in Europe, thanks to various side-documents and contracts.

With economic progress, the economies have become less regionally fragmented and instead more integrated and centralized. This development actually seems to have gone hand in hand with the growth of the large scale corporations and with increasing dependence on foreign markets and global forces. Thus the idea that the corporative consensus societies and the mixed economy were based on large-scale and inflexible solutions, and a 'top-down' steering, while the liberal market-based system is more flexible, more disintegrated and more entrepreneurial, is only partly right. Although flexible ways to communicate, produce and sell are evolving and supply chains, outsourcing and sub-contractors are new strategies to increase flexibility and avoid risk, the largest firms are today even larger than before. One reason is the cross-border mergers, very evident in the Nordic region. Some of the most important and recent examples are the Pan-Nordic bank, Nordea, the Swedish–Finnish telecoms company TeliaSonera and the case from this book, Stora-Enso (Chapter 6).

Some of the differences can also be ascribed to divergent stages of economic and societal development, and it appears that some of the institutional models and solutions have become more similar over time. Traditionally the Nordic countries look to each other for models, and they have co-operated on various levels and in various sectors, often with an aim to adjust and harmonise the institutional setting in order to facilitate economic interaction. However, it is also a fallacy that the Nordic countries' model of capitalism and institutional settings just follow each other, perhaps with a lag originating in economic development. All four countries have followed their own individual paths and individual characteristics have existed.

The role of the state in Nordic business systems

The role of the state is a factor we have particularly stressed in our analysis as we regard it as being of utmost importance for understanding the formation of capitalism. Moreover, the role of the state is much more complex and multifaceted than is often presented in the literature. The question about an 'active' versus a passive 'state' and the 'strong' versus the 'weak' state is generally simplified and somewhat superficially dealt with. From a careful reading of the chapters of this book it is evident that the state's actions and government policies can take a multitude of variations. In all the countries the state has been a significant actor, but its role and influence have changed over time.

This is well exemplified by the era of transition from mercantilist to economic liberalism in the second half of the nineteenth century; the state was in all countries fairly passive with respect to direct intervention in the economy. However, that did not mean that the state has to be regarded as altogether passive, nor that it was weak. The state actively promoted reforms and introduced legislative and institutional modernization, which was important for economic progress in all four countries. While the state was fairly passive in other respects in Denmark, it was in the three other countries fairly active with respect to infrastructural investment and the promotion of industrialization, through the building of railways, roads and canals, and by introducing educational and other reforms.

In the inter-war period the role of the state grew, but the development paths diverged somewhat. In both Denmark and Sweden the state's direct steering of the economy grew after the 1930s. In Finland direct intervention was still avoided, although the first state companies emerged immediately after independence. Self-regulation was the key principle concerning business activities, wage-setting, etc. However, at the same time the state had policies to support industrialization as part of nation-building, which indicated a transformation towards a more active state. This was also the case in Norway, separated from Sweden in 1905 when the union was dissolved. The Norwegian government was very active in introducing and supporting reforms – e.g. educational reforms and infrastructural investments promoting industrialization during the first decades of full independence. In Norway and Finland industrialization, as a national project, seems to have been more pronounced, typical of small newly independent states. However, in Norway these policies promoted small-scale industrialization, while in Finland 'big business'. The political aspects of industrialization are also important, not the least when evaluating the role of the state.

In relation to the more active state, this period also meant the birth of the welfare state and corporatism and consensus policies on the labour market in Denmark, Norway and Sweden. The 1930s saw the birth of the concept of *folkhemmet*, of the 'Swedish model' or of the 'Nordic model', whatever concept is used. In Denmark, the state gained a pronounced role on the labour market as a result of the Official Conciliator's Act, while in Sweden the *Saltsjöbaden* agreement marked the start of a collective bargaining system and consensus policies. Also in Norway labour market practices were transformed and a system of collective bargaining appeared. The co-operative or collaborative features increased in all the countries, taking the form of 'systematic co-operation', as Iversen and Andersen have called the period in the case of Denmark. But this concept also could fit the Swedish and Norwegian cases. During this period Finland stands out as a exception, as the 'Nordic model' in this form did not come about until during the war and in reality it was not until the post-war era that it took a similar form as in the other Nordic countries. Tendencies towards new labour market practices can be observed at the end of the 1930s and the relationship and collaboration between government and business was also intimate.

Today, the state is more withdrawn, but still very visible. It is also quite strong, governing market forces through legislation and monitoring, perhaps most observable in competition policies and financial supervision.

A 'Nordic' model internationally embedded

We claim that the capitalistic models in the four Nordic countries studied here are fairly similar, and have perhaps become increasingly so over time.

The four Nordic countries are among themselves clearly more similar than, for example, Denmark and Japan, or Sweden and Britain. Although foreign models and influences have been significant in the Nordic countries, the common institutional, historical and cultural heritage have put their stamp on the countries' development until today. Thus, foreign models and ideas, for example neo-liberalism in the 1980s, have been reshaped and adjusted to fit the existing cultural pattern.

Although the Nordic countries have several features that can be seen as specifically 'Nordic', many of the institutional solutions discussed in the country chapters can also be found at various periods of time in other European countries, particularly in some of the small open economies like the Netherlands and Austria, but also in larger countries like Germany and France. For example social reforms, an income-based pension systems, regulative policies, strong unions and state-owned companies were common in post-war Europe, although they took various forms. Liberalistic trends during the late nineteenth century, which occurred in all the four countries at about the same time, were part of broader development trends in the liberalistic and international environment of the so-called 'first globalization era', marked by expanding trade and capital flows and an international monetary order (i.e. the international Gold Standard). The liberalization of recent decades has also been a fairly general phenomenon in Europe after the end of the 'Golden Era' (1950–73), although taking place at a divergent pace and time, but following a similar path. Institutional change does not occur in isolation, but is often part of international trends.

It would also be fruitful to expand the comparisons with other European countries. The American economic historian, Joel Mokyr, has highlighted the remarkable economic growth in a number of so-called Small Successful European Economies (SSEEs), such as Austria, Finland, Ireland and the three Scandinavian countries.[4] Mokyr points to three important characteristics of these SSEEs, namely a combination of efficient, stable and democratic public institutions, a long-term insistence on liberal, open economic principles and finally the ability to define and exploit global niches. The Nordic chapters in this book confirm Mokyr's characteristics and it is thus likely that some of the characteristics of the 'Nordic' economies are not necessarily exclusive Nordic but rather common to a number of small successful, open European economies.

The German business historian, Harm Schröter, has studied small European countries and concludes that the Nordic countries – with the

Netherlands and Switzerland – have been fairly similar in their co-operative models. Schröter focuses particularly on co-operation and co-ordination within and between industries. Co-operation provides an efficient tool to protect small domestic players and make them more competitive on international markets, as we have seen in the individual country chapters. But as we can see, co-operation and collaboration within other sectors – for example, on the labour market – was also motivated by other arguments: it was often in the national interest to reach consensus and avoid harmful conflict. In spite of their similarities, however, Schröter concludes that small states in Europe did not develop a similar form of capitalism – a 'small-state capitalism'.[5] According to him, the dependence on international trade and markets did not necessarily give rise to similar institutional solutions. However, our results point in another direction.

Another factor which is often overlooked – and perhaps also given too little attention in this book – is regional differences in the business systems *within* an individual country. There has been an increasing debate on the fruitfulness of taking the nation state as the focus for investigations. In many cases the business systems in Helsinki, Oslo, Copenhagen and Stockholm are perhaps more similar, than for example the business systems in Helsinki and Kuopio (a city situated in the east of Finland) or in Oslo and Hammerfest (in the north of Norway). Likewise, the counties in northern Sweden have more in common with north parts of Norway and Finland than with the south of Sweden, where the landscape and regional economy reminds one of Denmark. In a similar way, Finland and eastern Sweden take part in the expansion of regional economy around the Baltic Sea, including countries such as Russia, the Baltic countries, Germany and Poland. At the same time, partly thanks to a bridge between Malmö and Copenhagen, a strong regional economy has been developed around the Sound (Öresund). Other strong local or regional economies have been developed along the border linking Norway with Sweden and around the Gulf of Bothnia, i.e. across the northern borders of Finland and Sweden.

These regional variations are of course reflected in business structure, as a majority of natural-based industries, such as mining, timber, paper and pulp, are located in certain parts of Finland and Sweden while Denmark and southern Sweden host many firms in the dairy industry. However, the vast majority of research is still carried out on a national level. One obvious reason is, of course, the availability of statistical data, which is primarily collected on a national level; the legal and institutional framework are also mostly nation-bound. But, as we can see from some of the individual chapters, business systems can and do vary regionally.

Understanding mechanisms of renewal

Our company cases are all different. Not only do they represent various sectors, the firms studied are also different in terms of size, age and degree of international orientation. However, they have one thing in common: they all illustrate how certain principles of renewal can be applied in business. The basic reason for renewal in a private business is to make profits in the long run. The cases show that this can be done in many ways, in order to guarantee a high level of innovation, entrepreneurship and strong leadership. In the case of the Bonnier and the Wallenberg groups, key principles of renewal helped family-based groups to stay in business for 150 years (Chapter 3). Somewhat paradoxically, the groups retained their family traditions at the same time as they demonstrated an ability to adapt to change and stay competitive in a modern market economy. Thus, as active long-term controlling owners, they do not seem to have been restricted by their family traditions in the renewal process. During the last fifty years they have also recruited non-family members to top-level positions. Therefore, the case on Bonnier and Wallenberg shows that comparative advantages can appear as a consequence of low information costs in hierarchical but less bureaucratic business groups. We also gain the insight that family-based large firms operating in mature industries did not disappear with earlier industrial revolutions, something suggested in many deterministic models. In fact, large family firms are still successfully organizing long-term, profit-generating enterprises, not only in the Nordic countries.

The case of ASEA/ABB (Chapter 4) points to the importance of management and strong leadership for transformation, where the merger in 1988 took the renewal process to a higher level. The case clearly shows the need for looking beyond three-pronged investments in marketing, manufacturing and managerial hierarchies, as noted by Alfred D. Chandler, Jr. A feature of ASEA/ABB, and many other major Swedish industrial enterprises from the second industrial revolution, is their success through innovation and technological development. Not only does the industrial enterprise need to reap the advantages of scale and scope in operation; the ability to continuously move the 'production function frontier' in dynamic markets is also a necessity for survival. This implies both product innovations that can increase the value of products for customers but also, as the case shows, process and organizational innovations that can cut costs below those of competitors. Moreover, ASEA/ABB exemplifies the transformation from a home-country-based (in terms of both R&D, manufacturing plants and corporate management) exporting engineering firm quite typical of the Swedish corporate landscape in the twentieth century, to a truly TNC with R&D and manufacturing facilities all over the world and corporate management originating in many countries. In order to overcome obstacles associated with this process ASEA/ABB had to reinvent its managerial approach, with regard both to organizational structures (where the M-form was never a conspicuous feature) and to abandoning the Swedish hegemony at the strategic apex of the organization.

The first Finnish company case, on Enso-Gutzeit (Chapter 6), shows how the renewal process can be treated by the state as the major owner of a listed company. In the start-up phase of the company, ownership by the state was necessary to secure vital resources. The organic growth through large-scale investments in production and technology continued in the post-war period with diversification into more or less related lines of business. The de-diversification starting in the 1980s was also representative of business in Finland, as it was of the entire industrialized world at this time. The domestic consolidation in the 1980s and 1990s was followed by a Nordic-based one after the merger with STORA, one of the leading Swedish pulp and paper companies. Both STORA and Enso had had a bad experience in entering the North American market, where they had had establishments in the 1960s. It took more than ten years for STORA to make a profitable plant in Nova Scotia, while only a third of the long period that Enso stayed in Canada was profitable. Together they made a new effort in 2000 by buying the US-based Consolidated Paper. Since the synergy effects were weak, they decided to exit North America in 2007. Thus, the case of Enso gives us a hint of the limits to FDI as a key to successful renewal. Although this branch experienced problems globally at the turn of the millennium, the problems of StoraEnso are most likely a broader indicator of such limitations.

The comparison of the two large-scale Finnish conglomerates, Nokia and Tampella, is a fascinating story of how two enterprises started under similar conditions in the same sector and with same institutions, and then developed in diametrically opposite ways (Chapter 7). Before that, they were also hit by the same financial crisis at the turn of the 1990s. When Bank of Finland saved Tampella from bankruptcy the old company ceased as an independent entity, while the survival and success of Nokia is known to everybody.

The main difference here is the choice of strategy. Nokia was differently diversified than Tampella, which was bound to many mature industries with high capital costs. But Nokia was also more effective in divesting from their unprofitable lines of business – i.e. implementing structural and organizational changes. The 'creative destruction' in the early 1990s was enhanced by a previous symbiotic relationship with the government, spurred by a Soviet trade with overpriced, large-scale orders based on predetermined annual quotas. This applies to both Tampella and Nokia. As co-ordinated by state representatives, these arrangements provided stability and predictability in the business environment. However, as non-market strategies they only led to market power, not economic efficiency and innovations. On the other hand, neither the break-up of the Soviet Union nor emerging liberalization can fully explain the success story of Nokia. The take-off in the 1990s started with a strategic decision in the 1960s, to hold on to electric engineering. This was followed up by R&D and investments in mobile phones and networks, even during later periods of de-diversification and reconstructions. Such a renewal by making a 'strategic turn' failed in Tampella.

Although the Danish business system has been liberal, the state involvement has been profound in many economic sectors. The case of Arla (Chapter 9) shows that state policies and business transformation tend to follow each other in a complex but corporative manner. In the nineteenth century, the support from the government was decisive for the breakthrough of the dairy industry. From the 1930s, the state had to strongly regulate the sector and today regulation has become international and primarily rooted in international organizations such as the EU and the WTO. The long transition from a decentralized organization to an MNE shows that large-scale companies and concentration of capital is not always necessary to create a successful development of capitalism and industry. Instead, the Arla case shows how renewal can emanate from co-operative arrangements, internal competition among small and independent actors, fuelled by a strong export market (primarily the UK). The case also illustrates how the renewal of Danish economy has been closely connected to the international development of both capitalism and markets. Finally, the case suggests that is less fruitful to distinguish between the agriculture and industry sectors, since their renewal processes are highly interdependent.

In the case of Carlsberg (Chapter 10), the process of renewal went hand in hand with the internationalization of the business. After the merger between the two largest Danish breweries in 1970, Carlsberg and Tuborg, growth strategies took the new company from an export-oriented MNC to a world-wide operating firm. Today, the firm has a transnational focus on globally consistent brand, production and management systems. However, this process started in the 1880s, when both companies began to export their beers to Asia and the Middle East through trading companies such as the East Asiatic Company and various merchant houses operating out of Hamburg. The cartel agreement between Carlsberg and Tuborg that lasted from 1903 to 1970 and regulated prices and market conditions coincided with a slower process of internationalization (though strong regulation does not necessarily mean less FDI). Various price arrangements continued to exist even after 1970, but in 1988 competition agreements were dissolved after the breweries began to violate the cartel-like norm by increasing their internal competition. The new institutional setting, with a renaissance of liberal ideas, paved the way for a stronger internationalization. Here the case shows how Carlsberg/Tuborg took advantage of being a profitable exporter to gradually expand the 'home market' to cover the four largest Nordic countries. Recently, acquisitions in Eastern Europe, Germany and China have triggered the renewal process and made Carlsberg to one of the fastest-growing international beer brands in the early twenty-first century. In that sense, the Carlsberg case illustrates how market shares for a relatively simple product can be won by aggressive branding in combination with horizontal integration through acquisitions.

All the firms studied here are large, which require an organization of some 250 employees according to the latest classification by the EU. However, the firms here are all significantly larger than this, which means that our focus is primarily entrepreneurship in 'big business'. The firms are also quite old, which means that they have changed their structure and strategies more than once over the years. This also applies to Elkem, the Norweigan electro-metallurgic company that started in 1904 (Chapter 12). The first entrepreneur was Norwegian, Sam Eyde, while the financial capital came from Sweden, the Wallenberg group. For many decades the company expanded thanks to a genius invention, the Söderberg electrode. In the beginning, the firm was a creator and seller of knowledge, technology and whole enterprises. Then it slightly changed its business to become an important producer of goods, supported by a government that facilitated investment opportunities in the post-war regulated economy. The development of the last decade reveals an ambition to return to its innovative roots. The case shows some distinctive factors behind a successful renewal process. First, a relatively high level of

R&D, which enables the firm to benefit from innovations and diffusions of technology and knowledge, both nationally and internationally. Second, a strategic choice of locating core knowledge in an international environment in order to speed up the innovation process. Third, a focus on excellence, to recruit appropriate competence and reach the highest level of knowledge. For obvious reasons, the Elkem case is important for our understanding of how firms rooted in a specific national context are able – on a regular basis – refresh their innovative capacity.

The final case study highlights the relation between an effective financial system and growth in the non-financial sector (Chapter 13). The Christiania Bank has been an important player by financing innovative Norwegian business since 1848. This commercial bank has contributed to economic growth in the country for over 150 years. The case treats both macro- and micro-perspective. On the macro-level, it is obvious how the mix of a large number of local savings banks and commercial banks reflects the structure of Norwegian society and business, with strong regions and few large mature industries. As a late-comer to industrialization, Norway did not develop universal banks like Germany and Sweden. In fact, it was only quite recently that commercial banks in Norway started to incorporate different types of financial services and products into their businesses. On the micro-level, the case proves that Christiania Bank has played a vital if indirect, role, in fostering the transformation of business. The size and activity of the bank has been appropriate to meet the demands from innovative and growth-oriented enterprises. The latest step has been to build a pan-Nordic bank, Nordea. Thus, the case of Christiania is an illustration of the 'third wave' of mergers in the banking market, a process that started with mergers between local actors in the nineteenth century, followed by mergers between national giants in the post-war period and more recently, mergers between Nordic banks.

To sum up, the case studies illustrate various principles and processes of renewal. A key notion is that access to the Nordic market has been a prerequisite for further expansion; very often, agents or FDI in one of the neighbouring countries have paved the way for a broader international take-off. Likewise, the Nordic market has been important for testing goods and services. Another aspect that binds the cases together is the flow of knowledge and competence across borders. In fact, Nordic business history is full of creative network relationships and financing of innovative joint ventures. If our textbook had included Iceland, the fifth largest Nordic economy, the notion of such collaborations would have increase further. It is also clear that modern activity in Nordic-based M&A is not a new phenomenon, rather a renaissance of the activity going on during the 'first wave' of globalization around the turn of the nineteenth century.

Tools to study capitalism, entrepreneurship and structural change

Our point of departure in this book was the 'Business Systems' and the 'Varieties of Capitalism' traditions, although we did not follow strictly any line of thought.[6] In particular, we adopted some of the concepts and tools to study the larger institutional setting from these traditions. However, we also started out by criticising these two traditions for being unhistorical, although they have lately been dealing more explicitly with institutional change.[7] Recently, it has been asked why different systems evolve, become established and – perhaps more importantly – why a certain system is reproduced over time.[8] One reason for this newly awakened interest in change has been the scholarly criticism of these approaches as being unhistorical, static and coping badly with transformation. The interest in change has also grown as a result of perceived transformations, mainly ascribed to globalization and increasing economic integration. The effect of globalization on the individual systems during the recent period is also evident in the country chapters of this book.

Another issue that has been addressed by scholars is whether systems transform rapidly or if change happens gradually, mainly through small incremental steps. This 'revolution versus evolution' question is also addressed here, and touched upon in the individual chapters. External shocks have often been a force giving rise to or speeding up the process of change, as Chapter 5 on Finland tells us. However, it has also been put forward that there has been a lack of tools to handle a process of gradual change. In the absence of such tools, there has been a tendency either to (over)stress the role of shocks and radical ruptures, which often leads to a simple two-stage model with static periods in between or, alternatively, to see transformation as a smooth, even process. Most likely, the process of change is much more complicated, with periods of radical ruptures alternating with periods of transformative changes and fairly stable periods of smaller, incremental change.[9] In relation to these discussions, our aim has been to bring history to our analysis of the Nordic countries and at the same time try to cope with transformations, and track down driving forces of transformations. Important tools have been the concept of 'business systems' and 'formative phases'. So, have these concepts helped us to grasp and understand the Nordic model and its change any better?

We introduced a 'diamond' model to cover the segments that constitute a business system (see Figure 1.1, p. 10). Throughout the book we use this model with boxes to discuss what constitutes the business system and entrepreneurship during various periods in the specific country. The original Whitley model has been complemented with a box for the state, reflecting a certain depth of activity from the government side in all four Nordic countries. With this model we have been able to establish substantial similarities between the development paths of the Nordic countries. Very often, the four countries have met the same type of institutional changes at the same time – for example, regarding reforms in the labour market and re-regulations in the financial market. The differences in development paths we have observed are limited to time lags – for example, a late rather than a semi-late industrial breakthrough.

We have also been able to discuss structural changes by applying the concept of 'formative phases'. This concept highlights the fact that the pace of transformation has not been perfectly regular. Sometimes the business system has taken a leap in a certain direction, and left the old institutional framework and techno-economic paradigm behind. We have also observed that such irregular shifts have been followed by phases of stability. Our periodization of the economic history has enabled us to establish certain 'layers' or 'inertias', which have underlain every new emerging formative phase. As an example, the institutions from the liberal era in the middle of the nineteenth century did not vanish with the dominance of a social democratic regime in Sweden, Norway and Denmark from the 1930s. Likewise, the international, market-oriented economy today bears strong marks of the regulated welfare economy in the early post-war period. Thus, we do not see any periods of an 'institutional vacuum'. Instead, the implication is that the transformation of the business system has been an evolutionary process where later phases of innovations and institutional shifts are continuously being prepared in an earlier stage, though remaining dormant during a phase of structural stability.

We also observe an interplay between institutions and dominant techno-economic paradigms. This interaction involves a tension between various interest groups, for example labour unions and employers' association in relation to urban factories in the late nineteenth century or between open (i.e. export industries) and closed sectors (domestic market industries) with respect to currency policies in the post-war period. The trade-off between the interests and the compromises that actors are willing to make in these ideological battles or battles over dominance in agenda-setting determine not only the pace of the transformation but also the direction of new development paths.

We also establish that the developments paths have been less different between the four Nordic countries over history. In that sense, the countries have converged, which confirms that suggestion of *one* Nordic business system instead of four national-based business systems. It is difficult to say anything about causation – i.e. if political reforms have led to less economic differences, or vice versa. However, on a lower level of analysis we can confirm tracks that have been decisive for this type of convergence. First of all, the Nordic region has been the most important export and import market for all four countries. Second, nearly all firms have started their international expansion by making FDI in another Nordic country. Third, an increasing number of project-based activities and M&As have taken place between Nordic firms. Fourth, many Nordic-based associations have contributed to integration processes in the Nordic region, including the recent rapid and economically successful transformation in Iceland. Fifth, membership in the EU has implied a certain conformism and determinism for the development of the Nordic business system, by ruling out alternative and national-based governance mechanisms. This process of convergence has been driven by a simultaneous interplay of institutions, market forces and entrepreneurship. Our results also show that this integration process has been highly substantial in countries with partly overlapping business structures, such as Finland and Sweden, and Denmark and Sweden.

Another possible reason for convergence is that the implementation of institutions and other changes in country-specific business systems have followed international modes of transformation. If so, convergence should be viewed as a *shared response* to an international process of renewal. We already know that the integration process in Europe has resulted in less dominance for the national state, including a dissolution of certain governance systems. The latest 'formative phase' carries policies on a supra-national level and urges a deliberate implementation of more or less federal norms. Likewise, businesses have risen from the national level and taken advantage from lower labour costs and emerging markets all over the world. We have shown how this expansion of Nordic MNCs has been less dependent on national restrictions in recent times. In fact, the strongest growth of employment in Nordic MNCs appears to be outside the Nordic region, in the Baltic countries, in Eastern Europe and in various Asian countries, including China.

We have stated that there is a Nordic business system. Where is the system going now? Will it be dissolved in a (one and only) global, market-based capitalistic system? If so, will it lose some of its cultural roots and national specificities? Or will it continue to be recognized as a distinctive business system among all economies in the world, i.e. continue to have certain characteristics that cannot be found in any other region? These are open questions for reflection by for all of us. As authors of this book, we are inclined to think that there are other business systems in the world that remind us of the Nordic one. For example, the mixed economies in south-east Asia seem similar to the Nordic ones, which implies the white Nordic swans have close friends in some Asian tigers on the other side of the globe.

Many countries look towards the north today. Because of stable and favourable growth figures, the Nordic business system has been attractive to policy-makers from all over the world. The system has also proved to be effective to carry out the delicate balancing act between an active state, high taxes and international competitive business. Most likely, the fascination about the Nordic business system emanates from the result of this balancing act, no matter if we measure the outcome as long peaceful periods, few conflicts on the labour market, low income differentials, international competitive businesses, good welfare systems or sustainable economic growth. Since this high-profile performance has persisted we are inclined to believe that the Nordic business system will continue be an inspiration for other small economies and emerging competitive peripheries in the world.

Notes

1. Kettunen (2006).
2. Childs (1936).
3. Olsson (2001).
4. Mokyr (2006).
5. Schröter (1997).
6. 'Varieties of capitalism' has become something of a standardized concept for a tradition emerging in the wake of the work by Hall and Soskice (2001), but a similar discussion about capitalism had occurred much earlier.
7. Streeck and Thelen (2005).
8. Morgan *et al.* (2005).
9. Streeck and Thelen (2005).

References

Childs, M. W. *Sweden, The Middle Way* (New Haven: Yale University Press, 1936).
Hall, P. A. and Soskice, D., *Varieties of Capitalism: The Institutional Foundation of Comparative Advantages* (Oxford: Oxford University Press, 2001).

Kettunen, P., 'The Power of International Comparison – A Perspective on the Making and Challenging of the Nordic Welfare State', in Christensen, N.F., Petersen, K., Edling, N. and Haave, P., *The Nordic Model of Welfare: A Historical Appraisal* (Copenhagen: Museum Tusculanum Press, University of Copenhagen, 2006).

Mokyr, J., 'Successful Small Open Economies and the Importance of Good Institutions', in Ojala, J., Eloranta, J. and Jalava, J. (eds), *The Road to Prosperity: An Economic History of Finland* (Helsinki: Suomalaisen Kirjallisuuden Seura, 2006).

Morgan, G., Whitely, R. and Moen, E. (eds), *Changing Capitalisms? Internationalization, Institutional Change, and Systems of Economic Organization* (Oxford: Oxford University Press, 2005).

OECD Unemployment Outlook, 2007, www.oecd.org/topicstatsportal

Olsson, U., *Furthering a Fortune* (Stockholm: Ekerlids förlag, 2001).

Schröter, H. 'Small European Nations: Cooperative Capitalism in the Twentieth Century', in Chandler, A. D., Jr, Amatori, F. and Hikino, T. (eds), *Big Business and the Wealth of Nations* (Cambridge: Cambridge University Press, 1997).

Streeck, W. and Thelen, K., 'Introduction', in Streeck W. and Thelen, K. (eds), *Beyond Continuity: Institutional Change in Advanced Political Economies* (Oxford: Oxford University Press, 2005).

The World Economy, 2007, www.adb.org/Documents/Books/ADO/2007/part01-world.pdf

WELFARE CAPITALISM: THE SWEDISH ECONOMY 1850–2005 ● ENTREPRENEURSHIP AND OWNERSHIP: THE ERM VIABILITY OF THE SWEDISH BONNIER AND WALLENBERG FAMILY BUSINESS GROUPS ● FROM ABB **statistical appendix** WAY ● GROWTH AND INVESTMENT: FINNISH CAPITALISM, 1850S–2005 ● FROM STATE OWNERSHIP TO MULTINATIONAL CORPORATION: THE PATH OF ENSO-GUTZEIT TO STORA-ENSO ● SUCCESS AND FAILURE OF A CONGLOMERATE FIRM: THE STRATEGIC PATHS OF NOKIA AND TAMPELLA IN THE LIBERALIZING FINNISH ECONOMY AFTER THE SECOND WORLD WAR ● CO-OPERATIVE LIBERALISM: DENMARK FROM 1857 TO 2007 ● ARLA – FROM DECENTRALIZED INDUSTRY TO MULTINATIONAL ENTERPRISE ● CARLSBERG AND THE SELF-REGULATION OF THE DANISH BEER MARKET ● NORWAY: A RESOURCE-BASED AND DEMOCRATIC CAPITALISM ● CONSTRUCTIVE POWER: ELKEM 1904–2004 ● FINANCE AND THE DEVELOPMENT OF NORWEGIAN CAPITALISM – THE CASE OF CHRISTIANIA BANK

Table A.1 **Population, 1860–2006 (1000s)**

Year	Denmark[1]	Finland	Norway[1]	Sweden
1860	1608	1747	1702	3860
1880	1969	2061	1919	4566
1900	2449	2656	2240	5136
1920	3104	3148	2649	5904
1940	3844	3695	3157	6371
1960	4585	4446	3591	7498
1980	5122	4788	4091	8318
2000	5330	5181	4478	8883
2006	5427	5255	4640	9047

Note: 1. Denmark 1900 refers to the census in 1901; Denmark 1920 refers to the Census in 1921, Southern Jutland not included; Norway 1860 to the census in 1865; Norway 1940 to the Census in 1946.
Sources: Christiansen, Niels Finn et al., The Nordic Model of Welfare. (Copenhagen: Museum Tusculanums förlag, 2006), p. 355; Nordic Statistical Yearbook 2006.

Table A.2 **Country size and population density, 2006**

	Denmark	Finland	Norway	Sweden
Land area (1000 km²)	42.7	304.5	324	410.3
Population (million)	5.42	5.26	4.64	9.05
Population per km² land area	127.1	17.3	15.2	22.0
Capital population incl. suburbs (million)	1.83	0.99	1.04	1.89

Source: Nordic Statistical Yearbook 2007.

Table A.3 **Population density, urban settlements with 2000 inhabitants or more, 1875–2000 (% of total)**

Year	Denmark	Finland	Norway	Sweden
1875	24.8	6.6	19.2	13
1900	38.3	11.9	31.2	22.6
1920	42.7	15.2	36.8	32
1940	55.2	26.6	42.3[1]	42.2
1960	62.4	38	48.7	60
1980	69.5	61.7	59.6	72.2
2000	71.5	75	65.1	73.3

Note: 1. Figures from 1946.
Source: The Nordic Model of Welfare, p. 356.

Table A.4 GDP Levels, 1850–2006 (million 1990 International Geary–Khamis dollars)

	1850	1870	1890	1900	1920	1940	1960	1980	1990	2000	2006
Denmark	2,649	3,782	5,788	7,726	12,942	19,606	40,367	78,010	94,863	122,580	135,563
Finland	1,483	1,999	3,265	4,415	5,782	11,909	27,598	61,890	84,103	100,952	121,321
Norway	1,331	2,360	3,414	4,185	7,217	12,005	25,798	61,595	78,333	112,907	128,061
Sweden	4,490	6,927	9,972	13,104	16,463	30,873	64,986	124,130	151,451	184,517	215,224
UK	63,342	100,180	150,269	184,861	212,938	330,638	452,768	728,224	944,610	1,205,155	1,389,948
US	42,583	98,374	214,714	312,499	593,438	929,737	2,046,727	4,230,558	5,803,200	8,019,378	9,320,104
Germany[1]	48,178	72,149	115,581	162,335	170,235	377,284	558,482	1,105,099	1,264,438	1,560,098	1,652,266

Note: 1. From 1945–90, West Germany only.
Sources: 1850–1940, Angus Maddison The World Economy: Historical Statistics, 1950–2006; Groningen Growth and Development Centre and the Conference Board, Total Economy Database, January 2007, http://www.ggdc.net.

Table A.5 **Average unemployment, 1910–2005**

Year	Denmark	Finland	Norway	Sweden
1910[3]	10.7	—	—	—
1920	19.3[1]	—	—	—
1930	13.9	—	16.6	11.8
1940	15.7	—	2.7[2]	11.8
1950	8.7	—	0.9	2.2
1960	4.3	1.5	1.4	1.4
1970	1.8	1.4	0.9	1.5
1980	8.4	4.6	1.6	2
1990	7.2	3.2	5.2	1.7
2000	4.3	9.8	3.4	5.6
2005	4.9	8.5	4.7	6

Notes: 1. Figures for 1922; 2. Figures for 1941; 3. Figures from 1910 to 1950 for unionised workers only.
Sources: *Danmark Statistik Yearbook, 1917, 1927, 1947 Yearbook of Nordic Statistics* 2006.

Table A.6 **Annual hours, worked, per person employed, 1870–2006**

Year	Denmark	Finland	Norway	Sweden
1870	2945	2945	2945	2945
1913	2553	2588	2588	2588
1950	2283	2035	2101	1951
1973	1742	1707	1721	1571
1990	1638	1668	1460	1508
1998	1664	1637	1428	1582
2006	1577	1721	1407	1583

Sources: *The World Economy: A Millennial Perspective*, p. 347, *OECD Unemployment Outlook*, 2007 p. 263.

Table A.7 Employment, by sector 1940–2005

	Agriculture	Manufacturing	Construction	Commerce	Communication	Services	Unknown
(a) Denmark							
1940	32.0	29.3	6.9	14.0	6.5	10.6	0.7
1960	17.8	29.7	7.3	14.3	7.0	21.0	3.0
1980 (81)	7.7	20.3	7.6	14.8	6.4	39.8	3.4
2000	3.2	17.5	6.2	30.5	6.7	35.6	0.4
2005	2.8	15.5	6.4	31.8	6.4	36.8	0.4
(b) Finland							
1940	59.8	13.9	2.2	4.4	3.5	8.8	7.4
1960	35.5	22.8	8.7	11.6	6.3	14.8	0.3
1980	12.6	27.2	7.1	16.7	7.9	26.2	2.2
2000	5.9	21.2	6.4	27.4	7.4	31.5	0.3
2005	4.6	19.3	6.6	29.1	7.1	33.0	0.2
(c) Norway							
1946	29.7	22.9	9.7	9.9	9.5	17.3	1.0
1960	19.5	26.9	9.5	14.4	11.9	17.4	0.4
1980	7.2	24.2	8.4	19.0	9.0	26.1	0.6
2000	4.1	15.2	6.5	29.8	7.4	36.9	0.1
2005	3.3	13.8	6.9	30.7	6.6	38.6	0.0
(d) Sweden							
1940	28.8	29.1	6.4	11.0	6.7	18.0	0.3
1960	13.8	36.0	9.1	13.5	7.5	19.8	0.3
1980	5.5	26.3	7.2	20.4	7.2	33.2	0.2
2000	2.4	19.1	5.4	29.4	6.7	36.9	0.1
2005	2.0	16.1	5.9	29.6	6.3	39.8	0.2

Sources: 1940–2000, The Nordic Model of Welfare, pp. 360–1, 2005 The Nordic Statistical Yearbook.

Table A.8   Economically active population, by sex, 1930–2005 (000)

		1930	1940	1950	1960	1970	1980	1990	2005
Denmark	Men	1588	1971	2063	1448	1466	1485	1448	1371
	Women	484	685	691	616	844	1140	1222	1237
Finland	Men	1715	2020	1984	1232	1226	1187	1289	1228
	Women	705	870	808	801	893	1035	1179	1150
Norway	Men	1168	–	1388	1084	1058	945	1115	1211
	Women	317	–	328	321	398	434	915	1078
Sweden	Men	2892	3000	3105	2278	2206	2149	2346	2225
	Women	896	810	819	966	1207	1604	2162	2038

Note: – Not available.
Source: Yearbook of Nordic Statistics, 1966, p. 19; 1973 p. 34; 1984, p. 47; 1992, p. 91; 2006 p. 145.

Table A.9   Labour productivity (GDP per hour worked), 1870–1998 (1990 international $ per hour)

	1870	1913	1950	1973	1990	1998	2006
Denmark	1.57	3.58	6.57	16.57	21.67	26.18	30.66
Finland	0.86	1.87	4.28	13.81	20.27	25.69	29.17
Norway	1.2	2.4	5.95	15.44	26.43	32.77	39.65
Sweden	1.22	2.58	7.08	18.02	22.49	26.27	30.85

Sources: 1870–1998, *The World Economy: A Millennial Perspective*, p. 35; for 2006, Groningen Growth and Development Centre and the Conference Board, Total Economy Database, January 2007, http://www.ggdc.net.

Index

Key: **bold** = extended discussion, f = figure, n = endnote/footnote, p = photograph;
t = table.

social engineering   45
'social engineers'   313
social equality   560
social insurance   294–5
Social Insurance Act (Denmark, 1892)   283
Social Liberal Party (Denmark)   285, 286,
      288, 294, 318
social liberal political-economic order
      (Norway, 1890–1920)   419
social liberalism   396, 397
Social Reform (Denmark, 1933)   294–5, 312
social responsibility   224, 234, 253
social security   58, 164, 183, 204
social stability   **435–8**
social tension (Finland)   **152–3**
socialism   6, 20, 22, 29, 43–4, 45, 151, 162,
      223, 282, 340, 397, 439, 440, 441, 559
socialist countries (former)   198
socialist trade block (SEV)   172, 250, 252
Society of Technical Schools (Tekniske
      Selskabs Skoler)   275
Soda Factories/Sodafabrikkerne   276t
Söderberg anode 511
Söderberg electrode   393, 444, 447, **495–503**,
      573
Söderberg system/principle 504–5, 507,
      510–17, 519, 524
Söderberg, C.W.   **500–2**
software   15t, 119, 472
Sogner, K.   **xvi**
soil   337, 393, 478
SOK (co-operative)   145
solar energy   495, 523, 524
Solberg family   508, 509
Solberg Spinning Mill   406–7
Solin, A.   245
Sonderweg (Nordic)   2
Sør-Trøndelag   424
Søral   445
Soskice, D.   481, 578(n6)
Soteva   245
South Africa   292, 515
South America   10–11, 495
South Asia   60
South Korea   4, 13, 139, 461
South-East Asia   578
southern Europe   48
Southern Manganese (Alabama)   503
Soviet Union *see* USSR
Spain   44, 112, 247, 318, 320n, 505, 515
Sparebank Venstre   536
Sparkasseloven av 4 October 1919 (savings
      bank law, Norway)   537
speciedaler (Norwegian currency)   402

speculation (financial)   20, 418, 540, 543, 545
speculative bubbles   54, 142, 154, 159,
      188–93, 541, 553
Stabburet   480
stability   **482**
Stadtholder (governor)   400
stagflation   68, 173
stagnation   295, 318
Standard Telefon- og Kabelfabrik   452, 464
Standard/ITT-Norway   552
standardization   121, 123, 431
Stanford Research Institute (SRI),   120
state, the   460, 560, 563, 576
      contextual arena   7f, **8**, 71–4f, 216–17f,
         332–4f, 491–3f
      corporatist   45
      passive versus active   566
      strength   263, 566
      'stronger' (Finland)   **160–2**
State Power Board (Norway)   465
state regulation   438–9
state role   45, 63, 137, 151, 153–4, 167, 204,
      208, 210, 269, 312
      Finland   **202–3**
      literature   566
      Nordic business systems   **566–7**
state-guided collaborative economy   **438–42**
state-owned company syndrome   234
state-owned enterprises (SOEs)   55, 160,
      162, 167, 174, 187–8, 203t, 203, 208, 319,
      449, 461, 462, 467, 472, 485, 550, 559,
      562, 568
      Enso-Gutzeit   **218–37**
      growing importance (Finland)   179–81
state-private combines
      disintegration (Norway)   **464–6**
State's Direct Financial Interest (SDFI,
      Norway, 1984)   467
Statfjord oil field   467–8
stationsbyer (new towns alongside railway)
      274
Statkraft   (Norway, 1991–)   465, 473, 484
Statoil (Stavanger, 1972–)   393, 421, 471, 472
      market capitalization and employees   468
      merger with Hydro (2006/7)   469
      partial privatization (2001)   467
      privatized (2001)   484
StatoilHydro (2007–)   469, 484
Stauning, T.   289, 293, 294
      '*Stauning eller Kaos*' (slogan)   294p
Stavanger   414, 433, 467
Stavanger University (2005–)   493f
steam engine   28, 369, 406, 408, 410

4377 296